A HISTORY

OF

THE DOCTRINE OF
THE HOLY EUCHARIST

BY

DARWELL STONE, M.A.

PUSEY LIBRARIAN

FORMERLY PRINCIPAL OF DORCHESTER MISSIONARY COLLEGE

IN TWO VOLUMES

VOL. II.

Wipf & Stock
PUBLISHERS
Eugene, Oregon

Wipf and Stock Publishers
199 W 8th Ave, Suite 3
Eugene, OR 97401

A History of the Doctrine of the Holy Eucharist
By Stone, Darwell
ISBN 13: 978-1-59752-973-0
ISBN 10: 1-59752-973-7
Publication date 9/20/2006
Previously published by Longmans, Green, and Co., 1909

CONTENTS.

VOLUME II.

CHAPTER IX.

THE PERIOD OF THE REFORMATION : PART I.

CHAPTER XIV.

POST-REFORMATION THEOLOGY : PART I.

CHAPTER XV.

POST-REFORMATION THEOLOGY : PART II.

CHAPTER XVI.

POST-REFORMATION THEOLOGY : PART III.

x CONTENTS

CHAPTER IX.

THE PERIOD OF THE REFORMATION.

PART I.

In the sixteenth century the history of Eucharistic doctrine in the West presents new features. These are closely connected with the circumstances of the time. Results of much thought and many events of the fourteenth and fifteenth centuries now made themselves felt. The invention of printing, the development of literature, the new methods of art, the revived study of Greek, the fresh access to the Fathers and to the sources of Church history, the progress of criticism, all that is associated with the work of the Humanists and the New Learning, the discoveries of explorers, the expansion of trade, social unrest, class hatreds, the growth of individualism in politics,—all these combined to produce in the early years of the sixteenth century a condition of affairs without previous parallel. The movement towards a wider learning, a more accurate scholarship, a greater fidelity to history, which had been begun by Robert Grosseteste and Roger Bacon in the thirteenth century, had made great advance. In the first twenty years of the sixteenth century there are notable landmarks of the study of theology in the printing of the Complutensian Polyglot under the directions of Cardinal Ximenes at Alcala in 1514, the publication by Erasmus of the first edition of his Greek Testament at Basle in 1516, the editing by Erasmus of St. Jerome and other Fathers, and the publication in 1516 of the *Utopia* of Sir Thomas More.

In the activity of enterprise and investigation, of discovery and thought, of new knowledge and new methods, it was impossible that what was established and old should escape criticism and challenge. It was natural to the men who were feeling the movement of the age to examine and question everything which they found. In the vigour and joy of their fresh life, their wealth of discovery, their power of achievement, only the most balanced could hope to avoid the insolence and self-confidence which are among the chief notes of the time.

The characteristics of the age may be seen in the treatment of the doctrine of the Holy Eucharist. The appeal to Scripture, the use of history, the impatience of mystery, the love of change, the attraction of mechanical and materialistic arguments, are in varying degrees powerful influences on one side ; on the other a steadfast conservatism, for the most part not less prone to be mechanical and formal, obtains different results from Scripture and tradition. Both at their worst are crude and impatient and overbearing; both at their best are eager to maintain what they believe to be the consequences of the life and work and revelation of Christ. Some of the most pleasing notes of character are seen in those whom it is difficult to place in any theological group.

I.

Among the pioneers of the New Learning was John Colet. He was born about 1466, and some seventeen years later went to Oxford, perhaps to Magdalen College, at that time " essentially the home of the Classical Renaissance in Oxford ".[1] After subsequent travels in France and Italy he returned to England about 1496, and was ordained deacon and priest. His work as a lecturer at Oxford probably began in the autumn of 1497 and ended in 1504, when he became Dean of St. Paul's Cathedral. In 1511 he was one of the judges for the trial of heretics in the diocese of Canterbury, and in the following year preached a notable sermon before Convocation on the ignorance and corruption of the bishops and clergy. In 1512 he founded St. Paul's School and appointed William Lilly head-master and John Ritwyse surmaster. About the same time he was charged with heresy by Fitzjames, the Bishop of London, on the grounds that he had denounced the worship of images and large episcopal revenues, and that he had raised objections to the use of written sermons in preaching. The charges were dismissed as frivolous by Warham, the Archbishop of Canterbury. In 1519 he died.

[1] Rashdall, *The Universities of Europe in the Middle Ages*, ii. 515.

The references to the Holy Eucharist in the writings of Colet are marked by great caution and restraint. There is an entire absence of the subtle questions in which the schoolmen delighted ; and the influence of the theology of the pseudo-Dionysius the Areopagite,[1] then still supposed to be a writer of apostolic times, is clearly shown. The treatise *On the Sacraments of the Church*, while dealing at considerable length with Orders and Matrimony and Penance, contains only very short statements on the Sacraments of Baptism, Confirmation, the Holy Communion, and Extreme Unction. In regard to the Sacraments in general a distinction is made, similar to that in St. Ambrose and other writers,[2] that "in heaven" "all things are after a heavenly manner and in reality," while "among us" they are "after the manner of an image".[3] On the Eucharist Colet says :—

"The Sacrament of Communion of flesh and blood in ordinary food, which is the Sacrament of union and unity, is the feeding and nourishment in common in Christ in supreme unity of those who have been confirmed and filled with the Spirit. For we are called that we may be cleansed and enlightened and perfected in spirit and nourished together and may live together and fight together and conquer together and be glorified together. This is the force of the love of spiritual men." [4]

Colet's lectures on the First Epistle to the Corinthians contain the following passages referring to the Eucharist :—

"In the blessed cup and the broken bread is the health-giving communication of the real body and blood of Jesus Christ itself, which is received by many in order that they may be one in Him. Many are united in the participation of One and by being re-made for this very purpose, that we may be conformed to Christ and may be in Him. This is what he says, 'We, who are many, are one bread and one body,'[5] all we, that is, who partake of the one bread and the one cup. The food on which we are fed is one, distributed to the whole society in order that it may be one body, that all men who are fed may be one in Him who is One, that is, in Him on whom they feed; not changing the food into themselves, but being transformed into

[1] See vol. i. pp. 138-40, *supra*.
[2] See, *e.g.*, vol. i. pp. 119, 226, 227, *supra*.
[3] C. 5 (Lupton's edition, p. 49).
[4] C. 9 (Lupton's edition, p. 93).   [5] 1 Cor. x. 17.

1 *

Him by the food, as by the stronger. For thus is effected the conformity and unity of all, because Christ, being received by different
persons, does not undergo change into the nature of those persons.
For they who receive Him are not stronger than Him whom they
receive ; but the different persons, being re-made into one by Christ,
who is the stronger, are happily united to that very Person on whom
they feed." [1]

  "The Supper of the Lord is the breaking of the bread and the
distribution of His own most sacred body. Also, together with the
bread there is the drinking of the blood of the Same, whereby the
new covenant and league of God with men is preserved. For by
the blood of holy offerings all things are consecrated and ratified.
By the redeeming and sanctifying blood of the sacrificed Lamb, the
spotless Christ, the league and new covenant of God with those who
are redeemed and sanctified to God is consecrated. That is, if
through Christ and in Christ, imitating Him, we serve God, then
from the compact and league which is ratified by the blood of Christ
we shall be fellow-sharers in the glory of the same Jesus Christ.
Otherwise the league would be void. This Supper of the Lord, the
eating of the bread and drinking of the cup, affords the commemoration and proclamation and representation of the death of Christ.
For it is the breaking of the body and as it were the shedding of
the blood. But the breaking and the shedding are in order that
the chosen may feed on that Victim, so that, by Christ dying in
them, they may live again in Him, that, having Jesus wholly in
themselves, they may be wholly and completely in Jesus, being
now incorporated and concorporated with Him by participation in
His uniting and life-giving body, who at His Supper, the Supper of
the Lord, bestows Himself wholly on us, that He may transform us
wholly into Himself and may make us fellow-members with Him,
so that there may be as it were one body in the union of Him as the
Head with His own, the body having God wholly and being wholly
in God, not only in their souls by the communication of deity but
also in their bodies by the communication of His body, that we may
be nourished into one body in Him. So He Himself, for He is the
Church, feeds on Himself, and the Church is not fed on any other
food than Christ Himself, all in Him being priests and fellow-sacri-
ficers and fellow-guests on the same Victim, the Church itself, certainly Christ Himself, being fed and nourished on Christ Himself
unto everlasting life. Jesus Christ was sacrificed and offered and
died that we may feed on this sacrifice until He come, and that in

---

[1] On chap. x. (Lupton's edition, p. 237).

feeding we may remember Him who died for us, being partakers of His death, that we may live in Him, being partakers of His life, that now we may be dead in Him and being raised from the dead may be alive in Him. Now we are in the temple, that we may all feed on the Victim, and may all be partakers of the altar of God, nay of God Himself who was offered on the altar of the cross, that, being crucified and offered together with Him and in Him, we may be sacrifices acceptable to God. So also the sharing in the Supper with the Lord is dying with Him. . . . He gave to His own His body, which was to be delivered up to death for them, of which He willed that they should partake in remembrance of His death, and that they should do this worthily, lest they should be guilty of the death of the Lord. If any eat unworthily, they kill Christ ; if they eat worthily, they themselves live in Him who has died, and being dead in Him they live in Him. . . . The disciples ate Jesus, who was about to die, being themselves about to die in Him, that they may rise with Him, when He shall come. In later times all receive the same Sacrament, being all about to die together with Him in Him, that at His coming they may rise together with Him." [1]

In Colet's abstract of the treatise of the pseudo-Dionysius the Areopagite *On the Hierarchy of the Church*, which appears to be as much an expression of his own opinions as a statement of the substance of the teaching of the pseudo-Dionysius, the following are the most important passages referring to the doctrine of the Eucharist :—

"The holy food of the Eucharist is given for union with the body, for the nourishment of the member, by which it is understood both that he is in the body and that in the body he is fed and spiritually nourished. No one is perfectly a member of the body of Christ until he is a partaker of the Holy Communion and the life-giving nourishment. By partaking of this he is united to the body. . . . The washing cleanses, the subsequent anointing with chrism gives enlightenment and brightness, the Eucharist completes and perfects in the perfect Christ, in whom all things are perfect, in whom nothing can be which is not perfect." [2]

"This Communion in the body and blood of Jesus Christ is the consummation of all Sacraments. All Sacraments indeed lead to communion, but they are nothing in comparison with this, in which is marvellous participation and union of life, since many become one

[1] On chap. xi..(Lupton's edition, pp. 242-44).
[2] P. 215 (Lupton's edition).

in the One whom they receive. For this men are prepared by other
Sacraments, which go before in order that they may be completed
by this. All Sacraments accomplish this, that there is unity and
likeness and simplicity in men. In this we make progress through
other Sacraments; by the Eucharist and Communion we are perfected." [1]

"The people and the less taught multitude are well and suitably
instructed, in the one bread and cup which are set forth and in the
reception by all of the same food, that being fed and nourished by
One they are all made one in concord and brotherly peace under
God the Father at the Table of God, and that they may understand
that, as there is one and like bread and a one and like cup which
all taste, so they themselves ought all to be one and like with one
another, and to be bound together in unity of love, which is the
bond of peace. This Communion has also the venerable representation of the Last Supper of the Lord with His disciples, in which He
gave Himself to be eaten by them, that they all might be united in
Him, and being incorporated in Him might be made one. . . . The
Saviour being set forth under the species of bread and wine, afterwards follows the commemoration of the saints, that they being
united to Jesus may be understood to be one with Him. . . . In the
early Church in the Mass the subordinates of the celebrant partook
with Him of the sacrificed Christ; before their eyes he sets forth the
consecrated Sacrament; he divides the holy bread into portions, and
administers together with the cup, and so multiplies One to many
that he may unite many in One. . . . Jesus . . . came forth from
the hidden place to the sight of men, the Invisible was made
visible, the One was made in some way many, that He might draw
together all things to His purpose. And this is the mystery which
the bringing forth of the one bread and cup from the hidden and
secret place and the showing and administration and reception of
them signify; for thus we may understand that, as the things of
sense being one are multiplied to bring about union, so the Invisible,
even Jesus, being One is multiplied to bring about the uniting of
multitudes in Him." [2]

In the doctrinal and devotional matter prefixed to the Latin
Accidence which Colet wrote for the use of the boys of St.
Paul's School a short statement on the seven Sacraments contains
the sentence about the Eucharist that—

[1] P. 216 (Lupton's edition).
[2] Pp. 221, 224, 227 (Lupton's edition).

" By gracious Eucharist, where is the very presence of the Person
of Christ under form of bread, we be nourished spiritually in God " ;
under the head of " Houselling " it is said—
    "As often as I shall receive my Lord in Sacrament, I shall with
all study dispose me to all cleanness and devotion " ;
and under the head of " In sickness " it is said—
    " When I shall die, I shall call for the Sacraments and rites of
Christ's Church betimes, and be confessed and receive my Lord and
Redeemer Jesu Christ." [1]

Thus, with the caution and restraint and mysticism which
mark the writings of Colet on this subject he appears to have
joined the acceptance of the main features of the traditional
theology of the Church.   It is not altogether easy to conjecture
what his attitude would have been towards the Eucharistic controversies of the sixteenth century, if he had lived until they
began, though it is probably not too much to say that he would
have been afraid alike of theories which might seem mechanical
or carnal and of contentions which might endanger the belief
that the consecrated elements are the body and blood of Christ.

Another pioneer of the New Learning was the Frenchman
Jacques Lefèvre, usually known as Faber Stapulensis, who was
born at Etaples in Picardy about 1440 or somewhat later.   He
was a member of the University of Paris, and afterwards studied
in Italy.   For a considerable part of his life he was a teacher of
arts ; and he translated many of the works of Aristotle into
Latin.   Later he devoted himself to the study of theology.   In
1512 he published a Latin translation of the Pauline Epistles,
including the Epistle to the Hebrews, with a commentary ; and
in 1523 he published a new French translation of the Gospels
and the rest of the New Testament, which however was ordered
to be burnt by the authorities in France in 1525.   In 1536 he
died at Nérac.   The commentary on the Pauline Epistles contains incidental references to the Eucharist, in which Lefèvre
lays stress on the need of communicating worthily if the reception of Communion is to benefit the soul, shows his belief in the
presence of Christ in the Sacrament, and speaks of the Eucharistic sacrifice as a memorial of the one sacrifice of Christ and
an opportunity for approach to His heavenly offering.

[1] In Lupton, *Life of John Colet*, pp. 287, 288.

"But a man will say, ' We have received the Holy Ghost, we
have been baptised in Christ, we have partaken of the body and
blood of Christ ; therefore we shall be made partakers of the Gospel,
therefore we shall receive the incorruptible crown '. Not so ; the
reality may be known from the figure ; if we have fallen into evil
and gluttonous desires, into covetousness which is idolatry, or into
any other kind of idolatry, into fornication, if we provoke Christ by
unbelief, if we murmur against His providence, if we do such unlawful and unholy deeds, although all those mysteries are ours, yet
we shall not receive that crown and we shall not in any wise enter
the kingdom of God. . . . The things which happened to the Jews
are types and figures ; the Jews are a figure of the people of Christ ;
the cloud, of the Holy Ghost ; the sea, of Baptism ; Moses, of Christ
as lawgiver ; the manna, of the body of Christ as heavenly bread
and the food of life ; the stream which flowed from the rock, of the
blood of Christ as life-giving drink. . . . Because the completion of
prayer and of all divine grace is union to God, and that union to
God and in God is accomplished by means of the spiritual reception
of the body and blood of Christ, therefore to that participation of
the divine body and blood which completes all we must approach
with the greatest reverence, purity, and holiness. . . . With great
reverence must we approach this most august mystery. . . . Who
dare approach to touch the Holy of holies unless he be clean, to receive the King of kings unless with awe, the Judge of all unless
with fear ? . . . If you were to receive as a guest an earthly king,
and your own king too, and should not prepare his dwelling place
or take pains to adorn it, but should put him in a mean place, . . .
would you not appear to despise the royal dignity, and thus to be
guilty of treason ? . . . But He is more to be revered than all the
kings of the earth, and His majesty not only by men but also by all
angels and powers in heaven and hell. Of how great an offence
are you guilty, if you do not receive Him with all the worthiness of
which you are capable ; for with the worthiness of which He Himself is worthy not heaven nor earth nor any creature can receive
Him." [1]

"Our High Priest is in heaven. . . . He is so really our High
Priest that all things are done by Him, even at our altars. He
was Man, and He is Man ; on behalf of men He is both in heaven
and on earth. In heaven, that He may give unveiled glory to
those of heaven ; on earth, that He may lead us strangers to immortality in heaven by His immortal food. . . . He is near at hand

[1] On 1 Cor. x. xi. (fo. 121 a, 123 a, 123 b, edition 1512).

on our altars, that no one may despair of pardon because of distance from the High Priest. He is God, that He may spare and have mercy. He is King, that He may reward and bestow grace. He is Brother, that He may embrace. Let us flee then to the throne of His majesty ; with the body, to Him who is near at hand before us on the altars, with the mind to His seat above the heavens, where He sits on the right hand of the Father of mercy. . . . Christ not for His own sins (for He did no sin neither was guile found in His mouth) but for the sins of the whole world satisfied by one offering, His one self and the one occasion being more power-ful than innumerable sacrifices repeated an infinite number of times. Therefore those things which are done daily in the ministry of His priesthood are not so much repeated offerings as the memorial and remembrance of the one same ·sacrifice, of that which was offered once only. . . . Once did He make satisfaction for all. Neither does it contain any other mystery than the memorial of that divine and all-saving offering and satisfaction through the presence of the body and blood formerly offered. . . . Christ once entered into heaven ; and that once endures even to the end of the world ; for He has never gone out and will not go out, except when going out without leaving He will come to judge the world. But having once entered into the holy of holies on high, He abides present before the face of God offering Himself without intermission for the salva-tion of all even unto the end of the world." [1]

II.

Martin Luther was born at Eisleben in Southern Prussia on November 10, 1483. He became a member of the University of Erfurt in 1501, entered an Augustinian monastery· at the same place in 1504, was ordained priest in 1507, and was appointed Professor of Philosophy in the University of Wittenburg in 1508. Controversies which began in 1517 led to his excommunication by Pope Leo X. in 1520, and to a sentence of outlawry decreed by the Emperor Charles V. and the Diet of Worms in 1521. In 1524 he renounced all monastic obligations; in 1525 he per-formed a ceremony of ordaining George Roesser deacon, and himself married a nun named Katherina von Bora. After spend-ing the rest of his life in the translation of the Bible, finished in 1534, the organisation and government of his adherents, and the formation of service books and instructions for their use, he died in 1546 at Eisleben.

[1] On Heb. iv. vii. ix. (fo. 236 b, 243 a, 249 a, edition 1512).

In the latter half of 1520 Luther published three works usually known as " The Three Great Reformation Treatises," which were entitled *To the Christian Nobility of the German Nation respecting the Reformation of the Christian Estate, Concerning Christian Liberty, On the Babylonish Captivity of the Church*. The third of these treatises, *On the Babylonish Captivity of the Church*, contained a section " Concerning the Lord's Supper ". This section affords a detailed statement of Luther's opinions on the subject of the Eucharist in 1520.

Luther begins by limiting the number of the Sacraments to " three, Baptism, Penance, and the Bread," though, he says, it would be " according to the usage of Scripture " to " hold that there was only one Sacrament, and three sacramental signs ". After setting aside the sixth chapter of St. John's Gospel " as not saying a single syllable about the Sacrament," he maintains at some length that the Eucharist ought to be received in both kinds by all.[1] He then proceeds to discuss the doctrine of the Sacrament with reference to the ordinary belief of the time that by the consecration the substance of the bread and wine is converted into the substance of the body and blood of Christ, and that only the accidents of the bread and wine remain.

" Formerly, when I was imbibing the scholastic theology, my lord the Cardinal of Cambray[2] gave me occasion for reflection by arguing most acutely, in the fourth book of the *Sentences*, that it would be much more probable, and that fewer superfluous miracles would have to be introduced, if real bread and real wine, and not only their accidents, were understood to be upon the altar, unless the Church had determined the contrary. Afterwards, when I saw what the Church was which had thus determined—namely, the Thomistic, that is, the Aristotelian Church—I became bolder ; and whereas I had been before in great straits of doubt, I now at length established my conscience in the former opinion, namely, that there is real bread and real wine, in which is the real flesh and real blood of Christ in no other manner and in no less degree than the other party assert them to be under the accidents. And this I did because I saw that the opinions of the Thomists, whether approved by the Pope or by a Council, remained opinions, and did not become

---

[1] *De Captiv. Bab.* (*Opera Latina*, Frankfort edition, v. 21-29) ; Wace and Buchheim, *Luther's Primary Works*, pp. 301-10.

[2] That is, Peter d'Ailly ; see vol. i. p. 371, *supra*.

articles of the faith, even were an angel from heaven to decree otherwise. For that which is asserted without the support of the Scriptures, or of an approved revelation, it is permitted to hold as an opinion, but it is not necessary to believe. Now this opinion of Thomas is so vague, and so unsupported by the Scriptures or by reason, that he seems to me to have known neither his philosophy nor his logic. For Aristotle speaks of accidents and subject very differently from St. Thomas; and it seems to me that we ought to be sorry for so great a man when we see him striving, not only to draw his opinions on matters of faith from Aristotle, but to establish them upon an authority whom he did not understand, a most unfortunate structure raised on a most unfortunate foundation." [1]

Thus, for himself, Luther rejects the scholastic doctrine of Transubstantiation on the grounds that it lacks support in revelation and is not the most reasonable way of asserting the presence of the real flesh and blood of Christ. He does not, however, claim that all others also should reject it. His contention is that, while it is lawful as an opinion, it may not be imposed as of faith.

"I quite consent, then, that whoever chooses to hold either opinion should do so. My only object now is to remove scruples of conscience, so that no man may fear being guilty of heresy if he believes that real bread and real wine are present on the altar. Let him know that he is at liberty, without peril to his salvation, to imagine, think, or believe in either of the two ways, since here there is no necessity of faith." [2]

After thus declaring the freedom of Christians to hold or to reject the scholastic doctrine of Transubstantiation, Luther goes on to repeat with great vehemence, and to defend, his "own opinion" that in the consecrated Sacrament the substance of the bread and wine remain, although the real flesh and blood of Christ are there also. Throughout his arguments he appears to have had constantly in mind the tendency of the Scotist divines to question or reject the Thomist philosophy of place and the Thomist assertions that it is impossible for two natural bodies to be in the same place at the same time or for the same natural body to be in two places at the same time. [3] The plain

---

[1] *Opera Latina,* Frankfort edition, v. 29, 30; Wace and Buchheim, *op. cit.* pp. 310, 311.

[2] *Ibid.* 30; Wace and Buchheim, *op. cit.* p. 311.

[3] See vol. i. pp. 331, 332, 340, *supra.*

literal sense of Scripture seems to him to postulate the continued existence of the bread and wine; the teaching of the Church "for more than twelve centuries" supports the same view; there is no more "peril of idolatry" if the unseen substance of the bread and the wine remains than if the seen accidents remain, "for if it is not the accidents which they adore, but Christ concealed under them, why should they adore the substance of bread, which they do not see?"; there is nothing contrary to reason in the substance of the bread co-existing together with the substance of the body of Christ.

"Why should not Christ be able to include His body within the substance of bread, as well as within the accidents? Fire and iron, two different substances, are so mingled in red-hot iron that every part of it is both fire and iron. Why may not the glorious body of Christ much more be in every part of the substance of the bread? Christ is believed to have been born of the inviolate womb of His mother. In this case, too, let them say that the flesh of the Virgin was for a time annihilated, or, as they will have it to be more suitably expressed, transubstantiated, that Christ might be enwrapped in its accidents and at length come forth through its accidents. The same will have to be said respecting the closed door and the closed entrance of the tomb, through which He entered, and went out without injury to them. . . . I rejoice greatly that at least among the common people there remains a simple faith in this Sacrament. They neither understand nor argue whether there are accidents in it or substance, but believe with simple faith that the body and blood of Christ are truly contained in it, leaving to these men of leisure the task of arguing as to what it contains. . . . As the case is with Christ Himself, so is it also with the Sacrament. For it is not necessary to the bodily indwelling of the Godhead that the human nature should be transubstantiated, that so the Godhead may be contained beneath the accidents of the human nature. But each nature is entire, and we can say with truth, This Man is God; this God is Man. Though philosophy does not receive this, yet faith receives it, and greater is the authority of the word of God than the capacity of our intellect. Thus, too, in the Sacrament it is not necessary to the presence of the real body and real blood that the bread and wine should be transubstantiated, so that Christ may be contained beneath the accidents; but, while both bread and wine continue there, it can be said with truth, This bread is My body; this wine is My blood, and conversely. Thus for the present will I understand the matter in honour of the holy words of God, which I will not allow to have violence done them by the petty reasonings of men, or to be distorted into meanings alien to them. I give leave, however, to others to follow the other opinion, which is distinctly laid down in the decretal, provided only, as I have said, they do not press us to accept their opinions as articles of faith." [1]

Up to this point the teaching of Luther about the Eucharist in this treatise is very clear. The consecrated bread and wine are the body and blood of Christ. They are still bread and wine as well as the body and blood. The body and blood are as really present as if the scholastic doctrine of Transubstantiation were true. Though Transubstantiation is not to be imposed on any as of faith, it may be held by those who so wish. In their "simple faith," "the common people" of the time believe the truth that "the body and blood of Christ are truly contained in" the Sacrament, without their troubling themselves with the subtleties of the theologians about substance and accident.

A long passage of great obscurity and difficulty follows. The main object in it is evidently to reject the idea that the celebration of the Eucharist is the performance of "a good work" and the offering of a "sacrifice".

"The third bondage [2] of this same Sacrament is that abuse of it—and by far the most impious—by which it has come about that at this day there is no belief in the Church more generally received or more firmly held than that the Mass is a good work and a sacrifice. This abuse has brought in an infinite flood of other abuses, until faith in the Sacrament has been utterly lost, and they have made this divine Sacrament a mere subject of traffic, huckstering, and money-getting contracts. Hence communions, brotherhoods, suffrages, merits, anniversaries, memorials, and other things of that kind are bought and sold in the Church, and made the subject of bargains and agreements ; and the entire maintenance of priests and monks depends on these things." [3]

[1] *Opera Latina*, Frankfort edition, v. 31-35 ; Wace and Buchheim, *op. cit.* pp. 313-17.

[2] The first " bondage " is Communion in one kind ; the second " bondage " is the requirement of belief in Transubstantiation as a matter of faith.

[3] *Opera Latina*, Frankfort edition, v. 35 ; Wace and Buchheim, *op. cit.* p. 317.

Against the idea that " the Mass is a good work and a sacrifice," Luther maintains that in the words of institution, "and absolutely in nothing else, lies the whole force, nature, and substance of the Mass "; that " the Mass or Sacrament of the altar is the testament of Christ, which He left behind Him at His death, to be distributed to those who believe in Him," and "a promise of the remission of sins made to us by God, and such a promise as has been confirmed by the death of the Son of God "; that it is therefore to be approached " by no works, no strength, no merits, but by faith alone "; that, though prayers are offered in connection with it, it is itself " a gift from " God, and not " a sacrifice offered to God ".[1]

"The bread and wine are presented beforehand to receive a blessing, that they may be sanctified by the word and prayer. But after being blessed and consecrated, they are no longer offered but are received as a gift from God. And in this matter let the priest consider that the Gospel is to be preferred to all canons and collects composed by men ; and the Gospel, as we have seen, does not allow the Mass to be a sacrifice."[2]

In the same treatise there is one passage which, in spite of the very definite assertions of the presence in the Sacrament of the real flesh and blood of Christ by which it is surrounded, appears to bear a greater resemblance to the writings of John Wessel[3] than to the teaching of the mediæval theologians on the possibility and value of Spiritual Communion.[4]

" In the Mass, that chief of all promises, He gave a sign in memory of so great a promise, namely, His own body and blood in the bread and wine, saying, ' Do this for My memorial '. Thus in Baptism He adds to the words of the promise the sign of immersion in water. Whence we see that in every promise of God two things are set before us, the word and the sign. The word we are to understand as being the testament, and the sign as being the Sacrament; thus in the Mass the word of Christ is the testament, the bread and wine are the Sacrament. And as there is greater power in the word than in the sign, so there is greater power in the testament than in the Sacrament. A man can have and use the word or testament without

[1] *Opera Latina*, Frankfort edition, v. 36-55 ; Wace and Buchheim, *op. cit.* pp. 317-39.

[2] *Ibid.* 52, 53 ; Wace and Buchheim, *op. cit.* p. 336.

[3] See vol. i. pp. 371-73, *supra*.

[4] See vol. i. pp. 316, 320, 331, 372, 383, *supra*.

the sign or Sacrament. 'Believe,' saith Augustine, 'and thou hast eaten'; but in what do we believe except in the word of Him who promises? Thus I can have the Mass daily, nay hourly, since, as often as I will, I can set before myself the words of Christ, and nourish and strengthen my faith in them; and this is in very truth spiritual eating and drinking." [1]

Luther's *Short Catechism* and his *Greater Catechism*, written in 1529, show the forms in which he put his doctrinal system for instruction of the most simple and of a less elementary kind. In the *Short Catechism* the section on the Eucharist is as follows:—

" The Sacrament of the Altar.

" How the master of the house should explain it simply to his household.

" What is the Sacrament of the altar?

" *Answer.* It is the real body and blood of our Lord Jesus Christ, under the bread and wine, for us Christians to eat and drink, according to the institution of Christ Himself.

" Where is this written?

" *Answer.* Thus say the holy Evangelists Matthew, Mark, Luke, and St. Paul. . . .

" What avails it to eat and drink thus?

" *Answer.* This is shown us by the words, 'Given and shed for you for the remission of sins,' namely, that in the Sacrament forgiveness of sins, life, and salvation are bestowed on us according to these words. For where forgiveness of sins is, there is also life and salvation.

" How can bodily eating and drinking accomplish these great things?

" *Answer.* Eating and drinking do not indeed accomplish this, but the words which stand there, 'Given and shed for you for the remission of sins'. These words, together with the bodily eating and drinking, are the most important part of this Sacrament, and whoever believes these words, he has what they say, and as they speak, namely, remission of sins.

" Who, then, are they who receive this Sacrament worthily?

" *Answer.* Fasting and bodily preparation are in truth a good external discipline, but he is truly worthy and prepared who believes the words, 'Given and shed for you for the remission of sins'. But

[1] *Opera Latina*, Frankfort edition, v. 43; Wace and Buchheim, *op. cit.* p. 326.

he who does not believe or doubts these words is unworthy and not prepared. For the words, ' for you,' demand truly believing hearts." [1]

The *Greater Catechism* contains a much longer treatment of the doctrine and use of " the Sacrament of the altar ". The most important parts of it which bear on the Eucharist are the following :—

" As the Ten Commandments, the Lord's Prayer, and the Creed retain their power and value whether we keep the commandments or not, whether we pray or not, and whether we have faith or not, so this most holy Sacrament remains unalterable ; it is not divested of anything, even though we receive it and treat it unworthily. Dost thou think that God takes into consideration our actions and belief, so as to change His ordinances because of them ? . . . Now, what is the Sacrament of the altar ? Answer : It is the real body and blood of our Lord Jesus Christ in and under the bread and wine, through Christ's word, appointed for us Christians to eat and drink. And, as we said when speaking of Baptism, that it is not mere water, so we say again here that the Sacrament is bread and wine, but not mere bread and wine such as is ordinarily placed before us at meals, but bread and wine comprehended in God's word and bound up in it. The word, I say, is what makes and distinguishes the Sacrament, so that it is not mere bread and wine, but is and is called the body and blood of Christ. . . . It is the word and ordinance not of a prince or an emperor but of the Most High God ; wherefore all His creatures should fall at His feet, saying, Yea, it shall be as He says, and shall be accepted in all honour, fear, and humility. With these words thou canst strengthen thy conscience and say, Even though a hundred thousand devils with all their fanatics were to come and ask, How can bread and wine be the body and blood of Christ, etc. ?—yet I know that all the spirits and learned men together are not as wise as is the little finger of the Almighty. And we have here Christ's own words, ' Take, eat; this is My body : drink ye all of it ; this is the new testament in My blood'. Let us hold to this, and see who can overcome Him, or make it different from what He said. It is certainly true that if the word be omitted, or it be regarded without the word, then we should have nothing but mere bread and wine, whereas if the word remains where it should and must be then by means of it we have the real body and blood of Christ. For as we have it from the mouth of Christ Himself, so it shall be, for He cannot

---

[1] *Der kleine Katechismus* (*Werke*, Erlangen edition, xxi. 19, 20) ; Wace and Buchheim, *op. cit.* pp. 17, 18.

lie or deceive. . . . Though it be a rogue who takes or gives the Sacrament, it is the right Sacrament—that is, Christ's body and blood —just as though he handled it with utmost reverence. For it is not based on the holiness of mankind but upon God's word; and since no saint on earth, yea, no angel in heaven, can make bread and wine into Christ's body and blood, so no one can change or alter it, though it be wrongly used. For neither the person nor the unbelief can falsify the word by which it became a Sacrament and was instituted as such. For He did not say, If ye believe or are worthy, ye have My body and blood, but, 'Take, eat and drink; this is My body and blood: this do' (that is, what I do now institute, give you, and bid you take). This is as much as to say, Whether thou art worthy or unworthy, thou hast here His body and blood by virtue of these words, which come to the bread and wine. . . . Because He offers and promises forgiveness of sins, it cannot be received otherwise than through faith. Such faith He Himself demands when He says, 'For you given and for you shed,' as though He would have said, I give it you and bid you eat and drink, that you may accept it and enjoy it. Now, he who takes this to heart, and believes it to be true, has it; whereas he who does not believe, has it not, for he allows it to be offered to him in vain, and cannot enjoy the gracious blessing. The blessing is opened to us and at every one's door, yes, on every one's table; still it is necessary that thou accept it and believe it faithfully, as given by the words. This is all that is required by a Christian, to prepare him for receiving the Sacrament worthily. For since this blessing is offered in the words, we cannot grasp or accept it otherwise than with our hearts; with our hand we could not grasp such a gift and everlasting blessing. Fasting, praying, etc., may perhaps serve as an outward preparation, and a discipline for the simple, so that our body be kept chaste and reverent towards the body and blood of Christ; but that which is given in and with it cannot be comprehended or obtained by our body. But the faith of the heart does it, as it recognises the blessing, and desires it." [1]

In his other writings Luther continuously maintains the same general position, that the continued existence of the bread and wine is consistent with the presence of our Lord's body and blood in them, that this presence of Christ is independent of the state and motives of the communicants who receive the Sacrament, that

[1] *Der grosser Catechismus* (*Werke*, Erlangen edition, xxi. 141-44, 146, 147); Wace and Buchheim, *op. cit.* pp. 143, 144, 145, 148.

the benefits of reception can be gained only through faith, and that the presence is a promise of the spiritual benefit which faith gains rather than a means of conveying it.

In 1523 Luther appears to have held that, while his doctrine of the presence of Christ in the Sacrament might logically be thought to imply a duty of adoring our Lord therein present, yet, since the purpose of the institution of the Sacrament is Communion, it is diverted from its proper purpose so far as adoration is made prominent. His two lines of thought may be seen in the following passage from his treatise *On the Adoration of the Sacrament*, which was published in 1523.

" He who does not believe that Christ is present in the Sacrament with His body and blood does rightly if he does not adore either with his spirit or with his body. But he who believes this— and it has been shown superabundantly that we ought so to believe —cannot possibly without sin deny reverence to the flesh and blood of Christ. For I must acknowledge that Christ is there present where His body and blood are present; His words tell me no lie and He cannot in any way be separated from His body and blood. . . . There is a difference between Christ sitting on high in heaven and His being present here in the Sacrament and in the hearts of the faithful. Certainly He ascended into heaven for this purpose, that we may adore Him there, and acknowledge that He is Lord over all things.[1] But in the Sacrament and in the hearts of the faithful He is properly present not for this purpose, that He wishes to be adored there, but that He may act with us and help us, as also He came to earth in the flesh, not that He should be adored, but to minister to us, as He Himself said, 'I have not come to be ministered unto, but to minister, and to give My life for many'.[2] . . . We are of opinion that those ought not to be condemned as heretics who do not adore the Sacrament. For this was not commanded, neither is Christ present for this purpose. Moreover, the Apostles are not recorded to have adored; for the bread and wine were given to them as they were reclining. But on the other hand, neither are those who adore the Sacrament to be condemned as heretics. For, although Christ did not command this, yet neither did He forbid it. Therefore either course may be adopted." [3]

---

[1] Phil. ii. 9-11.   [2] St. Matt. xx. 28 ; St. Mark x. 45.

[3] *Vom Anbeten des Sacraments des heiligen Leichnams Christi* (*Werke*, Erlangen edition, xxviii. 408-10).

Luther's retention of the ceremony of the elevation of the
consecrated Sacrament till 1544 does not tend in an opposite
direction from the passage which has just been quoted, when the
retention is viewed in the light of his allusion to the elevation in
1520 in his treatise *On the Babylonish Captivity of the Church*,
the reason given for retaining it in 1523 in his *Form of Mass and
Communion*, his opinion expressed in 1542 that this ceremony
was an indifferent action of no doctrinal importance, and his defence of the omission of it in 1545. In the treatise *On the Babylonish Captivity of the Church* he wrote, with reference to the
elevation prescribed in the canon of the Mass :—

"Since all these gifts were sanctified by the word and prayer
after the Hebrew rite, in accordance with which they were lifted on
high, as we read in Moses, the words and the practice of elevation,
or of offering, continued in the Church long after the custom had
died out of collecting and bringing together the gifts which were
offered or elevated. . . . For the same reason the priest elevates
the bread and the cup as soon as he has consecrated them ; but the
proof that he is not therein offering anything to God is that in no
single word does he make mention of a victim or an oblation. This
too is a remnant of the Hebrew rite, according to which it was customary to elevate the gifts which, after being received with giving
of thanks, were brought back to God. Or it may be considered as
an admonition to us, to call forth our faith in that testament which
Christ on that occasion brought forward and set 'before us, and also
as a display of its sign. . . . The priest ought to call forth our faith
by the very rite of elevation." [1]

In his *Form of Mass and Communion* of 1523 he wrote :—

"The bread and the cup are to be elevated, this ceremony being
still maintained for the sake of the weak, who might perhaps be
offended by a sudden change in this notable ceremony in the Mass,
especially when they have been taught by popular discourse what
is to be sought for at this elevation." [2]

In 1542, two years before he ceased to use the ceremony, he
wrote :—

[1] *Opera Latina*, Frankfort edition, v. 51, 52 ; Wace and Buchheim,
op. cit. pp. 335, 336.
[2] Sehling, *Die evangelischen Kirchenordnungen des sechszehnten Jahrhunderts*, i. (1) 6 ; *Opera Latina*, Frankfort edition, vii. 9.

" As to the elevation of the Sacrament, do what you like. In no such matter will I lay a snare for any one. So I write and have written and will write to all those who are vexing me with this question every day." [1]

In 1545 in his *Short Confession about the Holy Sacrament* he wrote with reference to the abandonment of the practice of elevation :—

" I hear it said that some people are moved to think that we are at one with the fanatics because we have given up and ceased to practise the elevation in our churches, as if we admitted that the body and blood of Christ are not in the Sacrament, and are not received with the mouth. But the matter stands thus. It is now twenty or twenty-two years since I began to condemn the Mass and made a strong assault on the papists, contending that the Mass is not an offering or a work of ours, but a gift and boon or testament of God, which we cannot offer to God, but must receive from God. . . . At that time I had it in mind to abolish the elevation because of the papists, who make of it an offering and a work offered by us to God, and have observed it in this way for over six hundred years. But, because at that time our doctrine was new, and was beyond measure scandalous to the whole world, I was obliged to act gently, and for the sake of the weak to leave much which I afterwards changed. So also the elevation was left, since it is capable of a good explanation, as I wrote in my little book *On the Babylonish Captivity*." [2]
Then, after saying that he would have abandoned the practice of elevation at an earlier date but for the false charge of Carlstadt and others that by retaining it he allowed that the Mass is a sacrifice, and that in it Christ is crucified and slain, Luther added :—

" The only reason why we have given up the elevation is this : For a long time most of the Churches have given up the elevation ; and therefore we have wished to be in union with them as to this, and that there may not be a difference on such a matter, which in itself is free and can be kept or left without any injury to the conscience." [3]

The consideration of these statements makes it clear that, while he retained the ceremony of elevation, Luther did not

---

[1] Letter of November 10, 1542, *Briefe*, v. 507 (ed. de Wette).

[2] *Kurzes Bekenntniss vom heiligen Sacrament* (*Werke*, Erlangen edition, xxxii. 420, 421).

[3] *Op. cit.* xxxii. 423.

intend thereby to commit either the ministers who used it or the congregation to adoration.

Luther's contention that the presence of the body and blood of Christ in the consecrated elements does not require the cessation of the existence of the bread and wine was to a large extent connected with the views about place developed by the Scotist theologians.[1] Some parts of his teaching would seem to imply that he regarded the presence as being of the body of Christ in its natural state and after a natural manner, a doctrine rejected by all schools of mediæval theologians.[2] He rejects as inadequate a view that the Eucharist affords a participation in the spiritual body of Christ;[3] and his use of language closely resembling that in the declaration imposed on Berengar by the Council of Rome of 1059[4] is, in all the circumstances of his history, somewhat difficult to account for, if he were intending to reject the carnal view which many have thought to be expressed by that language. Thus, in 1528 he maintained that it had been right to force Berengar to acknowledge that the real body of Christ is crushed by the teeth;[5] and he wrote in 1534 :—

" This is the sum of our opinion, that the body of Christ is really eaten in and with the bread, so that all which the bread does and suffers, the body of Christ does and suffers, so that it is divided and is eaten and is bitten with the teeth."[6]

On the other hand, he used language in 1527 and 1534 which appears to tend in an opposite direction. In 1527 he wrote :—

" We . . . are not so foolish as to believe that the body of Christ is present in the bread in the gross visible manner in which bread is in the basket, or wine in the cup, as the fanatics would lay to our charge " ;[7]

and in 1534 he wrote :—

[1] See vol. i. p. 340, vol. ii. pp. 10, 11, *supra*.

[2] See vol. i. pp. 316, 320, 331, 340, *supra*.

[3] *Vom Anbeten des Sacraments* (*Werke*, Erlangen edition, xxviii. 392-401).

[4] See vol. i. p. 247, *supra*.

[5] *Bekenntniss von Abendmahl Christi* (*Werke*, Erlangen edition, xxx. 297).

[6] Instruction to Melanchthon, 17th December, 1534, *Briefe*, iv. 572 (ed. de Wette).

[7] *Dass diese Worte Christi, Das ist mein Leib noch fest stehen wider die Schwarmgeister* (*Werke*, Erlangen edition, xxx. 65, 66).

"We hold that Christ is present with the bread in the Sacrament not only by way of operation. . . . We hold that Christ is present with the bread not only according to His Godhead. We hold that the body and blood of Christ are present with the bread and wine in the Sacrament by way of substance or essence. The fundamental point in the contrary opinion is this, that the body of Christ must be in one place locally, that is, by way of dimensions, and cannot be in any other way than locally, that is, by way of dimensions, and therefore the body cannot be at the same time in more places than one ; and also that it is impossible for the body to be present to several different bodies which are not in the same place, which also are not themselves together. In opposition to this, we hold that the body of Christ must not be in one place only locally, that is, by way of dimensions, but we hold that the body of Christ can also be at the same time in other ways in more places than one ; and we hold that the body and blood of Christ are really and substantially present in other places and bodies, where it is guaranteed that they are, than with the bread and wine in the Sacrament. And it is not true that the body of Christ cannot be in any other way than locally, that is, by way of dimensions. We hold also that, by virtue of this union, the body of Christ is present with the bread and wine in the Sacrament, although unworthy persons use and eat the Sacrament." [1]

It was partly in connection with the doctrine of the Eucharist that Luther developed his theory of the ubiquity of our Lord's body. His argument was that wherever Christ is as God, there He is also as Man ; that where He is as Man, there is His manhood ; that where His manhood is, there must His body be ; and that therefore, since He is everywhere present as God, His body must be present everywhere. Consequently, the uniqueness of the Eucharistic presence is not that the body of Christ is in the consecrated elements, for it is in every material thing, but that it is there sacramentally for special purposes under the promise of Christ. In 1528 he wrote :—

"The body of Christ can sit at the table and nevertheless be in the bread, as also He can be in heaven and wherever He wills and nevertheless in the bread. There is no barrier far or near to prevent Him from being at the table and at the same time in the bread. . . . Wherever God is present to me, there must His man-

---

[1] Memorandum of December 1534, *Briefe*, iv. 573 (ed. de Wette).

hood be present to me. . . . The manhood is more closely united with God than our skin with our flesh or our soul with our body. . . . He is God and Man, one Person, and the two natures are more closely united with one another than body and soul, so that Christ must be also as Man wherever He is as God. He is as God and Man in one place : does it therefore follow that He is not as Man and God also in another place ? He is as Man and God also in another place : does it therefore follow that He is not in a third and a fourth and a fifth and in every place ? " [1]

" It is a sacramental unity that the body of Christ and bread are given us in the Sacrament; it is not a natural or personal unity. . . . Where is the bread, there is the body of Christ." [2]

And in 1539 he wrote :—

" What is there absurd in believing that the body of Christ is at the same time in heaven and in the Sacrament ? Is that which seems to us incredible difficult to Almighty God ? In the third chapter of St. John it is said, ' No man hath ascended into heaven, but He that descended out of heaven, even the Son of man, which is in heaven '.[3] If then He was in heaven when He walked on earth, how shall He not be at the same time in different places ? If this is incredible to any one, how will he believe that God is Man ? How should true God be at the same time essentially in the Virgin's womb ? How should one Person of the wholly simple Godhead become incarnate without the Others ? . . . It is reason which demands that the same body cannot be in different places. But reason is blind ; and what is impossible to it is most easy to God. I have not the same body in heaven and on earth ; but what am I ? I have not a great body in a little particle of bread ; but who am I ? Nothing is impossible to God." [4]

It was not unnatural that from the view of a sacramental presence of the ubiquitous body and blood of Christ in the bread and wine for the purpose of Communion Luther should develop a theory limiting this sacramental presence to the time of the administration of the Sacrament ; and this theory, which was an important part of the belief of the later Lutherans, was expressed by him with some care in a letter written in 1543, in which he says :—

[1] *Bekentniss von Abendmahl Christi* (*Werke*, Erlangen edition, xxx. 199, 212, 222).

[2] *Op. cit.* xxx. 297.   [3] St. John iii. 13.

[4] Letter of 7th August, 1539, *Briefe*, v. 199 (ed. de Wette).

"Certainly Dr. Philip[1] has written rightly that there is no Sacrament outside the sacramental action ; but you define the sacramental action too sharply and abruptly. Wherefore you will bring it to pass that you will seem to have no Sacrament at all. For, if that excessive limitation of the action hold good, it will follow that after the utterance of the words, which is the chief and principal action in the Sacrament, no one will receive the body and blood of Christ because the action has ceased. This certainly Dr. Philip does not wish. And that definition of the action would produce boundless scruples of conscience and endless questions, like the discussion of the papists whether the body and blood of Christ are present at the first or the middle or the last syllables. . . . We will define the time or sacramental action as beginning from the beginning of the Lord's Prayer,[2] and lasting until all have communicated and they have emptied the cup and consumed the particles and the people have been dismissed and the departure from the altar has taken place. So we shall be safe and free from the scruples and scandals of endless questions. Dr. Philip defines the sacramental action in relation to what is external, that is, against the reservation and carrying about of the Sacrament ; he does not divide it within itself or define it against itself. Wherefore you must take care that whatever is left of the Sacrament be received either by some of the communicants or by the priest and minister himself, not that the deacon alone or some other simply drink what is left in the chalice, but that he give to others who also have partaken of the body, lest you should seem to set a bad example and divide the Sacrament or to handle the sacramental action irreverently. Such is my opinion, and such also is Philip's, I know."[3]

III.

The authoritative documents drawn up by the early Lutherans contain much the same Eucharistic doctrine as that in the writings of Luther himself. The articles of the Conference held at Marburg in October, 1529, will be considered later.[4] In 1530

---

[1] That is, Philip Melanchthon (Schwarzerd, born at Bretten in Baden in 1497, died at Wittenberg in 1560).

[2] In Luther's " Form of Mass and Communion " the recital of the institution was followed by the Sanctus with the Benedictus, during which the elevation took place, and the Lord's Prayer was then said. See Sehling, *Die evangelischen Kirchenordnungen des sechzehnten Jahrhunderts*, i. (1) 6 ; *Opera Latina*, Frankfort edition, vii. 9.

[3] Letter of 20th July, 1543, *Briefe*, v. 577, 578 (ed. de Wette).

[4] See p. 43, *infra*.

the Emperor Charles V. ordered the Lutheran princes to present a statement of their belief at a Diet to be held at Augsburg. Partly as a result of this command and partly in consequence of the need felt by the Lutheran teachers of some such document, the *Confession of Augsburg* was drawn up by Melanchthon, who utilised in the composition of it the articles of the Marburg Conference and the Schwabach Conference both held in October, 1529, and of the Torgau Conference held in March, 1530.[1] This *Confession* was sent to Luther for revision, and he expressed his approval of it in a letter dated 15th May, 1530.[2] On 25th June, 1530, it was read aloud at the Diet of Augsburg; and it was signed on 23rd August by John, Elector of Saxony; George, Margrave of Brandenburg; Ernest, Duke of Lueneburg; Philip, Landgrave of Hesse; John Frederick, Electoral Prince of Saxony; Francis, Duke of Lueneburg; Wolfgang, Prince of Anhalt; the Senate and Magistracy of Nuremberg; and the Senate of Reutlingen. The tenth article of the *Confession* was entitled "Concerning the Lord's Supper". It stated, according to the Latin text of the *Confession* :—

"Concerning the Lord's Supper they teach that the body and blood of Christ are really present, and are distributed to those who eat in the Lord's Supper; and they disapprove of those who teach otherwise." [3]

In the German text this statement is more explicit :—

"Concerning the Lord's Supper they teach that the real body and blood of Christ are really present under the form of bread and wine in the Lord's Supper, and are distributed and received. Wherefore also the opposite doctrine is rejected." [4]

In an Appendix on the Amendment of Abuses, the first article gave as the reasons for the reception of Communion in both kinds that the Sacrament had been so instituted by our Lord; that it had been so used in the time of St. Paul; and that it had been so received for a long time in the Church.[5] The

---

[1] The articles of Marburg, Schwabach, and Torgau are in Bretschneider and Bindseil, *Corpus Reformatorum*, xxvi. 122-200.

[2] *Briefe*, iv. 17 (ed. de Wette).

[3] Francke, *Libri Symbolici Ecclesiæ Lutheranæ*, i. 16.

[4] Bretschneider and Bindseil, *Corp. Reform.* xxvi. 559; Heppe, *Die Bekenntnisschriften der altprotestantischen Kirche Deutschlands*, p. 25.

[5] Francke, *Lib. Symb. Eccl. Luth.* i. 26, 27.

third article was headed "Concerning the Mass". It contained the following statements:—

"Our churches are falsely accused of abolishing the Mass. For the Mass is retained among us, and is celebrated with the greatest reverence. Moreover, almost all the customary ceremonies are preserved, except that in some places, in order to teach the people, we have added to what is sung in Latin some things sung in German. . . . It does not appear that Masses are more religiously celebrated among our adversaries than among us. But it is clear that for a long time this has been the public and much the most important complaint of all good men, that Masses are basely profaned by being used for gain. . . . Therefore, when the priests among us were admonished of this sin, private Masses were discontinued among us, since scarcely any private Masses had been celebrated except for gain. . . . There was added an opinion, which increased private Masses infinitely, that Christ by His passion satisfied for original sin, and appointed the Mass in which an offering should be made for daily sins, both mortal and venial. From this came a common opinion that the Mass is a work blotting out the sins of the living and the dead by the fact of its being offered (*ex opere operato*). As a result men began to discuss whether one Mass said for many people was of as great force as particular Masses said for particular persons. This discussion brought forth that infinite multitude of Masses. Concerning these opinions we have taught that they differ from Holy Scripture and injure the glory of the passion of Christ. For the passion of Christ was an offering and satisfaction not only for original sin but also for all other sins. . . . Also Scripture teaches that we are justified before God through faith in Christ, when we believe that our sins are forgiven for the sake of Christ. If the Mass blots out the sins of the living and the dead by the fact of its being offered (*ex opere operato*), then justification takes place by the work of Masses, not by faith, which Scripture does not allow. But Christ commands to 'do in remembrance of' Himself;[1] wherefore the Mass was instituted that faith in those who use the Sacrament may recollect the benefits received through Christ, and may raise and console the timid conscience. For this is to remember Christ, to remember His benefits and to perceive that they are really presented to us. Nor is it enough to recollect the history; because even the Jews and the wicked can recollect this. The Mass then is to be celebrated for this purpose, that in it the Sacrament may be given to those who have need of com-

[1] St. Luke xxii. 19.

fort. . . . And, since the Mass is such a giving of the Sacrament, one common Mass is kept up among us on all holy days and also on other days if any wish to use the Sacrament, and at these times the Sacrament is given to those who desire it." [1]

In December, 1536, partly with a view to negotiations with the adherents of the Pope, Luther drew up a series of articles which, after being submitted to Melanchthon and other Lutherans for their approval, was sent to the Elector of Saxony in January, 1537, and was subsequently signed by Luther and Melanchthon and other Lutheran theologians at Schmalkalden, in Thuringia, and became known as the *Articles of Schmalkalden*. The sixth of these articles was headed " Concerning the Sacrament of the Altar," and was as follows :—

" Concerning the Sacrament of the altar we are of opinion that the bread and wine in the Supper are the real body and blood of Christ, and they are given and taken not only by pious but also by impious Christians. And not one species only is to be given. For we do not need that far-fetched idea which maintains that under one species is as much as under both, as the sophists and the Council of Constance [2] teach. For, although it may perhaps be true that there is as much under one species as under both, yet one species is not the whole of what was ordained and instituted by Christ, and handed down and commanded. . . . We care nothing for the subtle sophistry concerning Transubstantiation, whereby they pretend that the bread and wine leave and lose their natural substance, and that only the species and colour of bread, and not real bread, remain. For it is most in agreement with Holy Scripture that the bread is present and remains, as Paul himself uses the word, ' the bread which we break,' and ' So let him eat of the bread '." [3]

In 1540, ten years after the first drawing up of the *Confession of Augsburg*, this *Confession* was revised by Melanchthon, partly as an attempt to find a means of agreement between the Lutherans and the followers of Zwingli. In this new edition the tenth article was modified so as to be :—

" Concerning the Lord's Supper they teach that together with the bread and wine the body and blood of Christ are really presented (*exhibeantur*) to those who eat in the Lord's Supper." [4]

[1] Francke, *Lib. Symb. Eccl. Luth.* i. 29-31.
[2] See Hardouin, *Conc.* viii. 381.
[3] Francke, *Lib. Symb. Eccl. Luth.* ii. 32, 33.   See 1 Cor. x. 16, xi. 28.
[4] Francke, *op. cit.* iv. 8.

In this altered form of the articles there were four important changes. The express assertion " together with the bread and wine " was added. The declaration "the body and blood of Christ are really present " was omitted. The statement that the body and blood of Christ " are distributed to those who eat in the Lord's Supper " was altered to a statement that they " are really presented to those who eat in the Lord's Supper," apparently to avoid what was held to be an assertion that the body and blood of Christ are given in the Sacrament to those who communicate unworthily as well as to those who communicate worthily. The words " they disapprove of those who teach otherwise " were omitted.

In the Appendix on the Amendment of Abuses in the *Confession of Augsburg* as revised in 1540 the section " Concerning the Mass " followed in an enlarged form the lines adopted in 1530. The passages in the original section on the retention of the Mass were little altered. The part relating to the theological ideas which had underlain the increase in the number of private Masses was modified so as to be in the following form :—

"We will point out whence those abuses arose. An opinion became prevalent in the Church that the Lord's Supper is a work, which being celebrated by a priest merits remission of sins and of guilt and of penalty to him who does it and to others, and this by the fact of its being offered (*ex opere operato*) without any good intention on the part of him who uses it. Also, that when applied on behalf of the dead it is a satisfaction, that is, it merits for them remission of the penalties of purgatory. So they interpret the sacrifice when they call the Mass a sacrifice, namely, to be a work, which when applied on behalf of others merits for them remission of guilt and of penalties, and this by the fact of its being offered (*ex opere operato*) without any good intention on the part of him who uses it. So they interpret that an offering is made by the priest in the Mass for the living and the dead. This notion being accepted, they went on to teach men to seek for remission of sins and good things of every kind, and to free the dead from penalties, by the benefit of the Mass. Nor did it make any difference by what kind of people the Masses were offered, because they taught that the Masses benefited others without any good intention on the part of the user. Then the question was debated whether one Mass said for many people was of as great benefit as particular Masses said for particular persons. This discussion increased infinitely the number and gain of Masses. But we are not now discussing the question of gain ; we are making an accusation of impiety. For we teach that this opinion about the merit and application of the Mass is false and impious. This is the position of this controversy. And a judgment on this matter is easy for pious people, if any one will weigh the arguments which follow. First, we have shown above that men obtain remission of sins freely by faith, that is, by confidence in mercy for the sake of Christ. Therefore it is impossible to obtain remission of sins because of the work of another, and indeed without any good intention, that is, without faith of one's own. This reason refutes clearly enough that monstrous and impious opinion about the merit and application of the Mass. Secondly, the passion of Christ was an offering and satisfaction not only for original guilt but also for all other sins. . . . This honour of the sacrifice of Christ ought not to be transferred to the work of a priest. . . . It is impious to transfer the confidence, which ought to rest on the offering and intercession of the High Priest Christ, to the work of a priest. Thirdly, in the institution of the Lord's Supper Christ does not command that priests offer for others living and dead. By what authority then has this rite been instituted in the Church without the command of God as an offering for sins ? It is much more absurd that the Mass is applied to freeing the souls of the dead. For the Mass was instituted to be a recollection, that is, that those who use the Lord's Supper may by the recollection of the benefit of Christ stablish and strengthen their faith and comfort their terrified consciences. Nor is the Mass a satisfaction for penalty, but it was instituted for the sake of remission of guilt, that is, not that it may be a satisfaction for guilt, but that it may be a Sacrament by the use of which we may be kept in mind of the benefit of Christ and the remission of guilt. . . . Fourthly, in the New Testament a ceremony without faith merits nothing either for him who performs it or for others. . . . Therefore the Mass does not merit remission of guilt or penalty by the fact of its being offered (*ex opere operato*). Fifthly, the application of the benefit of Christ takes place through one's own faith. . . . And this application takes place freely. Therefore no application of it takes place by the work of another or because of the work of another. . . . Sixthly, the institution of the Sacrament is against this abuse. For nothing is ordered about an offering for the sins of the living and the dead ; but it is ordered that the body and blood of the Lord be taken, and that this be done for the recollection of the benefit of Christ. Now the recollection signifies not only some representation of the history as in a show, as those dream who defend merit from the fact of the offering (*ex opere operato*); but it signifies the recollection by faith of the promise and benefit, the comforting of the conscience, and the giving of thanks for so great a benefit.   For the chief reason for the institution is that faith may there be aroused and exercised when we receive this pledge of grace.   Besides, the institution provides that there be the administration, that is, that the ministers of the Church give to others also the body and blood of the Lord." [1]

Like the writings of Luther himself, this statement in the revised form of the *Confession of Augsburg* appears to deny the Eucharistic sacrifice in any ordinary sense as well as to clear away perverted ideas about it.   And the sentence " The chief reason for the institution is that faith may be aroused and exercised when we receive this pledge of grace " seems to be an acceptance of one of the most puzzling elements in the teaching of Luther, the apparent dissociation of any grace from that which is received in the Sacrament in spite of the concurrent strong emphasis that the consecrated Sacrament is the body of Christ.

In 1551 an adaptation of the *Confession of Augsburg* was made by Melanchthon, with a view to its presentation to the Council of Trent, and was entitled the *Saxon Confession*.   It represents substantially the same position as the *Confession of Augsburg*.   The most noticeable features in it are an explanation of the sense in which the Eucharistic rite as a whole is regarded as sacrificial and the pains taken to emphasise the limitation of the sacramental character of the elements to their use in the service.   In a statement in the preface on the abuses which the Lutherans were repudiating it is said :—

" Very many sacrificing priests read and offer Masses, as they say, in complete ignorance of what they are doing; they only follow custom and serve their belly.   Other superstitious men, who think more about this work of theirs, pretend that they perform a work necessary to the whole Church, which merits remission of sins for him who performs it and for others.   Afterwards comes in the snatching at the greatest gain, sacrifices are offered for the dead, and the churches are more filled with funeral ceremonies than with the sound of sermons or the devotions of the living.   Nor are the people rightly taught about the use of the Sacrament among our

[1] Francke, *op. cit.* iv. 20-22.

opponents, because the monks teach that those who partake receive
from the performance of the work (*ex opere operato*), as they say,
remission of sins ; and one part of the Sacrament is taken away from
the people, ánd the other part is carried about outside the ordained
use, and is adored contrary to the nature (*rationem*) of the Sacrament ;
and many false opinions are added. They say nothing about the
righteousness of faith and about the right use of the Sacraments,
which are not merits but are testimonies confirming faith." [1]

In the section entitled " Concerning the Lord's Supper " the most
important parts relating to the use of the Sacrament and to the
sacrifice are the following :—

"That there may be greater reverence in the use of this Sacrament, the real reasons of the institution are to be considered, which
pertain to the public congregation and to the comfort of individuals. The first reason is : the Son of God wishes the sound of the
Gospel to be heard in a public and honourable congregation. The
bond of this congregation He wishes to be this reception, which
must be with the greatest reverence, since there is shown the testimony of the wonderful association of the Lord and of those who receive. . . . The second reason is that He wishes the assembly and
the rite itself to be beneficial for the preservation and propagation
of the memory of the passion and the resurrection and of His benefits. The third reason is that He wishes each one who receives to
establish individually by this testimony that he determines that the
benefits of the Gospel pertain to him, since the discourse is common ;
and by this testimony, by this reception, He shows that you are His
own member, and that you ·have been washed by His blood, and
that He makes this covenant, ' Abide in Me, and I in you,' and ' I in
them, and Thou in Me '.[2]   The fourth reason is that He wishes this
public reception to be a confession, whereby you may show that you
accept the kind of doctrine of the assembly to which you join your-
self; He wishes also that thanks be given publicly and privately in
this ceremony itself to God the eternal Father and to the Son and
to the Holy Ghost both for all other benefits and especially for the
immeasurable benefit of redemption and salvation ; He wishes also
that the members of the Church themselves may have a bond of
mutual kindness with one another. . . . We openly condemn the
monstrous error of the monks, who wrote that the reception merits
remission of sins, and this from the performance of the work (*ex
opere operato*) without any good intention on the part of the user.

[1] Francke, *op. cit.* iv. 72.   [2] St. John xv. 4, xvii. 23.

. . . We exhort also that men are not to think that because of this
work or this obedience sins are remitted, but that confidence-may
behold the death and merits of the Son of God and His resurrection,
and may determine that our sins are remitted for His sake and that
He wishes this faith to be confirmed by this remembrance and witness.
. . . Also men are taught that the Sacraments are actions ordained
by God, and that the things themselves have not the nature (*rationem*)
of a Sacrament outside the ordained use ; but that in the ordained
use Christ is really and substantially present in this Communion,
and that the body and blood of Christ are really presented (*exhiberi*)
to those who receive ; and that Christ bears witness that He is in
them and makes them His members, and that He has washed them
by His blood. . . . And since a rite outside the ordained use has
not the nature (*rationem*) of a Sacrament, let the devout and learned
consider what a service of idols takes place there [*i.e.* among the
opponents of the Lutherans]. It is also clear sacrilege to carry about
and adore part of the Lord's Supper, where in truth a part is put to
a use wholly different from that for which it was ordained." [1]

"Many before this time have written that there is an offering
in the Mass for the living and the dead, and that it merits for him
who offers it and for others remission of sins from the performance
of the work (*ex opere operato*). . . . We simply and truly set out the
word of God, which condemns those errors, and we affirm with all
our heart in the presence of God and the whole Church in heaven
and in earth that there is only one propitiatory sacrifice or sacrifice
whereby the wrath of the eternal Father towards the human race
was appeased, that is, the complete obedience of the Son of God,
our Lord Jesus Christ, crucified and risen. . . . And this sacrifice is
applied to individuals by their own faith, when they hear the
Gospel and use the Sacraments. . . . The ancient Church uses the
words sacrifice and offering, but thereby understands the whole
action, prayer, reception, recollection, faith, confession, and thanksgiving. This whole inner and outer action, in one converted
to God, and in the whole Church, is in very truth a sacrifice of
praise, or Eucharistic, and a reasonable service. . . . Certain persons are now craftily learning to lessen the absurdity. They say
that the offering is not merit but application ; they form plots by
means of words, and keep the same abuses. But I have already
said that each one applies to himself the sacrifice of Christ by his
faith both when he hears the Gospel and when he uses the Sacraments. . . . What then do the sacrificing priests now understand

[1] Francke, *op. cit.* iv. 94, 95, 97.

who say that they offer Christ? Antiquity did not so speak. They accuse us most savagely, and say that we destroy the continual sacrifice, as did Antiochus,[1] who is a type of Anti-Christ. We have already made answer that we retain the whole rite of the Church of the Apostles. And it is a continual sacrifice to proclaim the uncorrupted doctrine of the Gospel and to call on God rightly ; lastly, as the Lord says, to ' worship the Father in spirit and in truth '.[2] Here also we hold fast the right use of the Sacraments. Since we preserve all these things most faithfully, we preserve with the greatest reverence the continual sacrifice." [3]

About the same time as the formation of the *Saxon Confession*, the *Wurtemberg Confession* was drawn up by John Brenz, also for the purpose of presentation to the Council of Trent. The teaching contained in it closely resembles that in the *Saxon Confession*. The nineteenth article is on the Eucharist. Emphasis is laid on the continued existence of real bread and wine in the consecrated Sacrament and on the presence of the real body and blood of Christ. The Eucharist is allowed to be a sacrifice in a general sense, as a memorial of Christ's death, and as a means of applying the merits of His passion to communicants.

" Concerning the substance of the Eucharist, we believe and teach that the real body of Christ and His real blood are given ; and we reject the teaching of those who say that the bread and wine of the Eucharist are only the signs of the absent body and blood of Christ. We believe also that the almighty power of God is so great that He is able in the Eucharist to annihilate the substance of bread and wine, or to change it into the body and blood of Christ. But that God uses in the Eucharist this absolute almighty power of His does not seem to be declared in the certain word of God ; and it appears to have been unknown to the ancient Church. . . . When it is said of the bread, ' This is My body,' it is not necessary that the substance of the bread be changed into the substance of the substance of the body of Christ ; but it suffices to the reality of the Sacrament that the body of Christ be really present together with the bread, and therefore the very necessity of the reality of the Sacrament seems to require that real bread remains together with the real presence of the body of Christ."

" Since the word sacrifice is capable of very wide meaning, and signifies a holy worship in general, we willingly grant that the right

[1] See Dan. viii. 11, xi. 31 ; 1 Macc. i. 41-50.
[2] St. John iv. 23.   [3] Francke, *op. cit.* iv. 95-97.

and lawful use of the Eucharist may in this sense be called a sacrifice. And, if the Eucharist be celebrated according to Christ's
ordinance in such a way that the death of Christ is proclaimed
therein, and the Sacrament of Christ's body and blood dispensed to
the Church, it is rightly called an application of the merit of Christ's
passion, to them, that is, who receive the Sacrament. . . . Another
error is that the Eucharist is a sacrifice of such a kind that it ought
to be continually offered in the Church to expiate the sins of the
living and the dead, and to obtain for them other benefits both
bodily and spiritual. . . . Another error is that some think the
oblation, as they call it, not indeed to be in itself a propitiation
for sins, but to apply the propitiation and merit of Christ to the
living and dead. But it has been shown that the Eucharist is not
properly an oblation but is so called because it is a memorial of the
oblation once offered on the cross. Again the application of the
merit of Christ is not made by any other external instrument than
the preaching of the Gospel of Christ and the administration of the
Sacraments which Christ instituted for this purpose. And the merit
of Christ which is offered and applied is received only by faith.
. . . Another error is the carrying about and reserving of one
part of the Eucharist for the special worship of God. The Holy
Ghost forbids the institution of any worship of God without the
certain command of God. . . . It is clear that the bread which is
carried about and reserved for adoration is not reserved for the sick
but is at last consumed by those who consecrate it." [1]

In consequence of the controversies with the adherents of
the Pope, with the more extreme Reformers, and among the
Lutherans themselves, the *Formula of Concord* was drawn up in
1577, as a result of long and difficult negotiations. It was the
work of Martin Chemnitz of Brunswick, an eminent theologian,
a pupil of Melanchthon; Nicholas Selnecker of Leipsic, also a
follower of Melanchthon; Jacob Andreæ, Professor of Theology
and Chancellor of the University at Tuebingen, a pupil of Brenz;
Christopher Koerner, Professor of Theology at Frankfort on the
Oder, a follower of Melanchthon; David Chytraeus, Professor of
Theology at Rostock, a follower of Melanchthon; and Andreas
Musculus, Professor of Theology at Frankfort on the Oder, an
opponent of Melanchthon in those matters, chiefly relating to the
Incarnation, in which Melanchthon and Luther were opposed to

---

[1] Heppe, *Die Bekenntnisschriften der altprotestantischen Kirche Deutschlands*, pp. 514-20.

one another. In 1580 the *Formula of Concord* was published by
order of Augustus, Elector of Saxony, in the *Book of Concord*,
together with the Apostles' Creed, the enlarged Nicene Creed,
the Athanasian Creed, the *Confession of Augsburg*, Melanchthon's
Apology for the Confession of Augsburg, the *Articles of Schmalkalden*, and Luther's two *Catechisms*. In spite of this attempt to
place the *Formula of Concord* in the position of an authorised
Lutheran statement of doctrine, it was much attacked, and it never
attained to the authority of the *Confession of Augsburg*.[1] Its
teaching about the Eucharist, however, except in regard to the
ubiquity of the human nature of Christ, may be taken as representative of the Lutheranism of the time. The most important
parts of this teaching are the following :—

"We believe, teach, and confess that in the Lord's Supper the
body and blood of Christ are really and substantially present, and
that they are really distributed and taken together with the bread
and wine ; . . . that the bread does not signify the absent body of
Christ, and the wine the absent blood of Christ, but that on account
of the sacramental union the bread and wine are really the body
and blood of Christ ; . . . that the right hand of God is everywhere,
and that Christ, in respect of His manhood, is really and actually
seated thereat ; . . . that God knows and has in His power various
ways in which He can be any where, and is not limited to that single
way which philosophers usually call local or circumscribed ; . . .
that the body and blood of Christ are taken, together with the bread
and wine, not only spiritually through faith but also by the mouth,
yet not Capernaitically but after a supernatural and heavenly manner
by reason of the sacramental union ; . . . that not only those who
really believe in Christ and approach the Lord's Supper worthily but
also the unworthy and unbelieving take the real body and blood of
Christ, in such wise, nevertheless, that they receive thence neither
comfort nor life but rather that the reception turns to them for judgment and condemnation unless they are converted and penitent ;
. . . that no one who really believes, so long as he keeps a living
faith, takes the Holy Supper of the Lord to judgment, whatever be
the weakness of faith under which he labours ; . . . that the whole
worthiness of the guests at this heavenly Supper consists alone in
the most holy obedience and the most perfect merit of Christ, and
that we apply this to ourselves by real faith, and are made certain

[1] For a statement as to where the *Formula* was accepted, and where it
was rejected, see Schaff, *History of the Creeds of Christendom*, i. 331.

of the application of this merit and are confirmed in our minds by means of the Sacrament, and that the worthiness in no way depends on our virtues or on our inward or outward preparations." [1]

"We reject and condemn . . . the papistical Transubstantiation, namely, when it is taught among the papists that the bread and wine in the Holy Supper lose their substance and natural essence, and are thus annihilated, and that those elements are so changed into the body of Christ that nothing remains of them except the outward species ; the papistical sacrifice of the Mass, which is offered for the sins of the living and the dead ; . . . that the body of Christ in the Holy Supper is not taken by the mouth together with the bread, but that only bread and wine are received by the mouth, while the body of Christ is taken only spiritually, that is, by faith ; that the bread and wine in the Lord's Supper are only symbols or tokens whereby Christians mutually recognise one another ; that the bread and wine are only figures and similitudes and types of the body and blood of Christ very far absent from us ; . . . that Christ's body is so shut up in heaven that it can in no way whatever be at one and the same time in more places than one or in all the places on earth where the Lord's Supper is celebrated ; . . . that God, even with all His almighty power (a thing fearful to say and hear), cannot effect that the body of Christ be at one and the same time substantially present in more places than one ; . . . that the external and visible elements of bread and wine in the Sacrament are to be adored." [2]

The Saxon *Visitation Articles* were written in 1592 by Aegidius Hunnius, Professor of Theology at Marburg, a leading Lutheran divine, with the assistance of other Lutheran theologians. The acceptance of them was enforced in Saxony on all pastors and teachers and civil officers ; but they were never made a generally authoritative Lutheran document. In regard to the Eucharist, they state the main points of the Lutheran doctrine shortly and clearly in the following article, in which the use of

---

[1] Franke, *op. cit.* iii. 44-47.

[2] *Ibid.* 47-50. See also the expanded explanations in the second part of the *Formula of Concord* in Francke, *op. cit.* iii. 156-87. In this longer statement there is added to the repudiation of the adoration of the elements the explanation, "But that Christ Himself, true God and Man, who is really and substantially present in His Supper, that is, in the right use of it, as He is also in spirit and in truth in all other places, especially where His Church is gathered together, ought to be adored, no one but an Arian heretic would deny " ; see Francke, *op. cit.* iii. 186.

the phrases "natural body" and "natural blood" is of some importance :—

"The words of Christ . . . are to be understood in the simple and literal sense, as they sound. In the Sacrament there are two things, which are presented (*exhibentur*) and received together, the one earthly, which is bread and wine ; the other heavenly, which is the body and blood of Christ. This union and presentation (*exhibitio*) and reception takes place here below on earth, not above in heaven. The real and natural [1] body of Christ, which hung on the cross, and the real and natural blood, which flowed from the side of Christ, are presented (*exhibeatur*) and received. The body and blood of Christ are received in the Supper not only spiritually by faith, which can take place even apart from the Supper, but by the mouth together with the bread and wine, yet after a manner which is inscrutable and supernatural ; and this for a pledge and assurance of the resurrection of our bodies from the dead. The reception of the body and blood of Christ by the mouth is not only by the worthy but also by the unworthy who approach without penitence and real faith, though with different result. For the reception is by the worthy for salvation and by the unworthy for judgment." [2]

IV.

Huldreich Zwingli was a contemporary of Luther. He was born at Wildhaus in the canton of St. Gall in 1484 ; he entered the University of Vienna in 1499 ; after subsequently teaching and continuing his studies at Basle, he was ordained priest and became pastor at Glarus in 1506 ; he was a preacher at Einsiedeln in 1516 ; his preaching in Zurich Cathedral in 1519 and later years attracted much notice ; he was the leader of the Swiss Reformers ; he died in 1531 on the battlefield of Kappel, whither he had accompanied the troops of Zurich. Large parts of his many and lengthy writings are occupied with the Eucharistic controversy. He attacked unsparingly the opinions both of the papal theologians and of Luther. His claim that as a Reformer he was independent of Luther [3] was probably well founded. Like Luther, he dissented from the doctrine of Transubstantiation. To Luther's own view that the body and blood of Christ are present together with the bread and wine he was no less opposed.

[1] See note 2 on p. 66, *infra*.
[2] Francke, *op. cit.* iv. 116, 117.
[3] See, *e.g.*, *Opus Articulorum* (*Opera*, ed. 1581, i. 37, 38).

He interpreted our Lord's words at the institution of the Sacrament as figurative only, and regarded the consecrated elements
as merely symbols of the body and blood of Christ. As a rule
he speaks of the Sacraments as signs only; but there are some
passages in his writings which appear to imply or affirm a spiritual
feeding of the soul on Christ in connection with the reception
of the Sacrament. He rejected any idea of a Eucharistic sacrifice,
and explained the Eucharist as a commemoration, not itself
sacrificial, of the sacrifice of Christ.

The *Book of Articles*, published in 1523, shows an early
form of Zwingli's teaching. The eighteenth article of the series
was :—

"Christ, who offered Himself once for all on the cross, is for
ever the effectual sacrifice and victim for the sins of all the faithful.
From this it follows that the Mass is not a sacrifice but a commemoration of the sacrifice once for all offered on the cross, and as
it were a seal of the redemption afforded in Christ " ;

and in the course of the explanation of this article it was maintained that "the offering of Christ is impaired and blasphemed "
by the saying, "Since we daily sin, it is necessary to offer this
Sacrament of the altar daily "; to say that Christ "is offered "
in the Mass is the same as to say that he "dies" in it; the
Mass is a "testament," a "covenant," and a "commemoration,"
but not a "sacrifice"; it is "a ratifying to the weak that they
have been redeemed through Christ, so that they may be assured of the remission of sins and firmly believe that Christ made
satisfaction for sins on the cross, and in this faith may eat and
drink His body and blood and recognise that His body and
blood have been given to them that they may be assured of the
grace and favour of God"; "when they eat and drink the body
and blood of Christ in faith, their sins are remitted not otherwise than if Christ were now dying on the cross "; "Christ died
and by His death established His testament towards us so as
to give His own flesh for the food and His blood for the drink
of our souls, so that our hope might have here a sure pledge
and a sure sign that after death we also should be made partakers of that inheritance which by His blood He affirmed for
us"; "the blood of Christ is given to us for drink that we
may have a sign that what was once done on the cross holds

good and is effectual for ever "; the bread is "the figure of the body" and the wine is "the figure of the blood"; on the papal view "the blood or the body cannot fall to the ground even if the accidents fall"; "to take or approach unworthily does not mean to take while in a state of sin but to approach not duly, not with that faith which is required from those who are united into the body of Christ, not according to the institution of Christ"; "Christ's body and blood are the food of the soul when the soul firmly believes that the body and blood of Christ are its salvation, pledge, and price of redemption before God"; "the body and blood of Christ are nothing else than the word of faith, namely, that His body which died for us and His blood which was shed for us on the cross redeemed us and reconciled us to God"; "when we firmly believe this, our soul is nourished and refreshed by the body and blood of Christ"; "it ought to be enough for us to believe that Jesus Christ is our redemption, the food and consolation of the soul".[1]

The *Discussion on the Canon of the Mass*, published in 1523, and the *Reply to Emser*, published in 1524, contain the same teaching as that in the *Book of the Articles;* in the *Reply to Emser* it is allowed that "the Eucharist is spiritual food, whereby those who believe that the death of Christ is their life fasten and join and unite themselves mutually into the one body of Christ".[2]

In the treatise *On True and False Religion*, published in 1525, the same doctrine is taught. Noticeable features are the assertion that the ideas of the reception of a body and of eating spiritually are inconsistent with one another; the explanation of the word "is" in the sentence "This is My body" as meaning "signifies"; the denial that the Eucharist is more than a "commemoration" and the eating of a "sign" or "figure"; and the rejection of any other spiritual body of Christ than the Church and the faith of Christians.

"Nor do we think that those are to be heard who say, We indeed eat the real and bodily flesh of Christ, but after a spiritual manner. For they fail to see that to be a body and to be eaten after a spiritual manner are inconsistent with one another; for body

[1] *Opus Articulorum*, on Art. xviii. (*Opera*, ed. 1581, i. 28-37).
[2] *Opera*, i. 200.

and spirit are so different that, whichever you take, the other cannot be." [1]

"The whole difficulty lies not in the pronoun 'This' but . . . in the verb 'is'. For this word is often used in Holy Scripture in the sense of 'signifies'. . . . This word 'is' is used in this place in the sense of 'signifies' in our judgment, although this is not our judgment but the judgment of the eternal God, for we cannot glory in anything which Christ has not wrought in us." [2]

"The Eucharist or Communion or Lord's Supper is nothing else than a commemoration, whereby those who firmly believe that they have been reconciled to the Father by the death and blood of Christ announce this life-giving death, that is, praise it and glory in it and proclaim it." [3]

"To eat sacramentally can be nothing else than to eat the sign or figure." [4]

"They say, We adore and eat the spiritual body of Christ. What, by Great Jupiter, is the spiritual body of Christ? Is any other spiritual body of Christ anywhere found in Scripture than either the Church . . . or our faith, which believes that He paid the penalties for us on the cross and is assured of salvation through Him? Why do we load devout minds with words of this kind, which no understanding grasps? A spiritual body is just as much understood by a human being as if you spoke of a bodily mind or a fleshly reason. Do we not spiritually eat the body of Christ when we believe that He was slain for us, and trust Him? Are not spirit and life already in us? Why do we still join incompatiblef words simply to weave that long rope of strife? Let us plainly say, We eat spiritually when we come to Christ through the grace of God. Therefore, what else can spiritually eating the body of Christ be than trusting Christ?" [5]

Like teaching is contained in the *Aid Concerning the Eucharist*, published in 1525, and the *Clear Explanation of the Lord's Supper*, published in 1526. In the latter treatise the Eucharist is compared to a ring which reminds a wife of her absent husband and is the sign of her fidelity to him.

---

[1] *Opera*, ii. 206.

[2] *Ibid.* 209. Zwingli's friend Oecolampadius (John Hussgen, born in 1482 at Weinsberg near Wuerzburg, died in 1531 at Basle) reached the same result by interpreting the words "My body" to mean "the sign of My body"; see, *e.g.*, his *Reply to Luther, inter opera Zwinglii*, ii. 481.

[3] *Ibid.* 212.   [4] *Ibid.* 215.   [5] *Ibid.* 215.

"Our Lord Jesus Christ willed that there should be a figure and memorial, so that we might never forget that boundless kindness whereby He subjected His body to all kinds of insults and at length deigned to give it up even to death, and that we should not only hold the remembrance of this fixed in our breasts but should also celebrate this ineffable kindness by public praise and solemn thanksgiving. To provide for this both more easily and with stronger love in our hearts, He commanded us to eat and drink this Sacrament, that is, the sign of His passion and death. This action is the figure that Christ deigned to give up His body to death for us, and to shed His blood to wash away our sins. For Christ ordained it in these words, 'This is,' that is, signifies, 'My body,' and 'This is My blood'. This is just the same as if a wife, pointing to a ring of her husband which he had left with her, should say, This is my husband. When we celebrate the mystic action of this commemoration, we individually profess that we are of the number of those who place all the confidence of their souls in Christ Jesus." [1]

A somewhat similar comparison occurs in a sermon preached at Berne in 1528, in which Zwingli said :—

"A flower is more noble when it is put in the wreath of a bride than if it be used in some more common way, though as to its matter it is the same as the other flowers. One who takes from a king his signet ring is reckoned guilty of a far worse crime than if he had taken only so much gold, though the matter is no different at all. In like manner the matter of the bread is no different from all other ordinary bread, but the use of it and the dignity of the Supper give it an excellence far above that of ordinary bread." [2]

Further instances of the opinions of Zwingli may be taken from the *Nature of the Faith*, published in 1530, and the *Exposition of the Christian Faith*, published in 1531. In the *Nature of the Faith*, which was addressed to the Emperor Charles V., he wrote:—

"All Sacraments are so far from conferring grace that they do not even bring or dispense it. . . . Sacraments are given for a public testimony of that grace which is previously present to each individual. . . . By Baptism the Church publicly receives him who has previously been received by means of grace. Therefore Baptism does not bring grace, but it bears witness to the Church that he to whom

[1] *Opera*, ii. 293.   [2] *Ibid.* 532.

it is given has received grace. . . . A Sacrament is a sign of a sacred thing, that is, of grace which has been given. I believe that it is the visible figure or form of the invisible grace which has been given and bestowed by the gift of God, that is, it is the visible example, which nevertheless has some kind of analogy to the thing which is done by the Spirit. I believe that it is the public testimony. . . . In the Holy Eucharist, that is, the Supper of thanksgiving, the real body of Christ is present by the contemplation of faith, that is, those who give thanks to the Lord for the benefit conferred on us in His Son recognise that He took real flesh, that in it He really suffered, that He really washed away our sins by His blood, and so that everything done by Christ becomes as it were present to them by the contemplation of faith. But that the body of Christ essentially and actually, that is, the natural body itself, is either present in the Supper or is committed to our mouth and teeth, as the papists and certain people who look back to the fleshpots of Egypt maintain, this we not only deny but we constantly affirm that it is an error which is opposed to the word of God." [1]

In the *Exposition of the Christian Faith*, addressed to Francis I., King of France, Zwingli wrote:—

"The opinion which asserts that the body of Christ is eaten in the Supper corporally, naturally, essentially, and even by way of dimensions is irreligious because it is alien from the truth; and whatever is alien from the truth is impious and irreligious. . . . To eat the body of Christ spiritually is nothing else than to lean in spirit and mind on the mercy and goodness of God through Christ, that is, with unshaken faith to be assured that God will give us pardon for sins and the joy of eternal blessedness for the sake of His Son, who became wholly ours and by being offered for us reconciled to us the righteousness of God. . . . To eat the body of Christ sacramentally, since we wish to speak distinctively, is to eat the body of Christ in mind and spirit with the addition of the Sacrament. . . . When you come to the Lord's Supper together with the spiritual feeding and give thanks to the Lord for so great a benefit, for the deliverance of your soul, whereby you have been set free from the destruction of despair, and for the pledge whereby you have been assured of eternal blessedness, and together with the brethren partake of the bread and wine which are now the symbolical body of Christ, you eat distinctively sacramentally, when you do within

[1] *Opera*, ii. 541.

the same as you do without, when the mind is refreshed by this faith to which you bear witness by the figures." [1]

" We believe that the real body of Christ is eaten sacramentally and spiritually in the Supper by the religious and faithful and holy mind." [2]

The fifteenth of the articles drawn up at the conference held at Marburg in October, 1529, illustrates the agreement and the difference between the Zwinglians and the Lutherans. It is there said :—

" We all believe and hold concerning the Supper of our dear Lord Jesus Christ that we should use both kinds according to the institution of Christ, that the Sacrament of the altar is a Sacrament of the real body and blood of Jesus Christ, and that the spiritual enjoyment of the self-same body and blood is ordained for every individual Christian, with especial reference to the needs of each one, in the use of the Sacrament as has been given and instituted by the word of Almighty God so as to move the weak consciences to faith through the Holy Ghost. As at present however we have not been able to agree whether the real body and blood of Christ are in bodily fashion present in the bread and wine, each party is to show to the other Christian love, so far as conscience can allow, and both parties are to pray diligently to Almighty God that He will grant us a right understanding through His Spirit. Amen." [3]

This article, together with the others agreed to at Marburg, was signed by Luther, Justus Jonas, Melanchthon, Osiander, Stephen Agricola, John Brenz, Oecolampadius, Zwingli, Bucer, and Caspar Hedio.

V.

Martin Butzer, often called Bucer, was born at Schlettstadt in Alsace in 1491. He was educated at Udenheim, and, after joining the Dominican Order in 1506, at the University of Heidelberg. He was ordained priest. In 1521 he was dispensed from his monastic vows and transferred to the secular clergy. In 1522 he was made pastor of Landstuhl, and definitely severed himself from the papal side in the conflicts of the time by marrying a nun. He went to Strassburg in 1523, and continued to minister there till 1548, when his opposition to the *Interim*, by which the

[1] *Opera*, ii. 554, 555.   [2] *Ibid.* 563.
[3] Bretschneider and Bindseil, *Corpus Reformatorum*, xxvi. 126, 127

Emperor Charles V. endeavoured to prevent any change in
matters of religion except the administration of the chalice to
the laity and the allowance of the marriage of priests until a
general council should have been held, led to his being obliged
to leave. On the invitation of Cranmer he came to England
and was appointed Regius Professor of Divinity at Cambridge,
where he died in 1551.

In regard to the Eucharist, a large part of the aim of Bucer
was to discover a means of reconciliation between the doctrine of
Luther and that of Zwingli, although at times he attacked both.
Like Luther, he asserted that the communicant receives the body
and blood of Christ. Like Zwingli, he denied that'the body and
blood are united to the sacramental signs. His own view appears to have been that the communicants receive in the Sacrament only bread and wine; but that their faith, when they
receive the elements, uplifts them to a real spiritual participation
of the body and blood of Christ in heaven. A series of *Nine
Propositions Concerning the Holy Eucharist* which he set out in
1530 states his opinions in a short form. They are as follows :—

"i. We deny Transubstantiation.

" ii. We deny that the body of Christ is locally in the bread,
as if one were to imagine that the body is so contained in the bread
as wine is in a cup or as flame is in glowing iron.[1]

"iii. We affirm that the body of Christ is really in the Supper,
and that Christ actually present feeds us with His real body and
His real blood, using for this purpose His own words which the
ministers recite and the holy signs of bread and wine.

"iv. We confess that, as by Baptism there is the power of regeneration, so the very body and blood of Christ are presented
(*exhiberi*) by the symbols of the Eucharist.

"v. We say that these are received by faith alone and simple
and unfaltering,[2] as Doctor Cyril says, although we do not shrink
even from these words of Doctor Chrysostom, 'O mighty miracle, O
great kindness of God towards us, He who sits above with the Father
is at this hour held by the hands of all and gives Himself to those who

---

[1] Of these two comparisons, both of which Bucer thus repudiated in
1530, Luther had affirmed that of fire in red-hot iron in 1520 and had denied
that of wine in the cup in 1527. See pp. 12, 21, *supra*.

[2] *Inexquisita*, possibly for ἀνενδοιάστῳ in St. Cyril of Jerusalem, *Cat.*
xxiii. 20.

wish to surround and embrace Him,'[1] and any like sayings which are found in this and other writers.   But we understand these sayings, as Chrysostom himself also teaches, so as to cast away every carnal thought and to say that these things are done in the heavenly places and are seen only by the soul and by the mind.

" vi. We confess with Doctor Augustine that Christ is in some place in heaven because of the manner of His real body ; yet none the less we acknowledge that He is really and actually present in the Supper, nevertheless not locally but in a way peculiar to this Sacrament, which exists through words, but words that are believed, and symbols, but symbols that are received by faith.   For we confess that they are Sacraments only when they are in use.

" vii. The words of the Evangelists bear witness that the covenant, by which we believe that the body and blood of Christ are present and are offered to us when the bread and the wine are set before us, is made only with those for whom these were sacrificed.

" viii. We confess that those who are possessed of faith can yet be in such a relation not of faith to these sacred gifts that they become guilty of the body and blood not absent but present, as actually happened to the Corinthians.

" ix. The Sacraments of Christians are assuredly the signs and testimonies of Christ present, not absent." [2]

In a letter written in 1533 Bucer very emphatically maintained that he had not at any time denied that Christ is spiritually present in the Eucharist.

" In all my writings I bear witness that there is specially in the Holy Supper a presentation (*exhibitionem*) of the body and blood of Christ which is most real because it is heavenly and spiritual.   I have never attacked anything but impanation and carnal eating.   Never at any time have I denied that which is actual and efficacious.   Yet none the less there is a figure in the words of the Lord because more is understood than is said.   The bread is shown and given to the senses, and at the same time the body of the Lord, that is, the communion of the Lord, is presented (*exhibetur*) and given (*traditur*) to faith, so that we may be members of His flesh and of His bones.

---

[1] The passage is in *De Sac.* iii. 4.   The ordinary text adds, " This all do with the eyes of faith," but the right reading appears to be " This all then do with their eyes " ; see Dr. Nairn's edition of *De Sac.* p. 52.
[2] In *Martini Buceri Scripta Anglicana*, p. 611.

God forbid that I should say that Christ is absent from the Supper of Christians." [1]

Bucer was largely instrumental in promoting the temporary agreement between the Lutheran and the Swiss Reformers on the subject of the Eucharist at the convention held at Wittenberg in 1536. At this convention Bucer and his friends stated that they held that "the real body and real blood of Christ are presented (*exhiberi*) and given and taken together with the visible signs of bread and wine," and that "the body and blood of Christ are offered to all who receive the Sacrament by the minister of the Church, and are taken not only by the worthy, who receive them with heart and mouth to salvation, but also by the unworthy, who receive them with the mouth to their judgment and condemnation"; and Luther explained that "he did not unite the body and blood with the bread and wine by any natural bond, and did not locally enclose them in the bread and wine". As a result of these mutual explanations, a formula drawn up by Melanchthon was for the time agreed to by both parties.

"We have heard Doctor Bucer explaining his own opinion and that of others who are with him concerning the Sacrament of the body and blood of Christ as follows :—

"1. They confess according to the words of Irenaeus that the Eucharist consists of two things, an earthly and a heavenly. Therefore they hold and teach that together with the bread and wine there are really and substantially present and presented (*exhiberi*) and taken the body and blood of Christ.

"2. And although they deny that Transubstantiation takes place, and do not hold that any local inclusion is in the bread, or that there is any lasting conjunction outside the use of the Sacrament, yet they allow that the bread is the body of Christ by sacramental union, that is, they hold that, when the bread is offered to the communicants, the body of Christ is at the same time present and is really presented (*exhiberi*). For they hold that the body of Christ is not present outside the use, when the bread is reserved in the pyx or shown in processions after the custom of the papists.

"3. Moreover, they hold that this institution of the Sacrament

---

[1] *Ep. ad Michaelem N. Hisp. (op. cit.* p. 612). *Cf. Resp. adv. Axioma Cath. Robt. Ep. Abrin. (op. cit.* pp. 613-31); *Axiomata Apologetica (op. cit.* pp. 634-41).

is valid in the Church, and does not depend on the worthiness of the minister or the receiver. Wherefore, as Paul says [1] that the unworthy also eat, so they hold that the body and blood are really offered to the unworthy and that the unworthy take them when the words and institution of Christ are preserved. But such take to judgment, as Paul says, because they abuse the Sacrament, since they use it without repentance and without faith. For it is set out for this end, to bear witness that the benefits of Christ are applied to those who exercise repentance and raise themselves by faith in Christ, and that these are washed by the blood of Christ." [2]

In the same year 1536 Bucer published his two *Retractations*, in which he allowed that Luther did not hold "a natural union of the body of the Lord with the bread or a circumscribed inclusion of it in the bread," and that Zwingli and Oecolampadius did not hold that "in the Supper there are mere symbols without Christ".[3]

It is probable that in the statements of 1536 Bucer, in order to promote the reconciliation which he desired between the Lutherans and the Swiss Reformers, went to the furthest limit which he thought possible in a Lutheran direction, and that his mind is more fairly represented by the phraseology of the *Nine Propositions* of 1530 already quoted [4] and of his *Letter to Peter Martyr* [5] in 1549 and his *Confession Concerning the Holy Eucharist* [6] of 1550. In the latter he wrote :—

"Three things are bestowed and received, the symbols of bread and wine, the body and blood of the Lord, and the ratification of the new covenant and of the remission of sins. . . . Here is the presence of Christ, whether it is offered and testified only by words or also by Sacraments, not of place, not of sense, not of reason, not of earth, but of the spirit, of faith, of heaven, insofar as we through faith are raised to heaven and placed there together with Christ, and lay hold of Him in His heavenly majesty and embrace Him as He is shown and offered to us by the mirror and riddle of words and Sacraments discernible by sense. But the anti-Christs persuade the more simple from these words that we here receive and possess Christ present in some manner of this world or enclosed in or joined together with the bread and wine or under their accidents

---

[1] 1 Cor. xi. 27.   [2] Hospinian, *Hist. Sacr.* ii. 243, 244.
[3] In *Scripta Anglicana*, p. 646.   [4] See pp. 44, 45, *supra*.
[5] *Op. cit.* pp. 546-50.   [6] *Ibid.* 538-45.

in such a way that He ought to be adored and worshipped. Therefore the teachable are to be taught that there is no presence of
Christ in the Eucharist except in the lawful use of it and that
which is grasped and held only by faith." [1]

The *First Confession of Basle*, first drafted by Oecolampadius in 1531, modified to its present form by Oswald Geiss-
shuessler, usually known as Myconius, in 1532, and published in
1534, represents the Swiss theology as influenced by the lines of
thought which were characteristic of Bucer. It contains the following article on the subject of the Eucharist :—

"We confess that the Lord Jesus instituted His Holy Supper
for a memorial of His holy passion together with thanksgiving, to
proclaim His death, and to bear witness to Christian love and unity
and true faith. And, as in Baptism (in which cleansing from sins,
which nevertheless is accomplished only by the Father and the
Son and the Holy Ghost, is offered to us through the minister of the
Church) real water remains, so also in the Supper of the Lord (in
which the real body of the Lord and the real blood of Christ is represented and offered to us through the minister of the Church
together with bread and wine) the bread and wine remain. But
we believe firmly that Christ Himself is the food of believing souls
to eternal life, and that our souls through true faith in the crucified
Christ are given the flesh and blood of Christ as food and drink, so
that we, the members of His body our only Head, may live in Him,
and that He may live in us, who in the last day will rise through
Him and in Him to eternal joy and happiness. But we do not include in the Lord's food and drink the natural and real and substantial body of Christ, which was born of the pure Virgin Mary
and suffered for us and ascended into heaven. Therefore we do not
adore Christ in the signs of bread and wine, which we commonly
call the Sacraments of the body and blood of Christ, but in heaven
at the right hand of God the Father, whence He will come to judge
the living and the dead." [2]

The *Second Confession of Basle*, more often called the *First
Helvetic Confession*, was drawn up by a number of Swiss divines
in 1536, partly as a result of the efforts of Bucer and others to
promote unity between the Lutheran and the Swiss Reformers
and partly in view of the probable summoning of a general
council by the Pope. It probably bears the mark of Bucer's

---

[1] *Op. cit.* pp. 538, 540.   [2] *Sylloge Confessionum*, pp. 112, 113.

influence. In the twentieth article, which deals with the Sacraments in general, it is said :—

"These symbols of hidden things do not consist of bare signs but of signs together with things. . . . In the Eucharist bread and wine are the signs. But the thing is the communication of the body of Christ, the accomplished salvation, and the remission of sins, which indeed are received by faith, as the signs by the body, and in the thing itself is the whole fruit of the Sacraments. Wherefore we assert that the Sacraments are not only certain marks (*tesseras*) of the Christian society but also symbols of the grace of God, by which the ministers co-operate with the Lord to that end which He Himself promises and offers and effects ; yet in such a way that, as has been said of the ministry of the word, all the power of salvation is ascribed to the Lord alone." [1]

The twenty-second article is on the Eucharist. It is as follows :—

"The mystic Supper is that in which the Lord really offers His body and blood, that is, Himself, to His people, so that more and more He may live in them and they in Him ; not that the body and blood of the Lord are naturally united to the bread and wine, but that the bread and wine are ordained by the Lord to be symbols by which the real communication of His body and blood may be presented (*exhibeatur*) by the Lord Himself by means of the ministry of the Church not for food of the belly that shall perish but for the sustenance of eternal life. Therefore we often use this sacred food, since by His command, beholding the death of the Crucified and His blood with the eyes of faith, and contemplating our salvation not without taste of the life of heaven and a true sense of eternal life, we are re-made with ineffable sweetness by this spiritual and lifegiving and inner food, and we exult with joy which no words can describe because of the life which we have found, and we all with all our strength pour out thanksgiving for the wonderful kindness of Christ towards us. Therefore the opinion of some that we assign too little to the holy symbols is not at all deserved by us. For these are holy and venerable things as being instituted and used by the High Priest Christ, exhibiting in their own way, as we have said, the things signified, affording testimony to that which has been done, representing difficult realities, and bringing the most clear light to those mysteries by a certain wonderful analogy to the

[1] *Op. cit.* pp. 106, 107.

things that are signified. For these purposes they supply help and aid to faith itself, and finally they bind him who is initiated by them in lieu of an oath. So holily do we think of the sacred symbols. But we assign the force and power of the Quickener and Sanctifier to Him who is eternal, who is Life, to whom be praise for ever and ever." [1]

VI.

John Calvin, a native of Picardy, was born in 1509. In 1523 he received the tonsure, and was sent to Paris to prepare for the priesthood. Though holding and supported by ecclesiastical preferments, he gave most of his attention to law, which he studied at Paris and Orleans and Bourges. He never received Holy Orders. After 1532 he often preached at the meetings of the French Reformers. He spent some time in Angoulême, Poitiers, Orleans, Paris, Basle, and Strassburg, and eventually settled in Geneva in 1541 ; and he died at Geneva in 1564. The earliest and shortest form of his chief work, the *Institutes of the Christian Religion*, was published at Basle in 1536. Its most enlarged and final form appeared at Geneva in 1559, five years before his death. The fourth book of the *Institutes*, entitled " Concerning the External Means and Helps by which God Invites Us into the Society of Christ, and Keeps Us in it," contains six chapters on the Sacraments, of which two relate to the Eucharist. The teaching formulated by Calvin carried further the attempt of Bucer to find a middle position between Luther and the Zwinglians. He united a strong denial that the elements are by consecration the body and blood of Christ with a strong affirmation that the body and blood of Christ are received by the faithful communicant. In regard to the Eucharistic presence his ideas are clearly set out in the following passages :—

" There are two faults to be avoided, so that we may not unduly depreciate the signs and separate them from the mysteries to which in some way they are attached, or excessively exalt them and seem to obscure the mysteries themselves. That Christ is the Bread of life by which the faithful are nourished to eternal salvation no one who is not utterly irreligious would fail to admit. But there is not equal agreement as to what is the method of partaking of Him. For there are those who define eating the flesh of Christ and drinking

[1] *Op. cit.* pp. 107, 108.

His blood as nothing else than believing on Christ Himself. But to me Christ seems to have intended to teach something more express and lofty in that famous discourse in which He commends to us the eating of His flesh, namely, that we are quickened by a real participation of Him, which He described by the words eating and drinking so that no one should think that the life which we receive from Him is received merely by thought. For, as not the sight of bread but the eating of bread supplies the body with nourishment, so it is fitting that the soul should really and inwardly be partaker of Christ in order that by His power it may be quickened into spiritual life. Yet we acknowledge that this eating is the work of faith, as it cannot be imagined to be anything else. But between my statement and that of those whom I am opposing there is this difference, that to them to eat is only to believe, so that the flesh of Christ is eaten by believing that He is made ours by faith, whereas I say that this eating is the fruit and result of faith. Or, if you desire a clearer statement, to them eating is faith, to me it seems rather to ensue from faith. The difference may be small in words, but it is not unimportant in fact. For, though the Apostle teaches that Christ dwells in our hearts through faith,[1] yet no one would interpret this dwelling to be faith, but all perceive that the splendid result of faith is described, that through it the faithful attain to the possession of Christ abiding in them. After this manner, in calling Himself the Bread of life the Lord willed to teach not only that salvation is laid up for us in faith on His death and resurrection but also that a real communication of Himself brings to pass that His life passes into us and becomes ours, not otherwise than bread, when it is taken for nourishment, supplies strength to the body." [2]

"Let it be a conclusion that our souls are fed by the flesh and blood of Christ as our bodily life is guarded and sustained by bread and wine. For the analogy of the sign would not hold good if our souls did not find their nourishment in Christ, which cannot be unless Christ is really joined to us and refreshes us by the eating of His flesh and the drinking of His blood. And, though in so great distance of place it seems incredible that the flesh of Christ should reach to us so as to be our food, let us remember how greatly the hidden power of the Holy Ghost surpasses all our senses, and how foolish it is to wish that His limitless force should be measured by our standard. What then our mind does not understand, let faith receive, namely, that the Holy Ghost really unites what are divided in place. . . . I acknowledge that the breaking

[1] Eph. iii. 17.   [2] IV. xvii. 5.

4 *

of the bread is a symbol, not the thing itself. But when this has
been laid down, we shall rightly infer that in the presentation
(*exhibitione*) of the symbol the thing itself is presented (*exhiberi*).
. . . Why does the Lord give into your hands the symbol of His
body if it be not to assure you of real participation of Him ? But,
if it is true that a visible sign is bestowed on us to ratify the gift
of the invisible thing, let us believe that, when the symbol of the
body is received, the body itself is no less certainly given to us. I
say then, as has always been received in the Church and as all
right minded people teach to-day, that the mystery of the Holy
Supper consists of two things, the bodily signs which are set before
our eyes and represent to us invisible things in such way as our
weakness can grasp, and the spiritual reality which is both denoted
and presented (*exhibetur*) by the symbols." [1]

" There is no one of the writers of antiquity who does not acknowledge in explicit words that the holy symbols of the Supper are
bread and wine, although, as has been said, they sometimes dignify
them with various epithets to commend the dignity of the mystery.
For their saying that at the consecration there is a hidden conversion
so that there is now something else than bread and wine, as I have
just taught, does not mean that the bread and wine are reduced to
nothing but that they are to be regarded differently from common
food which is destined only to feed the body, since in them is presented (*exhibeatur*) to us the spiritual food of the soul. This is not
denied by us. . . . The nature of a Sacrament is overthrown unless
the earthly sign corresponds in the method of signifying to the
heavenly thing. And consequently, the reality of this mystery is
overthrown unless real bread represents the real body of Christ." [2]

" If these absurdities" (that is, "anything which does despite to the
heavenly glory of Christ" or "is inconsistent with His human nature,"
such as "binding Christ to the element of bread or enclosing Him in
the bread" or "saying that His body is infinite or is at the same time
in more places than one ") "are taken away, I gladly accept whatever
can mark the real and substantial communication of the body and
blood of the Lord, which is presented (*exhibetur*) to the faithful under
the holy symbols of the Supper, and in such a way that the faithful
are understood to receive not merely by the imagination and perception of the mind but to enjoy the thing itself for the nourishment
of eternal life." [3]

" They are greatly deceived who suppose that there is no presence
of Christ in the Supper unless it is placed in the bread. For by such

[1] IV. xvii. 10, 11.   [2] IV. xvii. 14.   [3] IV. xvii. 19.

an idea they leave nothing to the secret operation of the Spirit which
unites Christ Himself to us. Christ does not seem to them to be
present unless He descends to us, as if we did not equally possess
His presence if He draws us up to Him. Therefore the question
is only about the manner. They locate Christ in the bread; we do
not think it right for us to bring Him down from heaven. Let the
readers judge which is the more right. Only let the slander cease
that Christ is taken away from His Supper unless He is hidden under
the covering of bread. For, since this mystery is heavenly, to bring
Christ to earth is not necessary for uniting Him to us. If any one
asks me about the manner, I am not ashamed to confess that the
mystery is higher than my mind can grasp or my words express, and,
to speak more openly, beyond my understanding. And therefore I
here embrace without controversy the truth of God, in which I may
safely rest. He declares that His flesh is the food, and His blood
is the drink, of my soul. I give my soul to Him to be fed on such
food. In the Holy Supper He commands me to take and eat and
drink His body and blood under the symbols of bread and wine. I
do not doubt that He really gives and that I receive." [1]

   " A false charge is made against us that our teaching concerning
spiritual eating is opposed to real and actual eating, as they say, since
we are only considering the manner of eating, which with them is
carnal, since they enclose Christ in the bread, but with us is spiritual
because the hidden power of the Spirit is the bond of our union with
Christ. There is no more truth in the other objection that we treat
only of the fruit or result which the faithful receive from the eating
of the flesh of Christ. For we said before that Christ Himself is the
matter of the Supper, whence follows the result that we are expiated
from sins by the sacrifice of His death, washed by His blood, raised
by His resurrection to the hope of heavenly life. . . . The flesh itself
of Christ in the mystery of the Supper is no less a spiritual thing
than eternal salvation. Whence we infer that those who are
without the Spirit of Christ can no more eat the flesh of Christ than
one who cannot bear the taste can drink wine. . . . I acknowledge and maintain that the force of the mystery remains unimpaired although the impious may try to empty it as far as they
can. Yet it is one thing to be offered, another thing to be
received. Christ offers to all this spiritual food and spiritual
drink. Some feed on it eagerly; others reject it fastidiously. Will
the rejection cause the food and drink to lose their nature? Our
opponents will say that their opinion is helped by this comparison,

[1] IV. xvii. 31, 32.

namely, that the flesh of Christ, though it be tasteless, is none the less flesh.   But I deny that it can be eaten without the taste of faith, or, if it is more pleasing that I should speak with Augustine, I deny that men can take from the Sacrament more than they gather in the vessel of faith.   So nothing is lost from the Sacrament.   Its reality and efficacy remain unimpaired, although the impious depart empty after outwardly receiving it.. If they object again that despite is done to the words ' This is My body ' if the impious receive corruptible bread and nothing else, the answer is ready, that the true God does not wish to be acknowledged in the mere act of reception but in the persistence of His goodness, whereby He is prepared to bestow on, nay liberally offers to, the unworthy that which they reject. And this is the integrity of the Sacrament, which the whole world cannot violate, that the flesh and blood of Christ are given not less really to the unworthy than to the elect faithful of God ; yet it is also true that, as the rain which falls on a hard rock flows away because there is no possibility of it sinking into the stone, so the impious by their hardness drive away the grace of God and prevent it from entering into them.   Moreover, for Christ to be received without faith is no more reasonable than for a seed to sprout in the fire." [1]

"This thought will take us away from the carnal adoration, which some with perverse rashness have introduced in the Sacrament. . . . That pious minds may rightly lay hold of Christ, they must be raised to heaven.   But, if this is the office of the Sacrament, to raise the weak mind of man so that he may rise to grasp the height of spiritual mysteries, they who are detained in the outward sign wander from the right way of seeking Christ. . . . Rather is Christ to be adored spiritually in the glory of heaven than this so dangerous way of adoration devised, full of a carnal and gross idea of God. . . . What is idolatry if it is not to worship the gifts instead of the Giver?   In which there is doubly a sin ; for the honour is taken away from God, and bestowed on a creature ; and God Himself is dishonoured in His polluted and profaned gift, when from His Holy Sacrament a dreadful idol is made." [2]

Calvin rejected the doctrine of the sacrifice of the Mass as taught in his time, and described it as a " most pestilent error " and an " abomination ".[3]   In this rejection he repudiated any idea of a sacrificial offering in the Eucharist other than that which is to be found in all Christian prayer.   The following

[1] IV. xvii. 33.   [2] IV. xvii. 35, 36.   [3] IV. xviii. 1, 18.

passages are representative of the general position taken up in his long treatment of the subject :—

"The Levitical priests were commanded to typify the sacrifice which Christ was to offer; there was a victim, which was in the place of Christ Himself; there was an altar, on which it was offered; all things were done in such a way that there might be before men's eyes a likeness of the sacrifice which was to be offered in expiation to God. But, when the sacrifice was accomplished, the Lord instituted another method for us, namely, to bestow on the faithful people the fruit of the sacrifice offered to Him by His Son. Therefore He has given us a Table at which to feast, not an altar on which to offer a sacrifice; He has not consecrated priests to sacrifice but ministers to distribute the sacred banquet." [1]

"A sacrifice of expiation has as its object to appease the wrath of God and satisfy His judgment, and thus to cleanse and wash away sins, so that the sinner cleansed from the filth of them may be restored to the purity of righteousness and brought back to the favour of God Himself. Thus under the Law the sacrifices which were offered to expiate sin were so called, not because they were able to reconcile the grace of God and blot out iniquity, but because they foreshadowed the real sacrifice of this kind, which at length was actually offered by Christ alone, by Him alone, because it could not be offered by any other. And it was offered once for all, because the efficacy and power of that one sacrifice which was offered by Christ is eternal, as He Himself bore witness with His own mouth when He said that it was complete and fulfilled, that is, whatever was necessary to reconcile the grace of the Father, to obtain remission of sins, for righteousness, for salvation, all this was done and finished by that one offering of His; and therefore there is nothing lacking so as afterwards to leave room for another sacrifice to-day. . . . In the other kind of sacrifice, which we have called Eucharistic, are contained all the offices of love with which, while we embrace our brethren, we honour the Lord Himself in His members, then all our prayers, praises, thanksgivings, and whatever is done by us for the worship of God. And all these depend on the greater sacrifice by which we are consecrated in soul and body to be a holy temple unto the Lord. For it is not enough that our outward actions be applied to His service; but we ourselves first, and then all that is ours, must be consecrated and dedicated to Him, so that whatever is in us may serve His glory and be animated by the desire of increasing it:

[1] IV. xviii. 12.

This kind of sacrifice has nothing to do with appeasing the wrath of God, or obtaining remission of sins, or gaining righteousness, but it deals only with glorifying and exalting God; for nothing can be pleasing or acceptable to God which is not from the hand of those who have already received the remission of sins, whom He has otherwise reconciled to Himself and set free by expiation. . . . This kind of sacrifice the Lord's Supper cannot be without, in which, while we announce His death and return thanks, we offer nothing else than a sacrifice of praise. From this duty of sacrifice we Christians are all called a royal priesthood, because by means of Christ we offer to God that sacrifice of praise of which the Apostle speaks,[1] the fruit of lips which make confession to His name. For neither can we with our gifts appear in the presence of God without an Intercessor. Christ is He by whose intercession as our Mediator we offer our gifts to the Father. He is our High priest, who has entered into the sanctuary of the heaven and has opened a way of approach for us. He is the altar on which we lay our gifts, so that in Him we dare whatever we dare. ˋHe it is, I say, who has made us a kingdom and priests to the Father."[2]

The first draft of the *Gallican Confession of Faith* of 1559 was made by Calvin; in its final form it was the workˉ of his pupil Chandieu and a council of the French Reformers held at Paris in 1559. The teaching contained in it is the same as that in the writings of Calvin. The twenty-seventh and twenty-eighth articles are as follows:—

" We confess that the Holy Supper, which is the second Sacrament, is a witness to us of the union which we have with Jesus Christ, inasmuch as He not only died and rose for us once, but also really feeds and nourishes us with His flesh and His blood, so that we may be one with Him, and that His life may be in us. Although He is in heaven until He shall come to judge all the world, yet we believe that by the hidden and incomprehensible power of His Spirit He nourishes and quickens us with the substance of His body and His blood. We hold that this is done spiritually, not that we put imagination or fancy in the place of fact and reality, but because the height of this mystery surpasses the measure of our senses and the whole order of nature. In short, because it is heavenly, it can be apprehended only by faith. We believe . . . that in the Supper . . . God gives us actually and in fact that which is there represented;

---

[1] Heb. xiii. 15.
[2] IV. xviii. 13, 16, 17. *Cf.* 1 Pet. ii. 9; Rev. i. 6.

and that, consequently, besides the signs there is the real possession
and enjoyment of that which is there presented to us. And thus
all who bring to the Holy Table of Christ a pure faith, like a vessel,
really receive that which the signs represent; that is, the body and
the blood of Jesus Christ are no less the food and drink of the soul
than the bread and the wine are of the body." [1]

The *Belgic Confession* was drawn up in the first instance in
1561 by Guy de Brès, Adrian Saravia,[2] and others, and after
some revision was adopted by councils of Reformers held at Antwerp in 1566, at Wesel in 1568, at Emden in 1571, at Dort in
1574, at Middelburg in 1581, and at Dort in 1619. It became
a recognised statement of belief of the Dutch and Belgian
Reformers. The teaching of the thirty-fifth article, entitled
"Concerning the Lord's Supper," is the same as that of Calvin.
It contains the following sentences :—

"For the preservation of the spiritual and heavenly life which
the faithful possess God has sent living Bread, which came down
from heaven, namely, Jesus Christ, who nourishes and sustains the
spiritual life of the faithful, when He is eaten, that is, applied and
received in the spirit by means of faith. That He might represent
to us this spiritual and heavenly Bread, Christ has instituted earthly
and visible bread and wine as the Sacrament of His body and
blood, to testify to us that as really as we receive and hold this Sacrament in our hands, and eat and drink it with our mouths, whence
afterwards our life is maintained, so really do we by faith, which is
the hand and mouth of our soul, receive the real body and the real
blood of Christ our only Saviour in our souls, for the support of our
spiritual life. . . . We do not err when we say that what is eaten
is the identical and natural [3] body of Christ, and what is drunk is His
real blood. But the manner in which (*la manière par laquelle* in the
French text ; *instrumentum seu medium quo* in the Latin text) we eat
and drink is not the mouth but the spirit through faith. Thus Jesus
Christ always sits at the right hand of God the Father in heaven,
but none the less for that He communicates Himself to us through
faith. This feast is a spiritual table, at which Christ communicates
to us Himself with all His benefits, and causes us there to enjoy
both Himself and the merits of His passion and death, nourishing
and strengthening and comforting our poor afflicted souls, by the

[1] Schaff, *Creeds of Christendom*, iii. 380, 381.
[2] See pp. 220-25, *infra*.
[3] See note 2 on p. 66, *infra*.

eating of His flesh, and sustaining and renewing them by the drinking of His blood." [1]

The *Heidelberg Catechism* was drawn up through the influence of Frederic III. Elector of the Palatinate. It was largely the work of Zacharias Baer, usually known as Ursinus, and Caspar Olewig. It was published in 1563. Like the *Belgic Confession* it became a recognised statement of belief of the Dutch and Belgian Reformers as well as of the Germans who followed the Swiss rather than the Lutherans ; and it was of the widest influence among many Protestant bodies. It consists of 129 questions and answers, many of the answers being of considerable length. Eight of these relate to the Eucharist. The doctrinal teaching on this subject is the same as that in the writings of Calvin and in the *Belgic Catechism*. One of the questions with its answer, that of the " difference between the Lord's Supper and the Popish Mass," was added after the completion of the *Catechism* because of the orders of the Elector Frederic III. The five questions and answers which are of chief doctrinal importance are the following :—

"*Question* 75. How are you shown and confirmed that in the Lord's Supper you are partaker of the one sacrifice of Christ on the cross and of all His benefits ?

"*Answer*. Thus, that Christ has commanded me and all the faithful to eat of this broken bread, and to drink of this cup, for His memorial, and has joined therewith these promises: first, that His body was offered and broken on the cross for me, and His blood was shed for me, as certainly as I see with my eyes the bread of the Lord broken for me and the cup communicated to me ; and, further, that with His body which was crucified for us and with His blood which was shed for us He feeds my soul to eternal life as certainly as I receive from the hand of the minister, and taste with the mouth of my body, the bread and the cup of the Lord, which are given to me as certain tokens of the body and blood of Christ.

"*Question* 76. What is it to eat the crucified body of Christ and to drink His shed blood ?

"*Answer*. It is not only to embrace with a believing heart the whole passion and death of Christ, and thereby to obtain remission of sins and eternal life, but also to be united more and more to His

---

[1] *Sylloge Confessionum*, pp. 351, 352. The French text is in Schaff, *Creeds of Christendom*, iii. 429, 430.

blessed body by the Holy Ghost, who dwells both in Christ and in us, so that, though He is in heaven and we are on earth, we are nevertheless flesh of His flesh and bone of His bones, and live and are governed for ever by one Spirit, as the members of our body are by one soul.

"*Question* 78. Do then the bread and wine become the actual body and blood (*der wesentliche Leib und Blut* in German text ; *ipsum corpus et sanguis* in Latin text) of Christ ?

"*Answer*. No ; but as the water in Baptism is not changed into the blood of Christ, and does not become the washing away of sins itself, but is only a divine token and assurance thereof, so also in the Supper the holy bread does not become the body of Christ itself, though according to the nature and usage of Sacraments it is called the body of Christ.

"*Question* 79. Why then does Christ call the bread His body and the cup His blood or the new covenant in His blood, and St. Paul the communion of the body and blood of Jesus Christ ?

"*Answer*. Christ, speaks thus not without great cause, namely, not only to teach us thereby that like as bread and wine sustain this temporal life, so also His crucified body and shed blood are the true food and drink of our souls to eternal life, but much more by this visible sign and pledge to assure us that we are as really partakers of His real body and blood through the working of the Holy Ghost as we receive with the mouth of the body these holy tokens for His memorial, and that all His sufferings and obedience are as certainly our own as if we had ourselves suffered and done all in our own persons.

"*Question*. 80. What difference is there between the Lord's Supper and the Popish Mass ?

"*Answer*. The Supper testifies to us that we have full remission of all our sins by the one sacrifice of Jesus Christ, which He has Himself once for all accomplished on the cross, and that by the Holy Ghost we are ingrafted into Christ, who with His real body is now in heaven at the right hand of the Father, and wills there to be worshipped. But the Mass teaches that the living and the dead have not remission of sins through the sufferings of Christ unless Christ is still daily offered for them by the priests of the Mass, and that Christ is bodily under the form of bread and wine and is therefore to be worshipped therein. And thus the Mass at bottom is nothing else than a denial of the one sacrifice and passion of Jesus Christ and an accursed idolatry." [1]

[1] *Sylloge Confessionum,*. pp. 378-81   The German text is in Schaff, *Creeds of Christendom,* iii. 332-36.

The *Second Helvetic Confession* was composed by Henry Bullinger for his own use and to be a testimony after his death of the beliefs which he had held.   On being asked by the Elector Frederic III. for a statement of doctrine he sent this *Confession*, and in 1566 it was published and adopted both in Switzerland and Germany as an expression of belief on the part of those who followed the Swiss Reformers.   After the *Heidelberg Catechism*, it became the most authoritative of the documents of this school of Reformers.   On the subject of the Eucharist the position taken up in it is again the same as that of Calvin; and it may be sufficient to make a few extracts from the lengthy treatment in the twenty-first chapter.

"In this Holy Supper there is a pledge that the body of the Lord was really given up for us, and that His blood was shed for the remission of sins, that our faith may not fail.   And indeed that is outwardly and visibly represented in the Sacrament by means of the minister, and as it were is set out to be seen by the eyes, which is accomplished invisibly within in the soul by the Holy Ghost Himself. . . . The faithful receive that which is given by the minister of the Lord, and they eat the bread of the Lord, and they drink from the cup of the Lord; within by the operation of Christ through the Holy Ghost they receive the flesh and blood of the Lord, and they feed on them unto eternal life."

"Eating is not only of one kind.   There is bodily eating, whereby food is received in man's mouth and is crushed by the teeth and is swallowed into the stomach. . . . Neither did pious antiquity believe nor do we believe that the body of Christ is bodily or essentially eaten by the mouth of the body."

"There is also the spiritual eating of the body of Christ, not that indeed whereby we might think that the food itself is changed into spirit but that whereby, while the body and blood of the Lord remain in their essence and own nature, they are spiritually communicated to us, not in a bodily way but in a spiritual, through the Holy Ghost, who applies and grants to us those things which were obtained for us by the surrender to death of the flesh and blood of the Lord, that is, the remission of sins, deliverance, and eternal life, so that Christ lives in us and we live in Him, and He brings to pass that by true faith we receive Him in whom is this spiritual food and drink of ours, that is, our Life. . . . This eating of the flesh, and drinking of the blood of the Lord, is so necessary to salvation that without it no one can be saved.   And this spiritual eating and drinking can take place apart from the Supper of the Lord, and as often as, and wherever, a man believes in Christ."

"Besides the above-mentioned spiritual eating there is also the sacramental eating of the body of the Lord, whereby the believer not only spiritually and within partakes of the real body and blood of the Lord, but also by outwardly approaching the Table of the Lord receives the visible Sacrament of the body and blood of the Lord. Formerly, indeed, when the believer believed, he received the life-giving food, and he still enjoys it, but, when he now receives also the Sacrament, therefore he receives something. For he goes on in the communication of the body and blood of the Lord, and therefore is enkindled more and more, and faith increases, and he is refreshed with spiritual nourishment. For as long as we live faith has continual accessions. And he who receives the Sacrament outwardly with real faith does not receive the sign only, but enjoys the thing itself also, as we have said."

"We do not so join the body of the Lord and His blood with the bread and the wine that we say that the bread itself is the body of Christ in any but a sacramental fashion, or that the body of Christ lies hidden bodily under the bread, so that it ought to be adored even under the species of bread, or that every one who receives the sign receives also the thing itself. The body of Christ is in heaven at the right hand of the Father. And therefore our hearts are to be lifted up and not to be fixed on the bread, nor is the Lord to be adored in the bread. And yet the Lord is not absent from His Church celebrating the Supper. The sun is absent from us in the sky, yet is none the less efficaciously present to us ; how much more Christ the Sun of righteousness, absent from us in heaven in His body, is present to us, not indeed bodily but spiritually by life-giving operation." [1]

VII.

Erasmus ('Ερáσμιος) and Desiderius are the debased Greek and Latin forms of the name of the great scholar of the early part of the Reformation period, the illegitimate son of Gerhard Roger, whom his mother called Gerhard Gerhardsohn. He was born at Rotterdam in 1465 or a year or two later. Largely through pressure of various kinds he took the monastic vows among the Augustinian canons of Stein when he was about eighteen ; and in 1492 he was ordained priest. In later years he was released

[1] *Sylloge Confessionum*, pp. 82-86.

from the obligations of his vows by Pope Leo X. For the age he travelled widely, and visited France, England, and Italy. He resided for a time at Oxford and at Cambridge; and during one of his three visits to England he taught both divinity and Greek at Cambridge. After a life devoted to learning he died in 1536. He was a man of letters rather than a theologian, though his work touched theology at many points, and the revival of learning which so greatly affected the theology of the Reformation period owed much to him. In the controversies of the time he was distrusted and attacked by both sides, partly because of certain elements of indecision in his character, but still more because of his love of peace and the sensitive judgment which made him sadly conscious of the faults and mistakes both of the Reformers and of their opponents.

The genius of Erasmus and his cautious and tentative position in matters of theology give to a few references to the Eucharist contained in his writings an interest which they would not of themselves possess. He appears to have felt the attraction of views which represented the Eucharistic elements merely as symbols of spiritual gifts bestowed on the soul, but to have been influenced by Scripture and the authority of the Church and some general considerations to retain his belief that the consecrated bread and wine are the body and blood of Christ.

In his *Paraphrase on the First Epistle to the Corinthians*, published in 1517, Erasmus wrote :—

"Does not that sacred cup, which we receive and consecrate with thanksgiving for a memorial of the death of Christ, show our fellowship, that we have been alike redeemed by the blood of Christ? Again, that holy bread, which we divide among ourselves by the example and command of Christ, shows the covenant and the close fellowship which we possess as having been initiated by the same Sacraments of Christ. The bread is so made up of countless grains that they cannot be distinguished. The body so consists of different members that they are all inseparably united. Since then we are all sharers of the same bread, we declare that, however many we may be in number, yet in the consent of our minds we are one bread and one body." [1]

"Christ willed this feast to be a commemoration of His death and a symbol of the eternal covenant. . . . Mystic is the bread, of

[1] On 1 Cor. x. 16, 17.

which all ought to partake alike. Holy is the cup, which belongs to all alike, made ready not to assuage the thirst of the body but to represent a hidden thing, that we may not forget by what price we were redeemed from the sins of our former life. Therefore, as often as you come together to eat this bread and to drink from this cup, you are concerned with no affair of the belly, but you represent in a mystic rite the death of the Lord Jesus, that His abiding memory may keep you in your service until He Himself comes again to judge the world. Therefore, whoever shall eat this bread or drink of the cup of the Lord unworthily makes himself guilty of a serious crime, since he has treated the body and blood of the Lord otherwise than the Lord Himself commanded it to be treated. . . . Though the thing itself is the health-giving body and blood of the Lord, yet whoever eats or drinks unworthily, for him it is turned into plague and destruction, because he has approached so great a mystery irreverently and with an unwashed soul, not sufficiently pondering with how great awe the body of the Lord ought to be received." [1]

In the *Paraphrase on the Gospels*, published in 1522, he wrote :—

" In this Last Supper, which Jesus kept with His disciples before His death, He instituted this most holy symbol of His death, that there might be preserved among them an abiding reminder of His boundless love, whereby He did not hesitate to give His life to redeem our mortal race, and that our minds might never lose the remembrance of that divine sacrifice by which the most pure Lamb, the new and true Passover, offered Himself on the altar for us to God the Father, whose wrath towards us He propitiated by His blood, Himself for our offences paying the penalties which were due to our sins. . . . This sacrifice, this covenant, He willed to commend to the minds of His disciples before He was offered, that they might understand His death to be no common or ineffectual thing, but an efficacious sacrifice for the expiation of the sins not only of the Jews but also of all nations and ages. But, since the death of Christ was not to be repeated, to prevent men forgetting so great a benefit and the most holy covenant once entered and the Author of their salvation, He ordained that by the frequent Communion of the holy bread and cup the memory might be kept fresh among the professors of the Gospel Law. And He willed this most holy sign to be among His soldiers, and therefore to be reverenced, that, as much divine grace should be added to those who should receive the body and blood of

[1] On 1 Cor. xi. 25-29.

the Lord purely and worthily, so those who should receive unworthily should take to themselves great condemnation." [1]

In *Letters* written in 1525 and 1526 Erasmus wrote :—

" A new opinion has arisen that in the Eucharist there is nothing but bread and wine.   John Oecolampadius has made it most difficult to refute this, for he has fortified the view with so many proofs and arguments that even the elect seem able to be seduced." [2]

" The opinion of Oecolampadius would not displease me, if the consent of the Church was not an obstacle to accepting it.   For I do not see what good a body not discernible by the senses does, or that it would accomplish any good if it could be discerned, provided spiritual grace be present in the symbols.   And yet I cannot depart, and I never have departed, from the consent of the Church." [3]

" In certain matters concerning the Eucharist I as being too little learned should hesitate unless the authority of the Church held me fast.   And by the authority of the Church I mean the consent of Christian people throughout the world." [4]

" I allowed this to your [5] opinion that it seems to me more simple thus to avoid manifold labyrinths of difficulties, if it could be right for a Christian man to dissent from that which the authority of the councils and the consent of all Churches and nations have approved for so many ages.   I have always denied that I could bring my mind to this, especially as the words in the Gospels and of the Apostles so plainly speak of the body which is given and the blood which is poured out, and since moreover it agrees wonderfully with the ineffable love of God towards the human race that those whom He has redeemed by the blood and body of His Son He has willed to feed in a certain ineffable way with the flesh and blood of the same Son, and to console them with this hidden presence of the Son as a pledge till He shall come again in glory for all to behold.   These considerations would incline me to the belief of the Catholic Church even if nothing had ever been defined this way or that.   Now what madness it would be if I should not shrink from saying that there is

---

[1] On St. Matt. xxvi. 26.   *Cf.* on St. Mark xiv. 22 ; St. Luke xxii. 16, 19, 28 ; St. John vi. 52, 64.

[2] Letter 766, of 2nd October, 1525, in Erasmus, *Opera* (Leyden edition, 1703-06), iii. (1) 892.

[3] Letter 823, of 6th June, 1526, *op. cit.* iii. (1) 941.

[4] Letter 827, of 30th July, 1526, *op. cit.* iii. (1) 945.

[5] That is, of Pellikan (Kuersner), who became Professor of Hebrew at Zurich early in 1526, and had assured his friends there that Erasmus agreed with him in accepting the opinion of Oecolampadius.

nothing there but bread and wine! It is my custom together with learned friends, especially when those who are weak are absent, to discuss all kinds of things freely from love of inquiry and for the sake of tests and also for intellectual pleasure ; and perhaps in this I am more simple than I ought to be. But I would acknowledge that I am guilty of parricide if any mortal ever heard me say either in earnest or in jest that there is nothing in the Eucharist but bread and wine, or that the real body and blood of the Lord are not there. . . . Up to the present time together with all Christians I have adored in the Eucharist Christ who suffered for me. Nor do I now see any reason why I ought to abandon this opinion. By no human reasons can I be induced to depart from the agreement of the Christian world." [1]

Thomas de Vio was born at Gæta about fifty miles north of Naples in 1469. His baptismal name was James ; the name Thomas was assumed by him as a mark of his devotion to St. Thomas Aquinas. He is usually known as Cajetan from the name of his birthplace. He entered the Dominican Order at the age of sixteen ; he was made a cardinal by Pope Leo X. in 1517 ; he died in 1534. He was much less a scholar and man of letters than Erasmus, with whose life his was almost exactly contemporary ; but he was not uninfluenced by the New Learning. He was an active opponent of Luther, and, though some of his statements have not escaped censure, one of the most eminent of the papal theologians. His philosophical and theological writings were many and elaborate, and include a commentary on the *Summa Theologica* of St. Thomas Aquinas. His positive Eucharistic teaching may be best seen in his commentaries on the New Testament. He defends the doctrine of Transubstantiation, maintains that the body of Christ is actually received by communicants, lays stress on the need of receiving the Sacrament worthily if there is to be spiritual partaking of Christ, and closely follows the teaching of St. Thomas Aquinas that the Eucharist is a sacrifice as being the memorial of a sacrifice.

"The Church is compelled to confess the Transubstantiation of the bread into the body of Christ ; for it could not happen in any other way than by Transubstantiation that this substance is the

[1] Letter 847, written in 1526, *op. cit.* iii. (1) 965. *Cf.* Letters 845, 846, also written in 1526, to Pellikan, *op. cit.* iii. (1) 963, 965.

body of Christ ; for, if Transubstantiation does not take place, it is not true that this which was indicated when Christ spoke the pronoun ' This ' (that is, the substance which the pronoun denoted when He uttered it) is the body of Christ ; but this substance, which was then indicated, if it remains at the end of the consecration what it was before, is not the body of Christ but bread ; and, if it is annihilated, it is neither bread nor the body of Christ, but nothing." [1]

" That they may not understand Him to speak of a mystical or metaphorical body, He shows that it is His real and natural body by saying, ' which is given for you,' that is, it is the very same body which is given to the death of the cross." [2]

" This saying [that is, ' Except ye have eaten the flesh of the Son of Man and drunk His blood, ye have no life in you ' [3]] has a threefold sense. The first is concerning faith in the death of Christ. This sense is, Except ye have used the death of the Son of Man as food and drink, ye have not the life of the spirit in you. . . . The second sense is concerning faith in the Sacrament of the Eucharist, which is the memorial of the death of Christ. . . . For the chalice and the host signify the actual separation of the flesh and blood which took place on the cross. And the sense is, Except ye have spiritually eaten and drunk the Sacrament of the Eucharist, ye have no life in you. And this is a true sense in itself, since spiritually to eat and drink the Sacrament of the Eucharist, so far as the thing of the Sacrament is concerned, is nothing else than for one to abide in Christ and for Christ to abide in him, without which abiding it is clear that the life of the spirit cannot be. But whether this is intended is not plain ; nay, if the question is considered clearly, it appears that the formal saying is not concerning the Sacrament, but concerning the thing of the Sacrament and the fountain of the Sacrament. . . . The third sense is concerning the sacramental eating, yet the eating worthily. The sense is, Except ye have eaten the flesh of the Son of Man in the Sacrament of the host, and have drunk His blood in the Sacrament of the chalice, ye have not the life of the spirit in you. So an argument is derived from this sense that not only the Sacrament of Baptism but also the Sacrament of the Eucharist in both kinds is necessary to salvation.

[1] On St. Matt. xxvi. 26.

[2] On St. Luke xxii. 19. Cajetan here obviously uses the phrase "natural body" in the sense of the same body as that which died on the cross. See vol. i. pp. 378, 379, supra, vol. ii. pp. 37, 57, supra, pp. 111, 112, 117, 118, 135, 154, 162-79, 190-95, 198, 205, 318, 319, infra.

[3] St. John vi. 53.

From this sense has recently arisen the Bohemian sect who communicate even infants in both kinds. This sense is contradicted by the custom of the Church, which does not communicate infants and does not communicate the people in both kinds. And not only the custom but also the doctrine, since the Church teaches that it is sufficient for salvation to communicate under the species of bread. . . . The actual separation of the flesh and blood of Christ in the Sacrament is only after a representative fashion; but in the death of Christ it was in fact. . . . That it is a bad application of this passage to assert the necessity of giving Communion to all is shown by the fact that to eat the Sacrament presupposes natural eating, as to be born sacramentally presupposes to be born naturally. . . . Infants, therefore, who still cannot eat . . . are wrongly included under this precept, it being allowed for the sake of the argument though not acknowledged that the text speaks about the eating of the Sacrament. . . . It is clear that the literal sense of the saying [1] is not concerning eating and drinking the Sacrament of the Eucharist, but concerning eating and drinking the death of Jesus. . . . To feed on the death of Jesus is to have eternal life." [2]

" He [3] does not say, It signifies the Communion, but, It is the Communion; because there is really a Communion of the blood of Christ (not of wine) to those who partake of the chalice. . . . To those who receive sacramentally only, there is a Communion of the blood of Christ sacramentally only; and to those who receive both sacramentally and spiritually, there is the sacramental and spiritual Communion of the blood of Christ. . . . One and the same thing, that is, the real body of Christ, not the substance of bread, is communicated to all who eat, for whom it is broken." [4]

" Here it is clearly said that the Eucharist is a sacrifice ; for he explicitly enumerates the sacrifices of the Jews and the sacrifices of the Gentiles for no other purpose than to show that one cannot partake both of the sacrifice of Christians and of the sacrifice of Gentiles." [5]

" In commanding the Eucharist, He not only orders ' Do this,' but adds, ' for My memorial,' that we may understand that there is command for not only a Sacrament but also a sacrifice, since offerings and sacrifices are those things which are done for a memorial." [6]

---

[1] At this point, the comment has gone on to St. John vi. 54, "He that eateth My flesh and drinketh My blood hath eternal life".

[2] On St. John vi. 53, 54.   [3] St. Paul in 1 Cor. x. 16.

[4] On 1 Cor. x. 16.   [5] On 1 Cor. x. 21.   [6] On 1 Cor. xi. 24.

" From this theologians take the distinction between sacramental and spiritual eating or drinking. And hence it is rightly
held that some eat and drink sacramentally only, which Paul calls
to eat or drink unworthily; while others receive both sacramentally and spiritually, who are here called those who eat or drink
worthily." [1]

"The will of God is the will to cleanse us from sins; and this
cleansing was not effected by the ancient sacrifices but was effected
by the offering of the body of Christ Jesus on the cross, which was
not repeated, or to be repeated, but was once for all." [2]

"The direction of the writer's argument is that from the fact
that in the new law remission of sins has been accomplished through
the offering of Christ, there remains now no offering for sin. For
this would be an injury to the offering of Christ as insufficient. Nor
are you who are a novice to wonder on this account that the
sacrifice of the altar is daily offered in the Church of Christ; for
this is not a new sacrifice, but that which Christ offered is commemorated, as He Himself commanded, ' Do this for My memorial '.
For all the Sacraments are nothing else than applications of the
passion of Christ to those who receive them. Now it is one thing
to repeat the passion of Christ, and another thing to repeat the
commemoration and application of the passion of Christ." [3]

"The Christian altar is the altar of the body and blood of
Christ; for this is the only altar which we have." [4]

VIII.

After the formation of the *Confession of Augsburg* in 1530 [5]
a reply was drawn up on behalf of the papal party by John
Maier von Eck, the Professor of Theology in the University of
Ingolstadt, and other divines, and after some revision to please
the Emperor was read in the Diet on 3rd August, 1530. The
comment on the tenth article of the *Confession of Augsburg* was
as follows :—

"The tenth article is not verbally hurtful, because they acknowledge that in the Eucharist after consecration lawfully made the
body and blood of Christ are substantially and really present, if

[1] On 1 Cor. xi. 27.   [2] On Heb. x. 10.
[3] On Heb. x. 18. The same position is taken by Cajetan in his treatise
against Luther entitled *On the Sacrifice of the Mass*, 6 ; see *Opuscula*, iii.
287, edition 1562.
[4] On Heb. xiii. 10.   [5] See pp. 24-27, *supra*.

only they would believe that the whole Christ is present under each species, so that the blood of Christ is no less under the species of bread by concomitance than it is under the species of wine, and the body of Christ under the species of wine. Otherwise, the body of Christ in the Eucharist would be dead and bloodless. . . . One very necessary addition to the article of the *Confession* is that they should believe the Church rather than any who wrongly teach differently, so as to acknowledge that by the almighty word of God in the consecration of the Eucharist the substance of bread is changed into the body of Christ. . . . They are to be praised because they condemn the Capernaites who deny that the reality of the body and blood of our Lord Jesus Christ is in the Eucharist."[1]

In the course of a lengthy defence of existing practices in the celebration of the Mass, the following statements on important doctrinal matters occur :—

"Neither can the assumption be properly understood that Christ made satisfaction by His passion for original sin and instituted the Mass for actual sin ;[2] for this idea was never heard of by Catholics, and very many of them on now being asked strongly deny that there has been any such teaching. For the Mass does not blot out sins, which are removed by means of Penance as it were by a special medicine, but it blots out the penalty due for sin ; it supplies satisfactions ; and it confers increase of grace and healthful protection on souls that are in life ; lastly, to certain needs and necessities of ours it affords hope of comfort and divine aid."[3]

"Neither are St. Paul's words to the Hebrews, that 'by one offering we have been justified once for all by Christ,'[4] contrary to the offering of the Mass. For St. Paul is speaking of the offering of the victim, that is, of the bloody sacrifice, of the slain lamb, to wit, on the altar of the cross. This offering certainly was made once for all ; and from it all the Sacraments and also the sacrifice of the Mass have their efficacy. Therefore He was offered once only on the cross with shed blood ; to-day He is offered in the Mass as a peaceful and sacramental victim. Then He was offered in a passible manner in visible form ; to-day He is offered in the Mass impassibly, veiled in mysteries, as in the Old Testament He was sacrificed typically and figuratively."[5]

[1] Francke, *Lib. Symb. Eccl. Luth.* iv. 48.
[2] Referring to the *Confession of Augsburg :* see p. 26, *supra.*
[3] Francke, *op. cit.* iv. 60. [4] Heb. x. 14.
[5] Francke, *op. cit.* iv. 61.

With the repudiation in this manifesto of the papal party
of the idea that the sacrifice of the cross availed only for original
sin, and that the sacrifice of the Mass was a separate and new
sacrifice for actual sins, may be compared a statement written
a little later by the eminent theologian Albert Pighi, the Provost
of the Church of St. John at Utrecht, in his treatise *On the
Sacrifice of the Mass*. Referring to the *Confession of Augsburg*,
he wrote :—

"They are to be told that they have not acted candidly, and do
not so act, in ascribing to us in their *Confession* the 'opinion which
increased private Masses infinitely, namely, that Christ by His passion
made satisfaction only for original sin, and instituted the Mass, in
which there should be an offering for daily mortal and venial sins'.[1]
In truth I, who for very many years have had experience of the
schools, which are open to all kinds of discussions and examinations
of the truth and assertions, have yet never heard or read of any one
advancing an opinion of this kind before I read their *Confession*.
Nor do I think that they will be able to produce any one, whether
a schoolman or anybody else, who puts forth an opinion of this kind ;
and, even if they had found any such person, they still would not
have acted candidly in ascribing the stupidity of one man to us all,
who never heard or read of any such thing among ourselves ; and
by monstrosities of this kind they asperse our doctrine, and defile it,
and misrepresent it among a populace ignorant of these matters and
ready to believe them." [2]

Yet some justification for the opinion of the Reformers that
a doctrine was held which regarded the Sacrifice of the Mass as a
separate and independent sacrifice may be seen in the writings of
Lancelot Politi, usually known as Ambrose Catharinus, a skilful
if somewhat eccentric theologian whose life extended from 1487
to 1553. In some passages in his works he writes as if he thought
the efficacy of the redemption accomplished on the cross to be
limited to sins committed before Baptism ; and this was understood to be his meaning not only by anti-Roman Catholic controversialists such as Bishop Jewel,[3] but also by Roman Catholic

---

[1] Quoted from the *Confession of Augsburg*. See p. 26, *supra*.

[2] Pighi, *Controver. Ratispon.* fol. 92 *b*, edition 1545. In the later
Lutheran documents the accusation of this notion does not appear. See
pp. 28-30, *supra*. Cf. also p. 69, *supra*, and pp. 71-75, 146, 213, 236, *infra*.

[3] *The Defence of the Apology of the Church of England*, II. xv. 2 (p. 558,
Parker Society's edition).

divines, notably Melchior Cano, Vasquez, and Suarez.[1] In other passages, however, he very distinctly represents the sacrifice of the Mass as deriving its efficacy from the sacrifice of the cross. The following quotations afford instances of both types of language, and supply two interesting allusions to the heavenly presentation of the Eucharistic sacrifice.

In his *Commentary on the Epistle to the Hebrews* Catharinus writes :—

"When they [that is, the Lutherans] object 'Where there is remission of sins, there is no more offering for sins,'[2] I answer that the Apostle is speaking of the sins which were under the first covenant, as was original sin, and the sins which had their source in it. . . . And so it is necessary that sacrifice should remain for faults which are admitted after the remission of the old sins and the reception of grace. . . . .They [that is, the Levitical priests] offered sacrifices for that original sin, which returns no more if once taken away. Wherefore it was not right that, when this was once removed, they should sacrifice any more for it. But we, since we offer sacrifice for continual sins, are not forbidden, or rather are obliged, continually to sacrifice and at the same time continually to supplicate, so that those sins which are continually committed may be continually expiated by sacrifice. For the sacrifice is not always offered by us for the same sins. . . . We say that the priests who are now on earth are not without occupation, because He is in the presence of God in heaven and makes intercession for us. . . . The holy of holies is in heaven, whither our High Priest has now entered with His own blood in the midst, that one offering whereby it was brought about that expiation was made for the former faults which were under the first covenant, and that for the new faults which should arise under the new covenant the ancient useless priesthood should be removed, and a new priesthood appointed for doing away with the faults which are continually repeated under the new covenant. . . . We have blood, and real blood, which we offer to appease God for the new faults, because without blood there is no remission; and the outpouring of this blood, which took place once, ought always to be of profit, provided it is continually offered. Nor is it offered only for those faults which are committed but also for the thanksgiving and the praise which we owe to God. And not only to do away the sins which have been committed but also to obtain benefits and to prevent their being lost. For as often as we offer, so often that blood is poured out

----

[1] See pp. 359, 364, 371, *infra*.   [2] Heb. x. 18.

before the face of God, that is, so often it affords the efficacy of that
outpouring ; because, when there is a memorial of that outpouring
(for we do it for His memorial), in a kind of way it is renewed.
For so did the Lord most wisely institute.   For it is needful, in
order that it may profit, for that sacrifice to be applied to us.   Now
in respect of the former faults, which were under the old covenant,
it is applied by means of Baptism.   But in respect of the new faults
it is applied by means of this new sacrifice, and by means of the
other Sacraments, which would not avail without this sacrifice as
neither would Baptism avail without that sacrifice of Christ. . . . Since
then these reasons for sacrifice undoubtedly remain under the
new covenant, this one bloodless sacrifice of the body and blood
of Christ was ordained for us, that it might be sufficient for all
purposes, that is, for rendering praise and thanksgiving to God,
and for obtaining new benefits, and for blotting out fresh sins ;
yet it has force from that one offering which was made by
Christ, which is renewed in our offerings.   For, as it is right for us
to pray for ourselves and also for the whole body of the Church (although Christ prayed for us all), so it is right for us also to sacrifice
for ourselves, although Christ sacrificed for us and for the whole
world, because we thus apply to ourselves both His prayer and
His sacrifice." [1]

" This place also [2] smites our opponents [that is, the Lutherans]
hard.   For from this it is seen that for the sins committed under
the new covenant after the reception of the efficacy of the saving
sacrifice in Baptism we have not for sin that offering which Christ
offered for the sin of the world and for the offences preceding
Baptism.   For He died only once, and therefore that sacrifice is
only once applied to this effect.   Nevertheless another way of remission by means of Penance is not excluded, Christ being present
in heaven and making intercession for us, provided we also make
satisfaction for the penalties that are due." [3]

With these quotations from the *Commentary on the Epistle to
the Hebrews* the following extracts from the treatise *Concerning
the Reality of the Bloodless Sacrifice* [4] should be compared.

[1] On x. 14 (pp. 503-5, edition 1566).   [2] Heb. x. 26.
[3] On x. 26 (p. 506, edition 1566).
[4] There is a copy of this extremely rare treatise in the Lambeth Palace
Library. It constitutes columns 146-82 of the volume (shelfmark 15. E. 12)
with the title-page *Enarrationes R. P. F. Ambrosii Catharini Politi Senensis
Archiepiscopi Compsani In quinque priora capita libri Geneseos.   Adduntur
plerique alii Tractatus et Quaestiones rerum variarum ac scitu dignissimarum,*

"This is the Catholic and most holy truth, that in the new covenant and the law of grace there has been instituted by the word of the Lord an outward and sensible sacrifice to be offered visibly on the altar by the priests and ministers of God for the expiation of their own sins and the sins of others both living and departed. This sacrifice is the body and blood of our Lord Jesus Christ hidden in the Sacrament." [1]

"To effect this result—which is to be set free from sin and to be justified and to enter into Christ and so into the way to wage war, as He Himself waged war and conquered, all which are signified and come to pass in Baptism—there never has been, and there is not, and there will not be, any other priest except Him alone, or any other sacrifice except the bloody sacrifice of His body alone, or any other offering except that one offering made by Him on the cross with prayer and tears. . . . That one offering was sufficient for the redemption of those transgressions which were under the first covenant, which signifies nothing else but what we have said, original sin together with its fruits, since they who were under original sin were shut up guilty of death under the first covenant. . . . But at this point some one will attack us and say, If the thing is so, that Christ by His bloody offering wrought redemption for us only for the preceding offences, which are under the first covenant, it seems to follow that in the new covenant either there are no offences or, if there are any, they are inexpiable ; and, if so, that the heresy of Novatus is here again, . . . from which heresy if we shrink, it seems to remain that we say (as the new heretics lay down) either that after Baptism there are no transgressions, because there is no law, or that, if there are any, God does not care about them, but considers them to have been expiated by that first bloody offering of the Lord, and so does not now impute them to believers, so that they be expiated by faith and assurance alone without any sacrifice. . . . It is altogether false and irrational to say that the sins committed in the new covenant are not imputed because of the bloody sacrifice of Christ already once for all offered, which, as has been said, pertained to the faults of the first covenant. . . . But that the sins committed under the new covenant are inexpiable is a perverse opinion, long

quarum catalogum versa pagina indicabit. . . . Cum gratia et privilegio Julii Tertii Pontificis Maximi. Romae Apud Antonium Bladum Camerae Apostolicae typographum, MDLII. The author had searched vainly for the treatise in many libraries, and at last learnt of the copy in the Lambeth Palace Library from the Bishop (J. Wordsworth) of Salisbury's *De validitate ordinum Anglicanorum*, p. 23.

[1] Col. 146.

ago condemned and refuted by the Church.   Since then there are
sins, and they are expiable, and they do not pertain to the bloody
sacrifice of Christ, inquiry must be made in what way they are expiated, whether it is without sacrifice. . . . We say that sacrifice is
altogether necessary, since without sacrifice there could not be any
Sacrament. . . . Now, as the sins which are committed under the
new covenant are of a different kind from those of old, so they
ought to have their own proper sacrifice and priesthood and offering
and suitable oblations, not one only, as those which were under the
former covenant ; because all the sins which were under that were
in a sort of way reckoned as one, as being derived from that one sin
which was committed once in Paradise. Wherefore it required only
one offering to expiate it, as we have said. For those sins which
are committed under the new covenant are considered individually
by themselves, and each one demands its own expiation." [1]

"This sacrifice . . . is the sacrifice of the new covenant, which
presupposes, as I have said, the redemption by and the acceptance
of that bloody sacrifice." [2]

"This new and bloodless sacrifice has its efficacy from that
bloody sacrifice of which it is the commemoration. . . . Although
that first bloody offering of Christ freed the whole world from the
ancient sin and the guilt of it, and consequently from all the guilt
of the sins which have been mentioned, yet, as we have said, it did
not free in such a way that there be no necessity of the merits of
that sacrifice being applied to each individual." [3]

"There is not one power of the Sacrament and another of the
sacrifice, but by means of the Sacrament of the Eucharist itself the
power of the bloodless sacrifice is applied, which we obtain (mutua-
mur) from the bloody sacrifice, as by means of Baptism the power of
the bloody sacrifice is applied without any other sacrifice being intermediate." [4]

"Insofar as we are priests, what should we have to offer unless
He has given Himself as a sacrifice? And with what face could
we hope to make the sacrifice acceptable when offering it on earth,
unless we had received with a sure faith that the same sacrifice is
borne by Him or His angel to the altar on high in heaven, which is
the glorious presence of the Holy Trinity, and is presented by Him,
as we declare in the canon ? " [5]

"We entreat that our sacrifice may be borne by the angel, that
is, by Christ, that the spiritual thing which we offer on the earthly

[1] Col. 160-162.   [2] Col. 165.   [3] Col. 170, 71.
[4] Col. 172.   [5] Col. 176.

altar, may be brought by the hands of the Holy Angel Himself to the altar of the Most Holy Godhead."[1]

Whatever the right explanation of the meaning of Catharinus may be, it is easy to understand that some of the passages which have been quoted were thought to indicate a doctrine that the efficacy of the sacrifice of the cross was limited to the sphere of sins remitted in Baptism ; and there are not wanting slight signs elsewhere either of a popular teaching or of a popular misunderstanding of teaching to this effect. Whatever may be the truth of the belief of the authorities at Nuremberg in 1524 that a friar had taught that " Christ suffered only for original sin and for the actual sins committed before He came,"[2] or in the popular accusation against Johann Rode, the Rector of the Church of Our Lady at Luebeck, in 1529 that he had maintained that the death of Christ was effectual only for men of former times,[3] they may afford evidence, if not of misconceptions of this kind in popular teaching, at least of what some uninstructed persons supposed to be taught.[4]

A statement made in defence of the sacrificial character of the Mass at the second Disputation at Zurich held in October, 1523, by Martin Steinly, a representative from Schaffhausen, is not without interest. Steinly in his thesis in opposition to Zwingli gave four reasons why the Mass is a sacrifice. First, the universality of sin prevents the sacrifice of themselves offered by individual Christians, or the sacrifice of itself offered by the Church, from being a pure and holy and spotless sacrifice ; and the words of the prophet Malachi[5] show that there is to be a " pure offering " not only in Jerusalem, like the sacrifice on the cross, but also " in every place ". " That pure offering which is offered among the Gentiles is nothing else than the sacrifice of the altar, which the Christian Church, established among the

[1] Col. 179.

[2] Spalatin, *Annales, s. ann.* 1524 ; see Menckenius, *Scriptores Rerum Germanicarum,* ii. 634.

[3] See Regkmann, *Lubeckische Chronick,* col. 131-33 ; *cf.* Ranke, *History of the Reformation,* iii. 427 (English translation).

[4] The author has to thank the Rev. Dr. Kidd, of Keble College, Vicar of St. Paul's Church, Oxford, not only for his learned and accurate book, *The Later Mediæval Doctrine of the Eucharistic Sacrifice,* but also for valuable suggestions on this subject.

[5] Mal. i. 11.

Gentiles and dispersed throughout every place, is wont to offer by means of her ministers to the Name of God." Secondly, the institution of the Eucharist was the fulfilment by our Lord of the type of Melchizedek, who offered bread and wine; and the priesthood after the order of Melchizedek, as distinct from that of Aaron, is an abiding priesthood, the exercise of which remains in the Mass. "The Priest after the order of Melchizedek abides for ever in such a way that He sacrifices after the pattern of Melchizedek; and this takes place invisibly daily in the Mass, when the Church sacrifices His flesh and blood under the species of bread and wine." Thirdly, in view of the promise of our Lord that the Holy Ghost, who is the Spirit of truth, shall be with the Church, the unvarying Christian tradition proves that the Mass is a sacrifice. "Whatever has been received with unanimous consent by the Church of the living God, the pillar and ground of the truth, which contains both sheep and shepherds, ought to be received as delivered by the Holy Ghost, who rules the Church." Fourthly, the Mass was instituted by our Lord to be in remembrance of Him; and it is a commemoration of His passion, in which there is both the sign and the reality of sacrifice. "Since that same blood of Christ, and that same body which hung on the cross, and that same Christ who suffered on the cross, are actually a sacrifice in the Mass itself, the Mass is assuredly a sacrifice actually as well as in name, and it is both a sacrifice and the commemoration of a sacrifice."

IX.

The course of events at Cologne in the fourth and fifth decades of the sixteenth century afford important illustrations of current teaching. In 1536 a provincial council was held under the authority of Hermann von Wied, the Archbishop of Cologne, partly with a view to meeting the circumstances brought about by the early stages of the Reformation. The decrees of the council are thought to have been largely the work of John Groepper, who was a canon of Cologne. The more important of those relating to the Eucharist are as follows :—

"The people are to be taught to believe with most assured faith that in this Sacrament is the real body and real blood of

[1] *Acta Disputationis Secundæ*, printed in Zwingli, *Opera*, ii. 623-46 (edition 1581). The disquisition referred to above is in ii. 635, 636.

Christ Jesus. . . . In the Eucharist is the whole Christ, although He is there in the form (*sub ratione*) of food and drink. For He who has given His real body and blood without doubt has given them alive. Wherefore, if we believe that in the tomb the divine nature was not separated from the dead body, how much more shall we believe that in the Sacrament it is not separated from the living body!" [1]

"The parish priest is to teach . . . that the body and blood of the Lord are completely in one species by itself, so that the layman, who communicates in the species of bread, receives not only the body but also the blood of the Lord no less than one who partakes in both species of bread and wine." [2]

"Since Christ is contained in this Sacrament, the people are to be exhorted that, coming with awe to this mystery, they are to bow reverently when the health-giving host is elevated in the celebration of the Mass, to bend their bodies to the ground, and with their minds to adore the Crucified, and that they are to do the same when the priest carries the Eucharist to the sick." [3]

"The people are to be taught the nature of the sacrifice of the Mass, namely, that it is representative. Christ died once, the just for the unjust. . . . True God and true Man hung once only on the cross, offering Himself to the Father as a sacrifice living, passible, immortal, accomplishing the redemption of quick and dead. . . . And yet He is sacrificed daily in the Sacrament. Not that Christ is thus often slain; but that the one sacrifice is daily renewed by mystic rites, and that by the daily remembrance of the death of the Lord, by which we have been set free, in eating and drinking the flesh and blood which have been offered for us, this very deed which formerly was accomplished may be represented; and this sacramental offering admonishes us to gaze as it were on the Lord on the cross and draw thence for ourselves from that inexhaustible source the grace of salvation ; and we offer sacrifice for the living and the dead when we implore the Father for them through the death of the Son." [4]

In the proceedings of this council fuller instruction was promised in an *Enchiridion* or *Handbook* to be published later. This appeared as the work of Archbishop Hermann; but, like the decrees of the council, it is thought to have been largely the

[1] VII. 14 (Hardouin, *Conc.* ix. 2004, 2005).
[2] VII. 15 (*op. cit.* ix. 2005).
[3] VII. 16 (*op. cit.* ix. 2005).
[4] VII. 27 (*op. cit.* ix. 2007, 2008).

work of Groepper. The doctrine of the Eucharist is treated at great length. Among the more important of the passages on this subject are the following :—

" By the power of the word of God the Sacrament of bread and wine is so changed that it is substantially different from what it was before, and what before the consecration were bread and wine are after the consecration in substance the flesh and blood of Christ. . . . The word of this Sacrament is the saying of Christ, by the power of which this Sacrament is made, by the efficacy of which the bread becomes the body of Christ and the wine mingled with water is changed into His blood." [1]

"When the flesh and blood of Christ are eaten not only sacramentally but also spiritually, they marvellously refresh and gladden and feed the inner man, since indeed he perceives that he through Christ has received all things, regeneration, justification, and eternal life." [2]

"The flesh of Christ is offered for the salvation of the body, and His blood for our soul. . . . Yet under either species the whole Christ is taken, nor is He taken more under both species or less under one only. . . . Under the species of bread by force of the Sacrament, as they say, the body of Christ is contained, and the blood by concomitance. Under the species of wine the blood of Christ is contained by force of the Sacrament, and the body by concomitance." [3]

"When the health-giving host is broken, this fraction takes place only in the species of bread, which remains after the consecration without a subject ; but Christ remains unbroken and whole in every fragment." [4]

"The adversaries pretend that the orthodox have defined that the offering in the Mass is a sacrifice which when applied on behalf of the living and the dead merits for them remission of guilt and penalty, and that too from the work wrought (*ex opere operato*) although the faith of those to whom it is to be applied be not added. They pretend, that is, that the orthodox impair the work of Christ, and that they crucify the Son of God again, in withdrawing the sanctification for our sins from the offering once made on the cross and assigning it to the Mass or rather to the outward work of the priest. But these calumnies of the adversaries ought not to offend any one in the Church, because the mind and judg-

[1] Fo. 49 *b*, 50 *a*, edition 1558.   [2] Fo. 52 *b*.
[3] Fo. 54 *a*, 54 *b*.   [4] Fo. 57 *a*.

ment of the orthodox always have been and are altogether different from what they pretend. All the devout from the beginning of the world unto this day have known by the help and teaching of the Holy Ghost that there is only one propitiatory and satisfactory sacrifice for our sins and for those of the whole world, namely, Christ the Lord, the Lamb without spot, who was offered for us on the cross, who is described as having been slain from the beginning of the world." [1]

"It is clear from what has been said that sacrifice is of two kinds. There is a propitiatory sacrifice which is offered for the remission of sins to appease the wrath of God and to reconcile us to God. There is also a sacrifice of praise and thanksgiving and obedience which we pay to God as the honour and service which are rightly due to Him. Again, because this sacrifice of praise had failed after the fall of Adam and the corruption of nature, it is clear that the propitiatory sacrifice was promised at the first and at length fulfilled in Christ that He might inaugurate the Eucharistic sacrifice. . . . It follows that these sacrifices are so united that the later could not be without the former, but that the former is the cause and foundation of the later. Again, it is clear that the propitiatory sacrifice in the second sense is called propitiatory in the same signification as were those of the Old Testament, the burnt offering and sacrifice for sin and for guilt ; but that in the first sense is actually real, and was signified by the sacrifices of the old law. Hence it is shown that in every sacrifice there are two things, the thing that is offered and the act of offering itself. . . . And so in the Mass there are both the thing that is offered and the act of offering. Again, the thing that is offered is twofold, namely, the real body of Christ and the mystical body of Christ. If we consider the real body of Christ which by the power of the almighty word of God is contained in the most holy Eucharist, who denies that this body can rightly be called a propitiatory sacrifice not by reason of the act of offering which the priest makes but by reason of that act of offering which has once taken place, having been made on the cross, the force of which, as being ever of the same power and efficacy, lasts for ever ? . . . Though in this way the body of the Lord on the altar is not with absolute propriety (*non omnino proprie*) [2] called a sacrifice, but is rather a Sacrament or the substance (*res*) of the Sacrament, since a Sacrament and a sacrifice seem to differ in this that a Sacrament is a holy sign by means

---

[1] Fo. 58 *a* ; see Rev. xiii. 8.
[2] *Proprie* is here used in its technical sense.

of which God presents something to us, and a sacrifice is that which we offer to God. Yet, as we have said, the fathers did not hesitate to call this body of Christ on the altar a sacrifice and a health-giving victim, not by reason of the sacrifice which consists in the action of the priest or of those who take part in the Mass or of the Church, but by reason of the sacrifice which was once offered on the cross, in which Christ is Himself the Priest and the offering which is of power for ever. . . . Thus in this Sacrament there is nothing which is the priest's own, but Christ does all, who even to this day creates and sanctifies and blesses and distributes to those who take it devoutly this His most real and most holy body. . . . When you see the priest give you the body, think not of the hand of the priest but of the hand of Christ as stretched out to you. . . . Insofar as the Church offers to God the Father the real body and real blood of Christ, the sacrifice is simply representative of that which was once accomplished on the cross. Insofar as the Church offers herself (and she is the mystical body of Christ), and dedicates herself and all that is hers to God through Christ, the sacrifice is real but spiritual, that is, the Eucharistic sacrifice of praise and thanksgiving and the obedience that is properly due to God. But you will say, How does it happen that the real body of Christ is again offered on the altar when the Apostle says that Christ by one offering has perfected for ever them that are sanctified?[1] Who has given this power to the Church? We answer, Christ in the manifestation of His body and the showing of His limbs has offered Himself once unto death in His mortal flesh, that He might de-stroy death, and restore to us life by rising again. But none the less the Church daily offers Him, not in death, because Christ once rising from the dead dieth no more, but in the remembrance of His death, that she may be filled with the fruit of His passion and death."[2]

"Christ is sacrificed on the altar, but sacramentally and mysti-cally, because in the Sacrament there is made a remembrance of that which was once done."[3]

"For this, to repeat the same thing over and over again, the whole Church clearly professes, that remission of sins or justification is ascribed only to the offering which was made on the cross. For this alone is the ransom for our sins, and for those of the whole world, and in the case of adults this is applied only to those who accept it by their own faith."[4]

[1] Heb. x. 14.   [2] Fo. 65 a-66 b.
[3] Fo. 67 a.   [4] Fo. 70 b.

Some three years after the Council of Cologne of 1536 Arch-bishop Hermann came under the influence of Melanchthon and Bucer.[1] A result of this and of other influence was that he adopted opinions of a different character from those which he had defended in the Council of Cologne and in the *Enchiridion*. In 1546 he was excommunicated; in 1547 he was deprived of his offices; from that time until his death in 1552 he lived in re-tirement. A famous book, thought to have been largely the work of Melanchthon and Bucer, appeared as his in 1543 under the title of *Einfaltigs Bedencken warauff*. A Latin version was published in 1545 entitled *Simplex ac pia Deliberatio*. In 1547 an English translation was issued with the title *A Simple and Religious Consultation*, of which a revised edition appeared in 1548. In the chapter "Of Holy Oblations" Hermann spoke of Christ as "that only acceptable and propitiatory sacrifice through which we obtain of God grace, salvation, and all bene-fits"; of "our bodies and our souls" as "an acceptable sacrifice through faith"; of "repentance" as "a sacrifice unto God"; of the "sacrifices of praying, magnifying God, and giving of thanks, the sacrifice of liberality towards our neighbours".[2] In the chapter "Of the Lord's Supper," the opinions adopted ap-pear to be Lutheran; and Hermann made against the teaching inherited from the middle ages in the sixteenth century the charges from which he had defended it at the Council of Cologne and in the *Enchiridion*.

"We certainly believe that our Lord Jesus Christ Himself is here present in the midst of us, and that He Himself, though it be by the ministry of the Church, doth truly give us His body and blood and together all things whatsoever He obtained and deserved by the offering of His body on the cross, I mean remission of sins, the everlasting covenant of God's grace, the blessed adoption of God that we be the sons and heirs of God and His co-heirs."[3]

"The pastors shall warn the people that they doubt nothing but the Lord Himself is present in the midst of them, and giveth them His very body and blood, that they ever may more fully live

---

[1] See pp. 25-35, 43-50, *supra*.

[2] Signatures s. vii *b*, s. viii *a*, s. viii *b*, English edition of 1547. Any difference in any passages quoted between the German, the Latin, and the two English editions does not affect doctrine.

[3] Signature Cc. iv *a*.

in Him, and He in them, and that they may daily grow more and more into Him, which is the Head, and be moved of Him as His lively and uncorrupt members."[1]

"By this only thing, that Christ on the cross offered His holy body and blood to the Father for our sins, we be reconciled to God and delivered from the power of Satan, being made the sons and heirs of God."[2]

"Before all things, the pastors must labour to take out of men's minds that false and wicked opinion whereby men think commonly that the priest in Masses offereth up Christ our Lord to God the Father after that sort that with his intention and prayer he causeth Christ to become a new and acceptable sacrifice to the Father for the salvation of men, applieth and communicateth the merit of the passion of Christ, and of the saving sacrifice whereby the Lord Himself offereth Himself to the Father a sacrifice on the cross, to them that receive not the same with their own faith."[3]

"Men are everywhere in this error, that they believe, if they be present when the priest sayeth Mass, and take part of the Mass only with their presence, that this very work and sacrifice of the priest whereby he offereth the Son to the Father for their sins, that is to say, setteth Him before the Father with his intention and prayer, is of such efficacy that it turneth all evil from them, and bringeth them all felicity of body and soul, though they continue in all manner of sins and mischiefs against God and their conscience, and neither perceive or receive the Sacraments out of the Mass but only behold the outward action as a spectacle, and honour it with bowing of knees and other gestures and signs of veneration."[4]

"Through this work of the Mass they are made more careless and stronger in their sins and contempt of Christ, thinking that by that ceremony the wrath of God is turned from them, and all other evils."[5]

"Before all things then the Lord offereth unto us His flesh and His blood, and biddeth us to take the same."[6]

"The Lord Jesus truly offereth unto us this His sanctifying flesh and blood in His Holy Supper with visible signs of bread and wine by the ministry of the congregation, and exhibiteth the same unto the remission of sins, to be meat of everlasting life, to confirm the covenant of God's adoption and of everlasting life."[7]

"The most holy Supper of our Lord Jesu Christ, wherein He

[1] Signature Cc. v a.   [2] Ibid. b.   [3] Ibid. vii b.
[4] Ibid. viii b.   [5] Ibid. Dd. i a.
[6] Ibid. vii b.   [7] Ibid. viii b.

hath given us His flesh for meat and His blood for drink, to confirm our faith and very Christian life." [1]

"He then that eateth of this bread after this sort and drinketh of the cup, and firmly believeth these words, which he heareth of the Lord, and signs, which he receiveth, eateth truly and wholesomely the flesh of Christ and drinketh His blood, and more fully receiveth into himself whole God and Man with all His merits and favour wherewith the Father embraceth Him, with the right and participation of everlasting life, he abideth in Christ the Lord, and the Lord in him, and he shall live for ever." [2]

In 1544 a book was published at Cologne in the name of the chapter of Cologne Cathedral as an answer to the work of Hermann, entitled *Antididagma or a Defence of the Christian and Catholic Religion*. Like the decrees of the Council of Cologne of 1536,[3] and the *Enchiridion*,[4] it is thought to have been largely the work of John Groepper.[5] It contains a lengthy statement and vindication of the traditional doctrines received from the middle ages. A few extracts will illustrate the general position which is elaborately maintained in the book.

"The Catholic Church has taught that this most sacred Sacrament is made and consecrated by the Almighty word of Christ, by which the invisible Priest in His holy ministry converts and changes the visible creatures into the substance of His body and blood." [6]

"Since the Sacrament of the Eucharist is always consecrated for this purpose, that it may eventually be consumed, the Catholic Church has taught to this day that in the Sacrament, when the consecration has taken place, the real body and real blood of Christ are contained under the species of bread and wine, and are really there, and remain until the Sacrament is consumed." [7]

"Since Christ makes Himself present in the Sacrament, it has always been observed in the Church that He Himself as really present is to be adored there with kneeling and most reverently and with the greatest devotion in spirit and in truth." [8]

"The Church ought not to be condemned for being content, in her faith and devotion with thanksgiving to God, to administer one species only, containing as it does the body and the blood. For it

[1] Signature Ee. ii b.   [2] *Ibid.* iii b.
[3] See pp. 76, 77, *supra*.   [4] See pp. 77-80, *supra*.
[5] See pp. 76-78, *supra*, and p. 100, note 1, *infra*.
[6] Fo. xlii a, edition 1544.   [7] Fo. xliii a.   [8] Fo. xliv b.

6 *

is most true that this Sacrament was instituted rather that we should spiritually receive it than for its outward species. . . . Wherefore we ought not in this Sacrament to be too much concerned about the species, whether they are many or few, small or great; but we should consider rather the virtue of the mystery, especially as the whole Christ, body and blood, is in each species of bread and wine." [1]

"Christ offered a sacrifice of a twofold kind when He went from this world to the Father. One was the bloody sacrifice on the cross, where by the offering of His body and the shedding of His precious blood He obtained for us remission of sins and eternal redemption. . . . This sacrifice of the new law, offered once only on the cross, is offered no more in like manner. That is the one sacrifice which has merited for us remission of sins and eternal life. . . . But, when the heavenly Father determined to establish with us by the death of His only-begotten Son a new covenant and league of grace, He took care also to provide that a sacrifice harmonious to such a covenant, whereby we might be continually kept in mind of the covenant and league, should be instituted and manifested to us. Wherefore Christ the Lord, when He had willed to offer Himself once for us a bloody sacrifice, on the very night in which He was betrayed, before His passion, after He had already determined to undergo it, instituted and left to us a kind of image of His sacrifice as a sacrifice whereby we might thenceforth again and again offer sacrifice in the Church. And this is that other sacrifice, not the bloody but the bloodless offering of remembrance and thanksgiving and praise. . . . He commanded that we should offer spiritually and by way of commemoration this most holy sacrifice to the heavenly Father again and again, and ever until He should come, not to merit remission of sins as if remission had not been fully and sufficiently obtained through Christ once on the cross for all believers, but for a memorial of that redemption of His, that is, that in these most holy mysteries we may ever mystically and in figure represent and set forth His passion and death to God the Father, and give Him thanks, that of His free grace He has given to us and to all the world His beloved only Son, and through Him remission of sins, and all His gifts, so that thus by spiritual representation and commemoration and thanksgiving of this kind, and particularly by the reception of His most holy Sacrament, we may apply and appropriate to ourselves those divine gifts which have been procured." [2]

<hr />

[1] Fo. xlv *b*.   [2] Fo. lvi *a*, lvi *b*.

" On the method of this sacrifice the Catholic Church has to this time taught that in every Mass four sacrifices are spiritually offered to God. First, by the command and institution of His Son our Lord Jesus Christ, by an eternal work but with a mystical signification, bread and wine mingled with water are offered. Secondly, there is offered the common sacrifice of praise and thanksgiving on behalf of the whole Catholic Church, nay, on behalf of all the world, for all the good deeds of God, whether known or unknown to us, which to all the world from the beginning unto now He has unceasingly shown, and daily shows. Thirdly, when the consecration has taken place, Christ Himself is offered, His body and His blood, and His most sacred passion by means of the commemoration and representation of it. And, fourthly, the Church herself and whole community of Christ is offered, which in this most sacred action dedicates and sacrifices herself wholly to God the Father through Christ our Lord, whose body she is. And, moreover, the holy fathers have taught that besides these four chief sacrifices very many others are offered. Such are the profession of belief, manifold prayers, entreaty and intercession for all men, and many other and devout desires and wishes. All these assuredly are kinds of real and spiritual sacrifices, and are set out in the Mass." [1]

" Although this sacrifice in the form in which it was offered on the cross has been offered once only, and the blood has been shed once only, so that in this way it cannot be offered again, yet none the less such a sacrifice is and abides perpetually accepted before God in its power and efficacy in such a way that the sacrifice once offered on the cross is no less prevailing and living in the presence of the Father to-day than on that day on which the blood and the water flowed from the wounded side. . . . The holy fathers call the body and blood of the Lord present on the altar at one time the satisfaction for our sins and for those of the whole world, at another time the price of our redemption. . . . God has given to us His Son our Lord Jesus Christ for this purpose, that we, who trust not in our strength and power and confess our sins, may present to the Father Him who is our Lord and Redeemer as the one sacrifice making satisfaction for our sins." [2]

" The schoolmen make this distinction between the work wrought (*opus operatum*) and the work working (*opus operans*). They say that the former is the work of God alone and of Christ, not consisting in the act of offering but in the consecration and sanctification of the Sacrament, and that it is always pure and holy,

---

[1] Fo. lviii *a*, lxviii *b*.   [2] Fo. lxiii *b*, lxiv *a*.

although God sometimes allows it to be outwardly performed by the hands of an unclean priest. . . . Of the work working (*opus operans*), which consists not in the consecration of the Sacrament but in the act of offering the sacrifice in thanksgiving and prayers and so on, they say that it is sometimes unclean, and that it is not of the same value whether it is offered by a religious man or one who is impious, by one who is good or one who is bad, nay, that it tends rather to the condemnation of a bad priest, although, as sometimes happens, it may be productive of good to those who are present, not indeed by reason of the priest but because of their own devotion which is theirs through their hearing of the prayers, especially as the prayer offered by means of the priest as a public minister is said in the name of all. . . . The Church has never taught that the outward work of a bad priest procures remission of sins for any one without faith and devotion." [1]

X.

The differing types of opinion in regard to the Eucharist held by different groups of Reformers were considered with great care at the Council of Trent by the Bishops who remained in communion with the Pope. Some years elapsed between the first project of this council and its actual meeting. Shortly after the accession of Pope Paul III. in 1534 he determined to summon a council to consider the affairs of the Church. It was at first ordered that the council should meet at Mantua in 1537. Various circumstances occurred to cause delay; and the first session was held at Trent in 1545. In 1547 the sittings of the council were transferred to Bologna; and in the same year they were suspended. Up to this point in the proceedings the chief subjects considered in all the sessions except the seventh were the Creed, Holy Scripture, and the doctrine of Grace. Between the sixth and the seventh sessions, both of which were held at Trent, the Sacraments in general, Holy Baptism, Confirmation, and the Holy Eucharist were very fully considered and discussed. At the seventh session the council affirmed thirteen canons on the Sacraments in general, fourteen canons on Baptism, and three canons on Confirmation. No further point than discussion was reached in regard to the Eucharist. In the canons on the Sacraments in general the number of the "Sacraments of the new law" was declared to be seven, all of which were "instituted by

[1] Fo. lxxi *b*, lxxii *a*.

our Lord Jesus Christ," of which the Eucharist is one ; views
placing the "Sacraments of the new law" on a level with those
of the Jews, making the seven Sacraments equal to one another,
and denying the necessity of them to salvation, were condemned ;
there were statements on the imprinting of "character" on the
soul in Baptism, Confirmation, and Orders, the need in ministers
of "the intention at least of doing what the Church does," the
valid nature of Sacraments administered by a sinful minister,
the incapacity of Christians in general to administer all the
Sacraments, and the lack of authority on the part of individual
ministers to alter "the received and approved rites of the Catholic
Church". On the relation of the Sacraments to grace the canons
were as follows :—

"If any one shall say that these Sacraments were instituted for
the purpose of nourishing faith alone, let him be anathema."

"If any one shall say that the Sacraments of the new law do
not contain the grace which they signify, or that they do not confer
grace itself on those who place no obstacle (*obicem*), as if they were
only external signs of the grace or righteousness which are received
by means of faith, and certain marks of Christian profession by
which the faithful are distinguished among men from the unbelievers, let him be anathema."

"If any one shall say that grace is not given by means of Sacraments of this kind always and to all, so far as the part of God is
concerned, even if they duly receive them, but sometimes and to
some, let him be anathema."

"If any one shall say that grace is not conferred from the work
wrought (*ex opere operato*) by means of the Sacraments of the new
law themselves, but that faith in the promise of God is sufficient by
itself for the reception of grace, let him be anathema." [1]

The eighth session was that which determined on the transference of the council to Bologna; and the ninth, tenth, and
eleventh sessions, which were held at Bologna, transacted little
but formal business.

. After the suspension of the sittings of the council in 1547
no further meeting was held during the Papacy of Paul III.   In
1549 Paul III. died, and in 1550 he was succeeded by Pope
Julius III.   In 1551 the new Pope summoned the council to
meet again; and the sittings were resumed at Trent in May.

[1] Hardouin, *Concilia*, x. 52-55.

Between this date and 28th April, 1552, when the proceedings were again suspended, the subjects of the Eucharist, Penance, and Extreme Unction were considered. In regard to the Eucharist a statement of the opinions of the different schools of Reformers had been drawn up as a basis of consideration at the earlier proceedings at Trent; and this statement, with some alterations, was now again submitted to the judgment of the theologians. It is of considerable importance as giving a brief abstract, apparently mostly made with great fairness, of the crucial points in the teaching of the Reformers, and as showing that the differences between the Lutherans and others were clearly understood by those who drew it up. It is as follows:—

" 1. In the Eucharist there is not really the body and blood or the Godhead of our Lord Jesus Christ, but only as in a sign. This is the error of Zwingli and Oecolampadius and the Sacramentarians.

" 2. In the Eucharist Christ is presented to the communicants (*exhiberi*), but only spiritually, to be eaten by means of faith, not sacramentally. This is an article of the above-mentioned heretics, especially Oecolampadius. . . . While they do not deny that Christ is really in the Eucharist, they assert that Christ cannot be eaten except by means of faith, and that only the morsel of bread is taken sacramentally.

" 3. In the Eucharist there is indeed the body and blood of our Lord Jesus Christ, but together with the substance of the bread and the wine, so that there is no Transubstantiation, but a hypostatic union of the humanity and the substance of the bread and the wine,[1] so that it is true to say, This bread is My body, and This wine is My blood. Martin Luther speaks thus. . . .

" 4. The Eucharist was instituted only for the remission of sins. This article . . . is Luther's.

" 5. In the Eucharist Christ is not to be adored, or to be worshipped on the feasts, or to be carried about in processions, or to be taken to the sick; and those who thus adore Him are real idolaters. Luther thus speaks.[2] . . . The same is also taught in the *Confession of Augsburg*.

" 6. The Eucharist is not to be reserved in the sanctuary, but is

---

[1] It may be questioned whether the phrase " hypostatic union " fairly represents the doctrine of Luther, whose teaching is here described. For his teaching about the continued existence of the bread and wine, see pp. 10-13, 23, *supra*.

[2] For Luther's teaching on this subject, see pp. 18-21, *supra*.

to be consumed at once, and given to those who are present; and those who act otherwise abuse this Sacrament. Nor is it lawful for any one to give Communion to himself. These statements are made in the book of reformation for the people of Cologne.

"7. The body of Christ does not remain in the consecrated hosts or particles after the Communion, but is there only while it is being received, not before or after reception. This article is Luther's.[1] . . .

"8. It is of the law of God to give Communion to the people and to little children under both kinds; and therefore they sin who compel the people to use one kind only. It is so stated in the *Confession of Augsburg*. . . . Luther also so speaks. . . .

"9. As much is not contained under one kind as under both, neither does a communicant under one kind receive as much as a communicant under both. John Eck says . . . Luther thus asserts. . . .

"10. Faith by itself is sufficient preparation for the reception of the Sacrament, neither is Confession before it necessary, but free, especially to the instructed. Nor are men under obligation to communicate at Easter. Luther thus speaks. . . ."[2]

This statement of the opinions of the Reformers was submitted to the consideration of a large number of theologians present at Trent. Their reports, as given by Angelo Massarello, the Bishop of Telese, the secretary of the council, are strongly hostile to the teaching described in it.[3] As a result of their consideration of the matter, all the theologians consulted advised the absolute condemnation of the first, third, fifth, seventh, and eighth propositions, and the first part of the sixth. Some of them suggested that the condemnation of the second, fourth, ninth, and tenth propositions, and the second part of the sixth, should be so worded as to show accurately in what sense the condemnation was passed.[4] The fathers of the council after lengthy discussions drew up a statement of doctrine and a number of canons;[5] and these were formally approved in the thirteenth session of the council.[6] In the statement of doctrine the reason for the institution of the Eucharist was described as being that

[1] For a letter written by Luther on this subject in 1543, see pp. 23, 24, *supra*.

[2] Theiner, *Acta Genuina SS. Oec. Conc. Trid.* i. 488, 489.

[3] *Op. cit.* i. 490-501.   [4] *Ibid.* 501, 502.

[5] *Ibid.* 502-29.   [6] *Ibid.* 530.

the memory of Christ might be preserved and His death proclaimed; that the Sacrament might be taken as "the spiritual food of souls, whereby they might be nourished and strengthened, living by the life of" Christ, and as an "antidote, whereby we might be set free from daily faults and preserved from mortal sins"; and that it might be a "pledge of our future glory" and a "symbol of that one body of which He Himself is the Head, to which He willed that we, as members, should be bound by the closest ties of faith and hope and love". It was declared that "after the consecration of the bread and wine our Lord Jesus Christ, true God and Man, is really and actually and substantially contained under the species of those sensible things"; that He is "ever at the right hand of the Father in heaven after a natural manner of being," but is also "present with us in many other places sacramentally in His substance according to that manner of being which is possible to God, though we can hardly express it in words". Of this supernatural presence of Christ it was further said that "immediately after the consecration the real body of the Lord and His real blood are under the species of bread and wine together with His soul and Godhead"; "the body under the species of bread and the blood under the species of wine from the force of the words"; "the body under the species of wine and the blood under the species of bread and the soul under both by the force of that natural connection and concomitance whereby the parts of the Lord Christ, who has now risen from the dead no more to die, are united with one another"; "the Godhead by reason of its wonderful hypostatic union with the body and the soul"; so that "the whole and complete Christ is under the species of bread and under every part of that species and also under the species of wine and under the parts of it". Of Transubstantiation it was said that "by the consecration of the bread and wine the conversion takes place of the whole substance of the bread into the substance of the body of our Lord Christ, and of the whole substance of the wine into the substance of His blood, which conversion is fittingly and rightly called Transubstantiation by the Holy Catholic Church". It was pointed out that the duty of adoring the Sacrament was not impaired by the fact that it was instituted for the purpose of Communion; and processions of the Sacrament and reservation of it and the carrying of it to the sick were approved. Stress was laid on the need of reverent approach to the Sacrament; and the custom that no one conscious of mortal sin should communicate without previous sacramental Confession was pronounced to be right. The traditional distinction of "three ways of receiving this holy Sacrament" was accepted, namely, the merely sacramental reception by which sinners partake of it; the reception spiritual only on the part of those "who desire to eat the heavenly bread and experience its fruit and benefit by living faith, which works by love"; and the reception which is both sacramental and spiritual by those "who first so prove and prepare themselves that they may approach this divine Table clad in the marriage robe". This doctrinal statement included an exhortation to Christians to "believe and venerate these holy mysteries of the body and blood of" "our Lord Jesus Christ" "with such constancy and firmness of faith, such dedication of mind, such godliness and devotion, that they may be able frequently to receive the supersubstantial bread, and that it may be really the life of their souls and the abiding health of their minds," so that "they may be able to attain to the heavenly country and receive without a veil the same Bread of angels of which they now eat under the sacred veils".[1] The canons put in a shorter form and made obligatory what was thus taught in the doctrinal statement. They were as follows :—

"1. If any one shall deny that in the most holy Sacrament of the Eucharist is contained really and actually and substantially the body and blood together with the soul and Godhead of our Lord Jesus Christ, and therefore the whole Christ, but shall say that He is in it only as in a sign or a figure or in power, let him be anathema.

"2. If any one shall say that in the most holy Sacrament of the Eucharist the substance of the bread and wine remains together with the body and blood of our Lord Jesus Christ, and shall deny that wonderful and unique conversion of the whole substance of the bread into the body and of the whole substance of the wine into the blood, the species of bread and wine only remaining, which conversion the Catholic Church most suitably calls Transubstantiation, let him be anathema.

"3. If any one shall deny that in the venerable Sacrament of the Eucharist the whole Christ is contained under each species, and

---

[1] Hardouin, *Concilia*, x. 79-82.

under every separate part of each species, when they are divided, let him be anathema.

"4. If any one shall say that in the wonderful Sacrament of the Eucharist the body and blood of our Lord Jesus Christ are not after consecration, but only in use while it is being received, and not before or after, and that the real body of the Lord does not remain in the consecrated hosts or particles which are reserved or are left over after Communion, let him be anathema.

"5. If any one shall say either that the chief fruit of the most holy Eucharist is the remission of sins or that no other effects result from it, let him be anathema.

"6. If any one shall say that in the most holy Sacrament of the Eucharist Christ the only-begotten Son of God is not to be adored with the worship due to God including the outward marks of such worship (*cultu latriæ etiam externo*); and therefore that the Sacrament is not to be venerated with a special festival commemoration, and is not to be solemnly carried about in processions according to the praiseworthy and universal custom and practice of the Church ; or that it is not to be shown to the people publicly for them to adore; and that those who adore it are idolaters, let him be anathema.

"7. If any one shall say that it is not lawful for the Holy Eucharist to be reserved in the sanctuary, but that it must necessarily be distributed after the consecration to those who are present ; or that it is not lawful for it to be borne with honour to the sick, let him be anathema.

"8. If any one shall say that Christ presented (*exhibitum*) in the Eucharist is eaten only spiritually and not also sacramentally and actually, let him be anathema.

"9. If any one shall deny that all and every one of the faithful people of Christ of both sexes, when they have come to years of discretion, are bound to communicate every year, at least at Easter, according to the precept of the Holy Church, let him be anathema.

"10. If any one shall say that it is not lawful for a priest who is the celebrant to administer the Communion to himself, let him be anathema.

"11. If any one shall say that faith by itself is sufficient preparation for receiving the most holy Sacrament of the Eucharist, let him be anathema. And in order that so great a Sacrament may not be received unworthily, and therefore to death and condemnation, this holy council appoints and declares that sacramental Confession must necessarily precede Communion in the case of those whose conscience is under the burden of mortal sin, however contrite they may consider themselves, if they have access to a confessor. If any one shall presume to teach or preach or persistently assert or even defend in a public disputation the contrary, let him thereby be counted excommunicate." [1]

In the congregation which preceded the thirteenth session of the council it had been decided that the practical questions as to Communion in one or in both kinds and as to the Communion of little children should be postponed ; [2] and most of the rest of 1551 was devoted to the consideration of the Sacraments of Penance and Extreme Unction. In December, 1551, the consideration of the sacrifice of the Mass was begun. As in the case of the doctrine of the Eucharistic presence, the first step was to draw up a statement of the opinions of the different types of Reformers, and to submit it to the judgment of the theologians attending the council. This statement was as follows :—

" 1. The Mass is not a sacrifice, nor an offering for sins, but only a commemoration of the sacrifice accomplished on the cross. Though it is metaphorically called a sacrifice by the fathers, yet it is not really and properly a sacrifice, but only a covenant and promise of the remission of sins. This article is asserted by Luther . . . and it is stated in the *Defence of Augsburg*.

" 2. The Mass is not of the Gospel and it was not instituted by Christ, but it was invented by men ; neither is it a good or meritorious work ; rather in it is committed manifest and multiple idolatry. This assertion is made in the *Defence of Augsburg* and by Calvin and Melanchthon. . . .

" 3. Blasphemous despite is done to the most holy sacrifice of Christ accomplished on the cross if any one believes that the Son of God is offered anew to God the Father by priests in the Mass. That Christ is mystically sacrificed and offered for us is nothing else than that He is given to us to be eaten. And in the words, ' Do this for My memorial ' [3] Christ did not ordain that the Apostles should offer His body and blood in the sacrifice of the Mass. Urban Rieger . . . Luther . . . Bucer. . . .

" 4. The canon of the Mass is full of mistakes and delusions, ought to be abolished, and is to be avoided no less than the worst abomination. This is stated in the *Defence of Augsburg* and by Zwingli and Bullinger and Melanchthon. . . .

[1] Hardouin, *Concilia*, x. 83, 84.
[2] Theiner, *op. cit.* i. 528.   [3] St. Luke xxii. 19.

"5. The Mass is not profitable as a sacrifice either to the living or to the dead ; and it is impious to apply it for sins, satisfactions, and other needs.   Melanchthon . . . Calvin . . . the *Defence of Augsburg* . . . Luther. . . .

"6. As no one communicates for another, or is absolved for another, so neither in the Mass can a priest offer sacrifice for another. This is stated in the *Defence of Augsburg*.

"7. Private Masses, that is, those in which the priest alone, and no other, communicates, did not exist before Gregory the Great, and are unlawful and to be abolished, and are opposed to the institution of Christ, and present excommunication rather than the Communion instituted by Christ.   The *Defence of Augsburg* and Calvin. . . .

"8. Wine is not the matter of this sacrifice.   Neither is water to be mixed with the wine in the cup.   So to mix it is contrary to the institution of Christ.   Bucer. . . .

"9. The rite of the Church of Rome by which the words of consecration are said secretly and in a low voice is to be condemned ; and the Mass ought to be celebrated only in a vernacular language which all understand ; and it is an imposture to assign certain Masses to certain saints.   This is asserted by Calvin. . . .

"10. In the celebration of Masses all ceremonies, vestments, and outward signs are incitements to impiety rather than offices of piety.   And as the Mass of Christ was most simple, so the nearer and the more like a Mass is to that first Mass of all the more Christian it is.   Luther. . . . "[1]

Reports on this statement of the opinions ascribed to the Reformers were made by the theologians.   They were strongly hostile to the whole tendency of the opinions described, though qualifications by careful distinctions were suggested in some of the condemnations proposed and it was pointed out that the statement " wine is not the matter of this sacrifice " did not appear to represent any current view.   Discussions took place in the council after the reception of the reports of the theologians ; and canons had been drawn up for examination and consideration on this subject and on the Sacrament of Orders when the proceedings of the council were again suspended on 28th April, 1552.[2]

In 1555 Pope Julius III. died.   His successor Pope Marcellus II. occupied the papal see for three weeks only.   Paul IV. was Pope from 1555 to 1559.   In 1559 Pope Pius IV. succeeded to

---

[1] Theiner, *op. cit.* i. 602, 603.   [2] *Ibid.* 603-60.

the Papacy, and in 1560 he ordered that the Council of Trent should again meet. Action was taken on the practical matters which had been postponed in 1551. In June, 1562, four canons were affirmed in the twenty-first session of the council denying the necessity of Communion in both kinds and of the Communion of little children.[1] To these canons a statement was added to the effect that the question of permitting Communion in both kinds in some places and circumstances was postponed for further consideration ; and after much discussion the council passed a decree by a majority in September, 1562, remitting this question to the Pope.[2] In July, 1562, the consideration of the sacrifice of the Mass, which had been interrupted by the suspension of the council in 1552, was resumed. A series of thirteen questions on the points raised by the propositions contained in the list drawn up in December, 1551, was submitted to the theologians. These questions were the following :—

" 1. Whether the Mass is only a commemoration of the sacrifice accomplished on the cross, and not a real sacrifice.

" 2. Whether the sacrifice of the Mass does despite to the sacrifice accomplished on the cross.

" 3. Whether in the words, ' This do for My memorial,'[3] Christ ordained that the Apostles should offer His body and blood in the Mass.

" 4. Whether the sacrifice which takes place in the Mass is. beneficial only to one who receives it, and cannot be offered for others, both living and dead, and for their sins and satisfactions and other needs.

" 5. Whether private Masses, that is, those in which the priest alone, and no other, communicates, are unlawful and to be abolished.

" 6. Whether it is contrary to the institution of Christ that water should be mixed with the wine in the Mass.

" 7. Whether the canon of the Mass contains errors and ought to be abolished.

" 8. Whether the custom of the Church of Rome by which the words of consecration are uttered secretly and in a low voice is to be condemned.

[1] Hardouin, *Concilia*, x. 122.
[2] *Ibid.* 22, 135 ; Theiner, *op. cit.* ii. 88, 96-116, 127-32.
[3] St. Luke xxii. 19.

" 9. Whether the Mass ought to be celebrated only in a vernacular language, which all understand.

" 10. Whether it is an abuse to assign certain Masses to certain saints.

" 11. Whether the ceremonies and vestments and outward signs which the Church uses in the celebration of Masses are to be done away.

" 12. Whether it is the same for Christ to be mystically offered for us and for Him to be given to us to be eaten.

" 13. Whether the Mass is only a sacrifice of praise and thanksgiving, or also a propitiatory sacrifice, both for the living and for the dead." [1]

After the submission of these questions, reports were made by the theologians, and lengthy discussions by the fathers of the council took place.[2] Eventually a statement of doctrine and canons giving effect to it were affirmed by the council in September, 1562, at the twenty-second session.[3] The statement of doctrine recounted that " our Lord Jesus Christ," " although He was about to offer Himself to God the Father on the altar of the cross by the intervention of death to accomplish there eternal redemption," " yet at the Last Supper left to His Church a visible sacrifice," " whereby that bloody sacrifice once for all to be accomplished on the cross might be represented, and His memorial might abide even unto the end of the world, and the saving power of the sacrifice of the cross might be applied to the remission of those sins which we daily commit "; and " declaring Himself appointed for ever a Priest after the order of Melchizedek, offered His body and blood under the species of bread and wine to God the Father "; and " appointed His Apostles priests of the new covenant "; and " commanded them and their successors in the priesthood to offer sacrifice ". The " visible sacrifice " thus appointed was declared to be " really propitiatory," so that " through it " those who " come to God with a true heart and right faith, with fear and reverence, in contrition and penitence, obtain mercy and find grace to help in time of need ". As to the relation of the sacrifice of the Mass to the cross it was said that in both alike " the Victim is one and the same," since He who " offered Himself on the cross " " now offers by the ministry of priests," " the method of offering alone being different "; that

---

[1] Theiner, *op. cit.* ii. 58.   [2] *Ibid.* 59-129.   [3] *Ibid.* 130, 131.

" the fruits of the bloody offering " on the cross " are most richly received by means of this bloodless offering "; and that consequently "no despite of any kind is done " to the work of Christ on the cross. It was added that the sacrifice of the Mass might rightly be offered "for the sins and penalties and satisfactions and other needs of the faithful still alive, and also for the departed in Christ who are not yet fully cleansed ". Approval was expressed of the connection of thanksgivings for the saints and prayers for their intercessions with Masses offered to God ; and of the canon and the ceremonies of the Mass. Of "private Masses " it was said that it was desirable for Communions to be made at every Mass "not only by spiritual affection but also by sacramental reception of the Eucharist," so that those thus communicating might have " the richer fruit of this most holy sacrifice " ; but that, failing communicants, Masses might be celebrated in which "the priest alone communicates sacramentally "; and that such Masses "ought to be accounted really general (*vere communes*), partly because in them the people communicate spiritually, and partly because they are celebrated by the public minister of the Church not only for himself, but for all the faithful who pertain to the body of Christ ". It was ordered that water should be mixed with the wine because of "the belief that this was done by the Lord Christ "; of the "flow of water together with blood from His side "; and of the "representation of the union of Christians with Christ their Head ". It was further laid down that the Mass was not to be said in the vernacular everywhere, but should be frequently explained to the people.[1] The canons which imposed the crucial points of the doctrinal statement were as follows :—

" 1. If any one shall say that in the Mass a real and proper sacrifice is not offered to God, or that no other offering is made than that Christ is given to us to be eaten, let him be anathema.

" 2. If any one shall say that in the words, ' Do this for My memorial,' [2] Christ did not appoint the Apostles priests, or did not institute that they and other priests should offer His body and blood, let him be anathema.

" 3. If any one shall say that the sacrifice of the Mass is only a sacrifice of praise and thanksgiving, or is a bare commemoration of the sacrifice accomplished on the cross and not propitiatory or that

[1] Hardouin, *Concilia*, x. 126-28.   [2] St. Luke xxii. 19.

it is of profit only to one who communicates, and that it ought not
to be offered for the living and the departed, for sins, penalties,
satisfactions, and other needs, let him be anathema.

"4. If any one shall say that by the sacrifice of the Mass any
blasphemy or despite is done to the most holy sacrifice of Christ
accomplished on the cross, let him be anathema.

"5. If any one shall say that it is an imposition to celebrate
Masses to the honour of the saints and to obtain their intercession
with God, let him be anathema.

"6. If any one shall say that the canon of the Mass contains
errors and ought therefore to be abolished, let him be anathema.

"7. If any one shall say that the ceremonies and vestments and
outward signs which the Catholic Church uses in the celebration of
Masses are incitements to impiety rather than offices of piety, let
him be anathema.

"8. If any one shall say that Masses in which the priest alone
communicates sacramentally are unlawful and are therefore to be
abolished, let him be anathema.

"9. If any one shall say that the custom of the Church of Rome
by which part of the canon and the words of consecration are said
in a low voice is to be condemned; or that the Mass ought to be
celebrated only in a vernacular language; or that water ought not
to be mixed with the wine in the cup that is to be offered as being
contrary to the institution of Christ, let him be anathema." [1]

The reports of the theologians and the discussions of the
fathers of the council show the grounds on which the enactments
of the Council of Trent in regard to the doctrines of the Eucharistic presence and of the Eucharistic sacrifice were based. Scripture and tradition alike were regarded as requiring the belief
that the consecrated Sacrament is the body and blood of Christ,
and that the Eucharist is a sacrifice. With this fundamental
position the more detailed statements to which the council was
committed were held to be inseparably connected. The affirmation of the Lateran Council of 1215 that "the bread is transubstantiated into the body and the wine into the blood" [2] was
viewed as a necessary consequence. The scholastic subtleties of
the middle ages and the philosophical questions as to the methods
of the change in consecration were to a large extent set aside;
and the definitions showed the reserve which is apt to characterise

[1] Hardouin, *Concilia*, x. 129.   [2] See vol. i. p. 313, *supra*.

statements of councils imposed as of faith as distinct from expressions of individual theologians which bind no one.   But the
conversion of the whole substance of the bread and the wine into
the body and blood of Christ, the doctrine of concomitance, the
lasting character of the presence beyond the time of administration, and the duty of adoration were expressly affirmed as matters
of faith ; and the distinction in the statement on doctrine on
which the canons were based between the natural method of the
presence of Christ in heaven and His sacramental presence in
the Eucharist followed the main principles of the lines of thought
which in the middle ages had characterised in particular the
Thomist theologians.[1]   In regard to the sacrifice it was maintained throughout the discussions that, since the same body and
blood which were offered on the cross are offered in the Eucharist,
the sacrifice of the Mass is one and the same as the sacrifice of
the cross, and that, consequently, there is in it, no addition to
the work done on the cross, but rather an application of the results of it.   For the most part any connection with the heavenly
offering of our Lord, such as that recognised by many of the
Fathers, by the mediæval Western liturgical writers, and by the
Greek theologians of the middle ages, was out of sight, though
in the consideration of the sacrifice in 1551 and 1552 three of
the theologians referred to this idea, two in terms of approval,
one in condemnation.

"Though the offering of the Eucharist is different in method from
the offering of the cross, yet it is the same offering, the same flesh,
and the same blood ; and it is offered for the same end, yet under
different forms.   That on the cross was bloody and was offered once ;
this on the altar is bloodless and is offered daily ; the heavenly
offering also, which is made by Christ in heaven in the presence of
the Father, is bloodless and is ever made ; for Christ continually
stands in the presence of the Father to appease the wrath of God,
making intercession for us.   Therefore the sacrifice of the altar is
one and the same as that of the cross." [2]

"The sacrifice of the Mass represents the invisible sacrifice of
Christ in the upper room, and the visible sacrifice on the cross, and
that which Christ continually does, making intercession for us to the

[1] See vol. i. pp. 321, 331, 332, 340, *supra.*
[2] Francis van den Velde (Somnius, died in 1576) in Theiner, *op. cit.* i.
612.

7 *

Father in heaven. Therefore the Mass represents all these sacrifices, and is a commemoration of them." [1]

"When it is said, 'Thou art a priest for ever,' [2] it is implied that in the Mass His body is continually offered by priests; and so also the priesthood of Christ is perpetuated in priests. But Christ offers Himself to the Father not only in the upper room and on the cross, but continually. Wherefore John [3] says that He ever makes Himself an advocate for us in the presence of the Father and intercedes for us, that is, presents His own body to the Father, who was wroth with us. Which, nevertheless, He does not in heaven, offering Himself a sacrifice, but by means of the Eucharist on the altar. And this sacrifice is applied to others, that is, it makes them partakers of the fruits and effects of the passion of Christ." [4]

The fathers of the Council of Trent for a time intended that a *Catechism* embodying the doctrines affirmed by them should be drawn up while the council was sitting and approved by it. It proved impossible to carry out this plan; and eventually it was determined in the twenty-fifth session of the council that the approval and issue of a *Catechism* should be placed in the hands of the Pope.[5] Pope Pius IV. gave instructions for the composition of the work to four theologians. It was drawn up by them with the assistance of others, including St. Charles Borromeo, and after examination by a commission was issued in 1566 by the command of Pope Pius V. It came to be known as the *Catechism of the Council of Trent*. This *Catechism* possesses very high authority in the Roman Catholic Church, though the teaching contained in it is not binding as a matter of faith. The treatment of the Holy Eucharist is long and elaborate. The general doctrinal characteristics are the same as those of the decisions of the Council of Trent; and, like those decisions, exhibit the desire to enforce the doctrines that the consecrated

---

[1] John Groepper (born in 1503, died in 1559, the author of a book entitled *On the Real and Actual and Permanent Presence of the Body and the Blood of Jesus Christ after the Consecration*, published at Cologne in 1548 : see also pp. 76-78, 83, *supra*) in Theiner, *op. cit.* i. 618.

[2] Heb. v. 6.   [3] 1 St. John ii. 1, 2.

[4] Ambrose Storch (Pelargus, born about 1493, died in 1561, the author of books against Oecolampadius entitled *Defence of the Eucharistic Sacrifice*, published at Basle in 1528, and *Hyperaspismus*, published at Basle in 1529) in Theiner, *op. cit.* i. 621.

[5] Hardouin, *Concilia*, x. 157, 191.

Sacrament is the body and blood of Christ and that the Eucharist is a sacrifice, and at the same time to preserve the spiritual nature of the Eucharistic presence and the completeness of our Lord's acts of redemption on the cross. The differences are such as follow from the *Catechism* being a manual of instruction as distinct from conciliar decisions, and not being binding of faith as distinct from terms of communion. In regard to the Eucharistic presence there is much more explanation, and there are more details and technicalities. The teaching of the identity of the Eucharistic body of Christ with that of His earthly and heavenly life is more strongly expressed, while the spiritual character of the presence is implied rather than explicitly stated. The treatment of the sacrifice is scanty and adds little to what is found in the decrees of the council itself. A few quotations will sufficiently illustrate these features.

"There are more things than one in this mystery to which sacred writers have sometimes applied the name Sacrament. For the name Sacrament is applied sometimes to both the consecration and the reception, and frequently to the body and blood of the Lord themselves, which are contained in the Eucharist. . . . In this way we assert that this Sacrament is to be adored, meaning thereby the body and blood of the Lord. But it is clear that in all these senses the word Sacrament is less properly used. It is the species of bread and wine that in a real and absolute sense are called by this name." [1]

"There are three things chiefly to be wondered at and received, which the Catholic faith without any doubt believes and confesses to be effected in this Sacrament by the words of consecration. The first is that the real body of Christ, that very same body which was born of the Virgin and sits at the right hand of the Father in heaven, is contained in this Sacrament. The second is that no substance of the elements remains in it, although nothing can seem more different and removed from sense. The third is, what may easily be gathered from the first two, although the words of consecration most of all express it, that the accidents, which are seen by the eyes or perceived by the other senses, are in a wonderful and inexplicable way without any subject. And though one can see all the accidents of bread and wine, yet they do not depend on any substance but exist in themselves, since the substance of bread and

[1] II. iv. 8.

wine is so changed into the very body of the Lord that the substance of bread and wine wholly ceases to be." [1]

"Not only the real body of Christ and whatever pertains to the
real state of a body, as bones and sinews, but also the whole Christ
is contained in this Sacrament. It must be taught that Christ is the
name of God and Man, that is, of one Person, in whom divine
nature and human nature are united. Wherefore He possesses each
substance, and what belongs to each substance, Godhead and whole
human nature, which consists of the soul and of all the parts of the
body and of the blood, all which must be believed to be in the
Sacrament. For since in heaven the whole humanity is united to
the Godhead in one Person and Subsistence, it is wicked to suppose
that the body, which is in the Sacrament, is separated from that
same Godhead. . . . Because the blood and the soul and the Godhead are united to the body, all these, as well as the body, will be
in the Sacrament, not indeed from the force of the consecration, but
as being united to the body. And they are said to be in the Sacrament from concomitance, by which consideration it is clear that the
whole Christ is in the Sacrament. For if any two things are actually
united, where one is, there the other also of necessity must be.
Therefore it follows that the whole Christ is contained in the species
of bread as in the species of wine, so that, as in the species of bread
not only body but also blood and the whole Christ are really present,
so on the other hand in the species of wine not only blood but also
body and the whole Christ are really present. . . . Not only in each
species but in every particle of each species the whole Christ is contained. . . . The substance of bread and wine does not remain
after consecration. This, though it rightly calls out the greatest
wonder, yet is a necessary consequence of what has already been
shown. For if the real body of Christ is under the species of bread
and wine after consecration, it is absolutely necessary, since it was
not there before, that this comes to pass either by change of place
or by creation or by the conversion of another thing into it. Now it
certainly cannot be that the body of Christ is in the Sacrament by
coming from one place into another; for in that case it would
happen that He would be absent from His abode in heaven, since
nothing is moved without leaving the place from which it is moved.
And it is still less credible for the body of Christ to be created, and
this cannot even be imagined. Therefore it remains that the body
of the Lord is in the Sacrament by the conversion of the bread into
it; wherefore of necessity no substance of bread remains. . . . The

---

[1] II. iv. 26.

Eucharist is usually called bread both because it has the species of bread and also because it still retains the power of sustaining and nourishing the body, which is a property of bread. . . . Christ the Lord is not in this Sacrament as in a place, for a place goes with things themselves as they are possessed of a certain size; but we do not say that Christ is in the Sacrament after such a manner as great or small, which pertains to bulk, but as substance." [1]

" As natural food does no good to dead bodies, so also the holy mysteries do no good to a soul which does not live by the spirit. . . . As the body is not only preserved by natural food but is also increased, and tastes daily of new pleasure and sweetness from it, so also the food of the Holy Eucharist not only supports the soul but adds strength to it and effects that the spirit is more and more moved by delight in divine things. . . . That the lighter sins, which are usually called venial, are remitted and pardoned by the Eucharist ought not to be doubted. . . . There is power in the sacred mysteries to keep us clean from offences and untouched by them, and to preserve us in safety from the assault of temptations, and to prepare the soul as by a heavenly medicine so as not to be easily infected or corrupted by the poison of deadly disturbance. . . . That all the advantages and benefits of this Sacrament may be comprehended in one word, it must be said that the chief power of the Holy Eucharist is for the obtaining of eternal glory." [2]

" Some receive only the Sacrament, as sinners, who are not afraid to receive the holy mysteries with impure heart and mouth. . . . These not only obtain no benefit but, on the testimony of the Apostle himself, ' eat and drink judgment to themselves '.[3]   Others are said to receive the Eucharist only spiritually; these are those who eat the heavenly food which desire and wish set before them, inflamed with living ' faith which worketh by love ' ; [4] and from this reception they obtain, if not all, yet certainly the chief beneficial fruits.   Lastly, there are others, who receive the Holy Eucharist sacramentally and spiritually, who, since they ' first prove themselves ' in accordance with the teaching of the Apostle,[5] and approach this divine Table adorned with a marriage garment, obtain from the Eucharist those richest fruits of which we have spoken before." [6]

" It has been appointed by the Church that any one who has not received Communion at least once every year at Easter is to be excommunicated.   Yet the faithful are not to consider it enough that

[1] II. iv. 31, 32, 34, 35, 38, 42.   [2] II. iv. 48, 49, 50, 51, 52.
[3] 1 Cor. xi. 29.   [4] Gal. v. 6.   [5] 1 Cor. xi. 28.   [6] II. iv. 53.

they pay attention to the authority of this decree and receive the
body of the Lord only once in the year; but they are to think
that the Communion of the Eucharist should be made more frequently.   Whether monthly or weekly or daily is the most expedient, cannot be laid down by a fixed rule for all. . . . It will be
the task of the parish priest frequently to exhort the faithful that,
as they think it necessary to supply the body with nourishment
every day, so also they will not reject daily care for the sustenance
and nourishment of the soul with this Sacrament; for it is clear
that the soul needs spiritual food no less than the body needs
natural food." [1]

"The Eucharist was instituted by Christ for two reasons.   The
first reason is that it may be the heavenly nourishment of our soul,
whereby we can protect and preserve spiritual life.   The second
reason is that the Church may have a continual sacrifice, whereby
our sins may be expiated, and the heavenly Father, often grievously offended by our wickedness, may be brought from anger to
mercy, from the severity of just punishment to pity. . . . When
our Saviour was about to offer Himself to God the Father on the
altar of the cross, He could give no clearer sign of His boundless
love for us than in His leaving to us a visible sacrifice, whereby
that bloody sacrifice a little later to be once for all offered on the
cross might be renewed, and the memory of it kept daily to the
end of the world by the Church throughout the whole world with
the greatest gain. . . . Although it has been the custom of the
Church sometimes to celebrate Masses in memory and honour of
saints, yet it has taught that the sacrifice is not offered to them but
to God alone, who crowned the saints with immortal glory. . . .
That which is done in the Mass and that which was offered on the
cross are one and the same sacrifice; as there is one and the same
Victim, Christ our Lord, who offered Himself on the altar of the
cross once for all only as a bloody sacrifice.   For the bloody and
the bloodless sacrifice do not make two sacrifices but one only.
. . . There is also one and the same Priest, Christ the Lord; for
the ministers who offer the sacrifice act not in their own persons
but in the person of Christ when they consecrate His body and
blood. . . . The most holy sacrifice of the Mass is not only a sacrifice of praise and thanksgiving, or a bare commemoration of the
sacrifice which was offered on the cross, but it is also really a propitiatory sacrifice, by which God is appeased and rendered propitious. . . . This is the power of this sacrifice that it is of benefit not

[1] II. iv. 57, 58.

only to him who offers and him who receives but also to all the faithful, whether still living with us on earth or being dead in the Lord and not yet fully expiated." [1]

The proceedings of the Council of Trent and the *Catechism* drawn up in consequence of the action at Trent show the rejection by the Church of Rome in the sixteenth century of the characteristic ideas about the Eucharist of the continental Reformers. The denial of Zwingli that the body and blood of Christ are received; the contention of Bucer and Calvin that, though there is spiritual reception of the body and blood of Christ by the faithful communicant, the consecrated elements are not that body and blood; the assertion of Luther that, while the consecrated elements are the body and blood of Christ, they are also as fully bread and wine as before consecration; the refusal of all of these to allow any other kind of sacrifice in the Eucharist than a mere commemoration or such as may be in any kind of prayer, were all put aside and condemned. In these condemnations the Church of Rome adhered closely to the main lines of the mediæval Western theology, though some features of that theology were but little emphasised or were obscured. The exigencies of controversy led to the emphasis on the spiritual nature of the presence being but slight; but the mediæval distinctions between the method of Christ's presence in heaven and that of His presence in the Eucharist, and between the method of the presence of a natural body in a place and that of the presence of the body of Christ under the Eucharistic species, were preserved, and the great safeguards of a spiritual way of regarding the Sacrament, the assertion of the possibility and value of Spiritual Communion and the denial of benefit to be obtained by unworthy reception, were maintained. The changed state of our Lord's body after the resurrection and in His heavenly glory was probably realised less by the divines of Trent than it had been by some writers of the Middle Ages; and the lack of attention to this supremely important factor may have had a good deal to do with the use of the words "as bones and sinews" in the description of the "real state of a body" in the *Catechism*. As regards the sacrifice, the properly and distinctively sacrificial character of the Eucharist was insisted

[1] II. iv. 68, 71, 74, 75, 76, 77.

on; there was marked restraint as to detailed explanation, and
such ideas as that of destruction in sacrifice, and matters about
which controversies had taken place between the Thomist and
the Scotist divines; the ideas of a commemoration and an application of the fruits of the passion were maintained; the doctrine,
closely connected with that of the presence of the body and
blood of Christ, of the identity of the sacrifice of the Mass with
the sacrifice of the cross was preserved with great care; the association with the heavenly offering of Christ, though not wholly
ignored by all the theologians, failed to find a place in the official
decisions of the Council of Trent or in the *Catechism.*

CHAPTER X.

THE PERIOD OF THE REFORMATION.

PART II.

An attempt has been made in the last chapter to point out some of the influences which were operative in the early years of the sixteenth century, to illustrate from the writings of John Colet a cautious attitude which may have been characteristic of some of the pioneers of the New Learning, to estimate the different opinions of typical representatives of the continental Reformers, and to sketch the attitude taken up by the Church of Rome towards them. Apart from what was said in regard to Colet, the course of events in England after the beginning of the Reformation has been hitherto ignored. It is necessary next to consider the discussions and actions which took place in England.

I.

In 1521 a book entitled *Assertion of the Seven Sacraments*, bearing the name of King Henry VIII., was printed in London. It was an answer to Martin Luther's *On the Babylonish Captivity of the Church*. Presented at Rome by John Clerk, the English ambassador, who was afterwards Bishop of Bath and Wells, it won for Henry the title of " Defender of the Faith," which by a strange history was thus originally conferred on the King of England by the Pope, was afterwards recalled by papal authority, and was eventually granted to the king in defiance of the Pope by an Act of Parliament (35 Hen. VIII. c. 3). In this book the king maintained the doctrine of Transubstantiation and the sacrificial character of the Mass. He laid stress on the words of Christ at the institution of the Sacrament, in which the consecrated elements are called His body and blood, not bread and wine. He explained St. Paul's use of the word bread to

denote the Sacrament [1] as "either following the custom of Scripture, which sometimes calls a thing not by the name of what it is,
but of what it was before, as when it says, The rod of Aaron
devoured the rods of the magicians,[2] which then were not rods
but serpents, or else perhaps content to call it what in species it
appeared to be".[3] The doctrine of Transubstantiation, he said,
was believed by the Church, not because of the scholastic disputations which Luther had ridiculed, but because she had believed it from the first, as was expressed in the writings of the
Fathers. He condemned as worthless Luther's arguments that
the Mass is not a sacrifice or a good work, and declared that its
sacrificial character, like the doctrine of Transubstantiation, is
taught by the Fathers. The positive teaching contained in the
treatise affirmed:—

"Christ in His most holy Supper, in which He instituted the
Sacrament, made of bread and wine His own body and blood, and
gave them to His disciples to be eaten and drunk. A few hours
afterwards He offered the same body and blood on the altar of the
cross, a sacrifice to His Father for the sins of the people, which
sacrifice being finished, the covenant was consummated. . . . He
who diligently examines this will find Christ to be the eternal
Priest, who, in the place of all the sacrifices which were offered by
the temporary priesthood of Moses's law, whereof many were but
the types and figures of this holy sacrifice, has instituted one sacrifice, the greatest of all, the plenitude of all, as the sum of all others,
that it might be offered to God and given for food to the people.
. . . On the cross He consummated the sacrifice which He began
in the Supper. And therefore the commemoration of the whole
thing, to wit, of the consecration in the Supper and the oblation on
the cross, is celebrated and represented together in the Sacrament
of the Mass, and therefore the death is more truly represented than
the Supper." [4]

"The most holy fathers, . . . amongst many other things,
with great care delivered to us this also, that the bread and the
wine do not remain in the Eucharist but are truly changed into the
body and blood of Christ. They taught the Mass to be a sacrifice
in which Christ Himself is truly offered for the sins of Christian

[1] 1 Cor. x. 16, 17 ; xi. 26-28.   [2] Ex. vii. 12.
[3] Pp. 30, 31, edition 1521 (pp. 20, 21 in T. W.'s translation, edition
1688).
[4] Pp. 45, 46, 47 (pp. 32, 33 in T. W.'s translation).

people. And so far as was lawful for mortals, they adorned this immortal mystery with venerable worship and mystical rites. They commanded people to be present so as to revere it whilst it is being celebrated for the procuring of their salvation. Finally, lest the laity by forbearing to receive the Sacrament should by little and little omit it for good and all, they have established that every man shall receive it at least once in the year." [1]

The chief interest of this treatise of King Henry VIII. is in connection with the personality of that monarch and as representing the ordinary ideas of the time. In itself it is of no special importance. More favourable specimens, though marred by intemperate language and tone, of controversial works on the same side as that of the king are the attacks on Luther and Oecolampadius by Bishop Fisher of Rochester in his *Refutation of the Assertion of Luther*, published at Antwerp in 1523, his *Defence of the Assertion of the King against the Babylonish Captivity*, published at Cologne in 1525, and his treatise *On the Reality of the Body and Blood of Christ in the Eucharist against Oecolampadius*, published at Cologne in 1527. Like King Henry VIII. Bishop Fisher advocated substantially the same doctrines as those afterwards affirmed by the Council of Trent. As regards the Eucharistic presence, it appears to have been a matter of course to them that the Scriptural and patristic descriptions of the consecrated Sacrament as the body and blood of Christ inevitably imply that the substance of the bread and wine is so converted into the body and blood of Christ that after consecration the only remaining substance is that of the body and blood. As to the Eucharistic sacrifice, the sacrificial language in the tradition of the Church and the identity of the body and blood in the Eucharist with the body and blood of our Lord's earthly life led to the close association of the Mass with our Lord's actions in the upper room and His death on the cross; with them, as with so many others at this time, the connection of the Eucharist with the high-priestly work of our Lord in heaven seems to have been out of sight.

An interesting but tragic instance of dissent from the current doctrine, which was thus supported in England against the opinions of different continental Reformers, was in the case of John Frith. Frith's own belief appears to have been much the same

---

[1] P. 59 (pp. 43, 44 in T. W.'s translation).

as that of Calvin; but the most noticeable point in his latest
teaching is the contention that Transubstantiation, whether
true or not, ought not to be required as an article of faith.   A
book written by him fell into the hands of Sir Thomas More,
who wrote an answer to it.   The continuance of the controversy
led to the arrest of Frith, and his trial before the bishops, and
eventually to his death by burning at Smithfield in 1533.   The
reasons for his condemnation were the opinions which he expressed about purgatory and the Eucharist.   On the latter subject he wrote in a letter which he sent to his friends when he was
a prisoner in the Tower:—

"The whole matter of this my examination was comprehended
in two special articles, that is to say, Of purgatory, and Of the substance of the Sacrament. . . . Secondly, they examined me touching the Sacrament of the altar, whether it was the very body of
Christ or no.   I answered that I thought it was both Christ's body
and also our body, as St. Paul teacheth us in 1 Cor. x.   For in that
it is made one bread of many corns it is called our body, which,
being diverse and many members, are associated and gathered together into one fellowship or body.   Likewise of the wine, which is
gathered of many clusters of grapes, and is made into one liquor.
But the same bread again, in that it is broken, is the body of
Christ, declaring His body to be broken and delivered unto death, to
redeem us from our iniquities.   Furthermore, in that the Sacrament is distributed, it is Christ's body, signifying that as verily as
the Sacrament is distributed unto us, so verily are Christ's body
and the fruit of His passion distributed unto all faithful people.
In that it is received, it is Christ's body, signifying that as verily
as the outward man receiveth the Sacrament with his teeth and
mouth, so verily doth the inward man through faith receive Christ's
body and the fruit of His passion, and is as sure of it as of the bread
which he eateth.

" Well (said they) dost thou not think that His very natural body,
flesh, blood, and bone, is really contained under the Sacrament, and
there present without all figure or similitude ?   No (said I) I do not
so think : notwithstanding I would not that any should count that I
make my saying (which is the negative) any article of faith.   For
even as I say that you ought not to make any necessary article of
the faith of your part (which is the affirmative), so I say again that
we make no necessary article of the faith of our part, but leave it
indifferent for all men to judge therein, as God shall open their

hearts, and no side to condemn or despise the other, but to nourish in all things brotherly love ; and one to bear another's infirmity. . . . This is a spiritual meat, which is received by faith, and nourisheth both body and soul unto everlasting life. . . . The cause why I die is this, for that I cannot agree with the divines and other head prelates that it should be necessarily determined to be an article of faith, and that we should believe under pain of damnation, the substance of the bread and wine to be changed into the body and blood of our Saviour Jesus Christ, the form and shape only not being changed. Which thing, if it were most true (as they shall never be able to prove it by any authority of the Scripture or doctors) yet shall they not so bring to pass that that doctrine, were it ever so true, should be holden for a necessary article of faith. For there are many things, both in the Scriptures and other places, which we are not bound of necessity to believe as an article of faith. So it is true that I was a prisoner and in bonds when I wrote these things, and yet for all that I will not hold it as an article of faith, but that you may without danger of damnation either believe it or think the contrary. But as touching the cause why I cannot affirm the doctrine of Transubstantiation, divers reasons do lead me thereto : first, that I do plainly see it to be false and vain, and not to be grounded upon any reason either of the Scriptures or of approved doctors. Secondly, for that by my example I would not be an author unto Christians to admit anything as a matter of faith more than the necessary points of their creed, wherein the whole sum of our salvation doth consist, especially such things the belief whereof hath no certain argument of authority or reason. . . . Thirdly, because I will not for the favour of our divines or priests be prejudicial in this point unto so many nations of Germans, Helvetians, and others, which altogether rejecting the Transubstantiation of the bread and wine into the body and blood of Christ are all of the same opinion that I am, as well those that take Luther's part as those that hold with Oecolampadius. Which things standing in this case, I suppose there is no man of any upright conscience who will not allow the reason of my death, which I am put unto for this only cause, that I do not think Transubstantiation, although it were true indeed, to be established for an article of faith." [1]

It is to be observed that the phrase "natural body" was used in the question addressed to Frith by the bishops. From this time on the word "natural" often occurs in such a context. [2]

---

[1] See Foxe, *Acts and Monuments*, v. 11-14 (edition 1843-9).
[2] On the use of it by some of the Reformers, see pp. 37, 57, *supra*.

The use of it was probably due to the exigencies of controversy which led men to seek for phrases which seemed definite and explicit; and the design in using it was probably to affirm that the body of Christ in the Eucharist was really the same body as that of His earthly life. But the use of it marked a tendency to forget the differences between the manner of the presence of Christ in heaven and the manner of His presence in the Eucharist on which the schoolmen had insisted,[1] and which the divines at Trent a little later were careful to maintain; [2] and also the failure to realise the changed state of our Lord's body after the resurrection and the ascension which seems to have been general among controversialists on all sides in the sixteenth century.

There is an account of Frith's condemnation and the reasons for it in a letter which Archbishop Cranmer addressed to Nicholas Hawkins, the Archdeacon of Ely, who was the English Ambassador at the court of the Emperor Charles V., on 17th June, 1533.

"One Frith, which was in the Tower of London, was appointed by the king's grace to be examined before me, my lord of London, my lord of Winchester, my lord of Suffolk, my lord Chancellor, and my lord of Wiltshire; whose opinion was so notably erroneous that we could not dispatch him but was fain to leave him to the determination of his Ordinary, which is the Bishop of London. His said opinion is of such nature that he thought it not necessary to be believed as an article of our faith that there is the very corporal presence of Christ within the host and Sacrament of the altar, and holdeth of this point most after the opinion of Oecolampadius. And surely I myself sent for him three or four times to persuade him to leave that his imagination; but for all that we could do therein, he would not apply to any counsel; notwithstanding now he is at a final end with all examinations, for my lord of London hath given sentence and delivered him to the secular power, where he looketh every day to go unto the fire." [3]

Andrew Hewet was burnt with Frith on 4th July, 1533. In his examination by the bishops he had said that he thought concerning the Eucharist "as John Frith doth," and that he

[1] See vol. i. pp. 305, 312, 321, 332, 333, *supra*.

[2] See pp. 90, 99, *supra*.

[3] *Miscellaneous Writings and Letters of Thomas Cranmer* (Parker Society), p. 246.

did not believe that the Sacrament is "really the body of Christ, born of the Virgin Mary ".[1]

At the meeting of the Convocation of Canterbury in 1536 the Lower House laid before the Upper House a list of "errors and abuses " which they regarded as " worthy of reformation ". These tenets were probably due to the teaching of the Lollards. Those of the " errors and abuses " which related to the Eucharist were the following :—

" 1. That it is commonly preached and discoursed to the slander of this noble realm, the disquiet of the people, and to the hindrance of their salvation, that the Sacrament of the altar is not to be regarded : for several profane and scandalous persons are neither ashamed nor afraid to say, ' Why should I see the sacring of the High Mass ? Is it anything else but a piece of bread, or a little pretty round robin ? ' "

" 6. That all those deserve the character of Antichrist who refuse to communicate the laity under both kinds."

" 7. That all who are present at the Mass and do not receive with the priest have no benefit by that office."

" 37. That it is a pity Mass, Matins, Vespers, or any other part of Divine Service, was ever made, or suffered to be read or sung in a church."

" 41. That all recommending prayers and offices, such as Dirges, Masses, distributions of charity, etc., for the souls of the departed signify nothing."

" 51. That the saying or singing of Mass, Matins, or Vespers, is no better than roaring and whistling, masquerading and leger-demain."

" 58. That the canon of the Mass is the comment of some illiterate foolish priest." [2]

It is not known what took place in the Upper House of Convocation as the direct result of the presentation by the Lower House of this list of censured propositions. But the document known as the *Ten Articles* appears to have been drawn up in consequence of the discussions arising out of the presentation. This document was issued with the authority of the king, and was signed by very many of the bishops and by a

[1] See Foxe, *Acts and Monuments*, v. 17 (edition 1843-49).
[2] See Collier, *An Ecclesiastical History of Great Britain*, iv. 337-41.

considerable number of the dignified clergy.[1] It was evidently the outcome of an attempt to formulate a statement upon which the more moderate advocates of the traditional doctrines and the more conservative adherents of the Lutheran theology could agree. The article entitled " The Sacrament of the Altar " was as follows :—

" As touching the Sacrament of the altar, we will that all bishops and preachers shall instruct and teach our people committed by us unto their spiritual charge, that they ought and must constantly believe that under the form and figure of bread and wine, which we there presently do see and perceive by outward senses, is verily, substantially, and really contained and comprehended the very self-same body and blood of our Saviour Jesus Christ, which was born of the Virgin Mary, and suffered upon the cross for our redemption ; and that under the same form and figure of bread and wine the very self-same body and blood of Christ is corporally, really, and in the very substance exhibited, distributed, and received of all them which receive the said Sacrament ; and that therefore the said Sacrament is to be used with all due reverence and honour, and that every man ought first to prove and examine himself, and religiously to try and search his own conscience before he shall receive the same." [2]

In view of the later history of opinion it is of some interest that among the episcopal signatories to the *Ten Articles* there were from the party most favourable to the Reformers Thomas Cranmer, Archbishop of Canterbury, and Hugh Latimer, Bishop of Worcester, and from the party most opposed to the Reformers John Stokesley, Bishop of London, and Cuthbert Tunstall, Bishop of Durham, while the name of Stephen Gardiner, Bishop of Winchester, does not appear in either of two existing copies of the list of signatures.[3] *The Institution of a Christian Man, Containing the Exposition or Interpretation of the Common Creed, of the Seven Sacraments, of the Ten Commandments, and of the Pater Noster, and the Ave Maria, Justification, and Purgatory,* usually known as the *Bishops' Book,* was composed in 1537 by

[1] See the signatures in Collier, *op. cit.* iv. 356-59 ; Lloyd, *Formularies of Faith Put Forth by Authority during the Reign of Henry VIII.* pp. 17-20.

[2] Collier, *op. cit.* iv. 350, 351 ; Lloyd, *op. cit.* pp. 11, 12 (*cf.* pp. xxv, xxvi).

[3] See the references in note 1, *supra.*

a committee consisting of all the bishops and some other divines. It was signed by all the members of the committee ; and it was issued by the king, with orders that portions of it should be read in church every Sunday and holy day during the three years following, though he stated that he had not minutely considered its contents.[1] A difference of some importance as regards general character between the *Bishops' Book* and the *Ten Articles* was that, while the *Ten Articles* had referred to the three Sacraments of Baptism, the Eucharist, and Penance without defining whether there are or are not other Sacraments, the *Bishops' Book* treated explicitly and at length the " seven Sacraments " of the usual list. The article on " the Sacrament of the Altar " was not changed except for very slight verbal alterations which did not in any way affect the meaning.[2]

In 1538 the desire of King Henry VIII. to obtain political support from Germany, coupled with the demand of the Lutheran princes that all who should enter into league with them should assent to the truth of the *Confession of Augsburg*, caused him to invite an embassy of the more conservative Lutheran divines to visit England. On their arrival he nominated a committee of three bishops—apparently Stokesley of London, Tunstall of Durham, and Sampson of Chichester—and four doctors, with Cranmer as president, to confer with them. A manuscript written in Latin, entitled *A Book Containing Divers Articles, de Unitate Dei et Trinitate Personarum, de Peccato Originali, etc.*, which was found by the late Dr. Jenkyns among a bundle of papers which belonged to Archbishop Cranmer, probably gives all the statements of doctrine on which the Lutheran and English divines were able to agree. It is usually known as the *Thirteen Articles*. Its historical importance is considerable, both as showing what at this time Cranmer and Tunstall could agree to assert and because it appears to have been the link between the *Confession of Augsburg* and the Articles which were eventually formed into the present Thirty-nine *Articles of Religion* of the Church of England. The article on the Eucharist was as follows :—

---

[1] *See Miscellaneous Writings and Letters of Thomas Cranmer* (Parker Society), pp. 469, 470 ; *cf.* pp. 83-114.

[2] Lloyd, *op. cit.* pp. 100, 101.

"Concerning the Eucharist we firmly believe and teach that in the Sacrament of the body and blood of the Lord, the body and blood of Christ are really and substantially and actually present under the species of bread and wine; and that under the same species they are really and actually presented (*exhibentur*) and administered to those who receive the Sacrament, both good and bad." [1]

In the same year as that of the drawing up of the *Thirteen Articles*, 1538, John Nicholson or Lambert engaged in a controversy about the Eucharist with Dr. Taylor, the Rector of St. Peter's, Cornhill; and, on being prosecuted by Archbishop Cranmer, appealed to the king. After trial before the king and discussions with the bishops, he was condemned to death, and was burned at Smithfield in November, 1538. The gist of his opinions may be seen from the following passage from his *Treatise upon the Sacrament*, which he addressed to the king :—

"I confess and acknowledge that the bread of the Sacrament is truly Christ's body, and the wine to be truly His blood, according to the words of the institution of the said Sacrament: but in a certain wise, that is to wit, figuratively, sacramentally, or significatively, according to the exposition of the doctors before recited and hereafter following. And to this exposition of the old doctors am I enforced both by the articles of my creed, and also by the circumstances of the said Scripture, as after shall more largely appear. But by the same can I not find the natural body of our Saviour to be there naturally, but rather absent both from the Sacrament and from all the world, collocate and remaining in heaven, where He by promise must abide corporally unto the end of the world." [2]

Before the German divines who had formed the embassy which together with the English divines drew up the *Thirteen Articles* left England they wrote a paper in which they recorded their condemnation of what they considered to be the abuses of Communion in one kind, private Masses, and the celibacy of priests; and it was suggested with some probability by the late Archdeacon Perry [3] that the king's annoyance at this document had something to do with the actions on his part which shortly

[1] *Miscellaneous Writings and Letters of Thomas Cranmer* (Parker Society), p. 475.

[2] Foxe, *Acts and Monuments*, v. 249 (edition 1843-9).

[3] *History of the English Church*, ii. 164.

followed.   In 1539 he sent a message to the House of Lords in which he expressed his wish for the appointment of a committee to examine different opinions about religion, and draw up articles of agreement for the consideration of the House.   The committee was appointed, but at the end of ten days had failed to reach any conclusion.   Thereupon the Duke of Norfolk proposed that six articles dealing with matters in dispute should be discussed in the whole House, and for this purpose submitted six questions, of which those relating to the Eucharist were the first, second, and fourth, namely, " Whether in the Holy Eucharist Christ's real body is present without any Transubstantiation " ; " Whether the laity are to communicate in this Sacrament under both kinds " ; and " Whether by the law of God private Masses ought to be celebrated ".   The same six questions were submitted to the Convocation of Canterbury, which declared that no substance of bread and wine remains in the Sacrament after consecration, that Communion in both kinds is not necessary, and that private Masses ought to be continued.   Latimer the Bishop of Worcester and Shaxton the Bishop of Salisbury, and two members of the Lower House, voted against this decision. Shortly afterwards the " Statute of the Six Articles " was passed by both Houses of Parliament, and received the royal assent.   It declared the agreement of Convocation and Parliament, and included the following statements among those which it was made penal to deny :—

" First. That in the most blessed Sacrament of the altar, by the strength and efficacy of Christ's mighty word (it being spoken by the priest) is present really under the form of bread and wine, the natural body and blood of our Saviour Jesu Christ, conceived of the Virgin Mary : and that after the consecration there remaineth no substance of bread or wine, or any other substance but the substance of Christ, God and Man."

" Secondly. That the Communion in both kinds is not necessary *ad salutem* by the law of God to all persons : and that it is to be believed and not doubted of but that in the flesh under the form of bread is the very blood, and with the blood under the form of wine is the very flesh, as well apart as though they were both together."

" Fifthly. That it is meet and necessary that private Mass be continued and admitted in this the king's English Church and congregation, as whereby good Christian people ordering themselves accordingly do receive both godly and goodly consolations and benefits : and it is agreeable also to God's law." [1]

In this Statute, as in the questions addressed by the bishops to John Frith six years earlier,[2] and in later documents of the sixteenth century,[3] the phrase " natural body " occurs.

The " Statute of the Six Articles " was enforced with less consistence and severity than might have been expected, but from time to time it was put in operation with the brutality which was characteristic of the age.

The book entitled *A Necessary Doctrine and Erudition for any Christian Man*, usually called the *King's Book*, a revision of the *Bishops' Book*, was the work of a commission of the two archbishops, six bishops, and twelve divines appointed by the king in 1540. In 1543 it was submitted to Convocation and approved ; and it was published in the same year with a commendatory preface by the king. It contained a long exposition of the Eucharist, in which the word Transubstantiation was avoided but the doctrine of the conversion of the substance of the bread and wine into the substance of the body and blood of Christ was taught. The most important parts of this section of the book are the following :—

" The Sacrament of the altar . . . among all the Sacraments is of incomparable dignity and virtue, forasmuch as in the other Sacraments the outward kind of the thing which is used in them remaineth still in their own nature and substance unchanged. But in this most high Sacrament of the altar the creatures which be taken to the use thereof, as bread and wine, do not remain still in their own substance, but by the virtue of Christ's word in the consecration be changed and turned to the very substance of the body and blood of our Saviour Jesu Christ. So that, although there appear the form of bread and wine after the consecration as did before, and to the outward senses nothing seemeth to be changed, yet must we, forsaking and renouncing the persuasion of our senses in this behalf, give our assent only to faith, and to the plain word of Christ, which affirmeth that substance there offered, exhibited, and received to be the very precious body and blood of our Lord, as it is plainly written by the Evangelists and also by St. Paul, where they entreating of the institution of this Sacrament, show how our Saviour Christ sit-

[1] Collier, *An Ecclesiastical History of Great Britain*, v. 38.
[2] See pp. 110-12, *supra*.   [3] See p. 66, note 2, *supra*.

ting at His Last Supper with His Apostles took bread and blessed it and brake it and gave it unto His disciples and said, 'Take ye and eat; this is My body'. And also when He gave the cup, He said, 'This is My blood of the New Testament, which shall be shed for many for the remission of sins'.[1] By these words it is plain and evident to all them which with meek, humble, and sincere heart will believe Christ's words, and be obedient unto faith, that in the Sacrament the things that be therein be the very body and blood of Christ in very substance. . . . Here is to be noted, as touching the receiving of this Sacrament, that although our Saviour Jesus Christ at the first institution thereof in His Supper did minister it unto His disciples then present under both the kinds of bread and wine, yet that fashion and manner of ministering is not so necessary to the receiver, except it be to the priest when he consecrateth, that without the due observation of that way man might not receive that blessed Sacrament to his salvation. For the benefit or hurt that cometh to a Christian man by receiving of this Sacrament standeth not in the fashion or manner of receiving of it under one or both kinds, but in the worthy or unworthy receiving of the same. For he that receiveth this Sacrament worthily under the one kind, as under the form of bread only, receiveth the whole body and blood of Christ, and as many and great benefits of Christ as he that receiveth it in both kinds. . . . Seeing it is the very body of our Saviour Christ, which is united and knit to His Godhead in one Person, and by reason thereof hath the very virtue and substance of life in it, it must needs consequently by the most holy and blessed participation of the same give and communicate life also to them that worthily receive it. And it endueth them with grace, strength, and virtue against all temptation, sin, and death, and doth much ease and relieve all the troubles, diseases, and infirmities of their soul. . . . This heavenly meat is not turned into our substance, as other corporal meat is, but by the godly operation thereof we be turned towards the nature of it, that is to say, of earthly, corruptible, and sinful we be made heavenly, spiritual, and strong against sin and all wickedness. . . . It is to be remembered that, as in the receiving of this Sacrament we have most entire Communion with Christ, so be we also joined by the same in most perfect unity with His Church, and all the members thereof. . . . It was thought good to the Apostles and the Universal Church, being moved with the Holy Ghost, for the more honour of so high a Sacrament, and for the more reverence and

[1] St. Matt. xxvi. 26-28; St. Mark xiv. 22-24; St. Luke xxii. 19, 20; 1 Cor. xi. 23-25.

devout receiving thereof, that it should always be received of Christian people when they be fasting, and before they receive any bodily sustenance, except it be in case of sickness or necessity. Wherefore, considering the most excellent grace, efficacy, and virtue of this Sacrament, it were greatly to be wished and prayed for that all Christian people had such devotion thereunto that they would gladly dispose and prepare themselves to the more often worthy receiving of the same. But seeing that in these last days charity is waxed cold, and sin doth abound (as Christ said in the Gospel that it should), yet if Christian men will avoid the great indignation of God, it shall be good for them, whensoever they receive this Sacrament themselves or be present when it is ministered or used, as specially in the time of Mass, to behave themselves reverently in pure devotion and prayer, and not to walk up and down, or to offend their brethren by any evil example of unreverence to the said Sacrament, except they will declare themselves to have small regard to our Saviour Christ there bodily present." [1]

An explanation of the rites of the Church or *Rationale*, which was drawn up about this time, may have been the work of the commission which formed the *King's Book*. This explanation was not published, but a copy of it survived and was printed early in the eighteenth century by the Nonjuror Jeremy Collier. It is entitled *Ceremonies to be used in the Church of England together with an Explanation of the Meaning and Significancy of Them*. The section on " Ceremonies used in the Mass " assumes the doctrine taught in the *King's Book* and expresses in a simple and practical form the view of the prayers and ceremonies of the Mass customary in the middle ages, by which they are regarded as a mystical representation of the incarnate life of Christ. The most important parts of this section are as follows :—

" The Mass is a remembrance of the passion of Christ, whose most blessed body and blood is there consecrated, and the ceremonies thereof are not dumb, but they be expressives and declaratives of the same passion, to the intent that by such signs and ceremonies they that be present thereat may the better be admonished and reduced into the memory of the same. And,

" First. It is to be understood that the priest is a common minister in the name and stead of the whole congregation ; and as the mouth of the same not only renders thanks to God for Christ's

[1] Lloyd, *Formularies of Faith Put Forth by Authority during the Reign of Henry VIII.* pp. 262-69.

death and passion but also makes the common prayers, and commends the people and their necessities in the same to Almighty God.

"The priest therefore when he shall say Mass says it not in his common apparel which he daily uses; but puts upon him clean and hallowed vestments, partly representing the mysteries which were done at the passion, partly representing the virtues which he himself ought to have that celebrates the Mass.   And,

"First. He putteth on the amice, which, as touching the mystery, signifies the veil with the which the Jews covered the face of Christ when they buffeted Him in time of His passion; and, as touching the minister, it signifies faith, which is the head, ground, and foundation of all virtues; and therefore he puts that upon his head first.

"Secondly. He puts upon him the albe, which, as touching the mystery, signifieth the white garment wherewith Herod clothed Christ in mockery when he sent Him to Pilate; and, as touching the minister, it signifies the pureness of conscience and innocency he ought to have, especially when he sings the Mass.

"The girdle, as touching the mystery, signifies the scourge with which Christ was scourged; and, as touching the minister, it signifies the continent and chaste living, or else the close mind which he ought to have at prayers when he celebrates.

"The stole, as touching the mystery, signifieth the ropes or bands that Christ was bound with to the pillar when He was scourged; and, as touching the minister, it signifieth the yoke of patience, which he must bear as the servant of God, in token whereof he puts also the phanon on his arm, which admonisheth him of ghostly strength and godly patience that he ought to have to vanquish and overcome all carnal infirmity.

"The overvesture or chesible, as touching the mystery, signifies the purple mantle that Pilate's soldiers put upon Christ after that they had scourged Him; and, as touching the minister, it signifies charity, a virtue excellent above all other.

"The minister the which shall celebrate in the beginning comes forth as from some secret place to the midst of the altar, signifying thereby that Christ, who is the High Priest, came forth from the secret bosom of His Father into this world to offer sacrifice for man's redemption.   And albeit that that sacrifice be a sufficient price and redemption for all the world, yet it is not efficient or effectual but only to them which knowledgeth themselves with penance to be sinners, whom He came to justify. . . . Therefore the minister in the beginning teacheth all men by his confession to humiliate and knowledge themselves sinners and ask remission to the intent they may be the more apt to participate of this high mystery. . . . Then after this followeth *Kyrie Eleison et Christe Eleison,* which be words of desire and to pray God for mercy, which mercy we cannot have of our deserts but of God's goodness and Christ's merits only ; and therefore the minister, proceeding to the midst of the altar, renders the glory unto God, singing the angels' hymn and song *Gloria in Excelsis Deo,* that is, glory be unto God in heaven, whereby we be learned not only to know that we receive all our benefits of God, being bound to give Him thanks for them, but also the means whereby we receive them, which is by the mediation of Christ, that is both God and Man, by whom the Father is pleased and reconciled, angels and men agreed. Then this song done, the minister and people with salutations exhort each other to prayers, in which he prays as well for the multitude as for himself. . . . After that prayer made, then the priest as a meet minister to teach the people reads the Epistle, which is a lesson taken out of the Old and New Testaments, and it precedes the Gospel, and prepares the mind thereunto, like as St. John prepared unto Christ, and the old law unto grace, and Christ sent the disciples into divers places to preach before His coming. . . . Next to the Epistle ensues the Graill, the which teacheth also such wholesome doctrine as was taught before in the Epistle, that they, proceeding in virtue by degrees, may proceed from virtue to virtue until such time as they may see Almighty God in His glory. . . . Then follows the Gospel, which is a glad message or tidings, for in it is contained the glad news of our salvation. . . . And forasmuch as faith springeth of the word of God, therefore divers days the Church (after the Gospel read) pronounces with a loud voice the Creed, expressing the faith with her mouth. . . . Then follows the Offertory, whereby we learn to prepare ourselves by God's grace to be an acceptable oblation to Him, to the intent we may be partakers of the blessed sacrifices which Christ offered for us upon the cross. At which time the minister, laying the bread upon the altar, makes the chalice, mixing the water with the wine, signifying thereby how that blood and water ran out of Christ's side in His passion, and admonishes us of the inseparable coupling and joining of Christ and His Church. Then after the Offertory done the priest washes his hands, knowledging himself not to be so clean but that he has ever need more to be washed. . . . Then after follows a prayer secretly said, which is called the Secret of the Mass, and that signifies Christ's secret and privy conversation which He kept with His disciples a

little before His passion. . . . Next after the Secret follows the
Preface, which is a prolocution or prayer which goes before the most
reverend consecration of Christ's body and blood, preparing the
minds of the faithful people to the reverence of the same, and moving
them to erect their hearts to Almighty God. . . . Then after this
Preface follows the Canon, which is said secretly of the priest, not
because it is unlawful to be heard, read, or known of the people (as
some fancy) but that it is expedient to keep silence and secrecy at
the time of such a high mystery, and that both the priest and people
may have the more devout meditations, and better attend about
the same.   Then the priest begins to represent in this sacrifice of
the Mass the most painful and bloody sacrifice once offered for
our salvation upon the cross, and prays the Father to accept these.
gifts prepared for the consecration, and, inclining his body, makes
a cross upon the altar and kisses it, signifying thereby the humble
inclining and obedience of Christ to His Father's will, to suffer His
passion upon the altar of His cross for our salvation.   And then
following the example of Christ, the High Bishop, which, approaching the time of His passion, gave Himself to prayer, and also according to the Apostle's doctrine to Timothy, the minister gives himself
to prayer. . . . He proceeds with all reverence to the consecration.
First.   Of the bread, taking it in his hands and giving thanks,
following the example of Christ, by virtue and power of whose words
the substance of bread is turned into the substance of the body of
Christ.   And likewise the substance of wine into His precious blood,
which he lifteth up both that the people with all reverence and
honour may worship the same, and also to signify thereby partly
Christ's exaltation upon the cross for our redemption, which was
figured by the serpent set up by Moses in the desert, and partly
signifying that triumphant advancement and exaltation whereto God
the Father because of His passion has exalted Him above all creatures, bidding the people to have it in remembrance as oft as they
shall do the same.   After the which the priest extends and stretches
forth his arms in form of a cross, declaring thereby that according
to Christ's commandment both he and the people not only have fresh
remembrance of the passion but also of His resurrection and glorious
ascension.   And so proceeds to the second *Memento*, in which he
prays for them that be dead in the faith of Christ and sleep in peace.
. . . Then he joins himself with the people, knocking himself upon
the breast, thereby teaching them that both he and they be sinners
and have need of mercy and grace purchased by Christ's passion.
. . . The priest then to the intent he may the more worthily receive
the blessed body and blood of Christ both to the comfort and

strength as well of him as of them that be present, saith the *Pater Noster*. . . . And so discovering the Chalice in token that Christ would the fruit of His passion to be opened and manifest to all the world, takes the host and breaks it and divides it in token of the distribution of it amongst His disciples at His Last Supper and the breaking of His body at the time of His passion, at which Supper above all things He commends to them peace and charity, saying, *Pacem meam do vobis, pacem relinquo vobis.*[1] And therefore the minister takes the kiss of peace from the blessed Sacrament, and sends it to the people. . . . Then saith the priest thrice, *Agnus Dei, etc.,* advertising us of the effects of Christ's passion ; whereof the first is deliverance from the misery of sin ; the second is from pain of everlasting damnation, wherefore he saith twice, *miserere nobis*, that is, have mercy on us ; and the third effect is giving everlasting peace, consisting in the glorious fruition of God, wherefore he saith, *Dona nobis pacem*, that is, give us peace. Then follows the commixtion of the body and blood of Christ together, signifying the joining together of His body and soul at the resurrection, which before were severed at the time of His passion. And albeit there be two consecrations, yet there is but one Sacrament, containing under the form the holy body and blood of Christ inseparably. Then follows the Communion, which is an exciting or a moving to the people to laud and praise God. And because in the primitive Church, when devotion was fervent, divers used many times to receive it together with the priest, therefore in the prayer called the Post-communion the priest in the name of them all prays and renders thanks unto God for their spiritual refection *per Dominum nostrum*, by whose passion exhibit the Mass has its strength and efficacy. Then the priest eftsoons turning his face to the people after the salutation says these words, *Ite, missa est*, that is, Go ye, the Mass is ended. And in that he bids them go is signified that we ought to follow Christ in His holy life, and always be going from virtue to virtue, and not to stand and tarry in the worldly pleasures, but diligently to haste us to life everlasting. And that we may be of the number of them to whom it shall be said, *Venite benedicti*, that is, Come ye blessed of My Father, and receive the kingdom, etc., the priest gives us at our departure sometimes the benediction in the name of the whole Trinity, signifying that last benediction which Christ gave to His disciples in the Mount of Olivet, when He ascended to His Father, where He sits on His right hand, a continual Intercessor for us." [2]

[1] St. John xiv. 27.
[2] See Collier, *An Ecclesiastical History of Great Britain*, v. 110-17.

It has seemed worth while to quote a considerable part of the section of this *Rationale* which refers to the Eucharist partly because of the additional illustration to that supplied by the *King's Book* which it affords of the doctrinal teaching in the closing years of the reign of King Henry VIII. of the conversion of the substance of the bread and wine into the body and blood of Christ at the consecration, and partly because it is an excellent instance of that way of regarding the prayers and ceremonies of the Mass which the sixteenth century inherited from the middle ages.

II.

On 28th January, 1547, King Henry VIII. died, and was succeeded by his son under the title of King Edward VI. Edward's reign was marked by great changes in theological belief among prominent men, and in the formularies of the Church of England. The transition of opinion which can be traced in the case of Archbishop Cranmer may have been representative of what took place in many minds. When Cranmer became Archbishop of Canterbury in 1533 he is not known to have dissented in any way from the customary doctrines about the Eucharist. In that year he tried to persuade John Frith to give up his opinions on this subject ; and, on failing to do so, appears to have regarded it as a matter of course that Frith must be burnt.[1] In 1536 and 1538 and 1539 and 1543 he assented to documents which asserted the presence of the body and blood of Christ in the consecrated elements, of which the *Six Articles* in 1539 and the *King's Book* in 1543 maintained that the substance of the bread and wine does not remain after consecration.[2] While it is probably the case that during the latter part of this period his own mind was more in the direction of a doctrine of the presence of Christ in the consecrated elements which did not require the cessation of the existence of the substance of bread and wine, he was able to continue to hold his office while persons were being burnt for denying the conversion of the substance at consecration. Largely owing to the influence of Ridley, he abandoned the belief that the consecrated Sacrament is the body and blood of Christ.[3]

[1] See p. 112, *supra*.   [2] See pp. 113-20, *supra*.

[3] See his statements at his examination in 1555 ; *Miscellaneous Writings and Letters of Thomas Cranmer* (Parker Society), p. 218.

In 1548 Cranmer published a *Catechism* which was translated from a Latin *Catechism*, which again had been translated in 1539 by the Lutheran Justus Jonas from an unknown German *Catechism*. It was entitled, *Catechismus. That is to say, A Short Instruction into Christian Religion for the singular commodity and profit of Children and Young People. Set forth by the Most Reverend Father in God Thomas Archbishop of Canterbury, Primate of All England and Metropolitan.* There is nothing in this *Catechism* to deny the doctrine that the consecrated Sacrament is the body and blood of Christ, and the body and blood are said to be taken by the "bodily mouth"; but there is no assertion of more than that they are received by the communicants, and a statement in the Latin Lutheran *Catechism* that the Sacrament "is really the body and blood" of Christ is altered to the statement that "in the Sacrament we receive truly the body and blood of Christ". The chief passages bearing on Eucharistic doctrine are the following :—

"By the Communion of the Holy Supper of the Lord we are preserved and strengthened, that we may be able steadfastly to stand and fight against the violent invasions of sin and the power of the devil. Wherefore, good children, forasmuch as ye be already planted in Christ by Baptism, learn also, I pray you, how ye may continually abide and grow in Christ, the which thing is taught you, in the use of the Lord's Supper. . . . We ought to believe that in the Sacrament we receive truly the body and blood of Christ.[1] . . . Believe the words of our Lord Jesus, that you eat and drink His very body and blood, although man's reason cannot comprehend how and after what manner the same is there present. . . . Doubt not but there is the body and blood of our Lord, which we receive in the Lord's Supper. . . . Christ causeth, even at this time, His body and blood to be in the Sacrament after that manner and fashion as it was at that time when He made His Maundy with His disciples. . . . Christ hath commanded us to do the self same thing that His disciples did, and to do it in the remembrance of Him, that is to say, to receive His body and blood, even so as He Himself did give it to His disciples. . . . Christ Himself doth give unto us His flesh and blood as His words doth evidently declare. . . . When ye do thus [that is, communicate after self-examination, acknowledgment of sin, penitence, forgiveness],

[1] The Latin Lutheran *Catechism* has here "Credere debemus quod vere corpus et sanguis eius sit".

then ye worthily receive the body and blood of Christ. And he that so receiveth it, receiveth everlasting life. For he doth not only with His bodily mouth receive the body and blood of Christ, but he doth also believe the words of Christ, whereby he is assured that Christ's body was given to death for us, and that His blood was shed for us. And he that this believeth, eateth and drinketh the body and blood of Christ spiritually. . . . When ye be asked, What is the Communion or the Lord's Supper? ye may answer, It is the true body and true blood of our Lord Jesus Christ, which was ordained by Christ Himself to be eaten and drunken of us Christian people under the form of bread and wine." [1]

By the year 1550 or possibly earlier Cranmer had reached the position maintained in his *A Defence of the True and Catholic Doctrine of the Sacrament of the Body and Blood of our Saviour Christ*, and more fully explained in his *An Answer unto a Crafty and Sophistical Cavillation, devised by Stephen Gardiner, Doctor of Law, late Bishop of Winchester, against the True and Godly Doctrine of the most Holy Sacrament of the Body and Blood of our Saviour Jesus Christ*, published in 1551. In these treatises Cranmer's ultimate belief about the Eucharist is very clearly stated, and is defended at great length. He denies Transubstantiation both in its more carnal and in its more spiritual form; he rejects the belief that the consecrated bread and wine are the body and blood of Christ; and he repudiates any sacrifice of Christ's body and blood in the Eucharist. He allows that the bread and wine may be called the body and blood of Christ; that Christ may be said to be present in the Sacrament; and that the word sacrifice may be applied to the Eucharist. But he shows that the meaning which he attaches to this terminology is, in his mind, consistent with the denials which have been mentioned. According to that meaning, the faithful communicant receives the virtue and grace of Christ's body and blood, which are themselves absent; Christ is present in the Sacrament as He is present in Baptism or during prayer, or as the sun is present wherever its warmth is felt; and the sacrificial character of the Eucharist is that there are in

---

[1] This *Catechism* and the Latin Lutheran *Catechism* from which it was translated were edited by Dr. Edward Burton in 1829 with the title *A Short Instruction into Christian Religion, being a Catechism set forth by Archbishop Cranmer in 1548*.

it a remembrance of Christ's sacrifice, a sacrifice of praise and thanksgiving, and an oblation of those who take part in the service. Consequently, Cranmer rejects the opinions of Luther and Calvin and Bucer as well as those of the theologians of the middle ages and the adherents of the papal doctrine in the sixteenth century. On the other hand, he is opposed to the teaching contained in some parts of the writings of Zwingli and Oecolampadius, which made the Eucharist a merely commemorative rite. By an intermediate position between any kind of assertion of the reception of the actual body and blood of Christ and any merely figurative view, he maintained the opinion which had sometimes been described as Virtualism, namely, that the faithful communicant sacramentally receives those effects of Christ's life and death which would be conveyed if there were a beneficial reception of His actual body and blood. When his phraseology is carefully examined, and his statements viewed in their context, and his general line of argument observed, this teaching is found throughout his books; and it is expressed with great clearness in the preface to the *Answer to Gardiner*.

"Where I use to speak sometimes (as the old authors do) that Christ is in the Sacraments, I mean the same as they did understand the matter; that is to say, not of Christ's carnal presence in the outward Sacrament but sometimes of His sacramental presence. And sometime by this word Sacrament I mean the whole ministration and receiving of the Sacraments either of Baptism or of the Lord's Supper; and so the old writers many times do say that Christ and the Holy Ghost be present in the Sacraments, not meaning by that manner of speech that Christ and the Holy Ghost be present in the water, bread, or wine, which be only the outward visible Sacraments, but that in the due ministration of the Sacraments according to Christ's ordinance and institution Christ and His Holy Spirit be truly and indeed present by their mighty and sanctifying power, virtue, and grace, in all them that worthily receive the same. Moreover, when I say and repeat many times in my book that the body of Christ is present in them that worthily receive the Sacrament, lest any man should mistake my words, and think that I mean that, although Christ be not corporally in the outward visible signs, yet he is corporally in the persons that duly receive them, this is to advertise the reader that I mean no such thing; but my meaning is that the force, the grace, the virtue and benefit of Christ's body that was crucified for us and of His blood that was shed for us be really and effectually present with all them that duly receive the Sacraments; but all this I understand of His spiritual presence, of the which He saith, 'I will be with you until the world's end,' and 'Wheresoever two or three be gathered together in My name, there am I in the midst of them,' and 'He that eateth My flesh and drinketh My blood dwelleth in Me, and I in him'.[1] Now no more truly is He corporally or really present in the due ministration of the Lord's Supper than He is in the due ministration of Baptism." [2]

The history of Cranmer's opinions in regard to the Eucharist has much more than a merely individual importance in view of the changes made in the formularies of the English Church during the reign of Edward VI. On the death of Henry VIII. the official statement of belief was the *King's Book*, which in regard to the Eucharist, without using the word Transubstantiation, affirmed that the substance of bread and wine does not remain after consecration but is converted at the consecration into the substance of the body and blood of Christ; and the prayers and ceremonies of the order and canon of the Mass were unaltered, and implied throughout the doctrines that the consecrated Sacrament is the body and blood of Christ, and that the Eucharist is a sacrifice.

The Convocation of Canterbury met on 5th November, 1547. On 30th November Archbishop Cranmer sent down to the Lower House an "ordinance" "for the receiving of the body of our Lord under both kinds, namely, bread and wine"; and on that day this ordinance was accepted by the prolocutor, John Taylor, the Dean of Lincoln, and some other members of the Lower House. On 2nd December "this session, all this whole session, in number sixty-four, by their mouths did approve the proposition made the last session of taking the Lord's body in both kinds, *nullo reclamante*".[3] In the same month an Act of Parliament was passed and received the royal assent, by which the authority of the State was given for the administration in both kinds. This Act made provision for the punishment of

---

[1] St. Matt. xviii. 20, xxviii. 20; St. John vi. 56.

[2] P. 3 (Parker Society's edition).

[3] Strype, *Memorials of Cranmer*, i. 220, 221 (edition 1840); *cf.* Wilkins, *Concilia*, iv. 16.

those who despised or reviled the Sacrament; and enacted that
it was to be administered in both kinds to the people.

"The institution of which Sacrament being ordained by Christ,
as is beforesaid, and the said words spoken of it here before rehearsed being of eternal, infallible, and undoubted truth, yet the
said Sacrament (all this notwithstanding) hath been of late marvellously abused by such manner of men before rehearsed, who of
wickedness or else of ignorance and want of learning, for certain
abuses heretofore committed of some in misusing thereof, have condemned in their hearts and speech the whole thing, and contemptu-
ously depraved, despised, or reviled the same most holy and blessed
Sacrament, and not only disputed and reasoned unreverently and
ungodly of that most high mystery, but also in their sermons,
preachings, readings, lectures, communications, arguments, talks,
rhymes, songs, plays, or jests, name or call it by such vile and unseemly words as Christian ears do abhor to hear rehearsed : For
reformation whereof, Be it enacted by the king's highness with the
assent of the lords spiritual and temporal and of the commons in
this present Parliament assembled, and by the authority of the
same, that whatsoever person or persons from and after the first
day of May next coming shall deprave, despise, or contemn the
said most blessed Sacrament in contempt thereof by any contemptu-
ous words, or by any words of depraving, despising, or reviling, or
what person or persons shall advisedly in any otherwise contemn,
despise, or revile the said most blessed Sacrament, contrary to the
effects and declaration abovesaid, that then he or they shall suffer
imprisonment of his or their bodies, and make fine and ransom at
the king's will and pleasure."

"Forasmuch as it is more agreeable both to the first institution
of the said Sacrament of the most precious body and blood of our
Saviour Jesus Christ, and also more conformable to the common use
and practice both of the Apostles and of the primitive Church by
the space of 500 years and more after Christ's ascension, that the
blessed Sacrament should be ministered to all Christian people under
both the kinds of bread and wine ; and also it is more agreeable to
the first institution of Christ, and to the usage of the Apostles and
of the primitive Church, that the people being present should receive the same with the priest than that the priest should receive
it alone: therefore be it enacted by our sovereign lord the king,
with the consent of the lords spiritual and temporal and the commons in this present Parliament assembled, and by the authority of
the same, that the said most blessed Sacrament be hereafter com-

monly delivered and ministered unto the people within this Church of England and Ireland and other the king's dominions under both the kinds, that is to say, of bread and wine, except necessity otherwise require ; and also that the priest which shall minister the same shall, at the least one day before, exhort all persons which shall be present likewise to resort and prepare themselves to receive the same." [1]

A week after the giving of the royal assent to this Act of Parliament, a royal proclamation was issued on December 27, which referred to the continuance of "contentious and superfluous questions," and went on to say—

"which persons, not contented reverently and with obedient faith to accept that the said Sacrament, according to the saying of St. Paul, 'the bread is the communion,' or partaking, 'of the body of the Lord ; the wine,' likewise, 'the partaking of the blood of Christ,' [2] by the words instituted and taught of Christ : and that the body and blood of Jesu Christ is there ; which is our comfort, thanksgiving, love-token of Christ's love towards us, and of ours as His members within ourselves, search and strive unreverently whether the body and blood aforesaid is there really or figuratively, locally or circumscriptly, and having quantity and greatness, or but substantially and by substance only, or else but in a figure and manner of speaking, whether His blessed body be there, head, legs, arms, toes and nails, or any other ways, shape and manner, naked or clothed ; whether He is broken or chewed, or He is always whole ; whether the bread there remaineth as we see, or how it departeth ; whether the flesh be there alone, and the blood, or apart, or each in other, or in the one both, in the other but only blood ; and what blood, that only which did flow out of the side, or that which remaineth : and other such irreverent, superfluous, and curious questions, which, how and what, and by what means, and in what form, may bring into them. . . . The king's highness, by the advice of the lord protector and other his majesty's council, straitly willeth and commandeth that no man nor person from henceforth do in any wise contentiously and openly argue, dispute, reason, preach, or teach, affirming any more terms of the said blessed Sacrament than be expressly taught in the Holy Scripture, and mentioned in the aforesaid Act, nor deny none which be therein contained and mentioned, until such time as the king's majesty, by the advice of his highness's council and the clergy of this realm, shall define,

[1] 1 Edw. VI. c. 1.   [2] 1 Cor. x. 16.

declare, and set forth an open doctrine thereof, and what terms and
words may justly be spoken thereby other than be expressly in the
Scripture contained in the Act before rehearsed.   In the mean time
the king's highness's pleasure is, by the advice aforesaid, that every
his loving subjects shall devoutly and reverently affirm and take
that holy bread to be Christ's body, and that cup to be the cup of
His holy blood, according to the purport and effect of the Holy
Scripture contained in the Act before expressed, and accommodate
themselves rather to take the same Sacrament worthily than rashly
to enter into the discussing of the high mystery thereof." [1]

The condemnation in this proclamation of those who talked
irreverently about the Sacrament was evidently directed primarily
against the successors of the Lollards and the shocking profanities
of which they were guilty in their ridicule of the doctrine of the
Eucharist held in the Church.[2]   But it appears to have been
intended also to discourage any explicit teaching or defence of
Transubstantiation, and to have aimed at there being as little
definition as possible in regard to the Eucharist until further
action had been taken by the king and the council.

In January, 1548, a commission of six bishops and six divines
with Cranmer as president was appointed by the council to com-
pose an *Order of Communion* in English which might give effect
to the determination of Convocation and Parliament that the
Sacrament was to be administered in both kinds.   This *Order*
was not submitted either to Convocation or to Parliament, and
was therefore without any proper authority either from the Church
or from the State.   It was authorised on its publication in March,
1548, by a royal proclamation.   No change in doctrine was asserted or implied in it.   Though doubts as to the doctrine of
concomitance may have been in the minds of some who were
responsible for it, the desirability of Communion in both kinds
had been based in the documents already quoted not on any
matter of doctrine but on the facts of the method of the institution of Christ and of the usage of the primitive Church.   The

---

[1] Wilkins, *Concilia*, iv. 18, 19.   The spelling in this proclamation, as
in other documents of the period, has been modernised above.

[2] For an instance see the verses entitled *A Pore Help*, purporting to be
an attack on the Lollard preachers but really in that guise ridiculing the
doctrines to which they were opposed, printed in Strype, *Memorials of
Edward VI.*, vol. ii. part ii. pp. 333-37 (edition 1822).

prayers and ceremonies of the order and canon of the Mass were for the present left unaltered ; and the new *Order* was simply to be inserted, after the communion of the priest, for use in communicating the people. And in the *Order* itself, while there was no elaboration of doctrinal teaching, the consecrated Sacrament was regarded and described as the body and blood of Christ. In one of the exhortations it was said :—

"To the end that we should always remember the exceeding love of our Master and only Saviour Jesus Christ thus doing for us, and the innumerable benefits which by His precious blood-shedding He hath obtained to us, He hath left in these holy mysteries, as a pledge of His love and a continual remembrance of the same, His own blessed body and precious blood, for us spiritually to feed upon, to our endless comfort and consolation " ;

the prayer before Communion included the words :—

"Grant us therefore, gracious Lord, so to eat the flesh of Thy dear Son Jesus Christ, and to drink His blood, in these holy mysteries, that we may continually dwell in Him, and He in us, that our sinful bodies may be made clean by His body, and our souls washed through His most precious blood " ;

the consecrated bread and wine were called "the Sacrament of the body of Christ" and "the Sacrament of the blood" as well as "the bread" and "the wine"; the words of administration, closely following the old form, were :—

"The body of our Lord Jesus Christ, which was given for thee, preserve thy body unto everlasting life " ;

"The blood of our Lord Jesus Christ, which was shed for thee, preserve thy soul unto everlasting life " ;

and in the rubric directing that each one of the "consecrated breads" should be broken into two pieces or more, it was said :—

"Men must not think less to be received in part than in the whole, but in each of them the whole body of our Saviour Jesu Christ."

The retention of the order and canon of the Mass of the old rite and the character of the *Order of Communion* alike show that up to this point no doctrinal change about the Eucharist was made in the formularies. Yet it should be noted that, though it was explicitly ordered that no " other rite or ceremony in the Mass" should be varied except what was provided for the communion of the people, it was directed that, in the event of a necessity for the consecration of more wine, there was not to be "any elevation or lifting up" of the chalice at this additional consecration.

The use of the *Order of Communion* together with the order and canon of the Mass was only intended as a temporary expedient; and in September, 1548, a number of bishops and divines met at Chertsey and Windsor to compile a complete book for public worship. In December, 1548, a debate took place in the House of Lords concerning the Eucharist. Besides some discussion as to the extent of the agreement of the bishops to the "book which was read touching the doctrine of the Supper," the debate went on for three days on the general subject of Eucharistic doctrine. A contemporary manuscript giving an account of this debate still exists, from which it is clear that very distinct differences of opinion were expressed. The arguments used by Cranmer do not appear to have been much nearer the traditional theology than his treatise published in 1551.[1] In a discussion which sprang out of a statement of Bishop Tunstall of Durham that "there is the very body and blood of Christ both spiritual and carnal,"[2] he maintained that "the spirit and body are contrary"; and the contentions ascribed to him include that "our faith is not to believe Him to be in bread and wine, but that He is in heaven"; "Christ when He bids us eat His body it is *figurative;* for we cannot eat His body indeed"; "to eat His flesh and drink His blood is to be partaker of His passion, as water is water still that we are christened withal or that was wont to be put into the wine"; "the change is inward, not in the bread but in the receiver. To have Christ present really here, when I may receive Him in faith, is not available to do me good. Christ is in the world in His divinity, but not in His humanity. The property of His Godhead is everywhere, but His manhood is in one place only"; "it was natural bread, but now no common bread for it is separated to another use. Because of the use it may be called bread of life. That which you see is bread and wine. But that which you believe is the body of Christ. We

---

[1] See pp. 127-29, *supra.*

[2] "Carnal" appears to be here used in the sense of "of the real flesh," not as equivalent to "gross".

must believe that there is bread and the body." The statements ascribed to Ridley include "*Communicatio* is the true mystery and sign of the body that was given for us"; "concerning the outward thing it is very bread. But according to the power of God is ministered the very body"; "the manhood is ever in heaven; His divinity is everywhere present"; "Christ sits in heaven and is present in the Sacrament by His working"; "the bread" "is converted into the body of Christ" as we are "turned in Baptism"; "the bread" "is more than a figure, for besides the natural bread there is an operation of divinity"; "of the common bread before it is made a divine influence". On the other hand, Bishop Tunstall of Durham maintained that "His body is in bread and wine"; Bishop Day of Chichester that "the verity of Christ's body" "is in the Sacrament," that "the form and accidents of the bread" "remain, but not very bread," that "like as in the humanity of Christ the Godhead was, even so the presence of His very body is in the Sacrament"; Bishop Thirlby of Westminster that "the adoration to be left out he never consented"; and Bishop Sampson of Lichfield that he "thought the doctrine of the book very godly. For he never thought it to be the gross body of Christ, so grossly as divers there alleged; nevertheless he took it to be the glorified body of Christ"; that the right word was not "Transubstantiation" but "Transmutation"; and that "it is no gross body, but a natural body [1] that is glorified and not only in virtue and spirit; but faith receiveth both the virtue and the natural body also".[2]

On the day after this debate in the House of Lords was over, the first Act of Uniformity, giving legal effect to the book which had led to the debate was introduced into the House of Commons. On 21st January, 1549, this Act had passed through all the stages in both Houses of Parliament; it received the royal assent on 14th March; it authorised the use of the book on Whitsunday, which in that year fell on 9th June, or earlier if copies could be procured. Whether the book, the use of which was thus made

---

[1] The context shows that "natural body" is not here used to denote a "gross" presence, but that it is the actual body of Christ; *cf.* p. 66, note 2, *supra*.

[2] This MS. is printed in Gasquet and Bishop, *Edward VI. and the Book of Common Prayer*, pp. 397-443; *cf.* Tomlinson, *The Great Parliamentary Debate*.

the law of the land, had been submitted to Convocation is a disputed point, as to which there is something to be said on both sides. A suggestion of Mr. Frere, that, though not formally passed through the proper stages in Convocation, it " was held to have the assent of the bishops by their votes in the House of Lords, and was further submitted to the Lower Houses of Convocation, and won the assent of the clergy through their representatives there," [1] is perhaps more likely to be correct than either the view that it was not in any way brought into touch with Convocation or that it had the full and formal sanction of that body. As regards the action of the bishops in the House of Lords, eighteen bishops took part in the division, of whom ten voted for the Act and eight against it.

The new book, with the addition of the Ordinal published a year later, was intended to be a complete manual of public worship in the English language. It was entitled *The Book of the Common Prayer and Administration of the Sacraments, and other Rites and Ceremonies of the Church : after the Use of the Church of England.* The office for the Eucharist was headed, *The Supper of the Lord, and the Holy Communion, commonly called the Mass.* This new office did not contain any sign of a change of doctrine. It was directed that " the priest that shall execute the holy ministry shall put upon him the vesture appointed for that ministration, that is to say, a white albe plain, with a vestment or cope ". The phrases " Lord's Table " and " altar " are both used. The exhortations contained the sentences :—

" the benefit is great, if with a truly penitent heart and lively faith we receive that holy Sacrament ; for then we spiritually eat the flesh of Christ, and drink His blood, then we dwell in Christ, and Christ in us, we be made one with Christ, and Christ with us " ;

" He hath left us in those holy mysteries as a pledge of His love, and a continual remembrance of the same, His own blessed body and precious blood, for us to feed upon spiritually, to our endless comfort and consolation " ;

" He hath not only given His body to death and shed His blood, but also doth vouchsafe in a Sacrament and mystery to give us His said body and blood to feed upon spiritually."

In the prayer of consecration, the recital of the institution was preceded by the invocation :—

[1] *A New History of the Book of Common Prayer,* p. 52.

" Hear us (O merciful Father) we beseech Thee ; and with Thy Holy Spirit and word vouchsafe to bl✠ess and sanc✠tify these Thy gifts and creatures of bread and wine, that they may be unto us the body and blood of Thy most dearly beloved Son Jesus Christ."

The prayer of oblation contained the words :—

" Humbly beseeching Thee that whosoever shall be partakers of this Holy Communion may worthily receive the most precious body and blood of Thy Son Jesus Christ, and be fulfilled with Thy grace and heavenly benediction, and made one body with Thy Son Jesu Christ, that He may dwell in them, and they in Him."

The prayer before Communion, as in the *Order of Communion* of 1548, had the petition :—

"Grant us therefore, gracious Lord, so to eat the flesh of Thy dear Son Jesus Christ, and to drink His blood, in these holy mysteries, that we may continually dwell in Him, and He in us, that our sinful bodies may be made clean by His body, and our souls washed through His most precious blood."

At the administration the consecrated elements are called " the Sacrament of the body of Christ," and "the Sacrament of the blood " ; and the words of administration remained unaltered except that " thy body and soul " was said in connection with the administration in both kinds instead of " thy body " with the species of bread and " thy soul " with the species of wine. In the thanksgiving after Communion are the words :—

" We most heartily thank Thee for that Thou hast vouchsafed to feed us in these holy mysteries with the spiritual food of the most precious body and blood of Thy Son our Saviour Jesus Christ."

As in 1548, the rubric directing the dividing of each piece of the consecrated bread into two or more parts stated :—

"Men must not think less to be received in part than in the whole, but in each of them the whole body of our Saviour Jesu Christ."

As regards the sacrificial aspect of the Eucharist, the prayer of oblation included the passages :—

"Wherefore, O Lord and heavenly Father, according to the institution of Thy dearly beloved Son, our Saviour Jesu Christ, we Thy humble servants do celebrate and make here before Thy divine majesty, with these Thy holy gifts, the memorial which Thy Son hath willed us to make : having in remembrance His blessed passion, mighty resurrection, and glorious ascension, rendering unto Thee most hearty thanks for the innumerable benefits procured unto us by the same, entirely desiring Thy fatherly goodness mercifully to accept this our sacrifice of praise and thanksgiving, most humbly beseeching Thee to grant that by the merits and death of Thy Son Jesus Christ, and through faith in His blood, we and all Thy whole Church may obtain remission of our sins and all other benefits of His passion.   And here we offer and present unto Thee, O Lord, ourselves, our souls and bodies, to be a reasonable, holy, and lively sacrifice unto Thee. . . . And, although we be unworthy, through our manifold sins, to offer unto Thee any sacrifice, yet we beseech Thee to accept this our bounden duty and service, and command these our prayers and supplications, by the ministry of Thy holy angels, to be brought up into Thy holy tabernacle before the sight of Thy divine majesty."

In the order for the Communion of the Sick the ordinary mediæval teaching about Spiritual Communion [1] was repeated in the rubric :—

"If any man either by reason of extremity of sickness or of lack of warning given in due time to the curate, or by any other just impediment, do not receive the Sacrament of Christ's body and blood, then the curate shall instruct him that, if he do truly repent him of his sins, and steadfastly believe that Jesus Christ hath suffered death upon the cross for him, and shed His blood for his redemption, earnestly remembering the benefits he hath thereby, and giving Him hearty thanks therefor, he doth eat and drink spiritually the body and blood of our Saviour Christ profitably to his soul's health, although he do not receive the Sacrament with his mouth."

In all these respects the Prayer Book of 1549, in spite of the differences of belief among the bishops and clergy and the divisions of opinion as to the advisability of the use of the Book, would be naturally understood as giving expression to the same doctrine as that contained in the order and canon of the Mass, while, like the order and canon of the Mass and liturgical works generally, it did not commit those who used it to one opinion or to another as to whether the substance of the bread and wine remains after consecration or as to the exact nature of the Eucharistic sacrifice.   On the other hand, the prohibition of

_____
[1] See vol. i. pp. 320, 331, 372, 383, *supra*.

" any elevation or showing the Sacrament to the people" at the consecration was a prominent and important departure from a usage closely connected with the doctrine of the Sacrament.

It is probable that the Prayer Book of 1549 represented rather what it was thought safe to put out at the time than what Archbishop Cranmer and those who were acting with him wished, and that at the time of the publication of the Book they already had in view a revision of it which would approach much more nearly the position of the extreme Reformers. At any rate projects of revision went on from this time; and in 1552 the Second Prayer Book of Edward VI. was completed. There is no evidence that this Book was ever submitted to Convocation; it had the authority of Parliament in the second Act of Uniformity, which passed both Houses of Parliament in April, 1552, the five peers who voted against its third reading in the House of Lords including Bishop Thirlby of Norwich and Bishop Aldridge of Carlisle. This new Book bore evident marks of the opinions to which Cranmer was now committed. The word "Mass," which had been retained in 1549, was omitted from the title of "The Order for the Administration of the Lord's Supper or Holy Communion". Instead of the provision of the 1549 Book that at the Holy Communion the priest should wear "a white albe plain with a vestment or cope" was the rubric that—

"the minister at the time of the Communion, and at all other times in his ministration, shall use neither alb, vestment, nor cope: but being archbishop or bishop he shall have and wear a rochet; and being a priest or deacon he shall have and wear a surplice only."

The office was broken up with obviously controversial intentions, so as to interrupt the action of the rite. The words preceding the recital of the institution were altered to—

"Hear us, O merciful Father, we beseech Thee: and grant that we receiving these Thy creatures of bread and wine, according to Thy Son our Saviour Jesu Christ's holy institution, in remembrance of His death and passion, may be partakers of His most blessed body and blood."

The order that the priest was to "take the bread into his hands" and to "take the cup into his hands" in connection with the words of institution was omitted, an omission which, if designed, may imply that the recital of our Lord's action at the Last Supper was regarded rather as a mere historical account than as an act of consecration, although it must be observed that the recital was still embedded in a prayer. The old words of administration, which with slight additions had been preserved in the Order of Communion of 1548 and the Prayer Book of 1549, were abandoned; and in their place were substituted the sentences :—

" Take and eat this in remembrance that Christ died for thee ; and feed on Him in thy heart by faith, with thanksgiving " ;

"Drink this in remembrance that Christ's blood was shed for thee ; and be thankful."

The descriptions of the consecrated elements as " the Sacrament of the body of Christ," "the Sacrament of the blood," and as having " in each of them the whole body of our Saviour Jésu Christ" were omitted, as was the sentence " we " " do celebrate and make here before Thy divine majesty with these Thy holy gifts the memorial which Thy Son hath willed us to make, having in remembrance His blessed passion, mighty resurrection, and glorious ascension ". The phrase in the prayer of humble access, " so to eat the flesh of Thy dear ·Son Jesus Christ, and to drink His blood," still remained, and still by the word " so " implied that the consecrated Sacrament was the flesh and blood of Christ, independently of the faith of the communicant ; [1] but, while in 1549 this phrase had been harmonious with the whole office of which it formed part, in the new Book it stood alone as a survival. There was nothing indeed explicitly to deny the doctrines which were preserved in the Book of 1549 ; but the new Book, as a revision of that of 1549, could hardly have been the work of men who believed those doctrines, and the general impression conveyed by it is well represented by the changes made in the prayer of consecration and in the words of administration. Thus the Book may be regarded as having been designed to teach some form of receptionist or even virtualist doctrine, such as that now held by Cranmer. [2]

[1] It has, however, been maintained that " so to eat . . . that our sinful bodies " is simply a different way of expressing "to eat . . . so that our sinful bodies" : see An English Presbyter [N. Dimock], *Papers on the Doctrine of the English Church concerning the Eucharistic Presence*, pp. 436-39 ; Dowden, *Further Studies in the Prayer Book*, pp. 339-43.

[2] See pp. 127-29, *supra*.

After the Prayer Book of 1552 had been printed, but before most of the copies had been issued by the printer, a declaration on kneeling when receiving the Holy Communion was added on the authority of the council. This declaration was as follows :—

"Although no order can be so perfectly devised but that it may be of some, either for their ignorance and infirmity or else of malice and obstinacy, misconstrued, depraved, and interpreted in a wrong part : and yet because brotherly charity willeth that, so much as conveniently may be, offences should be taken away : therefore we willing to do the same, Whereas it is ordained in the Book of Common Prayer, in the administration of the Lord's Supper, that the communicants kneeling should receive the Holy Communion : which thing being well meant for a signification of the humble and grateful acknowledging of the benefits of Christ given unto the worthy receiver, and to avoid the profanation and disorder which about the Holy Communion might else ensue : lest yet the same kneeling might be thought or taken otherwise, we do declare that it is not meant thereby that any adoration is done, or ought to be done, either unto the sacramental bread or wine there bodily received, or to any real and essential presence there being of Christ's natural flesh and blood. For, as concerning the sacramental bread and wine, they remain still in their very natural substances, and therefore may not be adored, for that were idolatry to be abhorred of all faithful Christians. And, as concerning the natural body and blood of our Saviour Christ, they are in heaven and not here. For it is against the truth of Christ's true natural body to be in more places than in one at one time."

Very much of the phraseology used in this declaration is capable in itself of being explained in harmony with the belief that the consecrated Sacrament is the body and blood of Christ. That "it is against the truth of Christ's true natural body to be in more places than one at one time" might not be more than an acceptance of the Thomist and Dominican philosophy as against the speculations of the Scotist and Franciscan divines.[1] That "the natural body and blood of our Saviour Christ" "are in heaven and not here" might not amount to more than such a distinction between the natural method of our Lord's being in heaven and the supernatural and sacramental method of His being in the Eucharist as was frequently made in the middle ages [2] and

[1] See vol. i. pp. 332, 333, 340, *supra*.

[2] See vol. i. pp. 305, 316, 321, 322, 331-33, 341, *supra*.

as had been insisted on a year before at the Council of Trent.[1]
That "the sacramental bread and wine" "remain still in their
very natural substances, and therefore may not be adored " might
not be more than a denial of Transubstantiation and a repudiation of adoration of the bread and wine which would be entirely
consistent with an assertion that the consecrated Sacrament is
the body and blood of Christ, and that Christ Himself there
present is to be adored.   Even the statement that no " adoration
is done, or ought to be done," " to any real and essential presence
there being of Christ's natural flesh and blood," can be interpreted
so as not to be inconsistent with a belief that the consecrated
Sacrament is the spiritual manhood of our Lord's risen and
ascended life, and that He Himself is there to be adored.   Such
an explanation of the declaration would be following lines of
thought and of language which were very customary in the
middle ages and must have been familiar to theologians in the
sixteenth century.   But, when the declaration is viewed in relation to the known opinions of Cranmer, to the whole character
of the Prayer Book to which it was affixed, and to the object of
the addition as described in the declaration itself as being to
assure the extreme Reformers of the innocence, from their point
of view, of kneeling when receiving the Holy Communion, a
method of interpretation, which as a mere matter of language is
in the abstract possible, becomes incredible.   Historically considered, the declaration added by the council to the Book of
1552 must be regarded as a denial of the doctrine that the consecrated Sacrament is the body and blood of Christ.

The two Acts of Uniformity passed in 1549 and 1552 in connection with the First and the Second Prayer Books of King
Edward VI. were characteristic signs of the intolerant and per-
secuting spirit of the age.   The formation of a series of articles,
dealing both with central and with very many subordinate doctrines, to which assent was to be required as a condition of ministering in the Church of England and of holding certain positions,
was similarly in harmony with the time.   On December 27, 1549,
John Hooper, afterwards Bishop of Gloucester, wrote to Henry
Bullinger, one of the Swiss Reformers, who had succeeded Zwingli
as chief pastor at Zurich in 1531:—

[1] See pp. 90, 99, *supra*.

" The Archbishop of Canterbury entertains right views as to the nature of Christ's presence in the Supper, and is now very friendly towards myself. He has some articles of religion, to which all preachers and lecturers in divinity are required to subscribe, or else a licence for teaching is not granted them ; and in these his sentiments respecting the Eucharist are pure and religious and similar to yours in Switzerland." [1]

Six weeks later, in another letter to Bullinger, Hooper wrote :—

" The Bishops of Canterbury, Rochester, Ely, St. Davids, Lincoln, and Bath are all favourable to the cause of Christ ; and, as far as I know, entertain right opinions in the matter of the Eucharist. I have freely conversed with all of them upon this subject, and have discovered nothing but what is pure and holy. The Archbishop of Canterbury, who is at the head of the king's council, gives to all lecturers and preachers their licence to read and preach : every one of them, however, must previously subscribe to certain articles, which, if possible, I will send you ; one of which, respecting the Eucharist, is plainly the true one, and that which you maintain in Switzerland." [2]

In 1551 the king and the council ordered Cranmer to draw up articles of religion, to be published with the authority of the State ; and Cranmer's articles, still in a tentative stage, were submitted by him to other bishops; a year later he laid them before the council ; and on their being returned made some additions and sent them to Sir William Cecil and Sir John Cheke and to the king, and subsequently to the six royal chaplains. At this stage they were forty-five in number, and were written in Latin. The following are those which relate to the Eucharist :—

" xxvi. Of the Sacraments.

" Our Lord Jesus Christ hath knit together a company of new people with Sacraments most few in number, most easy to be kept, most excellent in signification. As is Baptism and the Lord's Supper, which two only have been ordained in the Church by Christ the Lord as Sacraments, and which alone have the proper nature of Sacraments.

" Sacraments were not ordained by Christ to be gazed upon, or to be carried about, but that we should duly use them. And in those only who worthily receive them, they have a wholesome effect,

[1] *Original Letters Relative to the English Reformation* (Parker Society). i. 71, 72.
[2] *Op. cit*, i. 76.

and yet not that of the work wrought (*ex opere operato*), as some men speak, which word, as it is strange and unknown to Holy Scripture, so it engenders no godly but a very superstitious sense. But they that receive unworthily purchase to themselves damnation, as St. Paul saith.

"Sacraments ordained by the word of God are not only marks of profession among Christians, but rather they are certain sure witnesses and effectual signs of grace and God's good will towards us, by which He doth work invisibly in us, and doth not only quicken but also strengthen our faith in Him."

"xxix. Of the Lord's Supper.

"The Supper of the Lord is not only a sign of the love that Christians ought to have among themselves one to another; but rather it is a Sacrament of our redemption by Christ's death. And therefore to such as duly and worthily and with faith receive the same, the bread which we break is a partaking of the body of Christ, and likewise the cup of blessing is a partaking of the blood of Christ."

"xxx. Of Transubstantiation.

"Transubstantiation of the bread and wine in the Eucharist cannot be proved by Holy Writ, but is repugnant to the plain words of Scripture, and has given occasion to many superstitions."

"xxxi. Of the bodily presence of Christ in the Eucharist.

" Forasmuch as the truth of man's nature requires that it cannot be at the same time in many places but in some certain and fixed place, therefore the body of Christ cannot be present at the same time in many and diverse places. And because, as Holy Scripture doth teach, Christ was taken up into heaven, and will there remain until the end of the world, no one of the faithful ought either to believe or openly to confess the real and bodily presence, as they term it, of His flesh and blood in the Eucharist."

"xxxii. The Sacrament of the Eucharist not to be kept.

" The Sacrament of the Eucharist was not by Christ's ordinance kept, or carried about, or lifted up, or worshipped."

"xxxiii. Of the one perfect offering of Christ made on the cross.

" The offering of Christ made once for all is the perfect redemption, propitiation, and satisfaction for all the sins of the whole world both original and actual, and there is no other expiation for sins but that alone. Wherefore the sacrifices of Masses in which it was commonly said that the priest did offer Christ for the quick and the dead are fables and dangerous deceits." [1]

---

[1] Hardwick, *A History of the Articles of Religion*, pp. 284-86 (edition 1890).

In 1553 a series of articles known as the *Forty-two Articles* was issued with a title stating that they had received the approval of Convocation. This statement appears to have been an " official fiction " ; [1] and there is no reason to suppose that this document had any other explicit authority than that of the king and the council. In June, 1553, a royal mandate was issued, requiring the subscription of clergy, schoolmasters, and members of the universities on taking their degrees to the *Forty-two Articles*. They differ little from the forty-five articles of the draft already mentioned. In the case of those concerning the Eucharist, the sentence "which two only have been ordained in the Church by Christ the Lord as Sacraments, and which alone have the proper nature of Sacraments," was omitted ; the four articles " Of the Lord's Supper," " Of Transubstantiation," " Of the bodily presence of Christ in the Eucharist," and " The Sacrament of the Eucharist not to be kept," were combined into one article under the title "Of the Lord's Supper" ; the statement "it cannot be at the same time in many places " was altered to " the body of one and the self same man cannot be at one time in diverse places " ; and the words " to have remission of pain or sin " were added after " did offer Christ for the quick and the dead ". Both in the draft and in the articles as officially issued, the extreme form of Zwinglianism, Transubstantiation, and belief in " the real and bodily presence " were condemned ; " a partaking of the body of Christ " and " of the blood of Christ " by those who " duly and worthily and with faith receive" was affirmed, probably rather in the sense of the Virtualism which Cranmer had by this time come to believe than in the sense of an actual reception of the body and blood of Christ by the faithful communicant according to the view of Calvin. A result of the combination of four articles in the draft into one article in those eventually decided on was the omission of the heading " The Sacrament of the Eucharist not to be kept," so that there was no explicit prohibition of the reservation of the Sacrament but only the statement that "the Sacrament of the Lord's Supper " (in the Latin text " *Sacramentum Eucharistiæ* ") " was not com-

---

[1] Gairdner, *The English Church in the Sixteenth Century*, p. 311. See also Dixon, *History of the Church of England*, iii. 512-16 ; Gibson, *The Thirty-nine Articles of the Church of England*, pp. 12-20 ; Kidd, *The Thirty-nine Articles*, p. 29.

manded by Christ's ordinance to be kept," which did not necessarily mean more than that reservation was not an essential part
of obedience to the institution of Christ.   As to the Eucharistic
sacrifice, both the draft and the official form condemned any
opinion which might conflict with the complete efficacy of " the
offering of Christ made once for ever," and in particular any view
that the sacrifice of the cross was offered for original sin only,
and that the sacrifice of the Mass was a distinct and parallel
sacrifice for actual sins;[1] when it is remembered how easy it
would have been to find phraseology which would have unmis-
tably repudiated any doctrine of the Eucharist as a sacrifice of
Christ's body and blood, it appears probable that this article was
intended to leave open any further questions than those necessarily involved in the explicit condemnations which it contains.

Some copies of the *Forty-two Articles* had added to them a
brief treatise entitled *A Short Catechism; or Plain Instruction,
Containing the Sum of Christian Learning*.   This *Catechism*
appears to have been the work of John Poynet,[2] who had succeeded Gardiner as Bishop of Winchester on the deposition of
the latter in 1551.   The printing of it was authorised by royal
letters patent dated 25th March, 1553.   The part relating to
the Eucharist conveys either a receptionist or a virtualist doctrine.

" *Master.* What is the use of the Lord's Supper ?

" *Scholar.* Even the very same that was ordained by the Lord
Himself. . . . This was the manner and order of the Lord's Supper,
which we ought to hold and keep, that the remembrance of so great
a benefit, the passion and death of Christ, be alway kept in mind ;
that, after that the world is ended, He may come, and make us to
sit with Him at His own Board.

" *Master.* What declareth and betokeneth the Supper unto us,
which we solemnly use in the remembrance of the Lord ?

" *Scholar.* The Supper, as I have showed a little before, is a certain thankful remembrance of the death of Christ, forasmuch as the
bread representeth His body, betrayed to be crucified for us, the
wine standeth in stead and place of His blood, plenteously shed for

---

[1] See pp. 26, 69-75, *supra.*

[2] See a letter of Sir John Cheke to Bullinger, written on 7th June,
1553, in *Original Letters Relative to the English Reformation* (Parker
Society), i. 142.

us. And, even as by bread and wine our natural bodies are sustained and nourished, so by the body, that is, the flesh and blood of Christ, the soul is fed through faith and quickened to the heavenly and godly life.

"*Master.* How come these things to pass?

"*Scholar.* These things come to pass by a certain secret mean, and lively working of the Spirit, when we believe that Christ hath once for all given up His body and blood for us, to make a sacrifice and most pleasant offering to His heavenly Father, and also when we confess and acknowledge Him our only Saviour, high Bishop, Mediator, and Redeemer, to whom is due all honour and glory.

"*Master.* All this thou dost well understand. For methinketh thy meaning is that faith is the mouth of the soul, whereby we receive this heavenly meat, full both of salvation and immortality, dealt among us by the means of the Holy Ghost." [1]

III.

Cranmer's treatises of 1550 and 1551, the Prayer Book of 1552, the *Forty-two Articles* of 1553, and the *Short Catechism* published in 1553, may be taken as illustrating the opinions about the Eucharist which were in favour at the court during the last part of the reign of King Edward VI. The same facts may be illustrated in a different manner from the history and writings of Stephen Gardiner. Gardiner, after being private secretary to Cardinal Wolsey and in the service of King Henry VIII. became Bishop of Winchester in 1531. After the accession of Edward VI. his opposition to the removal of images from churches and to the Injunctions and Homilies of 1547 led to his committal to the Fleet prison on 25th September, 1547. From that imprisonment he was released on 8th January, 1548; but a little later was confined as a prisoner in his own house. After being again at liberty various charges of resistance or disrespect to the Council were brought against him; and to afford him an opportunity of showing his innocence he was ordered to preach before the king. Cecil, afterwards Lord Burleigh in Elizabeth's reign, was sent to him by the Duke of Somerset to try to induce him not to speak of Transubstantiation or the Mass. To this Gardiner replied, according to his own account of his words:—

[1] *The Two Liturgies and other Documents set forth by Authority in the Reign of King Edward VI.* (Parker Society), pp. 516, 517.

10 *

"I will preach the very presence of Christ's most precious body and blood in the Sacrament, which is the Catholic faith, and no doubtful matter, nor yet in controversy, saving that certain unlearned speak of it they wot not what." [1]

On receiving from Cecil a report of his interview, Somerset wrote a letter to Gardiner on 28th June, 1548, in which, after referring to his prohibition "to entreat upon those principal questions which remain amongst the number of learned men in this realm as yet in controversy concerning the Sacrament of the altar and the Mass," he went on to say :—

"Your answer hereunto our said servant hath declared unto us in this manner, Ye can nowise forbear to speak of the Sacrament, neither of the Mass, this last being the chief foundation, as you say, [2] of our religion, and that without it we cannot know that Christ is our sacrifice. . . . We reply very shortly . . . charging you . . . to abstain in your said sermon from treating of any matter in controversy concerning the said Sacrament and the Mass." [3]

On the following day, St. Peter's Day, Gardiner preached his sermon in the presence of the king. In the course of it he made the following references to the Holy Eucharist :—

"Christ was sent to be our Messias, our Saviour, He was sent to be our Bishop and also our Sacrifice. He was sent from the Trinity, to be our Mediator between God and us, and to reconcile us to the favour of God the Father. He was the Bishop that offered for our sins, and the Sacrifice that was offered. And as He is our Bishop, so is He our mean to pacify God for us. . . . And as He was our sacrifice, so is He our reconciliation to God again. But we must confess and believe Him thoroughly, I say, for as He was our Bishop then, so is it He that still keepeth us in favour with God. And like as His sacrifice then made was sufficient for us, to deliver us from our sins and bring us in favour with God, so, to continue us in the same favour of God, He ordained a perpetual remembrance of Himself. He ordained Himself for a memory of Himself at His Last Supper, when He instituted the Sacrament of the altar. Not for another redemption, as though the first had not been sufficient, nor as though the world needed a new redemption from sin ; but that

---

[1] Foxe, *Acts and Monuments*, vi. 70 (edition 1843-9).

[2] Gardiner afterwards denied that he had applied this expression to the Mass : see p. 156, *infra*.

[3] Foxe, *op. cit.* vi. 86 ; Wilkins, *Concilia*, iv. 28.

we might thoroughly remember His passion, He instituted this
Sacrament by His most holy word, saying, 'This is My body,' which
word is sufficient to prove the Sacrament, and maketh sufficiently
for the substance thereof. And this daily sacrifice He instituted to
be continued among Christian men, not for need of another redemption or satisfaction for the sins of the world (for that was sufficiently
performed by His sacrifice of His body and blood, done upon the
cross), neither that He be now our Bishop for need of any further
sacrifice to be made for sin, but to continue us in the remembrance
of His passion suffered for us, to make us strong in believing the
fruit of His passion, to make us diligent in thanksgiving for the
benefit of His passion, to establish our faith, and to make us strong
in acknowledging the efficacy of His death and passion suffered for
us. And this is the true understanding of the Mass, not for another
redemption, but that we may be strong in believing the benefit of
Christ's death and bloodshedding for us upon the cross. . . . Where
I said of the Mass that it was a sacrifice ordained to make us the
more strong in the faith and remembrance of Christ's passion, and
for commending unto God the souls of such as be dead in Christ
(for these two things are the special causes why the Mass was instituted), the Parliament very well ordained Mass to be kept ; and
because we should be the more strong in the faith and devotion
towards God, it was well done of the Parliament, for moving the
people more and more with devotion, to ordain that this Sacrament
should be received in both kinds. Therefore I say that the Act of
Parliament for receiving of the Sacrament of the altar in both kinds
was well made. I said also that the proclamation which was made
that no man should unreverently speak of the Sacrament, or otherwise speak of it than Scripture teacheth them, was well made ; for
this proclamation stoppeth the mouths of all such as will unreverently speak of the Sacrament. For in Scripture there is nothing to
be found that maketh anything against the Sacrament, but all
maketh with it. . . . But here it may be said unto me, 'Why, Sir,
is this your opinion? It is good, you speak plainly in this matter,
and halt nothing, but declare your mind plainly without any colour-
ing or covert speaking. The Act for the dissolving and suppressing
of the chantries seemeth to make against the Mass, how like you
that Act ? What say you of it ? Or, what would you say of it, if
you were alone ? ' I will speak what I think of it. I will use no
colourable or covert words. I will not use a devised speech for a
time and afterward go from it again. If chantries were abused
by applying the Mass for the satisfaction of sin, or to bring men to

heaven, or to take away sin, or to make men, if wicked, just, I like the Act well ; and they might well be dissolved ; for the Mass was not instituted for any such purpose. . . . As for the chantries themselves, if there were any such abuse in them concerning the Mass, it is no matter if they be taken away. King Henry VIII., a noble and wise prince, not without a great pain maintained the Mass ; and yet in his doctrine it was confessed that Masses of *Scala coeli*[1] were not to be used or allowed, because they did pervert the right use and institution of the Mass. For when men add unto the Mass an opinion of satisfaction, or of a new redemption, then do they put it to another use than it was ordained for. I, that allow Mass so well, and I, that allow praying for the dead, as indeed the dead are of Christian charity to be prayed for, yet can agree with the realm in that matter of putting down chantries. But yet ye would say unto me, 'There be fewer Masses by putting away the chantries'. So were there when abbeys were dissolved ; so be there when ye unite many churches in one. So this is no injury nor prejudice to the Mass. It consisteth not in the number, nor in the multitude, but in the thing itself. . . . I like well the Communion,[2] because it provoketh men more and more to devotion. I like well the proclamation, because it stoppeth the mouths of all such as unreverently speak or rail against the Sacrament. I like well the rest of the king's majesty's proceedings concerning the Sacrament. I have now told you what I like ; but shall I speak nothing of that I mislike ? Ye will then say I speak not plainly. I will therefore show my conscience plainly. I mislike that preachers which preach by the king's licence, and those readers which by the king's permission and sufferance do read open lectures, do openly and blasphemously talk against the Mass and against the Sacrament." [3]

Noticeable features of this sermon of Gardiner's are its great care and restraint, the recognition of abuses and the expression of willingness for the reform of them, the approval of the provision for the reception of Communion in both kinds, and the assertion of the Eucharistic sacrifice in such a way as to avoid any risk of

[1] That is, the *Scala coeli* at Rome. In the section " Of prayer for souls departed " in the *King's Book* one of the " fond and great abuses " condemned was " that Masses said at *Scala coeli*, and other prescribed places, phantasied by men, did there in those places more profit the souls than in another ". See Lloyd, *Formularies*, pp. 376, 377.

[2] That is, Communion in both kinds.

[3] Foxe, *op. cit.* vi. 88-90, 92.

impairing the efficacy and sufficiency of the sacrifice of the cross. But it was regarded by the council as the climax of all his offences; and on the following day, 30th June, 1548, he was committed to the Tower. During the earlier years of his imprisonment Gardiner was allowed the use of his pen; and on the publication of Cranmer's *A Defence of the True and Catholic Doctrine of the Sacrament of the Body and Blood of our Saviour Christ* in 1550, he quickly produced an answer entitled *An Explication and Assertion of the True Catholic Faith touching the most Blessed Sacrament of the Altar, with Confutation of a Book Written against the Same*, which was published in France. In this treatise Gardiner asserted " the truth of the presence of the substance of Christ's body, as the true Catholic faith teacheth"; and as a " consequent " and " necessity " thereof the doctrine of Transubstantiation.[1] In regard to the Eucharistic sacrifice he taught that—

" The oblation and sacrifice of our Saviour Christ was, and is, a perfect work, once consummate in perfection without necessity of reiteration, as it was never taught to be reiterate, but a mere blasphemy to presuppose it. It is also in the Catholic teaching, grounded upon the Scripture, agreed that the same sacrifice once consummate was ordained by Christ's institution in His most holy Supper to be in the Church often remembered and showed forth in such sort of showing as to the faithful is seen present the most precious body and blood of our Saviour Christ under the forms of bread and wine, which body and blood the faithful Church of Christian people grant and profess, according to Christ's words, to have been betrayed and shed for the sins of the world, and so in the same Supper represented and delivered unto them, to eat and feed of it according to Christ's commandment, as of a most precious and acceptable sacrifice, acknowledging the same precious body and blood to be the sacrifice propitiatory for all the sins of the world, whereunto they only resort and only account that their very perfect oblation and sacrifice of Christian people, through which all other sacrifices necessary on our part be accepted and pleasant in the sight of God. And this manner of showing Christ's death and keeping the memory of it is grounded upon the Scriptures, written by the evangelists and St. Paul, and according thereunto preached, believed, used, and fre-

[1] P. 239, in *Writings and Disputations of Thomas Cranmer relative to the Lord's Supper* (Parker Society).

quented in the Church of Christ universally and from the beginning." [1]

"The Catholic doctrine teacheth not the daily sacrifice of Christ's most blessed body and blood to be an iteration of the once perfected sacrifice on the cross, but a sacrifice that representeth that sacrifice, and showeth it also before the faithful eyes, and refresheth the effectual memory of it; so as in the daily sacrifice, without shedding of blood, we may see with the eye of faith the very body and blood of Christ by God's mighty power without division distinctly exhibit, the same body and blood that suffered and was shed for us, which is a lively memorial to stir up our faith, and to consider therein briefly the great charity of God towards us declared in Christ. The Catholic doctrine teacheth the daily sacrifice to be the same in essence that was offered on the cross once, assured thereof by Christ's words when He said, 'This is My body that shall be betrayed for you'. The offering on the cross was, and is, propitiatory and satisfactory for our redemption and remission of sin, whereby to destroy the tyranny of sin. . . . The daily offering is propitiatory also, but not in that degree of propitiation as for redemption, regeneration, or remission of deadly sin, which was once purchased, and by force thereof is in the Sacraments ministered, but for the increase of God's favour, the mitigation of God's displeasure provoked by our infirmities, the subduing of temptations, and the perfection of virtue in us. All good works, good thoughts, and good meditations may be called sacrifices, and the same be called sacrifices propitiatory also, for so much as in their degree God accepteth and taketh them through the effect and strength of the very sacrifice of Christ's death, which is the reconciliation between God and man, ministered and dispensed particularly as God hath appointed, in such measure as He knoweth. . . . Because the priest in the daily sacrifice doth as Christ hath ordered to be done for showing forth and remembrance of Christ's death, that act of the priest done according to God's commandment must needs be propitiatory, and provoke God's favour, and ought to be trusted on to have a propitiatory effect with God to the members of Christ's body particularly, being the same done for the whole body in such wise as God knoweth the dispensation to be meet and convenient; according to which measure God worketh most justly and most mercifully, otherwise than man can by his judgment discuss and determine. To call the daily offering a ' sacrifice satisfactory ' must have an understanding that signifieth not the action of the priest,

[1] P. 344.

but the presence of Christ's most precious body and blood, the very sacrifice of the world once perfectly offered being propitiatory and satisfactory for all the world; or else the word 'satisfactory' must have a signification and meaning, as it hath sometime, that declareth the acceptation of the thing done, and not the proper contrevail of the action, after which sort man may satisfy God that is so merciful as He will take in good worth for Christ's sake man's imperfect endeavour, and so the daily offering may be called a sacrifice satisfactory because God is pleased with it, being a manner of worshipping Christ's passion according to Christ's institution. But otherwise the daily sacrifice, in respect of the action of the priest, cannot be called satisfactory ; and it is a word indeed that soundeth not well so placed, although it might be saved by a signification, and therefore think that word rather to be well expounded than by captious understanding brought in slander when it is used, and this speech to be frequented that the only immolation of Christ in Himself upon the altar of the cross is the very satisfactory sacrifice for reconciliation of mankind to the favour of God. . . . Finally man by any of his action to presume to satisfy God by way of countervail is a very mad and furious blasphemy. . . . Christ liveth ever, and therefore is a perpetual everlasting Priest, by whose authority priesthood is now in this visible Church, . . . which priests, visible ministers to our invisible Priest, offer the daily sacrifice in Christ's Church, that is to say, with the very presence, by God's omnipotency wrought, of the most precious body and blood of our Saviour Christ, showing forth Christ's death, and celebrating the memory of His Supper and death according to Christ's institution, so with daily oblation and sacrifice of the self-same sacrifice to kindle in us a thankful remembrance of all Christ's benefits unto us. " [1]

Gardiner, while very distinctly affirming Transubstantiation and that the Eucharist is a sacrifice of Christ's body and blood, appears to have avoided possible misconceptions of these doctrines. His belief about the sacrifice, as the passages which have been quoted show, necessitates and does not impair the efficacy of the sacrifice of the cross. His teaching about the presence includes the repudiation of carnal ideas as well as the acceptance of Transubstantiation. Thus, he says :—

" When we acknowledge by faith Christ's body present, although we say it is present truly, really, substantially, yet we say our

[1] Pp. 360, 361, 363.

senses be not privy to that presence, or the manner of it, but by instruction of faith ; and therefore we say Christ's body to be not locally present nor by manner of quantity, but invisible, and in no sensible manner, but marvellously in a Sacrament and mystery truly, and in such a spiritual manner as we cannot define and determine, and yet by faith we know His body present, the parts of which be in themselves distinct one from another in their own substance but not by circumscription of several places to be comprehended of our capacity ; which parts we can by no demonstration place, nor by imagination displace, diminish, alter, or confound." [1]

"The word 'corporally' may have an ambiguity and doubleness in respect and relation ; one is to the truth of the body present, and so it may be said, Christ is corporally present in the Sacrament ; if the word 'corporally' be referred to the manner of the presence, then we should say, Christ's body were present after a corporal manner, which we say not, but in a spiritual manner ; and therefore not locally nor by manner of quantity, but in such manner as God only knoweth, and yet doth us to understand by faith the truth of the very presence, exceeding our capacity to comprehend the manner 'how'." [2]

"No Catholic teaching is so framed with such terms as though we should eat Christ's most precious body grossly, carnally, joining those words so together. For else 'carnally' alone may have a good signification, as Hilary useth it ; but contrariwise, speaking in the Catholic teaching of the manner of Christ's presence, they call it a spiritual manner of presence, and yet there is present by God's power the very true natural body and blood of Christ,[3] whole God and Man, without leaving His place in heaven ; and in the holy Supper men use their mouths and teeth, following Christ's commandment in the receiving of that holy Sacrament, being in faith sufficiently instruct that they cannot nor do not tear, consume, or violate that most precious body and blood, but unworthily receiving it are cause of their own judgment and condemnation." [4]

In the year 1551 Gardiner's treatise was answered at length and paragraph by paragraph in Cranmer's *Answer unto a Crafty and Sophistical Cavillation ;* [5] but before it appeared

---

[1] P. 62.   [2] P. 89.   [3] See p. 66, note 2, *supra.*

[4] P. 112. At Gardiner's trial Lord Paget accused him of having taught "a carnal presence, a Transubstantiation" in his sermon in 1548 : see Foxe *op. cit.* vi. 163. Paget probably regarded "a carnal presence" and Transubstantiation as equivalent.

[5] See pp. 127-29, *supra.*

Gardiner had been tried, deprived of his bishopric, and again committed to the Tower, where he remained for the rest of the reign of Edward VI. In the course of his trial he put in his book as part of his case, and in general maintained the doctrines of the presence of Christ's body and blood in the Sacrament and of the Eucharistic sacrifice. His defence of the lawfulness of the doctrines which he held included the following statement:—

"The Bishop of London that now is, then being Bishop of Rochester,[1] did openly in his sermon made at Paul's Cross in the month of November or December or thereabouts in the first year of the king's majesty's reign that now is, very earnestly and vehemently preach and teach the true presence of Christ's most precious body and blood to be in the Sacrament of the altar. . . . Dr. Redman in a sermon which he preached before the king's majesty in Lent, the second year of his majesty's reign, did preach and teach to be believed for the true Catholic faith that the true presence of Christ's body and blood was in the Sacrament of the altar. . . . My Lord Archbishop of Canterbury about the time that the Bishop of Winchester aforesaid preached a sermon on St. Peter's Day at Westminster before the king's majesty, in a book by him translated, called *Catechism*, did affirm, publish, and set forth the true presence of Christ's most precious body and blood to be in the Sacrament of the altar. . . . In the months November and December in the second year of the king's majesty's reign the Bishops of Durham, Carlisle, London, Chichester, Worcester, Norwich, Hereford, and Westminster, being of the most ancient bishops and best learned in this realm, did openly in the Parliament then kept at Westminster defend the very and true presence of Christ's body and blood to be in the Sacrament of the altar.[2] . . . In sundry open and solemn disputations made as well in the University of Oxford as of Cambridge the third year of the king's majesty's reign the same true presence of the very body and blood to be in the Sacrament of the altar was maintained and defended by the great number of the chief and well learned of the said Universities. . . . The truth of Christ's most precious body and blood in the Sacrament of the altar hath not been nor was impugned by any famous clerk or yet by any named learned man in any part of all Christendom, either in the Greek or in the Latin Church, by our time; specially at the time of the letters sent by the same Duke of Somerset to the said bishop mentioned in this matter aforesaid, but only by Oecolampadius, Zuinglius, Vadianus, and

[1] Ridley.   [2] See pp. 134, 135, *supra*.

Carolostadius, the impugning whereof was most manifest error ; and
in England no learned man named had, or yet did, openly defend
or favour that error. . . . The said bishop said not to Master Cecil
that the Mass was the chief foundation of our religion, for Christ
Himself is the only foundation ; and in the Mass, as now in the
Communion, is the showing forth of Christ's death, which is a
sacrifice recordative of that only sacrifice of the cross, used in the
Church according to Christ's institution till His coming, the substance
of the sacrifice being all as one, and the manner of the offering only
differing." [1]

The deprivation and imprisonment of Gardiner afford an additional proof to those already mentioned that in the later years
of the reign of Edward VI. the opinions which were in favour
in high quarters in Church and State did not allow a doctrine
of the presence of the body and blood of Christ in the Holy
Eucharist other than of a receptionist or virtualist kind. Gardiner, though disliking some parts of the Prayer Book of 1549 and
in particular the prohibition of the elevation of the Sacrament,
was willing to accept that Book as containing " the most true
Catholic doctrine of the substance of the Sacrament " and as being " not distant from the Catholic faith ".[2] Between his beliefs
and those openly expressed and embodied in formularies before
the end of Edward's reign the difference was serious and acute.

IV.

By the directions of the Provincial Council of the Scottish
Church which met at Edinburgh in January, 1552, Archbishop
John Hamilton, the Archbishop of St. Andrews and Metro-
politan and Primate of Scotland, issued a *Catechism* in 1552.
Without entering into the more subtle questions concerned,
the *Catechism* teaches the doctrines of Transubstantiation and
of the sacrificial commemoration of the passion of Christ in the
Eucharist.

" This precious Sacrament contains Him which is the Fountain,

---

[1] Foxe, *op. cit.* vi. 125, 126.
[2] *An Explication and Assertion of the True Catholic Faith touching the
most Blessed Sacrament of the Altar*, pp. 55, 92 ; *cf.* pp. 79, 83, 84 ; and Foxe,
op. cit. vi. 114, 169.

the Well, and Giver of grace and sanctification, our Saviour Jesus Christ, in body and blood, soul and Godhead." [1]

"It is called the sacrifice of the altar because it is a quick and special remembrance of the passion of Christ." [2]

"It is the word of our Saviour Jesus Christ by whose virtue the Sacrament is consecrated; and by the might of that same word the bread is turned into the body of Christ, and the wine mixed with water is turned into the very blood of Christ." [3]

"After the words of consecration we see with our eyes the figure of bread and wine, we smell with our nose the savour of bread and wine, we taste with our mouth the gust of bread and wine, we feel with our touching the hardness of bread and the liquor of wine, yet there is no substance of bread and wine in that Sacrament, but only the substance of the body and blood of our Saviour under the form of bread and wine." [4]

"When we receive this Sacrament in remembrance of His passion, in deed we confess and grant that He died for us, that by His death we might get remission of our sins and eternal life." [5]

"Believe firmly and doubt not that under the form of bread which thou seest with thy bodily eyes there is contained the true body of Christ Jesu, the same body that was born of the Virgin Mary, that was crucified upon the cross, that rose from the dead the third day, that ascended to heaven, and sits at the right hand of God the Father Almighty. . . . Believe firmly that the whóle body of Christ is in the whole host and also in each part of the same; believe firmly there is but one body of Christ that is in many hosts, that is in sundry and many altars, that is in heaven sitting at the right hand of God, and that is in the Sacrament really present, it is one and the same body. . . . Trow firmly that after the words of consecration pronounced by the priest (by institution of our Saviour) the substance of the bread is turned into the substance of the body of Christ, remaining only the accidents, that is to say, the figure of bread, the sweetness of bread, the whiteness of bread with such like, so that there is not in the Sacrament the substance of bread. . . . When thou receivest in the Sacrament the body of Christ, believe also constantly that thou receivest a living body. . . . Thou receivest also His soul, and also His blood, for every living body has both soul and blood. . . . Trow surely that when thou receivest the body of Christ that thou

---

[1] Fo. cxxxix *b*. The author has used the facsimile edition published by Dr. Mitchell in 1882, but has modernised the spelling.
[2] Fo. cxl *b*.   [3] Fo. cxlii *a*.   [4] Fo. cxlii *b*.   [5] Fo. cxlvi *a*.

receivest also His Godhead. . . . Thou receivest both the body and blood of Christ in one form of bread as well as the priest receives them and each of them in two forms of bread and wine." [1]

" First, come with a right intention. Secondly, come with a whole faith. Thirdly, come with a clean conscience clad with perfect love of God and thy neighbour. And, last of all, come with devout prayers and orisons. And after the receiving of the Sacrament, with all thy heart give thanks to God for all His gifts, and specially that He has given to thee His own self to be thy spiritual refection and eternal salvation." [2]

---

[1] Fo. cxlvii *a*, cxlvii *b*, cxlviii *a*.   [2] Fo. cxlix *b*.

CHAPTER XI.

THE PERIOD OF THE REFORMATION.

PART III.

ON 6th July, 1553, King Edward VI. died. After the incident of Lady Jane Grey, Mary, Henry VIII.'s daughter by Catherine of Aragon, became queen, and she was proclaimed in London on 19th July. Her accession involved the reversal of the position of theological parties in England. Gardiner was released from prison, restored to his see of Winchester, and appointed Lord Chancellor. In like manner Bonner, the deprived Bishop of London, Heath, the deprived Bishop of Worcester, Day, the deprived Bishop of Chichester, and Tunstall, the Bishop of Durham, were set free; and resumed the occupancy of their sees. Cranmer and many other advocates of reforming opinions were imprisoned and put to death. The English formularies of Edward's reign were swept away; the Latin Mass was restored; a return was made to the doctrinal position of the reign of Henry VIII.

I.

The attitude of those who now became dominant may be seen by collecting some of the more official and authorised doctrinal statements of the time. The doctrine of the Eucharist was considered in both the Upper and the Lower House of the Convocation of Canterbury in October, 1553. In the Upper House the four following statements were agreed to :—

"Concerning the Sacrament of the altar.

"In the Sacrament of the altar duly administered we teach that by the words of Christ the real and actual substance of the body and blood of the Lord are present and contained under the species of the bread and the wine mixed with water. And since

Christ can no longer be divided, or His blood separated from His flesh, because He dieth no more, therefore we believe that the whole Christ, God and Man, is contained under either species, and is as much received by the faithful under one species as under both. And therefore we affirm that the praiseworthy custom of communicating the laity, and clergy who are not celebrating, under one species, which was introduced by the Church for great reasons and has been observed for a very long time, is to be retained in our churches and is not to be altered without the authority of the Catholic Church.

"Concerning Transubstantiation.

"Since Christ declared that the one sacrifice and unique mystery, which He instituted at the Last Supper and commanded to be received by the faithful, is His body which was betrayed for us, we do not believe that this is only bread, or that the body of Christ is with the bread or in the bread, apart from our calling it the Bread of life who came down from heaven. And since the manner of existing there is by the Transubstantiation and transition of the substance of bread and wine into the substance of the body and blood of the Lord, the accidents of bread and wine meanwhile remaining for the sake of our weakness and the signification of the mystery, the pastors of the Church lawfully assembled in the Lateran Council fittingly expressed the ancient truth of the Catholic faith by the new word Transubstantiation, as the fathers of the Nicene Council declared that the Son is of the same substance with the Father by the new word Consubstantial.

"Concerning the adoration and reservation of the Eucharist.

"Since we confess that the real body and real blood of Christ, and therefore the whole Christ, are in the Eucharist, how shall we do otherwise than adore Him who never has been and never ought to be without adoration among Christians? And the Sacrament which has once been consecrated for the use of the sick, that they may not depart hence without Communion—a practice which the most ancient authors and councils show to have been customary in antiquity—remains the Sacrament and body and blood of the Lord until it is consumed, so long as the species are uncorrupted.

"Concerning the substance of the sacrifice of the Church, and the intention of it, and by whom and for whom and to whom it is to be offered.

"We celebrate the holy and life-giving and bloodless offering in the churches, not believing that what is offered is the body of some one ordinary man, but that it is the body which the Word

who gives life to all things made His own, being at once the medicine for healing weaknesses and the burnt offering for cleansing
offences ; and we hold that on the Holy Table is placed the Lamb
of God, who takes away the sin of the world, who is sacrificed by
the priests without shedding of blood.   And this new offering of
the new covenant instituted and commanded by Christ, the Church,
receiving from the Apostles, offers throughout the whole world not
to angels, or to martyrs, or to any holy soul (for this would be
idolatry, since the obligation of sacrifice pertains to the worship of
supreme adoration), but only to God the Father and to the Son
and to the Holy Ghost, although she offers the sacrifice at the
memorials of the martyrs and in their memory, that they may pray
for us, not for those who are not incorporated in Christ but for
those who are the members of Christ, for the whole Church, for
kings, for priests, for the absent and the present, for the spirits of
the departed in Christ, that God may be propitious to their sins,
for plenty, for fruitfulness, for the fruits of the whole world, for
peace, for prosperity, for the sins and ignorances of the people, for
their salvation, and for the daily restoring which their weakness
needs, knowing that with such a sacrifice God is well pleased, and
that He forgives great sins." [1]

In the Lower House of Convocation the subject was discussed
at great length for some days.   Almost all the members were
agreed on the truth of the doctrine of Transubstantiation ; but at
the outset of the proceedings Philips, the Dean of Rochester,
Haddon, the Dean of Exeter, Philpot, the Archdeacon of Winchester, Cheyney, the Archdeacon of Hereford, and Ailmer, the
Archdeacon of Stow, refused to sign a declaration affirming it,
the discussion turned mainly on Transubstantiation, and formal
statements of opinion on the part of Philips, Haddon, Cheyney,
and Philpot, which are alike in having been carefully drawn so
as not to affirm it, have been preserved, apparently through a
quotation from the destroyed Journals of Convocation.   They
are as follows :—

"The opinion of Walter Philips, Dean of Rochester.
"In the consecrated bread and wine the faithful really and actually and substantially eat with the faith of the heart the real body
of Christ, which sits at the right hand of God the Father ; and with
the mouth they eat the Sacrament of the body of Christ.

[1] Strype, *Ecclesiastical Memorials*, III. i. 73-75 (1822 edition).

"The opinion of James Haddon, Dean of Exeter.

"The body of Christ is actually present in the Sacraments of His body and blood when administered rightly (*vere*) and in accordance with the institution of Christ. By actually understand really and not in pretence, sacramentally not carnally.

"The opinion of Richard Cheyney, Archdeacon of Hereford.

"In the Sacrament of the altar by the power of the word of God spoken by the priest the body of Christ which was conceived of the Virgin Mary is actually present. Also His natural blood.

"The opinion of John Philpot, Archdeacon of Winchester.

"I say that by means of the holy symbols of the Lord's Supper, administered in accordance with the institution recorded in the Gospels, the body and blood of Christ are really presented (*exhiberi*) by the Holy Ghost to those who receive in faith; and therefore that very body and blood in which Christ fulfilled all obedience for our salvation, in order that we might be joined together into one body together with Him, and might also perceive His power in the partaking of all good things." [1]

These four statements, as has been mentioned, are alike in having been carefully drawn so as not to affirm Transubstantiation. Apart from this one point they differ considerably from one another. Those of Philips and Philpot appear to express forms of receptionism. That of Haddon appears to follow the Lutheran idea of the presence of the body and blood of Christ in the consecrated elements during the administration. That of Cheyney seems most consistent with a belief that in the consecrated elements are the body and blood of Christ; and it is to be observed that he used the phrase "natural blood".[2] With few exceptions then the Lower House of the Convocation of Canterbury, like the Upper House, accepted the doctrine of Transubstantiation.

In 1554 Convocation ordered the three following propositions to be submitted to Cranmer, Ridley, and Latimer as a basis of a discussion to take place at Oxford :—

"i. In the Sacrament of the altar by the power of the word of God uttered by the priest the natural body of Christ which was conceived of the Virgin Mary is actually present under the species of bread and wine; also His natural blood.

"ii. After the consecration the substance of bread and wine does

---

[1] Collier, *Ecclesiastical History of Great Britain*, ix. 300, 301 (1846 edition).

[2] See p. 66, note 2, *supra*.

not remain, neither any other substance except the substance of Christ, God and Man.

"iii. In the Mass the life-giving sacrifice of the Church is propitiatory for the sins both of the living and of the dead." [1]

These propositions were also sent by Convocation to the University of Cambridge with the request that if held to be true they might be approved. They were so approved ; and the University decided to send Cambridge divines to take part in the discussion with the Cambridge men, Cranmer, Ridley, and Latimer, at Oxford.[2]

In 1555 Gardiner, as Chancellor of the University of Cambridge, put out a series of fifteen articles, subscription to which was to be made a condition of admission to any degree. Of these articles the eighth was as follows :—

"We believe that in the Sacrament of the Eucharist by the power of the word of God uttered by the priest the natural body of Christ which was born from the Virgin is actually present, and also His natural blood, and that the substance of bread and wine does not remain any longer, nor any other substance than that of Christ, God and Man. Wherefore we hold with sure faith that it is a holy act for us to adore the Eucharist whether in the Mass or outside the Mass. And we declare that in the Mass is the life-giving sacrifice of Christ, which is propitiatory both for the living and for the dead ; and that Communion under both species is not necessary to salvation ; and that the power of consecrating the body and blood of Christ has been granted only to priests lawfully ordained by Christ according to the rite of the Catholic Church." [3]

A declaration of doctrine set forth in 1556 by Cardinal Pole as papal legate included a statement about the Eucharist.

" The form of this Sacrament consists of the words of the Saviour in which He consecrated this Sacrament. For the priest consecrates this Sacrament speaking in the person of Christ ; for by the power of these words the substance of the bread is converted into the body of Christ, and the substance of the wine is converted into His blood, yet in such a way that the whole Christ is contained under the species of bread, and the whole Christ under the species of wine,

[1] Strype, *Memorials of Cranmer*, i. 479 (1840 edition); Wilkins, *Concilia*, iv. 98.
[2] Strype, *op. cit.* i. 479, 480, ii. 940-44 ; Wilkins, *Concilia*, iv. 98,
[3] Wilkins, *Concilia*, iv. 127.

and that the whole Christ is under every part of the consecrated
host and the consecrated wine, when a division is made. The effect
of this Sacrament, which it produces in the soul, is the union to
Christ of the man who receives it worthily." [1]

In the same year, 1556, Injunctions given by Cardinal Pole
in connection with the visitation of the diocese of Gloucester
contained an order—

"That all parishioners shall at the time of the elevation reverently kneel in such places of the church where they may both see
and worship the Blessed Sacrament " ; [2]

and in 1557 the articles of inquiry drawn up by him for his
visitation of the diocese of Canterbury included a question—

"Whether any person do hold, affirm, or say, that in the Blessed
Sacrament of the altar there is not contained the real and substantial
presence of Christ; or that by any manner of means do contemn
and despise the said Blessed Sacrament, or do refuse to do reverence or worship thereunto." [3]

II.

Another source of information as to the opinions held by the
now dominant party is in the articles presented against those
who were prosecuted and in many cases put to death. The
statements drawn up by Convocation in 1554 with a view to the
trial of Cranmer, Ridley, and Latimer have already been quoted.[4]
To these may be added a few representative instances from the
indictments of less famous prisoners.

The interrogatories administered by Bishop Bonner to William
Pigot and John Laurence in February, 1555, included the question—

"Whether do you think and steadfastly believe that it is a Catholic, faithful, Christian, and true doctrine to teach, preach, and say
that in the Sacrament of the altar under the forms of bread and
wine there is without any substance of bread and wine there remaining by the omnipotent power of Almighty God and His holy word
really, truly, and in very deed the true and natural body and blood
of our Saviour Jesus Christ, the self-same in substance, though not
in outward form and appearance, which was born of the Virgin Mary
and suffered on the cross." [5]

[1] Wilkins, *Concilia*, iv. 796.   [2] *Ibid.* 147.   [3] *Ibid.* 169.
[4] See pp. 162, 163, *supra*.   [5] Foxe, *op. cit.* vi. 737.

The articles of Bishop Bonner against John Taylor, or Cardmaker, in May, 1555, contained statements that—

"The belief of the Catholic Church is that in having the body and blood of Christ really and truly contained in the Sacrament of the altar is to have by the omnipotent power of Almighty God the body and blood of Christ there invisibly and really present under the said Sacrament, and not to make thereby a new God, or a new Christ, or a new body of Christ. . . . The body of Christ is visibly and truly ascended into heaven, and there is, in the visible form of His humanity; and yet the same body in substance is invisibly and truly contained in the said Sacrament of the altar. . . . Christ at His Last Supper, taking bread into His hands, blessing it, breaking it, giving it to His Apostles, and saying, 'Take, eat, this is My body,' did institute a Sacrament there, willing that His body really and truly should be contained in the said Sacrament, no substance of bread and wine there remaining, but only the accidents thereof." [1]

In the articles objected by Bishop Bonner against John Warne in the same month, May, 1555, were the following accusations :—

"Thou . . . hast believed, and dost believe, firmly and steadfastly, that in the Sacrament commonly called the Sacrament of the altar there is not the very true and natural body of our Saviour Christ in substance under the forms of bread and wine. . . . Thou hast believed, and dost believe, that after the words of consecration spoken by the priest there is not, as the Church of England doth believe and teach, the body of Christ, but that there doth only remain the substance of material bread as it is before the consecration, and that the said bread is in no wise altered or changed. . . . Thou hast said and dost believe that, if the Catholic Church do believe and teach that there is in the Mass now used in England, and in other places in Christendom, a sacrifice wherein there is a Sacrament containing the body and blood of Christ really and truly, then that belief and faith of the Church is naught and against God's truth and the Scripture. . . . Thou didst both then [2] and also before believe no otherwise than at this present thou dost believe, that is to say, that in the Sacrament of the altar there is neither the very true body or blood of Christ nor any other sub-

---

[1] Foxe, op. cit. vii. 79.

[2] That is, at the time of a former prosecution of John Warne in 1546, during the reign of Henry VIII., when he had been condemned to death but pardoned.

stance but the substance of material bread and wine; and to receive the said material bread and wine, and to break it and to
distribute it among the people only is the true receiving of Christ's
body, and no otherwise, so that thy faith and belief is that in the
said Sacrament there is no substance of Christ's material body and
blood, but all the thing that is there is material bread and the receiving thereof as afore, and that the substance of the natural and
true body of Christ, born of the Virgin Mary, is only in heaven and
not in the Sacrament of the altar." [1]

The indictments against William Wolsey and Robert Pigot
presented by Fuller, the Chancellor of Ely, in May, 1555, included the following charges :—

"You have said, affirmed, and holden opinions many times and
in divers companies in 1553, 1554, and 1555 that the natural body
and blood of our Saviour Jesus Christ is not really present in the
Sacrament of the altar (which he called an idol). . . . He obstin-
ately and persistently kept to his perverse opinion, publicly and
shamelessly saying in English words, The Sacrament of the altar is
an idol; and the natural body and blood of our Saviour Jesus Christ
is not really present in the said Sacrament. . . . You said you
could not away with processions, with bearing and following of the
cross nor with the Sacrament of the altar, which you cannot believe
nor will do any reverence or worship to it. . . . You will not believe the real presence after consecration." [2]

In January, 1556, seven persons, Thomas Whittle, priest,
Bartlet Green, gentleman, John Tudson, artificer, John Went,
artificer, Thomas Browne, Isabel Foster, wife, Joan Warne or
Lashford, maid, were prosecuted under one indictment by Bishop
Bonner. The indictment included the charge—

"Thou, . . . misliking and not allowing the sacrifice of the
Mass and Sacrament of the altar, hast both refused to come to thy
parish church to hear Mass and to receive the said Sacrament, and
hast also expressly said that in the said Sacrament of the altar there
is not the very body and blood of our Saviour Christ really, substantially, and truly, but hast affirmed expressly that the Mass is
idolatry and abomination, and that in the Sacrament of the altar
there is none other substance but only material bread and material

---

[1] Foxe, *op. cit.* vii. 80, 81.

[2] The two indictments are printed from the Ely Register in Dixon,
History of the Church of England, iv. 439-42. *Cf.* Foxe, *op. cit.* vii. 402-6.

wine, which are tokens of Christ's body and blood only, and that the substance of Christ's body and blood is in no wise in the said Sacrament of the altar." [1]

The articles administered in July, 1556, to Joan Waste by Bayne, the Bishop of Lichfield, included :—

"She did hold the Sacrament of the altar to be but only a memory or representation of Christ's body, and material bread and wine, but not His natural body, unless it were received. And that it ought not to be reserved from time to time over the altar, but immediately to be received. . . . She did hold, in the receiving of the Sacrament, she did not receive the same body that was born of the Virgin Mary and suffered upon the cross for our redemption. . . . She did hold that Christ at His Last Supper did not bless the bread that He had then in His hands but was blessed Himself; and by the virtue of the words of consecration the substance of the bread and wine is not converted and turned into the substance of the body and blood of Christ." [2]

With the indictments in prosecutions may be compared the recantation made by Sir John Cheke in 1556. In the declaration which he himself drew up he stated :—

" I do profess and protest that, whatsoever mine opinion of the Blessed Sacrament of Christ's body and blood, and of the sense of Christ's words spoken of the same, hath been heretofore, I do now . . . . believe firmly the real presence of Christ's very body and blood in the Sacrament, and none other substance there remaining, moved thereunto by invincible reasons of the Catholic doctors against the Arians of Christ's very true and natural being in us, and also by the consent of Christ's Catholic Church." [3]

This declaration being thought insufficient, a longer form of recantation was written by Cardinal Pole and made by Sir John Cheke before the court. In this longer form Sir John Cheke spoke of his former "arrogant blindness" and "great madness" and "pernicious sentence"; of his consent to "confess and re-tract" what he had previously thought ; and of his willingness "for an assured token that I say with my mouth that which I think with my heart," since he had "fallen into the error which Berengarius fell into," to "make the self-same confession that he did". Cheke then recited the declaration made by Berengar at

---

[1] Foxe, *op. cit.* vii. 716.   [2] *Ibid.* viii. 248.
[3] Strype, *Life of Sir John Cheke*, p. 115 (1821 edition).

the Council of Rome in 1059,[1] including the statement that " the real body and blood of our Lord Jesus Christ" "are held and broken by the hands of the priests, and are crushed by the teeth of the faithful ".[2]

It is to be noticed that in the formal statements of belief and in the articles of indictment the phrases "natural body" and "material body" of Christ occur in descriptions of the body which is present in the Eucharist ; and that the recantation imposed on Sir John Cheke contained the assertion that the body of Christ is "broken" in the Sacrament.   The phrases "natural body" and "material body" were probably used, like the phrase "natural body " in some of the formularies of foreign Reformers,[3] to emphasise that the body in the Eucharist is the same body as that which was born of the Virgin and suffered on the cross ; the expression that the body of Christ is "broken" to emphasise that the consecrated Sacrament is the body.   As in the Berengarian controversy, the influence of panic produced by denials of what was held dear may have had much to do with the choice of language which would not be congenial to the more careful advocates of Transubstantiation.   That the phraseology "natural body" and "material body" begins after the widespread denials of Transubstantiation and of the Real Presence in the reign of Edward VI., and that the phrase declaring the body of Christ to be "broken" should have been revived at this particular time after being laid aside for centuries, tends to indicate that such an influence was at work.   But this is not the whole explanation of the use of such language.   That the body of Christ was said to be "broken" denotes much forgetfulness of the philosophic teaching by the aid of which the doctrine of Transubstantiation was developed in the thirteenth century ; and the application of the words "natural" and "material" to the body of our Lord in its present state shows that the change in the condition of His body at the resurrection, which had been much emphasised in the middle ages, was but little remembered.[4]   The use of the

[1] See vol. i. p. 247, supra.

[2] Strype, op. cit. pp. 119, 122, 123.

[3] See pp. 37, 57, supra.

[4] Yet Thomas Collins, Sir John Baker's chaplain, at the trial of Edmund Allin in 1557, laid stress on the glorified state of our Lord's body, though without much theological accuracy, if the report of his words can be relied on. See Foxe, op. cit. viii. 324. Cf. pp. 170, 173, infra.

phrase "natural body" by Gardiner in a passage where he is at great pains to maintain the spiritual character of the presence of Christ's body in the Sacrament [1] is a sign that it does not necessarily imply a carnal view of the presence on the part of those who used it ; at the same time, it is a phrase which would readily lend itself to such a view.

III.

Very interesting examples of Eucharistic teaching on the part of those in favour in the reign of Mary are supplied by the writings of Bishop Tunstall and Bishop Watson.

Cuthbert Tunstall or Tonstall was born at Hackforth in the North Riding of Yorkshire in 1474. In 1491 he entered the University of Oxford, possibly at Balliol College, but left Oxford because of the prevalence of the plague, and migrated to King's Hall, which was afterwards merged in Trinity College, at Cambridge. He subsequently graduated as LL.D. at Padua. After filling various benefices and holding many offices, he became Bishop of London in 1522, and Bishop of Durham in 1530. The part played by him in the debate in the House of Lords in 1547 has already been mentioned.[2]   In 1552, after lengthy proceedings, he was deprived of his bishopric, and the bishopric of Durham itself was dissolved by Act of Parliament. Tunstall was a prisoner from the end of 1551 until the accession of Queen Mary in 1553. At Mary's accession he was released ; and in 1554 the bishopric of Durham was re-established by Act of Parliament, and he was restored to it. After the accession of Queen Elizabeth in 1558, he refused to take the oath of supremacy, or to consecrate Parker. He was deprived of his bishopric on 28th September, 1559. On 18th November, 1559, he died. His treatise *Concerning the Reality of the Body and Blood of Our Lord Jesus Christ in the Eucharist* was finished in 1551, as is shown by a note at the end of it and by the date of the preface ; the first known edition is that printed at Paris in 1554. In this treatise very definite and explicit teaching that the consecrated bread and wine are the body and blood of Christ is united with some deprecating of too curious inquiries into the exact manner of the presence. A few extracts will show sufficiently the position which is consistently maintained.

[1] See p. 154, *supra*.   [2] See pp. 134, 135, *supra*.

"These words [that is, the words of Christ at the institution of the Sacrament], which from the first beginning of the Catholic Church after the passion of Christ have always been understood by the consent of all the orthodox without any allegory or metaphor or trope or figure, clearly declare that the body of Christ, not only figuratively, not only by way of representation (as the authors of perverse opinions say), but the very real and natural body of Christ, although now spiritual, is under the species of bread ; and that the real and natural blood of Christ, although now spiritual, is present under the species of wine in fact, actually, and in reality.[1] . . . This body after His resurrection is now a spiritual body. . . . And in the Sacrament the very spiritual body is given invisibly and spiritually, and is received by the faithful ; in like manner also the blood which is now spiritual is given in the Sacrament in an invisible and spiritual way yet really, and is received by the faithful." [2]

"Those who are of opinion that the body of Christ in the Eucharist is not to be adored show themselves to the world as unbelievers, without faith in the words of Christ, since to their carnal eyes there seems to be nothing but bread and mingled wine." [3]

"From the beginning of the infant Church nowhere has any Catholic admitted to Baptism doubted concerning the presence of Christ in the Sacrament of the Eucharist ; but all, before being admitted to the font of the laver, have been so taught, and have confessed that they believe, as Justin Martyr bears witness in his *Second Apology* against the heathen.[4] But in what way the bread which was common before the consecration becomes (*transiret in*) His body by the ineffable sanctification of the Spirit, the most learned of the ancients thought inscrutable, lest, with the people of Capernaum failing to believe the words of Christ but asking how this should be, they should try to be wise above what is right, transgressing soberness of mind. But it seemed to them enough and more than enough to believe firmly in the almighty power and the words of Christ, who is faithful in all His words, and who alone with the Father and the Holy Ghost knows the manner of the working of His wonderful works. Before the time of Innocent III., the Bishop of Rome, who presided at the Lateran Council, those who made somewhat curious inquiries thought that this might happen in three

---

[1] The word "natural" is here plainly used by Tunstall in the sense of "actual", not in the sense of "in a natural condition". He used "carnal" in the same way at the debate in the House of Lords in 1547 : see pp. 134, 135, *supra*. See also p. 66, note 2, *supra*.

[2] Fo. 9 *b*, 10 *a*, 10 *b* (edition 1554).   [3] Fo. 41 *b*.

[4] St. Justin Martyr, *Apol.* i. 66 ; see vol. i. p. 34, *supra*.

ways.   Some thought that the body of Christ is present with the bread or in the bread, as fire in a mass of iron, which Luther seems to have followed.   Others thought that the bread is reduced to nothing, or is corrupted.   Others thought that the substance of the bread is changed into the substance of the body of Christ, which Innocent seems to have followed, rejecting the other methods at this council, although those who make somewhat curious investigations think that no fewer miracles but rather more result in this method than in those which he rejected.   But those who with Innocent were present at this council thought that to the almighty power of God, to whom nothing is impossible, all miracles yield, and that this method is most in accordance with the words of Christ, ' This is My body,' ' This is My blood '.   For John Scotus in the fourth book of the *Sentences,* the eleventh distinction, the third question, referring to Innocent, says there were three opinions, one that the bread remains, and that yet the body of Christ is really with the bread ; a second that the bread does not remain, and yet is not converted, but ceases to be, either by annihilation, or by being resolved into matter, or by corruption into something else ; a third that the bread is transubstantiated into the body, and the wine into the blood.[1]   The intention of each of these was to preserve the common element, that the body of Christ is really there, because to deny that is clearly contrary to the faith.   For it has been part of the verity of the faith expressed from the institution of the Eucharist that the body of Christ is really and actually contained there. . . . But whether it would have been better to have imposed silence on all curious persons, that they might not examine the method in which this happens, since the ways of the Lord are unsearchable, . . . or to have left each curious person to his own conjecture, as it was free before the council, provided he acknowledged that the reality of the body and blood of the Lord is in the Eucharist, . . . or out of the three methods mentioned above to choose the one which should agree best with the words of Christ, and to reject all the rest, lest in no other way should there be an end of the contentions among the too curious men of that age, since in no other way could silence be imposed on the curious tongues of that contentious time, I think it right that in matters of this kind, since the Church is the pillar of the truth, its definite decision should be wholly observed." [2]

Thomas Watson was born in the diocese of Durham in 1513. He graduated from St. John's College, Cambridge, in 1534, and

---

[1] See also vol. i. p. 340, *supra.*   [2] Fo. 45 *b*, 46 *a*, 46 *b*, 47 *a*.

was afterwards Fellow, and later Master.   He filled several benefices, and became Dean of Durham in 1553, and Bishop of Lincoln in 1556.   He was one of the commissioners sent by the
University of Cambridge in 1534 to dispute with Cranmer, Ridley,
and Latimer at Oxford, where he was incorporated D.D.   On
the accession of Queen Elizabeth he refused to take the oath of
supremacy, and was deprived of his bishopric.   He was several
times committed to the Tower ; and, after being in custody in
various places, died at Wisbech Castle on 27th September, 1584.
He took part in the conference about the Eucharist which was
held at Sir Richard Morison's house on 3rd December, 1551, and
maintained that communicants receive the "true substance" of
the flesh of Christ, and are "naturally united" to Him, being
partakers of His "natural flesh".[1]   He took part also in the debate in Convocation in October, 1553, in which he appears to
have maintained the doctrine of Transubstantiation.[2]   His belief about the Eucharist is more fully set out in his work *Wholesome and Catholic Doctrine concerning the Seven Sacraments of
Christ's Church, expedient to be known of all men set forth in
manner of Short Sermons to be made to the people*, which was
published in 1558.   This book consists of thirty sermons, of which
the seventh to the thirteenth are entitled " Of the Real Presence
of Christ's Body in the Sacrament of the Altar," " Of the
Change of the Bread and Wine, that is to say, of Transubstantiation," " Of the Effects of Christ's Body and Blood in the
Worthy Receiver," " An Exhortation for the Worthy Receiving
of the Holy Sacrament," " How a Man may Come Worthily to
Receive the Blessed Sacrament," " Of the Sacrifice of the New
Testament, which is Called the Mass," " Of the Godly Prayers and
Ceremonies used in the Sacrifice of the Mass ".   In these sermons
the doctrines of Transubstantiation and of the Eucharistic sacrifice are carefully expounded in their bearings on spiritual life
with the aim of making them popularly understood and devotionally helpful.   Features which may be noticed are the references
to the spiritual character of our Lord's body in its glorified state,
the contrast between the being of Christ's body in heaven and

[1] See the document in the Corpus Christi College, Cambridge, MSS. No.
cii. quoted in Strype's *Life of Sir John Cheke*, pp. 82, 83.

[2] See the document printed in Dixon, *History of the Church of England*,
iv. 81-85, from the Harleian MS. 422, vol. xxxviii.

its presence in the Sacrament, the emphasis on the need of communicating worthily and the advantage of frequent Communion, the distinction that adoration is of the body and blood of Christ and not of the visible qualities of the bread, and the representation of the Eucharistic sacrifice as the commemoration of the death of Christ and the same act on the part of the Church on earth as is performed by Christ Himself in heaven.

"Our Saviour Christ . . . doth still vouchsafe to nourish us so redeemed and brought to life with the sweet and wholesome milk of His own blood, and giveth us His flesh to eat, and His blood to drink, that we might be fed and nourished for the continuance of our spiritual life with the same precious things that we were redeemed withal before. And because our souls be as yet joined with our bodies, therefore for the time of this life our Saviour Christ giveth unto us His invisible graces in sensible Sacraments. . . . In the Sacrament of the altar under the visible forms of bread and wine is given unto us the substance of all grace, which is Christ Himself, that is to say, His body and His blood, which, though they be corporal things in their own nature, yet now being glorified they be spiritual, and therefore not sensible, but where it pleaseth our Saviour by miracle to have them appear. This is then most certainly and constantly to be believed of us all upon pain of damnation that in this blessed Sacrament of the altar . . . is verily and really present the true body and blood of our Saviour Christ which suffered upon the cross for us, and is received there corporally by the services of our mouths, not in the same form of His body as it was upon the cross, but in the forms of our daily and special nutriments of bread and wine, the substance of which bread and wine is converted and changed into the substance of Christ's body and blood by the omnipotent and secret power of His word assisting the due administration of His minister. . . . After the speaking of those words by Christ or by His minister in His person sufficiently authorised so to do by His commandment is made present the natural [1] body and blood of our Saviour Christ, there to be received of His faithful people, to the increase of all grace and immortality both of body and soul. . . . The oblations be consecrate by God's power and grace, who is now there present, and sanctifieth the creatures, and changeth them, by

_____
[1] "Natural " is evidently used by Bishop Watson in the sense of "actual " not as equivalent to "in a natural way " ; cf. the use of this word by Bishop Tunstall, p. 170, supra. See also p. 66, note 2, supra, pp. 174, 176, infra.

the invisible working of the Holy Ghost, which miraculous change must be imputed to Christ." [1]

"In the Sacrament there be two graces to be considered, the one is the substantial grace of Christ's body there present and contained, the other is the accidental grace only signified and not contained, which is wrought in the soul of the worthy receiver, whereby he is more inwardly joined to Christ's mystical body, not only spiritually by faith and charity, but also by natural [2] and corporal participation with Christ and His Church." [3]

"Ye ought to mark diligently that I have said concerning the two manners of being of Christ's body, the one in heaven at the right hand of His Father manifestly without all cover of Sacrament, the other the same moment of time here in earth among us in a Sacrament, to be received of us for our spiritual sustenance, in which thing we may not consider the nature of a man's body, but the invisible power of God that can do with His body what He will, and doth with it what He saith." [4]

"The inward substance of bread and wine is changed into the substance of the body and blood of Christ, the outward forms of the said bread and wine with the quantity and qualities of the same still remaining unchanged. . . . The Holy Ghost overshadoweth this mystery, and maketh present the body of Christ above the speech and reason of man, and changeth the bread and the wine into Christ's body and blood, the outward forms remaining still, so that now there be not two substances remaining, but one and the self same that was given for our redemption, otherwise the manner of it is not searchable. . . . It is most certain that the whole body and blood of Christ is as truly contained under the one kind of bread as under both the kinds of bread and wine, seeing that Christ's living body cannot be without His blood, nor His lively blood without His body. And it is also most certainly true that, if the outward element of bread be divided into small parts, there is the whole body of Christ contained in every part as it was in the whole element before it was divided, even as the soul of man is but one and whole in the whole body, and is likewise one and whole in every part of the body." [5]

"This spiritual meat of Christ's body and blood may not be given to him that is spiritually dead in his soul by deadly sin, for

---

[1] Fo. xxxvi *a*, xxxvi *b*, xxxvii *a*, xxxviii *a*.
[2] See p. 173, note 1, *supra*.
[3] Fo. xxxix *a*.   [4] Fo. xl *a*, xl *b*.
[5] Fo. xlii *b*, xliii *a*, xliv *b*, xlv *a*, xlvi *a*, xlvi *b*,

then he receiveth it unworthily to his further judgment and condemnation, being guilty as Judas was of the body and blood of
Christ. . . . Because a man doth daily offend, and so decayeth in
his spiritual life, therefore ought he often to receive this spiritual
medicine, which is called our daily bread, and thereby to recover
that health and strength he had lost before. . . . The oftener he
cometh, the better it is, and the more is he nourished to everlasting
life. And the better a man is, the more desirous is he to be joined
to God corporally by this Sacrament. . . . The body of our Saviour
Christ, which is every day both offered to God the Father for the
sins and infirmities of the people, and also is prepared and offered
to all them that will with a pure heart receive it." [1]

"Let every man or woman, when he seeth this Sacrament in
the priest's hands, direct the eye of his faith and his intent to
honour only that substance of Christ, God and Man, which he seeth
not with his bodily eyes, but believeth it most certainly to be there
present, and let him not fix his thought upon the visible whiteness
or roundness of the bread, which be sensible creatures reserved
there for the use of this mystery, and may in no wise be adored
and worshipped with godly honour, but let him intend to honour
the body and blood of Christ, and yet not those as only creatures,
but as they be united to the Godhead and made one Person in
divinity, for only God is to be honoured with godly honour, which
we do when we honour Christ, God and Man, present in the blessed
Sacrament." [2]

"We believe to be saved only by the merits of our Saviour
Christ, and that He bearing our sins in His body upon the cross,
and being the innocent Lamb of God without all sin Himself, shed
His most innocent blood for us sinners, and by the voluntary sacrifice of His own body and blood made satisfaction for all the sins
of the whole world, and reconciled the wicked world to the favour
of God again. This bloody sacrifice made Christ our Saviour upon
the altar of His cross but once, and never but once, and it is the
propitiatory sacrifice and a sufficient price and ransom for the sins
of all people from the beginning of the world to the last end. . . .
Christ our Saviour willeth that the sacrifice of this redemption
should never cease, but be always to all men present in grace, and
always be kept in perpetual memory. For which cause He hath
given and committed unto His Church the most clean and pure
sacrifice of His body and blood under the forms of bread and wine,
and hath commanded it to be offered to God, and received of us in

---

[1] Fo. xlix a, lxi b, lxii a,   [2] Fo. lxv b, lxvi a,

the remembrance of His passion till His last coming. Which thing the Church most faithfully and obediently observeth and useth, not by presumption taking upon itself to offer that sacrifice of our Saviour which is far above the dignity of man, but by commission and warrant of His most holy word authorised to offer Christ, God's Son to God the Father, that is to say, to represent to the Father the body and blood of Christ, which by His omnipotent word He hath there made present, and thereby to renew His passion, not by suffering of death again, but after an unbloody manner, not for this end that we should thereby deserve remission of sins, and deliverance from the power of the devil, which is the proper effect of Christ's passion, but that we should by our faith, devotion, and this representation of His passion obtain the remission and grace already deserved by His passion, to be now applied unto our profit and salvation, not that the passion of Christ is imperfect, or needeth any work of ours to be added to supply the imperfection of it, but to comfort and relieve our imperfection, that some drop of grace may be drawn and brought unto us out of the fountain of all grace, and wellspring of His passion, not that we can apply the merits of Christ's death as we list, and to whom we list, but that we by this representing of His passion, most humbly make petition and prayer to Almighty God to apply unto us that remission and grace which was purchased and deserved by Christ's passion before, after the measure of His goodness, to all those whose faith and devotion be known unto Him. So that the host or the thing that is offered both in the sacrifice of Christ upon the cross and in the sacrifice of the Church upon the altar is all one in substance, being the natural [1] body of Christ our High Priest, and the price or ransom of our redemption; but the manner and the effects of these two offerings be diverse; the one is by shedding of Christ's blood extending to the death of Christ, the Offerer, for the redemption of all mankind; the other is without shedding of His blood, only representing His death, whereby the faithful and devout people are made partakers of the merits of Christ's passion and divinity. . . . As Christ upon the cross, being the Head of all us His mystical body, the Church, offering there Himself, did also offer all us that be of the Church to God the Father for the pacifying of His wrath and indignation against our sin, so we, being His mystical body, do use to offer to God the Father Christ our Head, and by His merits do beg pardon for our offences, knowing that God, who spared not His only begotten Son but gave Him to us for our redemption, will now deny

[1] See p. 173, note 1, *supra*.

us nothing for His sake that we have need upon, who is now also at the right hand of God, and maketh intercession for us. So that Christ in heaven and all we, His mystical body in earth, do both but one thing. For Christ, being a Priest for evermore, after His passion and resurrection entered into heaven, and there appeareth now to the countenance of God for us, offering Himself for us, to pacify the anger of God with us, and representing His passion and all that He suffered for us, that we might be reconciled to God by Him. Even so the Church, our Mother, being careful for all us her children that have offended our Father in heaven, useth continually by her public minister to pray and to offer unto God the body and blood of her Husband Christ, representing and renewing His passion and death before God, that we thereby might be renewed in grace, and receive life, perfection, and salvation. . . . Whereas sacrifice is the greatest and chiefest kind of adoration that can be, pertaining to godly honour called Latria, therefore we do make sacrifice to no creature, neither to saint nor angel, but only to the Holy Trinity, which is the only and true God." [1]

" The special and substantial part of the Mass consisteth in these three points, in consecrating the bread and wine into the body and blood of Christ, in offering of the same body and blood of Christ to God the Father, and in receiving of the same by the devout and faithful people." [2]

" Thus doth the Church offer Christ her Head to God the Father as a worthy sacrifice of praise and thanks for her redemption, for the hope of health and salvation, and for all His other benefits ; and also it offereth Him as a sacrifice propitiatory by the virtue of His passion, for all her sins and offences, that we in this world might live in peace with God, and afterward be delivered from eternal damnation, and with His elect be rewarded in the kingdom of heaven." [3]

IV.

The opinions which those in authority in the reign of Mary desired to crush may be sufficiently illustrated from statements of Cranmer, Ridley, and Latimer, and by a few brief extracts from sayings of others who suffered.

1. The changes of belief on the part of Cranmer so far as the end of the reign of Edward VI. have already been shown. [4]

[1] Fo. lxviii b-lxxiii a.   [2] Fo. lxxv a.
[3] Fo. lxxviii a.   [4] See pp. 125-29, supra.

It does not appear that there was any material alteration in his opinions during the reign of Mary. About August, 1553, a rumour was widely prevalent that he had authorised the restoration of the Latin Mass in Canterbury Cathedral. This rumour stung him to write a *Declaration* in which he sharply contrasts the Latin Mass with the recently issued English Prayer Book.

" As the devil, Christ's ancient adversary, is a liar and the father of lying, even so he hath ever stirred up his servants and members to persecute Christ and His true word and religion, which lying he feareth not to do most earnestly at this present. For whereas a prince of famous memory, King Henry VIII., seeing the great abuses of the Latin Mass, reformed some things therein in time, and after our late sovereign lord Edward VI. took the same wholly away for the manifold errors and abuses thereof, and restored in the place thereof Christ's Holy Supper according to Christ's institution and as the Apostles in the primitive Church used the same in the beginning, now goeth the devil about by lying to overthrow the Lord's Holy Supper again, and to restore his Latin satisfactory Mass, a thing of his own invention and device. And to bring the same more easily to pass, some of his inventors have abused the name of me, Thomas, Archbishop of Canterbury, bruiting abroad that I have set up the Mass again in Canterbury, and that I offered myself to say Mass at the burial of our late sovereign prince King Edward VI., and also that I offered myself to say Mass before the queen's highness at Paul's church in London, and I wot not where. . . . This is to signify to the world that it was not I that did set up the Mass at Canterbury, but it was a false, flattering, and lying monk, with a dozen of his blind adherents, which caused the Mass to be set up there, and that without mine advice or counsel. The Lord reward him in that day. And as for offering myself to say Mass before the queen's highness at Paul's, or in any other place, I never did it, as her grace very well knoweth. But if her grace will give me leave, I will and by the might of God shall be ready at all times to prove against all that would say the contrary that all that is said in the Holy Communion set forth by the most innocent and godly prince, King Edward VI., in his Court of Parliament is conformable to that order that our Saviour Christ did both observe and command to be observed, which also His Apostles and primitive Church used many years, whereas the Mass in many things not only hath no foundation of Christ's Apostles nor the primitive Church, but also is manifestly contrary to the same, and containeth in it many horrible abuses.

. . . Where they boast of the faith of the Church in the olden time these fifteen hundred years, we will join with them in this point that that doctrine and usage is to be followed which was in the Church fifteen hundred years past. And we shall prove that the order of the Church set out in this realm by our said sovereign lord King Edward VI. by Act of Parliament is the same that was used fifteen hundred years past. And so shall they never be able to prove theirs." [1]

Cranmer intended to place this *Declaration* on the doors of St. Paul's Cathedral and of other London churches; but before he had done so, a copy which Scory, the deprived Bishop of Chichester, obtained from him was multiplied, and the *Declaration* circulated. As a result, he was summoned before the council and was committed to the Tower. Of the different charges brought against him, he received the queen's pardon for the treason of which he was accused for his share in the attempt to place Lady Jane Grey on the throne, but the charge of heresy was persevered in. In March, 1554, he was removed from the Tower to Windsor, and thence to Oxford. In April, 1554, the disputation at Oxford between the representatives of the Universities of Oxford and Cambridge and Cranmer, Ridley, and Latimer, already alluded to,[2] took place. The three propositions set out as the basis of discussion have previously been quoted.[3] In brief, they asserted the presence of the natural body of Christ in the Sacrament, the absence of any other substance than that of Christ, and that the Mass is a propitiatory sacrifice. The details of the disputation, with the sharpness on the one side of accusers acting like cross-examining counsel and the devices on the other side of men fighting for their lives, are unpleasant and unprofitable reading; and the fairest way of showing Cranmer's position at this point in his history is to quote from a paper which he put in on the first day of the disputation as his statement of his case.

" 1. Our Lord and Saviour Jesus Christ at the holy passover, being about to die for our sakes, that He might redeem us from eternal

---

[1] *Writings of Cranmer relative to the Lord's Supper* (Parker Society), pp. 428, 429 ; Strype, *Memorials of Cranmer*, i. 437, 438 (1840 edition). Foxe, *op. cit.* vi. 539, 540. Different copies of this Declaration differ verbally, the differences probably being due to many hurried copies of it having been made when Bishop Scory obtained possession of it.

[2] See pp. 162, 163, *supra*.   [3] *Ibid.*

death, forgive us all our sins, and blot out the handwriting which
was against us, instituted an abiding memorial of His passion to be
celebrated among Christians in bread and wine, to prevent us from
ever ungratefully forgetting His death. . . . Whoever for the sake
of a tradition of men deny the cup of the blood to laymen are the
open enemies of Christ, forbidding that which Christ commanded to
be done. . . . The sacramental and mystic bread, being broken and
distributed after the institution of Christ, and the mystic wine, being in the same way drunk and received, are not only Sacraments
of the flesh of Christ which was wounded for us and of His shed
blood, but are most certain Sacraments to us and as it were seals of
the promises and gifts of God, that is, of our communion with Christ
and all His members, of the heavenly nurture by which we are
nourished unto eternal life and the thirst of our boiling conscience
is quenched, of the ineffable joy by which the hearts of the faithful
are filled and are strengthened for all the duties of godliness. . . .
Real bread and real wine remain in the Eucharist until they are
consumed by the faithful, that, as signs annexed to the promises of
God, they may assure us of the gifts of God. And Christ remains
in those who eat His flesh and drink His blood, and they remain in
Him. . . . Christ remains in those who worthily receive the outward Sacrament, and does not depart at once when the Sacrament
has been consumed, but remains continually, feeding and nourishing us so long as we remain bodies and members of that Head. I
recognise no natural body of Christ that is only spiritual and the
subject of mind and not of sense and is not divided into any limbs
or parts ; but I recognise and worship only that body which was
born of the Virgin, which suffered for us, which is visible and palp-
able, which has all the form and shape and parts of the organic body
of man.

"2. Christ spoke not these words of any uncertain substance, but
of the certain substance of bread, . . . and likewise of the wine.
. . . Ancient writers describe Christ's way of speech as figurative,
tropical, anagogical, allegorical, which they interpret that, although
the substance of bread and wine remains and is received by the faithful, yet Christ changed the name and called the bread by the name
of flesh and the wine by the name of blood not in reality of fact but
in the significance of mystery, that we should consider not what
they are but what they signify, and should understand the Sacraments not carnally but spiritually, and that we should not attend to
the visible nature of the Sacraments, and should not look down to
the bread and cup, and should not think to see with our eyes any-

thing but bread and wine, but should lift up our minds and behold
the body of Christ with faith and touch it with the mind and drink
it in with the inner man; that, being like eagles in this life, we
should fly up with our hearts to heaven itself, where at the right hand
of the Father sits that Lamb who takes away the sins of the world,
by whose love we are healed, by whose passion we are filled at this
Table, whose blood we drink from His divine side and thereby live
for ever, and being made the guests of Christ we have Him dwelling in us by the grace and power of His real nature and by the
efficacy of His whole passion; and we are no less sure that we are
fed spiritually unto eternal life by the crucified flesh and the shed
blood of Christ, the necessary food of souls, than that our bodies are
fed with food and drink in this life. And the mystic bread and the
mystic wine, administered and received according to the institution
of Christ at the Table of Christ, are the remembrance, the pledge,
the token, the Sacrament, the sign to us of this thing. This is the
reason why Christ did not say, ' This is My body ; eat,' but after
commanding to eat added, ' This is My body, which shall be given
for you '. For this is just as if He should have said, ' In eating
this bread, regard it not as common but as mystic ; do not look at
that which is set before the eyes of your body, but see what feeds
you within. Behold My body which was crucified for you ; with
your minds feed eagerly on it ; be ye filled with My death. This
is the true food, this is the inebriating drink, whereby being really
filled and inebriated ye may live for ever. Those things which are
set before your eyes, the bread and the wine, are only tokens of Me ;
but I Myself am the eternal food. Therefore, when ye see the
Sacraments at My Table, look not so much at them as at that which
I promise you through them, Myself, the food of eternal life.'

" 3. The only offering of Christ, whereby He offered Himself unto
death to God the Father once for all on the altar of the cross for
our redemption, was of so great efficacy that there is no need of any
other sacrifice for the redemption of the whole world ; but He took
away all the sacrifices of the ancient law, giving in actual fact what
they figured and promised. Whoever, therefore, has placed the
hope of his salvation in any other sacrifice, falls from the grace of
Christ and despises the holy blood of Christ. . . . Whoever seeketh
any other propitiatory sacrifice for sins makes the sacrifice of Christ
to be without validity or efficacy. For, if this is sufficient for the
remission of sins, there is no need of any other ; for the need of
another implies the weakness and insufficiency of this. God Almighty grant that we may rightly (vere) lean on the one sacrifice of

Christ, and again return to Him our sacrifices,—thanksgiving, praise, the confession of His name, true contrition and repentance, kindness to neighbours, and all other duties of godliness. For by such sacrifices we shall show ourselves neither thankless towards God nor unworthy of the sacrifice of Christ." [1]

There is much in this statement which theologians of very differing opinions may agree to admire; if it is remembered that it was the nearest approach to the theology of the dominant party which Cranmer could conscientiously make when his life was at stake, there will probably be agreement also that it is not the outcome of any different beliefs than the form of receptionism or virtualism expressed in his treatises of 1550 and 1551.

Under the pressure of fear Cranmer yielded, and signed no fewer than six recantations. In the first three of these, all executed early in 1556, there was simply a general submission to the Catholic Church, and the Pope, and the king and queen. In the fourth, executed on 16th February, 1556, there was an expression of belief " as concerning the Sacraments of the Church " " in all points as the said Catholic Church doth and hath believed from the beginning of Christian religion ". The fifth was much longer, and contained the following sentences about the Eucharist :—

" I anathematise the whole heresy of Luther and Zwingli. . . . Concerning the Sacraments, I believe and worship in the Sacrament of the Eucharist the real body and blood of Christ most really contained under the species of bread and wine without any trope or figure, the bread and the wine being converted and transubstantiated into the body and blood of the Redeemer by the power of God."

The sixth recantation was longer even than the fifth. It contained the following passage :—

" I am greatly tortured in mind because I attacked the Sacrament of the Eucharist with so many blasphemies and insults, denying that the body and blood of Christ are really and actually contained under the species of bread and wine ; and I published books in which I strove with all my might against the truth ; and in this I was not

---

[1] The above is translated from the Latin document handed in by Cranmer as given in the official report of the disputation in the British Museum, printed in *Writings of Cranmer relative to the Lord's Supper* (Parker Society), pp. 396, 397. There is an English version in the same book, and in Foxe, *op. cit.* vi, 446-48.

only worse than Saul and the robber, but I was the most wicked of all whom the earth ever bore. O Lord, I have sinned against heaven and against Thee ; against heaven, which through me is without so many heavenly inhabitants, and because I most shamefully denied this heavenly gift presented to us ; I have sinned also against earth, which so long has miserably lacked this Sacrament, and against the men whom I have drawn away from this supersubstantial food, being the murderer of as many men as have perished from want of it. I have defrauded the souls of the departed of this continual and most splendid sacrifice."

The paper written by Cranmer a little before his death to be publicly read by him, which is sometimes called the seventh recantation, ended as follows :—

"And now I come to the great thing that so much troubleth my conscience, more than any other thing that ever I did ; and that is setting abroad untrue books and writings contrary to the truth of God's word, which now I renounce and condemn, and refuse them utterly as erroneous, and for none of mine. But you must know also what books they were, that you may beware of them, or else my conscience is not discharged ; for they be the books which I wrote against the Sacrament of the altar since the death of King Henry VIII. But, whatsoever I wrote then, now is time and place to say truth ; wherefore renouncing all those books, and whatsoever in them is contained, I say and believe that our Saviour Christ Jesu is really and substantially contained in the Blessed Sacrament of the altar under the forms of bread and wine." [1]

These recantations did not save Cranmer from condemnation as a heretic and from sentence of death by burning. At the time of his death he read to the crowd the paper of which the last quotation is the concluding paragraph, but for this paragraph he substituted the following :—

"And now I come to the great thing which so much troubleth my conscience, more than anything that ever I did or said in my whole life ; and that is the setting abroad of a writing contrary to the truth, which now here I renounce and refuse as things written with my hand contrary to the truth which I thought in my heart, and written for fear of death, and to save my life if it might be ; and that is all such bills and papers which I have written or signed with my hand since my degradation, wherein I have written many

[1] *Miscellaneous Writings of Cranmer* (Parker Society), pp. 563-66.

things untrue. And forasmuch as my hand offended, writing contrary to my heart, my hand shall first be punished therefore ; for, may I come to the fire, it shall be first burned. And as for the Pope, I refuse him as Christ's enemy and anti-Christ, with all his false doctrine. And as for the Sacrament, I believe as I have taught in my book against the Bishop of Winchester, the which my book teacheth so true a doctrine of the Sacrament that it shall stand at the Last Day before the Judgment of God, where the papistical doctrine contrary thereto shall be ashamed to show her face." [1]

Apart from the recantations, then, which were extorted from him through the fear of death, the belief of Cranmer concerning the Eucharist remained the same from the publication of his book in the latter part of the reign of Edward VI. to his death in 1556.

2. It has been mentioned that Cranmer's abandonment of belief in the doctrine that the consecrated Sacrament is the body and blood of Christ was due in the first instance to Nicolas Ridley.[2] Ridley was born in Northumberland early in the sixteenth century ; he became chaplain to Archbishop Cranmer in 1534, Master of Pembroke College, Cambridge, and chaplain to King Henry VIII. in 1540, Bishop of Rochester in 1547, and Bishop of London in 1550. On the accession of Queen Mary in 1553 he was arrested and imprisoned on a charge of treason for his support of Lady Jane Grey. Though, like others, he was pardoned for this offence, he remained in prison and was eventually condemned to death for heresy ; and he was burnt at Oxford on 16th October, 1555. It has been supposed that Ridley first read the treatise of Ratramn on the Eucharist [3] about 1545 ; and he himself said at Oxford in 1555 that it was this which "first " "pulled me by the ear, and that first brought me from the common error of the Romish Church".[4] In the debate in the House of Lords in December, 1548, he appears to have maintained not only that the bread and wine wholly remain after consecration but also that the presence of the body and blood of Christ is a presence by way of grace and power.[5] In a disputation held at Cambridge in June, 1549, he seems to have maintained much the same position. Among his statements then made are the following :—

[1] Foxe, *Acts and Monuments*, viii. 88 (edition 1843-49).
[2] See p. 125, *supra*.   [3] See vol. i. pp. 226-33, *supra*.
[4] *Works of Ridley* (Parker Society), p. 206.
[5] See pp. 134, 135, *supra*.

"By the word of God the thing hath a being that it had not before; and we do consecrate the body that we may receive the grace and power of the body of Christ in heaven by this sacramental body."

"I grant that there is a mutation of the common bread and wine spiritually into the Lord's bread and wine by the sanctifying of them in the Lord's word.   But I deny that there is any mutation of the substances; for there is no other change there indeed than there is in us, who, when we do receive the Sacrament worthily, then are we changed into Christ's body, bones, and blood, not in nature but spiritually and by grace.   Much like as Isaiah saw the burning coal, even so we see not there the very simple bread as it was before the consecration ; for a union cannot be but of two very things.   Wherefore, if we be joined to Christ, receiving the Sacrament, then there is no annihilation of bread."

"Say what you list, it is but a figurative speech, like to this, 'If you will receive and understand, he is Elias,' for a property; for indeed he was not Elias, but John the Baptist.   And so in this place Christ calleth it His body when it was very bread.   But better than the common bread because it was sanctified by the word of Christ."

"He was betrayed and crucified in His natural body substantially and really in very deed ; but in the Sacrament He is not so, but spiritually and figuratively only."

"There is no change either of the substances or of the accidents ; but in very deed there do come unto the bread other accidents, insomuch that whereas the bread and wine were not sanctified before nor holy, yet afterwards they be sanctified, and so do receive then another sort or kind of virtue which they had not before."

"Grace is there communicated to us by the benefit of Christ's body sitting in heaven. . . . We be not consubstantial with Christ ; God forbid that.   But we are joined to His mystical body through His Holy Spirit ; and the communion of His flesh is communicated to us spiritually, through the benefit of His flesh in heaven."

"Ye dream of a real presence of Christ's body in the Sacrament by the force of the words spoken, which the Holy Scripture doth impugn."

"Christ dwelleth in us by faith, and by faith we receive Christ, both God and Man, both in spirit and flesh ; that is, this sacramental eating is the mean whereby we attain to the spiritual eating ; and indeed for the strengthening of us to the eating of this spiritual food was this Sacrament ordained.   And these words,

'This is My body,' are meant thus, By grace it is My true body, but not My fleshly body, as some of you suppose."

"We are joined to Christ; that is, we are made partakers of His flesh and of immortality. And so in like case is there a union between man and woman; yet there is no transubstantiation of either or both."

"The flesh indeed is fed with the body and blood of the Lord when our bodies by mortification are made like to His body; and our body is nourished when the virtue and power of the body of Christ doth feed us. The same Tertullian is not afraid to call it flesh and blood, but he meaneth a figure of the same." [1]

In his *Determination* at the close of the disputations Ridley said :—

"This Transubstantiation is clean against the words of the Scripture and consent of the ancient Catholic fathers. . . . They which say that Christ is carnally present in the Eucharist do take from him the verity of man's nature. . . . They that defend Transubstantiation ascribe that to the human nature which only belongeth to the divine nature. . . . These Scriptures [2] do persuade me to believe that there is no other oblation of Christ, albeit I am not ignorant there are many sacrifices, but that which was once made upon the cross." [3]

In connection with his Visitation of the diocese of London in 1550, Ridley drew up a paper of reasons why "instead of the multitude of their altars, one decent Table" should be "set up" "in every church". Of these reasons the first was :—

"The form of a table shall more move the simple from the superstitious opinions of the popish Mass unto the right use of the Lord's Supper. For the use of an altar is to make sacrifice upon it ; the use of a table is to serve for men to eat upon. Now, when we come unto the Lord's board, what do we come for? To sacrifice Christ again, and to crucify Him again, or to feed upon Him that was once only crucified and offered up for us? If we come to feed upon Him, spiritually to eat His body, and spiritually to drink His blood, which is the true sense of the Lord's Supper, then no man can deny but the form of a table is more meet for the Lord's board than the form of an altar." [4]

---

[1] Foxe, *op. cit.* vi. 312-15, 318, 325, 329, 332.
[2] Heb. ix. 11-28, x. 14.
[3] *Works of Ridley* (Parker Society), pp. 171, 175, 176, 178.
[4] *Op. cit.* p. 322.

The three propositions set forth by Convocation for the disputations at Oxford in April, 1554, asserted the presence of the natural body and blood of our Lord in the Sacrament under the forms of bread and wine ; the absence of any other substance than that of the body and blood of Christ ; and that the Mass is a propitiatory sacrifice.[1] From the very lengthy discussions around Ridley's denial of these propositions the following statements made by him are selected :—

" Of Christ's real presence there may be a double understanding. If you take the real presence of Christ according to the real and corporal substance which He took of the Virgin, that presence being in heaven cannot be on the earth also.   But if you mean a real presence *secundum rem aliquam quæ ad corpus Christi pertinet*, that is, according to something that appertaineth to Christ's body, certes the ascension and abiding in heaven are no let at all to that presence. Wherefore Christ's body after that sort is here present to us in the Lord's Supper, by grace, I say, as Epiphanius speaketh it."

" I grant that Christ did both, that is, both took up His flesh with Him ascending up, and also did leave the same behind Him with us, but after a diverse manner and respect.   For He took His flesh with Him after the true and corporal substance of His body and flesh ; again, He left the same in mystery to the faithful in the Supper, to be received after a spiritual communication, and by grace. Neither is the same received in the Supper only, but also at other times, by hearing the Gospel, and by faith."

" I also worship Christ in the Sacrament, but not because He is included in the Sacrament, like as I worship Christ also in the Scriptures, not because He is really included in them.   Notwithstanding I say that the body of Christ is present in the Sacrament, but yet sacramentally and spiritually, according to His grace, giving life, and in that respect really, that is, according to His benediction, giving life.   Furthermore, I acknowledge gladly the true body of Christ to be in the Lord's Supper in such sort as the Church of Christ, which is the spouse of Christ and is taught of the Holy Ghost and guided by God's word, doth acknowledge the same. But the true Church of Christ doth acknowledge a presence of Christ's body in the Lord's Supper to be communicated to the godly by grace and spiritually, as I have often showed, and by a sacramental signification, but not by the corporal presence of the body of His flesh."

[1] See pp. 162, 163, *supra*.

"There is a deceit in the word *adoramus*. We worship the symbols when reverently we handle them. We worship Christ wheresoever we perceive His benefits; but we understand His benefits to be greatest in the Sacrament. . . . We adore and worship Christ in the Eucharist. And if you mean the external Sacrament, I say, that also is to be worshipped as a Sacrament."

"It is His true blood which is in the chalice, I grant, and the same which sprang from the side of Christ. But how? It is blood indeed, but not after the same manner after which manner it sprang from His side. For here is the blood, but by way of a Sacrament. Again, I say, like as the bread of the Sacrament and of thanksgiving is called the body of Christ given for us, so the cup of the Lord is called the blood which sprang from the side of Christ; but that sacramental bread is called the body because it is the Sacrament of His body. Even so likewise the cup is called the blood also which flowed out of Christ's side because it is the Sacrament of that blood which flowed out of His side, instituted of the Lord Himself for our singular commodity, namely, for our spiritual nourishment, like as Baptism is ordained in water to our spiritual regeneration."

"The blood of Christ is in the chalice indeed, but not in the real presence, but by grace, and in a Sacrament."

"That heavenly Lamb is, as I confess, on the Table, but by a spiritual presence by grace, and not after any corporal substance of His flesh taken of the Virgin Mary."

"We worship, I confess, the same true Lord and Saviour of the world, which the wise men worshipped in the manger; howbeit we do it in a mystery, and in the Sacrament of the Lord's Supper, and that in spiritual liberty, as saith St. Augustine,[1] not in carnal servitude, that is, we do not worship servilely the signs for the things, for that should be, as he also saith, a part of a servile infirmity. But we behold with the eyes of faith Him present after grace, and spiritually set upon the Table; and we worship Him which sitteth above, and is worshipped of the angels. . . . This assistance and presence of Christ, as in Baptism it is wholly spiritual, and by grace, and not by any corporal substance of the flesh, even so it is here in the Lord's Supper, being rightly and according to the word of God duly ministered."[2]

[1] *De Doct. Christ.* iii. 10.

[2] *Works of Ridley* (Parker Society), pp. 213, 222, 235, 236, 237, 238, 249, 251.

Ridley's treatise *A Brief Declaration of the Lord's Supper* was written while he was in prison about the same time as that of the Disputation in 1554. Its devotional temper, earnest tone, and evident desire for truth give this treatise a high place among the writings of the Reformation period ; but the recognition of and emphasis on a common ground does not prevent Ridley from writing with great hostility towards the doctrines held by those who for the time were in authority in the Church of England.

" Whosoever receiveth this holy Sacrament thus ordained in remembrance of Christ, he receiveth therewith either death or life. In this, I trust, we do all agree. . . . The partaking of Christ's body and of His blood unto the faithful and godly is the partaking or fellowship of life and immortality. . . . He that eateth and drinketh unworthily thereof [that is, of the bread and the cup] eateth and drinketh his own damnation, because he esteemeth not the Lord's body ; that is, he reverenceth not the Lord's body with the honour that is due unto Him. And that which was said, that with the receipt of the holy Sacrament of the blessed body and blood of Christ is received of every one, good or bad, either life or death, it is not meant that they which are dead before God may hereby receive life, or the living before God can hereby receive death. For as none is meet to receive natural food, whereby the natural life is nourished, except he be born and live before, so no man can feed (by the receipt of the holy Sacrament) of the food of eternal life except he be regenerated and born of God before ; and on the other side no man here receiveth damnation which is not dead before. Thus hitherto, without all doubt, God is my witness, I say, so far as I know, there is no controversy among them that be learned among the Church in England concerning the matter of this Sacrament ; but all do agree, whether they be new or old, and to speak plain, and as some of them do odiously call each other, whether they be Protestants, Pharisees, Papists, or Gospellers. And as all do agree hitherto in the aforesaid doctrine, so all do detest, abhor, and condemn the wicked heresy of the Messalians, which otherwise be called Euchites, which said that the holy Sacrament can neither do good nor harm ; and do also condemn those wicked Anabaptists which put no difference between the Lord's Table and the Lord's meat and their own. . . . The controversy (no doubt) which at this day troubleth the Church (wherein any mean learned man, either old or new, doth stand in) is not whether the holy Sacrament of the body and blood of Christ is no better than a piece of common bread, or no; or whether the Lord's Table is no more to be regarded than the table of any earthly man; or whether it is but a bare sign or figure of Christ and nothing else, or no. For all do grant that St. Paul's words do require that the bread which we break is the partaking of the body of Christ; and all also do grant him that eateth of that bread or drinketh of that cup unworthily to be guilty of the Lord's death, and to eat and drink his own damnation, because he esteemeth not the Lord's body. . . . Thus then hitherto yet we all agree. But now let us see wherein the dissension doth stand. . . . In the matter of this Sacrament there be divers points wherein men counted to be learned cannot agree; as, Whether there be any Transubstantiation of the bread, or no; any corporal and carnal presence of Christ's substance, or no; whether adoration only due unto God is to be done unto the Sacrament, or no; and whether Christ's body be there offered in deed unto the heavenly Father by the priest, or no; or whether the evil man receiveth the natural body of Christ, or no. . . . All five aforesaid points do chiefly hang upon this one question, which is, What is the matter of the Sacrament? whether it is the natural substance of bread or the natural substance of Christ's own body. The truth of this question, truly tried out and agreed upon, no doubt will cease the controversy in all the rest. For if it be Christ's own natural body born of the Virgin, then . . . (seeing that all learned men in England, so far as I know, both new and old, grant there to be but one substance) . . . they must needs grant Transubstantiation, that is, a change of the substance of bread into the substance of Christ's body; then also they must grant the carnal and corporal presence of Christ's body; then must the Sacrament be adored with the honour due unto Christ Himself for the unity of the two natures in one Person; then, if the priest do offer the Sacrament, he doth offer indeed Christ Himself; and finally the murderer, the adulterer, or wicked man, receiving the Sacrament, must needs then receive also the natural substance of Christ's own blessed body, both flesh and blood. Now, on the other side, if, after the truth shall be truly tried out, it be found that the substance of bread is the material substance of the Sacrament; although, for the change of the use, office, and dignity of the bread, the bread indeed sacramentally is changed into the body of Christ, as the water in Baptism is sacramentally changed into the fountain of regeneration, and yet the material substance thereof remaineth all one, as was before; if, I say, the true solution of that former question, whereupon all these controversies do hang, be that the natural substance of bread is the material substance in the Sacrament of Christ's blessed body ; then must it follow of the former proposition (confessed of all that be named to be learned, so far as I do know in England) which is that there is but one material substance in the Sacrament of the body, and one only likewise in the Sacrament of the blood, that there is no such thing indeed and in truth as they call Transubstantiation, for the substance of bread remaineth still in the Sacrament of the body. Then also the natural substance of Christ's human nature, which He took of the Virgin Mary, is in heaven, where it reigneth now in glory, and not here enclosed under the form of bread. Then that godly honour, which is only due unto God the Creator, may not be done unto the creature without idolatry and sacrilege, is not to be done unto the holy Sacrament. Then also the wicked, I mean the impenitent, murderer, adulterer, or such-like, do not receive the natural substance of the blessed body and blood of Christ. Finally, then doth it follow that Christ's blessed body and blood, which was once only offered and shed upon the cross, being available for the sins of all the whole world, is offered up no more in the natural substance thereof, neither by the priest nor any other thing. But here, before we go further to search in this matter, and to wade, as it were, to search and try out as we may the truth hereof in the Scripture, it shall do well by the way to know whether they that thus make answer and solution unto the former principal question do take away simply and absolutely the presence of Christ's body and blood from the Sacrament ordained by Christ and duly ministered according to His holy ordinance and institution of the same. Undoubtedly they do deny that utterly, either so to say or so to mean. . . . What kind of presence do they grant, and what do they deny ? Briefly they deny the presence of Christ's body' in the natural substance of His human and assumed nature, and grant the presence of the same by grace ; that is, they affirm and say that the substance of the natural body and blood of Christ is only remaining in heaven, and so shall be unto the latter day, when He shall come again in glory accompanied with the angels of heaven, to judge both the quick and the dead. And the same natural substance of the very body and blood of Christ, because it is united in the divine nature in Christ, the second Person of the Trinity, therefore it hath not only life in itself but is also able to give and doth give life unto so many as be or shall be partakers thereof ; that is, to all that do believe on His name, which are not born of blood, as St. John saith,[1] or of the

[1] St. John i. 13.

will of the flesh, or of the will of man, but are born of God, though the self-same substance abide still in heaven, and they for the time of their pilgrimage dwell here upon earth ; by grace I say, that is, by the gift of this life mentioned in John [1] and the properties of the same meet for our pilgrimage here upon earth, the same body of Christ is here present with us. Even as, for example, we say the same sun, which in substance never removeth his place out of the heavens is yet present here by his beams, light, and natural influence where it shineth upon the earth. For God's word and His Sacraments be as it were the beams of Christ, which is *sol justitiae*, the Sun of righteousness." [2]

On this statement of the case, Ridley gives his judgment that the second of the two sets of alternative answers to the five questions is true, since on the main question which governs the five he determines—

"the natural substance of bread and wine is the true material substance of the holy Sacrament of the blessed body and blood of our Saviour Christ. . . . Christ did take bread and called it His body for that He would thereby institute a perpetual remembrance of His body, specially of that singular benefit of our redemption which He would then procure and purchase unto us by His body upon the cross. But bread, retaining still its own very natural substance, may be thus by grace and in a sacramental signification His body, whereas else the very bread which He took, brake, and gave them could not be in any wise His natural body, for that were confusion of substances. And therefore the very words of Christ, joined with the next sentence following, both enforce us to confess the very bread to remain still, and also open unto us how that bread may be and is thus by His divine power His body which was given for us." [3]

At Ridley's last examination before the commissioners on 30th September, 1555, he spoke as follows about the Eucharist :—

" In a sense the first article [4] is true, and in a sense it is false ; for if you take really for *vere*, for spiritually by grace and efficacy, then it is true that the natural body and blood of Christ is in the Sacrament *vere et realiter*, indeed and really ; but if you take these terms

[1] St. John vi. 33.
[2] *Works of Ridley* (Parker Society), pp. 8-13.
[3] *Op. cit.* pp. 15, 16.
[4] The first article referred to is that charging Ridley with maintaining that "the true and natural body of Christ after the consecration of the priest is not really present in the Sacrament of the altar ".

so grossly that you would conclude thereby a natural body having motion to be contained under the forms of bread and wine *vere et realiter*, then really is not the body and blood of Christ in the Sacrament no more than the Holy Ghost is in the element of water in our Baptism."

" Both you and I agree herein, that in the Sacrament is the very true and natural body and blood of Christ, even that which was born of the Virgin Mary, which ascended into heaven, which sitteth on the right hand of God the Father, which shall come from thence to judge the quick and the dead ; only we differ *in modo*, in the way and manner of being : we confess all one thing to be in the Sacrament, and dissent in the manner of being there. I, being fully by God's word thereunto persuaded, confess Christ's natural body to be in the Sacrament indeed by spirit and grace, because that whosoever receiveth worthily that bread and wine receiveth effectually Christ's body and drinketh His blood, that is, he is made effectually partaker of His passion; and you make a grosser kind of being, enclosing a natural, a lively, and a moving body under the shape or form of bread and wine. Now this difference considered, to the question thus I answer, that in the Sacrament of the altar is the natural body and blood of Christ *vere et realiter*, indeed and really, for spiritually by grace and efficacy ; for so every worthy receiver receiveth the very true body of Christ. But if you mean really and indeed so that thereby you would include a lively and a movable body under the forms of bread and wine, then in that sense is not Christ's body in the Sacrament really and indeed. . . . In the Sacrament is a certain change in that that bread, which was before common bread, is now made a lively presentation of Christ's body, and not only a figure but effectually representeth His body ; that even as the mortal body was nourished by that visible bread, so is the internal soul fed with the heavenly food of Christ's body, which the eyes of faith see, as the bodily eyes see only bread. Such a sacramental mutation I grant to be in the bread and wine, which truly is no small change, but such a change as no mortal man can make, but only the omnipotency of Christ's word. . . . The true substance and nature of bread and wine remaineth, with the which the body is in like sort nourished as the soul is by grace and Spirit with the body of Christ. Even so in Baptism the body is washed with the visible water, and the soul is cleansed from all filth by the invisible Holy Ghost, and yet the water ceaseth not to be water but keepeth the nature of water still ; in like sort in the Sacrament of the Lord's Supper the bread ceaseth not to be bread."

"Christ, as St. Paul writeth,[1] made one perfect sacrifice for the sins of the whole world, neither can any man reiterate that sacrifice of His, and yet is the Communion an acceptable sacrifice to God of praise and thanksgiving.   But to say that thereby sins are taken away (which wholly and perfectly was done by Christ's passion, of the which the Communion is only a memory) that is a great derogation of the merits of Christ's passion ; for the Sacrament was instituted that we, receiving it, and thereby recognising and remembering His passion, should be partakers of the merits of the same.   For otherwise doth this Sacrament take upon it the office of Christ's passion, whereby it might follow that Christ died in vain." [2]

In one of his farewell letters, written between his condemnation on 1st October, 1555, and his death on 16th October, Ridley wrote :—

"In the stead of the Lord's Table they give the people, with much solemn disguising, a thing which they call their Mass, but . . . I may call it a crafty juggling, whereby these false thieves and jugglers have bewitched the minds of the simple people, that they have brought them from the true worship of God into pernicious idolatry, and make them to believe that to be Christ our Lord and Saviour which indeed is neither God nor man, nor hath any life in itself, but in substance is the creature of bread and wine, and in use of the Lord's Table is the Sacrament of Christ's body and blood ; and for this holy use, for the which the Lord hath ordained them in His Table to represent unto us His blessed body torn upon the cross for us and His blood there shed, it pleased Him to call them His body and blood." [3]

In the course of a rhetorical address to the see of London, which forms part of the same letter, Ridley exclaims :—

"O thou now wicked and bloody see, why dost thou set up again many altars of idolatry which by the word of God were justly taken away?   O why hast thou overthrown the Lord's Table?   Why dost thou daily delude the people, masking in thy Masses in the stead of the Lord's holy Supper, which ought to be common as well . . . to the people as to the priest?   How darest thou deny to the people of Christ, contrary to His express commandment in the Gospel, His holy cup? . . . Thy god, which is the work of thy hands and whom thou sayest thou hast power to make, that thy deaf and dumb god,

[1] Heb. x. 12.   [2] *Works of Ridley* (Parker Society), pp. 273-75.
[3] *Op. cit.* p. 401.

I say, will not indeed nor cannot, although thou art not ashamed to call him thy maker, make thee to escape the avenging hand of the high and Almighty God." [1]

To ascertain Ridley's exact meaning in many passages of his writings is by no means an easy task. The ambiguity of the word "natural" in connection with the body of our Lord, and the possibility of interpreting it either as descriptive of our Lord's body being in a natural state or as denoting that His body in the Eucharist is the same body as that of His natural life on earth, is a constantly disturbing factor in the attempt to reach his thought. Possibly, he was not always consistent. But a comparison of his statements about the Eucharist with one another, and an examination of his teaching as a whole, lead to the conclusion that the doctrine which he rejected was not simply some carnal notion which the divines at Trent would have themselves repudiated, but the belief that the consecrated Sacrament is by the power of God made to be the risen and ascended and glorified body and blood of our Lord ; and that the doctrine which he held was not in principle different from the later teaching of Cranmer that the presence of the body of Christ in the Eucharist is a presence of power and of grace proceeding from the body not the presence of the body itself. From this position would naturally follow, as he himself saw, the rejection of Transubstantiation, of Eucharistic adoration, of belief in the reception of the body of Christ by those who receive the Sacrament unworthily, of the sacrificial character of the Eucharist as the oblation of the body and blood of Christ.

3. Hugh Latimer was born in Leicestershire in the fifteenth century ; he became Fellow of Clare Hall, Cambridge, in 1509 ; after attaining some fame as a preacher and being a royal chaplain, he was appointed Bishop of Worcester in 1535 ; he resigned his bishopric in 1539 in consequence of the passing of the Statute of the Six Articles, and lived in the country till 1540, when he was imprisoned in the Tower. On the accession of Edward VI. in 1547 he was released ; and during Edward's reign he preached frequently at Paul's Cross. When Mary came to the throne in 1553, he was summoned before the council, and was committed to the Tower for seditious behaviour. Eventually he was charged

[1] *Op. cit.* p. 409.
13 *

with heresy, moved to Oxford, tried there, and burnt at the same time as Ridley on 16th October, 1555.

In his sermon on the parable of the marriage feast preached in 1552 [1] Latimer explained the food at the feast to be the body and blood of Christ spiritually received.

"What manner of meat was prepared at this great feast? . . . What was the feast dish? Marry, it was the bridegroom Himself; for the Father, the feast-maker, prepared none other manner of meat for the guests but the body and blood of His own natural Son. And this is the chiefest dish at this banquet; which truly is a marvellous thing, that the Father offereth His Son to be eaten. Verily, I think that no man hath heard the like. And truly there was never such kind of feasting as this is, where the Father will have His Son to be eaten and His blood to be drunk. . . . The Almighty God, which prepared this feast for all the world, for all those that will come unto it, He offereth His only Son to be eaten, and His blood to be drunken. . . . Our Saviour, the Bridegroom, offereth Himself at His Last Supper which He had with His disciples His body to be eaten and His blood to be drunk. And to the intent that it should be done to our great comfort, and then again to take away all cruelty, irksomeness, and horribleness, He showeth unto us how we shall eat Him, in what manner and form, namely, spiritually, to our great comfort, so that whosoever eateth the mystical bread and drinketh the mystical wine worthily according to the ordinance of Christ, he receiveth surely the very body and blood of Christ spiritually, as it shall be most comfortable unto his soul. . . . To be short : whosoever believeth in Christ putteth his hope, trust, and confidence in Him, he eateth and drinketh Him ; for the spiritual eating is the right eating to everlasting life, not the corporal eating, as the Capernaites understood it. For that same corporal eating on which they set their minds hath no commodities at all ; it is a spiritual meat that feedeth our souls. . . . It was ordained for our help, to help our memory withal, to put us in mind of the great goodness of God in redeeming us from everlasting death by the blood of our Saviour Christ, yea, and to signify unto us that His body and blood is our meat and

---

[1] Earlier references to the Eucharist on the part of Latimer are his condemnation of the abuses in the sale of Masses in his sermon before Convocation in June, 1537 (*Sermons of Latimer*, Parker Society, pp. 55, 56), and his statement in a sermon before King Edward VI. in April, 1549, that the meeting of Christians for Holy Communion in connection with dead friends in the primitive Church was not " to remedy them that were dead " (*op. cit.* pp. 236, 237).

drink for our souls, to feed them to everlasting life. . . . To the intent that we might better keep it in memory, and to remedy this our slothfulness, our Saviour hath ordained this His Supper for us, whereby we should remember His great goodness, His bitter passion and death, and so strengthen our faith, so that He instituted this Supper for our sake, to make us to keep in fresh memory His inestimable benefits. . . . Our Saviour, knowing our weakness and forgetfulness, ordained this Supper to the augmentation of our faith, and to put us in remembrance of His benefits." [1]

In a report published in 1556 of conferences which took place between Latimer and Ridley when they were in prison, Latimer is represented as saying:—

" I have read over of late the New Testament three or four times deliberately; yet can I not find there neither the popish consecration, nor yet their Transubstantiation, nor their oblation, nor their adoration, which be the very sinews and marrow-bones of the Mass." [2]

At the disputation at Oxford in April, 1554, with the representatives of the Universities of Oxford and Cambridge, Latimer put in a written paper in which he gave his answer to the three propositions of the presence of the natural body of Christ in the Eucharist, the absence of the substance of bread and wine, and the propitiatory character of the Eucharistic sacrifice.[3] On the first proposition he said that " there is none other presence of Christ required than a spiritual presence"; that " the same presence may be called a real presence because to the faithful believer there is the real or spiritual body of Christ ". The second proposition he explicitly rejected as having " no stay nor ground of God's holy word," and as being " a thing invented and found out by man, and therefore to be reputed and had as false ". In rejecting the third proposition, he referred at some length to the perfection of the sacrifice of the cross; and spoke of the studies of the New Testament by Cranmer, Ridley, Bradford, and himself when prisoners in the Tower in these terms:—

" We could find in the testament of Christ's body and blood no other presence but a spiritual presence, nor that the Mass was any sacrifice for sins; but in that heavenly book it appeared that the

[1] *Sermons of Latimer* (Parker Society), pp. 457-60.
[2] *Works of Ridley* (Parker Society), p. 112.
[3] See pp. 162, 163, *supra*.

sacrifice which Christ Jesus our Redeemer did upon the cross was
perfect, holy, and good, that God the heavenly Father did require
none other, nor that never to be done again, but was pacified with
that only omnisufficient and most painful sacrifice of that sweet slain
Lamb Christ our Lord for our sins." [1]

In his examination before the commissioners in September,
1555, Latimer said :—

" I do not deny . . . that in the Sacrament by spirit and grace
is the very body and blood of Christ, because that every man by receiving bodily that bread and wine spiritually receiveth the body
and blood of Christ, and is made partaker thereby of the merits of
Christ's passion.   But I deny that the body and blood is in such sort
in the Sacrament as you would have it."

After this statement Latimer replied to the inquiry of White
the Bishop of Lincoln whether he acknowledged his rejection of
the presence of the natural body of Christ in the Eucharist—

" Yes, if you mean of that gross and carnal being which you do
take."

On the subject of Transubstantiation, he said :—

" There is . . . a change in the bread and wine, and such a
change as no power but the omnipotency of God can make, in that
that which before was bread should now have the dignity to exhibit
Christ's body ; and yet the bread is still bread, and the wine still
wine.   For the change is not in the nature but in the dignity,
because now that which was common bread hath the dignity to exhibit Christ's body ; for, whereas it was common bread, it is now no
more common bread, neither ought it to be so taken, but as holy
bread sanctified by God's word."

On the subject of the sacrifice, he said :—

" Christ made one perfect sacrifice for all the whole world, neither
can any man offer Him again, neither can the priest offer up Christ
again for the sins of man which He took away by offering Himself
once for all . . . upon the cross, neither is there any propitiation
for our sins saving His cross only." [2]

It is not much easier to estimate Latimer's belief about the
Eucharist than it is to ascertain that of Ridley.   Some of his

---

[1] *Remains of Latimer* (Parker Society), pp. 252, 253, 259.
[2] *Op. cit.* pp. 285-87.

sayings could be interpreted to be a rejection only of a carnal presence; some of them could be understood to be laying stress, like many of the mediæval writers, on the spiritual character of the body of Christ and on the spiritual manner of His presence in the Eucharist. But, when all his language is weighed, and when it is considered in relation to the circumstances in which it was uttered, the probability appears to be that he, like Ridley, had reached the acceptance of the same doctrinal position as that of Cranmer in his later years.

4. It may be convenient to quote a few instances of statements about the Eucharist made by less well-known persons who were put to death during the reign of Mary. Richard Woodman, who was burnt with nine others in June, 1557, expressed his belief about the Eucharist as follows :—

"I do believe that when I come to receive the Sacrament of the body and blood of Jesus Christ, if it be truly ministered according to Christ's institution, I coming in faith, as I trust in God I will, whensoever I come to receive it, I believing that Christ was born for me, and that He suffered death for the remission of my sins, and that I shall be saved by His death and bloodshedding, and so receive the Sacrament of bread and wine in that remembrance, that then I do receive whole Christ, God and Man, mystically by faith." [1]

Thomas Spurdance, who was burnt in November, 1557, spoke thus :—

"It is no sacrifice; for St. Paul [2] saith that Christ made one sacrifice once for all ; and I do believe in none other sacrifice but only in that one sacrifice that our Lord Jesus Christ made once for all. . . . I believe that, if I come rightly and worthily, as God hath commanded me, to the Holy Supper of the Lord, I receive Him by faith by believing in Him. But the bread, being received, is not God ; nor the bread that is yonder in the pyx is not God. . . . You do very evil to cause the people to kneel down and worship the bread ; for God did never bid you hold it above your heads, neither had the Apostles such use." [3]

Elizabeth Young was examined nine times in 1558, and was severely rebuked for her statements :—

"I believe that in the holy Sacrament of Christ's body and blood, which He did institute and ordain, and left among His dis-

---

[1] Foxe, *Acts and Monuments*, viii. 372 ; *cf.* p. 361 (edition 1843-49).
[2] Heb. x. 12.   [3] Foxe, *op. cit.* viii. 431.

ciples that night before He was betrayed, when I do receive the Sacrament in faith and spirit, I do receive Christ. . . . These words, 'really' and 'corporally,' I understand not ; as for 'substantially,' I take it ye mean I should believe that I should receive His human body, which is upon the right hand of God, and can occupy no more places at once ; and that believe not I."

Eventually she was released after stating :—

"When I receive, I believe that through faith I do receive Christ. . . . I believe that He is there, and by faith I do receive Him. . . . I believe Christ not to be absent from His own Sacrament." [1]

[1] Foxe, *op. cit.* viii. 540, 541, 547.

CHAPTER XII.

THE PERIOD OF THE REFORMATION.

PART IV.

QUEEN MARY died on 15th November, 1558, and was succeeded by her half-sister Elizabeth, the daughter of King Henry VIII. and Anne Boleyn.

I.

One of the first proceedings of the reign in matters of religion was in connection with the Book of Common Prayer. A paper drawn up at this time contains a suggestion that "such learned men as be meet to show their minds herein" should compile a book, which, after being submitted to and approved by the queen, might be brought before Parliament.[1] Nothing is known as to any action of this kind ; but it is possible that a letter written by Edmund Guest, afterwards Bishop of Rochester and later Bishop of Salisbury, to William Cecil, afterwards Lord Burghley, had reference to a draft book so formed. In this letter Guest advocated the use of the surplice at the Communion as well as at other times for the reason that "if we should use another garment herein, it should seem to teach us that higher and better things be given by it than be given by the other service, which we must not believe" ; the division of the Communion into two parts, so that only those about to receive the Sacrament should be allowed to remain in the church for the celebration ; the disuse of " praying for the dead " " in the Communion because it doth seem to make for the sacrifice of the dead, and also because, as it was used in the First Book,[2] it makes some of the faithful to be in heaven and to need no mercy, and some of them to be in another place and to lack help and mercy " ; the disuse of the petition

---

[1] Cardwell, *Conferences*, p. 47.
[2] That is, the Prayer Book of 1549.

beginning "Hear us, O merciful Father," in the prayer of consecration in the Book of 1549 "because it is taken to be so
needful for the consecration that the consecration is not thought
to be without it, which is not true, for petition is no part of
consecration," and, secondly, because "it prays that the bread
and wine may be Christ's body and blood, which makes for the
popish Transubstantiation"; and that the Sacrament should be
received in the hands of the people, and either standing or kneeling.[1] This letter of Guest's is sufficient to show the existence of a
party of divines in favour of a return to some of the formularies
of the reign of Edward VI. and regarding the general features
of the Book of 1552 as preferable to those of the Book of 1549.[2]

Meanwhile, an opposite line was being taken by Convocation.
In January, 1559, the Lower House of the Convocation of Canterbury drew up *articuli cleri* for presentation to the Upper House,
asserting the three propositions which had been affirmed in 1554
in connection with the trial of Cranmer, Ridley, and Latimer, declaring the real presence of the natural body and blood of Christ
under the species of bread and wine, the absence of any substance
of bread and wine in the consecrated Sacrament, and that a propitiatory sacrifice is offered in the Mass.[3]   A little later the propositions received the approval of the bishops.[4]

At a provincial council of the Scottish Church, held in March
and April, 1559, a careful statement of the traditional doctrine
was made in view of the circumstances of the time.   It included
the following articles about the Eucharist :—

"On the existence of the body and blood of Christ in the Sacrament of the Eucharist.   In the Sacrament of the Eucharist the real
body of our Lord Jesus Christ is actually present; that is, His real
flesh and real blood, nay the whole Christ, God and Man.   Wherefore in it we rightly adore, not the bread, not the wine, not the
species which are presented to the bodily eyes, but our Lord Jesus
Christ who was crucified, whether in the Mass or outside the Mass,

[1] Cardwell, *op. cit.* pp. 50-54.

[2] Since the above was in type the author has read Dr. Gee's *The Elizabethan Prayer Book and Ornaments*, on pp. 1-53 of which it is contended
that this letter of Guest was written in 1552.

[3] Wilkins, *Concilia*, iv. 179, 180.   For the text of the propositions, see
pp. 162, 163, *supra*.

[4] *Ibid.* 180.

wherever the Eucharist has been placed, or whenever it is carried about by the priest in the public acts of prayer.

"On the Communion of the laity in one kind only. Communion in both kinds is not necessary to salvation for the laity ; but in accordance with the lawful permission of the Church it is enough to give the Sacrament in one kind only, that of bread ; and it must be believed that the flesh and blood, and therefore the whole Christ, are received under one kind by itself.

"On the utility of the Mass. The sacrifice of the Mass, which was instituted for the remembrance of the passion of Christ, is of profit to the living and the dead by the virtue of His passion." [1]

A *Godly Exhortation* issued by Archbishop Hamilton in 1559 in consequence of the action of this Provincial Council of the Scottish Church, which came to be known as *The Two-penny Faith*, contains the following statement of doctrine as part of an exhortation to receive the Sacrament worthily :—

"Under the form of bread, which I am now presently to minister to you, is contained truly and really our Saviour Jesus Christ, whole in Godhead and manhood, that is, both His body and blood and soul conjoined with His Godhead, who in His mortal life offered Himself upon the cross to the Father of heaven an acceptable sacrifice for our redemption from the devil, sin, eternal death, and hell. And now in His immortal life sits at the right hand of the eternal Father in heaven, whom in this Blessed Sacrament invisibly contained under the form of bread I am to minister to you." [2]

II.

In spite of the attitude of the English Convocation in January, 1559, the plan for a Book of Common Prayer to some extent on the lines advocated by Guest went forward. On 16th February, 1559, a bill was introduced in the House of Commons, and read a first time, but appears to have been dropped. On 18th April and the two following days a Bill of Uniformity to authorise a Prayer Book like the Second Prayer Book of Edward VI., with certain alterations, was read three times in the House of Commons,

---

[1] Wilkins, *Concilia*, iv. 213.

[2] Only one copy of this *Godly Exhortation* is known to exist. It was discovered by the Rev. George Griffith, of New Abbey, in a volume of tracts the property of the Rev. Henry Small, of Dumfries. A facsimile was printed at the end of the facsimile edition of Archbishop Hamilton's *Catechism* published by Dr. Mitchell in 1882. *Cf.* pp. 156-58, *supra*.

apparently without serious opposition; and it was sent up to the House of Lords. Here it met with strenuous opposition. The third reading was passed by a majority of three votes, nine bishops and nine other peers voting against the Bill, the remainder of the bishops being absent. The "Order for the Administration of the Lord's Supper, or Holy Communion" thus authorised by Parliament was the same as that in the Second Prayer Book of Edward VI. except that the words of administration were composed of those of the Book of 1549[1] added to those of the Book of 1552,[2] and that the declaration on kneeling[3] was omitted. And the rubric at the beginning of Morning Prayer directed the wearing of the Eucharistic vestments at the administration of the Holy Communion by ordering that "the minister at the time of the Communion, and at all other times in his ministration, shall use such ornaments in the church as were in use by authority of Parliament in the second year of the reign of King Edward the VI. according to the Act of Parliament set in the beginning of this Book," referring to the provision in the Act of Uniformity "that such ornaments of the church, and of the ministers thereof, shall be retained and be in use as was in this Church of England, by authority of Parliament, in the second year of the reign of King Edward the VI. until other order shall be therein taken by the authority of the queen's majesty, with the advice of her commissioners appointed and authorised under the great seal of England, for causes ecclesiastical, or of the metropolitan of this realm ". This retention of the Eucharistic vestments is of some importance in view of Guest's criticism of the use of them; and the change in the words of administration in combining those that were associated with the doctrine that the consecrated Sacrament is the body and blood of Christ with those which were most congenial to the deniers of this doctrine may be taken as significant of the policy which was to mark the reign of Elizabeth. The speeches of Feckenham, the Abbot of Westminster, and of Scott, the Bishop of Chester, delivered in the House of Lords against the Bill have been preserved.[4] The general line of both is that the Missal

---

[1] See pp. 133, 137, *supra.*   [2] See p. 140, *supra.*
[3] See p. 141, *supra.*
[4] They are printed in Cardwell, *Conferences,* pp. 98-117; Strype, *Annals of the Reformation,* I. ii. 431-50 (edition 1824).

used in Mary's reign gave effect to the traditional doctrines of the presence and sacrifice in the Eucharist and that the proposed Prayer Book did not. In the course of his speech, Bishop Scott said :—

"Let them glory as much as they will in their Communion, it is to no purpose, seeing that the body of Christ is not there, which, as I have said, is the thing that should be communicated. There did yesterday a nobleman in this House say that he did believe that Christ is there received in the Communion set out in this Book ; and, being asked if he did worship Him there, he said, No, nor never would so long as he lived. Which is a strange opinion, that Christ should be anywhere and not worshipped. They say they will worship Him in heaven but not in the Sacrament ; which is much like as if a man would say that, when the emperor sitteth under his cloth of estate princely apparelled, he is to be honoured ; but, if he come abroad in a frieze coat, he is not to be honoured ; and yet he is all one emperor in cloth of gold under his cloth of estate and in a frieze coat abroad in the street. As it is one Christ in heaven in the form of man and in the Sacrament under the forms of bread and wine. . . . As concerning this matter, if we would consider all things well, we shall see the provision of God marvellous in it. For He provideth so that the very heretics and enemies of the truth be compelled to confess the truth in this behalf. For the Lutherans writing against the Zwinglians do prove that the true natural body of our Saviour Christ is in the Sacrament. And the Zwinglians against the Lutherans do prove that then it must needs be worshipped there. And thus in their contention doth the truth burst out whether they will or no. Wherefore, in my opinion of these two errors, the fonder is to say that Christ is in the Sacrament and yet not to be worshipped than to say He is not there at all. For either they do think that either He is there but in an imagination or fancy, and so not in very deed, or else they be Nestorians and think that there is His body only and not His divinity, which be both devilish and wicked. Now, my lords, consider, I beseech you, the matters here in variance, whether your lordships be able to discuss them according to learning, so as the truth may appear, or no ; that is, whether the body of Christ be by this new Book consecrated, offered, adored, and truly communicated, or no ; and whether these things be required necessarily by the institution of our Saviour Christ, or no ; and whether Book goeth nearer the truth." [1]

[1] Cardwell, *op. cit.* pp. 113-14 ; Strype, *op. cit.* I. ii. 446-48.

In 1559 a "Declaration and Confession" was presented to the queen by some of the reforming party, consisting of a series of articles to a large extent following the *Forty-two Articles* of 1553.[1] The fourteenth and fifteenth of these articles are as follows :—

"Of the Lord's Supper.

"The Supper of the Lord is not only a sign of the love that Christians ought to have among themselves one to another, but rather it is a Sacrament of our redemption in Christ's death, insomuch that to such as rightly, worthily, and with faith receive the same the bread which we break is the communion of the body of Christ. Likewise the cup of blessing is the communion of the blood of Christ. So that in the due administration of this holy Supper we do not deny all manner of presence of Christ's body and blood ; neither do we think or say that this holy Sacrament is only a naked and a bare sign or figure, in the which nothing else is to be received of the faithful but common bread and wine, as our adversaries have at all times most untruly charged us. And yet do we not allow the corporal, carnal, and real presence which they teach and maintain, affirming Christ's body to be sensibly handled of the priest, and also corporally and substantially to be received with the mouth as well of the wicked as of the godly. For that were contrary to the Scripture, both to remove Him out of heaven where concerning His natural body He shall continue to the end of the world, and also by making His body bodily present in so many sundry and several places at once to destroy the proprieties of His human nature. Neither do we allow the fond error of Transubstantiation or change of the substances of bread and wine into the substances of the body and blood of Christ, which, as it is repugnant to the words of the Scriptures and contrary to the plain assertions of ancient writers, so doth it utterly deny the nature of a Sacrament. But we affirm and confess that, as the wicked in the unworthy receiving of this holy Sacrament eateth and drinketh his own damnation, so to the believer and worthy receiver is verily given and exhibited whole Christ, God and Man, with the fruits of His passion. And that in the distribution of this holy Sacrament, as we with our outward senses receive the sacramental bread and wine, so inwardly by faith and through the working of God's Spirit we are made partakers *vere et efficaciter* of the body and blood of our Saviour Christ, and are spiritually fed therewith unto everlast-

[1] See pp. 145, 146, *supra*.

ing life. And we also confess, and ever have done, that by the celebrating and right receiving of this mystery and holy Sacrament we enjoy divers and singular comforts and benefits. For herein we are assured of God's promises of the forgiveness of sins, of the pacifying of God's wrath, of our resurrection and everlasting life. Herein also by the secret operation of God's Holy Spirit our faith is increased and confirmed, we are made one with Christ and He with us, we abide in Him and He in us, we are stirred up to unity and mutual charity, to joyfulness of conscience and patient suffering for Christ's sake, and finally to continual thanksgiving to our merciful heavenly Father for the wonderful work of our salvation purchased in the death and bloodshed of our Redeemer and Saviour Jesus Christ."

" Of the perfect oblation of Christ made upon the cross.

"The offering of Christ made once for ever is the perfect redemption, the pacifying of God's displeasure, and satisfaction for all the sins of the whole world both original and actual ; and there is none other satisfaction for sin but that alone. Wherefore the sacrifice of the Masses, in the which it is commonly said that the priest did offer Christ for the quick and the dead, to have remission of pain or sin, are forged fables and dangerous deceits." [1]

In 1559 or 1560 a series of *Eleven Articles* was compiled by Parker, the Archbishop of Canterbury, Young, the Archbishop of York, and other bishops. Assent to them was required from all clergy on admission to cures and twice a year afterwards. They had no formal sanction from Convocation, no authority from Parliament, and no ratification from the Crown. They were designed as a temporary measure until some formal action could be taken ; and as such were drawn up and used by the bishops. The articles relating to the Eucharist were as follows :—

"9. Moreover, I do not only acknowledge that private Masses were never used amongst the fathers of the primitive Church, I mean,

[1] This *Declaration* exists in a MS. belonging to Corpus Christi College, Cambridge (MSS. cxxi. No. 20). It is referred to in Strype, *Annals of the Reformation,* I. i. 166-73 (edition 1824) ; Hardwick, *History of the Articles of Religion,* p. 117 (edition 1890). Considerable parts are printed in Dixon, *History of the Church of England,* v. 107-15. The thanks of the author are due to Mr. C. W. Moule, Librarian of Corpus Christi College, for his kindness in allowing him to copy the above Articles from the MS.

public ministration and receiving of the Sacrament by the priest
alone without a just number of communicants according to Christ's
saying, 'Take ye and eat ye,' etc., but also that the doctrine that
maintaineth the Mass to be a propitiatory sacrifice for the quick and
the dead, and a mean to deliver souls out of purgatory, is neither
agreeable to Christ's ordinance, nor grounded upon doctrine apostolic, but contrariwise most ungodly and most injurious to the precious
redemption of our Saviour Christ, and His only sufficient sacrifice
offered once for ever upon the altar of the cross.

"10. I am of that mind also that the Holy Communion or
Sacrament of the body and blood of Christ, for the due obedience to
Christ's institution, and to express the virtue of the same, ought to
be ministered unto the people under both kinds ; and that it is
avouched by certain fathers of the Church to be a plain sacrilege to
rob them of the mystical cup for whom Christ hath shed His most
precious blood, seeing He Himself hath said, 'Drink ye all of this,'
considering also that in the time of the ancient doctors of the Church,
as Cyprian, Hierom, Augustine, Gelasius, and others, six hundred
years after Christ and more, both the parts of the Sacrament were
ministered to the people." [1]

In these articles the most remarkable feature is the absence of
any statement concerning the presence of Christ in the Sacrament.

In 1563 the *Forty-two Articles* of 1553 were considered by
Convocation ; and in a revised form and reduced in number to
thirty-eight were published with the assent of Convocation and
the ratification of the queen. The alterations bearing on the
Eucharist were considerable. In what is now the twenty-fifth
article the repudiation of the operation of the Sacraments " of the
work wrought" was omitted. For the paragraph in the article
" Of the Lord's Supper" condemning belief in "the real and
bodily presence" the following paragraph was substituted :—

" The body of Christ is given, taken, and eaten in the Supper only
after an heavenly and spiritual manner. And the mean whereby the
body of Christ is received and eaten in the Supper is faith."

The article " Of the Perfect Oblation of Christ made upon the
Cross" was unaltered except that "forged fables" was strengthened into "blasphemous fables". An article was added declaring that the laity ought to receive Communion in both kinds.

[1] Hardwick, *History of the Articles of Religion*, pp. 358, 359 (edition
1890).

A new article on reception by the wicked was in the draft submitted to Convocation by Archbishop Parker, and agreed to by that body; but did not occur in the articles as finally published. In 1571 the articles of 1563 were sanctioned by both Houses of Parliament and were subsequently again revised by Convocation, ratified by the queen, and issued in their present form, thirty-nine in number. The only alteration of moment touching the Eucharist was that the present twenty-ninth article, which had been struck out of the articles of 1563 between their acceptance by Convocation and the publication of them with the ratification of the queen, was re-inserted. The title is " Of the Wicked which do not Eat the Body of Christ in the Use of the Lord's Supper ". Its words are :—

"The wicked and such as be void of a lively faith, although they do carnally and visibly press with their teeth (as Saint Augustine saith)[1] the Sacrament of the body and blood of Christ, yet in no wise are they partakers of Christ, but rather to their condemnation do eat and drink the sign or Sacrament of so great a thing."

The change in the article " Of the Lord's Supper " is of high importance. The article of 1553 had distinctly denied " the real and bodily presence (as they term it) of Christ's flesh and blood ". The article of 1563 and 1571 did not contain this denial, and in the place of it had the words quoted above.[2] There is contemporary evidence as to the significance attached to the change at the time. In July, 1566, the extreme Reformers Laurence Humphrey and Thomas Sampson wrote to Henry Bullinger at Zurich :—

[1] The reference is to St. Augustine, *In Joan. Ev. Tract.* xxvi. 18, quoted i. 93, 94, *supra.* The passage in its original form is, " he who does not abide in Christ and in whom Christ does not abide without doubt neither eats His flesh nor drinks His blood, but rather eats and drinks the Sacrament of so great a thing to his own judgment ". In the middle ages the passage was expanded so as to be, "he who does not abide in Christ and in whom Christ does not abide without doubt neither eats His flesh spiritually nor drinks His blood spiritually, though he carnally and visibly press with his teeth the Sacrament of the body and blood of Christ, but rather eats and drinks the Sacrament of so great a thing to his own judgment, because he presumes to come unclean to the Sacraments of Christ which no one receives worthily except he who is clean " (see vol. i. p. 200, *supra*). The sentence quoted in the article is from the interpolation.

[2] See p. 208, *supra.*

" The article composed in the time of Edward VI. respecting the spiritual eating, which expressly oppugned and took away the real presence in the Eucharist, and contained a most clear explanation of the truth, is now set forth among us mutilated and imperfect." [1]

On 22nd December, 1566, Edmund Guest the Bishop of Rochester, who in 1548 had attacked the canon of the Mass and the doctrine of a propitiatory sacrifice in the Mass and the practice of Eucharistic adoration,[2] and in 1559 had advocated dividing the Order of Holy Communion into two parts and excluding from the Offertory onwards those who were not about to communicate, and had opposed the use of the prayer that the elements may be the body and blood of Christ,[3] wrote to Sir William Cecil :—

" I suppose you have heard how the Bishop of Gloucester [4] found himself grieved with the placing of this adverb 'only' in this article, 'The body of Christ is given, taken, and eaten in the Supper after an heavenly and spiritual manner only,' because it did take away the presence of Christ's body in the Sacrament, and privily noted me to take his part therein, and yesterday in mine absence more plainly vouched me for the same, whereas between him and me I told him plainly that this word 'only' in the aforesaid article did not exclude the presence of Christ's body from the Sacrament, but only the grossness and sensibleness in the receiving thereof. For I said unto him though he took Christ's body in his hand, received it with his mouth, and that corporally, naturally, really, substantially, and carnally, as the doctors do write, yet did he not for all that see it, feel it, smell it, nor taste it. And therefore I told him I would speak against him therein, and the rather because the article was of mine own penning. And yet I would not for all that deny thereby anything that I had spoken for the presence. And this was the sum of our talk. And this that I said is so true by all sorts of men that even D. Harding writeth the same, as it appears more evidently by his words reported in the Bishop of Salisbury's book, pagina 325,[5] which be these, 'Then ye may say that in the Sacrament His very body is present, yea really, that is to say, in deed; substantially, that is, in substance ; and corporally, carnally, and naturally; by the which words is meant that His very body, His very flesh, and

[1] *Zurich Letters* (Parker Society), i. 165.
[2] In his *Treatise against the Privy Mass in the Behalf and Furtherance of the Most Holy Communion.*
[3] See pp. 201, 202, *supra.*   [4] That is, Richard Cheyney.
[5] That is, John Jewel.

His very human nature is there, not after corporal, carnal, or natural wise, but invisibly, unspeakably, supernaturally, spiritually, divinely, and by way unto Him only known'. This I thought good to write unto your honour for mine own purgation."[1]

In May, 1571, after the *Thirty-nine Articles* had been agreed to by Convocation and before they were ratified by the queen, Guest wrote a further letter to Cecil, in which he said on this subject :—

"In the article 'Of the Lord's Supper' it is thus said, 'The body of Christ is given, taken, and eaten in the Supper after a heavenly and spiritual manner only'. Though it be true that the body of Christ cannot be given, taken, and eaten in His Supper but it must needs be truly given, taken, and eaten in the Supper, yet, because some men for a more plainness would have added this word 'truly' or 'indeed' in this wise, 'The body of Christ is indeed given, taken, and eaten in the Supper,' it were well to put it in, and Calvin agreeth thereunto, for thus he writeth in his commentaries upon these words of Paul, '*hoc est corpus meum,*' '*concludo realiter ut vulgo loquuntur hoc est vere nobis dari in coena corpus Christi*'. And my lord of Salisbury [2] hath these words, 'That we undoubtedly receive Christ's body in the Sacrament it is neither denied nor in question'. In that in the book [3] it is further said, 'after a spiritual and heavenly manner only,' some be offended with this word 'only,' as my lord of Gloucester,[4] as though this word 'only' did take away the real presence of Christ's body, or the receiving of the same by the mouth, whereas it was put in only to this end, to take away all gross and sensible presence, for it is very true that, when Christ's body is taken and eaten, it is neither seen, felt, smelt, nor tasted to be Christ's body ; and so it is received and eaten but only after a heavenly and spiritual and no sensible manner. And because it is said, 'Because the mouth receiveth Christ's body, therefore it is sensibly received,' the consequent is not true, because the mouth in receiving Christ's body doth not feel it, nor taste it, nor we by any other sense do perceive it. Yet for all this, to avoid offence and contention, the word 'only' may be well left out as not needful. My lord of Gloucester is pronounced excommunicate by my lord of Canterbury, and shall be cited to answer before him and other bishops to certain errors which he is accused to hold.

---

[1] This letter is printed in Hodges, *Bishop Guest*, pp. 22, 23.
[2] That is, John Jewel.   [3] That is, of the Articles.
[4] That is, Richard Cheyney.

14 *

I think if this word 'only' were put out of the book for his sake, it were the best. It followeth in the book, 'But the mean whereby the body of Christ is received and eaten in the Supper is faith '. If this word 'profitably' were put hereunto in this sort, 'But the mean whereby the body of Christ is profitably received and eaten in the Supper is faith,' then should the occasion of this question, 'Whether the evil do receive Christ's body in the Sacrament' because they lack faith, which riseth of the aforesaid words and causeth much strife, should be quite taken away, for that hereby is not denied the unfruitful receiving of Christ's body without faith, but the fruitful only affirmed." [1]

In the same letter Guest went on to express his wish that the article " Of the wicked which do not eat the body of Christ in the use of the Lord's Supper " might not be ratified by the queen. On this subject he writes :—

" My lord's grace of Canterbury is purposed to present to the queen's majesty the first copy of the book of articles, to which the most part of the bishops have subscribed, to have it authorised by her majesty, and there is this article, 'Evil men receive not the body of Christ,' which article is not in the printed books either Latin or English. If this article be confirmed and authorised by the queen's grace it will cause much business, because it is quite contrary to the Scripture and to the doctrine of the fathers, for it is certain that Judas as evil as he was did receive Christ's body, because Christ said unto him, ' Take, eat, this is My body '. It is not said, If thou be a good or faithful man, take, eat, this is My body, but simply, without any such conditions, 'Take, eat, this is My body,' so that to all men which be of the Church and of the profession of Christ, whether they be good or bad, faithful or unfaithful (for to them only Christ spake these words, ' Take, eat, this is My body,' and not to the Jew, Turk, miscreant beast or bird), Christ's body is given and they do receive it. This is the cause that St. Paul saith, ' Whosoever shall eat of this bread and drink of this cup of the Lord unworthily shall be guilty of the body and blood of the Lord, for he that eateth and drinketh unworthily eateth and drinketh his own damnation, because he maketh no difference of the Lord's body '.[2] Note these words, 'the Lord's body '. It is not here said, 'The sign or Sacrament of the Lord's body, nor the grace or fruit of the Lord's body, nor the memory of the Lord's passion,' but plainly

---

[1] In Hodges, *op. cit.* pp. 24, 25.
[2] 1 Cor. xi. 27-29.

'the Lord's body,' to teach us that the evil men of the Church do receive Christ's body." [1]

The objections which Guest thus felt to the twenty-ninth article did not prevent him from eventually subscribing it ; [2] and it is probable that more careful attention to the phrase " partakers of Christ " led him to see that, however much he might dislike the article, he did not by subscribing necessarily say more than that those who communicate unworthily do not profitably receive the body of Christ. His explanations of the twenty-eighth article seem to make it clear that he intended this article as completed by him to assert that the actual body of Christ is really present after consecration and received by the communicants in a spiritual manner, while the article is explicit in its rejection of views of a carnal presence ; of Transubstantiation, probably understood in a carnal sense ; and of a merely symbolic representation. It is likely that, at the time of their being compiled and since, the twenty-eighth and twenty-ninth articles have been subscribed in good faith by those who have held almost all possible ideas of the Eucharistic presence between a carnal form of Transubstantiation and a wholly symbolic view, by those who have thought that the wicked receive the body of Christ to judgment and by those who have believed that the wicked do not receive the body of Christ at all. Similarly the article " Of the one oblation of Christ finished upon the cross " appears to have been worded in such a way as to make subscription possible both for those who denied any sacrifice of the body and blood of Christ in the Eucharist and for those who held any doctrine of the Eucharistic sacrifice which did not conflict with the unique and complete character of the sacrifice of Calvary or make a sacrifice of the Mass which as a separate offering might be parallel and supplementary to the work of Christ on the cross.

In the reign of Edward VI. a Book of *Homilies* for public reading in church had been published, and had received a general commendation in the *Forty-two Articles.* On the accession of Elizabeth a Second Book of *Homilies* was compiled. It was approved by Convocation in 1562, ratified by the queen after some delay in 1563, and declared to " contain a godly and wholesome doctrine and necessary for these times " in the *Thirty-*

[1] In Hodges, *op. cit.* pp. 25, 26,   [2] See Hodges, *op. cit.* p. 37.

eight and the *Thirty-nine Articles.* It is agreed by eminent commentators on the Articles,[1] and was affirmed by a judgment of the Court of Arches in 1838, that this statement of the thirty-fifth article does not commit the Church of England to every part of the doctrines which the *Homilies* contain ; but they are of interest and importance as showing the kind of teaching which Elizabethan divines wished English Church people to receive.   One of these *Homilies* is entitled *A Homily of the Worthy Receiving and Reverent Esteeming of the Sacrament of the Body and Blood of Christ.*[2]   It shows a strong sense of the existence of evils connected with the celebration of the Eucharist in the past ; of the importance of reverence and devotion and reality in the reception of the Sacrament ; and of the necessity of ministering it like our Lord and the Apostles and the primitive Church.   The statements that "every one of us must be guests and not gazers, eaters and not lookers," and that " we must be ourselves partakers of this Table and not beholders of others," appear to deprecate presence at the celebration of the Sacrament without Communion.   The caution—

"We must then take heed lest of the memory, it be made a sacrifice ; lest of a Communion, it be made a private eating ; lest of two parts we have but one ; lest applying it for the dead, we lose the fruit that be alive,"

apparently condemns the offering of the Eucharist for the departed ; the restriction of the Communion of others than the celebrant to the species of bread ; celebrations in which the priest alone communicated ; and at any rate some forms which the Eucharistic sacrifice had taken, or was thought to have taken. Because of the sacrifice on Calvary and the promise of Christ, it is said :—

" Herein thou needest no other man's help, no other sacrifice or oblation, no sacrificing priest, no Mass, no means established by man's invention."

On the other hand, it is explicitly stated that—

[1] See *e.g.* Browne, *An Exposition of the Thirty-nine Articles,* p. 777 ; Gibson, *The Thirty-nine Articles,* pp. 726-28 ; Maclear and Williams, *An Introduction to the Articles,* pp. 394, 395.

[2] In the announcement of a future Second Book of *Homilies* at the end of the First Book in 1547 the title of this *Homily* was given as *Of the Due Receiving of His Blessed Body and Blood under the Form of Bread and Wine.*

" In the Supper of the Lord there is no vain ceremony, no bare sign, no untrue figure of a thing absent " ;

the effects of Communion are said to be—

" the tranquillity of conscience, the increase of faith, the strengthening of hope, the large spreading abroad of brotherly kindness, with many other sundry graces of God " ;

the " meat " " in this Supper " is described as—

" spiritual food ; the nourishment of our soul ; a heavenly refection, and not earthly ; an invisible meat, and not bodily ; a ghostly substance, and not carnal " ;

it is said that—

" we receive not only the outward Sacrament, but the spiritual thing also ; not the figure, but the truth ; not the shadow only, but the body " ;

and the communicant is exhorted :—

" Take then this lesson, O thou who art desirous of this Table, of Emissenus, a godly father,[1] that when thou goest up to the reverend Communion, to be satisfied with spiritual meats, thou look up with faith upon the holy body and blood of thy God, thou marvel with reverence, thou touch it with the mind, thou receive it with the hand of thy heart, and thou take it fully with thy inward man."

It is probable that the writer of the *Homily* believed that faithful communicants receive the body and blood of Christ present in their Communion with spiritual reality. Whether he held also that the body and blood are present in the consecrated elements before Communion it seems impossible to say. Nor can it be determined whether in the denials of sacrifice he meant to deny any doctrine of the sacrifice of the body and blood of Christ in the Eucharist, or only those ideas which were perversions of the doctrine.

A *Catechism* chiefly taken from that of Poynet[2] was drawn up by Alexander Nowell, the Dean of St. Paul's, was welcomed by Archbishop Parker, was altered by the Lower House of the Convocation of Canterbury with a view to its acceptance, but never received the approval of the bishops. This *Catechism* consists of four parts. The fourth part is on the Sacraments. In regard to the Eucharist there are the following questions and answers :—

[1] See vol. i. pp. 129-31, *supra*.   [2] See pp. 146, 147, *supra*.

" *Master.* . . . Tell me the order of the Lord's Supper.

" *Scholar.* It is even the same which the Lord Christ did institute. . . . This the form and order of the Lord's Supper, which we ought to hold, and holily to keep till He come.

" *Master.* For what use ?

" *Scholar.* To celebrate and retain continually a thankful re- membrance of the Lord's death, and of that most singular benefit which we have received thereby ; and ·that as in Baptism we were once born again, so with the Lord's Supper we be alway fed and sustained to spiritual and everlasting life.

. . . .

" *Master.* Dost thou say that there are two parts in this Sacra- ment also, as in Baptism ?

" *Scholar.* Yea.   The one part, the bread and wine, the outward signs, which are seen with our eyes, handled with our hands, and felt with our taste ; the other part, Christ Himself, with whom our souls, as with their proper food, are inwardly nourished.

. . . .

" *Master.* Why would the Lord have here two signs to be used ?

" *Scholar.* First, He severally gave the signs both of His body and blood, that it might be the more plain express image of His death which He suffered, His body being torn, His side pierced, and all His blood shed, and that the memory thereof so printed in our hearts should stick the deeper.   And moreover, that the Lord might so provide for and help our weakness, and thereby manifestly de- clare that, as the bread for nourishment of our bodies, so His body hath most singular force and efficacy spiritually to feed our souls ; and, as with wine men's hearts are cheered, and their strength con- firmed, so with His blood our souls are relieved and refreshed ; that certainly assuring ourselves that He is not only our meat but also our drink, we do not anywhere else but in Him alone seek any part of our spiritual nourishment and eternal life.

" *Master.* Is there then not an only figure, but the truth itself of the benefits that thou hast rehearsed, delivered in the Supper ?·

" *Scholar.* What else ?   For, since Christ is the truth itself, it is no doubt that the thing which He testifieth in words, and re- presenteth in signs, He performeth also in deed, and delivereth it unto us ; and that He as surely maketh them that believe in Him partakers of His body and blood as they surely know that they have received the bread and wine into their mouth and stomach.

" *Master.* Since we be in the earth, and Christ's body in heaven, how can that be that thou sayest ?

"*Scholar.* We must lift up our souls and hearts from earth, and raise them up by faith to heaven, where Christ is.

"*Master.* Sayest thou then the mean to receive the body and blood of Christ standeth upon faith?

- "*Scholar.* Yea. For, when we believe that Christ died to deliver us from death, and that He rose again to procure us life, we are partakers of the redemption purchased by His death, and of His life, and all other His good things ; and, with the same conjoining wherewith the head and members are knit together, He coupleth us to Himself by secret and marvellous virtue of His Spirit, even so that we be members of His body, and be of His flesh and bones, and do grow into one body with Him.

"*Master.* Dost thou then, that this conjoining may be made, imagine the bread and wine to be changed into the substance of the flesh and blood of Christ?

"*Scholar.* There is no need to invent any such change. For both the Holy Scriptures and the best and most ancient expositors do teach that by Baptism we are likewise the members of Christ, and are of His flesh and bones, and do grow into one body with Him, when yet there is no such change made in the water.

"*Master.* Go on.

"*Scholar.* In both the Sacraments the substances of the outward things are not changed, but the word of God and heavenly grace coming to them, there is such efficacy that, as by Baptism we are once regenerate in Christ, and are first as it were joined and grafted into His body, so, when we rightly receive the Lord's Supper, with the very divine nourishment of His body and blood, most full of health and immortality, given to us by the work of the Holy Ghost, and received of us by faith, as by the mouth of our soul, we are continually fed and sustained to eternal life, growing together in them both into one body with Christ.

"*Master.* Then Christ doth also otherwise than by His Supper only give Himself unto us, and knitteth us to Himself with most straight conjoining.

"*Scholar.* Christ did then principally give Himself to us to be the Author of our salvation when He gave Himself to death for us, that we should not perish with deserved death. By the Gospel also He giveth Himself to the faithful, and plainly teacheth that He is that lively bread that came down from heaven to nourish their souls that believe in Him. And also in Baptism, as is before said, Christ gave Himself to us effectually, for that He then made us Christians.

"*Master.* And sayest thou that there be no less straight bands of conjoining in the Supper?

"*Scholar.* In the Lord's Supper both that communicating which I spake of is confirmed unto us and is also increased, for that each man is both by the words and mysteries of God ascertained that the same belongeth unto himself, and that Christ is by a peculiar manner given to him, that he may most fully and with most clear conjunction enjoy Him, insomuch that not only our souls are nourished with His holy body and blood as with their proper food, but also our bodies, for that they partake of the Sacraments of eternal life, have as it were by a pledge given them a certain hope assured them of resurrection and immortality, that at length, Christ abiding in us, and we again abiding in Christ, we also by Christ abiding in us may obtain not only everlasting life but also the glory which His Father gave Him.   In a sum I say thus : as I imagine not any gross joining, so I affirm that same secret and marvellous communicating of Christ's body in His Supper to be most near and straight, most assured, most true, and altogether most high and perfect. '

"*Master.* Of this thou hast said of the Lord's Supper, meseems, I may gather that the same was not ordained to this end, that Christ's body should be offered in sacrifice to God the Father for sins.

"*Scholar.* It is not so offered.   For He, when He did institute His Supper, commanded us to eat His body, not to offer it.   As for the prerogative of offering for sins, it pertaineth to Christ alone, as to Him which is the eternal Priest, which also, when He died upon the cross, once made that only and everlasting sacrifice for our salvation, and fully performed the same for ever.   For us there is nothing left to do but to take the use and benefit of that eternal sacrifice bequeathed to us by the Lord Himself, which we chiefly do in the Lord's Supper.

"*Master.* Then I perceive the Holy Supper sendeth us to the death of Christ, and to His sacrifice once done upon the cross, by which alone God is appeased towards us.

"*Scholar.* It is most true.   For by bread and wine, the signs, is assured unto us that, as the body of Christ was once offered a sacrifice for us to reconcile us to favour with God, and His blood once shed to wash away the spots of our sins, so now also in His Holy Supper both are given to the faithful, that we may surely know that the reconciliation of favour pertaineth to us, and may take and receive the fruit of the redemption purchased by His death.

"*Master.* Are then the only faithful fed with Christ's body and blood ?

"*Scholar.* They only.   For to whom He communicateth His body, to them (as I said) He communicateth also everlasting life.

" *Master.* Why dost thou not grant that the body and blood of Christ are included in the bread and cup, or that the bread and wine are changed into the substance of His body and blood ?

"*Scholar.* Because that were to bring in doubt the truth of Christ's body, to do dishonour to Christ Himself, and to fill them with abhorring that receive the Sacrament, if we should imagine His body either to be enclosed in so narrow a room, or to be in many places at once, or His flesh to be chewed in our mouth with our teeth, and to be bitten small, and eaten as other meat.

" *Master.* Why then is the communicating of the Sacrament damnable to the wicked, if there is no such change made ?

" *Scholar.* Because they come to the holy and divine mysteries with hypocrisy and counterfeiting, and do wickedly profane them, to the great injury and dishonour of the Lord Himself that ordained them." [1]

III.

The study of individual theologians of the reign of Elizabeth shows that the policy of comprehension then adopted met with success in the way of securing the inclusion within the English Church of those who held considerably differing beliefs about the Eucharist. A few instances may be sufficient to illustrate this fact.

Bernard Gilpin was born in 1517. He died in 1584. He was successively Vicar of Norton in Durham, Archdeacon of Durham, and Rector of Houghton-le-Spring. He refused the Bishopric of Carlisle. His attitude towards the Reformation movements and formularies gives special interest to his opinions. Bishop Lightfoot described him as " the true product of the English Reformation," "the exponent, the noblest exponent, of the teaching of the Reformation "; and wrote of him that " while the Reformers were in power under Edward he still clung to the old. When the Roman reaction set in under Mary he espoused the new." [2] Because of this special interest of his life and character it is worth while to mention the scanty evidence as to his beliefs in regard to the Eucharist. When accused of false doctrine during

---

[1] The original *Catechism* was in Latin. The above passages are quoted from the English translation by Thomas Norton, published in 1570.

[2] Lightfoot, *Leaders in the Northern Church*, pp. 130, 131. Yet Gilpin said in his letter to George Gilpin (see below) that after the death of Queen Mary he " began to explain " his "mind more fully ",

the reign of Mary, Bishop Tunstall was obliged to examine him about the Eucharist.

"In Transubstantiation he would not trouble me; only he inquired concerning the real presence, which I granted, and so was freed out of that danger. And as touching the real presence I found not myself fully resolved. I suppose that therein lay hid a mystery above my capacity. Nevertheless my conscience did sometimes chide me for that I had before them yielded in express words to a point which seemed unto me doubtful. But I hoped God would pardon mine ignorance, and in time bring me to a greater light of knowledge."

After the accession of Elizabeth his "tender conscience," he says, was "wounded" by a sermon in which Dr. Sandys [1] "seemed utterly to deny a real presence"; he subscribed the Eleven Articles [2] only after much hesitation; and after subscribing them sent to Sandys a "protestation touching those two points which had troubled" him. In 1575 he quoted with apparent approval an opinion ascribed to Dr. Chedsey that the right solution of Eucharistic controversies was to be found by granting "a real presence of Christ in the Sacrament" and in allowing the rejection of "the opinion of Transubstantiation," used the phrase "the fiction of Transubstantiation," and showed his dislike of the prevalent enforcement of elaborate formularies by saying that from the time of his ordination he had "resolved to be sworn to no writings but with this exception, so far only as they are agreeable to the word of God". In 1580 he described Transubstantiation as "a mere fiction without any foundation of Scripture".[3]

Adrian Saravia was a Flemish pastor who was born in 1530. After ministering in Flanders and Holland, he became persuaded of the divine institution of episcopacy, and was therefore obliged to sever himself from the Protestant religious bodies in those countries. He visited Guernsey early in the reign of Elizabeth, and became domiciled in England in 1588. He was appointed Prebendary of Canterbury in 1595, and of Westminster in 1601. He died in 1612, and was buried in Canterbury Cathedral. His

---

[1] See pp. 232-35, infra.   [2] See pp. 207, 208, supra.

[3] Gilpin's letters to George Gilpin (1575 A.D.) and Thomas Gelthrop (1580 A.D.) are in Bishop Carleton's Life of Mr. Bernard Gilpin (1629 A.D.), reprinted in Wordsworth, Ecclesiastical Biography (iv. 123-34, 137-50, edition 1810).

Latin book, entitled *A Treatise on the Holy Eucharist*, is dedicated to James I. and was probably presented to that king in 1604 or 1605. Saravia explicitly rejects Transubstantiation and any theory of a natural process by which the bread and wine become the body and blood of Christ. "The Romanists have wholly transformed into a foul idol the new covenant in the flesh and blood of our Lord"; "the Romanists take away the bread and wine, and leave us empty images of the bread and wine without their substance," "against the institution of the Lord, the nature of the things themselves, and the judgment of the old fathers, who knew nothing of this monstrous existence of accidents without subject"; "the substance of the wine and the bread is not changed, and the bread remains that which it was before, as also does the wine"; "it is a mistake to make that a change of substance which is one of quality"; that which is effected takes place "not naturally but sacramentally".[1] He believed that a ground of agreement among Christians could be found in the acceptance of the *Confession of Augsburg*.[2]   His assertions that the consecrated Sacrament is the body and blood of Christ are many and clear; and they are carried out to the conclusions that if the wicked communicate they receive the body of Christ, and that our Lord is to be adored as present in the consecrated species.

"The bread without the body of Christ is not a Sacrament, neither is the body of Christ without the bread. The Sacrament of the Eucharist may be defined thus, that there is under the form of bread and wine the Communion of the body of our Lord Jesus Christ once offered for us on the altar of the cross and of His blood of the new covenant shed for the remission of sins; and there is the commemoration of His death. We have here, as Irenaeus teaches, the two parts which make up the whole nature of the Sacrament, the earthly and the heavenly, namely, the bread and the wine, together with the crucified body of the Lord and His shed blood. The third thing which I wish noted is the remission of sins and eternal life, which is the virtue of the Sacrament, distinct from those two parts of it." [3]

"Of those who partake of the Eucharist, all eat the same

---

[1] Pp. 4, 24, 76 (Denison's edition).
[2] P. 16. For the *Confession of Augsburg*, see pp. 25-27, *supra*.
[3] P. 22.

spiritual food, and all drink the same spiritual drink; but it is certain that it has not happened, and does not happen, to all to do this to salvation. . . . Some eat and drink to salvation, and some to judgment, the same spiritual food, namely, the flesh and blood of Christ. . . . Those who eat and drink unworthily partake of the real and complete Supper of the Lord. . . . It seems to me no more absurd that the flesh of Christ be really eaten in the Sacrament by the wicked than that the ark of God could be handled and carried by the wicked sons of Eli, or taken into the temple of Dagon by the Philistines and set there side by side with an idol, or than that the Son of God should be kissed by the traitor Judas and crucified by sinners." [1]

"I exhort and admonish that we be holy before God both in soul and in body so often as we are about to receive the body and blood of the Lord. God, who is the Creator and Saviour of both parts of man, is to be worshipped and adored by both. There is a fear in the present day, which has never been before, that the bread may be adored if the Eucharist be received kneeling, and people contend that the Sacraments are not to be adored. Whence comes this fear? Who has ever taught that the bread of the Eucharist is to be adored? The Pope's men themselves, though they adore the bread, teach that it is not the bread which is the object of adoration. . . . They warn the people that the object of adoration is not the outward forms, which they say are accidents without subject, but that the object of adoration is That which lies hidden under those visible forms. The German theologians, who affirm that the very body of Christ is in the bread, or under the bread, or with the bread, have never said that the bread is to be adored; nor have I ever heard or read that any theologian has so taught, unless, perhaps, some one has said that Christ has taken the nature of bread as He is believed to have taken the nature of flesh. Whence, I ask, comes this fear of adoration? Is it from a desire that the custom of adoration be avoided when the Holy Communion is received? For my own part, I think it should much more be feared that a man should not adore That which is there and then presented for the adoration of the faithful. When some men say that Sacraments are not to be adored, this is to be understood of the outward symbols, which are created things." [2]

"So great is the majesty of this Sacrament that if a man by faith consider what That is which he holds in his hands and lifts to his mouth when he receives the bread or the cup, namely, that it is the

[1] Pp. 98, 100.   [2] Pp. 194, 196.

crucified flesh of Christ his Lord, and the shed blood of the new
covenant, and therefore the new covenant itself, shall he not be
struck by wonder that such things should be, and prostrate his
whole self before the throne of God's grace ?   What ! do we fear to
adore here on our knees, lest we seem to adore the material bread,
and not rather lest by sitting we seem not to adore Christ the Bread
of life ?   The great theologian Augustine thought otherwise.   'No
one,' he says, ' eats that flesh without first adoring.' [1]   In my judgment, where the true doctrine of the Sacraments prevails, there is no
room for fearing any excess of reverence either inward of the mind
or outward of the body." [2]

Like the theologians of the middle ages and of the Council of
Trent, Saravia distinguishes between the method of the presence
of Christ in heaven and that of His presence in the Eucharist,
and describes the latter as "divine," "spiritual," "heavenly,"
"supernatural".   Some passages show a tendency to restrict the
sacramental presence within the limits of the Eucharistic service.
A characteristic idea is the repeated contention that it is not
the glorified but the crucified body and blood which are present
in the Sacrament.

"Many discuss the Sacraments of the new covenant as if they
were things which had an existence apart from their use, or were
compounded of different substances, or were transformed either by
one substance being actually transformed into another or by a
transition in the first substance going away and another coming in
its place ; whereas the conjunction of the parts of the Sacrament
is one of relation, not of substance, as is the condition of a sign in
regard to the thing signified, and of a picture in regard to the thing
expressed by drawing and colours.   For the bread which is made
the Sacrament of the body of Christ has a relation to His body,
and the wine to His blood, by the institution of God, so that he
who has the bread has certainly and really the body, and he who
has the wine has the blood.   Not indeed that these are present absolutely and simply as they are now locally and circumscribed in
one place in heaven, but in a certain figure by a necessary relation
to the body and blood and by sacramental union therewith.   There
is one manner of presence of the body of Christ in heaven ; there is
another in the Sacrament.   A question is raised concerning the real
and actual presence of the body and blood of the Lord in this Sacra-

[1] St. Augustine, *Enar. in Ps.* *xcviii.* 9, quoted vol. i. p. 109, *supra.*
[2] Pp. 198, 200.

ment; and it is said that this presence cannot be exhibited at the same time in more places than one, because this would be contrary to the manner and nature of a real body, which is circumscribed locally by its dimensions, and that if you take away these you take away thereby the nature of a body. The answer to this argument is, that it does not show that He who is God, and created all things out of nothing, cannot make Himself present in His body in more places than one, wheresoever He wills, in a supernatural and divine manner. It is certain that this does not happen in the order of nature but by that power of God which is above all the order of nature. . . . In these thoughts concerning the divine and spiritual and heavenly and supernatural presence of the body of Christ in more places than one without any multiplication or extension of the body I see no impiety to call for rebuke. . . . Why must he be thought to sin who believes that the Lord from heaven, sitting at the right hand of God the Father, really and actually feeds us here on earth with His crucified flesh and His shed blood by the power of His deity; and that for this purpose there is no need that He place His flesh and His blood locally here on earth at that point of space where the mysteries are celebrated? And, on the other hand, how does another sin who believes that the love of Christ the Lord towards us is so great that He wills to be present in His mysteries with His body, and to enter the roof of our mouth in a divine and spiritual and heavenly and supernatural manner, so that His body thus present may fill the whole man with His deity? If there is any error here, it is a pious error. If it is maintained that it cannot happen, there is no impiety in my judgment in believing that it does happen. The horrible deductions which are drawn about the going down into the belly and to the draught may be urged against the papists; but they are blasphemous calumnies against those who maintain this presence in the action of the mystery only, that is, while the mystery is eaten and drunk, and do not believe or think of any other actual or local presence of the body." [1]

"Since this Sacrament is a commemoration of the death and passion of the Lord, it follows that the bread is not related to the flesh simply, such as the flesh is now in glory, but such as it was on the altar of the cross; and in like manner that the wine is related to the blood, not to that which is now in the glorified body of the Lord, but to that which flowed from the wounds of the body of the Lord." [2]

"The blessed state of glory has nothing in common with the

[1] Pp. 26-32.   [2] P. 40.

symbols of Christ's crucified body and shed blood ; for in this Sacrament is the showing forth of the death of the Lord, not of His glory and resurrection." [1]

" In vain is the bread believed to be transubstantiated into the body of Christ glorious and endowed with immortality, to be carried about in processions and reserved in secret places and adored, since the Sacrament is a Sacrament of His death and passion, not of glory and immortality. . . . It is clear that the spiritual and heavenly part of the Eucharist is not any kind of body of the Lord but the bloody and sacrificed body ; and so it is not any blood that is to be understood but so far as it is the blood of the new covenant shed for the remission of sins." [2]

John Jewel was born in 1522. The date of his ordination is not known. In 1551 he received a preaching licence. About that time, while resident in Oxford, he held the cure of Sunningwell near Abingdon. During the latter part of Mary's reign he was a refugee at Frankfort, Strasburg, and Zurich. On the accession of Elizabeth he returned to England. In 1560 he was consecrated Bishop of Salisbury. In 1571 he died. His most important writings are his sermon preached at Paul's Cross in 1560, his Letters to Dr. Cole of the same date ; and the *Reply unto M. Harding's Answer*, the *Apologia Ecclesiae Anglicanae*, and the *Defence of the Apology of the Church of England*, all published between 1562 and 1571.

Jewel's works, like those of his opponent Harding, are marked by unseemly language and a controversial spirit, and, though learned and acute, are painful reading. His teaching concerning the Eucharist closely resembles that of Bucer ; [3] and, while denying that the consecrated Sacrament is the body of Christ, he expresses belief in a specific participation of the body of Christ in heaven by faith through the reception of the Sacrament.

" We feed not the people of God with bare signs and figures, but teach them that the Sacraments of Christ be holy mysteries, and that in the ministration thereof Christ is set before us even as He was crucified upon the cross ; and that therein we may behold the remission of our sins, and our reconciliation unto God, and, as Chrysostom briefly saith, ' Christ's great benefit, and our salvation '. Herein we teach the people, not that a naked sign or token, but

[1] P. 46.   [2] Pp. 54, 56.   [3] See pp. 43-48, *supra*.

that Christ's body and blood indeed and verily is given unto us; that we verily eat it; that we verily drink it; that we verily be relieved and live by it; that we are bones of His bones, and flesh of His flesh; that Christ dwelleth in us, and we in Him. Yet we say not, either that the substance of the bread or wine is done away; or that Christ's body is let down from heaven, or made really or fleshly present in the Sacrament. We are taught, according to the doctrine of the old fathers, to lift up our hearts to heaven, and there to feed upon the Lamb of God. . . . Spiritually and with the mouth of our faith we eat the body of Christ and drink His blood, even as verily as His body was verily broken, and His blood verily shed upon the cross. . . . The bread that we receive with our bodily mouths is an earthly thing, and therefore a figure, as the water in Baptism is likewise also a figure; but the body of Christ that thereby is represented, and there is offered unto our faith, is the thing itself, and no figure. And in respect of the glory thereof, we have no regard unto the figure. . . . We put a difference between the sign and the thing itself that is signified. . . . We seek Christ above in heaven, and imagine not Him to be present bodily upon the earth. . . . The body of Christ is to be eaten by faith only, and none otherwise." [1]

"The bread of the Sacrament is one thing. . . . The flesh of Christ is another. The bread entereth only into the bodily mouth: Christ's flesh entereth only into the soul. Without eating of that bread of the Sacrament we may be saved: without eating of Christ's flesh we can never be saved." [2]

"So great difference is there between the Sacrament and the body of Christ. The Sacrament passeth into the belly: Christ's body passeth into the soul. The Sacrament is upon earth: Christ's body is in heaven. The Sacrament is corruptible: Christ's body is glorious. The Sacrament is the sign: Christ's body is the thing signified. . . . This banquet . . . is not the outward or bare Sacrament, but Christ's very body and blood, which are represented unto us by the Sacrament." [3]

"Bread and wine are holy and heavenly mysteries of the body and blood of Christ, and . . . by them Christ Himself, being the true Bread of eternal life, is so presently given unto us as that by faith we verily receive His body and His blood. . . . Christ doth truly

[1] *A Reply unto M. Harding's Answer, Works*, i. 448, 449, Parker Society's edition.
[2] *The Defence of the Apology, op. cit.* iii, 448, 449.
[3] *Ibid*, 472, 473.

and presently give His own self in His Sacraments; in Baptism, that we may put Him on; and in His Supper, that we may eat Him by faith and spirit, and may have everlasting life by His cross and blood. . . . Christ Himself altogether is so offered and given us in these mysteries that we may certainly know we be flesh of His flesh and bones of His bones, and that Christ continueth in us and we in Him. And therefore in celebrating these mysteries the people are to good purpose exhorted, before they come to receive the Holy Communion, to lift up their hearts, and to direct their minds to heavenward, because He is there by whom we must be full fed and live."[1]

"The patriarchs and prophets and people of God, which lived before the birth of Christ, did by faith eat His flesh and drink His blood. . . . Whosoever believed in Christ, they were nourished by Him then, as we are now. They did not see Christ; He was not yet born; He had not yet a natural body; yet did they eat His body; He had not yet any blood; yet did they drink His blood. They believed that it was He in whom the promises should be fulfilled, that He should be that blessed Seed in whom all nations should be blessed. Thus they believed, thus they received and did eat His body. . . . If they did eat the same meat, if the things, that is, the matter of their Sacraments were all one with ours, if their faith were all one with our faith, what difference is there between their and our eating? As they did eat Christ by faith, and not by the mouth of the body, so we eat Christ by faith, and not by the mouth of our body. . . . A Sacrament is a figure or token: the body of Christ is figured or tokened. The Sacrament-bread is bread, it is not the body of Christ: the body of Christ is flesh, it is no bread. The bread is beneath: the body is above. The bread is on the Table: the body is in heaven. The bread is in the mouth: the body is in the heart. . . . The Sacrament is eaten as well of the wicked as of the faithful: the body is only eaten of the faithful."[2]

In Harding's *Answer to M. Jewel's Challenge* he had distinguished between the presence of Christ in heaven and the presence of Christ in the Mass in the following terms:—

"The body of Christ . . . according unto His word by His power . . . is made present in the blessed Sacrament of the altar

[1] *Apologia Ecclesiae Anglicanae*, op. cit. iii. 13, 14, 63, 64.
[2] *A Treatise of the Sacraments Gathered out of Certain Sermons which Bishop Jewel Preached at Salisbury*, op. cit. ii. 1119-21.

under the form of bread and wine, wheresoever the same is duly
consecrated according to His institution in His holy Supper; and
that not after a gross or carnal manner, but spiritually and supernaturally, and yet substantially; not by local but by substantial
presence; not by manner of quantity, or filling of a place, or by
changing of place, or by leaving His sitting on the right hand of
the Father, but in such a manner as God only knoweth, and yet doth
us to understand by faith the truth of His very presence, far passing all man's capacity to comprehend the manner how. . . . He is
verily both in heaven at the right hand of the Father in His visible
and corporal form, very God and Man, after which manner He is
there and not here; and also in the Sacrament invisibly and
spiritually, both God and Man in a mystery; so as the granting of
the one may stand without denial of the other, no contradiction
found in these beings, but only a distinction in the way and manner
of being." [1]

On this distinction, in which Harding followed the lines of
the mediæval theologians [2] and of the Council of Trent, [3] the
terms of which resembled Gardiner's words in his *Explication
and Assertion of the True Catholic Faith Touching the Most
Blessed Sacrament of the Altar*, [4] Jewel comments with much
scorn and ridicule. It is, he says, "a sweet mist, to carry away
the simple in the dark," "a new-devised difference"; to make it
is to "dissemble in dark speeches"; it is "a very toy, only meet
to beguile children"; "unless this man were fast asleep, he
could never fall into so deep a dream". [5]

Consistently with his opinion that the consecrated Sacrament is not the body of Christ, Jewel repudiates adoration
of the Sacrament or of the body of Christ there present, and
limits the adoration of Christ to the adoration of Him in
heaven.

"The body of Christ, sitting above all heavens, is worshipped of
us, being here beneath in earth. . . . The eating thereof and the
worshipping must join together. But where we eat it, there must
we worship it; therefore must we worship it sitting in heaven. . . .

---

[1] Harding, *An Answer to M. Jewel's Challenge* in Jewel's *Works*, *op.
cit.* i. 480, 481.

[2] See vol. i. pp. 305, 321, 322, 331-33, 340, *supra.*

[3] See pp. 90, 99, *supra.*   [4] See pp. 153, 154, *supra.*

[5] *A Reply unto M. Harding's Answer*, *op. cit.* i. 483-85.

Christ's body is in heaven; thither therefore must we direct our hearts; there must we feed; there must we refresh ourselves; and there must we worship it." [1]

"Touching the adoration of the Sacrament, M. Harding is not able to show neither any commandment of Christ nor any word or example of the Apostles or ancient fathers concerning the same. . . . The matter is great, and cannot be attempted without great danger. To give the honour of God to a creature that is no God, it is manifest idolatry. . . . The bread of the Sacrament is not that bread of which Christ speaketh in the sixth of St. John, but very material bread indeed." [2]

"If M. Harding will . . . demand wherefore we adore not the Sacrament with godly honour, the godly simple man may make him this answer : Because it was ordained reverently to be received, and not to be adored, as a Sacrament, and not as God. For in all the Scriptures and holy fathers we have neither commandment to force us hereto nor example to lead us hereto. We adore the body of Christ, not only for the turning of a hand, while the priest is able to hold up the Sacrament, and that with doubt of ourselves, whether we do well or no; which thing is utterly uncomfortable and dangerous and full of terror to the conscience ; but we worship that blessed and glorious body, as that blessed martyr St. Stephen did, being in heaven at the right hand of the power of God, and therefore without doubt and danger, and that at all times and for ever." [3]

"Neither do we only adore Christ as very God, but also we worship [4] and reverence the Sacrament and holy mystery of Christ's body ; and, as St. Augustine teacheth us, 'We worship the Baptism of Christ, wheresoever it be'.[5] We worship the word of God, according to this counsel of Anastasius, "Let them diligently hear and faithfully worship the words of God'.[6] Briefly, we worship all other like things in such religious wise unto Christ belonging. But these things we use and reverence as holy, and appointed

[1] *Sermon at Paul's Cross, op. cit.* i. 12.
[2] *A Reply unto M. Harding's Answer, op. cit.* i. 516.
[3] *Ibid.* 551, 552.
[4] The context shows that the word " worship " is here used in the sense of " reverence ".
[5] St. Augustine, *Ep.* lxxxvii. 9, " Baptismum Christi ubique veneramur ".
[6] Pseudo-Anastasius I., quoted in *Decret.* III. i. 68, " Non sedentes sed venerabiliter curvi in conspectu Evangelii stantes Dominica verba intente audiant et fideliter adorent ".

or commanded by Christ; but we adore them not with godly honour, as Christ Himself." [1]

Jewel's doctrine of the Eucharistic sacrifice is harmonious with his doctrine of the presence. He denies that there is on the altar a sacrifice of the body and blood of Christ. He affirms a remembrance of Christ's death made to Christians in the Eucharist, and a sacrifice of praise and thanksgiving.

"The priest in the canon . . . saith. that he offereth and presenteth up Christ unto His Father, which is an open blasphemy. For, contrariwise, Christ presenteth up us, and maketh us a sweet oblation in the sight of God His Father." [2]

"This sacrifice [that is, of Christ on the cross] is revived, and freshly laid out before our eyes in the ministration of the holy mysteries."

"The ministration of the holy mysteries, in a phrase and manner of speech, is also the same sacrifice; because it layeth forth the death and blood of Christ so plainly and so evidently before our eyes. . . . Thus may the sacrifice of the Holy Communion be called Christ; to wit, even so as the ministration of the same is called the passion or the death of Christ."

"We offer up Christ, that is to say, an example, a commemoration, a remembrance of the death of Christ. This kind of sacrifice was never denied; but M. Harding's real sacrifice was yet never proved."

"The ministration of the Holy Communion is sometimes of the ancient fathers called an 'unbloody sacrifice,' not in respect of any corporal or fleshly presence that is imagined to be there without blood-shedding, but for that it representeth and reporteth unto our minds that one and everlasting sacrifice that Christ made in His body upon the cross. . . . This remembrance and oblation of praises and rendering of thanks unto God for our redemption in the blood of Christ is called of the old fathers 'an unbloody sacrifice'. . . . Our prayers, our praises, our thanksgiving unto God for our salvation in the death of Christ is called an unbloody sacrifice." [3]

Edmund Grindal was born in 1519. He was ordained in 1544 by the Bishop of Winchester. During the reign of Mary he took refuge at Strasburg and other places abroad. He re-

---

[1] *A Reply unto M. Harding's Answer, op. cit.* i. 514.

[2] *Sermon at Paul's Cross, op. cit.* i. 9.

[3] *A Reply unto M. Harding's Answer, op. cit.* i. 167, ii. 726, 729, 734, 735.

turned to England in December, 1558. In 1559 he was consecrated Bishop of London. In 1570 he became Archbishop of York, and in 1575 Archbishop of Canterbury. In 1583 he died. His opinions on the Eucharist, as expressed in his *Fruitful Dialogue between Custom and Verity*, much resembled those of Cranmer, though to some extent marked by the doctrine held by Bucer.

"It is not strange, nor a thing unwont in the Scriptures, to call one thing by another's name. So that you can no more of necessity enforce the changing of the bread into Christ's body in the Sacrament because the words be plain, 'This is My body,' than the wife's flesh to be the natural and real body and flesh of the husband because it is written, 'They are not two, but one flesh,'[1] or the altar of stone to be very God because Moses with evident and plain words pronounced it to be 'The mighty God of Israel'.[2] . . . Nothing is done in remembrance of itself. But the Sacrament is used in the remembrance of Christ. Therefore the Sacrament is not Christ. Christ never devoured Himself. Christ did eat the Sacrament with His Apostles. Ergo, the Sacrament is not Christ Himself."[3]

"Whereas I say that Christ's body must be received and taken with faith, I mean not that you shall pluck down Christ from heaven and put Him in your faith as in a visible place; but that you must with your faith rise and spring up to Him, and leaving this world dwell above in heaven, putting all your trust, comfort, and consolation in Him which suffered grievous bondage to set you at liberty and to make you free, creeping into His wounds, which were so cruelly pierced and dented for your sake. So shall you feed on the body of Christ; so shall you suck the blood that was poured out and shed for you. This is the spiritual, the very true, the only eating of Christ's body."[4]

"Seeing all the old fathers do constantly agree in one, that the body of Christ is ascended into heaven, and there remaineth at the right hand of the Father, and cannot be in more than one place, I do conclude that the Sacrament is not the body of Christ; first, because it is not in heaven, neither sitteth at the Father's right hand; moreover, because it is in a hundred thousand boxes, whereas Christ's body filleth but one place; furthermore, if the bread were turned into the body of Christ, then it would necessarily follow that sinners and unpenitent persons receive the body of Christ."[5]

---

[1] Gen. ii. 24; St. Matt. xix. 6.   [2] Gen. xxxiii. 20.
[3] Pp. 41-43 (Parker Society's edition).   [4] P. 46.   [5] P. 55.

Edwin Sandys was born in the same year as Grindal, 1519. In 1553, when Edward VI. died, he was Vice-Chancellor of the University of Cambridge. At the beginning of the reign of Mary he was imprisoned for nearly nine months. On being released, he took refuge abroad. On hearing the news of Queen Mary's death in 1558, he returned to England. In 1559 he was consecrated Bishop of Worcester. He succeeded Grindal as Bishop of London in 1570, and as Archbishop of York in 1576. The passages in his *Sermons* treating of the Eucharist contain much the same doctrine as that of Grindal.

"In this Sacrament there are two things, a visible sign and an invisible grace : there is a visible sacramental sign of bread and wine, and there is the thing and matter signified, namely, the body and blood of Christ : there is an earthly matter and an heavenly matter. The outward sacramental sign is common to all, as well the bad as the good. Judas received the Lord's bread, but not that bread which is the Lord to the faithful receiver. The spiritual part, that which feedeth the soul, only the faithful do receive. For he cannot be partaker of the body of Christ which is no member of Christ's body. This food offered us at the Lord's Table is to feed our souls withal ; it is meat for the mind, and not for the belly. Our souls, being spiritual, can neither receive nor digest that which is corporal ; they feed only upon spiritual food. It is the spiritual eating that giveth life. 'The flesh,' saith Christ, 'doth nothing profit.'[1] We must lift up ourselves from these external and earthly signs, and like eagles fly up and soar aloft, there to feed on Christ, which sitteth on the right hand of His Father, whom the heavens shall keep until the latter day. From thence and from no other altar shall He come in His natural body to judge both quick and dead. His natural body is local, for else it were not a natural body : His body is there, therefore not here : for a natural body doth not occupy sundry places at once. Here we have a Sacrament, a sign, a memorial, a commemoration, a representation, a figure effectual, of the body and blood of Christ. . . . Seeing then that Christ in His natural body is absent from hence, seeing He is risen and is not here, seeing He hath left the world and is gone to His Father, 'How shall I,' saith St. Augustine, 'lay hold on Him which is absent ? How shall I put my hand into heaven ? Send up thy faith, and thou hast taken hold' ; 'Why preparest thou thy teeth ?

[1] St. John vi. 63.

Believe, and thou hast eaten.'[1] Thy teeth shall not do Him
violence, neither thy stomach contain His glorious body. Thy
faith must reach up into heaven. By faith He is seen, by faith
He is touched, by faith He is digested. Spiritually by faith we
feed upon Christ, when we steadfastly believe that His body was
broken, and His blood shed for us, upon the cross, by which sacrifice, offered once for all, as sufficient for all, our sins were freely
remitted, blotted out, and washed away. This is our heavenly
bread, our spiritual food. This doth strengthen our souls and
cheer our hearts. Sweeter it is unto us than honey when we are
certified by this outward Sacrament of the inward grace given unto
us through His death, when in Him we are assured of remission of
sins and eternal life. . . . Time will not suffer me to let you see
the absurdities of the popish unsavoury opinions in this matter,
neither to confute their vain allegations and false collections, abus-
ing the Scriptures, dreaming evermore with the gross Capernaites
of a carnal and a fleshly eating. Behold the one part of this Sacrament consecrated is termed bread, the other a cup, by the Apostle
himself."[2]

"In the Eucharist or Supper of the Lord our corporal tasting of
the visible elements bread and wine showeth the heavenly nourishing of our souls unto life by the mystical participation of the glorious
body and blood of Christ. For inasmuch as He saith of one of
these sacred elements, 'This is My body which is given for you,'
and of the other, 'This is My blood,' He giveth us plainly to understand that all the graces which may flow from the body and blood
of Christ Jesus are in a mystery here not represented only but presented unto us. So then, although we see nothing, feel and taste
nothing, but bread and wine, nevertheless let us not doubt at all
but that He spiritually performeth that which He doth declare and
promise by His visible and outward signs; that is to say, that in
this Sacrament there is offered unto the Church that very true and
heavenly bread which feedeth and nourisheth us unto life eternal,
that sacred blood which will cleanse us from sin and make us pure
in the day of trial. Again, in that He saith, 'Take, eat: drink ye
all of this,' He evidently declareth that His body and blood are
by this Sacrament assured to be no less ours than His, He being
incorporate into us, and as it were made one with us. That He
became Man, it was for our sake: for our behoof and benefit He

[1] St. Augustine, *In Joh. Ev. Tract.* l. 4, xxv. 12; *cf.* vol. i. p. 92, *supra.*

[2] Pp. 88, 89 (Parker Society's edition).

suffered: for us He rose again: for us He ascended into heaven; and finally for us He will come again in judgment. And thus hath He made Himself all ours; ours His passions, ours His merits, ours His victory, ours His glory; and therefore He giveth Himself and all His in this Sacrament wholly unto us. The reason and course whereof is this. In His word He hath promised and certified us of remission of sins, in His death; of righteousness, in His merits; of life, in His resurrection; and in His ascension, of heavenly and everlasting glory. This promise we take hold of by faith, which is the instrument of our salvation; but because our faith is weak and staggering through the frailty of our mortal flesh, He hath given us this visible Sacrament as a seal and sure pledge of His irrevocable promise, for the more assurance and confirmation of our feeble faith. . . . To bear with our infirmity, and to make us more secure of His promise, to His writing and word He added these outward signs and seals, to establish our faith, and to certify us that His promise is most certain. He giveth us therefore these holy and visible signs of bread and wine, and saith, 'Take and eat, this is My body and blood,' giving unto the signs the names which are proper to the things signified by them; as we use to do even in common speech, when the sign is a lively representation and image of the thing." [1]

"In the time of the Gospel the Apostles had, and at this day also Christians have, their sacrifices, which, being faithfully offered, are graciously accepted in the sight of God. Sacrificing is a voluntary action whereby we worship God, offering Him somewhat in token that we acknowledge Him to be the Lord, and ourselves His servants. . . . In the Scriptures I find a threefold priesthood allowed of God, —a Levitical priesthood such as that of Aaron and his sons, a royal priesthood figured in Melchizedek and verified in Christ, a spiritual priesthood belonging generally to all Christians. . . . Where the popish priesthood taketh footing, in what ground the foundation thereof is laid, 1 cannot find in the Scriptures. Antichrist is the author of that priesthood: to him they sacrifice, him they serve. . . . There remaineth no other sacrifice to be daily offered but the sacrifice of 'righteousness' which we must all offer. At the hands of the minister it is required that he feed the flock committed unto his charge; this is righteousness in him, it is his sacrifice. . . . Let magistrates . . . execute justice without fear or favour when need requireth, and so shall they offer up the sacrifice. . . . We must all sacrifice unto the Lord with our goods, with our minds, and

[1] Pp. 302-4.

with our bodies. . . . Let us . . . offer Him sacrifice, as of our bodies, so likewise of our minds, repentance and praise. . . . The other sacrifice of the mind is praise, which consisteth in thanksgiving and petition. . . . The second part of this our sacrifice of praise is to pour out requests and supplications." [1]

Sandys thus affirms, like Cranmer, that faithful communicants receive the grace and virtue of the body of Christ. He appears to have held, like Bucer, that they are so uplifted by faith in the reception of the Sacrament as to have actual participation of the body of Christ in heaven. He leaves no room for a sacrifice in the Eucharist other than such as there may be in all good actions, repentance, praise, thanksgiving, and prayer.

Thomas Becon supplies a representative of the most extreme type of the English Reformers. He was born in 1511 or 1512; he was ordained about 1538; he became Vicar of Brensett in Kent. On the accession of Edward VI. he was appointed Rector of St. Stephen, Walbrook, and Archbishop Cranmer made him one of his chaplains and one of the six preachers of Canterbury Cathedral. When Mary became queen, he was deprived of his benefice and was imprisoned as a seditious preacher. After seven months' imprisonment he was released, and took refuge at Strasburg. On the death of Queen Mary he returned to England, and was re-instated in his preferments; and afterwards became Rector of Buckland in Hertfordshire, Vicar of Christ Church, Newgate Street, and Rector of St. Dionis Backchurch. He died about 1570. Most of his writings belong to the reign of Elizabeth.

The violence of Becon's language, and its frequently unseemly and sometimes indecent character, have tended to discredit his works. Yet he was a man of learning and ability, and his writings, painful reading as they are, are well worth study as illustrating lines of thought of his day. His repudiation of the sacrifice of the Mass included a rejection of any "proper" or "propitiatory" or "satisfactory" or "expiatory" sacrifice in the Eucharist; as to the Eucharistic presence, he appears to have wavered between Virtualism, such as that held by Cranmer, and the Zwinglian opinion that the Sacrament is merely symbolical of Christ.

[1]Pp. 410-15.

"The papists cannot be content with this doctrine, that the Supper of the Lord (which they more gladly term 'the Mass') should be a memorial or remembrance of that sacrifice which Christ Himself offered on the cross; but they will have it the self-same sacrifice, of the same virtue, strength, efficacy, might, and power, to save the souls both of the quick and dead. . . . They say that they offer up Christ the Son of God unto His heavenly Father, for a sacrifice both for the sins of the quick and of the dead. . . . To stablish a new sacrifice to take away sin is nothing else than to affirm and grant that the old sacrifice (I mean the death of Christ) is either of no force or else it is imperfect. For if the death of Christ be of full force and sufficiently perfect, yea, and to the uttermost able to take away the sins of the whole world (as it is indeed), what need we the Missal sacrifice lately brought in by the devil and antichrist? . . . Forasmuch as the celebration of the Lord's Supper is a certain representative image of the passion of Christ, which is the alone true sacrifice, therefore the holy fathers many times call the Lord's Supper a sacrifice. Now, if the Lord's Supper be not properly a sacrifice, but only a memorial of the true sacrifice, which is the passion and death of Christ, how can the Massing priests brag that their Mass (in the which many things are done contrary to the institution of Christ) is a propitiatory, satisfactory, and expiatory sacrifice for the sins of the quick and of the dead? . . . The Lord's Supper, although an holy institution or ordinance of Christ, is not a sacrifice to put away sin, but a memorial of that one and alone true sacrifice which Christ Himself offered on the cross for the abolishing of the world's sin; and . . . the Mass, which is but the invention of man, and containeth in it many absurdities, abuses, and errors, is no propitiatory, expiatory, or satisfactory sacrifice, as the adversaries brag, to put away the sins of the quick and of the dead, or, as some write, necessary *ad salutem*." [1]

"The Massmonger is become so impudent and without shame that he feareth nothing most ungodly and wickedly to affirm, teach, and hold that Christ by His death did only put away original sin; [2] and as for all other sins, saith he, they must be purged, cleansed, and put away by the sacrifice of the Mass: which is so great a blasphemy against the Son of God, against His one and alone everlasting sacrifice, against His passion, death, and blood, whereby alone we are for ever and ever sanctified, made holy, and sealed up

[1] *A New Catechism, Works*, ii. 246-51, Parker Society's edition.
[2] See pp. 26, 68-75, *supra*.

unto everlasting life, that none of Satan himself can be devised or imagined greater or more heinous." [1]

"The Lord's Supper . . . after the definition of St. Paul . . . is the partaking of the body and blood of Christ. . . . The Lord's Supper is an holy and heavenly banquet, in the which the faithful Christians, besides the corporal eating of the bread and the outward drinking of the wine, do spiritually through faith both eat the body of Christ and drink His blood, unto the confirmation of their faith, the comfort of their conscience, and the salvation of their souls. . . . The Supper . . . is a spiritual food, in which Christ Jesus the Son of God witnesses that He is the living Bread, wherewith our souls are fed unto everlasting life. . . . The Supper of the Lord is an Holy Sacrament instituted of the Lord Jesu, to be a commemoration and a perpetual remembrance of His body-breaking and blood-shedding, yea, of His passion and death on the altar of the cross, that the faithful communicants, eating and receiving those holy mysteries (I mean the bread and wine sanctified in the body and blood of Christ), should earnestly set before their eyes the death of Christ and all the benefits which they have received through the same ; that is to say, the grace, favour, and mercy of God, remission of sins, quietness of conscience, freedom from the captivity of Satan, from the curse of the law, from the sting of death, and from everlasting damnation, the gift of the Holy Ghost, and assurance of eternal life ; and that by this means they should be provoked and stirred up to magnify and praise our heavenly Father, for this His unoutspeakable kindness and exceeding great love. Or on this wise briefly : The Supper of the Lord is a memorial of Christ's death." [2]

"The doctrine of Transubstantiation . . . is a papistical, wicked, and devilish error. . . . As the doctrine of Transubstantiation is vain and false . . . so likewise the doctrine of Christ's corporal presence in the Sacrament is most vain, false, and erroneous. . . . Forasmuch as the body of Christ, although immortal and glorified, is, remaineth, and abideth still a creature, and is not swallowed up, as I may so speak, of the divine nature, but, being joined to the divine nature, abideth still a creature, and very Man, it therefore followeth most certainly that Christ's body, taken up into heaven, neither is, neither can be, both in heaven and in earth at once. . . . As touching His bodily presence, Christ is in heaven, yea, in heaven only." [3]

[1] *A Comparison between the Lord's Supper and the Pope's Mass, op. cit.* iii. 368.

[2] *A New Catechism, op. cit.* ii. 228, 229.   [3] *Ibid.* 270-72.

"Christ calleth the bread His body, not that it is His natural body indeed but because it representeth, signifieth, declareth, preacheth, and setteth forth His body unto us; and hath also, as I may so speak, certain properties with the body of Christ. For as the bread is broken of the faithful in the action of the Lord's Supper, so was Christ's body broken on the altar of the cross. And as the bread nourisheth, preserveth, and comforteth the body, when it is eaten, so likewise the body of Christ nourisheth, preserveth, and comforteth both the body and the soul of the faithful communicants. . . . The Sacrament of Christ's body and blood is called the body and blood of Christ, not that they be the things themselves, but they be so called because they be the figures, Sacraments, and representations of the things which they signify, and whereof they bear the names." [1]

"Christ is truly present at the holy banquet of His most holy body and blood, not in His humanity but in His divinity, not corporally but spiritually, not in quality and quantity but in virtue and majesty. . . . Christ . . . is none otherwise eaten and received of the godly communicants than after a spiritual and divine manner. . . . The true eating of the body of Christ, and the drinking of His blood in the Sacrament, is not corporal but spiritual, not done with the mouth of the body but with the faith of the soul." [2]

"The Sacrament of Christ's body and blood is not the very self real and natural body and blood of Christ, but an holy sign, figure, and token of His blessed body and precious blood. For this word 'Sacrament' is as much to say as a sign of a holy thing. Now that which is the sign of a thing cannot be the thing itself. And though Thy Son called the bread His body, and the wine His blood, because the disciples should the better remember the breaking of His body and the shedding of His blood (as He likewise called Himself a vine, a door, a rock, when notwithstanding He was neither natural vine, material door, or stony rock, but only likened unto them for certain properties which He hath with the vine, door, and rock), yet is neither the bread His natural body nor the wine His natural blood, as divers of the ancient doctors do declare and prove, but only a figure of His body and blood. The bread is called Christ's body because it visibly preacheth and bringeth to our remembrance the breaking of Christ's body. The wine also is called Christ's blood because it putteth us in remembrance of the shedding of Christ's blood." [3]

---

[1] *A New Catechism, op. cit.* ii. 282, 283.
[2] *Certain Articles of Christian Religion, op. cit.* iii. 430.
[3] *The Flower of Godly Prayers, op. cit.* iii. 67.

IV.

A philosophical and devotional basis for the Elizabethan policy of including in the Church of England the holders of differing opinions about the Eucharist was supplied by Richard Hooker. Hooker was born in 1553; was ordained in 1581; was successively Rector of Drayton Beauchamp, Master of the Temple, Rector of Boscombe, and Rector of Bishopsbourne; and died in 1600. His treatise *Of the Laws of Ecclesiastical Polity* contains a chapter on the Eucharist. Of Hooker's own belief concerning the Eucharistic presence it is impossible to make any detailed explicit statement. He insisted that by means of the Sacrament there is a real participation in the body and blood of Christ, and consequently in Christ Himself. So far as his own belief was concerned, he rejected Transubstantiation. Of set and deliberate purpose he abstained from expressing his own opinion as to whether the body and blood of Christ are present in the consecrated elements or are only communicated to the souls of the recipients of the Sacrament; and maintained with great clearness that, so long as men are agreed that the faithful communicant receives "the real presence of Christ's most blessed body and blood," there is no reason for parting communion because they cannot define alike the method of that presence, or its relation to the consecrated elements. Hooker's position is rather that of the Book of Common Prayer than that of the Thirty-nine Articles. The Prayer Book, as is natural in such a work, says nothing about Transubstantiation, either in the way of approval or in the way of disapproval. The Articles contain an explicit condemnation of it. Hooker contends that neither the affirmation nor the denial of Transubstantiation is of supreme importance, if only it can be agreed about the elements "that to me which take them they are the body and blood of Christ".

"Some did exceedingly fear lest Zwinglius and Oecolampadius would bring to pass that men should account of this Sacrament but only as of a shadow, destitute, empty, and void of Christ. But seeing that by opening the several opinions which have been held they are grown for aught I can see on all sides at the length to a general agreement concerning that which alone is material, namely, the real participation of Christ and of life in His body and blood by means of this Sacrament, wherefore should the world continue still distracted and rent with so manifold contentions, when there remaineth now no controversy saving only about the subject where Christ is ? Yea, even in this point no side denieth but that the soul of man is the receptacle of Christ's presence. Whereby the question is yet driven to a narrower issue, nor doth anything rest doubtful but this, whether when the Sacrament is administered Christ be whole within man only, or else His body and blood be also externally seated in the very consecrated elements themselves. . . . Is there any thing more expedite, clear, and easy than that, as Christ is termed our life because through Him we obtain life, so the parts of this Sacrament are His body and blood for that they are so to us who receiving them receive that by them which they are termed ? The bread and cup are His body and blood because they are causes instrumental upon the receipt whereof the participation of His body and blood ensueth. For that which produceth any certain effect is not vainly nor improperly said to be that very effect whereunto it tendeth. Every cause is in the effect which groweth from it. Our souls and bodies quickened to eternal life are effects the cause whereof is the Person of Christ, His body and blood are the true wellspring out of which this life floweth. So that His body and blood are in that very subject whereunto they minister life not only by effect or operation, even as the influence of the heavens is in plants, beasts, men, and in every thing which they quicken, but also by a far more divine and mystical kind of union, which maketh us one with Him even as He and the Father are one. The real presence of Christ's most blessed body and blood is not therefore to be sought for in the Sacrament, but in the worthy receiver of the Sacrament. And with this the very order of our Saviour's words agreeth, first, 'take and eat' ; then 'this is My body which was broken for you' ; first 'drink ye all of this' ; then followeth 'this is My blood of the New Testament which is shed for many for the remission of sins'. I see not which way it should be gathered by the words of Christ when and where the bread is His body or the cup His blood but only in the very heart and soul of him which receiveth them. As for the Sacraments, they really exhibit, but for aught we can gather out of that which is written of them they are not really nor do really contain in themselves that grace which with them or by them it pleaseth God to bestow. If on all sides it be confessed that the grace of Baptism is poured into the soul of man, that by water we receive it, although it be neither seated in the water nor the water changed into it, what should induce men to think that the grace of the Eucharist must needs be in the Eucharist before it can

be in us that receive it? The fruit of the Eucharist is the participation of the body and blood of Christ. There is no sentence of
Holy Scripture which saith that we cannot by this Sacrament be
made partakers of His body and blood except they be first contained
in the Sacrament or the Sacrament converted into them. 'This is
My body' and 'this is My blood' being words of promise, since we
all agree that by the Sacrament Christ doth really and truly in us
perform His promise, why do we vainly trouble ourselves with so
fierce contentions whether by Consubstantiation or else by Transubstantiation the Sacrament itself be first possessed with Christ or no?
A thing which no way can either further or hinder us howsoever it
stand, because our participation of Christ in this Sacrament depend-
eth on the co-operation of His omnipotent power which maketh it
His body and blood to us, whether with change or without alteration of the element such as they imagine we need not greatly to care
nor inquire. Take therefore that wherein all agree, and then consider by itself what cause why the rest in question should not rather
be left as superfluous than urged as necessary. It is on all sides
plainly confessed, first, that this Sacrament is a true and a real participation of Christ, who thereby imparteth Himself even His whole
entire Person as a mystical Head unto every soul that receiveth Him,
and that every such receiver doth thereby incorporate or unite Himself unto Christ as a mystical member of Him, yea, of them also
whom He acknowledgeth to be His own ; secondly, that to whom
the Person of Christ is thus communicated, to them He giveth by
the same Sacrament His Holy Spirit to sanctify them as it sanctifieth Him which is their Head ; thirdly, that what merit, force, or
virtue soever there is in His sacrificed body and blood, we freely,
fully and wholly have it by this Sacrament ; fourthly, that the effect
thereof in us is a real transmutation of our souls and bodies from
sin to righteousness, from death and corruption to immortality and
life ; fifthly, that because the Sacrament being of itself but a corruptible and earthly creature must needs be thought an unlikely
instrument to work so admirable effects in man, we are therefore to
rest ourselves altogether upon the strength of His glorious power
who is able and will bring to pass that the bread and cup which He
giveth us shall be truly the thing He promiseth. . . . Variety of
judgments and opinions argueth obscurity in those things where-
about they differ. But that which all parts receive for truth, that
which every one having sifted is by no one denied or doubted of,
must needs be matter of infallible certainty. Whereas therefore
there are but three expositions made of 'this is My body,'—the

first, 'this is in itself before participation really and truly the natural
substance of My body by reason of the coexistence which My omnipotent body hath with the sanctified element of bread,' which is the
Lutherans' interpretation ; the second, 'this is in itself and before
participation the very true and natural substance of My body, by
force of that deity which with the words of consecration abolisheth
the substance of bread and substituteth in the place thereof My
body,' which is the popish construction ; the last, 'this hallowed
food, through concurrence of divine power, is in verity and truth
unto faithful receivers instrumentally a cause of that mystical participation, whereby as I make Myself wholly theirs, so I give them in
hand an actual possession of all such saving grace as My sacrificed
body can yield, and as their souls do presently need, this is to them
and in them My body,'— of these three rehearsed interpretations
the last hath in it nothing but what the rest do all approve and acknowledge to be most true, nothing but that which the words of
Christ are on all confessed to enforce, nothing but that which the
Church of God hath always thought necessary, nothing but that which
alone is sufficient for every Christian man to believe concerning the
use and force of this Sacrament, finally nothing but that wherewith
the writings of all antiquity are consonant and all Christian confessions agreeable.   And as truth in what kind soever is by no kind of
truth gainsayed, so the mind which resteth itself on this is never
troubled with those perplexities which the other do both find, by
means of so great contradiction between their opinions and true
principles of reason grounded upon experience, nature, and sense.
. . . Where God Himself doth speak those things which either for
height or sublimity of matter or else for secrecy of performance we
are not able to reach unto, as we may be ignorant without danger,
so it can be no disgrace to confess we are ignorant.   Such as love
piety will as much as in them lieth know all things that God commandeth, but especially the duties of service which they owe to God.
As for His dark and hidden works, they prefer as becometh them in
such cases simplicity of faith before that knowledge which curiously
sifting what it should adore, and disputing too boldly of that which
the wit of man cannot search, chilleth for the most part all warmth
of zeal, and bringeth soundness of belief many times into great
hazard.   Let it therefore be sufficient for me presenting myself at
the Lord's Table to know what there I receive from Him, without
searching or inquiring of the manner how Christ performeth His
promise ; let disputes and questions, enemies to piety, abatements
of true devotion, and hitherto in this cause but over patiently

heard, let them take their rest; let curious and sharpwitted men beat their heads about what questions themselves will, the very letter of the word of Christ giveth plain security that these mysteries do as nails fasten us to His very cross, that by them we draw out, as touching efficacy, force, and virtue, even the blood of His gored side, in the wounds of our Redeemer we there dip our tongues, we are dyed red both within and without, our hunger is satisfied and our thirst for ever quenched; they are things wonderful which he feeleth, great which he seeth, and unheard of which he uttereth, whose soul is possessed of this Paschal Lamb and made joyful in the strength of this new wine; this bread hath in it more than the substance which our eyes behold, this cup hallowed with solemn benediction availeth to the endless life and welfare both of soul and body, in that it serveth as well for a medicine to heal our infirmities and purge our sins as for a sacrifice of thanksgiving, with touching it sanctifieth, it enlighteneth with belief, it truly conformeth us unto the image of Jesus Christ; what these elements are in themselves it skilleth not, it is enough that to me which take them they are the body and blood of Christ, His promise in witness hereof sufficeth, His word He knoweth which way to accomplish; why should any cogitation possess the mind of a faithful communicant but this, ' O my God, Thou art true, O my soul, thou art happy'." [1]

In the tract entitled *A Christian Letter of Certain English Protestants*, published in 1599, two years after the publication of the fifth book of Hooker's work, one of the points on which he was attacked was the description of the doctrine of Transubstantiation as "a thing which no way can either further or hinder us howsoever it stand," and the statement that "we need not greatly to care nor inquire" whether the presence of Christ in the Eucharist is "with change or without alteration in the element"; and it was observed that Transubstantiation had been described as "a thing contrary to the plain words of Scripture, overturning the nature of the Sacrament," and called "monstrous doctrine," and that Cranmer, Ridley, Hooper, Latimer, Rogers, Bradford, and others had "given their lives in witness against it".[2] A copy of this tract, preserved in the Library of Corpus Christi College, Oxford, is annotated in the margin by Hooker's own hand. These marginal notes include the following:—

"Whereas popish doctrine doth hold that priests by words of

<hr/>

[1] V. lxvii. 2, 5, 6, 7, 12.   [2] P. 34.

consecration make the real, my whole discourse is to show that God
by the Sacrament maketh the mystical body of Christ ; and that seeing in this point as well Lutherans as Papists agree with us, which
only point containeth the benefit we have of the Sacrament, it is
but needless and unprofitable for them to stand, the one upon
Consubstantiation, and upon Transubstantiation the other, which
doctrines they neither can prove nor are forced by any necessity to
maintain, but might very well surcease to urge them, if they did
heartily affect peace, and seek the quietness of the Church."

"Not to be stood upon or contended for by them, because it
[Transubstantiation] is not a thing necessary, although, because it
is false, as long as they do persist to maintain and urge it, there is
no man so gross as to think in this case we may neglect it.   Against
them it is therefore said, They ought not to stand in it as in a
matter of faith, nor to make so high account of it, inasmuch as
the Scripture doth only teach the Communion of Christ in the Holy
Sacrament, and neither the one nor the other way of preparation
thereunto.   It sufficed to have believed this, and not by determining
the manner how God bringeth it to pass, to have entangled themselves with opinions so strange, so impossible to be proved true." [1]

With this description of Transubstantiation as "false" may
be compared a sentence in a later chapter of the *Laws of Ecclesiastical Polity* than that already quoted, where Hooker says :—

"The greatest difference between us and " "popish communicants " "is the Sacrament of the body and blood of Christ, whose
name in the service of our Communion we celebrate with due
honour, which they in the error of their Mass profane.   As therefore on our part to hear Mass were an open departure from that sincere profession wherein we stand, so if they on the other side receive
our Communion, they give us the strongest pledge of fidelity that
man can demand." [2]

The present writer cannot agree either with those who have
claimed Hooker as himself accepting a doctrine which connects
the presence of the body of Christ with the consecrated elements
previous to reception [3] or with those who consider that he definitely intended to avow a receptionist doctrine. [4]   The sentence,

---

[1] On pp. 33, 34.   The above passages are quoted in Keble's notes on
V. lxvii. 6.
[2] V. lxviii. 8.   [3] See *e.g.* Staley, *Richard Hooker*, pp. 150, 151.
[4] See *e.g.* Bayne, *Of the Laws of Ecclesiastical Polity : the Fifth Book*,
pp. cvii-cxx.

"The real presence of Christ's most blessed body and blood is not therefore to be sought for in the Sacrament, but in the worthy receiver of the Sacrament," when viewed in its whole context, is plainly seen to demand an emphasis on the words "sought for," and to mean that the point to be considered is not as to the presence in the Sacrament but as to the presence in the communicant. On the other hand, the sentence, "This bread hath in it more than the substance which our eyes behold," is precluded by the rest of the passage in which it stands from implying a presence previous to Communion. Hooker's object was to concentrate attention on the fact of the reception of Christ by the faithful communicant on which he thought all might agree, and to avoid controversy about the further question as to the relation of the presence of Christ to the external elements.[1]

The subject of the Eucharistic sacrifice is nowhere discussed at length by Hooker; and in the few references to it there is considerable obscurity.

"They which honour the Law as an image of the wisdom of God Himself are notwithstanding to know that the same had an end in Christ. But what? Was the Law so abolished in Christ that after His ascension the office of priests became immediately wicked, and the very name hateful, as importing the exercise of an ungodly function? No, as long as the glory of the Temple continued, and till the time of that final desolation was accomplished, the very Christian Jews did continue with their sacrifices and other parts of legal service. That very law therefore which our Saviour was to abolish did not so soon become unlawful to be observed as some imagine; nor was it afterwards unlawful so far that the very name of altar, of priest, of sacrifice itself, should be banished out of the world. For though God do now hate sacrifice, whether it be heathenish or Jewish, so that we cannot have the same things which they had but with impiety, yet unless there be some greater let than the only evacuation of the Law of Moses, the names themselves may (I hope) be retained without sin in respect of that proportion which things established by our Saviour have unto them

---

[1] The ablest and most impartial treatment of Hooker's Eucharistic doctrine is in the present Bishop of Oxford's (Dr. Paget) *An Introduction to the Fifth Book of Hooker's Treatise Of the Laws of Ecclesiastical Polity*, pp. 172-83, 199, 200. The passage least easy to harmonise with the Bishop's exposition, which is followed above, is that in V. lxviii. 8, quoted on p. 244, *supra*.

which by Him are abrogated. And so throughout all the writings of the ancient fathers we see that the words which were do continue ; the only difference is that, whereas before they had a literal, they now have a metaphorical use, and are as so many notes of remembrance unto us that what they did signify in the letter is accomplished in the truth. And as no man can deprive the Church of this liberty, to use names whereunto the Law was accustomed, so neither are we generally forbidden the use of things which the Law hath, though it neither command us any particular rite, as it did the Jews a number, and the weightiest which it did command them are unto us in the Gospel prohibited." [1]

" It serveth as well for a medicine to heal our infirmities and purge our sins as for a sacrifice of thanksgiving." [2]

" For anything myself can discern herein, I suppose that they which have bent their study to search more diligently such matters do for the most part find that names advisedly given had either regard unto that which is naturally most proper ; or if perhaps to some other speciality, to that which is sensibly most eminent in the thing signified ; and concerning popular use of words that which the wisdom of their inventors did intend thereby is not commonly thought of, but by the name the thing altogether conceived in gross, as may appear in that if you ask of the common sort what any certain word, for example, what a priest doth signify, their manner is not to answer, a priest is a clergyman which offereth sacrifice to God, but they show some particular person whom they use to call by that name. And, if we list to descend to grammar, we are told by masters in those schools that the word priest hath his right place ἐπὶ τοῦ ψιλῶς προεστῶτος τῆς θεραπείας τοῦ Θεοῦ, ' in him whose mere function or charge is the service of God '. Howbeit, because the most eminent part both of heathenish and Jewish service did consist in sacrifice, when learned men declare what the word priest doth properly signify according to the mind of the first imposer of that name, their ordinary scholies do well expound it to imply sacrifice. Seeing then that sacrifice is now no part of the Church ministry, how should the name of priesthood be thereunto rightly applied ? Surely even as St. Paul applieth the name of flesh [3] unto that very substance of fishes which hath a proportionable correspondence to flesh, although it be in nature another thing. Whereupon when philosophers will speak warily, they make a difference between flesh in one sort of living creatures and that other substance in the rest which hath but a kind of analogy to flesh :

[1] IV. xi. 10.　　　[2] V. lxvii. 12.　　　[3] 1 Cor. xv. 39.

the Apostle contrariwise having matter of greater importance whereof to speak nameth indifferently both flesh. The fathers of the Church of Christ with like security of speech call usually the ministry of the Gospel priesthood in regard of that which the Gospel hath proportionable to ancient sacrifices, namely the Communion of the blessed body and blood of Christ, although it have properly now no sacrifice." [1]

In some sense then Hooker regarded the Eucharist as having a sacrificial aspect. He calls it " a sacrifice of thanksgiving "; and by describing it as " proportionable to ancient sacrifices," and as having a " proportion " to the sacrifices of the Mosaic Law, appears to have attached some fuller meaning to this phrase than was attached to it by the continental Reformers in general. Yet he says that "sacrifice is now no part of the Church ministry," and that " the Gospel " has " properly now no sacrifice," and repudiates " heathenish " and " Jewish " " sacrifice " as hated by God. Probably this obscure treatment is intentional. To assign small importance to the sacrificial aspect of the Eucharist would be harmonious with the position taken up in regard to the Eucharistic presence. If only the Communion aspect of the Eucharist is emphasised, it is easy to maintain that the one important question is that of what the communicant receives; as the sacrificial aspect is considered, the importance of the question whether the presence of the body of Christ is to be connected with the consecrated elements before reception is great.

In his Sermon on Justification, preached in 1586, twelve years before the publication of the fifth book of the *Laws of Ecclesiastical Polity*, Hooker uses the word " heresies " to describe the doctrines of the Church of Rome concerning Transubstantiation and the propitiatory sacrifice in the Eucharist; and contends that the holding of such " heresies " is no bar to salvation only because of ignorance on the part of those who hold them, and because in this ignorance the " heresies " did not prevent them from keeping " the foundation of faith ".

"In the Church of Rome it is maintained . . . that the bread in the Eucharist is transubstantiated into Christ; that it is to be adored, and to be offered up unto God as a sacrifice propitiatory for quick and dead. . . . Some heresies do concern things only believed, as

transubstantiating of sacramental elements in the Eucharist ; some
concern things which are practised also and put in ure, as adoration
of the elements transubstantiated." [1]

"The heresies of the Church of Rome, their dogmatical positions
opposite unto Christian truth, what man among ten thousand did
ever understand ? Of them which understand Roman heresies, and
allow them, all are not alike partakers in the action of allowing." [2]

"They be not all faithless that are either weak in assenting to
the truth, or stiff in maintaining things any way opposite to the truth
of Christian doctrine.   But as many as hold the foundation which is
precious, though they hold it but weakly, and as it were by a slender
thread, although they frame many base and unsuitable things upon
it, things that cannot abide the trial of the fire, yet shall they pass the
fiery trial and be saved, which indeed have builded themselves upon
the rock, which is the foundation of the Church.   If then our fathers
did not hold the foundation of faith, there is no doubt but they
were faithless.   If many of them held it, then is there herein no
impediment but that many of them might be saved." [3]

Obviously, these allusions to the Eucharistic doctrines of the
Church of Rome are much more hostile to those doctrines than
the more balanced attitude of the *Laws of Ecclesiastical Polity* ;
and this hostility is emphasised by the fact that they occur in a
context where Hooker is maintaining that many who have held
the doctrines of the Church of Rome may be saved.

In one of the two sermons on the Epistle of St. Jude, as
to which there is considerable doubt whether they are Hooker's
work,[4] there is a passage which to some extent recalls his positive
teaching in the *Laws of Ecclesiastical Polity* on the blessedness
of Communion.

"Blessed and praised for ever and ever be His name, who per-
ceiving of how senseless and heavy metal we are made hath instituted
in His Church a spiritual Supper, and an Holy Communion to be
celebrated often, that we might thereby be occasioned often to
examine these buildings of ours, in what case they stand. . . . This
Supper is received as a seal unto us that we are His house and His
sanctuary ; that His Christ is as truly united to me, and I to him, as
my arm is united and knit unto my shoulder ; that He dwelleth in

[1] *Serm.* ii. 11.   [2] *Ibid.* 12.   [3] *Ibid.* 14.
[4] See Keble's edition of Hooker, vol. i. pp. xlvii-xlix ; Paget, *Introduction to Hooker, Book v.,* p. 265.

me as verily as the elements of bread and wine abide within me. . . .
Receiving the Sacrament of the Supper of the Lord after this
sort (you that are spiritual judge what I speak) is not all other wine
like the water of Marah, being compared to the cup which we bless?
Is not manna like to gall, and our bread like to manna? Is there
not a taste, a taste of Christ Jesus in the heart of him that eateth?
Doth not he which drinketh behold plainly in this cup that his soul
is bathed in the blood of the Lamb? O beloved in our Lord and
Saviour Jesus Christ, if ye will taste how sweet the Lord is, if ye
will receive the King of glory, 'build yourselves'." [1]

V.

The facts which have been recounted 'make it possible to
attempt a general summary of Eucharistic doctrine in England
during the reigns of Henry VIII., Edward VI., Mary, and Elizabeth. The doctrine of the Eucharistic presence which for the
sake of convenience may be described as that of the Council of
Trent, including the affirmation of Transubstantiation either
verbally or without the name, is found in the writings of King
Henry VIII. and Bishop Fisher, the *Six Articles* of 1539, and
the *King's Book* of 1543; in the writing of Bishop Gardiner and
others in the reign of Edward VI.; in the official acts of the
reign of Mary; and in the proceedings of the Convocation of
Canterbury in 1559. Teaching that the consecrated elements
are the body and blood of Christ without the assertion of Transubstantiation is found in the *Ten Articles* of 1536, the *Bishops'
Book* of 1537, the *Thirteen Articles* of 1538, the First Prayer
Book of Edward VI., and the Scottish Provincial Council of
1559. A receptionist or virtualistic doctrine is suggested by
some features in the Second Prayer Book of Edward VI., by the
draft *Forty-five Articles* of 1551, by the *Forty-two Articles* of
1553, by Poynet's *Catechism* of 1553, and by the writings of
Ridley, Cranmer, and Latimer. The Prayer Book of Elizabeth
is patient of a doctrine that the elements become the body and
blood of Christ at consecration, or of a doctrine that the faithful
communicants receive the body and blood of Christ without these
having been present before reception, though perhaps nearest
the former belief. The tendency of the *Thirty-eight Articles* of
1563 and the *Thirty-nine Articles* of 1571 and of the *Homilies*

[1] *Serm.* vi. 10, 11.

of 1563 is to deny Transubstantiation and Zwinglianism alike, to assert the real reception of the body and blood of Christ, and to leave open whether the body and blood are present at consecration or only at Communion. The writings of individuals in the reign of Elizabeth afford further indications of the toleration of differing beliefs as to the Eucharistic presence. The subject of the Eucharistic sacrifice is less prominent; as a general rule the belief that the consecrated Sacrament is the body and blood of Christ carried with it the recognition of the specifically sacrifical character of the Eucharist, and in proportion as this belief was rejected there was a tendency to deprive the Eucharist of any fuller sacrificial nature than that of a mere memory of the sacrifice of the cross or such as is to be found in all prayer.

CHAPTER XIII.

THE PERIOD OF THE REFORMATION.

PART V.

THE English Reformation cannot be regarded as completed in the reign of Elizabeth. The Prayer Book of 1559 was not in any sense final. Like questions to those of Elizabethan times had to be considered and dealt with in later reigns. If the Reformation in England is to be viewed as having been finished at all, its completion must be looked for in the work of the divines of 1661. Consequently, the theology of the period from 1603 to 1662 may be taken in close connection with that of the sixteenth century.

I.

The accession of James I. in 1603 made possible the holding of the Hampton Court Conference between the king and representatives of the bishops, and the king and representatives of the Puritan party, in 1604. One of the results of this Conference was the addition to the Catechism of the questions and answers about the Sacraments. This addition was based on the *Catechism* of Dr. Alexander Nowell.[1] It is usually thought to have been written by Dr. John Overall, then Dean of St. Paul's and Prolocutor of the Convocation of Canterbury, afterwards Bishop of Coventry and Lichfield, and later Bishop of Norwich.

In the new part of the Catechism the reply to the question " Why was the Sacrament of the Lord's Supper ordained?" is " For the continual remembrance of the sacrifice of the death of Christ, and of the benefits which we receive thereby ". This answer does not compel the acceptance of any definite opinion in regard to the Eucharistic sacrifice. It can be used by those

---

[1] See pp. 215-19, *supra*.

who regard the memorial in the Eucharist simply as a reminder
to Christians of Christ's death and work, and no less by those
who believe that the Church's remembrance of Christ in the
Eucharist is also a presentation of Him before God in the
Church's prayer.

On the Eucharistic presence the Catechism has three questions
and answers :—

" *Question.* What is the outward part or sign of the Lord's Supper ?

" *Answer.* Bread and wine, which the Lord hath commanded to
be received.

" *Question.* What is the inward part, or thing signified ?

" *Answer.* The body and blood of Christ, which are verily and
indeed taken and received by the faithful in the Lord's Supper.

" *Question.* What are the benefits whereof we are partakers thereby ?

" *Answer.* The strengthening and refreshing of our souls by the
body and blood of Christ, as our bodies are by the bread and wine."

The Catechism thus explicitly asserts that the body and blood
of Christ are received in Communion. "The inward part, or
thing signified," it is said, " is the body and blood of Christ, which
are verily and indeed taken and received by the faithful." The
phrase that the body and blood of Christ are "taken" as well as
"received," and the division into "the outward part or sign,"
"the inward part, or thing signified," and "the benefits,"—
corresponding to the division into the "signum Sacramenti," the
"res Sacramenti," and the "virtus Sacramenti,"—may not unnaturally be taken to imply that Christ is present in the Sacrament as a result of the consecration and prior to Communion.
But this is not stated in so many terms ; and it may still be said
of the Church of England at the outset of the reign of James I.
that no action was taken to exclude the holders of any belief
about the Eucharist which was consistent with the repudiation of
Transubstantiation and Zwinglianism.

With this teaching contained in the Church Catechism may
be compared a statement by its supposed author, Bishop Overall,
who wrote as follows :—

" In the Sacrament of the Eucharist or the Lord's Supper the
body and blood of Christ, and therefore the whole Christ, are indeed
really present, and are really received by us, and are really united
to the sacramental signs, as signs which not only signify but also

convey, so that in the right use of the Sacrament, and to those who
receive worthily, when the bread is given and received, the body
of Christ is given and received; and when the wine is given and
received, the blood of Christ is given and received; and therefore
the whole Christ is communicated in the Communion of the Sacrament.
Yet this is not in a carnal, gross, earthly way by Transubstantiation
or Consubstantiation, or any like fictions of human reason, but in a
way mystical, heavenly, and spiritual, as is rightly laid down in our
Articles." [1]

The canons of 1640 were the work of the members of the
Convocations of Canterbury and York, and received the assent
of the Crown. On 5th May, 1640, Parliament was dissolved by
King Charles I. It was thought by some that the dissolution would
of necessity carry with it the cessation of the sittings of Convocation; but Archbishop Laud signified to the Convocation of
Canterbury that they would continue to sit. On the legality of
this course being challenged, a legal opinion was obtained from
the Lord Chancellor and six judges that "Convocation" "doth
continue until it be dissolved by writ or commission under the
great seal, notwithstanding the Parliament be dissolved". Instead of this opinion being acted on, however, a new writ was
issued authorising the Convocations of Canterbury and York,
under the name of synods, to sit and act. The seventh of the
canons subsequently drawn up by the Canterbury Synod and

[1] Overall, *Praelectiones seu Disputationes de Patrum et Christi anima
et de Antichristo.* This treatise is printed on pp. 203-26 of Archibald
Campbell, *The Doctrines of a Middle State between Death and the Resurrection, of Prayers for the Dead, and the Necessity of Purification.* The passage
quoted above is on pp. 212, 213. As printed by Campbell the words "in
the bread rightly given and received" (in recte dato et accepto) occur
instead of "in the right use of the Sacrament, and to those who receive
worthily, when the bread is given and received" (in recto usu sacramenti,
digneque recipientibus, dato et accepto pane) as quoted above. The passage is similarly quoted and ascribed to Overall, but without reference,
in Alexander Knox, *Remains,* ii. 162, 163. Probably Knox took it from
Campbell. As stated in his *Papers on the Doctrine of the English Church
concerning the Eucharistic Presence,* No. vi. pp. 297-99, "An English
Presbyter" [Mr. N. Dimock] has examined Bishop Overall's account of
what he said in the Harleian MS. No. 3142 in the British Museum, and
has found that Overall gave his words as quoted above. Probably Campbell
accidentally omitted the words "usu sacramenti, digneque recipientibus"
in copying.

assented to by that of York contained statements bearing on
the doctrine of the Holy Eucharist. It was ordered that the
holy tables should stand at the east end of churches; and it
was added :—

"We declare that this situation of the holy table doth not imply
that it is, or ought to be esteemed, a true and proper altar, whereon
Christ is again really sacrificed ; but it is and may be called an altar
by us in that sense in which the primitive Church called it an altar,
and in no other."

Provision was made for railing in the holy tables, for the administration of Communion near the holy table, and for "doing
reverence and obeisance" on entering and leaving church. In
regard to this last practice it was added :—

"The reviving therefore of this ancient and laudable custom we
heartily commend to the serious consideration of all good people,
not with any intention to exhibit any religious worship to the communion table, the east, or church, and anything therein contained,
in so doing, or to perform the said gesture in the celebration of the
Holy Eucharist upon any opinion of a corporal presence of the body
of Jesus Christ on the holy table, or in mystical elements, but only
for the advancement of God's majesty, and to give Him alone
that honour and glory that is due unto Him, and no otherwise ; and
in the practice or omission of this rite we desire that the rule of
charity prescribed by the Apostle may be observed, which is, that
they which use this rite despise not them who use it not, and that
they who use it not condemn not those that use it." [1]

These statements with their careful expressions rejecting " a
true and proper altar, whereon Christ is again really sacrificed," and
" any opinion of a corporal presence of the body of Jesus Christ
on the holy table, or in mystical elements," and their appeal to
the primitive Church, closely resemble much in the Reformation
documents of the Church of England, and may be compared in
particular with the thirty-first of the *Articles of Religion* [2] and
the *Declaration on Kneeling*. [3] The explanation of the phrases in
the mind of any reader will be determined by his view of the
documents as a whole.

[1] These canons are printed in Cardwell, *Synodalia*, i. 380-415. The
passages quoted above are on pp. 405, 406.
[2] See pp. 144, 146, 207, 208, *supra*.　　[3] See pp. 141, 142, 204, *supra*.

II.

As in the time of Elizabeth, so during the reigns of James I. and Charles I. there are instances of differing beliefs about the Eucharist held by eminent divines. It may be convenient to take in one group the writings of Andrewes, Laud, Mountague, and Herbert. Lancelot Andrewes was born in London in 1555. He was successively Vicar of Alton, Vicar of St. Giles, Cripplegate, Canon of St. Paul's, and Master of Pembroke Hall, Cambridge. He was a chaplain of Queen Elizabeth and of King James I.; and became Bishop of Chichester in 1605, Bishop of Ely in 1609, and Bishop of Winchester in 1618. In 1626 he died. His beliefs as to the doctrine of the Eucharist are expressed for the most part uncontroversially in his Sermons and Devotions, and are stated more explicitly in the course of several controversies.

Andrewes's Sermons contain many references to this Sacrament. It is the means by which pre-eminently we partake of the benefits of the Incarnation.

"Now ' the bread which we break, is it not the partaking of the body, of the flesh, of Jesus Christ ?' [1] It is surely, and by it and by nothing more are we made partakers of this most blessed union. A little before he said, 'Because the children were partakers of flesh and blood, He also would take part with them ' [2]—may not we say the same ? Because He hath so done, taken ours of us, we also ensuing His steps will participate with Him and with His flesh which He hath taken of us. It is most kindly to take part with Him in that which He took part in with us, and that to no other end but that He might make the receiving of it by us a means whereby He might ' dwell in us, and we in Him '; He taking our flesh, and we receiving His Spirit ; by His flesh which He took of us receiving His Spirit which He imparteth to us ; that, as He by ours became *consors humanae naturae,* so we by His might become *consortes divinae naturae,* 'partakers of the divine nature '.[3] Verily, it is the most straight and perfect 'taking hold' that is. No union so knitteth as it. Not consanguinity ; brethren fall out. Not marriage ; man and wife are severed. But that which is nourished, and the nourishment wherewith, they never are, never can be severed, but remain one for ever. With this act then of mutual 'taking,' taking of His flesh as He has taken ours, let us seal our duty to Him." [4]

[1] 1 Cor. x. 16.   [2] Heb. ii. 14.   [3] 2 St. Pet. i. 4.
[4] *Sermons (Anglo-Catholic Library),* i. 16, 17.

It is the application of the sacrifice of Christ to the souls of the communicants.

"He is given to us *in pretium*, 'for a price'. A price either of ransom, to bring us out *de loco caliginoso ;* or a price of purchase of that where without it we have no interest, the kingdom of heaven. For both He is given ; offer we Him for both. We speak of *quid retribuam ?* We can never retribute the like thing. He was given us to that end we might give Him back. We wanted, we had nothing valuable ; that we might have, this He gave us as a thing of greatest price to offer for that which needeth a great price, our sins, so many in number, and so foul in quality. We had nothing worthy God ; this He gave us that is worthy Him, which cannot be but accepted, offer we it never so often. Let us then offer Him, and in the act of offering ask of Him what is meet ; for we shall find Him no less bounteous than Herod, to grant what is duly asked upon His birthday. He is given us, as Himself saith, as 'the living bread from heaven,' which Bread is His 'flesh' born this day,[1] and after ' given for the life of the world'.[2] For look how we do give back that He gave us, even so doth He give back to us that which we gave Him, that which He had of us. This He gave for us in sacrifice, and this He giveth us in the Sacrament, that the sacrifice may by the Sacrament be truly applied to us."[3]

The elements are both tokens of, and means of conveying, the body and blood of Christ ; and the Eucharistic presence is not of Christ's Godhead only but also of His flesh.

"How shall we receive Him ? Who shall give Him us ? That shall One that will say unto us within a while, *Accipite,* 'Take, this is My body,' 'by the offering whereof ye are sanctified,' [4] 'Take, this is My blood,' by the shedding whereof ye are saved. Both in the holy mysteries ordained by God as pledges to assure us and as conduit pipes to convey into us this and all other the benefits that come by this our Saviour."[5]

"How may we better establish our hearts with grace, or settle our minds in the truth of His promise, than by partaking these the conduit pipes of His grace, and seals of His truth unto us ? Grace and truth now proceeding not from the Word alone, but even from the flesh thereto united ; the fountain of the Word flowing into the

---

[1] Preached on Christmas Day.
[2] St. John vi. 51.
[3] *Sermons, op. cit.* i. 30, 31.
[4] Heb. x. 10.
[5] *Sermons, op. cit.* i. 83.

cistern of His flesh, and from thence deriving down to us this grace and truth, to them that partake Him aright."[1]

"'Immanuel, God with us'[2] requires *Immelanu*, 'us with God,' again. He 'with us' now, I hope, for 'where two or three are gathered together in His name, there is He with them'.[3] But that is in His Godhead. And we are with Him; our prayers, our praises are with Him; but that is in our spirits whence they come. These are well, but these are not all we can; and none of these the proper 'with Him' of the day.[4] That hath a special *cum* of itself, peculiar to it. Namely, that we be so with Him as He this day was 'with us'; that was in flesh, not in spirit only. That flesh that was conceived and this day born (*corpus aptasti mihi*[5]), that body that was this day fitted to Him. And if we be not with Him thus, if this His flesh be not 'with us,' if we partake it not, which way soever else we be with Him, we come short of the *Im* of this day. . . . This, as it is most proper, so it is the most straight and near that can be, the surest being withal that can be. *Nihil tam nobiscum, am nostrum, quam alimentum nostrum,* 'nothing so with us, so ours, as that we eat and drink down,' which goeth, and groweth one with us. For *alimentum et alitum* do *coalescere in unum,* 'grow into an union'; and that union is inseparable ever after. This then I commend to you, even the being with Him in the Sacrament of His body, that body that was conceived and born, as for other ends so for this specially, to be 'with you'; and this day, as for other intents so even for this, for the Holy Eucharist."[6]

The presence and gift in the Sacrament is that of Christ Himself, as Christ Himself was laid in the manger when He became incarnate.

"Of the Sacrament we may well say, *Hoc erit signum.* For a sign it is, and by it *invenietis Puerum,* 'ye shall find this Child'.[7] For finding His flesh and blood, ye cannot miss but find Him too. And a sign, not much from this here. For Christ in the Sacrament is not altogether unlike Christ in the cratch. To the cratch we may well liken the husk or outward symbols of it. Outwardly it seems little worth, but it is rich of contents, as was the crib this day [8] with Christ in it. For what are they but *infirma et egena ele-*

---

[1] *Sermons, op. cit.* i. 100.
[3] St. Matt. xviii. 20.
[5] Ps. xl. 6; Heb. x. 5.
[7] St. Luke ii. 12.
VOL. II.

[2] Isa. vii. 14; St. Matt. i. 23.
[4] Preached on Christmas Day.
[6] *Sermons, op. cit.* i. 151, 152.
[8] Preached on Christmas Day.

17

menta, ' weak and poor elements ' [1] of themselves ?   Yet in them find
we Christ.   Even as they did this day *in præsepi jumentorum panem
angelorum,* ' in the beasts' crib the food of angels,' which very food
our signs both represent and present unto us." [2]

The bread and wine and the body and blood of Christ are alike
as real as His manhood and His Godhead ; and they are united
without either of them being changed, as the two natures of our
Lord were united in the Incarnation.

"We shall the better dispense the season, if we gather to prayers
to God's word, if we begin with them, if with the dispensation of
His holy mysteries gather to that specially.   For there we do not
gather to Christ or of Christ, but we gather Christ Himself; and
gathering Him we shall gather the tree and fruit and all upon it.   For
as there is a recapitulation of all in heaven and earth in Christ, so there
is a recapitulation of all in Christ in the holy Sacrament.   You may
see it clearly : there is in Christ the Word eternal for things in
heaven ; there is also flesh for things on earth.   Semblably, the
Sacrament consisteth of a heavenly and of a terrene part (it is Irenæus'
own words) ; [3] the heavenly—there the word too, the abstract of
the other ; the earthly—the element. . . . The gathering or vin-
tage of these two in the blessed Eucharist is as I may say a kind of
hypostatical union of the sign and the thing signified, so united together as are the two natures of Christ.   And even from this sacramental union do the fathers borrow their resemblance to illustrate by
it the personal union in Christ ; I name Theodoret [4] for the Greek, and
Gelasius [5] for the Latin Church, that insist upon it both, and press
it against Eutyches.   That even as in the Eucharist neither part is
evacute or turned into the other, but abide each still in his former
nature and substance, no more is either of Christ's natures annulled,
or one of them converted into the other, as Eutyches held, but each
nature remaineth still full and whole in his own kind.   And back-
wards ; as the two natures in Christ, so the *signum* and *signatum* in
the Sacrament, *e converso.*   And this latter device of the substance
of the bread and wine to be flown away and gone, and in the room
of it a remainder of nothing else but accidents to stay behind, was
to them not known ; and had it been true had made for Eutyches
and against them." [6]

[1] Gal. iv. 9.   [2] *Sermons, op. cit.* i. 213.
[3] See vol. i. p. 35, *supra.*   [4] See vol. i. pp. 99-101, *supra.*
[5] See vol. i. pp. 101, 102, *supra.*   [6] *Sermons, op. cit.* i. 281, 282.

With the reception of the body of Christ in the Sacrament there is also the reception of the Holy Ghost.

"I will show you a way how to say *Accipite Spiritum* to all, and how all may receive It. And that is by *Accipite corpus Meum*. For *Accipite corpus*, upon the matter, is *Accipite Spiritum* inasmuch as they two never part, not possible to sever them one minute. Thus, when or to whom we say *Accipite corpus*, we may safely say with the same breath *Accipite Spiritum;* and as truly every way. For that body is never without this Spirit: he that receives the one receives the other ; he that the body, together with it the Spirit also. And receiving It thus, it is to better purpose than here in the text[1] it is. Better, I say, for us. For in the text It is received for the good of others, whereas here we shall receive It for our own good. Now whether is the better, remission of sins, to be able to remit to others, or to have our own remitted ? To have our own, no doubt. And that is here to be had. To the stablishing of our hearts with grace, to the cleansing and quieting our consciences. Which spiritual grace we receive in this spiritual food, and are made to drink (I will not say of 'the spiritual rock,' but) of the spiritual 'vine' that followeth us, which 'vine' is Christ.[2] To that then let us apply ourselves. Both are received, both are holy, both co-operate to the 'remission of sins'. The 'body'—Matthew the twenty-sixth. The Spirit, here evidently. And there is no better way of celebrating the feast of the receiving the Holy Ghost than so to do, with receiving the same body that came of It at His birth, and that came from It now at His rising again."[3]

The opinion of many in England that in the Eucharist there is no actual partaking of the true body of Christ is contrary to the constant belief of the Church.

"To a many with us it is indeed so *fractio panis* as it is that only and nothing beside ; whereas the 'bread which we break is the partaking of Christ's' true 'body,'[4] and not a sign, figure, or remembrance of it. For the Church hath ever believed a true fruition of the true body of Christ in that Sacrament."[5]

---

[1] St. John xx. 22.   [2] 1 Cor. x. 4.

[3] *Sermons, op. cit.* iii. 278, 279.   [4] 1 Cor. x. 16.

[5] *Sermons, op. cit.* v. 67. For similar statements to those in this and the preceding quotations, see also *e.g.* i. 62, ii. 134, 298, 382, iii. 34-38, 58, 352.

17 *

"Sacrifice," "offer," and "altar" are all words which may be
used rightly about the Eucharist, though there is a sense in which
each one of them must be refused.

"Many among us fancy only a Sacrament in this action, and look
strange at the mention of a sacrifice, whereas we not only use it as
a nourishment spiritual, as that it is too, but as a mean also to renew
a 'covenant' with God by virtue of that 'sacrifice,' as the psalmist
speaketh.[1] So our Saviour Christ in the institution telleth us, in
the twenty-second chapter of Luke and twentieth verse, and the
Apostle, in the thirteenth chapter of Hebrews and tenth verse. And
the old writers use no less the word sacrifice than Sacrament, altar
than table, offer than eat ; but both indifferently, to show there is
both." [2]

"Two things Christ there gave us in charge : 1. ἀνάμνησις,
'remembering,' and 2. λῆψις, 'receiving'. The same two St. Paul,
but in other terms, 1. καταγγελλία, 'showing forth' ; 2. κοινωνία, 'communicating'. Of which, 'remembering' and 'showing forth' refer
to celebremus, 'receiving' and 'communicating' to epulemur here.[3]
The first, in remembrance of Him, Christ. What of Him ? Mortem
Domini, His death, saith St. Paul, 'to show forth the Lord's death '.[4]
Remember Him. That we will and stay at home, think of Him
there. Nay, show Him forth ye must. That we will by a sermon of
Him. Nay, it must be hoc facite. It is not mental thinking or
verbal speaking, there must be actually somewhat done to celebrate
this memory. That done to the holy symbols that was done to Him,
to His body and His blood in the passover ; break the one, pour out
the other, to represent κλώμενον, how His sacred body was 'broken,'
and ἐκχυνόμενον, how His precious blood was 'shed '. And in corpus
fractum and sanguis fusus there is immolatus. This is it in the
Eucharist that answereth to the sacrifice in the passover, the memorial to the figure. To them it was, hoc facite in Mei præfigurationem,
'do this in prefiguration of Me ' : to us it is, 'do this in commemoration of Me '.[5] To them prenuntiare, to us annuntiare ; there is the
difference. By the same rules that theirs was, by the same may ours
be termed a sacrifice. In rigour of speech, neither of them ; for to
speak after the exact manner of divinity, there is but one only sacrifice, veri nominis, 'properly so called,' that is, Christ's death. And that
sacrifice but once actually performed at His death, but ever before

[1] Ps. l. 5.   [2] Sermons, op. cit. v. 66, 67.
[3] 1 Cor. v. 8.   [4] 1 Cor. xi. 26.
[5] St. Luke xxii. 19 ; 1 Cor. xi. 26.

represented in figure, from the beginning; and ever since repeated in memory, to the world's end.   The only absolute, all else relative to it, representative of it, operative by it.   The Lamb, but once actually slain in the fulness of time, but virtually was from the beginning, is and shall be to the end of the world.   That the centre, in which their lines and ours, their types and our antitypes do meet. While yet this offering was not, the hope of it was kept alive by the prefiguration of it in theirs.   And after it is past, the memory of it is still kept fresh in mind by the commemoration of it in ours.   So it was the will of God, that so there might be with them a continual foreshowing, and with us a continual showing forth, the 'Lord's death till He come again '.   Hence it is that what names theirs carried, ours do the like, and the fathers make no scruple at it; no more need we.   The Apostle in the tenth chapter compareth this of ours to the *immolata* of the heathen;[1] and to the Hebrews *habemus aram*,[2] matcheth it with the sacrifice of the Jews.   And we know the rule of comparisons, they must be *ejusdem generis*."[3]

In a passage of some obscurity Bishop Andrewes connects the body of Christ which is received in the Eucharist with the state in which it was on the cross.

" *Epulemur* doth here[4] refer to *immolatus*.   To Christ, not every way considered, but as when He was offered.   Christ's body that now is.   True; but not Christ's body as now it is, but as then it was, when it was offered, rent, and slain, and sacrificed for us.   Not, as now He is, glorified, for so He is not, so He cannot be, *immolatus*, for He is immortal and impassible.   But as then He was when He suffered death, that is, passible and mortal.   Then, in His passible estate did He institute this of ours, to be a memorial of His *passibile* and *passio* both.   And we are in this action not only carried up to Christ (*sursum corda*), but we are also carried back to Christ as He was at the very instant, and in the very act of His offering.   So, and no otherwise, doth this text teach.   So, and no otherwise, do we represent Him.   By the incomprehensible power of His eternal Spirit not He alone, but He as at the very act of His offering is made present to us, and we incorporate into His death, and invested in the benefits of it.   If a host could be turned into Him now glorified as He is, it would not serve; Christ offered is it; thither we must look.   To the Serpent lift up, thither we must repair, even *ad cadaver ;* we must *hoc facere*, do that is then done.   So,

[1] 1 Cor. x. 21.   [2] Heb. xiii. 10.
[3] *Sermons, op. cit.* ii. 300, 301.   [4] 1 Cor. v. 8.

and no otherwise, is this *epulare* to be conceived.   And so, I think, none will say they do or can turn Him." [1]

In his Devotions Andrewes describes the Eucharist as being and affording—

"a token of the fellowship, a memorial of the dispensation, a showing forth of the death, a Communion of body and blood, a participation of the Spirit, remission of sins, a riddance of adversaries, quieting of conscience, blotting out of debts, cleansing of stains, healing of sicknesses of the soul, renewal of the covenant, provision for the journey of ghostly life, increase of enabling grace and winning comfort, compunction of repentance, illumination of mind, a preparatory exercise of humility, a seal of faith, fulness of wisdom, a bond of charity, a sufficient ground of almsgiving, an armour of endurance, alertness for thanksgiving, confidence of prayer, mutual indwelling, a pledge of resurrection, acceptable defence in judgment, a testament of inheritance, a stamp of perfectness " ;

as a remembrance of—

"the saving sufferings of Thy Christ, His quickening cross, right precious death, three days' burial, resurrection from the dead, ascension into heaven, session at the right hand of Thee the Father, glorious and fearful coming " ;

in which—

"we have held the remembrance of Thy death, we have seen the figure of Thy resurrection, we have been filled with Thine unending life, we have had fruition of Thine inexhaustible delight." [2]

In his first *Answer to Cardinal Perron* Andrewes repudiates alike the Zwinglian doctrine that the elements are only signs of the body and blood of Christ and the " carnal presence " which he thought to be implied in Cardinal Perron's phrase, "la vraye et reelle presence et manducation orale du corps de Christ au Sacrement sous les especes et dans les especes sacramentales " ; declares " the Sacrament to be venerable and with all due respect to be handled and received," and that, while " no divine adoration

---

[1] *Sermons, op. cit.* ii. 301, 302. Compare the teaching of Rupert of Deutz on vol. i. p. 292, *supra*, and of Saravia on vol. ii. pp. 223-25, *supra*.

[2] Medd, *The Greek Devotions of Lancelot Andrewes* (the Greek text), pp. 183-87; Brightman, *The Preces Privatæ of Lancelot Andrewes* (translation into English), pp. 122-24.

can be used to" "the symbols so abiding" "in their former substance, shape, and kind," "no Christian man" ought ever to "refuse" "to adore the flesh of Christ"; and explains the Eucharistic sacrifice in the following terms:—

"1. The Eucharist ever was, and by us is, considered both as a Sacrament and as a sacrifice. 2. A sacrifice is proper and appliable only to divine worship. 3. The sacrifice of Christ's death did succeed to the sacrifices of the old Testament. 4. The sacrifice of Christ's death is available for present, absent, living, dead (yea, for them that are yet unborn). 5. When we say the dead, we mean it is available for the Apostles, martyrs, and confessors, and all (because we are all members of one body): these no man will deny. 6. In a word, we hold with St. Augustine in the very same chapter which the Cardinal citeth, ' quod hujus sacrificii caro et sanguis ante adventum Christi per victimas similitudinum promittebatur; in passione Christi per ipsam veritatem reddebatur; post adventum [leg. ascensum] Christi per sacramentum memoriae celebratur'.[1] . . . If we agree about the matter of sacrifice, there will be no difference about the altar. The Holy Eucharist being considered as a sacrifice (in the representation of the breaking the bread and pouring forth the cup), the same is fitly called an altar, which again is as fitly called a Table, the Eucharist being considered as a Sacrament, which is nothing else but a distribution and an application of the sacrifice to the several receivers. The same St. Augustine that in the place alleged doth term it an altar[2] saith in another place, ' Christus quotidie pascit. Mensa Ipsius est illa in medio constituta. Quid causae est, O audientes, ut mensam videatis et ad epulas non accedatis ? '[3]   The same Nyssen in the place cited with one breath calleth it θυσιαστήριον, that is, an altar, and ἱερὰ τράπεζα, that is, the holy Table.[4] Which is agreeable also to the Scriptures; for the altar in the Old Testament is by Malachi called Mensa Domini.[5] And of the Table in the New Testament by the Apostle it is said, Habemus altare.[6] Which, of what matter it be, whether of stone, as Nyssen,[7] or of wood, as Optatus,[8] it skills not. So that the matter of altars make no difference in the face of our Church."[9]

---

[1] St. Augustine, C. Faust. xx. 21.   [2] Ibid.
[3] Ibid. Serm. cxxxii. 1.
[4] St. Gregory of Nyssa, De Bapt. Christi, quoted on vol. i. p. 68, supra.
[5] Mal. i. 7.   [6] Heb. xiii. 10.
[7] See above, and vol. i. p. 68, supra.
[8] Optatus, De schis. Donat. vi. 1.
[9] Works (Anglo-Catholic Library), xi. 7, 13, 14, 16, 17, 19, 20, 21.

In the *Responsio ad Apologiam Cardinalis Bellarmini* Andrewes maintains that the Anglican controversy with Rome is not as to the reality but as to the method of the presence of Christ ; that neither the word nor the doctrine of Transubstantiation is to be found in the fathers ; that not the Sacrament but Christ Himself really present in it is to be adored ; that the Eucharist is a commemorative sacrifice ; and that, if the doctrine of Transubstantiation should be abandoned, there would no longer be dispute as to the sacrifice.

"Christ said, 'This is My body'. He did not say, 'This is My body in this way'. We are in agreement with you as to the end ; the whole controversy is as to the method. As to the 'This is,' we hold with firm faith that it is. As to the 'This is in this way' (namely, by the Transubstantiation of the bread into the body), as to the method whereby it happens that it is, by means of In or With or Under or By transition there is no word expressed. And because there is no word, we rightly make it not of faith ; we place it perhaps among the theories of the school, but not among the articles of the faith. . . . We believe no less than you that the presence is real. Concerning the method of the presence, we define nothing rashly, and, I add, we do not anxiously inquire, any more than how the blood of Christ washes us in our Baptism, any more than how the human and divine natures are united in one Person in the Incarnation of Christ." [1]

"It is perfectly clear that Transubstantiation, which has lately been born in the last four hundred years, never existed in the first four hundred. . . . In opposition to the Jesuit, our men deny that the fathers had anything to do with the fact of Transubstantiation any more than with the name. He regards the fact of Transubstantiation as a change in substance (*substantialis transmutatio*). And he calls certain witnesses to prove this. And yet on this point, whether there is there a conversion in substance, not long before the Lateran Council the Master of the Sentences himself says 'I am not able to define'.[2] But all his witnesses speak of some kind of change (*pro mutatione, immutatione, transmutatione*). But there is no mention there of a change in substance, or of the substance. But neither do we deny in this matter the preposition *trans ;* and we allow that the elements are changed (*transmutari*). But a change in substance we look for, and we find it nowhere." [3]

---

[1] *Works, op. cit.* viii. 13.

[2] Peter Lombard, *Sent.* IV. xi. 1, quoted on vol. i. p. 305, *supra*.

[3] *Works, op. cit.* viii. 262.

"At the coming of the almighty power of the Word, the nature is changed so that what before was the mere element now becomes a divine Sacrament, the substance nevertheless remaining what it was before. . . . There is that kind of union between the visible Sacrament and the invisible reality (*rem*) of the Sacrament which there is between the manhood and the Godhead of Christ, where unless you want to smack of Eutyches, the manhood is not transubstantiated into the Godhead." [1]

"About 'the adoration of the Sacrament' he stumbles badly at the very threshold. He says, 'of the Sacrament, that is, of Christ the Lord present by a wonderful but real way in the Sacrament'. Away with this. Who will allow him this? 'Of the Sacrament, that is, of Christ in the Sacrament.' Surely, Christ Himself, the reality (*res*) of the Sacrament, in and with the Sacrament, outside and without the Sacrament, wherever He is, is to be adored. Now the King [2] laid down that Christ is really present in the Eucharist, and is really to be adored, that is, the reality (*rem*) of the Sacrament, but not the Sacrament, that is, the 'earthly part,' as Irenæus says, [3] the 'visible,' as Augustine says. [4] We also, like Ambrose, 'adore the flesh of Christ in the mysteries,' [5] and yet not it but Him who is worshipped on the altar. For the Cardinal puts his question badly, 'What is there worshipped,' since he ought to ask, 'Who,' as Nazianzen says, 'Him,' not 'it'. [6] And, like Augustine, we 'do not eat the flesh without first adoring'. [7] And yet we none of us adore the Sacrament." [8]

"Our men believe that the Eucharist was instituted by the Lord for a memorial of Himself, even of His sacrifice, and, if it be lawful so to speak, to be a commemorative sacrifice, not only to be a Sacrament and for spiritual nourishment. Though they allow this, yet they deny that either of these uses (thus instituted by the Lord together) can be divided from the other by man either because of the negligence of the people or because of the avarice of the priests. The sacrifice which is there is Eucharistic, of which sacrifice the law is that he who offers it is to partake of it, and that he partake by receiving and eating, as the Saviour ordered. For to 'partake by

[1] *Works, op. cit.* viii. 265.   [2] James I.
[3] St. Irenæus, *Adv. Hær.* IV. xviii. 5, quoted on vol. i. p. 35, *supra.*
[4] *Decret.* III. ii. 48.
[5] St. Ambrose, *De Spir. Sanc.* iii. 79, quoted on vol. i. p. 108, *supra.*
[6] St. Gregory of Nazianzus, *Orat.* viii. 18, quoted on vol. i. p. 106, *supra.*
[7] St. Augustine, *In Ps. xcviii. Enar.* 9, quoted on vol. i. p. 109, *supra.*
[8] *Works, op. cit.* viii. 266, 267.

sharing in the prayer,' that indeed is a fresh and novel way of partaking, much more even than the private Mass itself. . . . Do you take away from the Mass your Transubstantiation; and there will not long be any strife with us about the sacrifice. Willingly we allow that a memory of the sacrifice is made there. That your Christ made of bread is sacrificed there we will never allow." [1]

It is of interest to compare with the teaching of Bishop Andrewes about the Eucharistic sacrifice that contained in the sermon preached at his funeral by John Buckeridge, who had formerly been President of St. John's College, Oxford, was at that time Bishop of Rochester, and afterwards became Bishop of Ely. It is there taught that on the cross and in the Eucharist there is the "same sacrificed thing, that is, the body and blood of Christ," but not the same "action of sacrifice "; and that the Church offers in the Eucharist " the Church itself, the universal body of Christ," and does not "sacrifice the natural body of Christ otherwise than by commemoration ".

" As Christ's cross was His altar where He offered Himself for us, so the Church hath an altar also where it offereth itself, not *Christum in Capite*, but *Christum in membris*, not Christ the Head properly but only by commemoration, but Christ the members. For Christ cannot be offered truly and properly no more but once upon the cross, for He cannot be offered again no more than He can be dead again ; and dying and shedding blood as He did upon the cross, and not dying and not shedding blood as in the Eucharist, cannot be one action of Christ offered on the cross, and of Christ offered in the Church at the altar by the priest by representation only, no more than Christ and the priest are one person : and therefore, though in the cross and the Eucharist there be *idem sacrificatum*, the same sacrificed thing, that is, the body and blood of Christ offered by Christ to His Father on the cross, and received and participated by the communicants in the sacrifice of the altar, yet *idem sacrificium quoad actionem sacrificii*, or *sacrificandi*, it is impossible there should be the same sacrifice, understanding by sacrifice the action of sacrifice. For then the action of Christ's sacrifice, which is long since past, should continue as long as the Eucharist shall endure, even unto the world's end, and His *consummatum est* is not yet finished ; and dying and not dying, shedding of blood and not shedding of blood, and suffering and not suffering, cannot possibly be one action ; and the representation of an action cannot be the action itself. "

[1] *Works, op. cit.* viii. 250, 251.

"This then is the daily sacrifice of the Church in St. Augustine's resolute judgment, [1] even the Church itself, the universal body of Christ, not the natural body, whereof the Sacrament is an exemplar and a memorial only, as hath been showed. . . . We deny not then the daily sacrifice of the Church, that is, the Church itself, warranted by Scriptures and fathers. We take not upon us to sacrifice the natural body of Christ otherwise than by commemoration, as Christ Himself and St. Paul doth prescribe." [2]

William Laud was born at Reading in 1573. He was ordained deacon in 1600, and priest in 1601. He became President of St. John's College, Oxford, and Chaplain to King James I. in 1611, Bishop of St. Davids in 1621, Bishop of Bath and Wells in 1626, Bishop of London in 1628, Chancellor of the University of Oxford in 1630, and Archbishop of Canterbury in 1633. In 1640 he was accused of high treason; after many delays Parliament passed an act of attainder in which he was declared guilty, and he was beheaded on 10th January, 1645.

Most of Laud's teaching in regard to the Eucharist is to be found in his work entitled *A Relation of the Conference between William Laud, then Lord Bishop of St. Davids, now Lord Archbishop of Canterbury, and Mr. Fisher the Jesuite,* which he published in 1639.

Laud explicitly rejects Transubstantiation in at any rate the more obvious meaning of the word.

"Transubstantiation . . . was never heard of in the primitive Church, nor till the Council of Lateran, nor can it be proved out of Scripture ; and, taken properly, cannot stand with the grounds of Christian religion." [3]

"The primitive Church never . . . nor did it . . . dream of a Transubstantiation, which the learned of the Roman party dare not understand properly, for a change of one substance into another, for then they must grant that Christ's real and true body is made of the bread, and the bread changed into it, which is properly Tran-

[1] See vol. i. pp. 123, 124, *supra.*

[2] This sermon is printed in the edition of Andrewes's *Sermons* in the *Anglo-Catholic Library,* v. 257-98. The passages quoted above are on pp. 260, 265, 266. Compare Buckeridge's *Discourse Concerning Kneeling at the Communion,* added to his *Sermon Touching Prostration and Kneeling in the Worship of God,* preached at Whitehall on 22nd March, 1617, and published in 1618.

[3] *Works (Anglo-Catholic Library),* ii. 306.

substantiation ; nor yet can they express it in a credible way, as appears by Bellarmine's struggle about it, which yet in the end cannot be, or be called, Transubstantiation, and is that which at this day is a scandal to both Jew and Gentile, and the Church of God." [1]

Yet, in rejecting Transubstantiation as he understood it, he appears to have accepted the positive doctrine which the more theologically minded advocates of Transubstantiation had at heart.   He quotes Bellarmine's statement that—

"The conversion of the bread and wine into the body and the blood of Christ is substantial, but after a secret and ineffable manner, and not like in all things to any natural conversion whatsoever" ; [2]

and comments on it that—

"if he had left out ' conversion,' and affirmed only Christ's ' real presence' there, after a mysterious, and indeed an ineffable, manner, no man could have spoken better" ; [3]

and he allows "the true substantial presence of Christ ".[4]

In passages which to some extent recall the position of Hooker,[5] Laud recognises that Calvin affirmed the reception of "the true and real body of Christ" "in the Eucharist"; [6] points out that "the Church of England" "believes and teaches the true and real presence of Christ in the Eucharist"; [7] and makes an appeal, though perhaps somewhat grudgingly, for peace on the ground of the common belief that faithful communicants spiritually receive the body of Christ in the Sacrament.

"But, ' mark this,' how far you run from all common principles of Christian peace, as well as Christian truth, while you deny salvation most unjustly to us, from which you are farther off yourselves. Besides, if this were, or could be made, a concluding argument, I pray, Why do not you believe with us in the point of the Eucharist ? For all sides agree in the faith of the Church of England, That in the most blessed Sacrament the worthy receiver is by his faith made spiritually partaker of the 'true and real body and blood of Christ, truly and really,' and of all the benefits of His passion.   Your Roman Catholics add a manner of this His presence, 'Transubstantiation,' which many deny ; and the Lutherans, a manner of this presence,

---

[1] *Works, op. cit.* ii. 364, 365.
[2] On Bellarmine's teaching see pp. 364-67, *infra.*
[3] *Works, op. cit.* 322, 323.   [4] *Op. cit.* ii. 326, 327.
[5] See pp. 239-49, *supra.*   [6] *Op. cit.* ii. 328-31.   [7] *Ibid.* 328.

'Consubstantiation,' which more deny. If this argument be good, then, even for this consent, it is safer communicating with the Church of England than with the Roman or Lutheran; because all agree in this truth, not in any other opinion." [1]

Laud calls the doctrine of concomitance a "fiction of Thomas of Aquin," and rejects it because Christ instituted the Sacrament in both kinds, and because—

"the Eucharist is a Sacrament *sanguinis effusi*, of blood shed and poured out; and blood poured out, and so severed from the body, goes not along with the body *per concomitantiam*".[2]

Of the Eucharistic sacrifice, he writes:—

"As Christ offered up Himself once for all, a full and all-sufficient sacrifice for the sin of the whole world, so did He institute and command a memory of this sacrifice in a Sacrament, even till His coming again. For, at and in the Eucharist we offer up to God three sacrifices: One by the priest only, that is, the commemorative sacrifice of Christ's death, represented in bread broken and wine poured out.[3] Another by the priest and the people jointly, and that is the sacrifice of praise and thanksgiving for all the benefits and graces we receive by the precious death of Christ. The third, by every particular man for himself only, and that is the sacrifice of every man's body and soul, to serve Him in both all the rest of his life, for this blessing thus bestowed on him. Now, thus far these dissenting Churches agree, that in the Eucharist there is a sacrifice of duty, and a sacrifice of praise, and a sacrifice of commemoration of Christ. Therefore, according to the former rule (and here in truth too) it is safest for a man to believe the commemorative, the praising, and the performing sacrifice, and to offer them duly to God, and leave the Church of Rome in this particular to her superstitions, that I may say no more. And would the Church of Rome stand to A. C.'s rule, and believe dissenting parties where they agree, were it but in this, and that before, of the real presence, it would work far toward the peace of Christendom." [4]

A passage in Laud's *Speech Delivered in the Starr-Chamber on Wednesday, June 14, 1637, at the Censure of John Bastwick, Henry Burton, and William Prinn, Concerning Pretended Innova-*

---

[1] *Op. cit.* ii. 320, 321.   [2] *Ibid.* 338, 339.

[3] It should be observed that Laud regards the " commemorative sacrifice" as offered " by the priest only ".

[4] *Op. cit.* ii. 339-41.

tions in the Church bears on his Eucharistic doctrine. Speaking of the practice of bowing before the altar, he says :—

"And you, my honourable Lords of the Garter, in your great solemnities, you do your reverence, and to Almighty God, I doubt not ; but yet it is *versus altare*, towards His altar, as the greatest place of God's residence upon earth. (I say the greatest, yea, greater than the pulpit ; for there 'tis *Hoc est corpus Meum,* 'This is My body ' ; but in the pulpit 'tis at most but *Hoc est verbum Meum,* 'This is My word'. And a greater reverence, no doubt, is due to the body than to the word of our Lord. And so, in relation, answerably to the throne where His body is usually present than to the seat where His word useth to be proclaimed.) " [1]

In the same speech, in alluding incidentally to " bowing themselves and adoring at the Sacrament," he added, " I say, 'adoring at the Sacrament,' not 'adoring the Sacrament' ".[2]

Further illustration of Laud's belief may be seen in the Scottish Liturgy of 1637. On 21st October, 1610, three of the titular Scottish bishops—Archbishop Spotswood of Glasgow, Bishop Lamb of Brechin, and Bishop Hamilton of Galloway— were consecrated bishops in London by Bishop Abbot of London, Bishop Andrewes of Ely, Bishop Neile of Rochester, and Bishop Parry of Worcester. They consecrated other bishops, and in this way an episcopal succession was restored to Scotland. On 20th December, 1636, King Charles I. signed a document authorising the use of a Scottish Book of Common Prayer. In July, 1637, an unsuccessful attempt was made to introduce this Book in Scotland. It was supposed by many that the characteristic features of the Book were due to the influence of Laud ; and this was one of the charges brought against him at his trial. In the *History of the Troubles and Tryal of the Most Reverend Father in God William Laud, Lord Archbishop of Canterbury,* which he himself wrote during his imprisonment in the Tower, while not admitting that the Book was his work, he expresses his willingness to " bear the burden " of it,[3] and defends in detail

---

[1] *Op. cit.* vi. 57. Compare the account given by the Puritan Prynne of Laud's acts of reverence when approaching the altar and at the consecration of the Sacrament, in *Canterbury's Doom,* pp. 113, 114 (see, *e.g., Hierugia Anglicana,* ii. 82, 83, edition 1903).

[2] *Ibid.* 58.   [3] *Ibid.* iii. 336.

the parts of it which were attacked. The Scottish Liturgy followed the First Prayer Book of Edward VI. rather than the Second Book of Edward or the Book of Elizabeth, and thus suggested the doctrine of the presence of Christ in the consecrated elements, as distinct from the implied rejection of that doctrine in the Book of 1552, or the toleration of differing beliefs in the Book of 1559. The service was not broken up by the intermingling of the parts relating to Communion with the liturgical action, as in the Books of 1552 and 1559. The Eucharistic sacrifice was implied in the words—

" We Thy humble servants do celebrate and make here before Thy divine Majesty, with these Thy holy gifts, the memorial which Thy Son hath willed us to make, having in remembrance His blessed passion, mighty resurrection, and glorious ascension."

The invocation of the Holy Ghost was used before the recital of the institution :—

" Hear us, O merciful Father, we most humbly beseech Thee, and of Thy almighty goodness vouchsafe so to bless and sanctify with Thy word and Holy Spirit these Thy gifts and creatures of bread and wine that they may be unto us the body and blood of Thy most dearly beloved Son, so that we, receiving them according to Thy Son our Saviour Jesus Christ's holy institution, in remembrance of His death and passion, may be partakers of the same His most precious body and blood."

The words of administration were those used in the Book of 1549 :—

" The body of our Lord Jesus Christ, which was given for thee, preserve thy body and soul unto everlasting life,"
" The blood of our Lord Jesus Christ, which was shed for thee, preserve thy body and soul unto everlasting life,"

without the clauses substituted for these in 1552 and combined with them in 1559.[1]

Of the order of the prayers Laud wrote :—

" Though I shall not find fault with the order of the prayers as they stand in the Communion-book of England (for, God be thanked, it is well), yet, if a comparison must be made, I do think the order

[1] Hall, *Reliquiæ Liturgicæ*, ii. 148, 149, 152. The Book is also in Pickering's reprints of the Books of Common Prayer.

of the prayers as now they stand in the Scottish Liturgy to be the better, and more agreeable to use in the primitive Church; and I believe they which are learned will acknowledge it." [1]

Of the attack on the Book on the ground that "the corporal presence of Christ's body in the Sacrament is" "to be found here," he says :—

"They say, 'the corporal presence of Christ's body in the Sacrament is to be found in this Service-book'. But they must pardon me; I know it is not there. I cannot be myself of a contrary judgment, and yet suffer that to pass. But let's see their proof. 'The words of the Mass-book, serving to that purpose, which are sharply censured by Bucer in King Edward's Liturgy, and are not to be found in the Book of England, yet are taken into this Service-book.' I know no words tending to this purpose in King Edward's Liturgy, fit for Bucer to censure sharply; and therefore not tending to that purpose; for did they tend to that, they could not be censured too sharply. The words, it seems, are these: 'O merciful Father, of Thy almighty goodness, vouchsafe so to bless and sanctify with Thy word and Holy Spirit these Thy gifts and creatures of bread and wine that they may be unto us the body and blood of Thy most dearly beloved Son'. Well, if these be the words, how will they squeeze corporal presence out of them? Why, first, 'the change here is made a work of God's omnipotency'. Well, and a work of omnipotency it is, whatever the change be. For less than Omnipotence cannot change those elements, either in nature or use to so high a service as they are put in that great Sacrament. And therefore the invocating of God's almighty goodness to effect this by them is no proof at all of intending the 'corporal presence of Christ in this Sacrament'. 'Tis true this passage is not in the prayer of consecration in the Service-book of England; but I wish with all my heart it were. For though the consecration of the elements may be without it, yet it is much more solemn and full by that invocation. Secondly, 'these words,' they say, 'intend the corporal presence of Christ in the Sacrament because the words in the Mass are *ut fiant nobis*,' 'that they may be unto us the body and the blood of Christ'. Now for the good of Christendom I would with all my heart that these words *ut fiant nobis*,—that these elements might be 'to us,' worthy receivers, the blessed body and blood of our Saviour,—were the worst error in the Mass. For then I would hope that this great controversy, which to all men that are out of

the Church is the shame, and among all that are within the Church
is the division of Christendom, might have some good accommodation.
For if it be only *ut fiant nobis*, that they may be to us the body and
the blood of Christ, it implies clearly that they 'are to us' but are not
transubstantiated in themselves into the body and blood of Christ,
nor that there is any corporal presence in or under the elements.
And then nothing can more cross the doctrine of the present Church
of Rome than their own service. For as the elements after the
benediction or consecration are, and may be called, the body and
blood of Christ without any addition in that real and true sense in
which they are so called in Scripture ; so, when they are said to
become the body and blood of Christ *nobis*, to us that communicate
as we ought; there is by this addition, *fiant nobis*, an allay in the
proper signification of the body and blood : and the true sense, so
well signified and expressed that the words cannot well be understood otherwise than to imply not the corporal substance but the
real and yet the spiritual use of them. And so the words *ut fiant
nobis* import quite contrary to that which they are brought to
prove." [1]

Of the words of administration he says that he sees "no hurt
in the omission of those latter words, none at all," and quotes
with approval from Dr. Wetherborne's notes :—

"There is no more in King Edward VI. his first Book. And if
there be no more in ours, the action will be much the shorter.
Besides, the words which are added since, 'Take, eat, in remembrance, etc.,' may seem to relish somewhat of the Zwinglian tenet
that the Sacrament is a bare sign taken in remembrance of Christ's
passion." [2]

In regard to the charge that the Scottish Book contained
"the oblation of the body and the blood of Christ, which Bellarmine calls *Sacrificium laudis quia Deus per illud magnopere
laudatur*," he writes :—

"First, I think no man doubts but that there is and ought to be
offered up to God at the consecration and reception of this Sacrament *sacrificium laudis*, the sacrifice of praise ; and that this ought
to be expressed in the Liturgy for the instruction of the people.
And these words, 'We entirely desire Thy fatherly goodness mercifully to accept this our sacrifice of praise andthanks giving,' etc.,
are both in the Book of England and in that which was prepared

[1] *Op. cit.* iii. 353-55.   [2] *Ibid.* 357.

for Scotland. And if ' Bellarmine do call the oblation of the body
and the blood of Christ a sacrificium of praise,' sure he doth well in
it ; (for so it is) if Bellarmine mean no more by the oblation of the
body and the blood of Christ than a commemoration and a representation of that great sacrifice offered up by Christ Himself, as Bishop
Jewel very learnedly and fully acknowledges. But if Bellarmine go
further than this, and by ' the oblation of the body and the blood
of Christ' mean that the priest offers up that which Christ Himself
did, and not a commemoration of it only,[1] he is erroneous in that,
and can never make it good." [2]

The *Summary of Devotions Compiled and Used by Dr. William
Laud*, which was published in 1667 from his manuscript, illustrates
that Laud's theology was a deep influence in his life. The section
headed " Eucharistia " includes the following prayers :—

" O Lord, into a clean, charitable, and thankful heart give me
grace to receive the blessed body and blood of Thy Son, my most
blessed Saviour, that it may more perfectly cleanse me from all dregs
of sin."

"Behold, I quarrel not the words of Thy Son my Saviour's
blessed institution. I know His words are no gross unnatural con-
ceit, but they are spirit and life, and supernatural. While the
world disputes, I believe. He hath promised me, if I come worthily,
that I shall receive His most precious body and blood, with all
the benefits of His passion. If I can receive it and retain it (Lord,
make me able, make me worthy), I know I can no more die eternally
than that body and blood can die, and be shed again."

" How I receive the body and blood of my most blessed Saviour
Jesus Christ, the price of my redemption, is the very wonder of
my soul, yet my most firm and constant belief upon the words of
my Saviour."

" Lord, I have received this Sacrament of the body and blood
of my dear Saviour. His mercy hath given it, and my faith received
it into my soul. I humbly beseech Thee, speak mercy and peace
unto my conscience, and enrich me with all those graces which come
from that precious body and blood, even till I be possessed of eternal
life in Christ." [3]

---

[1] A note is here added : " Differentia est in modo ; illic enim Christus
vere occisus est: hic mortis fit repraesentatio [the difference is in the
method ; for in that case Christ was really slain : in this case His death
is set forth].—*Hugo Grot. in Consult. Cassandri ad Art.* 10, p. 25."

[2] *Op. cit.* iii. 358, 359.   [3] *Ibid.* 72-75.

Richard Mountague was born in 1577. After being Fellow of Eton, Rector of Stanford Rivers, Dean of Hereford, Canon of Windsor, Archdeacon of Hereford, and Rector of Petworth, he became Bishop of Chichester in 1628 and Bishop of Norwich in 1638. He died in 1641. His Eucharistic doctrine, as shown in his *A Gagg for the New Gospel?* No. *A New Gagg for an Old Goose* and *Appello Cæsarem : a Just Appeale from Two Unjust Informers*, published in 1624 and 1625, appears to have been much the same as that of Laud. He rejects Transubstantiation with great explicitness and vehemence, and calls it a "monster of monsters". He says that our Lord's teaching in the sixth chapter of St. John's Gospel is not contrary to "This is My body" but only to "This is My body by this means," that is, Transubstantiation; that some of St. Chrysostom's statements about the Eucharist "cannot be understood literally"; that there is "no difference" between the Church of England and the Church of Rome "in the point of real presence," but that the disagreement is "only in *de modo præsentiæ*"; that "change," "alteration," "transmutation," and "transelementation" are not to be denied; that the consecrated elements are "somewhat more than mere ordinary bread and wine," since there is "a sacramental being of them, and not only a natural, in their use and designment," and "no man otherwise believeth but that the natural condition of the bread consecrated is otherwise than it was; being disposed and used to that holy use of imparting Christ unto the communicants". He exhorts his Roman Catholic opponents, "Be contented with *That it is,* and do not seek nor define *How it is so ;* and we shall not contest or contend with you".[1] He maintains that the Eucharist is a "sacrifice," but that is "not propitiatory for the living and dead" and "not an external, visible, true, and proper sacrifice, but only representative, rememorative, and spiritual sacrifice"; and that there is "no such sacrifice of the altar," and there are "no such altars," as the Church of Rome teaches.[2]

George Herbert was born in 1593. He was a Fellow of Trinity College, Cambridge, and Public Orator at Cambridge. He was appointed to the Prebend of Layton Ecclesia in the diocese of Lincoln in 1625, and became Rector of Fugglestone

---

[1] *New Gagg*, pp. 12-15, 250-57 ; *Appello Cæsarem*, pp. 261, 262, 289, 293, 294.

[2] *Appello Cæsarem*, pp. 286, 287.

18 *

with Bemerton in 1630, three years before his death in 1633.
There are occasional allusions to the Eucharist in his poems, and
in his treatise, *A Priest to the Temple, or the Country Parson,
his character, and rule of holy life.*   In the *Priest to the Temple*
he writes :—

"The Country Parson being to administer the Sacraments is at
a stand with himself how or what behaviour to assume for so holy
things.   Especially at Communion times he is in a great confusion
as being not only to receive God but to break and administer Him.
Neither finds he any issue in this but to throw himself down at the
throne of grace, saying, 'Lord, Thou knowest what Thou didst when
Thou appointedst it to be done thus ; therefore do Thou fulfil what
Thou didst appoint ; for Thou art not only the Feast but the way to
it '." [1]

Herbert's poem entitled *The Holy Communion* is as follows :—

"Not in rich furniture, or fine array,
    Nor in a wedge of gold,
    Thou, who from me wast sold,
To me dost now Thyself convey ;
For so Thou should'st without me still have been,
    Leaving within me sinne :

But by the way of nourishment and strength,
    Thou creep'st into my breast :
    Making Thy way my rest,
And Thy small quantities my length ;
Which spread their forces into every part,
    Meeting sinnes force and art.

Yet can these not get over to my soul,
    Leaping the wall that parts
    Our souls and fleshly hearts ;
But as th' outworks, they may controll
My rebel-flesh, and carrying Thy name,
    Affright both sinne and shame.

Onely Thy grace, which with these elements comes,
    Knoweth the ready way,
    And hath the privie key,
Op'ning the souls most subtile rooms :
While those to spirits refin'd at doore attend
    Despatches from their friend.

[1] Chapter 22.

Give me my captive soul, or take
My body also thither.
Another lift like this will make
Them both to be together.

Before that sinne turn'd flesh to stone,
And all our lump to leaven;
A fervent sigh might well have blown
Our innocent earth to heaven.

For sure when Adam did not know
To sinne, or sinne to smother;
He might to heav'n from Paradise go,
As from one room t' another.

Thou hast restor'd us to this ease
By this Thy heav'nly blood,
Which I can go to, when I please,
And leave th' earth to their food."

One of the verses in the poem *The Priesthood* is—

" But th' holy men of God such vessels are,
As serve Him up, who all the world commands.
When God vouchsafeth to become our fàre,
Their hands convey Him, who conveys their hands:
O what pure things, most pure must those things be,
Who bring my God to me!"

The Invitation is as follows :—

" Come ye hither all, whose taste
Is your waste ;
Save your cost, and mend your fare.
God is here prepar'd and drest,
And the feast,
God, in whom all dainties are.

Come ye hither all, whom wine
Doth define,
Naming you not to your good:
Weep what ye have drunk amisse,
And drink this,
Which before ye drink is blood.

Come ye hither all, whom pain
                    Doth arraigne,
Bringing all your sinnes to sight :
Taste and fear not : God is here
                    In this cheer,
And on sinne doth cast the fright.

Come ye hither all, whom joy
                    Doth destroy,
While ye graze without your bounds :
Here is joy that drowneth quite
                    Your delight,
As a flood the lower grounds.

Come ye hither all, whose love
                    Is your dove,
And exalts you to the skie :
Here is love, which, having breath
                    Ev'n in death,
After death can never die.

Lord, I have invited all,
                    And I shall
Still invite, still call to Thee :
For it seems but just and right
                    In my sight,
Where is all, there all should be."

In *The Banquet* Herbert writes :—

"Welcome sweet and sacred cheer,
                    Welcome deare ;
With me, in me, live and dwell :
For Thy neatnesse passeth sight,
                    Thy delight
Passeth tongue to taste or tell.

O what sweetnesse from the bowl
                    Fills my soul,
Such as is, and makes divine !
Is some starre (fled from the sphere)
                    Melted there,
As we sugar melt in wine ?

Or hath sweetnesse in the bread
   Made a head
To subdue the smell of sinne,
Flowers, and gummes, and powders giving
   All their living,
Lest the enemy should winne ?

Doubtlesse neither starre nor flower
   Hath the power
Such a sweetnesse to impart :
Onely God, who gives perfumes,
   Flesh assumes,
And with it perfumes my heart.

But as Pomanders and wood
   Still are good,
Yet being bruis'd are better scented ;
God, to show how farre His love
   Could improve,
Here, as broken, is presented.

When I had forgot my birth,
   And on earth
In delights of earth was drown'd ;
God took blood, and needs would be
   Split with me,
And so found me on the ground.

Having rais'd me to look up,
   In a cup
Sweetly He doth meet my taste.
But I still being low and short,
   Farre from court,
Wine becomes a wing at last.

For with it alone I flie
   To the skie :
Where I wipe mine eyes, and see
What I seek for, what I sue ;
   Him I view
Who hath done so much for me.

> Lest the wonder of this pitie
>   Be my dittie,
> And take up my lines and life :
> Hearken under pain of death,
>   Hands and breath,
> Strive in this, and love the strife."

III.

Another group of writers who may conveniently be considered together consists of Crakanthorp, Morton, Sutton, Jackson, and Hammond.

Richard Crakanthorp was born at Strickland, a village in Westmoreland, in 1567. He was a Fellow of Queen's College, Oxford. He and Thomas Morton were chaplains to Lord Eure, the ambassador extraordinary to the Emperor at the end of Elizabeth's and beginning of James I.'s reign. In 1605 he was appointed Rector of Black Notley, and in 1617 of Paglesham also. He died in 1624. His most important work is the *Defensio Ecclesiæ Anglicanæ contra M. Antonii de Dominis, D. Archiepiscopi Spalatensis, Injurias.* In it he argues at great length against the doctrine of Transubstantiation.[1] Together with Transubstantiation he rejects what de Dominis, against whom he wrote, had called "the real and bodily presence of the body and blood of the Lord". He condemns the adoration of the body of Christ in the Sacrament, and contrasts the certainty of the presence of the Godhead of Christ in bread or wood or a stone or a priest or any man, in which cases no one suggests adoration, with the uncertainty of His presence as Man "in or under the species of bread". He explains the purpose of the consecration of the elements as being to make them an effectual sign and instrument to enable believers to receive the body and blood of Christ.

"Let us see how beautifully you prove that you are not idolaters in this [Eucharistic adoration]. You say, 'The real and bodily presence of the body and blood of the Lord in the most holy mysteries of the Eucharist is to us most certain'. Good heavens, 'most certain'? Concerning this you have not the certainty of faith, which is infallible. One might well discuss with you whether it is moral certainty; yet the 'certainty' you have here is hardly conjectural.

---

[1] *E.g.* ch. xlviii.

For listen to what I shall say seriously, and undertake to show by most sure and clear proofs when there is need. You have no certainty at all either that he who consecrates is a priest, or that he is baptised, or that he intends to do what the Church does, or that the bread is ever transubstantiated into the body of Christ, or that Transubstantiation is possible. . . . No one of these things do you know certainly and infallibly, nor can you know any one of them without a special revelation. I add that you either know or can know that it is not in accordance with Scripture, or the decrees and writings of the councils or fathers for six hundred years after Christ, or sense, or any reason, for the bread to be transubstantiated into the body of Christ; nay, the Scriptures and councils and fathers which I have cited, and reason and sense, assuredly show that the bread is not transubstantiated into the body of Christ. Yet you are 'most certain' concerning the bodily presence of Christ in the Eucharist, though your 'certainty' is not derived from Scripture, nor from the testimony of the ancient fathers, nor from sense, nor from reason; but about this you are cherishing an opinion that is merely vain, and is foolish and impossible, and paying court to it as the idol of your hearts. But what is your excuse for your idolatry? You say, 'We adore with real worship the body of Christ lying hid under the species, which is in itself adorable because of the personal union'. Well and significantly have you said, 'lying hid'. For of a surety it lies hid from the eyes of the body, the eyes of reason, the eyes of men, the eyes of angels, the eyes that are glorified, the eyes of others, the eyes of Christ Himself. . . . Tell me seriously, do you adore that hidden body of Christ 'in itself'? Is it 'in itself' adorable with worship? Take care lest you be men-worshippers, and come under the anathema of the holy Council of Ephesus. . . . Your words 'We adore the body of Christ itself,' and 'we adore the body in itself,' have a bad sound. I warn you, if your mind is right, to let your words be so also. In matters of faith I don't want tricks about words. Say then (what I think you meant) 'We adore Christ Himself, whose body is present in the species'. But there is something else which I very much want explained. Are we to think that the body of Christ itself is under the species, and that for this reason the body of Christ lying hid in them is to be adored by you in the host more than the deity of Christ itself lying hid in bread and in wood and in stone and in a priest and in any man is to be adored in them? The reason of your adoration is the presence of Godhead, because Christ who is God lies hid there. Since then there is the same reason for adoration in the other things of which

I spoke, since Christ who is God is really and actually in bread and in stone and in any man, why do you not fall at the feet of any priest, of any man, that you may show worship to Christ lying hid in them. Concerning the presence of Christ, in that He is God, in all these you are most certain; concerning the presence of Christ, in that He is Man, in or under the species of bread you are most uncertain." [1]

" See how easy and clear is our explanation of Christ's words. Christ took bread ; He blessed the bread ; by that blessing or prayer He consecrated it to this holy, lofty, heavenly, and mystic use, that it should be a sign not only signifying but also effectual and bestowing His body to believers instrumentally but spiritually. Of this bread so blessed, consecrated, and changed by the blessing of Christ . . . from common and ordinary use to this sacred and heavenly use He said, ' This is My body ' ; this which I have taken, which I have broken, which I have consecrated, ' This is My body '. . . . Because it is most certain that the bread is not the body of Christ properly speaking, it necessarily follows that the words of Christ are not literal but figurative and tropical, and that the bread was called His body by Christ because it is a sacred sign not only signifying but also bestowing the real body of Christ on believers instrumentally but spiritually. . . . There is no change in the substance, as there is none in the stones of the altar, or in a man elevated to the priesthood, or in water sanctified for Baptism ; [2] but the change is only accidental in the use, in the effect, in the power, in the office of the bread and wine, as is the change in the stones, in a priest, in the water of Baptism." [3]

Crakanthorp denies, though he evidently misunderstood, the doctrine of the Eucharistic sacrifice affirmed by the Council of Trent. He allows a commemorative sacrifice in the Eucharist.

" From what we have said about your Transubstantiation two, besides many other, consequences follow. First, the sacrifice of the Mass is not really a propitiatory sacrifice, as the Council of Trent defines, and your men teach ; but it is only Eucharistic and commemorative. A properly propitiatory sacrifice is one which makes God propitious to sinners of its own force without relation to anything else, and obtains the forgiveness of sins and the grace of God

---

[1] Ch. lxxi. §§ 2-5.

[2] Referring to the passage of St. Gregory of Nyssa, quoted on vol. i. pp. 68-70, *supra*. As there pointed out, this interpretation of St. Gregory's words is precluded by what he says elsewhere.

[3] Ch. lxxii. §§ 9, 19, ch. lxxiii. § 23.

of its own merit, value, price, and worth.[1] Such a sacrifice there never was or will be except Christ alone, offering His body and blood to God on the cross. He Himself, and no one besides Him, is ' the propitiation for our sins '.[2] Christ is not in the Eucharist bodily, as we have already shown ; and therefore His body and blood cannot be offered except in a figure and by way of commemoration. Therefore that which is offered actually and by the hands of the priest in the Mass cannot be really and properly a propitiatory sacrifice. Neither is there in the Mass any real and properly so-called sacrifice, not such as the Council of Trent defined and your men with one mouth profess. This is laid down as one of many requisites to the essence of a real and properly so-called sacrifice, and it is put in your own definition, that ' what is offered to God is changed ' ; that is, as Bellarmine himself explains, ' It is wholly destroyed, that is, it is so changed that it ceases to be' that which it was before,' in such a way that ' not only its use but also its substance is consumed '.[3] And in what way the substance of that which is offered is to be consumed he explains according to the differences in things which are offered. . . . See now on the showing of your own Cardinal either that, if Christ is not really, and actually slain, there is no real and proper sacrifice in the Mass, or that, if He is really and actually slain by the priests, your priests are really sacrilegious and slayers of God. . . . The second consequence of which I spoke is that the Church of Rome is really idolatrous, and all those who belong to it are properly and formally idolaters. For you adore with the service of worship the Eucharist and that body which is contained under the species of bread and wine. . That this body is in substance nothing else than bread and wine has already been abundantly shown. Therefore you give to bread and wine, that is, to creatures, the worship and service which are due to the Creator alone, than which there is nothing more properly idolatry." [4]

Thomas Morton was born at York in 1564. He was a Fellow of St. John's College, Cambridge ; and, after being chaplain to Lord Huntingdon and, together with Crakanthorp, to Lord Eure when acting as ambassador extraordinary to the Emperor, and holding several ecclesiastical preferments, including the Deaneries of Gloucester and Winchester, he became Bishop

[1] This sentence entirely, though probably unintentionally, misrepresents the Tridentine teaching : see pp. 96-100, *supra*.
[2] 1 St. John ii. 2.
[3] On Bellarmine's teaching, see pp. 364-67, *infra*.
[4] Ch. lxxiv. §§ 1-3.

of Chester in 1616, Bishop of Coventry and Lichfield in 1618, and Bishop of Durham in 1632. He died in 1659. Among his writings is an elaborate treatise entitled *Of the Institution of the Sacrament of the Blessed Body and Blood of Christ, (by some called) the Masse of Christ*, which was published in 1631. He denies Transubstantiation and the bodily presence of Christ; maintains that our Lord's words at the institution of the Sacrament were used in a figurative sense; and asserts that faithful communicants receive the body of Christ spiritually by faith.

"What necessity there is to inquire into the true sense of these words [This is My body] will best appear in the after examination of the diverse consequences of your own sense, to wit, your doctrine of Transubstantiation, corporal, and material presence, propitiatory sacrifice, and proper adoration. All which are dependants upon your Romish exposition of the former words of Christ. The issue then will be this, that if the words be certainly true in a proper and literal sense, then we are to yield to you the whole cause; but if it be necessarily figurative, then the ground of all these your doctrines being but sandy the whole structure and fabric which you erect thereupon must needs ruin and vanish. But yet know withal that we do not so maintain a figurative sense of Christ His speech concerning His body as to exclude the truth of His body, or yet the truly receiving thereof."[1]

"Ten reasons for proof of the necessity of interpreting the words of Christ figuratively. First, we have been compellable to allow a figurative sense by the confessed analogy of Scripture in all such sacramental speeches of both Testaments. . . . Secondly, we are challengeable hereunto by our article of faith, which teacheth but one natural body of Christ, and the same to remain now in heaven. Thirdly, we are enforced for fear of such heresies as have followed in other cases upon the literal sense. . . . Fourthly, we are necessarily moved to reject your literal sense by a confessed impossibility. . . . Fifthly, we are persuaded hereunto by the former alleged interpretation of the ancient fathers both of the Greek and Latin Church calling the Sacrament a figure, and expounding 'This is' by 'This signifieth'. Sixthly, we are urged by the rule set down by St. Augustine for the direction of the whole Catholic Church that, 'Whensoever the precept,' saith he, 'seemeth to command that which is heinous' (as to eat the flesh of Christ) 'it is figurative'.[2]

---

[1] II. i. *init.*

[2] St. Augustine, *De doct. Christ.* iii. 24, quoted on vol. i. p. 65, *supra.*

. . . Seventhly, a motive it must needs be to any reasonable man to defend the figurative sense by observing the misery of your disputers in contending for a literal exposition thereof. . . . Eighthly, your own unreasonableness may persuade somewhat, who have not been able hitherto to confirm any one of your five former objections to the contrary by any one father of the Church. Ninthly, for that the literal interpretation of Christ's words was the foundation of the heresy of the Capernaites, and hath affinity with divers other ancient heresies condemned by antiquity. Tenthly, our last persuasion is the consent of antiquity against the literal conversion of bread into Christ's body, which you call Transubstantiation, against the literal corporal presence, against literal corporal eating and union, and against a proper sacrifice of Christ's body subjectively. All which are fully presuasive inducements to enforce a figurative sense." [1]

"We, whom you call heretics, believe that the devout communicant, receiving Christ spiritually by faith, is thereby possessed of whole Christ crucified in the inward act of the soul." [2]

"There lieth a charge upon every soul that shall communicate and participate of this Sacrament, that herein he ' discern the Lord's body,' [3] which office of discerning (according to the judgment of Protestants) is not only in the use but also in the nature to distinguish the object of faith from the object of sense. The first object of Christian faith is the divine alteration and change of natural bread into a Sacrament of Christ's body ; this we call a divine change because none but the same omnipotent power that made the creature and element of bread can change it into a Sacrament. The second object of faith is the body of Christ itself sacramentally represented and verily exhibited to the faithful communicants. There are then three objects in all to be distinguished. The first is before consecration, the bread merely natural. Secondly, after consecration, bread sacramental. Thirdly, Christ's own body, which is the spiritual and supersubstantial bread truly exhibited by this Sacrament to the nourishment of the souls of the faithful." [4]

"There may be observed four kinds of truths of Christ His presence in this Sacrament. One is veritas signi, that is, truth of representation of Christ His body ; the next is veritas revelationis, truth of revelation ; the third is veritas obsignationis, that is, a truth of seal, for better assurance ; the last is veritas exhibitionis, the truth of exhibiting and deliverance of the real body of Christ to the faithful communicants. The truth of the sign in respect of the thing signified is to be acknowledged so far as in the signs of bread and wine

[1] II. iii. 6.   [2] I. iii. 10.   [3] 1 Cor. xi. 29.   [4] III. i. 1.

is represented the true and real body and blood of Christ, which truth and reality is celebrated by us and taught by ancient fathers in contradiction to Manichees, Marcionites, and other old heretics, who held that Christ had in Himself no true body but merely phantastical. . . . A second truth and reality in this Sacrament is called *veritas revelationis*, as it is a sign in respect of the typical signs of the same body and blood of Christ in the rites of the Old Testament, yet not absolutely in respect of the matter itself but of the manner, because the faithful under the Law had the same faith in Christ, and therefore their Sacraments had relation to the same body and blood of Christ, but in a difference of manner. . . . As . . . the truth of history is held to be more real than the truth of prophecy because it is a declaration of a real performance of that which was promised, so the evangelical Sacrament may be said to contain in it a more real verity than the Levitical. . . . Besides the former two, there is *veritas obsignationis*, a truth sealed, which maketh this Sacrament more than a sign, even a seal of God's promises in Christ. . . . A fourth reason to be observed herein, as more special, is *veritas exhibitionis*, a truth exhibiting and delivering to the faithful communicants the thing signified and sealed. . . . Vain therefore is the objection made by your Cardinal in urging us with the testimony of Athanasius [1] to prove that Christ His body is exhibited to the receivers, as though there were not a truth in a mystical and sacramental deliverance of Christ His body except it were by a corporal and material presence thereof, which is a transparent falsity, as any may perceive by any deed of gift which by writing, seal, and delivery conveyeth any land or possession from man to man, yet this far more effectually." [2]

" A Christian man consisting of two parts, the outward or bodily, and the inward which is spiritual, this Sacrament accordingly consisteth of two parts, earthly and heavenly, as Irenæus [3] spake of the bodily elements of bread and wine as the visible signs and objects of sense, and of the body and blood of Christ, which is the spiritual part. Answerable to both these is the double nourishment and union of a Christian, the one sacramental by communicating of the outward elements of bread and wine united to man's body in his taking, eating, digesting, till at length it be transubstantiated into him by being substantially incorporated in his flesh. The other, which is the

---

[1] Bellarmine, *De Euch.* ii. 11, citing St. Athanasius as quoted by Theodoret, *Dial.* ii. (t. iv. pp. 137, 138, Schulze ; *P.G.* t. lxxxiii. col. 180).

[2] IV. i. 2.

[3] St. Irenæus, *Adv. Hær.* IV. xxxi. 4, quoted on vol. i. p. 35, *supra*.

spiritual and soul's food, is the body and blood of the Lord (therefore called spiritual because it is the object of faith) by an union wrought by God's Spirit and man's faith, which (as hath been professed by Protestants) is most real and ineffable." [1]

"All our premised sections throughout this fifth book do clearly make up this conclusion that the body of Christ which Protestants do feed upon as their soul's food is the body of Christ once crucified and now sitting in glorious majesty in heaven; and that body of Christ believed by you is of corporal eating indeed and in truth of bread. . . . Wherefore let every Christian study with sincere conscience to eat the flesh of Christ with a spiritual appetite as his soul's food, thereby to have a spiritual union with Him proper to the faithful, not subject to vomitings or corruption and not common to wicked men and vile beasts, but always working to the salvation of the true receivers : so shall he abhor all your Capernaitical fancies." [2]

Morton denies that the Eucharist is a " proper sacrifice " on the ground that a "proper sacrifice" involves destruction. Misunderstanding, like Crakanthorp, the teaching of the Council of Trent, [3] and assuming that a "propitiatory sacrifice" must be propitious in its own force and of itself, he denies also that the Eucharist is a "propitiatory sacrifice". He allows that it is a spiritual and commemorative sacrifice, representing and applying the sacrifice of the cross.

"Every proper sacrifice is properly visible, of profane is made sacred, and properly suffereth destruction. (This is your own proposition in each part.) But the body of Christ in the Eucharist is neither properly visible, nor properly of profane made sacred, nor suffereth any proper destruction. (This is also your own assumption.) Therefore the body of Christ in this Sacrament is not a proper sacrifice nor properly sacrificed. This (except men have lost their brains) must needs be every man's conclusion. And that so much the rather because it cannot be sufficient that Christ's body be present in the Eucharist to make it a sacrifice without some sacrificing act. A sheep is no sacrifice whilst it remaineth in the fold, nor can every action serve the turn except it be a destructive act ; for the sheep doth not become therefore a sacrifice because it is shorn, nor yet can any destructive act be held sacrificing which is not prescribed by divine authority, which only can ordain a sacrifice,

[1] V. i. 1.   [2] V. ix. 4.   [3] See pp. 96-100, *supra*.

as hath been confessed.   But no such divine ordinance hath hitherto
been proved." [1]

"Protestants in their celebration profess four sorts of sacrifices.
For proof hereof we may instance in our Church of England, most
happily reformed and established.   First, the sacrifice of mortification in act, and of martyrdom in vow, saying, 'We offer unto Thee, O
Lord, ourselves, our souls and bodies, to be a holy, lively, and reasonable sacrifice unto Thee'.   Next, a sacrifice Eucharistical, saying,
'We desire Thy fatherly goodness mercifully to accept of our sacrifice of praise and thanksgiving'. . . . Thirdly, a sacrifice latreutical,
that is, of divine worship, saying, 'And although we be unworthy
to offer up any sacrifice, yet we beseech Thee to accept of our
bounden duty and service'.   This performance of our bounden
service is that which ancient fathers called an unbloody sacrifice.
. . . Now wherein and in what respect we may furthermore be said
to offer to God a sacrifice propitiatory, improperly, will after appear
when we consider Christ's body as the object herein." [2]

"Now we come to the last, most true, and necessary point, which
is the body and blood as the object of our commemoration.   Still,
still do you urge the saying of fathers where they affirm that we offer
unto God the same body and blood of Christ on this altar, even the
same which was sacrificed on the cross, which therefore you interpret
as being the same subject matter of our commemoration. . . . We
as instantly, and more truly, proclaim that we offer (commemoratively) the same, undoubtedly the very same body and blood of
Christ His all-sufficient sacrifice on the cross, although not as the
subject of His proper sacrifice, but yet as the only adequate object
of our commemoration. . . . It will be easy for us to discern the
subject sacrifice of Christ from ours, His being the real sacrifice on
the cross, ours only the sacramental representation, commemoration,
and application thereof." [3]

"First, although the whole act of our celebration in commemoration of Christ's death as proceeding from us be a sacrifice propitious,
as other holy acts of devotion, only by God's complacency and acceptance, yet the object of our commemoration being the death and
passion of Christ in His body and blood is to us, by the efficacy
thereof, a truly and properly propitiatory sacrifice and satisfaction
for a perfect remission of all sins.   Thus concerning Protestants.
As for you, if we consider your own outward acts of celebration
(where in ten circumstances we find ten transgressions of the institution of Christ, and therefore provocatory to stir up God's displeasure),

[1] VI. vi. 3.   [2] VI. vii. 3.   [3] VI. vii. 4.

we think not that it can be propitiatory so much as by way of God's acceptance. Next, when we dive into the mystery of your Mass, to seek out the subject matter of your sacrifice in the hands of your priest, which according to the faith of your Church is called a proper propitiatory sacrifice in itself, it hath been found (besides our proofs from Scriptures and your own principles) by ten demonstrations out of ancient fathers to be sacramental bread and wine, and not the body and blood of Christ. Wherefore the subject of your sacrifice can be no more properly (that is, satisfactorily) in itself propitiatory than natural bread can be Christ." [1]

Morton is careful to repudiate the notion of any who might lay such stress on the difference between the Church of England and Roman Catholics being only as to the manner of the presence of Christ's body in the Sacrament as to consider the Roman Catholic doctrines to be tolerable or open to reconciliation.

" It would be a wonder to us to hear any of our own profession to be so extremely indifferent concerning the different opinions of the manner of the presence of Christ's body in the Sacrament as to think the Romish sect therefore either tolerable or reconciliable upon pretence that the question is only *de modo*, that is, of the manner of being, and that consequently all controversy about this is but vain jangling. Such an one ought to enter into his second thoughts, to consider the necessity that lieth upon every Christian to abandon divers heresies, albeit their difference from the orthodox profession were only *de modo*. . . . That the Romish manner of eating Christ's body is Capernaitical ; her manner of sacrifice sacrilegious ; her manner of divine adoration thereof idolatrous ; and all these manners irreconcilable to the manner of our Church, is copiously declared in the books following." [2]

Christopher Sutton was born about 1565 ; he was a member of Lincoln College, Oxford ; he held a number of benefices and was Canon of Westminster and of Lincoln ; he died in 1629. His

---

[1] VI. xii. 2. Compare Morton's earlier work, *A Catholic Appeal for Protestants* (published in 1609), II. vii.

[2] IV. i. 1. In *A Catholic Appeal for Protestants*, II. ii. 1, Bishop Morton says, " Our difference is not about the truth or reality of presence, but about the true manner of the being and receiving thereof " ; but his meaning in the part of this treatise which relates to the Eucharist does not appear to be different from that expressed in the passages quoted above from *Of the Institution of the Sacrament.*

Godly Meditations upon the Most Holy Sacrament of the Lord's Supper, which was published in 1630, a year after his death, was one of the most popular devotional books of the seventeenth century. He strongly deprecates controversy about the Eucharist, and describes the true doctrine as a mean between Transubstantiation and a view that it is merely a badge and token and remembrance. He appears to have believed that there is no change in the elements at consecration except in regard to their use, but that those who receive them faithfully partake spiritually of the body and blood of Christ in a manner which passes human explanation and understanding.

"Consider the divine wisdom of the Son of God, who respecting our weakness hath conveyed unto us His body and blood after a divine and spiritual manner under the forms of bread and wine." [1]

"Consider the high and worthy effect of this heavenly food, which is not so much changed into the substance of the eater as it doth rather change the eater into the substance of it; the meat being divine doth make us also divine." [2]

"Now of long time, yea, too, too long, O holy Christ, have we Christians contended about Thy holy institution; from the fathers to Thy Apostles: yea, O blessed Saviour, we come with all reverence, and let us come hand in hand, to consider the first pattern instituted by Thyself. And here first, let the devout Christian call to mind that He that said of the wine, 'This is My blood,' and of the bread, 'This is My body,' said also of St. John the Baptist, 'This is that Elias,' and of Himself, 'I am the door,' 'the true vine,' etc. [3] These—'Receive My covenant in your flesh,' 'By Baptism we are buried with Him,' 'Being many, we are one bread, one body'—are usual phrases in Holy Writ. [4] Again, what more meet than in a spiritual food to admit a spiritual sense? 'We did all eat of the same spiritual meat,' saith the Apostle. [5] Was it not given after supper, and in small quantity? It is the Spirit that giveth life. I go forward, but by the way this pious consideration gathered out of the words of Christ our Saviour concerning His own institution doth easily show that to be the nourishment of our souls which is delivered in the Lord's Supper, and doth withal manifest the great excellency thereof. From the words of Christ I come unto the Apostle St. Paul, a good interpreter of the same words, one who wanted not care of stirring up the Corinthians to reverence and devotion about this mystery. Now, what

---

[1] IV. 3.　　　　[2] IV. 5.　　　　[3] St. John x. 7, xv. 1.
[4] Gen. xvii. 13; Rom. vi. 4; 1 Cor. x. 17.　　　　[5] 1 Cor. x. 3.

saith the Apostle? He commands no adoration; he speaks not a word of Transubstantiation; but only showeth the dignity thereof in showing both the Author and the end. . . . To break off the mentioning of the fathers, lest in multiplying their names we might seem ambitious, we hear them all, as it is meet, speaking with great reverence of so great a mystery : but for disputing or reasoning about Transubstantiation we hear not a word. Let their writings be read over, and read over again, and we shall find that they admit of a change, but what a one? of the substance? nothing less; for it remains the same : of the use? it is right, for sure in the Lord's Supper it is heavenly and divine. Whereas oftentimes in the fathers we meet with the words 'nature,' 'substance,' applying them to the efficacy of the Sacrament, we are to understand that by these words they intended, first, to draw the people from the outward signs to the substance, and next to kindle in their affections both reverence and love. Antiquity therefore is silent in the plea or the defence of Transubstantiation. Sure, yea, most sure it is that the figurative speeches of the ancient fathers do no way patronise this paradox. The sobriety of the same fathers let us, their posterity, praise and imitate. . . . We acknowledge that the dignity of this Sacrament is greater than words can express, yea, than the mind of man is able to conceive. If any will exact the efficacy of those five words, 'For this is My body,' we answer, It is a great mystery. Truly we give, and that justly, great respect and reverence to the Holy Eucharist ; for whereas bread and wine are elements naturally ordained for the sustenance of the body, by the power of divine benediction they do receive a virtue that, being received of the faithful, they become nourishment of the soul, nay, they become means whereby we are sanctified both in body and soul, and are made the members of Christ. But Christ, some say, in express words calleth the bread His body, and the wine His blood ; true, in express words also He calleth Himself a rock. Right well saith Eusebius Emisenus, ' Comest thou to the Sacrament, consider there the body and blood of Christ : wonder at it with reverence, touch it with thy mind, receive it with the hand of thy heart ' ;[1] do not say with the Capernaites, Master, how comest Thou hither? but with the disciples asking no question be glad thou dost enjoy Him. He is honoured in this mystery that was once offered upon the cross. Yea, but how can this be that Christ sitting at the right hand of God in heaven should dispose of His body to us poor inhabitants of earth? Take here the answer of the angel Gabriel, The Holy Ghost hath overshadowed it.[2] ' From hence,'

---

[1] See vol. i. pp. 129-31, *supra*.　　　[2] St. Luke i. 35.

19 *

saith St. Bernard, 'to search is temerity, to know is life eternal.'
Is it not a hard saying, 'Unless ye eat the flesh of the Son of God,'
etc.? It is a hard saying to them that are hard of believing. The
disciples hearing that of their Lord and Master, 'Take, eat, this is
My body,' they take, they eat, asking no question. . . . The Caper-
naite hearing dreameth of eating naturally, grossly; the godly are
assured of eating spiritually, and yet withal really. . . . The sun
remains a splendent body, though bats and owls cannot endure it;
the Holy Sacrament remains an unspeakable mystery, though the
carnal man doth not perceive it. In this case silence is the safest
eloquence, and the best expressing is not to express. A godly
meditation is safer than a Socratical disputing. Discourse of controversy doth often abate devotion : discourse of piety about this mystery is sweeter than the honey or the honey-comb. . . . To take a
survey of the beginning and progress of the doctrine of Transubstantiation, . . . one Berengarius in the year 1028 [1] was the first that
came upon the stage to act this tragedy, by him were kindled such
sparks as after brake out into great and fearful flames. . . . In the
year 1040 Berengarius abjured his former assertions : were his later
thoughts the wiser? This I stand not to discuss, dispute it that will.
The Church in the meanwhile, who ought to have followed the
counsel of St. Paul to Timothy in suppressing questions that cause
strife,[2] did clean contrary in adding more and more daily a multitude
of questions so long that those sparks kindled by Berengarius began
to increase, and set all as it were into a most hideous combustion.
. . . The Council of Lateran . . . promulgates a new and unheard
of doctrine of Transubstantiation. . . . After this the question comes
to be handled by the Master of the Sentences, whom the school
divines do follow. . . . At one time the doubt is about the power
of God, at another about His will ; now of the existing of substance
with accidents, then of accidents without a substance; sometimes
of annihilating of former natures, sometimes of transelementing the
same. In this chaos there is nothing found certain save that uncertain dream of Transubstantiation. . . . The Church of Rome was
happy while it enjoyed the presence of this holy mystery, had she
known her own happiness when for a thousand years together there
was never heard of the name of 'ubiquity,' 'sacramentary,' or the
like ; no division of the East against the West Church, or of the West
against the East ; all agreed about the truth of this holy mystery ;
but when once men would press into depths inaccessible, rend away

---

[1] For the actual dates see vol. i. pp. 245-57, *supra.*
[2] 1 Tim. i. 3, 4.

the veil, and intrude themselves into the Holy of Holies, good Lord, with what a spirit of giddiness were they whirled to and fro. . . . In this mean space all things now tossed and turmoiled there arise upon the contrary part a kind of men prone and apt not so much to the alteration as indeed to the utter ruinating of things. . . . Is the Communion celebrated well? A badge it is of our profession, a familiar assembly of guests, a remembrance of somewhat passed: Take ye, eat ye, stand ye, there is no other gesture required than what is used at public meetings ; what need any mention of the body of Christ, which was broken and given for us, of the blood of Christ, which was shed for us ? Take ye, eat ye, drink ye :—O blessed Paul, if thou didst live, thou wouldest tell these men they ought upon fear of judgment to discern the Lord's body. . . . Albeit then the manner be not of us over curiously inquired or searched after, yet the same presence of Christ is acknowledged which Christ Himself would have to be acknowledged. We say with St. Ambrose that there is not taken from bread the substance thereof, but that there is adjoined the grace of Christ's body after a manner ineffable. . . . Concerning the controversy about the Holy Eucharist, between two extremes, whereof we have heard, let us embrace the means, let us with a sincere faith apprehend the truth ; apprehending, let us keep it ; keeping, let us adore it with godly manners. . . . Let us forbear on both sides needless and unprofitable disputes. Unless thou, Lord, hadst said it, ' This is My body, This is My blood,' who would have believed it? Unless thou hadst said, O holy Christ, ' Take, eat, drink ye all of this,' who durst have touched it ? Who would have approached to so heavenly a repast, hadst Thou not commanded it, *hoc facite,* ' do ye this ' ; but Thou commanding, who would not joyfully come and communicate ? Let us then hold captive human reason, and prepare ourselves unto the fruit of this heavenly manna. Unnecessary disputes bring small profits ; we may with greater benefit wonder than argue. Then are the works of God most truly conceived when they are devoutly admired." [1]

Thomas Jackson was born in 1579. He was a Fellow of Corpus Christi College, Oxford, and was repeatedly Vice-President of that College. He held the benefices of Newcastle-on-Tyne and Winston in the diocese of Durham, and was Chaplain to Bishop Neile of Durham and to King Charles I. In 1630 he became President of Corpus Christi College, and held that office till his death in 1632. For some years he held also the benefice of Witney,

---

[1] LXX. 3, 4, 7-14, 18-24, 27, 32, 35-37.

and was Prebendary of Winchester and Dean of Peterborough. His chief work is a series of treatises which make up a commentary on the Apostles' Creed. The references to Eucharistic doctrine in it appear to give expression to a belief that the elements are not changed at consecration, but that by rightly partaking of them communicants spiritually receive the body and blood of Christ and the benefits of His sacrifice.

" In the Sacrament of Christ's body and blood there is a propitiation for our sins because He is really present in it, who is the propitiation for our sins. But it in no way hence follows that there is any propitiatory sacrifice for sin in this Sacrament. He becomes the propitiation for our sins, He actually remits our sins, not directly and immediately by the elements of bread and wine, nor by any other kind of local presence or compresence with these elements than is in Baptism. . . . Neither of these elements or sensible substances can directly cleanse us from our sins by any virtue communicated unto them or inherent in them, but only as they are pledges or assurances of Christ's peculiar presence in them, and of our true investiture in Christ by them. We are not then to receive the elements of bread and wine only in remembrance that Christ died for us, but in remembrance or assurance likewise that His body which was once given for us doth by its everlasting virtue preserve our bodies and souls unto everlasting life, and that His blood which was but once shed for us doth still cleanse us from all our sins, from which in this life we are cleansed or can hope to be cleansed. If we then receive remission of sins or purification from our sins in the Sacrament of the Eucharist (as we always do when we receive it worthily), we receive it not immediately by the sole serious remembrance of His death, but by the present efficacy or operation of His body which was given for us, and of His blood which was shed for us. . . . This present efficacy of Christ's body and blood upon our souls, or real communication of both, I find as a truth unquestionable amongst the ancient fathers and as a Catholic confession. The modern Lutheran and the modern Romanist have fallen into their several errors concerning Christ's presence in the Sacrament from a common ignorance ; neither of them conceive, nor are they willing to conceive, how Christ's body and blood should have any real operation upon our souls unless they were so locally present as they might *agere per contactum*, that is, either so purge our souls by oral manducation as physical medicines do our bodies (which is the pretended use of Transubstantiation), or so quicken our souls as sweet odours do the animal spirits, which were the more probable use of the Lutheran Consubstantiation. Both the Lutherans and Papists avouch the authority of the ancient Church for their opinions, but most injuriously. For more than we have said, or more than Calvin doth stiffly maintain against Zuinglius and other Sacramentaries, cannot be inferred from any speeches of the truly orthodoxical or ancient fathers. They all agree that we are immediately cleansed and purified from our sins by the blood of Christ, that His human nature by the habitation of the deity is made to us the inexhaustible fountain of life. But about the particular manner how life is derived to us from His human nature, as whether it sends its sweet influence upon our souls only from the heavenly sanctuary wherein it dwells as in its sphere, or whether His blood which was shed for us may have more immediate local presence with us, they no way disagree, because they in this kind abhorred curiosity of dispute. As for Ubiquity and Transubstantiation, they are the two monsters of modern times, brought forth by ignorance and maintained only by faction." [1]

"The truth . . . is . . . that Christ by His bloody sacrifice upon the cross was consecrated to be an everlasting priest; and that this consecration was not accomplished until His resurrection from the dead. For it is not conceivable that He should be an everlasting priest before He became an immortal Man, and by His rising, etc., opened the gate of everlasting life. After He was thus consecrated by death and by the resurrection from the dead to be an everlasting priest after the order of Melchizedek, He was not to offer any sacrifice; nor do we read that Melchizedek offered any. Wherein then did Melchizedek's priesthood consist? Only in the dignity of authoritative blessing. . . .. This exercise of Christ's spiritual priesthood in the heavenly sanctuary was foreshadowed by sundry services and sacrifices of the Law. . . . He consecrated the way itself by His bloody sacrifice upon the cross; from the very moment in which the veil did rend asunder the door was opened and the way prepared. But we must be qualified for walking in this way and for entering into this heavenly sanctuary by the present exercise of His everlasting priesthood, which is a priesthood of blessing not of sacrifice. And yet He blesseth us by communicating the virtue and efficacy of His everlasting sacrifice unto our souls. This participation and this blessing by it, the full expiation of our sins, we are to expect from His heavenly sanctuary. . . .. We may consecrate the elements of bread and wine, and administer them so consecrated as undoubted pledges of His body and blood, by which the new covenant was

[1] X. lv. 9, 12.

sealed and the general pardon purchased ; yet, unless He grant some actual influence of His Spirit, and suffer such virtue to go out from His human nature now placed in His sanctuary as He did once unto the woman that was cured of her issue of blood, unless this virtue do as immediately reach our souls as it did her body, we do not really receive His body and blood with the elements of bread and wine. We do not so receive them as to have our sins remitted or dissolved by them ; we do not by receiving them become of His flesh and of His bones. We gain no degree of real union with Him, which is the sole use or fruit of His real presence. Christ might be locally present as He was with many here on earth, and yet not really present. But with whomsoever He is virtually present, that is, to whomsoever He communicates the influence of His body and blood by His Spirit, He is really present with them, though locally absent from them. . . . As many as are healed from their sins, whether by the Sacrament of Baptism or the Eucharist, are healed by faith relatively or instrumentally. Faith is as the mouth or organ by which we receive the medicine ; but it is the virtual influence derived from the body and blood of Christ which properly or efficiently doth cure our souls and dissolve the works of Satan from us. . . . A matter as easy for the Son of God, or for the Man Christ Jesus ' in whom the Godhead dwelleth bodily,' [1] though still remaining at the right hand of God, to know the hearts and secret thoughts of all such as present themselves at His Table here on earth as well as He knew the secret thoughts of this woman which came behind Him. What need then is there of His bodily presence in the Sacrament, or of any other presence than the influence or emission of virtue from His heavenly sanctuary unto our souls ? He hath left us the consecrated elements of bread and wine to be unto us more than the hem of His garment. If we do but touch and taste them with the same faith by which this woman touched the hem of His garment, this our faith shall make us whole." [2]

" This distillation of life and immortality from His glorified human nature is that which the ancient and orthodoxal Church did mean in their figurative and lofty speeches of Christ's real presence, or of eating His very flesh and drinking His very blood in the Sacrament. And the sacramental bread is called His body, and the sacramental wine His blood, as for other reasons so especially for this, that the virtue or influence of His bloody sacrifice is most plentifully and most effectually distilled from heaven unto the worthy receivers of the Eucharist." [3]

[1] Col. ii. 9.   [2] X. lvi. 1, 2, 4.   [3] XI. iii. 12.

" All that are partakers of this Sacrament eat Christ's body and drink His blood sacramentally, that is, they eat that bread which sacramentally is His body, and drink that cup which sacramentally is His blood, whether they eat or drink faithfully or unfaithfully. . . . May we say then that Christ is really present in the Sacrament as well to the unworthy as to the faithful receivers? Yes, this must we grant; yet must we add withal that He is really present with them in a quite contrary manner, really present He is, because virtually present to both, because the operation or efficacy of His body and blood is not metaphorical but real in both. Thus the bodily sun, though locally distant for its substance, is really present by its light and heat as well to sore eyes as to clear sights, but really present to both by a contrary real operation ; and by the like contrary operation it is really present to clay and to wax, it really hardeneth the one, and really softeneth the other. So doth Christ's blood by its invisible but real influence mollify the hearts of such as come to the Sacrament with due preparation, but harden such as unworthily receive the consecrated elements. . . . When we say that Christ is really present in the Sacrament, our meaning is that as God He is present in an extraordinary manner, after such a manner as He was present before His Incarnation in His sanctuary ; . . . and by the power of His Godhead thus extraordinarily present He diffuseth the virtue or operation of His human nature either to the vivification or hardening of their hearts who receive the sacramental pledges. . . . No man can spiritually eat Christ but by believing His death and passion ; yet sacramental eating adds somewhat to spiritual eating, how quick and lively soever our faith be whilst we eat Him only spiritually. But though our faith were in both the same as well for degree as quality, yet the object of our faith is not altogether the same in sacramental and in spiritual eating. Christ's body and blood are so present in the Sacrament that we receive a more special influence from them in use of the Sacrament than without it, so we receive it worthily or with hearts prepared by spiritual eating precedent, that is, by serious meditation of Christ's death and passion." [1]

Henry Hammond was born at Chertsey in 1605. He was a Fellow of Magdalen College, Oxford, and afterwards Rector of Penshurst, Canon of Christ Church, and Chaplain to King Charles I. He was nominated one of the divines of the Westminster Assembly,[2] but never acted in that capacity, and his nomination was afterwards revoked. In 1648 he was Sub-dean of Christ

[1] XI. iv. 5, 10.   [2] See pp. 308-12, *infra*.

Church; but was expelled from his office, and for a short time imprisoned, under the commonwealth, when he was a great support to the deprived clergy. He died in 1660. His beliefs may be seen in his works *A Practical Catechism*, published in 1644, and *Of Fundamentals*, published in 1654. He regarded the Eucharist as a commemoration of the death of Christ and of the abiding sacrifice of Christ in heaven, and as a means whereby through the whole action of the rite God bestows on the faithful communicants the body and blood of Christ.

The treatise *A Practical Catechism* contains the following passages :—

"This Sacrament, which was after the commemorative passover, is so conceived a confederation of all Christians one with another, to live piously and charitably, both by commemorating the death of Christ, . . . and by making His blood, as it was the fashion in the eastern nations, a ceremony of this covenant, mutual betwixt God and us. . . . The full importance of the words ' Do this in remembrance of Me ' is, first, a commission to His Apostles to continue this ceremony now used by Him as a holy ceremony or Sacrament in the Church for ever.   Secondly, a direction that for the manner of observing it they should do to other Christians as He had now done to them, that is, ' take, bless, break this bread, take and bless this cup,' and then give and distribute it to others, settling this on them as part of their office, a branch of the power left them by Him, and by them communicable to whom they should think fit after them. Thirdly, a specifying of the end to which this was designed, a commemoration of the death of Christ, a representing His passion to God, and a coming before Him in His name, first, to offer our sacrifices of supplications and praises in the name of the crucified Jesus (as of old, both among Jews and heathens, all their sacrifices were rites in and by which they supplicated God.   See 1 Sam. xiii. 12), and, secondly, to commemorate that His daily continual sacrifice or intercession for us at the right hand of His Father now in heaven." [1]

"*Scholar*. . . . What now is that which is the more substantial difficulty to be explained in those Gospels ?

"*Catechist*. It is to resolve what is the meaning of Christ's words of institution, ' This is My body,' etc.

"*Scholar*. And what is that ?

"*Catechist*. Not that the bread was His body, and the wine His blood, in strict speaking, for He was then in His body when He so

---

[1] *Works (Anglo-Catholic Library)*, i. 378, 380, 381.

spake; and when His disciples distributed it among themselves, He was not bodily in every of their mouths. And now His body is in heaven, and there to be contained till the day of 'restitution of all things,'[1] and is not to be corporally brought down in every Sacrament, either to be joined locally with the elements or for the elements to be changed into it; many contradictions and barbarisms would be consequent to such an interpretation. Every loaf of consecrated bread would be the body of Christ, and so the same thing be two cubits long, and not two cubits long; and many the like contradictory propositions would be all true, which it is generally resolved to be impossible even for God, because it would make Him a liar, and be an argument not of power but imperfection. So, again, every communicant must carnally eat man's flesh and blood, which is so savage a thing that St. Austin saith that whensoever words of Scripture seem to sound that way, they must be otherwise interpreted.[2]

"*Scholar.* What sense then may or must be put upon them?

"*Catechist.* In answering this question, I shall first give you an observation taken from the Jewish phrases and customs used in this matter; and it is this, that the lamb that was dressed in the paschal supper, and set upon the table, was wont to be called the body of the passover, or the body of the paschal lamb; and that Christ seems to allude to this phrase when He saith, 'This is My body'; as if He should say, The paschal lamb, and the body of it, that is, the presentation of that on the table in the Jewish feast, the memorial of deliverance out of Egypt, and type of My delivering Myself to die for you, I will now have abrogated, and by this bread which I now deliver to you, I give or exhibit to you this other passover, My own self, who am to be sacrificed (My body which shall presently be delivered to death) for you, that you may hereafter, instead of that other, retain and continue to posterity a memorial and symbol of Me. This for the words, 'My body'; but then for the whole phrase or form of speech, 'This is My body,' it seems to be answerable to, and substituted instead of, the paschal form, 'This is the bread of affliction which our fathers ate in Egypt,' or 'This is the unleavened bread,' etc., or 'This is the passover'; not that it is that very identical bread which they then ate, but that it is the celebration of that anniversary feast which was then instituted, as when in ordinary speech we say on Good Friday and Easter Day, 'this day Christ died,' and

[1] Acts iii. 21.

[2] Referring to St. Augustine, *De Doct. Christ.* iii. 23, 24; *C. Advers. Leg. et Proph.* ii. 35. These passages are quoted on vol. i. p. 65, *supra.*

'this day Christ rose,' when we know that it was so many hundred years since He died or rose; which example is adapted to the point in hand by St. Austin in his *Epistles*.[1] Thus much for the phrase or form of speech; now for the sense or full importance of the words, 'This is My body,' I shall by the authority of the ancient fathers think myself obliged to acknowledge that the highest sense that will not be subject to those intolerable inconveniences mentioned in the answer to your last question may possibly be the sense of them; and that that which most belongs to other places of Scripture speaking of the same matter must in any reason be resolved to be the sense of them. For the former of these, it is certain that many of the ancient fathers of the Church conceived very high things of this Sacrament, acknowledged the bread and wine to be changed, and to become other than they were, but not so as to be transubstantiate into the body and blood of Christ, to depart from their own substance or figure or form, or to cease to be bread and wine by that change; and that the faithful do receive the body and blood of Christ in the Sacrament, which implies not any corporal presence of Christ on the Table, or in the elements, but God's communicating the crucified Saviour, who is in heaven bodily, and nowhere else, to us sinners on the earth, but this mystically and after an ineffable manner. And generally they make it a mystery, but descend not to the revealing of the manner of it, leaving it as a matter of faith but not of sense, to be believed but not grossly fancied or described. I shall leave these then, and apply myself to the latter sort, the other places of Scripture which speak of this matter, resolving that that must be the meaning of the words of Christ, 'This is My body,' which by examination shall appear to be most agreeable to those other places. And of this sort of places, you may first take the passages in the Gospels themselves, where Christ saith of the cup (not the wine but the cup, which refers to the action, the pouring out and drinking), that it is a new covenant in His blood which was shed for us. Which it seems is all one in sense with that other, 'This is My blood of the new covenant which is shed for many,' and in Matthew, 'This is My blood, that of the new covenant,' etc. Which being put together, as parallels to interpret one the other, will conclude that Christ's blood was truly shed for our benefit, particularly to seal a new covenant betwixt God and us, and that this Sacrament was the exhibiting that covenant to us, as when God saith to Abraham, 'This is the covenant that I will make with you, every male

---

[1] Referring to St. Augustine, *Ep.* xcviii. 9, 10. Part of the passage is quoted on vol. i. p. 84, *supra.*

among you shall be circumcised'; [1] this circumcision is in effect
called the covenant, as here the cup is the covenant, that is, not
only the sign of the covenant, but a seal of it, and an exhibition of
it, a real receiving me into covenant and making me partaker of the
benefits of it. And this you shall more fully see, if you proceed to
the places in St. Paul, especially that 1 Cor. x. 16. . . . I conceive
the literal notation of the words will bear this observation, that as
the word ' this ' in the latter words signifies not the bread but the
whole action or administration, ' do this,' that is, do you all that I
have done in your presence, take bread, break, bless it, give it to
others, and so commemorate Me. So the word ' this ' in the former
speech, ' This is My body,' may signify the whole action too, namely,
that the breaking and distributing, taking and eating this bread, is
the body of Christ, in what sense you shall see anon. . . . ' The cup
of blessing which we bless ' or, as the Syriac, ' the cup of praise,'
that is, the chalice of wine which is in the name of the people
offered up by the bishop or presbyter to God with lauds and thanksgivings, that is, that whole eucharistical action (and that expressed
to be the action of the people as well as the presbyter by their
drinking of it) is the communication of the blood of Christ, a service
of theirs to Christ, a sacrifice of thanksgiving, commemorative of that
great mercy and bounty of Christ in pouring out His blood for them,
and in making them—or a means ordained by Christ to make them
—partakers of the blood of Christ, not of the guilt of shedding it,
but, if they come worthily thither, of the benefits that are purchased
by it, namely, ' the washing away of sin in His blood '; so in like
manner the ' breaking and eating of the bread ' is a communication
of the body of Christ, a sacrifice commemorative of Christ's offering
up His body for us, and a making us partakers, or communicating
to us the benefits of that bread of life, strengthening and giving
us grace. . . . This ' breaking, taking, eating of the bread,' this
whole action, is the real communication of the body of Christ to me ;
. . . that, as verily as I eat the bread in my mouth, so verily God
in heaven bestows on me, communicates to me, the body of the
crucified Saviour. . . . God's part is the accepting of this our
bounden duty, bestowing that body and blood of Christ upon us,
not by sending it down locally for our bodies to feed upon, but
really for our souls to be strengthened and refreshed by it, as, when
the sun is communicated to us, the whole bulk and body of the sun
is not removed out of its sphere, but the rays and beams of it, and
with them the light and warmth and influences, are really and verily

[1] Gen. xvii. 10.

bestowed or darted out upon us. And all this is the full importance of 'This is My body,' or 'This is the communication of His body'." [1]

"In that Sacrament God really bestows, and every faithful prepared Christian as really and truly receives, the body and blood of Christ. As truly as the bishop or presbyter gives me the sacramental bread and wine, so truly doth God in heaven bestow upon me on earth the body and blood of Christ, that is, the crucified Saviour, not by local motion but by real communication, not to our teeth but to our souls, and consequently exhibits, makes over, reaches out unto us all the benefits thereof, all the advantages that flow to us from the death of Christ." [2]

In his treatise *Of Fundamentals* Hammond summarises five ways in which the "Sacrament of the body and blood of Christ" may be "considered" :—

"1. as an institution of Christ for the solemn commemorating of His death ; . . . 2. as a sacrifice eucharistical performed by the Christian to God ; . . . 3. as the κοινωνία 'communication' of the body and blood of Christ, the means of conveying all the benefits of the crucified Saviour unto all that come fitly prepared and qualified for them ; . . . 4. as a federal rite betwixt the soul and Christ, eating and drinking at His Table, and thereby engaging our obedience to Him ; . . . lastly, as an emblem of the most perfect divine charity to be observed among all Christians." [3]

IV.

Richard Field, one of the most famous and learned of post-Reformation English divines, was born at Hemel Hempstead in 1561. He was a member of Magdalen Hall, and later of Queen's College, Oxford. He was lecturer of Lincoln's Inn, Rector of Burghclere, and Prebendary of Windsor; and in 1610 was appointed Dean of Gloucester. In 1616 he died. The first four books of his work *Of the Church* were published in 1606; the fifth book appeared in 1610. A second edition considerably enlarged was issued posthumously in 1628. From allusions to the Eucharist in the course of this book, it appears that Field held that the bread and wine are changed in use at the consecration, so that they signify and exhibit and contain

---

[1] *Op. cit.* i. 382-85, 389, 393-95.
[2] *Ibid.* 396, 397.   [3] *Ibid.* ii. 178, 179.

and communicate the body and blood of Christ; and that the Eucharist is a sacrificial commemoration of the passion and death of Christ like to our Lord's presentation of Himself to God the Father in heaven.

"That body and blood which all true Christians do know to be mystically communicated to them in the Sacrament, to their unspeakable comfort."[1]

"The thing that is offered is the body of Christ, which is an eternal and perpetual propitiatory sacrifice, in that it was once offered by death upon the cross, and hath an everlasting and neverfailing force and efficacy. Touching the manner of offering Christ's body and blood, we must consider that there is a double offering of a thing to God. First, so as men are wont to do that give something to God out of that they possess, professing that they will no longer be owners of it, but that it shall be His, and serve for such uses and employments as He shall convert it to. Secondly, a man may be said to offer a thing unto God in that he bringeth it to His presence, setteth it before His eyes, and offereth it to His view, to incline Him to do something by the sight of it, and respect had to it. In this sort Christ offereth Himself and His body once crucified daily in heaven, and so intercedeth for us, not as giving it in the nature of a gift or present, for He gave Himself to God once, to be holy unto Him for ever, nor in the nature of a sacrifice, for He died once for sin, and rose never to die any more, but in that He setteth it before the eyes of God His Father, representing it unto Him, and so offering it to His view, to obtain grace and mercy for us. And in this sort we also offer Him daily on the altar in that, commemorating His death and lively representing His bitter passions endured in His body upon the cross, we offer Him that was once crucified and sacrificed for us on the cross, and all His sufferings, to the view and gracious consideration of the Almighty, earnestly desiring, and assuredly hoping, that He will incline to pity us and show mercy unto us for this His dearest Son's sake, who in our nature for us, to satisfy His displeasure, and to procure us acceptation, endured such and so grievous things. This kind of offering or sacrificing Christ commemoratively is twofold, inward and outward: outward, as the taking, breaking, and distributing the mystical bread, and pouring out the cup of blessing, which is the Communion of the blood of Christ; the inward consisteth in the faith and devotion of the Church and people of God so commemorating

[1] Book III. chap. xxxviii. (vol. i. p. 315, edition 1847).

the death and passion of Christ their crucified Saviour, and representing and setting it before the eyes of the Almighty, that they fly unto it as their only stay and refuge, and beseech Him to be merciful unto them for His sake that endured all these things, to satisfy His wrath, and work their peace and good." [1]

"We have altars in the same sort the fathers had, though we have thrown down popish altars; . . . we admit the Eucharist to be rightly named a sacrifice, though we detest the blasphemous construction the papists make of it." [2]

"All agree in this, that they understand such a mutation or change to be made that that which before was earthly and common bread by the words of institution, the invocation of God's name and divine virtue, is made a Sacrament of the true body and blood of Christ, visibly sitting at the right hand of God in heaven, and yet after an invisible and incomprehensible manner present in the Church; and that the body and blood of Christ are in the Sacrament, and exhibited and given as spiritual meat and drink for the salvation and everlasting life of them that are worthy partakers of the same." [3]

"The true presence of Christ's body and blood in the Sacrament, the exhibition of them to be the food of our souls, and such a change of the elements in virtue, grace, and power, of containing in them, and communicating to us, Christ's body and blood, as the nature of so excellent a Sacrament requireth." [4]

An interesting feature of Field's treatment of the Eucharist is his contention at length that the canon of the Mass as used in

---

[1] Book III. Appendix (vol. ii. pp. 61, 62). Just before this passage Field has rejected the idea that the Eucharist is a " propitiatory sacrifice for the quick and the dead " (p. 59).

[2] Appendix, part i. (vol. iv. p. 284).

[3] Appendix, part i. (vol. iv. p. 302), adopting a contention of Cassander ; cf. p. 466, infra.

[4] Appendix, part i. (vol. iv. p. 303). Cf. p. 408, where Field refers with approval to Zanchi's statement (Judicium de dissidio cœn. dom.) that the bread and wine are changed in use, and signify and exhibit and communicate the body and blood of Christ. Zanchi (born 1516, died 1590) was an Augustinian who became a Reformer. Cf. also Appendix, part ii. (vol. iv. pp. 487, 488), where Field repudiates the notion that, because he allowed that the " sanctified elements " " reserved " in the early Church " in reference to an ensuing receiving of them were the body of Christ, to wit, in mystery and exhibitive signification," he therefore allowed " the real, that is, the local presence of Christ's body in the Sacrament ".

the mediæval Church did not involve any doctrine contrary to that held since the Reformation.[1]

V.

In 1658 a very remarkable book called *Considerationes Modestæ et Pacificæ Controversiarum de Justificatione, Purgatorio, Invocatione Sanctorum, Christo Mediatore, et Eucharistia* was published in London. It was the work of William Forbes, a native of Aberdeen. He travelled abroad for some years, refused the professorship of Hebrew at Oxford, and held several offices, including that of Principal, in Marischal College at Aberdeen. He was consecrated Bishop of Edinburgh when that see was founded by Charles I. in February, 1634, but died shortly after his consecration on 12th April, 1634. The book entitled *Considerationes Modestæ et Pacificæ* is of the nature of an Eirenicon. All the subjects treated are handled with great learning and insight; and the author shows a valuable power of grasping the positive aspects of doctrine. The concluding part is on the Eucharist. Bishop Forbes rejects the Zwinglian doctrine of a merely figurative presence. He asserts that those who communicate worthily receive the body and blood of Christ really, though spiritually and imperceptibly; and that Christ is really present in the Sacrament. He maintains that Transubstantiation is not of faith, and that it is contrary to the teaching of Holy Scripture and of the fathers; but allows that neither Transubstantiation nor Consubstantiation is heretical, and argues that our limited knowledge does not warrant rash statements as to their impossibility. He commends the adoration of our Lord in the Sacrament. He denies that the Sacrament is a sacrifice of such a kind as involves destruction; but asserts that it is a sacrifice and is propitiatory in the sense of impetrating the propitiation which Christ has already made.

"The opinion of Zwingli, which the divines of Zurich tenaciously maintained and defended, namely, that 'Christ is present in the Eucharist only by the contemplation of faith; that there is no place to be given here to a miracle, since we know in what way Christ is present to His Supper, namely, by the quickening Spirit, spiritually and efficaciously; that sacramental union consists wholly in signifi-

[1] Book III. Appendix (vol. ii. pp. 5-104).

cation,' etc., is by no means to be approved, since it is most clearly contrary to Scripture and the common opinion of all the fathers." [1]

" The holy fathers . . . most firmly believed that he who worthily receives these mysteries of the body and blood of Christ really and actually receives into himself the body and blood of Christ, but in a certain spiritual, miraculous, and imperceptible way." [2]

" The opinion of those Protestants and others seems to be most safe and most right, who think, nay, who most firmly believe that the body and blood of Christ are really and actually and substantially present and taken in the Eucharist, but in a way which the human mind cannot understand, and much more beyond the power of man to express, which is known to God alone and is not revealed to us in the Scriptures, a way indeed not by bodily or oral reception, but not only by the understanding and merely by faith, but in another way known, as has been said, to God alone, and to be left to His omnipotence." [3]

" In the Supper by the wonderful power of the Holy Ghost we invisibly partake of the substance of the body and blood of Christ, of which we are made recipients no otherwise than if we visibly ate and drank His flesh and blood." [4]

" As regards Transubstantiation, many Protestants very perilously and too rashly deny that God is able to convert the bread substantially into the body of the Lord. For Almighty God can do many things above the understanding of all men, nay, even of the angels. All indeed allow that what implies contradiction cannot be done. But inasmuch as in the particular case it is not clear to any one what the essence of each thing is, and therefore what implies or does not imply a contradiction, it is certainly a mark of great rashness, on account of the weakness of our blind understanding, to prescribe limits to God, and stubbornly to deny that He can do this or that by His omnipotence." [5]

" Transubstantiation is not of faith, nay, is contrary to the Scriptures and the more ancient fathers, yet is by no means to be condemned as heretical." [6]

" The reasons by which the more rigid Protestants seem to themselves to have proved most clearly that each doctrine, both that of the Romanists and that of the Lutherans, is contrary to the articles

[1] *De Euch.* I. i. 2.   [2] I. i. 2.   [3] I. i. 7.
[4] I. i. 27.   [5] I. ii. 1.
[6] I. iii. heading to chapter. In this short sentence Bishop Forbes describes Transubstantiation as "contrary to the Scriptures," but he does not support this in detail.

of the faith and therefore heretical, impious, and blasphemous, have been abundantly refuted both by the maintainers of these opinions and by others who are anxious for the unity of the Church." [1]

"Take away the abuse of the modern Roman Church in reserving the host, which has been consecrated once for all, in ciboria for processions and theatrical pomp, as a thing which, not less apart from Communion than in Communion itself or in relation to it, is the real and substantial body of Christ, and continues such as long as the species endure (on the corruption of which, if so be, the body and blood of the Lord cease to be there); and this controversy may be removed without condemning the practice of the ancient Church as to reservation, which was then usual." [2]

"Gigantic is the error of the more rigid Protestants who deny that Christ is to be adored in the Eucharist with any but inward and mental adoration, and contend that He is not to be adored with any outward rite of worship, as by kneeling or some other like position of the body. Almost all these hold wrong views about the presence of Christ the Lord in the Sacrament, who is present in a wonderful but real manner." [3]

"As regards the first assertion of Bellarmine [4] about venerating the symbols with a kind of lesser worship, we admit it. But as regards his saying that the adoration of supreme worship, though in itself and properly it is due and given to Christ, yet belongs also to the symbols insofar as they are apprehended as one with Christ Himself whom they contain, and whom they cover and conceal like garments, it is false and is contrary to the opinion of many others." [5]

"The holy fathers say very often that the body of Christ itself is offered and sacrificed in the Eucharist, as is clear from almost numberless places, but not in such a way that all the properties of a sacrifice are properly and actually preserved, but by way of commemoration and representation of that which was performed once for all in that one only sacrifice of the cross whereby Christ our High Priest consummated all other sacrifices, and by way of pious prayer whereby the ministers of the Church most humbly beseech God the Father on account of the abiding Victim of that one sacrifice, who is seated in heaven on the right hand of the Father and is present on the Holy Table in an ineffable manner, to grant that the virtue and grace of this perpetual Victim may be efficacious and healthful to His Church for all the necessities of body and soul. . . . Assuredly, in every real sacrifice that is properly so called it is necessary that

---

[1] I. iv. 12.   [2] II. ii. 6.   [3] II. ii. 8.
[4] See p. 365, *infra.*   [5] II. ii. 9.

the victim should be consumed by a certain destructive change, as Romanists themselves universally admit.. But in the Mass the body of Christ is neither destroyed nor changed, as is clear." [1]

"The more moderate Romanists rightly affirm that the Mass is not only a sacrifice of thanksgiving and service or honour, but that it can also be called hilastic or propitiatory in a sound sense, not indeed as if it effected the propitiation and forgiveness of sins, for that pertains to the sacrifice of the cross, but as impetrating the propitiation which has already been made, as prayer, of which this sacrifice is a kind, can be called propitiatory." [2]

"The sacrifice which is offered in the Supper is not merely of thanksgiving, but is also propitiatory in a sound sense, and is profitable to very many not only of the living but also of the departed." [3]

VI.

The political events which overthrew the monarchy and set up the commonwealth led to the prohibition by the State of the use of the Prayer Book and to the establishment of new methods of worship. The Westminster Assembly of Divines was summoned in accordance with an ordinance of Parliament in 1643. The episcopalians appointed on this Assembly did not attend its meetings; of the puritans, the presbyterian element was the most influential, though there were also representatives of the Independents and some members of Erastian tendencies. The work of the Assembly which concerns the Eucharist may be seen in the parts of the *Confession of Faith*, the *Shorter Catechism*, and the *Larger Catechism* which relate to this subject. The *Confession of Faith*, with some omissions not affecting the present subject, was approved by the English Parliament in 1648 and 1660 ; it was adopted by the General Assembly of the Scottish Presbyterian Church in 1647 and approved by the Scottish Parliament in 1649 and again in 1690. The *Catechisms* were approved by the English Parliament in 1648, by the General Assembly of the Scottish Presbyterian Church in 1648, and by the Scottish Parliament in 1649. With these may be compared the *Directory for the Public Worship of God throughout the Three Kingdoms of England, Scotland, and Ireland*, to which the Westminster Assembly and the Scottish General Assembly agreed in

[1] III. i. 10, 12.   [2] III. ii. 2.   [3] III. ii. 17.

1644, the use of which instead of the Book of Common Prayer was ordered by the English Parliament in 1645. All these documents afford illustrations of the fact that the extreme form of Zwinglianism, according to which the Eucharist is only a badge or token, was still a discredited view even among those by whom, if by any, it might be anticipated that it would be held. The Eucharistic doctrine which they contain closely resembles that of Calvin.[1]

The chapter of the Westminster *Confession of Faith* entitled " Of the Lord's Supper " is as follows :—

" 1. Our Lord Jesus in the night wherein He was betrayed instituted the Sacrament of His body and blood called the Lord's Supper to be observed in His Church unto the end of the world, for the perpetual remembrance of the sacrifice of Himself in His death, the sealing all benefits thereof unto true believers, their spiritual nourishment and growth in Him, their further engagement in and to all duties which they owe unto Him, and to be a bond and pledge of their Communion with Him, and with each other, as members of His mystical body.

" 2. In this Sacrament Christ is not offered up to His Father, nor any real sacrifice made at all for remission of sins of the quick or dead, but only a commemoration of that one offering up of Himself by Himself upon the cross once for all, and a spiritual oblation of all possible praise unto God for the same, so that the popish sacrifice of the Mass, as they call it, is most abominably injurious to Christ's one only sacrifice, the alone propitiation for all the sins of the elect.

" 3. The Lord Jesus hath in this ordinance appointed His ministers to declare His word of institution to the people, to pray, and bless the elements of bread and wine, and thereby to set them apart from a common to an holy use; and to take and break the bread, to take the cup, and (they communicating also themselves) to give both to the communicants, but to none who are not then present in the congregation.

" 4. Private Masses, or receiving this Sacrament by a priest or any other alone, as likewise the denial of the cup to the people, worshipping the elements, the lifting them up, or carrying them about for adoration, and the reserving them for any pretended religious use, are all contrary to the nature of this Sacrament, and to the institution of Christ.

" 5. The outward elements in this Sacrament duly set apart to

---

[1] See pp. 50-56, *supra*,

the uses ordained by Christ have such relation to Him crucified as that truly, yet sacramentally only, they are sometimes called by the name of the things they represent, to wit, the body and blood of Christ, albeit in substance and nature they still remain truly and only bread and wine as they were before.

" 6. That doctrine which maintains a change of the substance of bread and wine into the substance of Christ's body and blood (commonly called Transubstantiation) by consecration of a priest, or by any other way, is repugnant not to Scripture alone but even to common sense and reason, overthroweth the nature of the Sacrament, and hath been, and is, the cause of manifold superstitions, yea, of gross idolatries.

" 7. Worthy receivers outwardly partaking of the visible elements in this Sacrament do then also inwardly by faith really and indeed, yet not carnally and corporally but spiritually, receive and feed upon Christ crucified and all benefits of His death, the body and blood of Christ being then not corporally or carnally in, with, or under the bread and wine, yet as really but spiritually present to the faith of believers in that ordinance as the elements themselves are to their outward senses.

" 8. Although ignorant and wicked men receive the outward elements in this Sacrament, yet they receive not the thing signified thereby, but by their unworthy coming thereunto are guilty of the body and blood of the Lord to their own damnation. Wherefore all ignorant and ungodly persons, as they are unfit to enjoy communion with Him, so are they unworthy of the Lord's Table, and cannot without great sin against Christ, whilst they remain such, partake of these holy mysteries or be admitted thereto."

In the Westminster *Shorter Catechism* there are the question and answer :—

" *Question* 96. What is the Lord's Supper ?

" *Answer.* The Lord's Supper is a Sacrament wherein by giving and receiving bread and wine according to Christ's appointment His death is showed forth, and the worthy receivers are, not after a corporal and carnal manner but by faith, made partakers of His body and blood with all His benefits to their spiritual nourishment and growth in grace."

The Westminster *Larger Catechism* expresses the same doctrine at somewhat greater length.

" *Question.* What is the Lord's Supper ?

" *Answer.* The Lord's Supper is a Sacrament of the New Testament, wherein, by giving and receiving bread and wine according to the appointment of Jesus Christ, His death is showed forth; and they that worthily communicate feed upon His body and blood to their spiritual nourishment and growth in grace, have their union and communion with Him confirmed, testify and renew their thankfulness and engagement to God, and their mutual love and fellowship each with other, as members of the same spiritual body."

"*Question.* How do they that worthily communicate in the Lord's Supper feed upon the body and blood of Christ therein ?

"*Answer.* As the body and blood of Christ are not corporally or carnally present in, with, or under the bread and wine in the Lord's Supper, and yet are spiritually present to the faith of the receiver no less truly and really than the elements themselves are to their outward senses, so they that worthily communicate in the Sacrament of the Lord's Supper do therein feed upon the body and blood of Christ not after a corporal or carnal but in a spiritual manner, yet truly and really, while by faith they receive and apply unto themselves Christ crucified and all the benefits of His death."

In the *Directory for the Public Worship of God* the minister is ordered—

"earnestly to pray to God, the Father of all mercies and God of all consolation, to vouchsafe His gracious presence and the effectual working of His Spirit in us ; and so to sanctify these elements both of bread and wine, and to bless His own ordinance, that we may receive by faith the body and blood of Jesus Christ crucified for us, and so feed upon Him that He may be one with us and we with Him, that He may live in us and we in Him and to Him, who hath loved us and given Himself for us " ;

and the instructions for the administration are as follows :—

"The elements being now sanctified by the word and prayer, the minister, being at the Table, is to take the bread in his hand, and say in these expressions (or other the like, used by Christ or His Apostle upon this occasion) :—

"According to the holy institution, command, and example of our blessed Saviour Jesus Christ I take this bread, and having given thanks I break it and give it unto you. (There the minister, who is also himself to communicate, is to break the bread and give it to the communicants.) Take ye, eat ye. This is the body of Christ, which is broken for you. Do this in remembrance of Him.

" In like manner the minister is to take the cup, and to say in these expressions (or other the like used by Christ or the Apostle upon the same occasion) :—

"According to the institution, command, and example of our Lord Jesus Christ I take this cup and give it unto you. (Here he giveth it to the communicants.) This cup is the New Testament in the blood of Christ, which is shed for the remission of the sins of many ; drink ye all of it." [1]

VII.

Much obscurity surrounds the history and authority of the document entitled *Articles of Religion Agreed upon by the Archbishops and Bishops, and the Rest of the Clergy of Ireland, in the Convocation Holden at Dublin in the Year of Our Lord God* 1615, *for the Avoiding of Diversities of Opinions, and the Establishing of Consent Touching True Religion.* But from 1615 to 1635 these Articles appear to have been at any rate a standard of belief in Ireland, whether they were subscribed by the clergy or not. In 1635 they practically ceased to have any authority by the adoption of the English Articles of 1563 and the failure of an attempt to induce the Irish Convocation to place them in a position co-ordinate to the English Articles. In regard to the Eucharist these Articles definitely adopted the doctrine of Calvin that those who communicate worthily receive the inward and spiritual gift of the body and blood of Christ, but that the elements are only symbols of His body and blood. The nine Articles grouped under the general heading " Of the Lord's Supper " are as follows :—

" 92. The Lord's Supper is not only a sign of the mutual love which Christians ought to bear one towards another, but much more a Sacrament of our preservation in the Church, sealing unto us our spiritual nourishment and continual growth in Christ.

" 93. The change of the substance of bread and wine into the substance of the body and blood of Christ, commonly called Transubstantiation, cannot be proved by Holy Writ, but is repugnant to plain testimonies of the Scripture, overthroweth the nature of a Sacrament, and hath given occasion to most gross idolatry and manifold superstitions.

" 94. In the outward part of the Sacrament the body and blood of Christ is in a most lively manner represented, being no otherwise present with the visible elements than things signified and

[1] Hall, *Reliquiæ Liturgicæ*, iii. 56, 57.

sealed are present with the signs and seals, that is to say, symbolically and relatively. But in the inward and spiritual part the same body and blood is really and substantially presented unto all those who have grace to receive the Son of God, even to all those that believe in His name. And unto such as in this manner do worthily and with faith repair unto the Lord's Table the body and blood of Christ is not only signified and offered but also truly exhibited and communicated.

"95. The body of Christ is given, taken, and eaten in the Lord's Supper only after an heavenly and spiritual manner; and the mean whereby the body of the Lord is thus received and eaten is faith.

"96. The wicked, and such as want a lively faith, although they do carnally and visibly (as St. Augustine speaketh) press with their teeth the Sacrament of the body and blood of Christ, yet in no wise are they made partakers of Christ, but rather to their condemnation do eat and drink the sign or Sacrament of so great a thing.

"97. Both the parts of the Lord's Sacrament according to Christ's institution and the practice of the ancient Church ought to be ministered unto God's people; and it is plain sacrilege to rob them of the mystical cup, for whom Christ hath shed His most precious blood.

"98. The Sacrament of the Lord's Supper was not by Christ's ordinance reserved, carried about, lifted up, or worshipped.

"99. The sacrifice of the Mass, wherein the priest is said to offer up Christ for obtaining the remission of pain or guilt for the quick and the dead, is neither agreeable to Christ's ordinance nor grounded upon doctrine apostolic, but contrariwise most ungodly and most injurious to that all-sufficient sacrifice of our Saviour Christ offered once for ever upon the cross, which is the only propitiation and satisfaction for all our sins.

"100. Private Mass, that is, the receiving of the Eucharist by the priest alone without a competent number of communicants, is contrary to the institution of Christ." [1]

VIII.

The teaching of John Hales needs separate treatment. Hales was born at Bath in 1584. He was a scholar of Corpus Christi College, Oxford, a Fellow of Merton, where he lectured in Greek,

[1] These Articles are printed in Hardwick, *A History of the Articles of Religion*, pp. 371-88, edition 1890,

and a Fellow of Eton. He was in Holy Orders, and was a Chaplain to Laud and a Canon of Windsor. In 1642 he was ejected from his canonry ; and in 1649 he was dispossessed of his Fellowship at Eton in consequence of his refusal to take the " Engagement ".[1] He died in 1656. His life was chiefly devoted to study ; and he was a pioneer of Latitudinarian thought, although there are good reasons for disbelieving the charge of Socinianism often brought against him.[2] His tract *On the Sacrament of the Lord's Supper, and concerning the Church's mistaking itself about Fundamentals* was probably published soon after 1635. He rejects " the doctrine of the Reformed Churches " concerning the presence of Christ in the Eucharist as well as the doctrine of " the Church of Rome ". Both err in supposing that at the words of consecration "something befalls that action which otherways would not ". It is a further mistake to say that the consecrated bread and wine are the body of Christ " not after a carnal but after a spiritual manner " ; for such a statement is " nonsense " whether made by the Reformers or by the divines of Rome. It is untrue to say that in the Communion " the body of God, into which the bread is transubstantiated," is given ; or that, " the same body, with which the bread is consubstantiated," is bestowed ; or that " the bread remaining what it was, there passes with it to the soul the real body of God in a secret unknown manner " ; or that " a further degree of faith is supplied us " ; or that " some degree of God's grace, whatever it be, is exhibited, which otherwise would be wanting ".[3] His own opinion he states clearly in the following passage :—

" First, In the Communion there is nothing given but bread and wine.

" Secondly, The bread and wine are signs indeed, but not of anything there exhibited, but of somewhat given long since, even of Christ given for us upon the cross sixteen hundred years ago and more.

" Thirdly, Jesus Christ is eaten at the Communion Table in no

[1] That is, an undertaking to " be true and faithful to the Government established without King and House of Peers ".

[2] See Tulloch, *Rational Theology and Christian Philosophy in England in the Seventeenth Century*, i. 206-8 ; Gordon in *Dictionary of National Biography*, xxiv. 31, 32.

[3] *Works*, i. 52-62, edition 1765,

sense, neither spiritually by virtue of anything done there nor really, neither metaphorically nor literally. Indeed that which is eaten (I mean the bread) is called Christ by a metaphor, but it is eaten truly and properly.

"Fourthly, The spiritual eating of Christ is common to all places as well as the Lord's Table.

"Last of all, The uses and ends of the Lord's Supper can be no more than such as are mentioned in the Scriptures, and they are but two.

"1. The commemoration of the death and passion of the Son of God, specified by Himself at the institution of the ceremony.

"2. To testify our union with Christ, and communion one with another, which end St. Paul hath taught us.

"In these few conclusions the whole doctrine and use of the Lord's Supper is fully set down; and whoso leadeth you beyond this doth but abuse you : 'Quicquid ultra quæritur, non intellitur'." [1]

Hales thus supplies an instance in the first half of the seventeenth century of avowedly Zwinglian belief concerning the Eucharist.

IX.

Ralph Cudworth was born at Aller in Somerset in 1617. He was a member of Emmanuel College, Cambridge, and became Fellow in 1639. He was appointed Master of Clare Hall in 1645 by the Parliamentary Visitors, who had ejected Dr. Paske from that office. In the same year he was made Regius Professor of Hebrew. In 1654 he was elected Master of Christ's College. He was appointed to the benefice of North Cadbury in Somerset in 1650, and to that of Ashwell in Hertfordshire in 1662 ; but it is not known whether he ever resided at either place. He died in 1688. He was a leader of the group of philosophical divines known as the " Cambridge Platonists ". In 1642, when he was only twenty-five, he published a short book of great learning entitled *A Discourse Concerning the True Nature of the Lord's Supper*. The main thought of the book is that "all great errors have ever been intermingled with some truth"; that falsehood is pure nonentity, and could not subsist alone by itself"; and that the "grand error of the papists concerning the Lord's Supper being a sacrifice" is no exception to this rule,

[1] *Works*, i, 62, 63.

but "perhaps at first did rise by degeneration from a primitive truth, whereof the very obliquity of this error yet may bear some dark and obscure intimation".[1] From this standpoint he traces out the custom of feasting on things sacrificed among Jews and heathens; and deduces the conclusions that the Eucharist is not a sacrifice but a feast upon the one true sacrifice once offered by Christ for us, and a federal rite between God and us.

"The right notion of that Christian feast called the Lord's Supper, in which we eat and drink the body and blood of Christ that was once offered up to God for us, is to be derived, if I mistake not, from analogy to that ancient rite among the Jews of feasting upon things sacrificed and eating of those things which they had offered up to God."[2]

"Having thus shown that both amongst the Jews under the law and the Gentiles in their pagan worship (for paganism is nothing but Judaism degenerate) it was ever a solemn rite to join feasting with sacrifice, and to eat of those things which had been offered up, the very concinnity and harmony of the thing itself leads me to conceive that that Christian feast under the Gospel called the Lord's Supper is the very same thing, and bears the same notion, in respect of the true Christian sacrifice of Christ upon the cross, that those did to the Jewish and heathenish sacrifices; and so is *epulum sacrificiale*, a sacrificial feast, I mean, a feast upon sacrifice, or *epulum ex oblatis*, a feast upon things offered up to God. Only this difference arising in the parallel, that because those legal sacrifices were but types and shadows of the true Christian sacrifice, they were often repeated and renewed as well as the feasts which were made upon them; but now, the true Christian sacrifice being come and offered up once for all, never to be repeated, we have therefore no more typical sacrifices left amongst us, but only the feasts upon the one true sacrifice still symbolically continued and often repeated in reference to that one great sacrifice, which is always as present in God's sight and efficacious as if it were but now offered up for us."[3]

X.

After the return to England of King Charles II. in 1660 a conference, known as the Savoy Conference, was held in 1661 between twelve bishops and twelve representatives of the Presbyterians, each side being assisted by nine other divines. A paper of "exceptions" against the Book of Common Prayer was

[1] Introduction.   [2] Chap. i.   [3] Chap. i.

drawn up and presented by the Presbyterian representatives. Among the requests contained in this paper, it was asked that the rubric concerning ornaments, which "seemeth to bring back the cope, albe, etc., and other vestments forbidden by the Common Prayer Book, 5 and 6 Edw. VI.," might be "wholly left out"; that the words in the Prayer of Humble Access, "that our sinful bodies may be made clean by His body, and our souls washed through His most precious blood," might be altered to "that our sinful souls and bodies may be cleansed through His precious body and blood," for the reason that they "seem to give a greater efficacy to the blood than to the body of Christ"; that it might "suffice to speak" the words of administration "to divers jointly," and that these words might be "the words of our Saviour as near as may be"; that kneeling at the reception of Communion might be optional as "being not that gesture which the Apostles used, though Christ was personally present amongst them, nor that which was used in the purest and primitive times of the Church"; and that the "declaration on kneeling," which the Council had added to the Prayer Book of 1552, which was omitted in the Prayer Book of 1559, might be "restored for the vindicating of our Church in the matter of kneeling at the Sacrament (though the gesture be left indifferent)".[1] In the reply of the bishops to these "exceptions," it was stated that they thought it "fit that the rubric" concerning ornaments "continue as it is"; that the words in the Prayer of Humble Access "can no more be said" to "give greater efficacy to the blood than to the body of Christ than when our Lord saith, 'This is My blood which is shed for you and for many for the remission of sins,' etc., and saith not so explicitly of the body"; and on kneeling at the reception of Communion and on the words of administration—

"The posture of kneeling best suits at the Communion as the most convenient, and so most decent for us, when we are to receive as it were from God's hand the greatest of the seals of the kingdom of heaven. He that thinks he may do this sitting, let him remember the prophet Malachi.[2] Offer this to the prince, to receive his

---

[1] Cardwell, *A History of Conferences and other Proceedings Connected with the Revision of the Book of Common Prayer*, pp. 310, 314, 320, 321, 322.

[2] Apparently a reference to Mal. i. 8.

seal from his own hand sitting, see if he will accept of it. When the Church did stand at her prayers, the manner of receiving was *more adorantium* (St. Augustine, *Ps. xcviii.;* Cyril, *Catech. Mystag.* 5)[1] rather more than at prayers, since standing at prayer hath been generally left and kneeling used instead of that (as the Church may vary in such indifferent things). Now to stand at Communion when we kneel at prayers were not decent, much less to sit, which was never the use of the best times."

"It is most requisite that the minister deliver the bread and wine into every particular communicant's hand, and repeat the words in the singular number, for so much as it is the propriety of Sacraments to make particular obsignation to each believer, and it is our visible profession that by the grace of God Christ tasted death for every man."

"Concerning kneeling at the Sacrament we have given account already ; only thus much we add, that we conceive it an error to say that the Scripture affirms the Apostles to have received not kneeling. The posture of the paschal supper we know ; but the institution of the holy Sacrament was after supper, and what posture was then used the Scripture is silent. The rubric at the end of the 1 Ed. C. that leaves kneeling, crossing, etc., indifferent is meant only at such times as they are not prescribed and required. But at the Eucharist kneeling is expressly required in the rubric following."

"This rubric [that is the 'declaration on kneeling'] is not in the Liturgy of Queen Elizabeth, nor confirmed by law ; nor is there any great need of restoring it, the world being now in more danger of profanation than of idolatry. Besides the sense of it is declared sufficiently in the twenty-eighth Article of the Church of England."[2]

In spite of this assertion of the bishops that there was not "any great need of restoring" the "declaration on kneeling," it was added, with one alteration of great significance, at the end of the Order of Holy Communion in the revised Prayer Book, which was drawn up by Convocation in 1661, and given the sanction of the State by the Act of Uniformity of 1662. The alteration made was by the substitution of the words "corporal presence" for the phrase "real and essential presence". It has already been pointed out that the declaration in the form adopted in 1552 was capable of an interpretation not inconsistent with

---

[1] The passages referred to are quoted on vol. i. pp. 106, 109, *supra.*
[2] Cardwell, *op. cit.* pp. 350, 351, 353, 354.

the doctrine affirmed by the Council of Trent if the stress was laid on the word "natural," but that it was not likely to have been drawn up by any who believed in the presence of the body and blood of Christ in the consecrated elements. In considering its meaning in the altered form in which it appeared in the Prayer Book of 1662, it is necessary to ask what reasons led the bishops to assent to the addition of the declaration after replying to the Presbyterian divines that it was unnecessary, and with what object the alteration of "real and essential presence" to "corporal presence" was made. On the one hand, it has been maintained that the alteration was made because by the time of the revision of the Prayer Book of 1662 the phrase "real and essential presence" had come to be used in the sense of a presence of Christ spiritually received by those who communicated worthily apart from any presence in the consecrated elements; and that the declaration was therefore altered simply so as to avoid condemning the assertion of such a presence in the communicants.[1] On the other hand, both general probability and an express testimony of Bishop Burnet in his *History of the Reformation of the Church of England* have been thought to indicate that the alteration was made for the purpose of limiting the condemnation in the declaration to such a gross and carnal presence as was contrary to the teaching of the mediæval theologians and the Tridentine divines.[2] Bishop Burnet's statement is as follows:—

"We know who was the author of that change, and who pretended that a corporal presence signified such a presence as a body naturally has, which the assertors of Transubstantiation itself do not, and cannot pretend is in this case; where they say the body is not present corporally but spiritually, or as a spirit is present. And he who had the chief hand in procuring this alteration had a very extraordinary subtlety, by which he reconciled the opinion of a real presence in the Sacrament with the last words of the rubric, 'That the natural body and blood of Christ were in heaven, and not here; it being against the truth of Christ's natural body to be at one time in more places than one'. It was thus: a body is in a place, if there is no intermediate body but a vacuum between it and the place; and he thought that by the virtue of the words of

[1] See Dimock, *Vox Liturgiae Anglicanae*, pp. 65-72, 128-35; Tomlinson, *The Prayer Book, Articles, and Homilies*, pp. 264, 265.

[2] See Pullan, *The History of the Book of Common Prayer*, pp. 316-18.

consecration there was a cylinder of a vacuum made between the elements and Christ's body in heaven ; so that, no body being between, it was both in heaven and in the elements." [1]

In the margin of this passage, opposite the words "the author of that change," the initials "D. P. G." occur, and have with much probability been supposed to denote Dr. Peter Gunning, one of the revisers of the Prayer Book, who was afterwards Bishop of Ely. Whatever the value of the "very extraordinary subtlety" which Burnet ascribes to him, Burnet's testimony that he was responsible for the alteration in the declaration, that he believed that the body of Christ "was both in heaven and in the elements," and that he understood the phrase "corporal presence" as condemned in the declaration to signify such a natural manner of presence as is rejected by "the assertors of Transubstantiation," is of very high importance. It must be added that Burnet in his *History of My Own Times* writes :—

"One important addition was made, chiefly by Gauden's [2] means. He pressed that a declaration explaining the reasons of their kneeling at the Sacrament, which had been in King Edward's Liturgy but was left out in Queen Elizabeth's time, should be again set where it had once been. The Papists were highly offended when they saw such an express declaration made against the real presence, and the Duke [3] told me that, when he asked Sheldon [4] how they came to declare against a doctrine which he had been instructed was the doctrine of the Church, Sheldon answered, Ask Gauden about it, who is a bishop of your own making ; for the king had ordered his promotion for the service which he had done." [5]

Putting all things together, it is most probable that at the time of the revision of the Prayer Book of 1662 there were among the revisers those who regarded the declaration as condemnatory

---

[1] Burnet, *The History of the Reformation of the Church of England,* vol. iii. preface, p. viii. (edition 1816).

[2] John Gauden was Master of the Temple in 1659, Bishop of Exeter in 1660, and Bishop of Worcester in 1662.

[3] Duke of York, afterwards King James II.

[4] Gilbert Sheldon was Bishop of London in 1660, and Archbishop of Canterbury in 1663.

[5] I. 185 (edition 1724). In a MS. draft of the *History of My Own Times,* in the British Museum (Harleian MSS. 6584), it is said that Sheldon opposed the addition of the declaration.

of the doctrine that the consecrated Sacrament is the body and blood of Christ, and also those who saw that it was not inconsistent with such ways of asserting that the body and blood of Christ are spiritually present in the consecrated elements as the mediæval theologians and the Tridentine divines had affirmed. Besides the addition of the declaration on kneeling in its altered form, no change bearing on the doctrine of the Eucharist was made in the Prayer Book of 1662. Moreover, the Articles of Religion remained unaltered.

XI.

Cosin and Taylor and Bramhall and Thorndike may be taken as representative divines of the period of the restoration.

John Cosin was born at Norwich in 1595. In 1616 he became librarian and secretary to Bishop Overall. After being Prebendary of Durham and Archdeacon of the East Riding of Yorkshire, he became Master of Peterhouse, Cambridge, in 1634, and Dean of Peterborough in 1640. He suffered in the troubled times which followed that year; and from 1643 to 1660 he was in France. In July, 1660, he returned to his deanery at Peterborough, and on 2nd December, 1660, he was consecrated Bishop of Durham. In January, 1672, he died.

In the Articles of Enquiry issued for his Visitation of the Archdeaconry of the East Riding in 1627 Cosin referred to the consecrated elements as " the body and blood of our Lord " in the question, " Doth he deliver the body and blood of our Lord to every communicant severally ? " [1]

About 1652, when he was in France, Cosin wrote a book called *Regni Angliæ Religio Catholica* at the request of Edward Hyde, afterwards Earl of Clarendon, with the object of giving Christians abroad a just idea of the doctrine and discipline of the Church of England. The English Church, he says, rejects "the fable of Transubstantiation," and "the repeated sacrifice of Christ to be offered daily by each priest for the living and the departed ". The Eucharist is celebrated on the greater festivals and on the first Sunday of each month; and, if those who can rightly communicate so wish, it can and therefore ought to be celebrated on any other Sunday, festival, or week-day. In describing the service,

[1] *Works (Anglo-Catholic Library)*, ii. 12.

he mentions the retention of the ancient ceremonies, prayers, and
vestments; that, after the Prayer for the Church Militant, those
who are not about to communicate leave the church; that the
communicants enter the chancel before the Confession; that at
the Prayer of Consecration the priest "blesses each symbol, and
consecrates them to be the Sacrament of the body and blood
of Christ"; that in the posture of kneeling at and after Communion the communicants "adore Christ, not the Sacrament";
and that this rite is "the solemn Eucharist or sacrifice of praise
of the Church, offered to God Most High as a commemoration
of the propitiatory sacrifice of Christ once for all offered on the
cross".[1]

Cosin wrote for the Countess of Peterborough *A Paper Concerning the Differences in the Chief Points of Religion betwixt the
Church of Rome and the Church of England*, which was printed
in 1705 by Dr. Hickes from the copy which Cosin had given to
the Countess. It contains lists of "the differences" and of "the
agreements" "between the Roman Catholics and us of the Church
of England". Among "the differences" are the Roman Catholic
beliefs—

"That the priests offer up our Saviour in the Mass as a real,
proper, and propitiatory sacrifice for the quick and the dead; and
that whosoever believes it not is eternally damned:

"That in the Sacrament of the Eucharist the whole substance
of bread is converted into the substance of Christ's body, and the
whole substance of wine into His blood, so truly and properly as
that after consecration there is neither any bread nor wine remaining there, which they call Transubstantiation and impose upon all
persons under pain of damnation to be believed."[2]

Among "the agreements" are that "Roman Catholics" and
"we are at accord"—

"In commemorating at the Eucharist the sacrifice of Christ's
body and blood once truly offered for us:

"In acknowledging His sacramental, spiritual, true, and real
presence there to the souls of all them that come faithfully and devoutly to receive Him according to His own institution in that holy
Sacrament."[3]

[1] *Op. cit.* iv. 347, 357-60.   [2] *Ibid.* 333.   [3] *Ibid.* 336.

In 1656, while he was at Paris, Cosin wrote his *Historia Transubstantiationis Papalis*, which was published in London in 1675 three years after his death. An English translation by Luke de Beaulieu appeared in the following year. In this treatise Cosin associates the doctrine of the Church of England with that of those foreign Reformers who followed Calvin in asserting a real presence of the body and blood of Christ to faithful communicants. A few passages at first sight seem to imply that the consecrated Sacrament is the body and blood of Christ before Communion; but, when these are examined closely and viewed in their context, the meaning of them appears to be that it is the office of the consecrated elements to enable the communicant to receive Christ's body and blood.

" The bread and the cup are in no way changed in substance, or removed, or destroyed; but they are solemnly consecrated by the words of Christ for this purpose, that they may most surely serve for the communication of His body and blood. . . . The words both of Christ and of the Apostle are to be understood sacramentally and mystically, and no gross or carnal presence of the body and blood can be supported by them. . . . It was the design of Christ to teach not so much what the elements of bread and wine are in their nature and substance as what they are in signification and use and office in this mystery; since not only are the body and blood of Christ most suitably represented by these elements, but also through their instrumentality Christ Himself by His own institution is most really presented (*exhibeatur*) to all, and is sacramentally or mystically eaten by the faithful. . . . None of the Protestant Churches doubt of the actual (*reali*), that is, the real (*vera*) and not imaginary presence of the body and blood of Christ in the Eucharist; nor is there any reason for suspicion that in this matter they have in the smallest degree departed from the Catholic faith. For it is easy to produce the consent of reformed writers and Churches by which it can be most clearly shown to all who have intellects and eyes that they are all most tenacious of this truth and that they have not in any way departed from the ancient and Catholic faith." [1]

After lengthy quotations from the documents of the English Church, English writers, the foreign Protestant *Confessions*, and from Calvin, Cosin goes on :—

[1] *Op. cit.* iv. 16-19.
21 *

" The result is that the body and blood of Christ are sacramentally united to the bread and wine in such a way that Christ is
really presented (*exhibeatur*) to believers, yet not to be considered
by any sense or by the reason of this world, but by faith resting
on the words of the Gospel.   Now the flesh and blood of Christ are
said to be united to the bread and wine because in the celebration
of the Eucharist the flesh is presented and received together with
the bread, and the blood together with the wine. . . . The papists
hold it an article of faith that in the Eucharist the substance of
bread and wine is annihilated, and that the body and blood of
Christ takes its place. . . . The Reformed are of a very different
mind.   Yet no Protestant altogether denies the conversion or
change of the bread into the body of Christ, and similarly of the
wine into His blood.   For they know and acknowledge that in
the Eucharist by virtue of the words and blessing of Christ the
bread is wholly changed in condition and use and office; that is,
of ordinary and common, it becomes our mystical and sacramental
food ; whereby they all assert and firmly believe that the real body
of Christ itself is not only signified and represented in a figure, but
is also presented (*exhiberi*) in actual fact, and is received in the
souls of those who communicate worthily." [1]

" The reformed Churches place the constitution (*formam*) of this
Sacrament in the union of the sign with the thing signified, that is,
the presenting (*exhibitione*) of the body of Christ, the bread remaining bread and being dedicated to sacramental uses, whereby these
two so become one by the appointment of God that, although this
union is not natural or substantial or personal or local (by the one
being in the other), yet it is so well adjusted (*concinna*) and real
that in the eating of the consecrated bread the real body of Christ
is given to us, and the names of the sign and of the thing signified
are reciprocally changed, and what is of the body is attributed to
the bread, and what is of the bread is attributed to the body, and
they are together in time, though separated in place.   For the
presence of the body of Christ in this mystery is opposed not to distance but to absence ; and absence, not distance, prevents the use
and enjoyment of the object.   Hence it is clear that the present
controversy between the reformed and the papists can be reduced
to four heads : first, concerning the signs ; secondly, concerning the
thing signified ; thirdly, concerning the union of the signs and the
things ; fourthly, concerning the participation in them.   As to the
first, we differ from them, because they make the accidents only to

<hr/>

[1] *Op. cit.* iv. 46.

be the signs, while we regard the substance of bread and wine as the signs in accordance with the nature of Sacraments and the teaching of Scripture. As to the second, we do not say that which they through misunderstanding our opinion ascribe to us. For we do not say that only the merits of the death of Christ are signified by the consecrated symbols, but that the real body itself which was crucified for us, and the real blood itself which was shed for us, are both represented and offered, so that our minds may enjoy Christ not less certainly and really than we see and receive and eat and drink the bodily and visible signs themselves. As to the third, since the thing signified is offered and presented (*exhibetur*) to us as really as the signs themselves, in this way we recognise the union of the signs with the body and blood of the Lord, and we say that the elements are changed into a different use from that which they had before. But we deny the assertion of the papists that the substance of bread and wine disappears, or is so changed into the body and blood of the Lord that there is nothing left but the bare accidents of the elements, which are united with the same body and blood. Further, we deny that the Sacrament outside the use appointed by God has the nature of a Sacrament so as to make it right or possible for Christ to be reserved or carried about, since He is present only to those who communicate. Lastly, as to the fourth point, we do not say that in this holy Supper we are partakers only of the fruit of the death and passion of Christ, but we join the ground with the fruits which come to us from Him, declaring with the Apostle, 'the bread which we break is a Communion of the body of Christ, and the cup a Communion of His blood,'[1] yea, in that same substance which He took in the womb of the Virgin and which He raised on high to heaven ; differing from the papists in this only, that they believe this eating and union to take place bodily, while we believe it to be not in any natural way or in any bodily manner, but none the less as really as if we were joined to Christ naturally and bodily. . . . The assertion of the papists that Christ gives us His body and His blood to be taken and eaten with the mouth and teeth, so that it is devoured not only by the wicked who are devoid of real faith but also by mice,—this we wholly deny with our mouths and our hearts and our minds."[2]

The fifth volume of the edition of Cosin's works in the *Anglo-Catholic Library* contains three series of notes on the Book of Common Prayer ascribed to Cosin. There is nothing in the

[1] 1 Cor. x. 16.   [2] *Op. cit.* iv. 48, 49.

second and third series, both of which are the work of Cosin, to suggest any different doctrine from that indicated in the foregoing quotations from his other writings. The most important passages are the following :—

"Christ can be no more offered, as the doctors and priests of the Roman party fancy Him to be, and vainly think that every time they say Mass they offer up and sacrifice Christ anew as properly and truly as He offered up Himself in His sacrifice upon the cross. . . . Without shedding of His blood and killing Him over again no proper sacrifice can be made of Him, which yet in their Masses the Roman priests pretend every day to do."[1]

"We do not hold this celebration to be so naked a commemoration of Christ's body given to death, and of His blood there shed for us, but that the same body and blood is present there in this commemoration (made by the Sacrament of bread and wine) to all that faithfully receive it: nor do we say that it is so nude a sacrifice of praise and thanksgiving but that by our prayers also added we offer and present the death of Christ to God, that for His death's sake we may find mercy, in which respect we deny not this commemorative sacrifice to be propitiatory. The receiving of which Sacrament, or participating of which sacrifice exhibited to us, we say is profitable only to them that receive it and participate of it ; but the prayers that we add thereunto, in presenting the death and merits of our Saviour to God, is not only beneficial to them that are present, but to them that are absent also, to the dead and living both, to all true members of the Catholic Church of Christ. But a true, real, proper, and propitiatory sacrificing of Christ, *toties quoties* as this Sacrament is celebrated, which is the popish doctrine, and which cannot be done without killing of Christ so often again, we hold not, believing it to be a false and blasphemous doctrine, founding ourselves upon the Apostle's doctrine,[2] that Christ was sacrificed but once, and that He dieth no more."[3]

"True it is that the body and blood of Christ are sacramentally and really (not feignedly) present when the blessed bread and wine are taken by the faithful communicants; and true it is also that they are not present but only when the hallowed elements are so taken, as in another work (the *History of the Papal Transubstantiation*) I have more at large declared. Therefore whosoever so receiveth

---

[1] *Op. cit.* v. 333.
[2] Rom. vi. 9, 10 ; Heb. ix. 28, x. 12.
[3] *Op. cit.* v. 336.

them, at that time when he receiveth them, rightly doth he adore
and reverence His Saviour there together with the sacramental
bread and cup, exhibiting His own body and blood unto them. Yet,
because that body and blood is neither sensibly present (nor otherwise at all present but only to them that are duly prepared to receive them, and in the very act of receiving them and the consecrated
species together, to which they are sacramentally in that act united),
the adoration is then and there given to Christ Himself, neither is
nor ought to be directed to any external sensible object, such as are
the blessed elements. But our kneeling, and the outward gesture
of humility and reverence in our bodies, is ordained only to testify
and express the inward reverence and devotion of our souls towards
our blessed Saviour, who vouchsafed to sacrifice Himself for us on
the cross, and now presenteth Himself to be united sacramentally
to us, that we may enjoy all the benefits of His mystical passion,
and be nourished with the spiritual food of His blessed body and
blood unto life eternal." [1]

"The Eucharist may by allusion, analogy, and extrinsical denom-
ination, be fitly called a sacrifice, and the Lord's Table an altar, the
one relating to the other, though neither of them can be strictly
and properly so termed. It is the custom of Scripture to describe
the service of God under the New Testament, be it either internal
or external, by the terms that otherwise most properly belonged to
the Old, as immolation, offering, sacrifice, and altar." [2]

Of the first series of these notes Dr. Barrow, the editor of the
edition of Cosin's works in the *Anglo-Catholic Library*, wrote,
"There can" "be no doubt that they are Bishop Cosin's"; and
he accounted for some peculiarities in them by the supposition
that they were written in the earlier part of Cosin's life, probably
before 1638.[3] It is, however, more probable that they are the
work of a different writer, possibly a nephew of Bishop Overall
named Hayward.[4] They explicitly connect the presence of the
body and blood of Christ in the Eucharist with the consecration ;
and they describe the Eucharist as a propitiatory sacrifice. The
following statements occur in them :—

[1] *Op. cit.* v. 345, 346.
[2] *Op. cit.* v. 347, 348. The passages of Scripture referred to are Isa.
lvi. 7 (the reference given, ii. 4, seems to be a mistake); Mal. i. 11 ; Rom.
xv. 16 ; Phil. ii. 17 ; Heb. xiii. 10.
[3] *Op. cit.* vol. v. pref. pp. xiv-xix.
[4] See a discussion on this point in some letters in the *Guardian* for
26th September, 3rd, 17th, 24th October, 1900.

"This is a plain oblation of Christ's death once offered, and a representative sacrifice of it, for the sins, and for the benefit, of the whole world, of the whole Church ; that both those which are here on earth and those that rest in the sleep of peace, being departed in the faith of Christ, may find the effect and virtue of it. . . . And in this sense it is not only an eucharistical, but a propitiatory, sacrifice. . . . Why should we then make any controversy about this ? They love not the truth of Christ, nor the peace of the Church, that make these disputes between the Church of Rome and us, when we agree, as Christian Churches should, in our liturgies : what private men's conceits are, what is that to the public approved religion of either Church, which is to be seen in their liturgies best of all ? " [1]

"It is confessed by all divines that upon the words of consecration the body and blood of Christ is really and substantially present, and so exhibited and given to all that receive it ; and all this not after a physical and sensual but after a heavenly and invisible and incomprehensible manner : but yet remains this controversy among some of them, whether the body of Christ be present only in the use of the Sacrament and in the act of eating, and not otherwise. They that hold the affirmative, as the Lutherans in *Conf. Sax.*,[2] and all Calvinists, do seem to me to depart from all antiquity, which place the presence of Christ in the virtue of the words of consecration and benediction used by the priest, and not in the use of eating of the Sacrament, for they tell us that the virtue of that consecration is not lost, though the Sacrament be reserved either for sick persons or other." [3]

Jeremy Taylor was born at Cambridge in 1613. He was a member, and became a Perse Fellow, of Gonville and Caius College. In 1636 he was made Fellow of All Souls College, Oxford, by Archbishop Laud ; in 1638 he became Rector of Uppingham ; and about the same time he was chaplain to the king. During the Commonwealth, being deprived of his benefice, he resided in Wales, London, and Ireland. On 27th January, 1661, he was consecrated Bishop of Down, Connor, and Dromore. He died in 1667. There are indications of his belief about the Eucharist in his *Life of Christ, Holy Living, The Worthy Communicant, Dissuasive from Popery, Letters to Persons Changed or Tempted to a Change in Their Religion,* and most fully in *The Real Presence and Spiritual of Christ in the Blessed Sacrament.* In the

---

[1] *Op. cit.* v. 119, 120.   [2] See pp. 30-33, *supra.*   [3] *Op. cit.* v. 131.

Life of Christ, published in 1649, Taylor, in referring to the
discourse at Capernaum, speaks of " the mysterious and symbolical manducation of Christ Himself " ; [1] in connection with the
Last Supper says that our Lord " gave His body and blood in
Sacrament and religious configuration " ; [2] and in his account of
the institution of the Sacrament writes :—

"We receive Him who is light and life, the fountain of grace,
and the sanctifier of our secular comforts, and the author of holiness
and glory. . . . The bread, when it is consecrated and made sacramental, is the body of our Lord ; and the fraction and distribution
of it is the communication of that body which died for us upon the
cross. He that doubts of either of the parts of this proposition
must either think Christ was not able to verify His word, and to make
' bread ' by His benediction to become to us to be ' His body ' or
that St. Paul did not well interpret and understand this mystery
when he called it 'bread '. . . . We see it, we feel it, we taste it,
and we smell it to be bread ; and by philosophy we are led into a
belief of that substance whose accidents these are, as we are to believe that to be fire which burns and flames and shines : but Christ
also affirmed concerning it ' This is My body ' ; and if faith can create
an assent as strong as its object is infallible, or can be as certain in
its conclusion as sense is certain in its apprehensions, we must at no
hand doubt but that it is Christ's body. Let the sense of that be
what it will, so that we believe those words, and (whatsoever that
sense is which Christ intended) that we no more doubt in our faith
than we do in our sense, then our faith is not reprovable. . . . They
that are forward to believe the change of substance can intend no
more but that it be believed verily to be the body of the Lord. And,
if they think it impossible to reconcile its being bread with the
verity of being Christ's body, let them remember that themselves
are put to more difficulties, and to admit of more miracles, and to
contradict more sciences, and to refuse the testimony of sense, in
affirming the special manner of Transubstantiation. And therefore
it were safer to admit the words in their first sense, in which we
shall no more be at war with reason, nor so much with sense, and
not at all with faith. And, for persons of the contradictory persuasion, who, to avoid the natural sense, affirm it to be only figurative, since their design is only to make this Sacrament to be Christ's
body in the sense of faith, and not of philosophy, they may remember that its being really present does not hinder but that all that

[1] III. xiv. 3.   [2] III. xv. 17.

reality may be spiritual; and, if it be Christ's body, so it be not affirmed such in a natural sense and manner, it is still only the object of faith and spirit; and, if it be affirmed only to be spiritual, there is then no danger to faith in admitting the words of Christ's institution, 'This is My body'. I suppose it to be a mistake, to think whatsoever is real must be natural; and it is no less to think spiritual to be only figurative: that is too much, and this is too little. . . . His power is manifest in making the symbols to be the instruments of conveying Himself to the spirit of the receiver: He nourishes the soul with bread, and feeds the body with a Sacrament; He makes the body spiritual by His graces there ministered, and makes the spirit to be united to His body by a participation of the divine nature. In the Sacrament, that body which is reigning in heaven is exposed upon the Table of blessing; and His body, which was broken for us, is now broken again, and yet remains impassible. Every consecrated portion of bread and wine does exhibit Christ entirely to the faithful receiver; and yet Christ remains one while He is wholly ministered in ten thousand portions. . . . Our wisest Master hath appointed bread and wine that we may be corporally united to Him; that, as the symbols becoming nutriment are turned into the substance of our bodies, so Christ being the food of our souls should assimilate us, making us partakers of the divine nature." [1]

In *The Rule and Exercises of Holy Living*, published in 1650, Taylor thus describes the consecration, and the benefits of receiving the Holy Communion worthily :—

" When the holy man stands at the Table of blessing and ministers the rite of consecration, then do as the angels do, who behold, and love, and wonder that the Son of God should become food to the souls of His servants; that He, who cannot suffer any change or lessening, should be broken into pieces and enter into the body to support and nourish the spirit, and yet at the same time remain in heaven while He descends to thee upon earth. . . . In the act of receiving, exercise acts of faith with much confidence and resignation, believing it not to be common bread and wine, but holy in their use, holy in their signification, holy in their change, and holy in their effect: and believe, if thou art a worthy communicant, thou dost as verily receive Christ's body and blood to all effects and purposes of the spirit as thou dost receive the blessed elements into thy mouth, that thou puttest thy finger to His hand, and thy hand

[1] III. xv. (discourse xix. 1, 2, 3, 4, 5).

into His side, and thy lips to His fontinel of blood, sucking life from His heart; and yet, if thou dost communicate unworthily, thou eatest and drinkest Christ to thy danger and death and destruction. Dispute not concerning the secret of the mystery, and the nicety of the manner of Christ's presence : it is sufficient to thee that Christ shall be present to thy soul as an instrument of grace, as a pledge of the resurrection, as an earnest of glory and immortality, and a means of many intermedial blessings, even all such as are necessary for thee, and are in order to thy salvation. And to make all this good to thee, there is nothing necessary on thy part but a holy life, and a true belief of all the sayings of Christ; amongst which, indefinitely assent to the words of institution, and believe that Christ in the Holy Sacrament gives thee His body and His blood. He that believes not this is not a Christian. He that believes so much needs not to inquire further nor to entangle his faith by disbelieving his sense." [1]

In *The Worthy Communicant*, which was published in 1660, there is teaching which closely resembles one part of the doctrine of Clement of Alexandria and Origen,[2] by which the Eucharistic flesh and blood of Christ are identified with His word and Spirit.

"The flesh of Christ is His word; the blood of Christ is His Spirit; and by believing in His word, and being assisted and conducted by His Spirit, we are nourished up to life; and so Christ is our food, so He becomes life unto our souls. . . . As the body or flesh of Christ is His word, so the blood of Christ is His Spirit in real effect and signification. . . . The word and the Spirit are the flesh and the blood of Christ, that is the ground of all. . . . The word and the Spirit are ministered to us in the Sacrament of the Lord's Supper. . . . Christ's body, His flesh and His blood, are therefore called our meat and our drink because by His Incarnation and manifestation in the flesh He became life unto us : so that it is mysterious indeed in the expression but very proper and intelligible in the event to say that we eat His flesh and drink His blood, since by these it is that we have and preserve life. But because what Christ began in His Incarnation, He finished in His body on the cross, and all the whole progression of mysteries in His body was still an operatory of life and spiritual being to us, the Sacrament of the Lord's Supper being a commemoration and exhibition of His death, which was the consummation of our redemption by His body and blood, does contain in it a visible word, the word in symbol and visibility and special manifestation. Consonant to which doctrine, the fathers by an elegant expression call the Blessed Sacrament 'the extension of the Incarnation '." [1]

In the *Real Presence and Spiritual* and the *Dissuasive from Popery*, which were published in 1654 and 1664 respectively, it is maintained at length that our Lord's words at the institution of the Sacrament were figurative, and that He is present in effect to the souls of faithful communicants. The following are representative passages :—

"The doctrine of the Church of England, and generally of the Protestants, in this article is, that after the minister of the holy mysteries hath rightly prayed, and blessed and consecrated the bread and the wine, the symbols become changed into the body and blood of Christ after a sacramental, that is, in a spiritual real manner: so that all that worthily communicate do by faith receive Christ really, effectually, to all the purposes of His passion : the wicked receive not Christ, but the bare symbols only, but yet to their hurt because the offer of Christ is rejected, and they pollute the blood of the covenant by using it as an unholy thing." [2]

"We say that Christ's body is in the Sacrament 'really but spiritually'. They [the 'papists'] say, it is there 'really but spiritually'. For so Bellarmine is bold to say that the word may be allowed in this question. Where now is the difference? Here, by 'spiritually' they mean 'present after the manner of a spirit'; by 'spiritually' we mean 'present to our spirits only'; that is, so as Christ is not present to any other sense but that of faith or spiritual susception ; but their way makes His body to be present no way but that which is impossible and implies a contradiction, a body not after the manner of a body, a body like a spirit, a body without a body, and a sacrifice of body and blood without blood, *corpus incorporeum, cruor incruentus*. They say that Christ's body is truly present there as it was upon the cross, but not after the manner of all or any body, but after that manner of being as an angel is in a place : that is there spiritually. But we by the real spiritual presence of Christ do understand Christ to be present as the Spirit of God is present in the hearts of the faithful by blessing and grace ; and this is all which we mean besides the tropical and figurative presence." [3]

"'Take, eat' and 'This do' are as necessary to the Sacrament as *Hoc est corpus ;* and declare that it is Christ's body only in the use and administration : and therefore not 'natural' but 'spiritual'." [4]

[1] I. ii. 3, 4.   [2] *Real Presence*, i. 4.   [3] *Ibid.* 8.   [4] *Ibid.* iv. 8.

"That the proposition is tropical and figurative is the thing, and that Christ's natural body is now in heaven definitively, and nowhere else; and that He is in the Sacrament as He can be in a Sacrament, in the hearts of faithful receivers as He hath promised to be there; that is, in the Sacrament mystically, operatively, as in a moral and divine instrument, in the hearts of receivers by faith and blessing." [1]

"His body figuratively, tropically, representatively in being, and really in effect and blessing." [2]

"The commandment to worship God alone is so express, the distance between God and bread dedicated to the service of God is so vast, the danger of worshipping that which is not God, or of not worshipping that which is God, is so formidable, that it is infinitely to be presumed that, if it had been intended that we should have worshipped the Holy Sacrament, the Holy Scripture would have called it 'God' or 'Jesus Christ,' or have bidden us in express terms to have adored it; that either by the first as by a reason indicative, or by the second as by a reason imperative, we might have had sufficient warrant direct or consequent to have paid a divine worship. Now that there is no implicit warrant in the sacramental words of 'This is My body,' I have given very many reasons to evince by proving the words to be sacramental and figurative." [3]

"We think it our duty to give our own people caution and admonition; 1. That they be not abused by the rhetorical words and high expressions alleged out of the fathers calling the Sacrament 'the body or the flesh of Christ'. For we all believe it is so, and rejoice in it. But the question is, After what manner it is so; whether after the manner of the flesh or after the manner of spiritual grace and sacramental consequence? We with the Holy Scriptures and the primitive fathers affirm the latter. The Church of Rome against the words of Scripture and the explication of Christ and the doctrine of the primitive Church affirm the former. 2. That they be careful not to admit such doctrines under a pretence of being ancient. . . . 3. We exhort them that they remember the words of Christ . . . that He tells us, 'the flesh profiteth nothing, but the words which He speaks are spirit and they are life'. [4] 4. That if those ancient and primitive doctors above cited say true, and that the symbols still remain the same in their natural substance and properties, even after they are

[1] *Real Presence*, vi. 1.   [2] *Ibid.* xi. 17.
[3] *Ibid.* xiii. 1.   [4] St. John vi. 63.

blessed, and when they are received, and that Christ's body and
blood are only present to faith and to the spirit, that then whoever
tempts them to give divine honour to these symbols or elements
(as the Church of Rome does) tempts them to give to a creature
the due and incommunicable propriety of God; and that then this
evil passes further than an error in the understanding; for it carries
them to a dangerous practice which cannot reasonably be excused
from the crime of idolatry." [1]

In the third of the three *Letters Written to a Gentleman that
was Tempted to the Communion of the Romish Church*, which is
dated 13th March, 1658, Taylor says :—

"We may not render divine worship to Him (as present in the
Blessed Sacrament according to His human nature) without danger
of idolatry: because He is not there according to His human nature,
and therefore you give divine worship to a *non ens*, which must
needs be idolatry. . . . He is present there by His divine power,
and His divine blessing, and the fruits of His body, the real effective consequents of His passion : but for any other presence, it is
idolum, it is nothing in the world. [2] Adore Christ in heaven; for
the heavens must contain Him till the time of the restitution of
all things." [3]

A comparison of the different parts of this teaching of
Jeremy Taylor about the Eucharistic presence makes it clear
that he held some such receptionist doctrine as that of Calvin, [4]
or virtualist doctrine as that of Cranmer. [5]

Taylor held a fuller doctrine concerning the Eucharistic sacrifice than might have been thought likely merely from the consideration of his views as to the presence of our Lord in the
Sacrament. And he laid stress on the connection of the Eucharist with the pleading of Christ's sacrifice in heaven which
was known to the fathers and Western liturgical and Greek
writers of the Middle Ages, which was to a large extent obscured
in the schoolmen and in the later Western theology.

In his *Life of Christ* he writes :—

"As it is a commemoration and representation of Christ's death,
so it is a commemorative sacrifice. . . . Whatsoever Christ did at

---

[1] *Dissuasive*, I. i. 5.　　　　　[2] See 1 Cor. viii. 4.
[3] In Taylor's *Works*, vi. 669, Eden's edition ; xi. 212, 213, Heber's
edition.
[4] See pp. 50-54, *supra*.　　　　[5] See pp. 127-29, *supra*.

the institution, the same He commanded the Church to do in re-membrance and repeated rites; and Himself also does the same thing in heaven for us, making perpetual intercession for His Church, the body of His redeemed ones, by representing to His Father His death and sacrifice. There He sits, a High Priest continually, and offers still the same one perfect sacrifice; that is, still represents it as having been once finished and consummate, in order to perpetual and never failing events. And this also His ministers do on earth; they offer up the same sacrifice to God, the sacrifice of the cross, by prayers, and a commemorating rite and representment, according to His holy institution. . . . Our very holding up the Son of God, and representing Him to His Father, is the doing an act of mediation and advantage to ourselves in the virtue and efficacy of the Mediator. As Christ is a priest in heaven for ever, and yet does not sacrifice Himself afresh, nor yet without a sacrifice could He be a priest, but by a daily ministration and intercession represents His sacrifice to God, and offers Himself as sacrificed, so He does upon earth by the ministry of His servants; He is offered to God; that is, He is by prayers and the Sacrament represented or 'offered up to God as sacrificed,' which in effect is a celebration of His death, and the applying it to the present and future necessities of the Church as we are capable by a ministry like to His in heaven. It follows, then, that the celebration of this sacrifice be in its proportion an instru-ment of applying the proper sacrifice to all the purposes which it first designed. It is ministerially and by application an instrument propitiatory; it is eucharistical, it is an homage, and an act of adora-tion; and it is impetratory and obtains for us, and for the whole Church, all the benefits of the sacrifice, which is now celebrated and applied; that is, as this rite is the remembrance and ministerial celebration of Christ's sacrifice, so it is destined to do honour to God, to express the homage and duty of His servants, to acknowledge His supreme dominion, to give Him thanks and worship, to beg pardon, blessings, and supply of all our needs. And its profit is en-larged not only to the persons celebrating, but to all to whom they design it, according to the nature of sacrifices and prayers and all such solemn actions of religion." [1]

In *The Rule and Exercises of Holy Living* he writes :—

" The celebration of the Holy Sacrament is the great mysterious-ness of the Christian religion, and succeeds to the most solemn rite of natural and Judaical religion, the law of sacrificing. For God

[1] III. xv. (discourse xix. 7).

spared mankind, and took the sacrifice of beasts together with our solemn prayers for an instrument of expiation. But these could not purify the soul from sin, but were typical of the sacrifice of something that could. . . . This the Son of God, Jesus Christ, God and Man, undertook, and finished by a sacrifice of Himself upon the altar of the cross. This sacrifice, because it was perfect, could be but one, and that once : but, because the needs of the world should last as long as the world itself, it was necessary that there should be a perpetual ministry established, whereby this one sufficient sacrifice should be made eternally effectual to the several new arising needs of all the world, who should desire it, or in any sense be capable of it. To this end Christ was made a priest for ever: He was initiated or conse-crated on the cross, and there began His priesthood, which was to last till His coming to judgment. It began on earth, but was to last and be officiated in heaven, where He sits perpetually representing and exhibiting to the Father that great effective sacrifice, which He offered on the cross to eternal and never-failing purposes. As Christ is pleased to represent to His Father that great sacrifice as a means of atonement and expiation for all mankind, and with special pur-poses and intendment for all the elect, all that serve Him in holiness : so He hath appointed that the same ministry shall be done upon earth too in our manner, and according to our proportion ; and there-fore hath constituted and separated an order of men who by ' showing forth the Lord's death ' by sacramental representation may pray unto God after the same manner that our Lord and High Priest does ; that is, offer to God and represent in this solemn prayer and Sacra-ment Christ as already offered ; so sending up a gracious instrument whereby our prayers may for His sake and in the same manner of intercession be offered up to God in our behalf, and for all them for whom we pray, to all those purposes for which Christ died.   As the ministers of the Sacrament do in a sacramental manner present to God the sacrifice of the cross by being imitators of Christ's inter-cession, so the people are sacrificers too in their manner ; for, besides that by saying Amen they join in the act of him that ministers, and make it also to be their own, so, when they eat and drink the con-secrated and blessed elements worthily, they receive Christ within them, and therefore may also offer Him to God, while in their sacrifice of obedience and thanksgiving they present themselves to God with Christ, whom they have spiritually received, that is, them-selves with that which will make them gracious and acceptable. The offering their souls and bodies and services to God in Him, and by Him, and with Him, who is His Father's well-beloved, and in whom He is well pleased, cannot but be accepted to all the purposes of blessing, grace, and glory. This is the sum of the greatest mystery of our religion; it is the copy of the passion, and the ministration of the great mystery of our redemption." [1]

In *The Worthy Communicant* he says :—

"When Christ was consecrated on the cross, and became our High Priest, having reconciled us to God by the death on the cross, He became infinitely gracious in the eyes of God, and was admitted to the celestial and eternal priesthood in heaven, where in the virtue of the cross He intercedes for us, and represents an eternal sacrifice in the heavens on our behalf. . . . Since it is necessary that He hath something to offer so long as He is a priest, and there is no other sacrifice but that of Himself offered upon the cross, it follows that Christ in heaven perpetually offers and represents that sacrifice to His heavenly Father, and in virtue of that obtains all good things for His Church. Now what Christ does in heaven, He hath commanded us to do on earth; that is, to represent His death, to commemorate this sacrifice, by humble prayer and thankful record; and by faithful manifestation and joyful Eucharist to lay it before the eyes of our heavenly Father, so ministering in His priesthood and doing according to His commandment and His example ; the Church being the image of heaven ; the priest the minister of Christ ; the Holy Table being a copy of the celestial altar ; and the eternal sacrifice of the Lamb slain from the beginning of the world being always the same ; it bleeds no more after the finishing of it on the cross ; but it is wonderfully represented in heaven and graciously represented here ; by Christ's action there, by His commandment here." [2]

John Bramhall was born near Pontefract in 1594. He was ordained about 1616. After holding several preferments in England, he became Archdeacon of Meath in 1633, and Bishop of Derry in 1634. During the Commonwealth, except for a short visit to Ireland, he was abroad, chiefly at Paris and Brussels and in Spain. In October, 1660, he returned to England; and on 18th January, 1661, he was translated from the see of Derry to the archbishopric of Armagh. He died on 25th June, 1663. His works, a large part of which treat of the controversy with Rome, contain many references to the doctrine of the Eucharist. His teaching on this subject differs considerably from that of

[1] IV. x. 1-6.   [2] I. iv. 4.

Cosin and of Jeremy Taylor, and at times shows a tendency to leave open both Transubstantiation and the question whether the presence of the body of Christ in the Sacrament is to be connected with the consecrated elements before Communion or restricted to the reception by the faithful communicants.

In his *Answer to an Epistle of M. de la Milletiere*, published in 1653, *A Just Vindication of the Church of England*, published in 1654, *A Replication to the Bishop of Chalcedon*, published in 1656, and in *Schism Guarded* and *Consecration of Protestant Bishops Vindicated*, both published in 1658, Bramhall writes in regard to the Eucharistic presence and to adoration as follows :—

" I find not one of your arguments that comes home to Transubstantiation, but only to a true real presence, which no genuine son of the Church of England did ever deny, no, nor your adversary himself.   Christ said, ' This is My body ' ; what He said, we do steadfastly believe.   He said not, after this or that manner, *neque con neque sub neque trans*.   And therefore we place it among the opinions of the schools, not among the articles of our faith." [1]

" We deny not a venerable respect unto the consecrate elements not only as love-tokens sent us by our best Friend but as the instruments ordained by our Saviour to convey to us the merits of His passion ; but [? and] for the Person of Christ, God forbid that we should deny Him divine worship at any time, and especially in the use of this Holy Sacrament ; we believe with St. Austin that ' no man eats of that flesh but first he adores ' ; [2] but that which offends us is this, that you teach and require all men to adore the very Sacrament with divine honour. . . . We dare not give divine worship unto any creature, no, not to the very humanity of Christ in the abstract (much less to the host), but to the whole Person of Christ, God and Man, by reason of the hypostatical union between the Child of the Blessed Virgin Mary and the eternal Son, ' who is God over all blessed for ever '. [3]   Show us such an union between the deity and the elements or accidents, and you say something. But you pretend no such things.   The highest that you dare go is this ; ' as they that adored Christ when He was upon earth did after a certain kind of manner adore His garments '. [4]   Is this all ?   This

---

[1] *Works (Anglo-Catholic Library)*, i. 8.
[2] The passage referred to is quoted on vol. i. p. 109, *supra*.
[3] Rom. ix. 5.
[4] Quoted from Bellarmine, *De Euch.* iv. 29.   See p. 365, *infra*. Bellarmine is speaking of the reverence due to the " Symbola ".

is 'after a certain kind of manner' indeed. We have enough. There is no more adoration due to the Sacrament than to the garments which Christ did wear upon earth. Exact no more. . . . We rest in the words of Christ, 'This is My body,' leaving the manner to Him that made the Sacrament. We know it is sacramental, and therefore efficacious, because God was never wanting to His own ordinances, where man did not set a bar against Himself: but whether it be corporeally or spiritually (I mean not only after the manner of a spirit but in a spiritual sense) ; whether it be in the soul only or in the host also ; and if in the host, whether by Consubstantiation or Transubstantiation ; whether by production or adduction or conservation or assumption or by whatsoever other way bold and blind men dare conjecture ; we determine not." [1]

"The Council of Trent is not contented to enjoin the adoration of Christ in the Sacrament (which we never deny), but of the Sacrament itself (that is, according to the common current of your schoolmen, the accidents or species of bread and wine), because it contains Christ. Why do they not add upon the same grounds that the pix is to be adored with divine worship because it contains the Sacrament? divine honour is not due to the very humanity of Christ as it is abstracted from the deity, but to the whole Person, deity and humanity, hypostatically united. Neither the grace of union nor the grace of unction can confer more upon the humanity than the humanity is capable of. There is no such union between the deity and the Sacrament neither immediately nor yet mediately *mediante corpore.*" [2]

"The opinions of the lawfulness of detaining the cup from the laity, and of the necessity of adoring the Sacrament, have by consequence excluded the Protestants from the participation of the Eucharist in the Roman Church." [3]

"Wherein then have we forsaken the communion of the Roman Church in Sacraments ? Not in their ancient communion of genuine Sacraments, but in their septenary number and supposititious Sacraments ; which yet we retain for the most part as useful and religious rites but not under the notion of Sacraments : not in their Sacraments, but in their abuses and sinful injunctions in the use of the Sacraments ; . . . as their injunction to all communicants to adore, not only Christ in the use of the Sacrament, to which we do readily assent, but to adore the Sacrament itself." [4]

"'The Sacrament is to be adored,' said the Council of Trent : that is, 'formally the body and blood of Christ,' say some of your

[1] *Op. cit.* i. 20-22.   [2] *Ibid.* 45.   [3] *Ibid.* 110.   [4] *Ibid.* ii. 35, 36.

22 *

authors; we say the same; 'the Sacrament,' that is, 'the species of bread and wine,' say others;[1] that we deny, and esteem it to be idolatrous." [2]

"Grossly is he mistaken on all sides when he saith that ' Protestants' (he should say the English Church if he would speak to the purpose) 'have a positive belief that the Sacrament is not the body of Christ,'[3] which were to contradict the words of Christ, 'This is My body'. He knows better, that Protestants do not deny the thing, but their bold determination of the manner by Transubstantiation, themselves confessing that the manner is incomprehensible by human reason. Neither do Protestants place it among the articles of the faith, but the opinions of the schools." [4]

"We ourselves adore Christ in the Sacrament, but we dare not adore the species of bread and wine." [5]

"They bring the very same objection against our priestly ordination,—'The form or words whereby men are made priests must express authority and power to consecrate, or make present, Christ's body and blood'. . . . Thus far we accord, to the truth of the presence of Christ's body and blood, so they leave us this latitude for the manner of His presence. Abate us Transubstantiation, and those things which are consequents of their determination of the manner of presence, and we have no difference with them in this particular. They who are ordained priests ought to have power to consecrate the Sacrament of the body and blood of Christ, that is, to make them present after such manner as they were present at the first institution, whether it be done by enunciation of the words of Christ, as it is observed in the Western Church, or by prayer, as it is practised in the Eastern Church, or whether these two be both the same thing in effect, that is, that the forms of the Sacraments be mystical prayers and implicit invocations. Our Church for more abundant caution useth both forms as well in the consecration of the Sacrament as in the ordination of priests. In the Holy Eucharist our consecration is a repetition of that which was done by Christ and now done by him that consecrateth in the person of Christ; otherwise the priest could not say, 'This is My body'." [6]

---

[1] Referring to Bellarmine, *De Euch.* iv. 29. See p. 365, *infra.*

[2] *Op. cit.* ii. 87.

[3] Referring to *A Survey of the Vindication of the Church of England,* vi. 6, by Richard Smith, titular Bishop of Chalcedon, who was in charge of the English Roman Catholics from 1625 to 1655.

[4] *Op. cit.* ii. 211. [5] *Ibid.* 494, 495.

[6] *Ibid.* iii. 165.

In the same works Bramhall explains the sense in which he considers that the Eucharist is to be regarded as a sacrifice, namely that it commemorates and represents the sacrifice of the cross, and is a means of obtaining and applying the benefits of the passion and death of Christ.

" You say we have renounced your sacrifice of the Mass. If the sacrifice of the Mass be the same with the sacrifice of the cross, we attribute more unto it than yourselves ; we place our whole hope of salvation in it. If you understand another propitiatory sacrifice distinct from that (as this of the Mass seems to be ; for confessedly the priest is not the same, the altar is not the same, the temple is not the same) ; if you think of any new meritorious satis-faction to God for the sins of the world, or of any new supplement to the merits of Christ's passion ; you must give us leave to renounce your sacrifice indeed, and to adhere to the Apostle, 'By one offering He hath perfected for ever them that are sanctified'.[1] Surely you cannot think that Christ did actually sacrifice Himself at His Last Supper (for then He had redeemed the world at His Last Supper ; then His subsequent sacrifice upon the cross had been superfluous) ; nor that the priest now doth more than Christ did then. We do readily acknowledge an Eucharistical sacrifice of prayers and praises : we profess a commemoration of the sacrifice of the cross : . . . we acknowledge a representation of that sacrifice to God the Father : we acknowledge an impetration of the benefit of it : we maintain an application of its virtue : so here is a commemorative, impetrative, applicative sacrifice. Speak distinctly, and I cannot understand what you can desire more. To make it a suppletory sacrifice, to supply the defects of the only true sacrifice of the cross, I hope both you and I abhor." [2]

" The Holy Eucharist is a commemoration, a representation, an application of the all-sufficient propitiatory sacrifice of the cross. If his sacrifice of the Mass have any other propitiatory power or virtue in it than to commemorate, represent, and apply the merit of the sacrifice of the cross, let him speak plainly what it is." [3]

" We acknowledge an eucharistical sacrifice of praise and thanks-giving ; a commemorative sacrifice, or a memorial of the sacrifice of the cross ; a representative sacrifice, or a representation of the passion of Christ before the eyes of His heavenly Father ; an im-petrative sacrifice, or an impetration of the fruit and benefit of His passion by way of real prayer ; and, lastly, an applicative sacrifice,

---

[1] Heb. x. 14.   [2] *Op. cit.* i. 54, 55.   [3] *Ibid.* ii. 88.

or an application of His merits unto our souls. Let him that dare go one step further than we do; and say that it is a suppletory sacrifice, to supply the defects of the sacrifice of the cross. Or else let them hold their peace and speak no more against us in this point of sacrifice for ever." [1]

"We have a meritorious sacrifice, that is, the sacrifice of the cross; we have a commemorative and applicative sacrifice, or a commemoration and application of that sacrifice in the Holy Eucharist. A suppletory sacrifice, to supply any wants or defects in that sacrifice, he dare not own; and unless he do own it, he saith no more than we say." [2]

Herbert Thorndike was born in 1598, probably in Suffolk, though he came of a Lincolnshire family. In 1618 or 1619 he was appointed minor Fellow, and in 1620 middle- or major Fellow, of Trinity College, Cambridge. He was ordained priest not later than 1627. He was University Preacher in 1631, Greek Reader of Trinity College in 1632, Senior Proctor in 1638, and Head Lecturer of Trinity College in 1639. He received the appointment of Prebendary of Layton Ecclesia in Lincoln Cathedral in 1636, but resigned this prebend because of a requirement of the College statutes in 1640. In 1639 he became Vicar of Claybrook, near Lutterworth, and in 1642 Rector of Barley in Hertfordshire. He was ejected from Barley in July, 1643, under the Commonwealth. In September, 1643, the Fellows of Sidney Sussex College elected him Master by a majority of one; but before the formalities of the election were completed the parliamentary soldiers interfered and forcibly took away one of the Fellows who had voted for Thorndike, with the result of a tie of votes and the eventual appointment of the other candidate, Richard Minshull, to the office of Master. Thorndike was ejected from his Fellowship at Trinity in May, 1646. Until the Restoration he probably lived chiefly in Cambridge and London. In 1660 he was reinstated as Fellow of Trinity and Rector of Barley. He resigned Barley on being appointed Prebendary of Westminster in September, 1661. He was a member of the Savoy Conference, and assisted in the revision of the Prayer Book. He died on 11th July, 1672.

Many references to the doctrine of the Eucharist are scattered about in Thorndike's very able writings. The most complete

---

[1] *Op. cit.* ii. 276.　　[2] *Ibid.* 642; *cf.* v. 188, 219-21.

and systematic treatment of this subject is contained in the
first five chapters of the third part of his great treatise entitled
*An Epilogue to the Tragedy of the Church of England, being
a Necessary Consideration and Brief Resolution of the Chief
Controversies in Religion that divide the Western Church ; occasioned by the Present Calamity of the Church of England:
in three books, viz. of I. The Principles of Christian Truth;
II. The Covenant of Grace; III. The Laws of the Church,*
which was published in 1659.

In this treatise Thorndike refers in somewhat slighting terms
to the "opinions" of the "factions" which maintain (1) Transubstantiation ; or (2) Zwinglianism, which he describes as "the
opinion of the Socinians" or of the "Sacramentaries"; or (3)
Calvinism ; or (4) Lutheranism. As it is of some importance to
observe exactly what he meant by Transubstantiation, his definition of that "opinion" may be quoted.

"The opinion of Transubstantiation . . . which importeth this,
—that, in celebrating this Sacrament, upon pronouncing of the words
with which our Lord delivered it to His disciples, 'This is My body,
this is My blood,' the substance of the elements, bread and wine,
ceaseth and is abolished, the substance of the body and blood of Christ
coming into their stead, though under the species of bread and wine ;
that is to say, those accidents of them, which our senses witness that
they remain." [1]

After describing these four "opinions," Thorndike proceeds
to affirm, and to support by arguments from Holy Scripture, the
statement, in opposition to Transubstantiation—

"that the bodily substance of bread and wine is not abolished nor
ceaseth in this Sacrament by virtue of the consecration of it." [2]

His next point is that, while "the nature and substance of
bread and wine" remain "in the Sacrament of the Eucharist even
when it is a Sacrament, that is, when it is received," yet it is
no less true and supported by Scripture that there is also the
presence

"of Christ's body and blood, brought forth and made to be in the
Sacrament of the Eucharist by making it to be that Sacrament." [3]

[1] *Works (Anglo-Catholic Library)*, iv. 4.
[2] *Op. cit.* iv. 6.   [3] *Ibid.* 11.

It is, he maintains, contrary to Scripture to hold either that "the Sacrament of the Eucharist is a mere sign of the body and blood of Christ without any promise of spiritual grace," or that the elements are not the body and blood of Christ "when they are received, but become so upon being received by living faith". Against these Zwinglian and Calvinistic views he asserts that—

"we receive the body and blood of Christ, not only when we receive the Sacrament of the Eucharist, but also by receiving it" ; that—

"the flesh and blood of Christ be" "in the Sacrament" "by virtue of the consecration of the elements into the Sacrament" ; and that—

"the flesh and blood of Christ is necessarily in the Sacrament when it is eaten and drunk in it, in which if it were not, it could not be eaten and drunk in it." [1]

Explaining his meaning more fully, he says :—

"Supposing the bread and the wine to remain in the Sacrament of the Eucharist, as sense informs and the word of God enforces ; if the same word of God affirm there to be also the body and blood of Christ, what remaineth but that bread and wine by nature and bodily substance be also the bodily flesh and blood of Christ by mystical representation (in that sense which I determined even now) and by spiritual grace ?" [2]

The "sense" of "representation" "determined even now" is thus stated :—

"Which kind of presence you may, if you please, call the representation of the sacrifice of Christ, so as you understand the word 'representation' to signify, not the figuring or resembling of that which is only signified, but as it signifies in the Roman laws, when a man is said *repræsentare pecuniam* who pays ready money : deriving the signification of it *a re præsenti*, not from the preposition *re ;* which will import, not the presenting of that again to a man's senses, which once is past, but the tendering of that to a man's possession, which is tendered him upon the place." [3]

He repeatedly emphasises that the presence is "mystical" ; that this "mystical" presence of the body and blood of Christ is

<hr />

[1] *Op. cit.* iv. 12-16.   [2] *Ibid.* 22.   [3] *Ibid.* 20.

a "means to convey His Spirit," and that the Holy Ghost "makes the elements" "the body and blood of Christ".[1] He rejects the view that the "mystical and spiritual presence of the flesh and blood of Christ in the elements" depends on the faith of the communicants.[2] Consequently, the body and blood of Christ are in some sense received even by those who communicate unworthily. "For," he says—

"that the body and blood of Christ should be sacramentally present in and under the elements (to be spiritually received of all that meet it with a living faith, to condemn those for crucifying Christ again that receive it with a dead faith), can it seem any way inconsequent to the consecration thereof by virtue of the common faith of Christians, professing that which is requisite to make true Christians, whether by a living or a dead faith?"[3]

He rejects also the doctrine ascribed to the Lutherans, that—

"the omnipresence of Christ's Godhead is communicated to His flesh by virtue of the hypostatical union, so that the body and blood of Christ, being everywhere present, necessarily subsisteth in the dimensions of bread and wine in the Eucharist."[4]

In a long and elaborate argument Thorndike maintains that the consecration is effected, not by the recital of the words, "This is My body," "This is My blood," but by the use of prayer. He supports this position by urging that when our Lord said these words He had already by His acts of blessing and thanksgiving made the elements to be His body and blood, and by pointing out that the ancient liturgies and the fathers agree in representing prayer as the means of consecration.[5]

After this, he repeats, in many varying ways of expression, his rejection of the "opinions" of the four "factions," and his affirmation of the presence of the body and blood of Christ. To quote passages which are representative of what he elaborates and illustrates at great length, he says :—

"If it can any way be showed that the Church did ever pray that the flesh and blood might be substituted instead of the elements under the accidents of them, then I am content that this be counted henceforth the sacramental presence of them in the Eucharist. But, if the Church only pray that the Spirit of God, coming down upon

---

[1] *Op. cit. e.g.* iv. 26, 27, 29, 32, 34, 47, 69, 77.   [2] *Ibid.* iv. 35, 36.
[3] *Ibid.* 38.   [4] *Ibid.* 43.   [5] *Ibid.* 50-68.

the elements, may make them the body and blood of Christ, so that they which received them may be filled with the grace of His Spirit; then is it not the sense of the Catholic Church that can oblige any man to believe the abolishing of the elements in their bodily substance : because, supposing that they remain, they may nevertheless become the instrument of God's Spirit, to convey the operation thereof to them that are disposed to receive it, no otherwise than His flesh and blood conveyed the efficacy thereof upon earth.   And that, I suppose, is reason enough to call it the body and blood of Christ sacramentally, that is to say, as in the Sacrament of the Eucharist.   It is not here to be denied that all ecclesiastical writers do with one mouth bear witness to the presence of the body and blood of Christ in the Eucharist.   Neither will any one of them be found to ascribe it to anything but the consecration; or that to any faith but that upon which the Church professeth to proceed to the celebrating of it.   And upon this account, when they speak of the elements, supposing the consecration to have passed upon them, they always call them by the name, not of their bodily substance, but of the body and blood of Christ which they are become." [1]

"The fathers . . . all acknowledge the elements to be changed, translated, and turned into the substance of Christ's body and blood; though as in a Sacrament, that is, mystically; yet therefore by virtue of the consecration, not of his faith that receives." [2]

"The canon of the Mass itself prays that the Holy Ghost coming down may make this bread and this cup the body and blood of Christ.[3]   And certainly the Roman Mass expresses a manifest abatement of the common and usual sense of the body and blood of Christ unto that sense which is proper to the intent and subject of them who speak of this Sacrament; when the Church in the consecration prays, *ut nobis corpus fiat dilectissimi Filii Tui Domini nostri Jesu Christi,* 'that they may become the body and blood of Thy most dearly beloved Son, our Lord Jesus Christ, to us'.   No man, that understands Latin and sense, will say it is the same thing for the elements to become the body and blood of Christ as to become the body and blood of Christ to those that receive; which imports no more than that which I have said.   And yet there is no more said in those liturgies which pray that the Spirit of God may make them the flesh and blood of Christ to this intent and effect, that

[1] *Op. cit.* iv. 69.   [2] *Ibid.* 73.

[3] A comparison of an earlier passage (iv. 57) seems to show that Thorndike here refers to the prayer in the canon of the Mass, "Command these to be borne by the hands of Thy Holy Angel to Thy altar on high," etc.

those which received them may be filled with the grace of His Spirit. For the expression of this effect and intent limits the common signification of the words to that which is proper to this action of the Eucharist ; as I have delivered it." [1] " As it is by no means to be denied that the elements are really changed, translated, turned, and converted into the body and blood of Christ (so that whoso receiveth them with a living faith is spiritually nourished by the same, he that with a dead faith is guilty of crucifying Christ), yet is not this change destructive to the bodily substance of the elements, but cumulative of them with the spiritual grace of Christ's body and blood ; so that the body and blood of Christ in the Sacrament turns to the nourishment of the body, whether the body and blood in the truth turn to the nourishment or the damnation of the soul." [2]

In the same treatise Thorndike discusses the nature of the Eucharistic sacrifice. He connects the sacrificial aspect of the Eucharist with the doctrine of the presence of the body and blood of Christ in the consecrated Sacrament which he has already maintained.

" Having showed the presence of the body and blood of Christ in the Eucharist because it is appointed that in it the faithful may feast upon the sacrifice of the cross ; we have already showed by the Scriptures that it is the sacrifice of Christ upon the cross in the same sense and to the same effect as it containeth the body and blood of Christ which it representeth ; [3] that is, mystically and spiritually and sacramentally (that is, as in and by a Sacrament) tendereth and exhibiteth. For seeing the Eucharist not only tendereth the flesh and blood of Christ, but separated one from the other, under and by several elements, as His blood was parted from His body by the violence of the cross ; it must of necessity be as well the sacrifice as the Sacrament of Christ upon the cross." [4]

In discussing " for what reasons the Sacrament of the Eucharist may be accounted and called a sacrifice," and " in what sense and for what reason it may be accounted propitiatory and impetratory without prejudice to Christianity," he explains that there are four distinct parts or stages in the sacrifice of the Eucharist. These four stages are : (1) the oblation of the unconsecrated ele-

---

[1] *Op. cit.* iv. 76, 77.   [2] *Ibid.* 81, 82.

[3] For Thorndike's use of the words " represent " and " representation," see p. 344, *supra.*

[4] *Op. cit.* iv. 98, 99.

ments in the offertory ; (2) the offering of prayer in connection with the intercession of Christ in heaven ; (3) the consecration ; and (4) the dedication to the service of God of the bodies and souls of those who receive the Sacrament.[1] Of these stages he writes :—

"Those species, set apart for the celebration of the Eucharist, are as properly to be called sacrifices of that nature which the Eucharist is of (to wit, commemorative and representative) as the same [2] are to be counted figurative under the Law from the time that they were deputed to that use. This is then the first act of oblation by the Church, that is, by any Christian that consecrates his goods, not at large to the service of God, but peculiarly to the service of God by sacrifice ; in regard whereof the elements of the Eucharist before they be consecrated, are truly counted oblations or sacrifices." [3]

"After the consecration is past, having showed you that St. Paul hath appointed that at the celebration of the Eucharist ' prayers, supplications, and intercessions, be made for all ' estates of the world and of the Church ; [4] and that the Jews have no right to the Eucharist (according to the Epistle to the Hebrews [5]) because, though eucharistical, yet it is of that kind the blood whereof is offered to God within the veil, with prayers for all estates of the world, as Philo [6] and Josephus [7] inform us : seeing the same Apostle hath so plainly expounded us the accomplishment of that figure in the offering of the sacrifice of Christ upon the cross to the Father in the highest heavens to obtain the benefits of His passion for us ; and that the Eucharist is nothing else but the representation [8] here upon earth of that which is done there : these things, I say, considered, necessarily it follows that whoso believes the prayers of the Church made in our Lord's name do render God propitious to them for whom they are made, and obtain for them the benefits of Christ's death (which he that believes not is no Christian), cannot question that those which are made by St. Paul's appointment at the celebration of the Eucharist, offering up unto God the merits and sufferings of Christ there represented must be peculiarly and especially effectual to the same purposes. And that the Eucharist

---

[1] *Op. cit.* iv. 106-118.
[2] The meal offering and drink offering of the Jewish Law.
[3] *Op. cit.* iv. 107.   [4] 1 St. Tim. ii. 1.
[5] Heb. xiii. 10.   [6] Philo, *De animal. sacr. idon.*
[7] Josephus, *C. Ap.* ii. 23.   [8] See pp. 344, 347, *supra.*

may very properly be accounted a sacrifice propitiatory and impetratory both in this regard—because the offering of it up to God with and by the said prayers doth render God propitious, and obtain at His hands the benefits of Christ's death which it representeth—there can be no cause to refuse, being no more than the simplicity of plain Christianity enforceth." [1]

" Having maintained that the elements are really changed from ordinary bread and wine into the body and blood of Christ mystically present as in a Sacrament; and that in virtue of the consecration, not by the faith of him that receives: I am to admit and maintain whatsoever appears duly consequent to this truth:— namely, that the elements so consecrate are truly the sacrifice of Christ upon the cross, inasmuch as the body and blood of Christ crucified are contained in them, not as in a bare sign, which a man may take up at his pleasure, but as in the means by which God hath promised His Spirit; but not properly the sacrifice upon the cross, because that is a thing that consists in action and motion and succession, and therefore once done can never be done again, because it is contradiction that that which is done should ever be undone. It is therefore enough that the Eucharist is the sacrifice of Christ upon the cross, as the sacrifice of Christ upon the cross is represented, renewed, revived, and restored by it, and as every representation is said to be the same thing with that which it representeth; taking ' representation ' here, not for barely signifying, but for tendering and exhibiting thereby that which it signifieth.[2] . . . Let it therefore have the nature of a sacrifice so soon as the consecration is past. It shall have that nature improperly, so long as it is not the sacrifice of Christ upon the cross ; though truly, so long as the Sacrament is not empty of that which it signifieth. . . . I will not therefore grant that this sacrificing (that is, this consecrating the elements into the sacrifice) is an action done in the person of Christ : though they are agreed that it is done by the rehearsing of the words of Christ. For the rehearsing of Christ's words is not an act done in the person of Christ ; nor do I take upon me His person whose words I recite. And I have showed that the consecration is done by the prayers of the Church immediately; though these prayers are made in virtue of Christ's order, commanding to do what He did, and thereby promising that the elements shall become that which He saith those which He consecrated are. . . . Having proved the consecration of the Eucharist to be the production of the body and blood of Christ crucified, or the causing of them to be mystically present in the elements thereof, as in a Sacrament representing them separated by the crucifying of Christ; and the sacrifice of Christ upon the cross being necessarily propitiatory and impetratory both; it cannot be denied that the Sacrament of the Eucharist, inasmuch as it is the same sacrifice of Christ upon the cross (as that which representeth is truly said to be the thing which it representeth), is also both propitiatory and impetratory by virtue of the consecration of it, whereby it becometh the sacrifice of Christ upon the cross." [1]

"Hereupon ariseth a fourth reason why this Sacrament is a sacrifice; to wit, of the bodies and souls of them who, having consecrated their goods to God for the celebration of it, do by receiving it profess to renew that consecration of themselves to the service of God according to the law of Christ, which their Baptism originally pretended." [2]

"Breaking, pouring forth, distributing, eating, drinking, are all parts of the sacrifice; as the whole action is that sacrifice, by which the covenant of grace is renewed, restored, and established against the interruption of our failures." [3]

After affirming that "the Sacrament of the Eucharist" is "a propitiatory and impetratory sacrifice by virtue of the consecration," Thorndike proceeds:—

"If from hence any man would infer that, seeing the Sacrament of the Eucharist (that is to say, the body and blood of Christ crucified there present by virtue of the consecration) is a propitiatory and impetratory sacrifice for the congregation there present, for their relations, and for the Church, therefore it is so whether they proceed to receive the Eucharist or not; therefore it is so, whether they proceed to offer up the Eucharist present by their prayers for the necessities of the Church or not; therefore it is so whether they pray with the Church or not; the consequence will straight appear to fail; because those reasons which make it such a sacrifice make it so in order to the receiving, or to the offering of it by the prayers of the Church in behalf of the Church." [4]

He maintains, further, that all the parts of the sacrifice are found in the Eucharist as celebrated in the Church of England in accordance with the Book of Common Prayer.[5]

In several passages in the early chapters of the third part of

[1] *Op. cit.* iv. 112, 113, 114, 115, 116, 117.   [2] *Ibid.* 118.
[3] *Ibid.* 119.   [4] *Ibid.* 120, 121.   [5] *Ibid.* 134, 135.

the *Epitome*, two of which have been quoted above, Thorndike closely connects the reception of the Holy Communion with participation in the Eucharistic sacrifice. In the latter of the two passages already quoted he does not seem to make the reception of Communion a necessity for share in the sacrifice if there is the offering of the Eucharist by prayer. In a later chapter he writes strongly on the need of all who are prepared receiving Communion at each celebration, but recognises that circumstances may justify some who are present at the Eucharist not communicating on all ·occasions.

" If the virtue and efficacy of these prayers be grounded upon nothing else than the fidelity of the congregation in standing to the covenant of Baptism (as, if Christianity be true, it consists in nothing else) ; and if the celebration of the Eucharist be the profession of fidelity and perseverance in it : what remaineth but that the efficacy of the sacrifice depend upon the receiving of the Eucharist ? unless the efficacy and virtue of Christian men's prayers can depend upon their perseverance in that covenant which they refuse to renew and to profess perseverance in it, that profession being no less necessary than the inward intention of persevering in the same. For the receiving of the Eucharist is no less expressly a renewing of the covenant of Baptism than being baptised is entering into it ; so that whosoever refuses the Communion of the Eucharist, inasmuch as he refuses it, refuses to stand to the covenant of his Baptism, whereby he expects the world to come. I say not, therefore, that whosoever communicates not in the Eucharist, so oft as he hath means and opportunity to do it, renounces his Christianity, either expressly or by way of construction and consequence. For how many of us may be prevented with the guilt of sin, so deeply staining the conscience that they cannot satisfy themselves in the competence of that conversion to God which they have time and reason and opportunity to exercise before the opportunity of communicating ? How many have need of the authority of the Church, and the power of the keys, not only for their satisfaction but for their direction, in washing their wedding garments white again ? How many are so distracted and oppressed with business of this world that they cannot upon all opportunities retire their thoughts to that attention and devotion which the office requires ? How many, though free of business which Christianity enjoineth, are entangled with the cares and pleasures of the world, though not so far as to depart from the state of grace, yet further than the renewing of the covenant of

grace importeth? Be it therefore granted that there is a great
allowance to be made in exacting the apostolical rule for all that are
present to communicate." [1]

The many references to the Eucharist elsewhere in Thorndike's voluminous writings add little to what is contained on this
subject in the third part of the *Epitome*, from which the above
quotations are all taken. But there are a few passages which
deserve notice for their bearing on special points.

In the twenty-fifth chapter of the treatise *The Reformation
of the Church of England better than that of the Council of
Trent*, written during the last two years of his life, Thorndike
endeavoured to find some common ground of agreement for
those who disagree in much as to the doctrine of the Eucharist.
This common ground he sought for, not, like Hooker,[2] in the reception of the body and blood of Christ by faithful communicants, but in the presence of the body and blood of Christ in the
Sacrament by virtue of the consecration in accordance with the
institution of our Lord.

"If this were agreed upon, which cannot be resisted but by
Socinians and Fanatics;—that the body and blood of Christ become
present in the Sacrament by the institution of our Lord, by celebrating the Sacrament, whereby His institution is executed by consecrating the elements to the purpose that the body and blood of
Christ may be received;—the whole dispute concerning the manner
of presence in the nature of the formal cause might be superseded.
For then all parties must agree that they are present sacramentally, as the nature of a Sacrament requireth. And that, as it would
be enough to make them 'guilty of the body and blood' of Christ
that 'eat and drink unworthily,' so it would still require living
faith to make that presence effectual to all that receive it; which
all parties are obliged to require to the effect as much as they are
obliged to require consecration to the sacramental presence of the
body and blood of Christ in the Sacrament."[3]

In the thirty-ninth chapter of the same treatise Thorndike
refers incidentally to the reservation of the Sacrament for the
Communion of the Sick.

"Thus far I will particularise as concerning the Eucharist, that
the Church is to endeavour the celebrating of it so frequently that

---

[1] *Op. cit.* iv. 569, 570.   [2] See pp. 239-49, *supra.*   [3] *Op. cit.* v. 544.

it may be reserved to the next Communion. For in the mean time it ought to be so ready for them that pass into the next world that they need not stay for the consecrating of it on purpose for every one. The reason of the necessity of it for all, which hath been delivered, aggravates it very much in danger of death. And the practice of the Church attests it to the utmost. Neither will there be any necessity of giving it in one kind only, as by some passages of antiquity may be collected, if common sense could deceive in a subject of this nature." [1]

In the forty-second chapter of the same treatise he condemns the practice of carrying the Sacrament through the streets for the purpose of adoration, and also the command of the Church of Rome for adoration at the consecration for the reason that this command was based on the enforcement of the acceptance of Transubstantiation in "commanding to believe that which was not delivered from the beginning"; but asserts that it is right and in accordance with patristic teaching for "reverence" to be "tendered to our Lord as present in the Sacrament," and allows adoration of our Lord in the Sacrament "when it passes the streets in order to Communion," since "it may be then so well understood that it may be then but due reverence to that great office".[2]

XII.

Matthew Wren was born in 1585; after being Master of Peterhouse, Cambridge, and Dean of Windsor, he was consecrated Bishop of Hereford in 1635, was appointed Bishop of Norwich in 1635 and Bishop of Ely in 1638; under the Commonwealth he was imprisoned; in 1660 he was released, and remained Bishop of Ely until his death in 1667. In a paper apparently prepared with a view to the revision of the Prayer Book, he refers scornfully to the "fancy of Transubstantiation" of "the Church of Rome"; and explains the "remembrance" in the Eucharist as being to put Christ in mind of Christians. He suggests the words "according to Thy Son our Saviour Jesus Christ's holy institution for a remembrance of Him by showing His death and passion" and "Do this for a remembrance of Me" in the Prayer of Consecration; and says of the first of these suggestions:—

[1] *Op. cit.* v. 578. [2] *Ibid.* 585, 586.

"This would be thus, first, because St. Paul's word is καταγγέλλετε, 1 Cor. xi. 26; and, secondly, because εἰς τὴν ἐμὴν ἀνάμνησιν being spoken by Christ does most properly signify, To put Me in mind of you; Christ of us, and not us in mind of Christ. For in that we do this, it appears we are mindful of Him. It is not done therefore only to put ourselves in mind of Him."[1]

In a similar paper Robert Sanderson expressed a different view, namely, that the Eucharistic remembrance is to Christians. Sanderson was born in 1587, was appointed Regius Professor of Divinity in the University of Oxford in 1642, was deposed from that office in 1648, was restored to it in 1660, and in the same year was consecrated Bishop of Lincoln. He died in 1663. He was one of the chief of the revisers of the Prayer Book in 1661. His words on this point are:—

"This Sacrament was ordained by our Saviour Jesus Christ Himself for this end especially, that the remembrance of His death, wherein He offered up Himself a sacrifice for our sins, and the innumerable benefits that we receive thereby, might be better remembered in the Christian Church to all succeeding generations."[2]

XIII.

Obscure as are some details, it is not difficult to state briefly the main lines of thought in regard to Eucharistic doctrine in England in the times of King James I., King Charles I., the Commonwealth, and King Charles II. The additions made to the Catechism in 1604 and the Prayer Book of 1662, like the Elizabethan Prayer Book, require a belief in the reception of the body and blood of Christ by faithful communicants, and incline towards the doctrine that the body and blood are present in the

---

[1] These notes are in a MS. in the Bodleian Library (MS. Bodl. Add. A. 213) which was given to Bishop Jacobson of Chester by Bishop Hamilton of Salisbury, whose father received it from Richard Terrick, who was Bishop of London from 1764 to 1777. There is a statement on the MS. that the notes are thought to be by Bishop Wren; and Bishop Jacobson was of opinion that a comparison with documents in Bishop Wren's handwriting established this without doubt. Bishop Jacobson published the notes in his volume *Fragmentary Illustrations of the Book of Common Prayer from Manuscript Sources*. The passages quoted above are on pp. 81, 82.

[2] This also is printed in Bishop Jacobson's *Fragmentary Illustrations of the Book of Common Prayer from Manuscript Sources*: see pp. 23, 24.

Sacrament at consecration and before reception without explicitly insisting on the acceptance of this doctrine. The existence during the reigns of James I. and Charles I. of a theology which included the rejection of Transubstantiation, the assertion of the presence of the body and blood of Christ in the Sacrament before reception, and the affirmation of sacrifice in the Eucharist may be known from the writings of Bishop Andrewes, Archbishop Laud, Bishop Mountague, George Herbert, and Bishop Forbes. With their teaching may be compared that of the divines of the restoration, Archbishop Bramhall and Herbert Thorndike. Instances of those who accepted some form of receptionism or virtualism have been seen in the times of King James I. and King Charles I. in Crakanthorp, Bishop Morton, Sutton, Jackson, and Hammond ; and among the divines of the restoration in Bishop Cosin and Bishop Jeremy Taylor. Cudworth suggested that the Eucharist is a feast on a sacrifice and a federal rite. The teaching of Hales was explicitly Zwinglian ; but it is significant of the extent to which the extreme form of Zwinglianism had become discredited that a receptionist doctrine is taught in the Westminster *Confession* and *Catechisms*, and in the *Directory for the Public Worship of God*, and in the Irish *Articles* of 1615.

CHAPTER XIV.

POST-REFORMATION THEOLOGY.

Part I.

The lines followed by the theologians of the Church of Rome in the period subsequent to the Reformation were those laid down by the Council of Trent. Thus, while in the case of English theology it is requisite for a due understanding of the facts to take the divines of the Caroline period in close connection with those of Edwardine and Jacobean and Elizabethan times, the Council of Trent affords the best point of division between the theology of the Reformation period and that to be regarded as post-Reformation in the Church of Rome. From the time of the Council until the present time Roman Catholic writers have dealt with the subject of the Eucharist with great fulness and learning and power; and in an historical survey such as is attempted in this book all that is possible is to select out of a literature of enormous extent and much complexity a few characteristic and representative instances of doctrinal teaching and methods of treatment.

I.

Melchior Cano, a theologian of great erudition and insight, was born at Tarancon in Spain in 1520, studied at Salamanca, was a teacher of theology at Alcala and Salamanca, was one of the divines who were present at the Council of Trent, and was appointed Bishop of the Canaries in 1552. He was a member of the Dominican order, and became provincial for Castille shortly after his appointment as Bishop. Consequently he never took possession of the see. He died at Toledo in 1560. His most important work, *De locis theologicis*, was completed at the time of his death, and was published in 1562. One of the chapters is devoted to the subject of the Eucharistic sacrifice. Most of it consists of a refutation in detail of arguments by which the denial of the sacrifice in the Eucharist had been supported. Incidentally, there is positive teaching that the elements are made to be the body and blood of Christ by means of the consecration, that "the real body of Christ is broken by the hands of the priests," and that the Eucharist is "really and properly" a "propitiatory sacrifice," which is a presentation of the passion and the sacrifice which Christ "always" and "really offers" "to the Father" "in heaven".[1] Following St. Thomas Aquinas,[2] he considers an essential part of sacrifice to be "the doing of something to the thing which is offered to God whereby the sacred thing itself is in a kind of way acted on";[3] and the nature of this action, as he understood it, is explained in a passage in which he describes the parts of the Eucharistic sacrifice as being four in number, namely, the consecration, the oblation of the consecrated elements, the fraction of the consecrated host, and the consumption of the Sacrament, and represents the fraction of the consecrated host as the needed "doing of something to the thing which is offered to God".

"It is clear that there are four parts of the Eucharistic sacrifice, first, the consecration of the body and blood, secondly, the oblation, thirdly, the fraction,[4] lastly, the consumption. For I will prove that any one who shall deny that our sacrifice is wholly completed (*redintegrari, confici, absolvi*) in these four parts has no learning or knowledge (*nihil didicisse, nihil quaesisse, nihil scire*) of the theory of a perfect sacrifice. . . . When the Holy Church breaks the host, it commemorates the sacrifice of Christ by signifying the breaking of the Lord's body on the cross. . . . The consumption of the species pertains to the complete signification of this sacrifice. . . . I do not forget that St. Thomas sometimes, as indeed appears to be the case, taught that the sacrifice is offered before the fraction of the host, and that the reception properly belongs to the Sacrament, and the oblation to the sacrifice;[5] and again asserted that the fraction of the host is not so necessary that, if it were omitted, the sacrifice would remain

---

[1] XII. xi. 25, 30, 42, 49, 71, 81.
[2] St. Thomas Aquinas, *S.T.* II.[2] lxxxv. 3, ad 3, quoted on vol. i., p. 324, *supra.*
[3] XII. xi. 16.   [4] That is, the fraction of the consecrated host.
[5] St. Thomas Aquinas, *S.T.* III. lxxxiii. 4.

incomplete, because the signification of this relates not to the real
body of Christ but to His mystical body ;[1] whence it follows that
the fraction is not to be reckoned among the parts of the sacrifice.
Now that the sacrifice is offered before the fraction it may be considered a great argument that immediately after the consecration
the priest says these words, 'We offer to Thy excellent majesty of
Thy bounties and gifts a pure offering,' etc. Therefore, while the host
is not yet broken there is both oblation and sacrifice. But whoever
cites St. Thomas against us makes St. Thomas to contradict both
himself and the true theory of sacrifice. For his words in the second
division of the second part are not obscure that the name sacrifice is
properly used when something is done in regard to the things that
are offered.[2] Which he supports by the illustration of the breaking
and eating of bread. Whence he infers that first fruits are offerings
but not a sacrifice, because no sacred act was performed in regard to
them. Therefore not only St. Thomas but also the Church speaks
of the sacrifice before the fraction in the way in which we speak of
a thing which is at hand and close by as if it were present. . . . The
bread itself we commonly call a host before consecration ; and St.
Thomas does not shrink from this way of speech. And the priest
before the consecration says that he offers 'holy and spotless sacrifices,' etc. But what theologian has ever been so utterly foolish as
to think that the sacrifice was offered before the host was consecrated ? And, that I may not say anything about the hidden and
inner sacrifice of the body and blood, the outward and mystic sacrifice certainly does not consist simply in the oblation. Therefore,
since in regard to the species nothing has been done of the sacrifice
before the fraction, the sacrifice has not been offered. Also, since
with the symbols of the realities, by the institution of Christ, we
ought to represent (*agere*) His death, if our sacrifice is real and complete and a perfect copy of that victim which Christ set forth on
the cross, and since there is no symbol of the realities until the
species are broken and mingled and consumed, we can receive a
most certain argument that the sacrifice is not yet complete before
the fraction. It remains therefore that not only the consecration
and the oblation but also the fraction and the consumption pertain
to the completeness of the outward sacrifice."[3]

Melchior Cano is at some pains to repudiate any idea of the
Mass as a merely mechanical means of the forgiveness of sins ;[4]

[1] St. Thomas Aquinas, *S.T.* III. lxxxiii. 6, ad 6.
[2] *Ibid.* II.[2] lxxxv. 3, ad 3, quoted on vol. i. p. 324, *supra.*
[3] XII. xi. 57, 58.   [4] XII. xi. 69-74.

and he stigmatises as "madness" the notion ascribed to Ambrose Catharinus [1] that the sacrifice of the altar as being for the remission of sins committed after Baptism is to be distinguished from the sacrifice of the cross as for sins committed before Baptism.

"Hence is manifest the madness of the idea of Ambrose Catharinus that sins committed before Baptism are remitted by means of the sacrifice of the cross, but all sins committed after Baptism by means of the sacrifice of the altar. For the sacrifice of the cross is the universal cause of the forgiveness of sins, whether committed before or after Baptism." [2]

Alphonso Salmeron was born at Toledo in 1515. He studied at Alcala and Paris. He was a member of the Society of Jesus. He was one of the divines who were present at the Council of Trent. Later he became provincial of the Jesuits in the kingdom of Naples. He died at Naples in 1585. He wrote voluminous expositions of Holy Scripture. In these incidental allusions to the Holy Eucharist often occur, and it is discussed at length in connection with the institution of the Sacrament. As regards the presence in the Eucharist there is nothing distinctive in his teaching that, while the accidents of the bread and the wine remain, the only substance after consecration is the substance of the body and blood of Christ. As regards the sacrifice, he considers the essential point to be the mystical offering to the Father of the body and blood of Christ present under the species of bread and wine, the crucial moment of the offering to be the consecration, and the distinctively sacrificial state of our Lord in the Sacrament to be the fact of His sacramental existence in a mystically divided method under the different species, whereby His death is represented in mystery, and the passion commemorated.

"In the Sacrament the most holy bread differs not at all from ordinary bread, not even to the taste ; and yet the body of Christ, which is glorious in heaven, is there, and in the hearts of the faithful." [3]

"It is customary in Scripture that, when things are changed, their former names are preserved. . . . In this way must be under-

---

[1] See pp. 70-75, *supra*.   [2] XII. xi. 75.
[3] *Comment.* III. xxxiv. (*Opera*, Cologne, 1602-4, iii. 297).

stood the Apostle's description of the Eucharist by the word bread, although it is bread no longer." [1]

"All the Sacraments of the new covenant are symbols of the grace which they confer; but in particular the Eucharist proclaims His death, that is, the separation of His soul from His body; and it represents the unity of the Church, for the Church is made up out of many men, as the bread and the vine are made up out of many grains; and it denotes the complete refreshment of our spirit." [2]

"In this wonderful mystery two things are contained. The first is the real and living body of Christ, which at the Last Supper was subject to suffering and death and yet was given in an impassible and immortal way, which after the resurrection is freed from death and all suffering and is given in a way equally incorruptible and immortal. The second is the representation and proclamation of the death of Christ." [3]

"In it the body of Christ is known to be present, and as the body of Christ is worshipped with the mind and adored with the body." [4]

"That the substance of the bread does not remain has been defined in the Church as an article of faith, and the word conversion or Transubstantiation has been approved, although the method of the conversion,—whether by the substance of the bread and wine ceasing to be and the body and blood of Christ entering in under the species that are left, or by the change of the substance of bread and wine into the substance of the body and blood of Christ,—has not yet been defined. For, however it happens, it can be called conversion or Transubstantiation." [5]

"Sacrifice . . . signifies a certain mystical action consecrating some external thing by applying it to the worship of God and by offering it to Him. . . . The form of sacrifice is the mystical action consecrating the thing by applying it to worship and by the offering whereby it is offered to God. . . . The primary efficient cause of sacrifice is God. . . . In a secondary way as the instrument the efficient cause is the priest. . . . Since in the sacrifice of the Mass four things are found, namely, the consecration, the oblation, the fraction, and the consumption, a doubt arises in which action of these four the sacrifice consists. In this matter there is no controversy with the heretics; for, since they deny the sacrifice, they

---

[1] Comment. I. xi. 33 (Opera, i. 205, 206).   [2] Ibid. xix. 6 (Opera, i. 345).
[3] Ibid. VIII. xxi. (Opera, viii. 158).   [4] Ibid. IX. xxiv. (Opera, ix. 179).
[5] Ibid. xvi. (Opera, ix. 108).

consequently deny that it can consist in any one of these, or in some, or in all. Therefore the dispute is between the theologians; and among them there are more opinions than one. The first opinion is that the sacrifice consists in all these four actions, so that, if any one of them were lacking, the sacrifice would not be complete. . . . The second opinion is that . . . in accordance with which there are three actions which are necessary to the sacrifice, and that among these the Communion is the chief. . . . The third opinion places the sacrifice in two things, namely, the consecration and the oblation. . . . The fourth opinion is that the sacrifice consists essentially only in the consecration, and that the other actions are rather means of explaining that the sacrifice is offered than means of it being a sacrifice. . . . Because this fourth opinion seems to be the most likely, and is held by the greater number of fathers, for the further explanation of it must be said: first, it is one thing to sacrifice, and another thing to offer that which is sacrificed, for the former happens once and the latter can happen very often, as we see in the case of Christ, who offers continually the body which was once sacrificed; secondly, there are three things in the consecration itself, namely, the desition (*corruptio*) of the bread and wine, the change of the substance of the bread and wine into the body of Christ, and the sacramental division of the body and blood of Christ. . . . Herein is the matter as an object of sense offered to God alone, namely Christ under the species of bread and wine, and by means of them an object of sense, although He abides herein in a way which the senses cannot discern; and the substance is acknowledged not in itself without accidents. But there is this special point that the matter is changed, and that the living victim is sacrificed not in actual fact but is said by the fathers to be sacrificed in mystery, that is, under the species of bread and wine." [1]

Gabriel Vasquez was born at Belmonte in Spain in 1551. He joined the Society of Jesus, and was eminent as a teacher of theology at Rome and at Alcala. He died at Alcala in 1604. His Eucharistic doctrine is explained at great length in his *Discussions* on the third part of the *Summa Theologica* of St. Thomas Aquinas.

In the philosophy underlying his theology concerning the Eucharistic presence Vasquez follows closely the main principles of the Thomist divines. For instance, as against the Scotists,

[1] *Comment.* IX. xxix. (*Opera*, ix. 217, 219, 220, 222, 223, 225).

he maintains that the natural presence, or presence by way of
extension, of a body cannot be at the same time in more places
than one.[1] Using this philosophy, he asserts the usual conclusions of the scholastic and Tridentine theologians as to the conversion of the substance of the bread and wine into the substance
of the body and blood of Christ, the continued existence of the
accidents, their capacity of corruption and their power of nourishing the body, the non-local character of the presence of the
body of Christ in the Sacrament so that, when the Sacrament
is moved, the body of Christ does not move, and on similar
questions.[2] Vasquez's teaching in regard to the Eucharistic
sacrifice is of a more distinctive character than his discussions
about the presence. While he allows that change is an element
in sacrifice, and recognises such a change as having taken place
in the sacrifice of the cross through our Lord's death, he does
not assert any kind of destruction in the sacrifice of the Mass.
In the "absolute sacrifice" on the cross destruction was a necessary element; in the "commemorative sacrifice" of the Mass
it is sufficient that the victim of the "absolute sacrifice" be
presented, and that there be some mark or sign of the destruction which then took place. This mark or sign is to be found
in the commemoration of the death of Christ which is supplied
by the mystic significance of the separate consecration of the
bread and the wine.

   "From what has been said we can shortly and easily collect
a right definition of sacrifice both by way of form and by way of
matter. First, by way of form, that is, by way of signification,
A sacrifice is a mark existing in a thing whereby we acknowledge
that God is the Author of life and death. . . . By way of matter
this is the definition, A sacrifice is a thing which is offered to God
by means of a change in itself, or a change in a thing which is
offered to God. . . . There are two kinds of sacrifice. One of them
is an absolute sacrifice, namely, that which is not the commemoration of another sacrifice, as the slaying of a sheep, or the consumption of something. The other is a relative or commemorative
sacrifice, the only example of which we have in the sacrifice of the
altar, which can be called a commemorative sacrifice; and, although
in this no change takes place in the thing which is offered in this
way, yet there is found a real sign and mark of the almighty power

----

[1] CLXXXIX. 5-8.   [2] CLXXX.-CXCV.

of God, as in an absolute sacrifice; and therefore this has the real nature of sacrifice no less than a bloody and absolute sacrifice." [1]

"The Catholic doctrine is that Christ is really and properly offered as a sacrifice in the Mass." [2]

"The right opinion is that the whole essence of this sacrifice consists of the consecration of the Sacrament alone in such a way that no other action belongs to its completeness, but that everything else which takes place in the Mass is either part of the preparation for the consecration or something which follows from and succeeds it. But, because the whole essence of this sacrifice is to be placed in the presentation of the death of Christ, which was a bloody sacrifice, and this is represented in the consecration not of one species only but of both taken together, therefore we say that the real and complete essence of the sacrifice exists in the consecration not of one species only but of both." [3]

"Although an absolute sacrifice, that is, one which is not commemorative of another, requires a change in the thing offered, yet the change is not formally of the nature of the sacrifice but a requisite by way of its matter. The formal nature of sacrifice was placed in the signifying of the almighty power of God as the Author of life and death. Therefore, if there be any offering by means of which without a real and actual change in the thing offered God can be denoted and worshipped as the Author of life and death, it ought to be called really and properly a sacrifice. Now the consecration of the body and blood of Christ is of this kind without any actual change in Christ Himself simply on account of the representation of His death; therefore it is really and properly a sacrifice." [4]

"The desition and conversion of the bread and wine have nothing to do with the nature of the sacrifice, but the sacrifice consists simply in the presence of the body and blood of Christ under the two species by the force of the words, and it would take place in the same way if the body and blood of Christ existed under the two species without any conversion of the bread and wine." [5]

"If the bloodless sacrifice which we priests offer in the Mass is compared with the sacrifice whereby Christ was offered on the cross, it is certain that it coincides with it, and is wholly the same, so far as concerns the victim and the thing offered, but differs in method and way of offering. . . . Though the same Christ offers in each sacrifice, yet He does not offer in the same way; for in the bloody sacrifice of the cross He offered directly, since by His own action He under-

[1] CCXX. 3.   [2] CCXXI. 3.   [3] CCXXII. 5.
[4] CCXXII. 8.   [5] CCXXIII. 4.

went suffering and death, in which the offering of that sacrifice consisted ; but in the sacrifice of the Mass He does not offer directly
and by His own action but by the ministry of the priests, whom He
has commanded to consecrate the Sacrament in His name and to
offer this bloodless sacrifice ; for Christ is now said to offer in this
sacrifice only in this way, that He commanded and instituted that
priests should offer in His name, and not because He Himself exercises the action of sacrificing." [1]

"Although Christ is said to offer this sacrifice remotely and only
because He instituted it, yet He is rightly called not only the offerer
but the principal offerer, whereby He immediately offers, since there
is no other who comes between offering principally. For not only
did He command it to be offered, but also by His institution He
gave it power by reason of His merits and death, so that from the
work wrought (*ex opere operato*), as Sacraments, it might accomplish
something in those for whom it should be offered, and also that it
might obtain something for them after the manner of an impetrative
cause. . . . Christ did not only command and institute that this
sacrifice should be offered, but also as High Priest out of the merits
of His works and sacrifice which He offered on the cross, gave it
power ; and so, though He offers remotely, none the less as priest,
and as chief or principal offerer, He is said to offer it." [2]

Like Melchior Cano,[3] Vasquez refers in terms of strong condemnation to the opinion ascribed to Catharinus,[3] that the efficacy
of the sacrifice of the cross is to be restricted to original sin, and
actual sins are expiated by the sacrifice of the Mass, calling it
"plainly absurd," and "directly contrary to the Catholic faith,"
and "opposed to the teaching of all schoolmen and fathers ".[4]

Robert Bellarmine was born in 1542 at Monte Pulciano near
Florence. He was the nephew of Cardinal Cervino, who in 1555
was Pope for twenty-one days, at the end of which he died,
with the title of Marcellus II. He entered the Society of Jesus
in 1560, in 1592 became Rector of the Jesuit College at Rome,
and in 1595 Provincial of the Order in the kingdom of Naples.
In 1599 he was made a cardinal by Pope Clement VIII. He
died in 1621. His works exhibit great learning and skill in controversy and power of exposition. His teaching on the subject
of the Eucharist is contained in the treatises *Concerning the*

---

[1] CCXXIV. 2.　　　[2] CCXXV. 3.　　　[3] See p. 359, *supra*.
[4] See pp. 70-75, *supra*.　　　[5] CCXXI. 4.

Eucharist and *Concerning the Sacrifice of the Mass.* As regards the Eucharistic presence his teaching follows the usual lines of the theologians who accepted the definitions of the Council of Trent. The body and blood of Christ are present after the consecration really and actually and substantially under the species of bread and wine.[1] This presence is of a sacramental, not of a local, character.[2] It exists because of the complete conversion of the substance of bread and wine into the body and blood of the Lord.[3] Though the bread is converted into the body, and the wine into the blood, yet the whole Christ, flesh and blood, body and soul, manhood and Godhead, is by concomitance under each species.[4] Christ, thus present in the Sacrament, is to be adored. On this last point he writes:—

"There is no Catholic who teaches that the outward elements are to be adored with the worship of latria in themselves and properly, but only that they are to be reverenced with a certain minor worship which is appropriate to all Sacraments; but we say that Christ is to be adored with the worship of latria in Himself and properly, and that this adoration pertains also to the elements of bread and wine insofar as they are considered as one thing with Christ Himself, whom they contain. In like manner, those who adored Christ on earth when clothed, did not adore Him apart, but after some kind of fashion they adored also His garments, for they did not bid Him be stripped of His garments before adoring Him, nor did they divide Him from His garments in mind and thought when they adored Him, but they simply adored Christ as He then was, yet the real object of adoration was not the garments, or even the manhood itself, but only the Godhead. Now, as to the way of speech, we confess that the Sacrament itself is said to be adored, as the Council of Trent says; but this is explained in two ways. For those who think that the Sacrament of the Eucharist is formally the body of Christ, as it is under those species, allow also that the Sacrament is said to be formally adored; but those who teach that the Sacrament of the Eucharist is formally the species of bread and wine, as they contain Christ, teach in consequence that the Sacrament of the Eucharist is to be materially adored. But, whatever is the case as to the method of speech, the only actual question is whether Christ in the Eucharist is to be adored with the worship of latria."[5]

[1] *De Sacr. Euch.* i. 2.　　[2] *Op. cit.* iii. 3.　　[3] *Ibid.* 18.　　[4] *Ibid.* iv. 21.
[5] *Op. cit.* iv. 29. Cf. *Apol. pro Resp.* (*Opera*, vii. 764, ed. 1617), where Bellarmine says, "Among novelties and new doctrines he places the adora-

In regard to the Eucharistic sacrifice the teaching of Bellarmine
has some characteristic features. His formal definition of sacrifice
does not include any explicit mention of destruction, but it contains the word " changed "; and in the explanation which follows
the definition destruction is spoken of as essential to sacrifice.

" Sacrifice is an outward offering made to God alone, wherein
for the recognition of human weakness and the profession of the
divine majesty some sensible and permanent thing is consecrated
and changed in a mystic rite by a lawful minister.

" We have said, 'and changed,' because it is required for a real
sacrifice that what is offered to God as a sacrifice be wholly destroyed,
that is, that it be so changed as to cease to be that which it was
before." [1]

In discussing the nature of the Eucharistic sacrifice, he lays down
that the oblation of the unconsecrated bread and wine, the oblation
of the consecrated Sacrament, and the fraction of the consecrated
host, though they are needed for the completeness of the sacrifice,
do not belong to its essence; that the consumption of the Sacrament by the priest who offers the sacrifice is " an essential part
but not the whole essence "; and that " the consecration of the
Eucharist belongs to the essence of the sacrifice ". As to the consecration, he further explains :—

" In the consecration of the Eucharist three things take place
in which the method of a real and actual sacrifice consists. First,
a profane thing becomes sacred; for the bread otherwise earthly
and common is turned by consecration into the body of Christ, that
is, the most sacred of all things. . . . Secondly, in the consecration
that thing which has been made sacred from being profane is offered
to God. . . . Thirdly, by means of the consecration the thing which
is offered is destined to a real, actual, and outward change and destruction, which has been declared necessary to the method of a
sacrifice. For by means of consecration the body of Christ receives
the form of food; and food is destined to be eaten, and in this way
to change and destruction." [2]

tion of the Sacrament of the Eucharist, that is, the adoration of the Lord
Christ present in the Sacrament in a wonderful but real manner ". In *De
Sacr. Euch.* iii. 24, Bellarmine defends in detail the terms of the Confession imposed on Berengar in 1059, quoted on vol. i. p. 247, *supra*, following the usual scholastic methods of interpreting the phrases, for which see,
e.g., vol. i. pp. 306, 310, 316, 324.

[1] *De Missa*, i. 2.   [2] *Op. cit.* i. 27.

On the reference to the "altar on high" in the canon of the Mass, he writes:—

"This is not to be understood so stupidly as to make us think that in heaven any bodily and sensible altar has been built, and that the Sacrament of the body of the Lord ought to be borne to it actually and bodily by the hands of angels; but that there is an altar, that is, a spiritual altar, in heaven, as also a tabernacle and a throne and incense and trumpets and crowns and palms and other things of this kind no one can deny without wishing to deny the Scriptures. . . . Of the same altar set in heaven Irenæus [1] and Augustine [2] have made mention. Therefore it is not a dream of Catholics, but the divine Scripture itself has set an altar in heaven. This heavenly altar signifies either Christ Himself, through whom our prayers and offerings go up to God; or certainly that there is said to be an altar in heaven, because the sacrifices which are offered to God on earth are received in heaven. And that our sacrifices are borne to God by the hands of the angel is nothing else than that our service and worship, which we desire to offer to God in sacrifice, are aided and commended to Him by the intercession of angels." [3]

Francis Suarez was born at Granada in 1548. At the age of seventeen he entered the Society of Jesus, and studied at Salamanca. He was afterwards a teacher at Segovia and Valladolid and Rome. From Rome he returned to Spain, and taught at Alcala and at Salamanca. In 1597 Philip II. appointed him principal professor of theology at the Portuguese University of Coimbra. In 1617 he died at Lisbon. His reputation as a teacher of the Aristotelian philosophy and of theology was of the highest; and he was the author of voluminous works of great ability. His *Commentaries and Disputations* on the third part of the *Summa Theologica* of St. Thomas Aquinas include lengthy and elaborate disquisitions on the Eucharist. As to the Eucharistic presence his teaching on important matters is that which is common to the Roman Catholic theologians of his time, although on some connected questions of philosophy he accepts the less usually held positions, and the influence of the Scotist theologians on his mind can be plainly seen. The body of Christ is really

---

[1] St. Irenæus, *C. Hær.* IV. xviii. 6, quoted on vol. i. p. 51, *supra*.

[2] St. Augustine, *Enar. in Ps. xxv.*, ii. 10, quoted on vol. i. pp. 120, 121, *supra*.

[3] *Op. cit.* ii, 24.

and actually and permanently present in the Sacrament by a presence of a sacramental kind differing from the nature and method of natural presence. While in the abstract it is possible for a natural body to be quantitively and by way of dimensions in more places than one at one time,[1] as a matter of fact the natural presence of the body of Christ is in heaven alone and is to be distinguished from the sacramental presence in the Eucharist. In the abstract, again, it would be possible for the body of Christ to be in the Sacrament together with the substance of the bread and wine;[2] but as a matter of fact the substance of bread and wine does not remain after consecration but is wholly converted into the substance of the body and blood of Christ. The substance of the body and blood of Christ is wholly present in both species by concomitance, and in each separate part of the species when divided. The body of Christ existing in the Eucharist cannot in itself be moved by any outward natural agency, though by way of accident Christ is moved by one who changes the place of the sacramental species. The body of Christ as it exists in the Eucharist cannot be seen by the eyes of the body; and in miraculous visions there is no physical sight of Christ or of His body or blood. In the consecrated Sacrament the accidents of bread and wine remain, and the consecrated species are capable of effecting or suffering anything which they could effect or suffer before consecration, as to nourish the body or to be corrupted. Christ is to be adored in the Eucharist with that supreme worship which would be His due if He were visibly present; and "not only Christ existing under the species but also the whole visible Sacrament, as it consists of Christ and of the species, is to be adored by one act of supreme worship". In order to be benefited it is necessary to receive the Sacrament worthily without knowledge of mortal sin and with a disposition to obtain grace.[3]

In regard to the Eucharistic sacrifice there is a distinctive feature of interest in the teaching of Suarez, which may possibly have been partly due to his Scotist leanings. His definition of sacrifice postulates some external action which involves a change,

[1] Suarez here follows the Scotist philosophy as distinct from the Thomist: see vol. i. p. 340, *supra*.

[2] Here again Suarez follows the Scotist philosophy: see vol. i. p. 340, *supra*.

[3] *Disp.* xlvi.-lxxii.

but this change does not necessarily consist in the destruction of the victim in the sacrifice; and in the case of the Eucharist it is to be found in the presence and·presentation of the body and blood of Christ on the altar as an offering made in honour of God.

"It is needful to gather from what has been said an explanation of a real and proper sacrifice, which can be given in two ways. The first is by way of physical definition, consisting of matter and form, so that a sacrifice is an offering made to God by means of the change of something to a sign, lawfully ordained, of the excellence of God and the reverence which pertains to Him. . . . A second way of defining can be if we say, A sacrifice is a sensible sign appointed expressly to denote the excellence of God and the worship due to Him by the change of some thing; or otherwise that it is an outward act ,of religion, containing the supreme worship of latria, and due to God alone. Where, that the definition may be adequate, one must understand by an outward act some outer action distinct from the utterance of words or praise and worship which is given in words." [1]

"For the explanation of sacrifice it is enough that there should be the Transubstantiation of the bread and wine into the body and ·blood of Christ, which takes place by means of the consecration; . . . and this is the unique and wonderful character of this sacrifice that in itself it is in the first instance rather for the sake of effecting than for the sake of destroying. For in every sacrifice, which takes place by means of an actual change, the destruction of something that is offered is found, from which there necessarily results something else, as it were rising up, and offered in honour of God. Yet there is a difference between the ancient sacrifices and this of ours, that they, because they were imperfect and took place by means of actions merely natural and human, consisted chiefly in the destruction of something, by which it was signified that God is the Author of all things, or something of the kind. . . . But in our sacrifice, because it is accomplished by means of supernatural and divine action, although the substance of bread and wine is destroyed,[2] yet that which is chiefly intended is the placing and pre-

[1] *Disp.* lxxiii. 6 (3).

[2] In here using this phrase, Suarez apparently meant it in the sense that the substance of the bread and wine is converted, not annihilated, since he held that the truer opinion is that maintained by most theologians, that the substance of the bread and wine is not annihilated : see *Disp.* l. 7 ; *cf.* vol. i. p. 329, *supra.*

senting (so to speak) of the body and blood of Christ on the altar of God in His honour. And therefore the thing which is offered in this sacrifice is principally and simply Christ, who is the end of such action." [1]

Thus, of the six chief actions in the Mass, the oblation of the unconsecrated bread and wine, the oblation of the consecrated Sacrament, the fraction and commixture after consecration, and the Communion of the people are not essential to the sacrifice; the Communion of the celebrant, though fitted for completing the sacrifice, is probably not of its essence; and the essential point in the sacrifice is the consecration.[2] In the sacrifice Christ is "the principal offerer, not only accidentally and remotely but also in some way He offers in act, though He offers by means of the priest".[3] The sacrifice has "some effect of the work wrought (*ex opere operato*), as being the proximate cause of the effect".[4] The power and efficacy of it are derived from the sacrifice of the cross.[5] The value of the sacrifice in itself, so far as it is offered by Christ, is infinite; but the effect from the work wrought (*ex opere operato*) and the value as offered in the person of the Church and as offered by an individual are finite.[6] It does not in any way derogate from the sacrifice of the cross:—

"First, because Christ on the cross satisfied sufficiently and abundantly for the sins not only of men who live under the law of grace but also of those who were under the old law and the law of nature; and they had propitiatory sacrifices without any injury to the cross of Christ, nay with simple faith in it; therefore we can do the same under the law of grace. Secondly, a like argument is derived from the institution of Sacraments, which were given under the law of grace for the remission of sins, and to confer grace, although Christ on the cross had sufficiently accomplished our salvation, and had merited most abundantly for us the remission of all sins. Thirdly, the reason of all is that Christ on the cross merited and satisfied infinitely so far as sufficiency is concerned, but not as concerns effective application, because that merit and satisfaction are not applied to us by means of the cross alone, and other means are necessary; and these are on our part dispositions and works performed with the aid of grace, and on the part of Christ Sacra-

---

[1] *Disp.* lxxv. 5 (6).   [2] *Ibid.* 2-5.   [3] *Ibid.* lxxvii. 1 (4).
[4] *Ibid.* lxxix. 1 (3).   [5] *Ibid.* 1 (10).   [6] *Ibid.* 11 (4-7).

ments, and also the propitiatory sacrifice, by which the fruit of His passion is applied to us ; therefore no injury is done to that passion, for that this application is necessary is not from the defect but rather from the power of the passion of Christ, because He was able not only to accomplish in Himself but also to give others power to accomplish ; and a method of provision of this kind was most suitable for the suitable rule of men." [1]

Leonard Leys, usually known by the Latin form of his name Lessius, was born at Brecht in Brabant in 1554. At the age of seventeen he became a member of the Society of Jesus. After his novitiate he was a teacher of philosophy at Douai, where he was ordained priest. Later he went to Rome, and there studied under Suarez. In 1585 he became a teacher of theology at Louvain ; and he died there in 1623. He is chiefly known in connection with controversies on the subjects of Holy Scripture and the doctrine of grace. His writings contain incidental allusions to the Eucharist, of which the fullest treatment is in his treatise *On the Perfections and Character of God*. As to the presence there does not appear to have been anything distinctive in his teaching. As to the sacrifice he regarded the essential point of the sacrifice as being in the separate consecration of the two species. His teaching about the presence may be seen in a passage in which he draws out with some detail the parallel between the Incarnation and the Eucharist.

" As in the mystery of the Incarnation the invisible Godhead was united to the visible manhood, so in the Eucharist the invisible flesh of Christ is united to the visible species. Secondly, as from that union one Christ is made, so from this union together with the species there is one Sacrament of the body and blood of Christ. Thirdly, as by means of the Incarnation the whole Word was united to the several parts of human nature, so by means of the consecration the whole body of Christ is united to the several parts of the species. Fourthly, as the Godhead remained unhurt and impassible when the manhood was hurt and suffered, so those vicissitudes (*passiones*) which take place in regard to the species cannot affect the body of Christ hidden under those species. Fifthly, as nevertheless on account of that union God was said to suffer, to be crucified, to die, when the manhood suffered, so on account of this union the body of Christ is said to be broken and to be taken when the

---

[1] *Disp.* lxxiv. 1 (12). *Cf.* the repudiation of Catharinus in lxxix. 1, and the whole treatment of the Eucharistic sacrifice in lxxiii.-lxxxviii.

species are broken and taken. For this union makes a kind of *communicatio idiomatum*. So also the body of Christ is said to be seen, to be touched, to be mixed, to be carried, by reason of the species ; and this visible thing is rightly called living, understanding, sanctifying, by reason of the body in it (*inclusi*). Sixthly, as the manhood of Christ had not its own natural way of existing but was sustained by the Word, so the species have not here their own natural way of existing but they are held together outside their own natural subject by the power of the body of Christ. Seventhly, as no created force can dissolve that union, so neither can any created force dissolve this union so long as the species continue to exist (*salvæ manent*)." [1]

His teaching as to the essential point in the sacrifice being the separate consecration may be seen in the following passages :—

" It does not seem doubtful that this sacrifice consists in the consecration. But in what way the consecration has the nature of sacrifice is not so easy to explain. It can be understood in two ways. First, that the consecration be thought to be the action of sacrificing insofar as by means of it the substance of the bread and wine is changed and converted into the body and blood as we have explained in the book entitled *Concerning Justice*.[2] Secondly, insofar as by means of it Christ is slain in a certain mystical way when after the manner of a slain victim His body and blood are shown separately on the altar by the force of the words ; and this way is easier to understand and corresponds better to the ordinary manner of sacrificing, which requires a victim and does not make it. According to this way, this sacrifice is accomplished not by an axe or a material sword, as of old the ancient sacrifices, but by the sword of the word of God, who is almighty. For as of old the sacrifice took place when the victim, being a lamb or a calf, was slain by the sword, and the blood was separated from the flesh, so now the sacrifice takes place when by the force of the words of consecration the body and blood of Christ are placed separately as the body of a thing slain and offered, the body under the species of bread, and the blood under the species of wine. Wherefore the words of consecration are like a sword ; the body of Christ, which now is living in heaven, is like a victim living and to be offered ; the body as placed under the species of bread, and the blood under the species of wine, are as the body and blood of a lamb which has now been offered. Wherefore they are as the end of the offering or action of sacrificing." [3]

[1] XII. xvi. 129.　　[2] See *De Iust*. II. xxxviii. 2.　　[3] XII. xiii. 95.

"The actual conversion of the substance of the bread and the wine insofar as it involves the desition of the bread and wine does not pertain to the essence of this sacrifice, because the sacrifice could take place even if the substance of the bread and wine remained, if God had so ordained." [1]

" It does not hinder the reality of this sacrifice that the separation of the blood from the flesh does not actually take place, because that is as it were accidental as a consequence of the concomitance of the parts. For so far as it is from the force of the words a real separation takes place, and the body alone, not the blood, is placed under the species of bread, and the blood alone, not the body, under the species of wine. And this is enough for the nature of the sacrifice, both that it be a real sacrifice (for there happens in regard to the victim, when the matter stands thus, a sufficient change, whereby we may declare that God has supreme power over all things), and that it be a commemorative sacrifice, representing to us the sacrifice of the cross and the death of the Lord." [2]

II.

The theologians who have so far been mentioned, while keeping carefully to the definition of the Council of Trent that the Mass is a "real and proper sacrifice," and assenting to the teaching of St. Thomas Aquinas that in a sacrifice " something is done to that which is offered," tend to make little of this latter point, and scrupulously avoid any doctrine which might seem to imply a repetition of the sacrifice of the cross or the death of Christ. This is alike true whether the sacrificial element is seen with Melchior Cano in the fraction of the consecrated host, with Salmeron and Vasquez and Lessius in the separate consecration of the two species, with Bellarmine in the consecration and Communion taken together, or with Suarez in the body of Christ being made present on the altar in honour of God. In all these explanations the element of destruction is either put out of sight altogether or is minimised.

The most famous representative of the opposite school of thought, that which makes much of the element of destruction, is Cardinal de Lugo. John de Lugo was born at Madrid in 1583. He entered the Society of Jesus in 1603. After teaching philosophy and theology in several colleges in Spain, he became professor of theology in the Jesuit College at Rome in 1621. Pope

[1] XII. xiii. 96. [2] XII. xiii. 97.

Urban VIII. made him a cardinal in 1643. In 1660 he died. During his life and ever since he has had a great reputation; and it would perhaps be impossible to find a better and more capable presentation of the later scholastic method in theology than is supplied by his writings. The discussions on the Eucharistic presence in his *Treatise on the Venerable Sacrament of the Eucharist*, with their minute and elaborate consideration of every detail which the theology of the subject suggests, may well be examined by any who wish to see the strength and the weakness of this method in its most complete development; but they do not present any conclusion which would do more than further illustrate beliefs of which many illustrations have already been given.[1] It is in his teaching concerning the Eucharistic sacrifice in the same treatise that De Lugo maintains a position which is of great interest and importance. He insists that destruction is an essential element in sacrifice, whether it is the destruction of the life of the person who offers the sacrifice or the destruction of something else as expression of his surrender, and that the destruction must affect that which is offered.[2] He rejects the views that the essential element in the Eucharistic sacrifice is the verbal oblation and that it is the fraction of the consecrated host, and accepts the opinion that the essential element is the consecration.[3] In discussing how the consecration makes the sacrifice, he rejects the opinions that the point of the sacrifice is the destruction of the bread and wine; that in this sacrifice a change of some kind is sufficient without any destruction; that, though destruction was necessary in the absolute sacrifice of the cross, it is not required in the Eucharist inasmuch as it is a commemorative sacrifice; that the needed feature is in the separate consecration of the body and blood of Christ; and that the sacrifice is to be seen in the change from the unsacrificed bread and wine to the sacrificed body of Christ.[4] Having thus cleared the ground by the rejection of the explanations which he thought wrong or inadequate, De Lugo, following out a suggestion already made by Bellarmine,[5] expands his own opinion that by consecration the body of Christ is brought into a lower state, being after a human fashion destroyed by being made useless for the ordinary purposes

---

[1] I.-XVIII. [2] XIX. i. [3] XIX. iii.
[4] XIX. iv. [5] See p. 366, *supra.*

of a human body and fit for food and drink, and that in this lowered state it is in the condition of a victim.[1] The sacrifice is offered by Christ, not in the sense that He actively concurs in the offering of it, but because He has commissioned His priests to offer it and acts through their agency, so that, if by an impossible hypothesis Christ did not know what was being done, the offering of the sacrifice could none the less take place.[2] Some of the more characteristic parts of De Lugo's teaching may be seen in the following quotations :—

" In the first place, sacrifice does not differ from other worship of God exactly in this, that it is a declaration of the supreme excellence of God, or of His power over life and death, as Vasquez said.[3] . . . Sacrifice denotes something else and in another way, by which it differs from all other worship, partly because of the thing signified in that it shows that God is worthy of our life being consumed in His honour, and partly because of the method in that it shows this by the destruction of something, by which we may express the desire for our own destruction, if it were lawful or necessary for the worship of God. Yet observe that it is not of the essence of the sacrifice that it be made by the destruction of some other thing, which may be substituted for us. For its essence could be preserved even better and more really if our life itself were sacrificed, as Christ our Lord on the cross offered to God a real sacrifice by His own destruction and death, which bore witness to the same excellence and dignity of God. We say then that it is of the nature of sacrifice that it be a declaration of that excellence of God, whereby He is worthy that our life be destroyed in His worship, whether this declaration be made by the actual destruction of one's own life or by the destruction of some other thing by which our desire is expressed, when our own destruction would not be lawful or expedient. Secondly, in every sacrifice there must be some destruction of the thing that is offered." [4]

" That we may explain how the consecration is substantially the act of sacrificing, I observe that, when we require the destruction of the victim for the nature of a real sacrifice, by the word destruction is not always understood the physical or metaphysical substantial corruption of the victim, but the destruction either physical or human, so that from the force of the act of sacrificing, so far as concerns the end of the action, it has some lower state, and ceases to be at least in human fashion. . . . Among the ancients, to whom, as it was more frequent, so also the essence of sacrifice was better known, we find that some things were wont to be sacrificed by such a human destruction: for instance, when there was a libation of wine by pouring it out from bowls on the earth in honour of God, that outpouring was called the act of libation and sacrificing; but it is certain that by the outpouring the wine was corrupted formally but not substantially, until afterwards it should gradually dry up and be consumed, while the sacrifice took place in the pouring out itself, because by the outpouring it was destroyed in human fashion, inasmuch as it now received some state useless for its former operations. . . . In which manner also they used to sacrifice when something was thrown into the sea or into a river, . . . because by that submersion the thing thrown in was destroyed in human fashion, although it was not substantially corrupted in its own existence. This being understood, it will be easy to explain how by the act of consecration itself the body of Christ is sacrificed; for, though it is not destroyed substantially by the act of consecration itself, yet it is destroyed in human fashion in so far as it receives a lower state of such a kind as to render it useless for the human purposes of a human body and suitable for other different purposes in the way of food. Wherefore in human fashion it is the same as if it were to become real bread and to be fitted and prepared for food. This change is sufficient for a real sacrifice; because for that to become eatable which was not eatable, and for it to become eatable in such a way as no longer to be useful for any other purposes but in the way of food, is a greater change than others which in the common judgment of men have been sufficient for a real sacrifice." [1]

"It is not required that Christ concur physically with the act of offering, or that Christ have in act some actual will physically existing whereby now to offer; for though Christ were now taking no notice, or did not know, nay, though whether possible or impossible He were asleep when this sacrifice is offered, it would still be said to be offered by Christ, as a king is said to show obedience to the pontiff when his ambassador shows it, though the king were at the moment asleep or not thinking about it. . . . It is not enough for this that there be a mere institution, but that there be an institution with the will that it be offered in His name; and much less is the application of His merits enough, for this application could be made at a sacrifice which was not in any sense offered in

[1] XIX. v. 65, 66, 67.

the name of Christ. Christ therefore now really offers because the priest by the institution of Christ offers in the name of Christ, which is enough for this action, morally speaking, to be called the action of Christ, as the reverence which the ambassador of a king shows to the pontiff is morally the reverence of the king towards the pontiff. So also Christ by means of the priest whom He has substituted as His ambassador and minister exercises this act of reverence and worship towards God, which consists in the offering of the sacrifice; and therefore this offering is deemed morally the action of Christ worshipping God by means of His minister." [1]

III.

It was observed in a former chapter that in the proceedings of the Council of Trent any idea of a connection between the Eucharistic sacrifice and the heavenly life of our Lord was almost wholly out of sight, although such an idea was referred to in the reports of three of the theologians made to the council, in two cases in terms of approval, in one case in terms of condemnation.[2] Any such idea is absent from the writings of the theologians whose teaching has so far been discussed in the present chapter except Melchior Cano; [3] and, while it would not be inconsistent with the explanations of the sacrifice given by Salmeron, Vasquez, Suarez, Bellarmine, and Lessius, it would be wholly precluded by the teaching of De Lugo with its assertion of the complete independence of the Eucharistic sacrifice of any present action of Christ. But in the same century in which De Lugo was developing and extending the idea of destruction as an essential element in the sacrifice, and was making the Eucharist wholly independent of the present life of our Lord in heaven, a very different way of regarding the sacrifice was receiving careful expression in France.

Charles de Condren was born in 1588 at Vauxbuin near Soissons. After studying at the Sorbonne he held the office of professor of philosophy at the University of Paris for a year. In 1614 he was ordained priest. In 1617 he entered the Congregation of the Oratory. In 1629 he succeeded Cardinal de Berulle, the founder of the Oratory, as General of the Congregation. In 1614 he died. The treatise *The Idea of the Priesthood and Sacrifice of Jesus Christ* was published in 1677 after his death;

. [1] XIX. vii. 93.   [2] See pp. 99, 100, *supra.*

[3] See, however, the passage concerning the "altar on high" quoted from Bellarmine on p. 367, *supra.* For Melchior Cano, see p. 357, *supra.*

and, though it may not in every part give his own actual words, it may be taken as indicating his teaching. Sacrifice is here described as having been instituted chiefly for four ends,—to honour God, to give Him thanks, to make satisfaction for sin, and to obtain gifts.[1] As a recognition of the sovereign dominion of God it requires the destruction of the victim. Of the spiritual and divine sacrifice of the Christian religion our Lord is the Priest, being the Mediator of the new covenant, exercising the functions of priesthood according to the order of Melchizedek. His first public act as Priest was on the cross; the priesthood there used was completed at the ascension; as High Priest He abidingly offers in heaven.[2] Between the cross and the ascension was His re-surrection, wherein His body was consummated as the victim in the sacrifice; and His resurrection thus corresponded in His sacrifice to the consuming of the body of the victim by fire in the burnt offerings of the Jews.[3] The sacrifice of the Mass, which the Church on earth offers by Christ is the same as the sacrifice which the risen and ascended Christ offers in heaven;[4] and this sacrifice thus now offered in heaven and on earth is the same as the sacrifice of the cross.[5] Our Lord Himself is the "altar on high," on which the offering made on the earthly altar is presented in heaven; and the angel whose hands bear the sacrifice to the "altar on high" is either our Lord or an angel of sacrifice representing Him and acting in His name and authority.[6] In the future this sacrifice of Christ will be the eternal offering of the courts of heaven.[7] The characteristic feature in this teaching—the close association of the earthly with the heavenly offering and the abid-ing activity of our Lord in the sacrifice—may be illustrated by the following quotations :—

"Jesus Christ being High Priest in heaven necessarily offers there. Since every priest is appointed to offer gifts and victims, He too must have something to offer. What can this be but that which He once offered on earth, the sacrifice of His own body, of which He perpetually renews and continues the oblation in heaven? The oblation of Jesus Christ has not been so completed and exhausted

---

[1] I. i. Cf. the devotional use of these four ends of sacrifice in the Paradisus animæ Christianæ, V. iv., of Jacques Merlo, usually known as Horstius, from his birthplace in Holland (born 1597, died 1644).

[2] I. v.   [3] I. viii.   [4] I. ix.

[5] I. x.   [6] II. iv. v.   [7] II. viii.-xi.

on earth as to have no further exercise in heaven; but rather it was only begun here below in order to be continued in heaven, where the perfection of sacrifice is found." [1]

"The spiritual Jews knew that the victim should be consumed in the most worthy way possible; for, besides the command of God to consume it by fire, they knew that fire was the symbol under which God was hidden; but only Christians know by faith the true fulfilment in the glorious resurrection of the body of Jesus Christ, the consummation of the adorable Victim in the truth which was symbolised by the fire. For after the immolation of His body on the cross and the destruction of His mortal life, it was still necessary that all the traces of mortality in the wounds which He had received, all disfigurement and lowliness and earthiness which He still retained, and all the likeness of the flesh of sin and of the infirmity of the children of Adam, should be entirely destroyed and consumed in glory. Thus the body of Jesus Christ as Victim was consummated and glorified in the resurrection. 'He rose from the dead by means of the glory of the Father.' [2] He was raised by the divine fire of the glory of the Father, by which was consumed all that in His body, mortal and dead on the cross, was not worthy of the body of God." [3]

"This great sacrifice which Jesus Christ in union with the saints offers to God in heaven, offering Himself with them, is the same sacrifice which the priest offers on earth, and which the whole Church offers by Him in the holy Mass. For the Victim which they offer is the same, being the body and blood of Jesus Christ really present, united to God, existing in the Word and in this mystery. It is the same Priest who offers it by His ministers; it is offered on the same altar, which is the Subsistence or Person of the Eternal Word, in the same temple, namely, the bosom of the Eternal Father, to the same God on earth as in heaven; and the Victim is not merely the same but is in the same state of consummation and glory. The only difference is that, though present here as really as in heaven, He is not so after a visible manner." [4]

"The sacrifice of the Mass is the same as that of the cross, inasmuch as the one contains the other; for it is Jesus Christ immolated on the cross who is present on the altar after the consecration, and is there offered as having been immolated for us. He has in the Mass the state of death which the Jews inflicted on Him in His crucifixion, inasmuch as He there offers Himself as once immolated on the cross; and it is in memory and in virtue of that immolation

[1] I. v.   [2] Ro. vi. 4.   [3] I. viii.   [4] I. ix.

that He is offered by the Church. This state of immolation and death is moreover shown and represented by the mystical separation of His body and blood under the different species of bread and wine separately consecrated; nevertheless the divine Victim is no longer there in the likeness of the flesh of sin but in glory and immortality." [1]

"The true altar of sacrifice in heaven is Jesus Christ. . . . In the canon of the Mass, . . . Jesus Christ is without doubt intended by the altar on high which is before the majesty of God. . . . The true altar of the great sacrifice is ·the Person or Subsistence of the Word, that is, of Jesus Christ. It was on this altar that the victim, His humanity, was laid in the mystery of the Incarnation. . . . On this altar all the parts of the sacrifice are carried out. . . . On this altar the oblation was made from the moment of the Incarnation. . . . On this altar the Victim was immolated, and the cross which bore Him in His death deserves to be called an altar only because it represented the invisible altar from which the sacred Victim was never separated. . . . On this altar the Victim was consummated and sanctified in the resurrection. . . . On this altar the blood of the Victim was carried into the invisible sanctuary by Him who is the High Priest when returning to His Father He re-entered as it were into His bosom. . . . Lastly, on this altar will the Victim, perfected by the union of all His members, be eternally presented to God, will adore Him, rendering to Him the love and praise and thanksgiving which are His due, and will continue for ever the sacrifice in which the eternal joy of the saints consists." [2]

John James Olier was born in Paris in 1608. At the age of eighteen he received the ecclesiastical preferments of the priory of the Holy Trinity at Clisson and the abbey of Our Lady at Pébrac. In 1633 he was ordained priest. He was the friend and disciple of De Condren. After De Condren's death in 1641 he attempted to form a seminary for priests at Chartres with a view to raising the standard of life among the French clergy, but the attempt failed. A further attempt of the same kind at Vaugirard in the outskirts of Paris was somewhat more successful, and in 1642 Olier was appointed curé of the parish of Saint Sulpice, where he founded the famous Congregation and Seminary of Saint Sulpice, and in 1646 began the building of the new church. In his work at Saint Sulpice he had much to do with the revival of a true spirit of priestly life in France. He died in

[1] I. x.   [2] II. iv.-vi.

1657. Olier's book entitled *Explanation of the Ceremonies of the Parochial High Mass* contains teaching concerning the Eucharist which closely resembles that of De Condren; and it will be sufficient to quote a few passages from it:—

"To understand the mystery of the most holy sacrifice of the Mass, . . . one must know that this sacrifice is the sacrifice of heaven. . . . It is a statement strange to a great part of the world to say that there is a sacrifice in heaven, I mean for people as a whole, since those who know in what religion and its first duty of sacrifice consist have no doubt that there is a sacrifice in heaven. . . . Our Lord, made a High Priest for ever after the order of Melchizedek, is with God His Father to offer to Him the sacrifice always. . . . There is a sacrifice in heaven, which is at the same time offered on earth, since the victim which is presented is borne to the altar in heaven; and the only difference is that here it is presented under veils and symbols, and there it is offered without cover or veil." [1]

"In heaven our Lord offers Himself in a glorious state; He does not present Himself to God as prepared for death, which is the first state of a victim, but as a victim once immolated and already completed in God." [2]

"On the day of the resurrection, finding His Son immolated in the tomb, the Father came in His light and divine glory to complete the sacrifice in Him, not leaving in Him any trace of His weakness and of His former state, of His state of carnal (*grossière*) and passible and mortal flesh, so as by wholly consuming it to make it pass into His divine state, as iron passes into the state of fire." [3]

"This victim [in the Jewish sacrifices] changed in the fire is raised towards heaven to signify that Jesus Christ, once completed in His Father at His resurrection, is afterwards raised to Him at His ascension." [4]

"The altar of the sacrifice is the Person of the Word, who bears Jesus Christ in His sacred manhood, and ever shows Him as smoking and consumed by the glory of God on His Person, as on an altar." [5]

---

[1] Preface (pp. 11, 12, 14, edition Paris, 1858).   [2] VII. i. (p. 380).
[3] VII. ii. (pp. 396, 397).
[4] II. iv. (p. 120); *cf.* VII. ii. (pp. 398, 399).
[5] Preface (p. 13). It is not without interest that, although with many theological differences, Jeremy Taylor was laying stress on the heavenly sacrifice of our Lord in the same century as De Condren and Olier: see pp. 334-37, *supra*.

Louis Thomassin was born in 1619 at Aix in the south of France. He was a member of the Congregation of the Oratory. He taught at Lyons and Saumur and Paris. He died in 1696. In the section of his great work *Theological Dogmas* entitled *On the Incarnation of the Word of God* there is a very full treatment of sacrifice, the sacrifice of Christ, and the Eucharistic sacrifice in connection with the priesthood of Christ. This treatment exhibits in a theological form with lengthy discussion and many patristic quotations the aspects of the sacrifice of Christ which were handled more devotionally than theologically by De Condren and Olier. The one sacrifice to which both nature and revelation looked forward is the death of Christ.[1] When He died, animal sacrifices became obsolete.[2] It was the purpose of the Incarnation that He who was God might be priest and victim in His death, and that there might be sacrifice as well as reconciliation to God.[3] The offering of the sacrifice was begun when God the Word became man.[4] The sacrifice offered in the death on the cross is abiding and eternal.[5] In a pre-eminent degree Christ entered on His priesthood after His resurrection, and He began its fullest exercise at His ascension.[6] The sacrifice which He offers in heaven is one and the same as the sacrifice of the cross.[7] In heaven He abidingly offers His cross to the Father, and with it the sufferings and acts of the righteous which are sprinkled from His cross.[8] By this heavenly priesthood the sacrifice of the cross, to which there was new life in the resurrection, is continually perpetuated.[9] Though it the once shed blood is ever offered to the Father ; and in His glorified manhood Christ continually offers a perpetual sacrifice.[10] With Himself He offers the Church.[11] In sacrifice there must be change, and the best kind of change is that which is for the better ; and the new life of the risen body supplies what thus is best.[12] For Christians the most real temple and sanctuary and altar are in heaven ; and their one real and proper sacrifice is that which is on the cross and in the Eucharist and in heaven.[13] In the Eucharist is Christ's most notable exercise of the priesthood of Melchizedek, since the Eucharist is more congruous than the cross with the bloodless sacrifice of Melchizedek.[14] The sacrifice

---

[1] X. vi. 5. [2] X. vii. 1. [3] X. viii. 1, 5. [4] X. ix. 16.
[5] X. x. 9, 10. [6] X. xi. 1. [7] X. xi. 8. [8] X. xi. 12.
[9] X. xii. 1, 2, 3. [10] X. xii. 6, xiii. 1, 2, 3. [11] X. xiv. 3.
[12] X. xiv. 9. [13] X. xiv. 9, 10. [14] X. xiv. 1, 4.

of the Eucharist, as being one and the same with the sacrifice of the cross, is a mystical repetition of it.[1] As it is essentially one with the cross as being of the same Victim, so this identity is outwardly shown by the ceremonial actions used.[2] In the Eucharist, as in heaven, the whole Church is offered to God as being the body of Christ.[3] The flesh of Christ is the same flesh as our own, but it is much more glorious and is now spiritual with the gifts of the risen life and the glory of the ascension.[4] The sacrifice is not now of His body in its mortal state, but of His immortal life.[5] The style of Thomassin is too lengthy and elaborate to lend itself readily to quotation, but a few extracts may be made to illustrate the summarised account of his teaching on the subject of the Eucharist which has been given.

"It is most clear that the sacrifice which the eternal law commands to be offered, which the will of God and the voice of nature and the consciousness of the soul destine for God, is offered only by means of the death of Christ. That one sacrifice is due to God, by it alone God is propitiated, by it alone the human race is cleansed."[6]

"When once the real sacrifice of the cross of Christ was offered, then at length all its shadows disappeared and the old and wonted practice of the nations everywhere of sacrificing beasts came to an end."[7]

"The object of this chapter is to show, first, that the purpose of the Incarnation of the Word was nothing else than the appointment of a Priest who could make expiation for the human race ; secondly, that Christ from the first beginning of His life had the dignity of priesthood ; and, lastly, that from this point His sacrifice began to be accomplished, and that the Incarnation itself was a sacrifice. . . . You see for what purpose mortal nature was joined to immortal Godhead in one Person, namely, that the immortal righteousness of the Godhead might become mortal by means of the mortal nature which was taken, and might by dying perform the offices of priest and victim. . . . There was need of this victim, in which the whole race of men should not only be reconciled to God, but should also be sacrificed. . . . It was necessary that in one Man, who should be Head of all and the union and universality of all, all of us as a universal but also a perpetual victim and an immortal sacrifice should

[1] X. xvii. 3.   [2] X. xviii. 1.   [3] X. xix. 1, 4.   [4] X. xxix. 1, 17.
[5] X. xxxi. 13.   [6] X. vi. 5.   [7] X. vii. 1.

be consecrated to God, that we all should be grafted into that One, all die with Him, all rise together with Him, all be immortally sacrificed together with Him by a continual sacrifice of love. This was afforded by the Incarnation, whereby One from among men was taken for Victim and Priest, set as Head and Leader to the rest, in whom all should be, in whom all should be grafted together in God to die and to live together. . . . God the Word abounded in all manner of rich life, but was in want of death, to obtain which He was conceived and born as Man. Therefore the Incarnation is the taking not of human life but of mortality and death. Therefore the Incarnation is a sacrifice. . . . The taking of mortality is already a kind of anticipation of death and a sacrifice. . . . This manhood from its first existence He began to show to the Father as a Victim, therefore to sacrifice." [1]

"The sacrifice of the cross is not only general or universal and spread over the whole world, but it is also ever continual. For once offered to God, it does not cease to be offered, and the whole race of men does not cease to have expiation by means of it. . . . The sacrifice of the cross of Christ is continual and eternal because to His one cross are fixed all the righteous, who, whether they are earlier or later members of His body, at whatever time they have lived, cleave to Him as their Head." [2]

"After His resurrection Christ most of all took to Himself the dignity and office of High Priest, as Paul testifies.[3] . . . He says that the Aaronic high priests were wont once in the year to enter into the innermost shrine of the temple not without blood, and that Christ, in order that He might illuminate and put to flight the shadows by the reality, entered once in the heavenly sanctuary by means of His own blood, as High Priest of good things to come." [4]

"The sacrifice of the cross and of heaven is the same and one. . . . No other is the sacrifice of heaven than the sacrifice of the cross; but here the victim is once slain, there through the veil, that is, His flesh, it is borne into the innermost sanctuary, that is, the most hidden deity, and there is consumed and is immortally devoured by the deity as by most pure and glowing fire. . . . Christ having been once slain, is incorruptibly consumed by fire that is not shadowy but real, I mean by God, and by means of His resurrection and immortality His human nature is devoured and received into the deity. . . . The sacrifice of Christ sitting at the right hand of the Father is universal, whereby the eternal High Priest ever

[1] X. viii. 1, 5, ix. 16.
[3] Heb. ix. 11, 12.
[2] X. x. 9, 10.
[4] X. xi. 1.

offers His cross to the Father and also eternally sacrifices as pieces of His cross and portions and complements of His own death the crosses and deaths of all the righteous and all their works unquestionably smeared and sprinkled with the blood and power of His cross. . . . His own abode and dwelling place is the heaven, and the sacrifice itself is altogether heavenly, because, although the victim is slain on earth, it is slain here in order that it may be placed there on its proper altar, and may be offered there for an eternal burnt offering." [1]

" He was made a sacrifice on the cross, but in the resurrection the Victim renewed and restored to life is consecrated as first fruits to God, and all we in it. . . . The immortal Priest ever offers to the Father the blood which was once shed. . . . Christ rising from the dead and ascending into heaven, as a sheaf of corn and as a lamb, is sacrificed to God for a sacrifice now bloodless, though bearing the smell and marks of His most recent offering. . . . The lamb once slain was not offered and sacrificed only when He was slain; but so long as the marks of His death remain and are presented to the Father, so long is He offered and sacrificed by the perpetuated sacrifice of the cross. . . . Christ entered heaven and sits at the right hand of the Father for this purpose, that He may show His shed blood, and present His passion and cross, and set forth His death and sacrificing as abiding. . . . That Christ in glorified manhood stands before the Father in heaven is the same as not to cease to offer a solemn sacrifice and to plead and to offer Himself, and without intermission to sacrifice a burnt offering and a perpetual sacrifice." [2]

" Christ would not be the universal and collective burnt offering unless with the Head Himself His body also, I mean His whole Church, were burning in the same fire." [3]

" Any sacrifice is a change of the victim. But a change has two kinds ; the one is for the worse ; the other is for the better. Which kind of change, I ask, does God most delight in ? . . . The most complete change of the whole man takes place by means of resurrection, wherein nothing is destroyed except destructibility, wherein soul and body are changed for the better to a form indescribably more glorious than their former state. This then will be a sweeter and more fitting sacrifice for God, whereby it shall come to pass that those things which are dedicated to Him are not destroyed but gain profit and honour. . . . These spiritual sacrifices [that is, prayer and love and martyrdom and virtue], although when com-

[1] X. xi. 8, 12, 13. [2] X. xii. 2, 6, xiii. 1, 2, 3. [3] X. xiv. 3.

pared with the Mosaic and other sacrifices, . . . they may seem to
be real and to be the more real in that they are more spiritual
and accepted by God, yet, when they are compared with the one
real and proper sacrifice of Christ on the cross, in the Eucharist,
in heaven, they are only improperly sacrifices, and only so at all so
far as they are parts of it, and derive from it whatever nature of
sacrifice they possess." [1]

"Of the most splendid priesthood of Christ from the prerogative of the order of Melchizedek the head and sum is found in the
sacrifice of the Eucharist, wherein He offered bread and wine, that
is, His body and blood. . . . To that bloodless and really Melchi-
zedekian sacrifice, which really is superior to the Aaronic sacrifice,
the Eucharist is more congruous than the cross, which represents
the gore and appearance of the Aaronic sacrifice." [2]

"One is the victim of the Eucharist and the cross, one is the
death of the victim, one is the oblation of the death. . . . The
sacrifice of the Eucharist is celebrated for a memorial of the cross ;
therefore it is not a different sacrifice from the cross, but it is a
mystic repetition of the cross. . . . On the cross the victim is put
to death, in the Eucharist it is at once set forth to be eaten ; that
putting to death is connected with this eating, this eating has relation to that putting to death ; the cross serves the Eucharist, the
Eucharist depends on the cross ; there is one sacrifice of the victim
slain on the cross, eaten on the altar. . . . This offering of the
sacrifice and death of Christ is not different from and like to that
first offering, but is one and the same with it, one and the same
past and present, or never past but ever present. . . . The whole
Christ with His whole cross is offered in the Eucharist as the
sacrifice, is distributed as the victim, is paid as the price. . . .
Not only is the same Christ, the same victim, the same passion and
death, the same offering contained inwardly, but outwardly also
the breaking of the host, the distribution, the eating, the pouring
out of His blood imitate most closely the savage sacrificing of the
cross." [3]

"The end and fruit of the priesthood of Christ are not only
that He offer Himself, but also that He offer the whole Church to
God in Himself. . . . Unless we depart from the very elements of
the Christian faith, there is no other sacrifice to God anywhere
than the body of Christ. How then do these three things agree,
that there is no other sacrifice than the body of Christ, that we ourselves are the most splendid sacrifice, that real and true virtues are

[1] X. xiv, 9, 10.   [2] X, xvi, 1, 4.   [3] X. xvii. 3, 4, 5, 7, xviii, 1,

a rich sacrifice to God ? Can these three agree in one, the flesh of Christ, we ourselves, the flock of virtues ? Certainly they can be united and coalesce into one victim. For the Church is the flesh of Christ ; we are members of Christ. Again, all virtues are united and joined together with Christ ; for this is the flesh of the Word, the flesh of righteousness, the body of wisdom and holiness." [1]

"The flesh of Christ is of the same substance with our own, but of far different glory ; in nature it agrees, but it surpasses by an infinite distance of majesty ; it is the most real flesh, but it is the dwelling place of all truth, the partner of deity, most rich in gifts of spiritual wealth, and a "spiritual body" far more splendid than that which we wait for, as the Apostle Paul testifies.[2] . . . Christ has ascended into heaven, that His flesh which is here eaten, and His flesh which is drunk, may be understood not carnally but spiritually. For that very flesh which sits at the right hand of the Father on high is sacrificed here. Is not that flesh which has been raised above all the ranks of angelic spirits spiritual ? . . . In that Christ died, He died to sin once ; but in that He liveth, He liveth to God ; wherefore mortal life could be sacrificed once, but immortal life returning in victory from death is now sacrificed for ever by a more blessed sacrifice. . . . The blessed and eternal Priest Christ after His resurrection continually and immortally sacrifices Himself and us all in Him to God ; and He sacrifices the Eucharist as a large portion even here of that blessed sacrifice on high and the sacrificed blessedness of God." [3]

IV.

The instances which have been given from theologians of the sixteenth and seventeenth centuries show sufficiently the tendencies in regard to the doctrine of the Eucharistic sacrifice which have been operative in the later theology of the Church of Rome. In the eighteenth and nineteenth and twentieth centuries there has been general agreement that the essential point in the sacrifice is the consecration. With that agreement as a basis, there have been different lines of thought as to the nature of the sacrifice ; and theologians may be divided into four groups, not all mutually exclusive. The great influence of the powerful mind of De Lugo has led to the acceptance by many of his opinion that in the Eucharistic sacrifice the manhood of our Lord is reduced to a lower state, and that the necessary element

[1] X. xix. 1, 4,   [2] 1 Cor. xv. 44.   [3] X, xxix, 1, 17, xxxi, 13.
25 *

of destruction is thereby supplied. The view of Salmeron and Vasquez and Lessius that a mystical destruction is enough, and that this consists in the separate consecration of the two species has had very many advocates. The contention of Suarez that no destruction is necessary, but that the production of the body and blood of Christ on the altar in honour of God is all the change that is needed for the sacrifice, has not been without its adherents. The assertion of the connection with the heavenly sacrifice of our Lord by Thomassin and others, which follows a wholly different line of thought from the theory of De Lugo but is not inconsistent with the opinions either of Vasquez or of Suarez, has been maintained by some. It may be convenient to mention a very few of the supporters of these four ways of re-garding the sacrifice.

1. The most notable advocate of the theory of De Lugo is Cardinal Franzelin. John Baptist Franzelin was born in the Tyrol in 1816. In 1834 he entered the Society of Jesus. After being a student and teacher at Rome, in 1848 he left that city because of the political troubles of the time, and for a short while was a teacher of Hebrew in France. Returning to Rome, he became a teacher of Oriental languages in the Jesuit College there. In 1857 he became Professor of Dogmatic Theology. In 1876 he was made a cardinal by Pope Pius IX. In 1886 he died. His treatise *On the Sacrament and Sacrifice of the Most Holy Euchar-ist* was first published in 1868. In the part of this treatise dealing with the sacrifice, Franzelin, after giving his reasons for thinking the opinions of Vasquez and Lessius and Suarez inadequate, and for accepting that of De Lugo,[1] and while carefully stating that what he says on this point is the expression of a theory only and not part of the doctrine of the Church, explains his own view of the lower state of our Lord's manhood which supplies the element of destruction as follows :—

"Let that state now be considered in which Christ the Lord, the High Priest, constitutes Himself as the victim by means of the consecration in His body and blood under the species of bread and wine. The First-begotten of all creation, the Head of the Church, holding in all things the pre-eminence,[2] gives Himself to His Church by means of His ministers the priests, to be constituted in His body and blood in such a mode of existence under the species of bread

---

[1] Pp. 390-403.   [2] Col. i. 15, 18.

and wine that He is really in the state of food and drink, so that
(formally in so far as He is constituted under these species) every
act connatural with the bodily life and dependent on the senses
ceases, so that He can do nothing connaturally as a body, so that
His body and blood, in so far as His presence is attached to the
species, is somehow granted to the will of creatures not otherwise
than if it were an inanimate thing ; but He has constituted Himself
in such a condition that He Himself, the High Priest, for the whole
Church whose Head He is, and the Church through Him, may express in His most sacred body and blood the supreme dominion of
God and the absolute dependence of every creature, of which Jesus
Christ Himself as Man is the First-begotten, and may at the same
time express and show forth the satisfaction for guilt formerly consummated on the cross in the surrender of this very body and the
shedding of this blood. · And yet such an ' exinanition,' [1] to express the majesty of the absolute dominion of God and the satisfaction for our guilt completed by death, is not sufficiently understood
simply as being really and properly sacrificial, but further with
the exception of the bloody sacrifice on the cross we can conceive
no more sublime or more profound method of real and proper
sacrifice. Therefore there is no doubt that in the sacramental way
of existence itself the fitness of the body and blood of Christ and,
granting the institution, the actual sacrificial signification, and consequently the inward method of a real and proper sacrifice, are not
only sufficiently but also eminently contained." [2]

2. In spite of the increased currency given to the theory of
De Lugo by the able advocacy of it by so weighty a theologian
as Franzelin, it is probable that the view still most widely held
in the Church of Rome is that the mystical destruction which
consists in the separate consecration under the two species is the
essential point in the sacrifice. One of the most distinguished
advocates of this theory in the nineteenth century was John
Perrone. Perrone was born in 1794 in Piedmont. He joined
the Society of Jesus in 1815. After teaching dogmatic theology at Orvieto and in the Jesuit College at Rome, he was obliged
to leave Italy in consequence of political troubles in 1848, and
took refuge in England. On his return to Italy he continued his

---

[1] The word *exinanitio* is connected with the phrase *semetipsum exinanivit*
(ἑαυτὸν ἐκένωσεν) used by St. Paul of our Lord in the Incarnation in Phil.
ii. 7.

[2] Pp. 404, 405.

work of teaching at Rome. He died in 1876. The *Theological Lectures* which he delivered in the Jesuit College at Rome contain a treatise *On the Eucharist.* In the section on sacrifice he clearly describes the teaching of Vasquez,[1] and then adds :—

" We do not at all contend that this is the only way of asserting the reality of our sacrifice ; but we say this one thing, that it seems to us more suitable for attaining the proposed end, whether because it removes the chief difficulty by which this reality is attacked, or because the words of the fathers are most in agreement with it, or lastly because the Protestants, if it is once established, have nothing more by which to be drawn away from the Catholic doctrine to be received concerning this article.   For in this opinion only two things are required, and are enough, in order that the reality of the sacrifice of the Mass be maintained, namely, the actual presence of Christ in the Eucharist, . . . and the representation of the sacrifice of the cross."[2]

With a slight modification, probably rather of expression than of thought, the theory of Vasquez has been accepted by the living writers Dr. Van Noort, the Professor of Theology in the seminary at Warmond in Holland, and the Roman Catholic Bishop (J. C. Hedley) of Newport.   Dr. Van Noort in his treatise *On the Sacraments* writes :—

" Many agree so far as to say that they think the sacrificial mark of the Mass is to be placed in the separate consecration of the body and blood of the Lord under the two species, of which one represents the body and the other the blood ; but they differ as to the further explanation.   Vasquez and Perrone are of opinion that the Mass is a real sacrifice of the present because the separate consecration represents the sacrifice of the cross.   But this certainly is not to the point ; for it seems impossible that any offering is formally a sacrifice of the present because it represents another sacrifice.   Lessius[3] with more followers lays down that it is counted a real sacrifice because the words of consecration of themselves tend towards making an actual separation of the body and blood of the Lord, which separation is nevertheless by accident hindered because Christ being now glorified dies no more.   But this, again, cannot be admitted ; for, to pass by other reasons, it is not understood how a sacrificing

---

[1] See pp. 361-64, *supra.*
[2] § 250 (vol. vi. pp. 268, 269, edition 1841).
[3] See pp. 372, 373, *supra.*

designed and, if one may say so, intended but hindered is sufficient for the nature of a sacrifice. Therefore keeping the common marrow of these opinions, Billot [1] has corrected their defective explanations by teaching that the Mass is a real sacrifice because in the consecration Christ is made present in the external guise of a violent death, inasmuch as His flesh and blood are so shown to our senses by means of the sacramental signs as if they were separated in death." [2]

Bishop Hedley writes in his book *The Holy Eucharist* :—

" In order then to understand—as far as we are permitted to understand—where the essential point of the sacrifice lies, and how a real 'immutation' can take place and yet the glorified body of Christ be in no way physically affected, we must carefully bear in mind that it is Christ in the Sacrament that is sacrificed, not Christ absolutely. . . . By the consecration of the bread, the bread is changed into the body of the Lord, the sacred blood, soul and divinity and the whole Christ becoming present at the same time by what is called concomitance, that is, because Christ can no longer be divided, or be without any part of His sacred being. But in the consecration of the chalice, it is not our Lord's body which is the object of Transubstantiation, but His precious blood. The wine is changed, not into the body, but into the blood. True, the body, soul, and divinity at once become present by concomitance. But the Transubstantiation is an entirely different Transubstantiation. . . . One's senses take note of certain visible appearances which one knows to be Christ's body (and the whole Christ) and others which one knows to be Christ's blood (also the whole Christ). This is visible ; and as there was first the action upon the bread and afterwards on the chalice, the separation of the blood from the body really effected *sub speciebus* may be well said to be visibly transacted. The second consecration has a plain, visible, and intended relation to the first. Thus the very thing in which the passion is represented carries in its inmost actuality the essentials of a true sacrifice. No one . . . maintains that our Blessed Lord in His natural glorified state dies again ; or even that so much as a tremor of the most delicate of the nerves or tissues of His sacred flesh is caused by the words of consecration. It is sufficient that in His sacramental state and as present under the species He should be the subject of some real occurrence which should congruously represent the blow of the sacrificial knife. . . . It is very probable that if Vasquez [3] had lived to answer the difficulties raised against

[1] *De Sacr.* I. liv.   [2] § 468 (pp. 373, 374).   [3] See pp. 361-64, *supra*.

his position by men who followed him, he would have made himself a little more explicit. He has been taken to mean that the mere presence on the altar of the body and blood of Christ under the two species, since it is the representation of the Lamb that is slain, is the sacrifice. But it is probable that he did not mean the mere presence, but the presence as brought about by the consecrating act. One thing may represent another thing, and one act may represent another act ; and if the matter which has to be represented is precisely the resultant of an action, the representation may be said to stand for the thing, but the representation will then itself include representative action. We cannot conceive that Vasquez would have maintained that the Mass was a mere representation of the cross. The Council of Trent had already defined. By 'representation,' therefore, he must have meant the consecrated species not precisely as they lie on the altar, but as the resultant of consecration. That is to say, the host and cup represent the slain Lamb, but it is the host and cup as consecrated, that is, as affected by an action done by the priest. That action is the production of the body, and then separately of the blood, by the words of consecration. And this seems to me to coincide with what I have called the plain Catholic tradition." [1]

Though not explicitly mentioned, the separate consecration of the two species was probably in view in the phrase " a mystic representation of the blood-shedding of Calvary," which occurred in a statement of the " Catholic doctrine on the sacrifice of the Mass" in a letter put forth by the Roman Catholic Archbishop and Bishops in England in 1898 under the title *A Vindication of the Bull " Apostolicæ Curæ "*. This statement is as follows :—

" The Mass, according to Catholic doctrine, is a commemoration of the sacrifice of the cross, for as often as we celebrate it ' we show the Lord's death till He come '. At the same time it is not a bare commemoration of that other sacrifice, since it is also itself a true sacrifice in the strict sense of the term. It is a true sacrifice because it has all the essentials of a true sacrifice : its Priest, Jesus Christ, using the ministry of an earthly representative ; its Victim, Jesus Christ, truly present under the appearances of bread and wine ; its sacrificial offering, the mystic rite of consecration. And it commemorates the sacrifice of the cross because, whilst its Priest is the Priest of Calvary, its Victim the Victim of Calvary, and its mode of offering a mystic representation of the blood-shedding of Calvary,

<hr>

[1] Pp. 162-64, 166, 167.

the end also for which it is offered is to carry on the work of Calvary, by pleading for the application of the merits consummated on the cross to the souls of men. It is in this sense that the Mass is propitiatory. To propitiate is to appease the divine wrath by satisfaction offered and to beg mercy and forgiveness for sinners. The sacrifice of the cross is propitiatory in the absolute sense of the word. But the infinite treasure of merit acquired on the cross cannot be diminished or increased by any other sacrifice. It was then offered once and for all, and there is no necessity of repeating it. That plenitude, however, of merit and satisfaction by no means excludes the continual application of such merit and satisfaction by the perpetual sacrifice of the Mass. Thus the sacrifice of the Mass is also propitiatory. And, as according to Catholic doctrine even the dead in Christ are not excluded from the benefits of this sacrifice, we call the Mass 'a propitiatory sacrifice for the living and the dead '." [1]

3. The theory of Suarez [2] that the essential point in the Eucharistic sacrifice is rather in what is positive than in what is negative, rather in the presence and presentation of the body and blood of Christ on the altar than in any kind of destruction however mystical, has received powerful advocacy from the very able theologians Joseph Scheeben, who was professor in the seminary of Cologne until his death in 1888, in his monumental treatise *Handbook of Catholic Dogmatic Theology*,[3] and Dr. Paul Schanz, the Professor of Theology in the University of Tuebingen, in his work *The System of the Holy Sacraments of the Catholic Church*,[4] which was published in 1893. This view of sacrifice with its elimination of the idea of destruction is adopted in the treatise giving for the most part the teaching of Scheeben in a shortened form entitled *A Manual of Catholic Theology*, the two volumes of which were published in 1890 and 1898 respectively, by Dr. Joseph Wilhelm and Dr. Thomas Scannell, without excluding the notion of the mystical commemoration of the death of Christ in the separate consecration under the two species. The passages in which Dr.

---

[1] Pp. 25, 26.   [2] See pp. 368-71, *supra*.

[3] III. 394-453, dealing with sacrifice in connection with the high priestly office of Christ, published by Dr. Scheeben before his death ; *cf.* iv. 632-66 of the continuation by Dr. Leonard Atzberger, Professor of Dogmatic Theology in the University of Munich, dealing with the Eucharistic sacrifice.

[4] Pp. 432-94.

Wilhelm and Dr. Scannell express this wider doctrine of sacrifice and their application of it to the Eucharist are so clear and careful as to justify somewhat lengthy extracts from them.

"Sacrifice is an act of worship in which God is honoured as the Beginning and End of man and of all things by the offering up of a visible creature, which, for this purpose, is submitted to an appropriate transformation by a lawful minister. An internal sacrifice is offered whenever man devotes himself to the service of God by either 'reforming or giving up' his life for God (Ps. l. 19).[1] No external sacrifice is perfect without an accompanying internal sacrifice, whereby the soul associates itself with the meaning and object of the external rite.

"1. The object of sacrifice is that of practical religion in general : to acknowledge God as the Beginning and End of man and of all things ; that is, to profess in deed our entire dependence on Him, both for existence and for ultimate happiness. Some post-Tridentine theologians have narrowed the idea of sacrifice to mean the expression of God's dominion over life and death, or of the divine power to dispose of all things, or of the divine majesty as exalted above all ; and have restricted its primary object to the atonement for sin.

"2. So, too, the external form of sacrifice—an appropriate transformation of the creature offered—has been limited by Vasquez and later theologians to the 'transformation by destruction '. Neither historical nor theological grounds can justify such limitations; for instance, the burning of incense, θυσία, which has furnished the Greek name for all sacrifices, is not so much the destruction of the incense as its conversion into 'an odour of sweetness,' the symbol of the soul of man transformed by the fire of charity. Similar remarks apply to all sacrifices without exception. In the sacrifice of the Mass, the *immutatio*, as the fathers technically call the sacrificial act, is not the destruction, but the production of the victim."[2]

"In Christ's sacrifice the immutation of the victim is brought about by an internal act of His will. . . . His death is the source of new life to Himself and mankind. The immutation, therefore, is spiritual, accomplished by the Eternal Spirit of the Sacrificer. This spiritual character is manifest in the glorious resurrection of Christ's body, and likewise in the Eucharistic sacrifice."[3]

[1] Ps. li. 17 in A.V. and R.V.
[2] II. 199, 200.   [3] II. 203.

"The sacrifice of the cross is chief amongst the sacerdotal functions of Christ, because it crowned His work on earth, and laid the foundation of His eternal priesthood in heaven. It alone realises all the aims and objects of the ancient sacrifices. . . . The sacrifice of the cross is also the central function of Christ's priesthood, inasmuch as all its other functions are based on this, and are only its consummation or perpetuation. It is virtually continued—not repeated—in heaven, where the sacrificial intention of the Priest and the glorified wounds of the Victim live for ever in the Divine Pontiff. One circumstance alone prevents the heavenly sacrifice from being actually the same as that of the cross : and that is the absence of any real immutation of the victim. . . . The ' odour of sweetness ' of the Saviour is His glorified Self ascending into heaven, and as the Lamb slain, standing in the midst of the throne before God, as an eternal sacrifice of adoration and thanksgiving. . . . From His heavenly throne Christ, through His priestly ministers on earth, continually consecrates and sacrifices in His Church, making Himself the sacrifice of the Church, and including the Church in His sacrifice. He thus brings down to earth the perennial sacrifice of heaven in order to apply its merits to mankind, and at the same time enables the Church to offer with Him and through Him a perfect sacrifice of adoration and thanksgiving. The Mass, then, like the eternal offering in heaven, completes the sacrifice of the cross by accomplishing its ends ; viz. the full participation of mankind in its fruits. Although the Eucharistic sacrifice is offered on earth and through human hands, it is none the less the formal act of Christ Himself as heavenly Priest. . . . The final consummation of Christ's sacrifice is the perfect participation in its fruits, in time and in eternity, by those on whose behalf it was offered. The sanctifying graces thus obtained consecrate the faithful with the Holy Ghost, and transform them into God's holy servants and priests, and make them members of the mystical body of Christ. With Christ they sacrifice and are sacrificed in the universal offering of the Holy City to God." [1]

"The notion of offering (oblatio, προσφορά) may be taken as the fundamental notion of all sacrifices. . . . The burning or outpouring of the gifts hands them over to God, and through their acceptance God admits the giver to communion with Him. For the essential character of the sacrificial gift is not its destruction, but its handing over and consecration to God. . . . The killing necessarily precedes the burning, but the killing is not the sacrifice. . . .

[1] II. 204, 205.

More importance attaches to the blood of the victim which is gathered and poured out at the altar. For, according to ancient ideas, the life, or the soul, is the blood. When, therefore, the blood is offered, the highest that man can give, namely, a soul or a life, is handed over to God. . . . The pouring out of the blood is the special function of the priest, whereas the killing . . . may be performed by a layman. . . . The eating of the victim accepted by God is simply the symbol of the union with God intended by those who offer the sacrifice. . . . The burning on the altar . . . was regarded as the means of conveying the victim to God, or, when the fire was kindled from heaven, it was God's acceptance of the sacrifice. Many of the Hebrew sacrifices may be described as things given to God to secure His favour, or to appease His wrath, or as thank and tribute offerings; but frequently also they meant an act of communion with God, either by means of a feast, which God was supposed to share with His worshippers, or by the renewal of a life-bond in the blood of a sacred victim. . . . These reasons justify the elimination of the element of destruction, real or equivalent, from the essential constitution of sacrifice in general. With Scheeben and Schanz we revert to the definitions commonly adopted before the time of Vasquez." [1]

"The Mass is a sacrifice 'relative to the sacrifice of the cross'. . . . The relation, external by institution and internal by nature, belongs uniquely to the Eucharistic sacrifice. . . . The mystical effusion consists in placing the divine body and blood on the altar under distinct and separate species. Of course Christ is wholly present under either species, yet so that the words of consecration which strike our ears, and the species which strike our eyes, convey a first impression (only to be rectified by reason and faith) of a divided presence. Considering the glorified state of the victim on the one hand, and on the other the manner in which the human memory is awakened by sense perceptions, it seems impossible to devise a better commemoration of the death on the cross. . . . The suspension of the lower life in Christ on the altar [that is, as asserted by Franzelin [2]] is a theological deduction not easily understood; at any rate, it is too dark to throw light upon other dark questions. Again, the state of meat and drink, and all the rest, do not produce in the real victim, that is, Christ glorified, any change for the worst which may be called, or likened to, destruction. Christ dieth no more. The painful efforts of some theologians to inflict at least a semblance of death on the Giver of life, are entirely due to

[1] II. 450-54.   [2] See pp. 388, 389, *supra*.

their narrow notion of sacrifice. If we eliminate the 'change for the worse' from the notion of 'victim,' and replace it by 'a change for the better,' we obtain a notion of the sacrificial act which throws new light upon all sacrifices. That we are justified in so doing, has been shown above." [1]

4. While the opinions thus expressed by Dr. Wilhelm and Dr. Scannell, following Scheeben and Schanz, postulate a very close association of the Eucharistic sacrifice with the sacrifice of our Lord in heaven, they fall short of affirming, though they are not necessarily inconsistent with, characteristic features of the teaching of De Condren and Olier and Thomassin concerning the oneness of the Eucharistic sacrifice with the sacrifice in heaven and the abiding priestly activity of our Lord alike in heaven and on earth. Recent instances of more definite and complete agreement with the French writers of the seventeenth century may be seen in the works of Thalhofer and the Abbé Lepin.

A very complete treatment of this subject occurs in the books *The Sacrifice of the Old and the New Covenants* and *Handbook of Catholic Liturgical Theology* by Dr. Valentin Thalhofer, a Bavarian theologian, who had been Professor of Pastoral Theology in the University of Munich, Director of the Munich Seminary, Dean of the Cathedral and Professor in the Seminary at Eichstætt, and died in 1891. In these treatises Thalhofer sets out his interpretation of the sacrifice of Christ, and supports it by lengthy and detailed discussions of the evidence on the subject from Holy Scripture and the writers of the Church. He regards surrender as an essential element in the offering of sacrifice. There was surrender on the cross when our Lord exhibited the outward acts of submission to death and the inward acts of dedication to the will of God the Father. It is shown in the offering of the same sacrifice in heaven as He maintains abidingly the inner submission which led Him to death and presents the marks of the wounds to which that death was due. It is found also in the Eucharist as He sets forth the same sacrifice in the sacramental separation between His body and His blood. From the Eucharistic sacrifice all sacramental grace and forgiveness of sins and sanctification for the present life of the Church are derived. The following quotations from the treatise *The Sacrifice of the Old and the New Covenants* illustrate his teaching on these points :—

[1] II. 454-458.

398 THE DOCTRINE OF THE HOLY EUCHARIST

"In His soul, in His will, He retains the wholly willing and obedient renunciatory act of the surrender of His life on earth ; and the willing act of His mediation on the cross abides in Him in the form of glory without strife or bitterness. . . . The inner sacrifice was manifested on the cross in the actual shedding of the blood as a visible surrender of the life of the body in death ; the sacrifice of Jesus must be a complete sacrifice, in which both soul and body are included, accomplished throughout the whole Man. That the heavenly sacrifice also relates to the bodily nature of the Lord, that the permanence of the sacrifice of obedience in the soul of Christ must also be manifested somehow in His glorified bodily nature, can be understood of itself ; probably the marks of the wounds which according to Scripture [1] and tradition [2] Christ still bears in His body on high in heaven, are to be considered as the visible, bodily manifestation of the one abiding sacrifice in the soul." [3]

"At the consecration the heavenly High Priest, and with Him His heavenly sacrifice, now enters into the earthly state of time and therefore into the earthly conditions of place ; when the words of transformation are spoken, He makes Himself present on the altar after the manner of the separation, in the form of sacrifice, He places on the altar, also in the state of time, essentially the whole identical sacrifice which He once placed on the cross and continually places on the heavenly altar. There is the same Priest of sacrifice as on the cross, there is the same Victim of sacrifice, namely His holy manhood in soul and body, there is the same act of sacrifice really maintained and renewed (*reproduzirt*) in relation. At the moment of consecration the soul of Jesus is moved by really the same sacrificial obedience and spirit of renunciation as at the time when the Saviour hung on the cross and in the visible shedding of blood accomplished and manifested His sacrificial obedience, as also at the moment of consecration each fibre of the body of Jesus is glowing through and through with really the same devouring sacrificial love as the burning pain that glowed and burnt in all the fibres of the bodily sacrifice hanging on the cross. And that the faithful may be assured, and may so far as is possible have a representation which the senses can discern, that at the consecration there happens what is essentially the same as at the time when the Saviour shed His blood, He is present at the consecration not only under the species of bread but after the manner of the separation. The mysti-

---

[1] Rev. v. 6.
[2] See St. Thomas Aquinas, *S.T.* III. liv. 4.
[3] P. 214.

cal separation of the flesh and blood in the act of the consecration
is the outward form for the invisible act of sacrifice that is identical
with the act of sacrifice on the cross, which Christ during the consecration places on the altar, and manifests Himself as the sensible
subject of the invisible act of sacrifice, as a proof and testimony.
First at the conjunction with the act of sacrifice that is invisible to
us, which Christ makes at the consecration, the separation of the
species has its whole meaning.   When the flesh and blood of Christ
are placed on the altar in a sacramental (not physical) separation,
the body of Christ is really and now surrendered to the sacrificial
death, the blood of Christ is so far shed, that Christ in the act of
the consecration effects essentially that same whole sacrificial action
which He once accomplished in the sensible surrender of His body
to death by means of the shedding of His blood.   In the act of the
consecration the Saviour exercises in His inner being on the altar
essentially the same sacrificial obedience, the same sacrificial love,
which He once exercised on the cross in the sacrifice of His body
and the shedding of His blood, and in this way He can say by His
minister at each holy Mass with literal truth, This is My body, which
(even now) is sacrificed ; this is My blood, that (even now) is shed.
When at the Last Supper Christ consecrated and instituted the
Eucharistic sacrifice, He had not yet outwardly sacrificed His body,
He had not yet visibly shed His blood ; but in His will He had
already decreed the sacrifice of His body and the shedding of His
blood as God required ; and just at the moment when He consecrated He aroused in Himself the intensive act of the sacrifice of
His body to death with the shedding of blood, and in this inner act,
so far as was then possible, He accomplished the sacrifice of His life,
He already actually destroyed it so far as it could come to outward
destruction in consequence of that inner act, in obedience to the
destruction of His life willed by God He entered on His determined act of will, already there was essentially the destruction of
His life; already the sacrifice of His body, the shedding of His
blood, so that the Saviour could say with entire conformity to
truth, 'the body which is being given for you, the cup which is
being poured out for you'.[1]   Since the Saviour could thus actually
anticipate the sacrifice of the cross, although it did not yet exist in
outward history, it is not in the least inconceivable that, when it has
been outwardly accomplished as an historical fact, He can essentially renew or continue (*recapituliren oder continuiren*) it in His will.
Anticipation and renewal (*Recapitulation*) exist only in their inner

[1] St. Luke xxii. 19, 20.

relation to the historical, sensible offering of sacrifice on the cross ;. if this had not followed that inner act of sacrifice which was accomplished at the Last Supper, the latter would have had no value, at least it would not have had the value of an act of sacrifice ; just so since the death of Jesus the act of consecration has the value and the meaning of an act of sacrifice only because of its inner relation to that sacrificial death, which as a willing surrender of life it affirms anew and continues (*continuirt*) and renews (*recapitulirt*). . . . In the days of His flesh Christ exercised His eternal priesthood by means of the shedding of His blood and the surrender and offering of His life.   At the act of consecration He places on our altars the same sacrificial action of the cross, and manifests Himself therein as the High Priest and Mediator of His Church on earth ; He is . . . the one and only Priest and High Priest of His Church." [1]

" From the Eucharistic sacrifice flows all the expiatory and sanctifying grace which is ministered by the Church and in the Church in Sacraments and sacramental rites. . . . The Eucharistic altar of sacrifice is the source of the birthplace of the new life ; the vanquishing of death and glorifying are grounded and ministered in Sacraments and blessings.   Be it never so impossible to establish the inner relation of the sacrifice to the Sacraments and the sacramental rites in detail and exactly, in general and on the whole it may stand unalterably fast that it is related to them as the source to the streams and brooks, which it feeds, as the beating heart to the veins, by which the life blood runs into all the limbs of the body." [2]

The teaching of Thalhofer on the Eucharistic sacrifice was the object of a very severe attack from Father Ferdinand Stentrup, a member of the Society of Jesus, a theological professor in the University of Innsbruck.[3]   As an advocate of the theory of De Lugo and Franzelin,[4] Stentrup was naturally strongly opposed to the ideas of Thalhofer on the sacrifice in heaven, and he went through Thalhofer's arguments in order and in detail with a view to refuting them ; further, he charged Thalhofer with resuscitating the error, which Stentrup like some older theologians ascribed to Catharinus,[5] of making the Eucharistic sacrifice independent of the sacrifice of the cross and of parallel value and power and application.[6]   A great part

---

[1] Pp. 261-63, 266.   [2] Pp. 267, 268.

[3] In his *Prælectiones Dogmaticæ de Verbo Incarnato*, II. ii. 173-532.

[4] See pp. 373-77, 388, 389, *supra*.   [5] See pp. 70-75, *supra*.

[6] Stentrup, *op. cit.* II. ii. 522, 523.

of the passage on which this last charge was based has been quoted above. It is probable that Stentrup's hostility to Thalhofer's teaching led him to an estimate of the meaning of the passage which he would have avoided if he had been more careful to remember the stress which Thalhofer lays on the value of the sacrifice of the cross, and the connection of the Eucharistic sacrifice with it as well as with the sacrifice in heaven.

The defence of the theory of De Condren and Olier closely associating the Eucharistic sacrifice with the sacrifice of our Lord in heaven by the Abbé Lepin, formerly Director of the Seminary of St. Sulpice at Issy near Paris and now Professor in the Seminary at Lyons, occurs in his book *The Idea of Sacrifice in the Christian Religion*, which was published in 1897. In his view the sacrifice of our Lord cannot be separated from any part of His human life. He was a Priest and a Victim, and He offered sacrifice, when He was conceived in the womb of His holy Mother, during His mortal life, on the cross, in His resurrection, and at His ascension. He now offers an abiding and eternal sacrifice in heaven ; and He offers sacrifice on the altar on earth in His Eucharistic life. In spite of all the separate acts involved, there is one sacrifice of the surrender of His manhood to God the Father in His dedication to do the Father's will.

"It is by His Incarnation that Jesus Christ received His essential characteristic of Mediator between God and man. It is by His Incarnation that He was constituted the supreme Priest, the High Pontiff of the true religion." [1]

" Being thus consecrated in His Incarnation by the anointing of the Holy Ghost eternal and perfect Priest after the order of Melchizedek, Jesus Christ is also constituted as the Victim of His priesthood." [2]

"Because He is about to expiate by His blood the sin of man, and to reconcile mankind to God by His death, Jesus Christ is a Victim devoted to be sacrificed at the first moment of His life. . . . At the first moment of His life . . . the Saviour offers Himself to promote the glory of His Father by His sufferings and by His death. . . . Jesus Christ is no sooner Priest and in possession of His Victim than He begins the formal act of His adorable sacrifice." [3]

" Inaugurated in the womb of Blessed Mary, the sacrifice of the Saviour continues throughout the different parts of His hidden life

[1] Pp. 89, 90.   [2] P. 94.   [3] Pp. 98, 99, 100.

and His public life. . . . The oblation of Himself which Jesus made at His entrance into the world, He continues thenceforth without ceasing." [1]

" From the Agony in the garden to the last breath on the cross Jesus continues His spiritual surrender of atoning worship, uninterrupted since the first moment of the Incarnation, and, as we have seen, inseparable from His holy soul. On the other hand, He does not cease to make to His Father that oblation of Himself which has marked every moment of His life. Lastly, the physical surrender, realised thus far in the humiliation and sufferings and mortality, continues and is completed in the supreme lowliness of the passion, the bloody sacrifice and death. . . . There is then, in spite of the novelty of the outward circumstances, the same offering infinitely acceptable to God, which we have seen inaugurated in the most pure womb of the Virgin, and continued without interruption throughout the mortal life of the Saviour. It is ever the same adorable sacrifice, the one and unceasing sacrifice of our Lord Jesus Christ." [2]

" The sacrifice of Jesus Christ continues during the time when His soul was separated from His body. From the hour when He breathed His last breath to the morning of the resurrection the work of His death really existed. . . . In the real sacrifice of our Lord Jesus Christ it is at the resurrection that the consummation of the Victim and the communion with God is fulfilled. . . . The mystery of the resurrection continues and completes, from an outward point of view, the adorable sacrifice of our Lord Jesus Christ. Still more, if we consider attentively the inner side of this great mystery, we shall find everything which is required for the continuation and completion of the real sacrifice. Certainly, the holy manhood of Jesus does not any more undergo an actual expiatory surrender ; the time of the actual expiation has passed ; the death and suffering and humiliation have no more place in it because it has been wholly glorified in God. The soul of the Saviour, none the less, continues that inner surrender of atoning worship which it has never ceased since the first moment of the Incarnation, and which it can henceforth rest on the infinite merits of the actual and physical surrender, realised during its mortal life. On the other hand, His holy body continues to undergo a kind of surrender, but a surrender new and infinitely honourable, in that it is absorbed by the glory and as it were loses its own nature in the fire of the Godhead. . . . This holy manhood, thus gloriously sur-

[1] P. 115.   [2] Pp. 140, 141.

rendered, Jesus, ever Priest, does not cease to offer to His Father.
. . . There is ever then, although in a new condition, the same
adorable sacrifice of our Lord Jesus Christ." [1]

"This perfect sacrifice of Jesus Christ, consummated in glory,
does not cease during the forty days when He still remained on
earth. It continues, ever actual, ever infinitely acceptable to God,
to the great day of the ascension. Nevertheless, this new mystery
completes, from an outward point of view, the work begun by the
resurrection, that is to say, the obvious consummation of the Victim,
and the manifestation of the communion with God." [2]

"The ascension of Jesus Christ to heaven fulfils the sacrificial
rite of the oblation of the blood, represented in the ancient sacrifices ; it completes the manifestation of the consummation of the
adorable Victim and also the Communion with God ; thereby it
brings the sacrifice of the Saviour to its perfection. But, does it
also mark the end ? Or, does the divine sacrifice continue in
heaven ? . . . The sacrifice of Jesus Christ continues eternally in
heaven. . . . On the day of the ascension Jesus Christ, His consummation being completed, entered on the possession of His
eternal priesthood. . . . This unceasing presentation by Jesus
Christ of His body marked with the scars of the passion, and of
His blood that was shed for us on the cross, is a really sacrificial
oblation, the eternal act of a real sacrifice. . . . In spite of the
change in the outward conditions of the Victim, it is ever the same
homage of perfect religion rendered by the incarnate Word to His
Father. It is ever the same and one sacrifice of our Lord Jesus
Christ, infinitely acceptable to the divine majesty. . . . This is the
great and sublime reality of the heavenly sacrifice. All is divine,
the Priest, the Victim, the Altar, the Temple." [3]

"The same Jesus Christ, High Priest, who in heaven fulfils
eternally the act of His sacrifice, likewise offers Himself here on
earth under the Eucharistic species, presenting to His Father the
infinite worship of His holy soul, and the satisfaction, ever real,
ever perfect, which He rests on the unceasing oblation of His holy
body. . . . The faith teaches us that Jesus Christ is present whole
and complete under the species of bread, whole and complete under
the species of wine ; and yet His body is represented to us as
separated from His blood. . . . The double consecration reproduces
mystically the sacrifice of the Saviour. . . . Absolute in other respects, the sacrifice of the Mass is also essentially relative to the

[1] Pp. 149, 151, 157, 158, 159, 160.   [2] P. 161.
[3] Pp. 167, 168, 169, 176, 188, 196.
26 *

sacrifice of Calvary, which it renews by a mystical representation.
. . . The inner essence of this sacrifice appears to reside, not exactly in the placing of Jesus Christ under the species, but in His
being under the two separate species in representation of the bloody
sacrifice of the cross. . . . The sacrifice of the Mass is ever the one
and unceasing sacrifice of our Lord Jesus Christ, the sacrifice begun
on earth from the Incarnation to the ascension; continued, so as
never to end, in heaven; brought to our altars in time, while we
wait for the blessed eternity. Throughout these three phases,
therefore, the sacrifice of Jesus Christ is one under the different
forms. As expiatory on earth, it was fulfilled in a physical surrender
of humiliation and suffering and death, begun at the Incarnation
and finished on the cross. In the resurrection and eternally in
heaven, it is continued in the consummation of glory, wherein it
has the real mark of the expiatory surrender of the past. In the
Eucharist, it is perpetuated on earth, through space and time, in an
outward real surrender, although without humiliation properly so
called and without suffering, yet with a real mark of the former expiatory offering. In other words, the Mass is the sacrifice of heaven
brought to the altar by the presence of Jesus Christ under the
Eucharistic species, but placed under a particular form which makes
it a real sacrifice specially for the Church militant." [1]

"With Jesus Christ surrendered under the species of bread and
wine and marked by the signs of His death our Communion with
the adorable Victim must be made here on earth. The Communion
is made according to the nature of the offering and the condition of
the communicants. In heaven, where the glorious manhood of Christ
has no veils to hide its glory from the gaze of the saints, and where
the saints themselves are freed from the bondage of the flesh, the
Communion is wholly spiritual. On earth, where the faithful are
still subject to sense, and where the divine Victim is presented in
a state fitted to their condition, the Communion is for the time
spiritual and bodily (*matérielle*). . . . We do not communicate only
with Jesus Christ incarnate; it is also with Jesus Christ sacrificed
for our salvation, raised for our justification; we communicate with
the Victim, offered and completed, of the real sacrifice. . . . The
Communion of the Eucharist begins to conform our body to the most
holy flesh of the Saviour, while we wait for our share in His glorious
consummation, of which it now gives us the pledge. Nevertheless,
the bodily eating is chiefly for the Communion of the spirit; and
the Jesus of the Eucharist comes to the body chiefly to reach the

[1] Pp. 202, 214, 215, 219, 229, 230.

soul. . . . . Wonderful Communion of time while we wait for that of eternity! Communion with Jesus Christ hidden under the species, while we wait for the Communion of heaven which shall be made without concealment or veil! The ancient law had only shadows ; the new has the reality together with the figure ; in heaven the reality will be unmingled. Here on earth we have the first-fruits ; there in heaven we shall have the fulness ; on the earth it is a foretaste ; the full delight will be in heaven."[1]

V.

In the period following the Council of Trent there has not been an absence of discussion and controversy on subtle questions as to the power of the celebrating priest to apply the benefits of the sacrifice of the Mass, and the conditions of the exercise of any such power. On these matters it may suffice to quote a very few representative theologians of the sixteenth and seventeenth centuries, the assertions of the Council of Pistoia and the condemnation of those assertions by Pope Pius VI. at the end of the eighteenth century, and a modern divine.

1. Melchior Cano[2] concluded, that, so far as "satisfaction"—as distinct from "impetration"—is concerned, a greater benefit might be bestowed through the offering of the sacrifice for one person individually than if it were offered for him as one among many.

"They who do not offer do not receive an equal part if the offering is made for many and if it is made for one only. So that, if a priest of his own accord without any request from any friend should sacrifice for those who are absent, I say that it does not avail as much to the many as it would avail to one, if it was offered for one of them individually. I speak as regards satisfaction ; for as regards impetration there is no less force in the sacrifice which is offered for many than in that which is offered for one alone. And this is common to all prayers, which suffer no loss as to impetration because they are made on behalf of many. But the helpers and hearers of Masses, those also who support the priest or in any way promote the sacrifice, really offer the sacrifice, and therefore each one receives a share of that offering in proportion to his devotion. Cer-

---

[1] Pp. 233, 234, 236, 239, 241, 242. *Cf.* the reference to the identity of the heavenly and the earthly sacrifice in M. Germain Breton's *La Messe*, pp. 55, 56.

[2] See p. 356, *supra.*

tainly the more closely the cause aiding the sacrifice is joined to the
principal cause of it, the more it satisfies for penalty, so that a priest
more than a deacon, a deacon more than a sub-deacon, a sub-deacon
more than an acolyte, an acolyte more than one of the congregation ;
but he who has given to the priest the necessary payment for his
sustenance excels each of these.   And these also will satisfy the
more, the more devoutly and religiously they perform, each their
own duty. . . . We see in the first cause of natural things that,
although it is itself of infinite power, yet by means of second causes
it produces finite effects so great and of such a kind as the power
and nature of the assisting causes require.   And the priest does not
impose limits on the sacrifice from his merit and holiness, but from
his intention and application, whereby he applies the power of the
sacrifice to this one or that, for whom he offers.   As by means of the
intention of the minister the blood of Christ is applied to little children who are baptised, and a fixed degree of grace is conferred, the
degree which is not assigned by the holiness of the minister but by
the will of Christ (for what degree it is, is unknown to mortals), so to
those for whom the sacrifice is offered, if they do not themselves at
the same time offer it, a fixed degree of penalty is remitted, a degree
of which we are ignorant, which Christ has appointed by His will.
But, as adults receive the more grace from Baptism, the more religiously and devoutly they receive it, so from the sacrifice he will
receive the greater advantage who shall offer it with greater holiness
and fervour.   To little children the washing by a particular minister
defines the power of the cross according to a fixed degree of grace,
which we believe to be equal in them all, because in them all the
disposition is equal ; but on adults, since in them there is not the
same disposition, but it differs in each individual, there is not the
same degree of grace conferred, but it differs in different cases.   So
the offering of the individual priest determines the universal and
infinite power of the sacrifice either to a fixed and equal remission
of penalty in those who are related to the sacrifice in the same way,
or also to an unequal remission in those who, since they are assisting
causes of the sacrifice, are affected in different ways, that is, well,
better, best."

Vasquez [2] expresses the opinion that the sacrifice is of as much
benefit to individuals if it is applied to a greater number as if it
is applied to fewer, for the reasons that

" a spiritual good, which belongs to the communication of itself, is

---

[1] *De loc. theol.* XII. xi. 86.   [2] See p. 361, *supra.*

like a spirit in relation to place, so that, as a spirit is whole in a whole place and whole in any part of a place, so also a spiritual good, such as is the fruit of the Mass, is entirely communicated whole to many and whole to individuals. Secondly, it is customary to explain and confirm this by the example of a bodily thing, because the same light of a lantern, when it is applied to many things on which it sheds light, does not give less light to each of them than it would if it were applied to fewer or to one only; and the same sound, when it is extended to many and is heard by them, affects the hearing of the individuals in the same way as if it were extended to a smaller number or to one only. Again, there is a proof from reason, because . . . by means of this Sacrament is applied to us the power of the merits of Christ, which, in that it is applied to many, does not benefit individuals less than if it were applied to fewer; therefore this sacrifice, by which it is applied, in the same way will benefit individuals, when it is offered for many, as if it were offered for fewer." [1]

Suarez [2] holds a different view from Vasquez, and maintains that a greater benefit is bestowed by means of a more individual offering of the sacrifice.

"I say, first, when many assemble together with the priest for an identical sacrifice, all and each, insofar as they are offerers, receive the whole fruit, not less than if one only were offering; whence in this sense the fruit of this sacrifice can in a kind of way be called infinite, or rather infinitely increasable so far as extension is concerned. . . . I say, secondly, the effect of the sacrifice answering to the offering of the priest, namely, that which he can offer on behalf of others, is finite and one only. Wherefore, if it be offered for many—whether with different special intentions or with one common intention only, as for the people or the community—the fruit will be lessened in individuals, and so much the more as they are more in number, supposing the application is uniform. . . . I say, thirdly, this sacrifice of itself has infinite worth for impetrating; and therefore, on its part, when it is offered on behalf of many, it does not benefit individuals less, so far as impetration is concerned, than if it were offered for one only, although it could happen differently so as not to benefit individuals equally." [3]

De Lugo [4] follows Suarez on this point, and in the course of his discussion bases an argument on the inferences which may be

---

[1] *In tert. part. S. Thom.* ccxxxi. 2. [2] See p. 367, *supra.*
[3] *In tert. part. D. Thom.* lxxix. 12 (4, 7, 8). [4] See pp. 373, 374, *supra.*

drawn from the practice of the Church. After mentioning
Vasquez's view,[1] he says :—

"The more common and truer opinion denies simply this in-
finity in the sacrifice of the Mass. . . . It is proved, because otherwise it would follow that the sacrifice is applied in vain or almost in
vain for some one departed person in particular ; for, if it is of so
great benefit to all and each as if it were applied for one only, why
are not all Masses applied for all the departed, nay, also for all the
living and for all other needs? Again, it would follow that the
priest who is under an obligation to say Mass for two or for three
could fulfil his obligation by offering one Mass for all, since it would
be of as much benefit to them as if it were offered for each of them
individually." [2]

2. The Council of Pistoia was held in September, 1786, being
summoned by Scipio de Ricci, the Bishop of Pistoia, largely
through the influence of Leopold, the Grand-Duke of Parma.
. . . The general attitude of this council was in the direction of
Jansenism and Gallicanism,[3] and of some reforms in practice, such
as the use of the vernacular in public worship. In the course of
statements in regard to the Eucharistic sacrifice, some share in the
sacrifice was allowed to those who might be present at Mass without communicating sacramentally on the ground of their Spiritual
Communion, and the belief that the celebrating priest can apply
the fruits of the sacrifice was condemned.

"Since the participation in the offering (*vittima*) is an essential
part of the sacrifice, the holy synod would desire that the faithful
should communicate every time that they are present. It does not
condemn as unlawful those Masses in which those who are present
do not communicate sacramentally, inasmuch as by receiving spiritually they participate, though in a less way, in the offering (*vittima*)." [4]

"We believe that the offering is universal, yet so that there
may be made in the liturgy a special commemoration of certain
persons both living and departed by praying to God especially for
them, yet not that we believe that it is in the power of the priest
to apply the fruits of the sacrifice to whom he will ; rather, we condemn this error as greatly offending against the laws of God, who

_____

[1] See pp. 406, 407, *supra*.   [2] *De Euch.* XIX. xii. 246.
[3] See *e.g.* Cheetham, *A History of the Christian Church since the Reformation*, pp. 99-109, 231.
[4] Martin and Petit, *Coll. Conc. Recent. Eccl. Univ.* ii. 1040.

alone distributes the fruits of the sacrifice to whom He will, and in what measure pleases Him." [1]

Eighty-five propositions of the Council of Pistoia were condemned by Pope Pius VI. in the Bull *Auctorem fidei*, dated 28th August, 1794. Among these, the two statements quoted above were condemned. The former of them—that relating to "the participation in the offering" as "an essential part of the sacrifice"—was described as "false, erroneous, suspected of heresy, and smacking of it,"

"insofar as it implies that any thing is lacking to the essence of the sacrifice in that sacrifice which is performed either with no one present or with those present who do not partake of the offering (*victima*) either sacramentally or spiritually, and as if those Masses are to be condemned as unlawful in which, while the priest alone communicates, there is no one present who communicates either sacramentally or spiritually." [2]

The latter of the two statements quoted above—that rejecting "the power of the priest to apply the fruits of the sacrifice to whom he will"—was described as "false, rash, destructive, hurtful to the Church, leading to error elsewhere condemned in the case of Wyclif,"

"being so understood that, besides the peculiar commemoration and prayer, the special offering or application of the sacrifice which is made by the priest is of no more benefit, other things being equal, to those on whose behalf it is applied than to others, as if no special fruit resulted from the special application, which the Church advises and orders to be made on behalf of fixed persons or orders of persons, particularly by pastors for their flocks." [3]

3. A statement by Dr. van Noort [4] may be quoted as representative of an attitude ordinarily taken by Roman Catholic divines at the present time on the subject of the application of the benefits of the sacrifice of the Mass.

"First, every Mass is offered, not only in the person of the whole Church, but also on behalf of the whole Church; therefore there is some fruit which pertains to the whole Church, that is, to each of its members, and indeed, as certainly seems to be the case, accord-

---

[1] Martin and Petit, *op. cit.* ii. 1041.   [2] *Ibid.* 1268, 1269.
[3] *Ibid.* 1269.   [4] See p. 390, *supra*.

ing to the measure both of disposition and of the hierarchical place which they severally fill in the Church, the general or universal fruit. Nay, since all men pertain to the Church at least potentially and as it were being owed, this fruit can in a sort of way benefit them all indirectly ; whence also we pray at the oblation of the chalice that the sacrifice ' may ascend with the odour of sweetness on behalf of our salvation and of that of the whole world '. Secondly, every Mass is offered in the person of Christ and of the Church by the priest as a public minister, whence it is easily understood that to this ministry as such there corresponds a peculiar part of the fruits the personal or special fruit. And the fruit of this kind, the proportion being preserved, pertains also to the faithful who share in the act of offering. Nor are you to think that this personal fruit of the celebrant and of those who offer with him is the same as that fruit which we have explained above. . . . For the fruit both general and personal no peculiar intention is required on the part of the priest, for they follow the very nature of the sacrifice, as it was instituted by Christ. Since then they are as it were applied by Christ the Institutor, they cannot be transferred to others. Moreover, it is certain that these fruits are not lessened to individuals because many persons receive them at the same time, for they are received by individuals as in some way offering them. Thirdly, we have it from the tradition of the Church that the sacrifice of the Mass can be specially offered on behalf of fixed persons, or to obtain a fixed end. It is clear, therefore, that, besides the general and personal fruit, there is given a certain intermediate fruit, which depends on the free disposition and application of the priest, the middle or intentional fruit, which is also called special, that is, which pertains to those on whose behalf the priest specially applies the Mass by his own intention. Concerning this fruit there is a difference of opinion whether it is finite in extension or not, that is, whether it is so limited that it is lessened for individuals if the Mass is applied on behalf of many persons at the same time. Since the matter depends on positive institution, the question cannot be solved by internal reasons alone. And yet the traditional practice of the Church so favours the limitation of the intentional fruit that the contrary opinion does not seem very probable. Certainly it is the custom of the Church that Mass should be offered, nay, should be offered most often, for one or a few persons only. Now, if the middle fruit were unlimited in extension, a practice of this kind would be very hurtful, since others without any reason would be excluded from participation in the fruit of it. Many theologians

restrict this limitation to the propitiatory effect alone,[1] understanding, if I am not mistaken, the appeasing of the divine wrath and
the remission of the penalty of time only ; but their reasons are not
of very great force ; wherefore we are of opinion that each effect,
both propitiatory and impetratory, is limited in extension." [2]

VI.

Separate notice may be taken of a theory of the Eucharistic
sacrifice which was suggested by the Spanish Jesuit theologian
Cardinal Cienfuegos, who was born in 1657 and died in 1739.
In his treatise entitled *The Life Hidden or Veiled by the Sacramental Species* Cardinal Cienfuegos followed the opinion of some
earlier theologians that, while our Lord does not use His bodily
senses in the Eucharist by any natural power, nevertheless He
does so act supernaturally.[3] Upon this opinion he built up a
theory that in the Eucharistic sacrifice our Lord offers this life
of the senses and suspends these vital actions until the mystical
representation of the resurrection in the commixture of the consecrated elements at the placing of a fragment of the host in
the chalice ; and that this suspension constitutes the sacrifice.

" This life Christ the Lord Himself as High Priest alone sacrifices
and offers inasmuch as by the sway of His human will He suspends
or removes the vital actions miraculously produced, and determines
not to elicit any further action or to use the instrumental power of
producing them according to His will, until by a kind of resurrection
in the commemoration of the resurrection in the commixture of the
body and the blood He resumes the actual life and free use of
instrumental power." [4]

The usual judgment on this theory is probably accurately
expressed by Cardinal Franzelin when he says that the prudent
theologian will beware of it.[5]

[1] See p. 405, *supra.*   Cf. Franzelin, *Tractatus de SS. Eucharistiæ
Sacramento et Sacrificio,* pp. 372, 373.
[2] *Tractatus de Sacramentis,* pp. 392, 393.
[3] See *e.g.* St. Bonaventura, *Sent.* IV. x. 1, 2, quoted on vol. i. pp. 337,
338, *supra ;* and *cf.* Suarez, *In tert. part. D. Thom.* liii. 3. Among recent
writers, this opinion has been described as " pious and very probable," though
needing caution, by Franzelin ; see his *Tract. de SS. Euch. Sacram. et
Sacrif.* pp. 178, 179. That our Lord in some way uses His senses in the
Eucharist is maintained at length in Dalgairns, *The Holy Communion,*
pp. 130-56.
[4] V. iii. 1 (num. 37), p. 359.   [5] *Op. cit.* p. 403.

VII.

It has been observed in passing that the great post-Tridentine theologians of the Church of Rome have adhered to the Tridentine teaching in regard to the Eucharistic presence; and it has not been necessary to dwell at any length on what they have thus said. The reality of the presence of the body and blood of Christ, the conversion of the whole substance of the bread and wine into the substance of the body and blood by Transubstantiation, the continued existence of the species of bread and wine without their natural substance but with their natural properties and forces, the spiritual and supernatural manner of the presence and change, have been steadily maintained. It remains to notice some bye-paths of thought and points of interest on the subject of the Eucharistic presence since the time of the Council of Trent.

1. The Council of Pistoia[1] affirmed the cessation of the existence of the whole substance of bread and wine, the presence of the whole Christ in each species and in every fragment of either species when divided, and the fact that in the Eucharist "the body of Christ is not a natural (*animale*) body but spiritual, and life-giving, and that it is in the Eucharist not after the manner of a natural (*naturale*) body but after a supernatural and spiritual manner". The word Transubstantiation was not used, and pastors were exhorted to avoid scholastic questions in instructing their people.[2] This statement was condemned by Pope Pius VI. in the Bull *Auctorem fidei*[3] because of the lack of any mention of Transubstantiation or conversion, and described as "hurtful, derogatory to the exposition of Catholic truth about the dogma of Transubstantiation, favouring heretics"—

"insofar as by an ill-advised and suspicious omission of this kind the knowledge both of an article pertaining to faith and of a word consecrated by the Church to protect its profession against heretics is taken away, and as it tends therefore to produce forgetfulness of it, as if it were a matter of a merely scholastic question."[4]

---

[1] See p. 408, *supra*.
[2] Martin and Petit, *Coll. Conc. Recent. Eccl. Univ.* ii. 1036.
[3] See p. 409, *supra*.   [4] Martin and Petit, *op. cit.* ii. 1269.

2. The Cartesian philosophy [1] with its theory of existence as dependent on consciousness was widely prevalent in the latter half of the seventeenth century. Such a theory not unnaturally affected the ideas about the Eucharist of those who held it, and the notion which Emmanuel Maignan [2] appears to have adopted, that the accidents were real only to consciousness and without actually existing were impressed on the senses by God, was due to it. Apart from certain difficult questions as to the method of the existence and influence of the accidents,[3] the theologians of the Church of Rome have been agreed ; and they have concurred in teaching, in accordance with the Tridentine Catechism,[4] that the accidents have real existence and entity. This fact may be illustrated by quoting from writers who do not altogether agree on the philosophical questions concerning the method of the existence and influence of the accidents, namely, Cardinal Franzelin, Dr. van Noort, Dr. Wilhelm and Dr. Scannell, and Bishop Hedley.

Cardinal Franzelin writes :—

" The fathers and the Universal Church constantly distinguish two things in the Sacrament, the visible part, which is the Sacrament only, and the invisible part, the body of Christ, which is both the Sacrament and the thing of the Sacrament. . . . The Sacrament is understood by all to be some sensible objective thing, not a modification in our senses and in surrounding objects. They gain nothing who say that the species are indeed something objectively real and not only a modification in our senses and in surrounding objects but that this objective reality is nothing else than the operation of God from that space where the bread was before. For the operation of God as distinct from its effect is nothing else than God Himself, and no one has said that God Himself, however He may be formally viewed as working, is a sacrament or sensible sign of a sacred thing ! On this hypothesis therefore no objective reality outside our senses and besides the modifications of surrounding bodies which can be called a Sacrament remains. . . . To this conviction of the objective reality of the visible part of the Sacra-

[1] Due to René Descartes, born 1596, died 1650.

[2] Born 1601, died 1676 ; see *e.g.* his *Philosophia Sacra*, XXII. iv. vi. (vol. i. pp. 866-71, 874-88).

[3] See *e.g.* Franzelin, *Tractatus de SS. Eucharistiæ Sacramento et Sacrificio*, pp. 286-92 ; van Noort, *Tractatus de Sacramentis*, pp. 282-88.

[4] See pp. 102, 103, *supra.*

ment not only does the general sense of the ordinary terminology of the Church correspond ; . . . but there are also in the fathers frequent and most skilful declarations of the physical reality of the sensible species and explanations of this in harmony with the desition of the substance of the bread and wine." [1]

Dr. van Noort says :—

" Since the accidents, which are the proper object of sensible cognition, really remain, and since the intellect, the proper object of which is the substance, is preserved from error by means of faith, there is no deception either of the senses or of the mind in the Holy Sacrament. Wherefore it is in an improper sense only that we sing, ' Sight, taste, touch in Thee are deceived '." [2]

Dr. Wilhelm and Dr. Scannell write :—

" We need not here enter into the philosophical or scientific bearings of Transubstantiation. We may observe that the doctrine is inconsistent only with idealism, and that it is not bound up with any ultra-realistic theories. The Council of Trent, when defining the change of substance, studiously avoids the use of the term ' accident,' the usual scholastic correlative of substance, and speaks of ' species ' ($\epsilon \hat{\iota} \delta o \varsigma$), appearances, or phenomena. It is commonly held, however, that these are not merely subjective impressions, but have some sort of corresponding reality." [3]

Bishop Hedley says :—

" After the consecration the qualities of the bread remain as external realities. It will not do to say that it is only our senses which continue—God being willing—to be affected just as if the bread were still there. Neither is it sufficient to say that the almighty power of God continues to excite in the air or the ether the same vibrations which were set in motion by the bread as long as it was there. Almighty God could certainly do all this. But the peremptory proof that this does not happen in the Holy Eucharist is that, if that were all, there would be no Sacrament. The Sacrament of the Eucharist lies in the consecrated species. Our Lord's body is contained by them ; but it is not that sacred

[1] *Tractatus de SS. Eucharistiæ Sacramento et Sacrificio*, pp. 272, 273.

[2] *Tractatus de Sacramentis*, p. 288. The quotation is from the hymn of St. Thomas Aquinas quoted on vol. i. 351, *supra*. The meaning of St. Thomas obviously was that the senses of sight and taste and touch cannot discern the reality of the presence of Christ.

[3] *Manual of Catholic Theology*, ii. 419, 420.

body in and by itself that is the Sacrament. For a Sacrament is an 'outward sign'; that is, it is something which is part of the world apprehended by sense. The species, therefore, which contain or present to sense that body which in itself is (in the Holy Eucharist) outside of and beyond all sensitive cognition, must be external and real. It would be impossible to understand how there could be a Sacrament if the vehicle of the Sacrament (so to speak) were only an excitation of the sense-nerve, or a motion of air-waves, seemingly produced by an external object, but really not so produced at all. It may be objected that after all the bread, which seems to produce them, is not there, and therefore there can be no reality producing them. But that is just the point. The substance of bread is no longer there; but what we hold is that the real qualities 'remain'. This too is, no doubt, miraculous—a transcendent miracle. But we are not here concerned to diminish the number of miracles. We have to save the reality of the Sacrament. . . . Although the doctrine of the real presence requires . . . that the species, qualities, or accidents which survive the conversion must be more than forms of the mind or affections of the sensitive apparatus, yet that doctrine does not require that we should hold any special theory of sense-operation. What we must maintain may be thus expressed: Material substance is objective and not merely subjective; material substance has certain means of impressing the human sense; in the Eucharistic conversion the impression-force of the substance of bread remains just as it was after the bread has ceased to be. The only opponents, therefore, that the Catholic doctrine has amongst physicists are those who deny either that material force is an objective reality or that its impression-force is an objective reality. It is in this sense that the 'accidents' must be said to persist. And persisting thus, they continue to play the same part in the physical universe as they, or the elements to which they belong, would have played had there been no Eucharistic conversion. They impress the senses as before. They affect other material substances just as if the bread or the wine were still there. They are themselves subject to physical alteration from their surroundings; and if such alteration goes so far as to destroy them, or to leave them no longer such as bread or wine naturally possesses and demands, the Eucharistic presence itself ceases to be there beneath them." [1]

3. Parallel to the care taken to insist on the reality of the accidents of bread and wine in the consecrated Sacrament has

[1] *The Holy Eucharist*, pp. 62-64.

been the rejection of views which have tended to minimise the Tridentine doctrine of the conversion of the whole substance of the elements of bread and wine. On 7th July, 1875, the Sacred Congregation issued a decree declaring that an explanation of Transubstantiation in the following terms was not to be tolerated :—

"1. As the formal state (*ratio*) of personality (*hypostasis*) is to be by itself (*per se*), or to exist by itself (*per se*), so the formal state (*ratio*) of substance is to be in itself, and not actually to be sustained in another as it were first subject ; for these two are rightly to be distinguished : to be by itself (*per se*), which is the formal state (*ratio*) of personality (*hypostasis*), and to be in itself, which is the formal state (*ratio*) of substance.

"2. Wherefore, as the human nature in Christ is not personal (*hypostasis*), because it does not exist by itself (*per se*), but was assumed by a higher divine Person (*hypostasis*), so finite substance, for instance the substance of bread, ceases to be substance by this only, and without any other change of itself, that it is sustained supernaturally in something else so as no longer to be in itself but in something else as in a first subject.

"3. Hence the Transubstantiation or conversion of the whole substance of bread into the substance of the body of Christ our Lord can be explained in this way, that the body of Christ, while it is substantially present in the Eucharist, sustains the nature of bread, which simply by this and without any other change of itself ceases to be substance, because it is no longer in itself but in something else sustaining it ; and therefore the nature of bread indeed remains, but the formal state (*ratio*) of substance ceases in it ; and therefore there are not two substances, but one only, namely, that of the body of Christ.

"4. Therefore in the Eucharist the matter and form of the elements of bread remain ; but now, supernaturally existing in something else, they have not the state (*ratio*) of substance, but they have the state (*ratio*) of supernatural accident, not as if they should affect the body of Christ after the manner of natural accidents, but in this only that they are sustained by the body of Christ in the way which has been described." [1]

---

[1] Denzinger, *Enchiridion*, §§ 1684-87. The decree does not state by whom this explanation of Transubstantiation was suggested. It is ascribed to Father Bayma in van Noort, *De Sacr.* p. 276. The author has examined all the works of Father Joseph Bayma, of the Society of Jesus (born 1816,

On 14th December, 1887, the Sacred Congregation issued a decree condemning forty propositions extracted from the works of Antonio Rosmini Serbati,[1] of which the following concerned the Eucharist:—

" In the Sacrament of the Eucharist the substance of bread and wine becomes the real flesh and real blood of Christ, when Christ makes it the end of His principle of perception (*eam facit terminum sui principii sentientis*), and quickens it with His life, much in the way in which bread and wine are transubstantiated into our flesh and blood, because they become the end of our principle of perception (*fiunt terminus nostri principii sentientis*).

" When the Transubstantiation is completed, it can be understood that there is added to the glorious body of Christ some part incorporated in it, undivided, and equally glorious.

" In the Sacrament of the Eucharist, by the force of the words the body and blood of Christ is only in that measure which corresponds to the quantity of the substance of bread and wine which is transubstantiated ; the rest of the body of Christ is there by concomitance.

" Since he who does not eat the flesh of the Son of Man and drink His blood has not life in him, and since none the less they who die with the Baptism of water or of blood or of desire undoubtedly attain eternal life, it must be said that to those who in this life have not eaten the body and blood of Christ this heavenly food is supplied in the future life at the very moment of death. Hence also to the saints of the Old Testament Christ could communicate Himself under the species of bread and wine when descending to hell, in order to make them fit for the vision of God." [2]

died 1892), which he has been able to find, but has not discovered any statement on the subject of Transubstantiation. He has never seen either the privately printed edition or the corrected and enlarged manuscript of the *Realis Philosophia*. There is an account of Father Bayma by Father Rickaby in *The Catholic Encyclopædia*, ii. 360.

[1] The founder of the Congregation of the Institute of Charity, born at Rovereto in 1797, died at Stresa in 1855.

[2] Denziger, *Enchiridion*, §§ 1764-67. The passages are from *L'Introduzione del Vangelo secondo Giovanni*, pp. 238, 285, 286, 287. For Rosmini's Eucharistic teaching, see also *Antropologia Soprannaturale*, iii. 372-502. The writings of Rosmini have had a chequered history as regards the attitude of the ecclesiastical authorities. In 1849 his *Project of a Constitution for Italy* and *Five Wounds of the Church* were prohibited by the Congregation of the Index ; and he submitted to the prohibition. He was then charged with errors placed under 327 heads, and in 1854 was acquitted by

418 THE DOCTRINE OF THE HOLY EUCHARIST

A more recent speculation of the Abbé Georgel, to some extent resembling ideas of St. Gregory of Nyssa,[1] that the substance of the bread and wine are converted into the body and blood of Christ because the almighty power of God incorporates them into Christ in much the same way in which our Lord during His mortal life incorporated food into Himself, is not without affinities to the views thus condemned. In this more recent speculation a distinction is made between the glorious body of Christ in heaven and the sacrificial state of His Eucharistic body on earth.[2]

4. There has been an occasional tendency to deduce from the doctrine that the Eucharistic flesh and blood of our Lord are in very truth that sacred manhood which He received from the Blessed Virgin a theory of the presence and reception of the body of the Virgin in the Eucharist as well as of the body of her Son. A passage in the famous commentator Cornelis Cornelissen van den Steen, usually known as Cornelius a Lapide, who was born at Bocholt in 1567 and died at Rome in 1637, may have done something to encourage such an idea, although the writer probably did not mean more than that the flesh and blood in the Eucharist are of the body of which the Blessed Virgin is the mother. His words were:—

"As the saying 'Those who eat me, shall still hunger' is literally true of Christ, whom we eat in the Eucharist, and yet hunger for

the Congregation in the sentence "Dimittantur opera Antonii Rosmini Serbati". In January, 1882, Pope Leo XIII. sent a letter to the Bishops of Milan, Turin, and Vercelli deprecating the discussion of some philosophical questions in the journals of North Italy and was understood to refer to Rosmini in the sentence "Iamvero metuendum est, ne hæc animorum concordia dirimatur contrariis partium studiis, quibus materiam præbet quædam inter Insubres ephemerides, et doctrina clari unius viri, cuius inter recentiores philosophos nomen percrebuit": see *Acta Leonis XIII.* i. 251. In 1887, as mentioned above, forty propositions from his writings were condemned by the Sacred Congregation. There is considerable doubt how far the apparent meaning of them really represented what Rosmini meant. See Lockhart, *Life of Antonio Rosmini Serbati*, Appendix ii., inserted in 1888, after the publication in 1886, at the end of vol. ii.; and the elaborate discussion in Morando, *Esame Critico delle xl Proposizioni Rosminiane condonnate della S.R.U. Inquisizione*, of which pp. 573-678 relate to the propositions about the Eucharist.

[1] See vol. i. pp. 72, 73, *supra*.
[2] *Annales de phil. chret.* May, 1901, pp. 175-93.

Him, and desire again to eat Him, so in like manner can it be said truly and literally of the Blessed Virgin. This is wonderful, but true. For as often as we eat the flesh of Christ in the Eucharist, so often do we actually eat in it the flesh of the Blessed Virgin ; for the flesh of Christ is the flesh of the Blessed Virgin ; yea, the very flesh of Christ, before it was detached from the Blessed Virgin in the Incarnation, and given to Christ, was the Blessed Virgin's own flesh, and was informed and animated by her soul. As then we daily hunger for the flesh of Christ in the Eucharist, so also we hunger in it for the flesh of the Blessed Virgin, that we may drink in her virgin endowments and character, and incorporate them in ourselves. And not only priests and Religious, but also all Christians do this ; for the Blessed Virgin feeds all in the Eucharist with her own flesh no less than with the flesh of Christ." [1]

An instance of speculative theology tending to encourage the same idea may be seen in a passage by the popular devotional writer Frederick William Faber, who was born in 1814, was ordained priest in the Church of England in 1839, became a Roman Catholic in 1845, and died in 1863.

" There is some portion of the precious blood which once was Mary's own blood, and which remains still in our Blessed Lord, incredibly exalted by its union with His divine Person, yet still the same. This portion of Himself, it is piously believed, has not been allowed to undergo the usual changes of human substance. . . . He vouchsafed at Mass to show to St. Ignatius the very part of the host which had once belonged to the substance of Mary." [2]

The theory itself of the presence of the Blessed Virgin in the Eucharist has been actually formulated by some writers, of whom it may be sufficient to mention De Vega in the seventeenth century and Oswald in the nineteenth, and to quote the words of Oswald :—

" We maintain a presence of Mary in the Eucharist. . . . We are much inclined to believe an essential co-presence of Mary in her whole person, with body and soul, under the sacred species. . . . The blood of the Lord and the milk of His Virgin Mother are both present in the Sacrament." [3]

---

[1] On Ecclus. xxiv. 29.   [2] *The Precious Blood*, pp. 29, 30.
[3] Oswald, *Dogmat. Mariol.* pp. 177, 179, 183 ; *cf.* Christopher de Vega, *Theol. Mariana.* See Pusey, *Eirenicon*, i. 169-72.

This theory has been viewed with disfavour by the theologians and authorities of the Church of Rome;[1] it has at any rate on one occasion been condemned;[2] the book of Oswald from which the above quotation is taken was placed on the Index of prohibited books;[3] in a famous *Letter* Newman spoke of "the shocking notion that the Blessed Mary is present in the Holy Eucharist in the sense in which our Lord is present".[4]

5. Some of the theories which have been mentioned are not wholly without a tendency towards viewing the conversion in the Eucharist as a natural process and therefore towards a carnal way of regarding the Eucharistic presence. Traces of similar tendencies may be found elsewhere in occasional expressions or suggestions. Statements that our Lord in the Sacrament is "inseparably chained to the species" or "falls to the ground" if an accident takes place,[5] or speculations whether in the Sacrament He uses His "senses" "naturally," or "sees and hears in the natural manner,"[6] are not altogether free from such tendencies, however much they may as a matter of fact be guarded by careful definitions made elsewhere by the same writers. A theory that, at the conversion of the substance, atoms of the body of Christ take the place of the chemical atoms thereby removed[7] seems to indicate that the mental attitude underlying the theory is directed towards a natural process of a carnal kind.[8] Against any such ideas, the ordinary teaching of theologians has asserted the spiritual character of the change in Transubstantiation and of the presence of the body of Christ.

VIII.

Of teaching designed to vindicate the spiritual nature of Eucharistic doctrine illustrations may be given from the writings of Cardinal Manning, Cardinal Franzelin, Cardinal Newman, Dr.

[1] See Hurter, *Nomencl. Liter.* ii. 12, 13.

[2] See Lambertini, *De beatif. et canon.* IV. ii. 30 (29).

[3] *Appendix libr. proh.* 1852-58, p. 5.

[4] *A Letter to the Rev. E. B. Pusey, D.D., on his recent Eirenicon*, p. 113; see also pp. 156-59.

[5] Dalgairns, *The Holy Communion*, p. 124.   [6] *Op. cit.* pp. 137-56.

[7] Leray, *Le Dogme de l'Eucharistie*, pp. 14-16.

[8] Some readers will feel that the tendency of the use of physical analogies to justify Eucharistic doctrine in *e.g.* the Abbé Constant's *Le Mystère de l'Eucharistie* is in the same direction.

van Noort, and Bishop Hedley. Manning wrote in a letter dated 28th September, 1852 :—

" 1. The Council of Trent says that our Lord's humanity, *secundum naturalem existendi modum*, that is, in its proper dimensions, etc., is at the right hand of God only.

" 2. The Church therefore distinguishes natural presence from supernatural or sacramental presence. Of the modes of this sacramental presence it defines nothing. It is supernatural.

" 3. The presence being supernatural is not a subject of natural criteria or natural operations.

" 4. Within the sphere of natural phenomena and effects there is no change in the consecrated elements. But a change does take place in a sphere into which no natural criteria such as sense can penetrate." [1]

In his *Treatise on the Sacrament and Sacrifice of the Most Holy Eucharist*, the first edition of which was published in 1868, Franzelin said :—

" This mode of presence is altogether analogous to the mode of the presence of spirits ; and it cannot be realised or declared by us in any other way than according to this analogy. . . . The body of Christ is not in the Eucharist as in a place, if by this phrase circumscribed presence is understood, so that the parts of the body would correspond to distinct parts of space ; yet it is in a place, or more properly present to place, insofar as it is actually and substantially here and is not everywhere. Also it is not in the Eucharist definitively, if by this word is understood such definitiveness to this place that it would not also be elsewhere. Yet the presence can be called definitive in this sense that the body of Christ is necessarily within a space and is not everywhere. . . . No body can act by natural power on the body of Christ as it exists in the Eucharist; and the body in the sacramental state cannot be naturally perceived by any senses. . . . In this sacramental mode of existing He cannot by the natural power of His manhood perform acts which relate to other bodies ; nor can the soul of Christ, so far as natural power only is concerned, act on His own body to produce either movement or the exercise of outward senses." [2]

In a note added in 1877 to a letter which he had written in

[1] Purcell, *Life of Cardinal Manning*, ii. 31. This letter was written seventeen months after Manning had become a Roman Catholic.
[2] Pp. 163, 177, 178.

1838 when an Anglican, Newman said in explanation of the doctrine of the Church of Rome :—

" Our Lord in *in loco* in heaven, not (in the same sense) in the Sacrament. He is present in the Sacrament only in substance, *substantive*, and substance does not require or imply the occupation of place. But, if place is excluded from the idea of the sacramental presence, therefore division or distance from heaven is excluded also, for distance implies a measurable interval, and such there cannot be except between places. Moreover, if the idea of distance is excluded, therefore is the idea of motion. Our Lord then neither descends from heaven upon our altars, nor moves when carried in procession. The visible species change their position, but He does not move. He is in the Holy Eucharist after the manner of a spirit. We do not know how ; we have no parallel to the ' how ' in our experience. We can only say that He is present, not according to the natural manner of bodies, but sacramentally. His presence is substantial, spirit-wise, sacramental ; an absolute mystery, not against reason, however, but against imagination, and must be received by faith." [1]

In his *Treatise on the Sacraments*, published in 1905, Dr. van Noort wrote :—

" There is local movement when the dimension of a body touches successively different superficies which contain it ; since then the body of the Lord as it is in the Eucharist does not touch any superficies, it has no local movement, it is not moved properly or in itself. Nevertheless, because it is really present under the species of bread, which is moved, it is necessary that it changes its place at the local movement of the host, and successively acquires and loses presence in separate places, through which the host passes, and in this sense it is said to be moved by way of accident. . . . Many histories record that the flesh or blood of the Lord in the Eucharist have sometimes sensibly appeared. The Church for the most part passes no judgment at all as to the historical truth of such narratives, and never absolutely warrants it. Prudence forbids alike to reject all such accounts together as a matter of course and to allow them all promiscuously ; for, even when all deceit is set aside, I could easily believe that a natural hallucination has sometimes had its share in visions of this kind. But, supposing the reality of the fact, it is inquired how the event can be explained. It must be said that those

---

[1] *Via Media,* ii. 220.

things which are seen in this case are not the flesh and blood of Christ themselves; for, first, since Christ is present in heaven after the circumscribed manner, and since a circumscribed presence in many places is a contradiction, He cannot be seen in another place; and, moreover, those things which are said to have appeared often do not agree with the glorious state of the body of the Lord, whose blood, for instance, cannot flow out of His veins or be corrupted afterwards. Therefore theologians are of opinion either that by the power of God the intended appearances are produced on the organs of those who behold them or that by the same power some figure is formed representative of Christ, which is attached either to the consecrated species themselves or to neighbouring objects, such as the corporal.[1] No deception is asserted in this explanation, for in it the miraculous appearance is stated to be formed to show the reality of the actual presence. . . . The predicates which express presence only apart from the mode of it are properly applied to the body of the Lord itself, as to be on the altar, to remain in the tabernacle, to be taken by the mouth. The predicates which express presence but also denote the contact of quantity or local movement properly belong to the species only, yet they are usually applied improperly[2] to the body of Christ, as to lie on the altar, to be touched, to be seen, to be placed on a throne, to be elevated, to be carried. The predicates which belong properly to the species only, but are used concerning them exactly insofar as they are signs of the body and blood of the Lord, still improperly but with somewhat more right are transferred to the body and blood themselves. In this way it is said that the body of the Lord is eaten, and broken, and that the blood of the Lord is poured out. For to be eaten (that is, not only to come into the mouth and thence into the stomach but also to be assimilated into the substance of the recipient) belongs properly to the species alone; but, because this eating was ordained only for a sign of the spiritual nourishment which the soul through it derives from the body of the Lord itself, it is customary to say that the body of Christ is eaten and His blood drunk. Further, it is often said to be really eaten, to be really drunk, but the more accurate meaning is: the body and blood of the Lord really come into our mouth and stomach, and so our soul is really nourished from them. Also, the species alone are properly broken and poured out, but where and sofar as the words breaking and pouring out are used to

[1] *Cf.* vol. i. p. 330, *supra*.
[2] Throughout this passage the words " proprie " and "improprie " are used in their technical senses.

symbolise the Lord's passion, they are rightly transferred to the body and blood themselves. The predicates which belong to the species exactly as they are something distinct from the Lord's body cannot in any way be used of the body and blood themselves, as to be round or to be white or to be warmed or to be corrupted." [1]

In his book *The Holy Eucharist*, published in 1907, Bishop Hedley said :—

" Our Lord's body is not touched or circumscribed or bounded by the species. Its parts have no point of contact in any point with the host. . . . It has . . . its natural parts as in heaven, one related to the other. It has its natural figure ; it has head, trunk, limbs, heart, and hands. But you cannot compare them with this or that point or portion of the host. . . . The peculiar and marvellous mode of the Eucharistic presence is that it is neither that of a spirit nor that of ordinary material things. Our Lord's body is not a spirit; and, although it is truly said to be in the Holy Eucharist after the manner of a spirit, yet this statement is of analogy only. It is in place after the manner of a material substance deprived of actual dimensions, actual shape, actual extended parts ; of a substance therefore which has no point of contact with any material surroundings ; a substance of which place in its formal sense cannot be predicated. Therefore it can be in many places at once, because the truth is, that it is (properly) in none of them. It cannot be moved from one place to another, because it is in no place to begin with. It is wholly in every particle or division of the species, because the species do not contain it as a stone is contained by the clay in which it is embedded, or a man's body by its surroundings, but in a way quite special to the Holy Eucharist, namely, as substance with no dimensive relation. It has no relation to this or that portion of the host's superficies or quantity, to this point or that line or that curve. . . . It cannot be touched by the hand or seen by the sense, because touch and other sensations can only be affected by contact, and the contact is with the species, whilst the qualities or properties of our Lord's sacred body are out of touch, not only with the lips of men, but with the species themselves. It cannot be broken or divided ; it is only the species that can be broken. It cannot be affected by injury from man, from animals, or from the elements. Whatever may chance, whatever devotion or impiety, care or violence, may bring about in the world into which He has deigned to enter, in the Sacrament He is unchanged, always safe,

[1] Pp. 303-6.

always undisturbed. . . . In the Eucharist the body of our Lord, by the wonderful and unique way in which it has taken the place of the substance of the bread, has adopted for outward purposes the bread's qualities. This makes it possible to say with truth that that host is the Lord's body, and justifies the worshippers in adoring. This also, as we have seen, makes it possible to assert that our Blessed Lord in the Eucharist is moved from place to place when, literally speaking, only the species are moved, because He is really contained therein. Thus also we are justified in saying that He is touched, seen, broken, eaten, etc. Under these and similar aspects the species have been assumed by our Lord expressly to signify His beneficent purpose in the Eucharistic dispensation. But if we were to say that the Lord's body was smooth or white or round or fragrant because the host possessed these qualities, we should be at variance with Catholic feeling, because it is not in these respects that the species are intended to serve as the means of making the sacred body capable of being dealt with by the senses and faculties of men."[1]

These quotations are very representative of recent Roman Catholic theology; and they exhibit the same characteristics as the teaching of the great theologians of the middle ages in the desire to preserve as co-ordinate beliefs the reality of the bodily presence of Christ in the Eucharist and the spiritual nature of that presence. Like earlier writers, those of recent times appear both to use philosophical systems and positions as a help to emphasising that the body of Christ is present after a spiritual manner and to be hampered by the technicalities involved in their definitions.

IX.

The doctrine of the Eucharist has not been wholly untouched by the "Liberal" movement which has been a marked feature of the life of the Church of Rome in the early years of the twentieth century. For the most part the discussions raised by this movement have concerned questions relating to the institution and history of the Sacrament rather than the subject of doctrine; but these discussions have not been without doctrinal results.

In the most moderate section of those theologians to whom the "Liberal" movement has been due may be placed M. P.

[1] Pp. 53, 54, 55, 64.

426 THE DOCTRINE OF THE HOLY EUCHARIST

Pourrat, Professor of Theology in the Seminary at Lyons, M. J.
Tixeront, Dean of the Catholic Faculty of Theology at Lyons,
and Mgr. Pierre Batiffol, formerly Rector of the Catholic
Institute at Toulouse, who has ceased to hold his office in consequence of action resulting from the Encyclical *On the Teaching
of the Modernists* issued in 1907 by Pope Pius X.   M. Pourrat
in his book *The Theology of the Sacraments*, published in 1906,
maintained that "not all the Sacraments were given to the
Church by the Saviour fully constituted," and that the form taken
by some of them was due to a process of development ; but that
Baptism and the Eucharist were completely explained by our
Lord, so that the Church at the first had full and complete knowledge of these two rites, and so that " Jesus directly and explicitly
instituted Baptism and the Eucharist, and directly but implicitly
instituted the other five Sacraments ".[1]   M. Tixeront in his *Ante-
Nicene Theology*, published in 1904 as the first volume of a contemplated *History of Dogma*, referred to the Eucharist as personally instituted by our Lord ; and in the course of the book
treated scantily, but with considerable power of touching the
main point, teaching about the Eucharist found in a few writers
of the ante-Nicene Church, noticing among other matters
characteristic features of the doctrine of Clement of Alexandria
and Origen.[2]   Mgr. Batiffol in his book *The Eucharist, the Real
Presence, and Transubstantiation*, published in 1905, ascribed the
institution of the Eucharist to the personal ministry of our Lord,
and supplied a history of the salient points in the development
of the doctrine of Transubstantiation as defined by the Council
of Trent, in which he showed great skill and honesty and courage
in disentangling and stating the different lines of thought which
have been found within the Church.   None of these writers appear to have questioned the definitions of the Council of Trent ;
and in stating that the Church has affirmed "the conversion of
the substance of the bread and the substance of the wine into
the body and blood under the continuance of the appearances or
species of bread and wine," [3] Mgr. Batiffol seems to be declaring
that which he himself believes.

[1] Pp. 274, 288, 363.
[2] Pp. 73, 92, 105, 143, 144, 150, 151, 245, 258, 259, 275, 276, 301, 302,
326, 348, 389, 405, 426.
[3] P. 383.

Among the more extreme promoters of the "Liberal" movement are to be numbered M. Alfred Loisy, M. Edward le Roy, and the Italian priests who published anonymously a letter entitled *What we want.* In considering this more extreme group, it may be convenient to state first the opinions of M. Loisy expressed before the publication of the *Syllabus* and *Encyclical* of Pope Pius X., then those of M. le Roy and of the group of Italian priests also prior to the *Syllabus* and *Encyclical,* then the statements of the Pope bearing on the subject, and lastly the teaching of M. Loisy since the *Syllabus* and the *Encyclical* appeared.

M. Loisy published *The Gospel and the Church* in 1902, and *Round about a Little Book* and *The Fourth Gospel* in 1903. In *The Gospel and the Church* he wrote :—

"Jesus in the course of His ministry did not either prescribe to His Apostles or Himself practise any rule of outward worship which has characterised the Gospel as religion. He no more laid down a rule for the progress of Christian worship than He made formal rules for the constitution and doctrines of the Church. . . . The Eucharistic Supper appears then as the symbol of the kingdom which the sacrifice of Jesus was to bring. The Eucharist, on the day of its first celebration, signified rather the abrogation of the ancient worship and the near approach of the kingdom than the institution of a new worship ; the outlook of Jesus did not directly embrace the idea of a new religion, of a Church to be founded, but always the idea of the kingdom of heaven to be realised. It was the Church which came into the world, and which by the force of circumstances placed itself more and more outside Judaism. By it Christianity became a distinct religion, independent and complete ; as a religion, it needed a worship, and it had one. It had such a worship as its origins permitted or commanded it to have. This worship was at first imitated from Judaism insofar as it had outward forms of prayer, and also certain important rites such as Baptism, anointing with oil, and the laying on of hands. The chief act, the Eucharistic meal, was indeed the work of Jesus. This was, in the Church of the Gentiles, the great mystery, without which it would not have been considered that Christianity was a complete religion. There was already an organised worship in the apostolic communities, and the readiness with which it constituted itself shows clearly that it corresponded to a close and unavoidable necessity of a new establishment. The impossibility of gaining converts to a religion without outward forms and without sanctifying actions was

complete; it was necessary for Christianity to be a worship or else
cease to exist. Therefore it was in its origin the most living worship
which can be imagined. Let us try only to realise the Baptisms
with the laying on of hands and the outward manifestations of the
divine Spirit, the breaking of the bread and the meal at which they
perceived the presence of the Master who had left the earth, the
songs of thanksgiving which flew from their hearts, the signs, sometimes strange, of an overflowing enthusiasm. Is it not true that, if
there is there no cold and abstract belief, there is no more any rite
which is simply symbolic and as the material expression of that belief? All is living, both the faith and the rites, both the Baptism
and the breaking of the bread; the Baptism is the Spirit, and the
Eucharist is Christ. No one considers the sign, no one speaks of the
physical efficacy of the Sacrament in Baptism or of Transubstantiation in the Eucharist; but what they believe and say comes very
near to these theological assertions. The worship of this age cannot be defined; it is a kind of spiritual realism which knows nothing
of mere symbols, which is essentially sacramental by the place which
the rite holds as the means of conveying the Spirit and the instrument of divine life. St. Paul and the author of the Fourth Gospel
are witnesses. . . . In matters of worship, the religious feeling of
the main body of Christians always preceded the doctrinal definitions
of the Church on the object of the worship. This fact is full of
significance; it shows the law which cries out for a worship appropriate to all the circumstances of life and to the character of the
believing people. The real communion with Christ in the Eucharist
was as imperiously demanded by the Christian conscience as the
divinity of Jesus; but the divinity of Christ is not a dogma conceived in the spirit of Jewish theology, and the Eucharist is no
more a Jewish rite. . . . The primitive Church knew only two
principal Sacraments, Baptism, with which Confirmation was connected, and the Eucharist; the number of the lesser Sacraments
was undetermined. This want of determination would be inexplicable if Christ in the course of His mortal life had directed
the attention of His disciples to seven distinct rites, destined to
be the foundation of Christian worship in all the centuries. The
Sacraments were born from a thought and an intention of Jesus,
interpreted by the Apostles and by their successors in the light
and under the pressure of circumstances and facts. . . . The development of the Eucharist has been above every thing theological
and liturgical. The basis of the doctrine and of the rite has
been no more different than in the case of Baptism. The Supper

of the first Christians was a memorial of the passion and an anticipation of the Messianic feast, at which Jesus was present. There was no very marked difference between the Pauline conception of the Eucharist and the idea which is held to-day by simple Christians, strangers to the speculations of theological knowledge (*gnose*), who believe that they enter into real communion with the divine Christ by their reception of the consecrated bread. Christian worship was developed wholly round the Eucharistic Supper. The simple blessing and distribution of the bread and the wine, separated from the agape, surrounded by readings and prayers and hymns, became the sacrifice of the Mass. Since the death of Christ was regarded as a sacrifice, the act commemorating His death had to share in the same character. The liturgical rite also helped to give it this sacrificial character by the actual oblation of the bread and the wine with the reception of consecrated food (*mets sanctifiés*) by all the faithful, as in the ancient sacrifices. Hence emerged the idea of a commemorative sacrifice, which simply perpetuated that of the cross without taking away anything from its meaning and value, and which was offered for all the intentions which the common prayer of the Church included, interests spiritual and temporal, the salvation of the living and the dead. The Christian feeling which guarded in one sense the divinity of Jesus against certain speculations of learned metaphysics, protected the Eucharist from those of an abstract symbolism. And, as the development of Penance ended by bringing about confessions of devotion, so the development of the rite of the Eucharist came to private Masses for priests and to Communions of devotion for the faithful." [1]

On the reading of *The Gospel and the Church* being prohibited by the Archbishop of Paris and other bishops, M. Loisy explained some parts of his meaning more fully in the work *Round about a Little Book*. Some of his explanations had to do with the Eucharist. In regard to it he wrote :—

" It is still easily seen in the New Testament that the Church was founded and that the Sacraments were instituted, properly speaking, only by the glorified Saviour. It follows that the institution of the Church and the Sacraments by Christ is, like the glorifying of Jesus, an object of faith, not of historical demonstration. . . . The Council [of Trent] decreed that Christ is actually and wholly present in the Eucharist ; that the substance of the bread and of the wine does not remain under the species after the conse-

[1] Pp. 225-28, 234, 238, 239, 243-45.

cration, but that there is a Transubstantiation, that is, a change, by the conversion of the whole substance of the bread into the body, and of the whole substance of the wine into the blood, of Christ; that the Mass is a real sacrifice instituted by the Saviour; that the Apostles were made priests by the words, 'Do this in remembrance of Me'; and that Jesus thus instituted a visible and perpetual priesthood. Here are views of faith, . . . and of a faith which is defined according to the philosophical ideas of the Middle Ages. Do you think that the Apostles, during the Last Supper, had a clear-cut idea of Transubstantiation, of the presence of the whole Christ under the species of bread and wine, that they knew that henceforth they were priests who should fill the place in the new covenant of the priesthood of Aaron and the ministry of the Levites ? And ourselves, do we now know as well as the fathers of Trent what is substance and what is accident, and can we form an idea of a bodily substance without appearance and an appearance without substance as easily as they did ? Is it not clear that the philosophical definition of the real presence was slowly elaborated and finally defined in view of heresies which tended more or less to make the Sacrament a mere symbol, and that the reality of the sacrifice of the Mass ought to be understood in connection with a particular idea of sacrifice, which the theologians themselves had some difficulty in explaining ? . . . I cannot here go into the criticism of the accounts of the Last Supper. The most complete is that of St. Paul,[1] but, when one examines it closely, it is very difficult to distinguish exactly what may come from the primitive tradition, what may be the relation of the Last Supper according to those who were present at it, from the theological and moral commentary of the Apostle. St. Paul is the theologian of the cross, of the atoning death ; and he plainly interprets the Supper as commemorative of the death according to his theory of universal redemption."[2]

After a brief discussion of the accounts of the institution, of the discourse in the sixth chapter of the Fourth Gospel, and of the appearances of our Lord after His death, M. Loisy goes on :—

"This discourse [that is, the discourse in the sixth chapter of the Fourth Gospel] takes the place in the Fourth Gospel of the simple account of the Supper which John has not wished to reproduce. Let us listen here to the voice of Christ glorified, the

[1] 1 Cor. xi. 23-25.   [2] Pp. 227, 235-37.

voice of the Church and of the Christian faith. He completes the accounts of the resurrection, because he makes us see in the immortal Christ the Eucharistic Christ, the bread of life. Here then, from the point of view of history, the faith in the Eucharist is attested almost by the same testimonies and in the same way as the faith in the resurrection; the two were born together and were together established by the same causes, the preceding faith in Jesus as Messiah and the appearances which followed the passion; the faithful ones of Jesus received at the same time the persuasion that their Master was ever living and that He was with them, among them (*avec eux, à eux*), in the breaking of the bread; and, as the faith in Jesus as the Messiah supported the faith in Jesus as immortal, so the recollection of the Last Supper supported and decided the faith in Jesus present in the breaking of the bread." [1]

In the treatise *The Fourth Gospel* M. Loisy explained at length his theory that this Gospel was never intended as an account of historical facts, but is an allegorical presentation in the form of events and discourses of what Christian faith had come to believe. From this point of view he writes :—

"The Johannine conception of the Eucharist corresponds to that of Baptism. We have seen above the reasons which explain the anticipation of the Eucharistic Supper in the multiplication of the loaves. The thought of the Eucharist does not cease to inspire the Johannine account of the Last Supper; it is called back in the passion, together with Baptism, by the water and the blood which flowed from the side of Jesus. The connection of the Eucharist with the passover and the death of the Saviour is not out of sight in the Fourth Gospel; the presentation of it is different from that in the Synoptics and in St. Paul, since it is subordinated to the general idea of the spiritual life which is maintained by union with Christ, and which is manifested in love. In the account of the multiplication of the loaves as well as in that of the Last Supper, the Evangelist thinks of the agape at the same time as of the Eucharist, and, thinking of the agape, he thinks of love, of which the agape both in name and in fact is the traditional expression. He places together in his symbolic view the bread and the wine, merely signs of invisible realities, the flesh and the blood of Christ, represented directly by the bread and wine, the spirit and the life which are the flesh and blood of the glorious Christ, the communion in the spirit and in the life, which is effected in the

[1] Pp. 243, 244.

reception of the bread and wine, flesh and blood of Christ, the manifestation of the spirit and of the life in Christian love, a manifestation
which has its act and its mystery, its sensible representation and its
source in the agape-Eucharist. The thought of death is no more
absent than that of love ; the Eucharist is a gift, it is Christ who is
given ; on the side of Christ it is love, and the love of Him who
has given His life for His friends, it is love even unto death ; and
it unites the faithful in that fulness of love which becomes their
law. But the death of Jesus is not considered in itself as something to be remembered, or even as an expiatory sacrifice as a
source of gain ; it is above all a proof of love ; on this title it retains its commemorative place in the Sacrament of love.

"These are the ideas which the discourse on the bread of life
and the discourse after the Supper sum up. It is of importance to
observe carefully the connection and the bearing, if we are not to
maim the meaning of these important passages. Thus, it cannot
be said without many qualifications that the Eucharistic doctrine
of John is dominated by the recollection of the multiplication of
the loaves, while that of Paul is dominated by the recollection of
the Last Supper ; that John separates the Eucharist from the
passion, and that he makes it a happy meal in which Jesus appears
as the principle of life, while Paul preserves the connection with
the Last Supper and the death of Jesus ; that John neglects
almost wholly the recollection of the passover, while Paul gives
force to it. All these antitheses have more appearance than reality. The author of the Fourth Gospel sees in the multiplication
of the loaves a symbol of the Eucharist, but his picture of the Last
Supper is no less Eucharistic, if we notice carefully, than the accounts and discourse of the sixth chapter, he realises also the
Eucharist as a memorial of the death of Christ, and he bases the
teaching of the Last Supper on these two ideas, the death and
love, the passion and the agape-love-Eucharist ; as he associates the
typical character of the passover directly with the account of the
passion, he thus retains, however less definitely expressed, the connection of the Eucharist with the paschal feast. Has he not also
taken pains to note that the multiplication of the loaves happened
near the passover ? What is true is that in the Fourth Gospel the
death of Christ has not the same significance ; it does not inspire
the kind of natural horror which we feel in the Synoptics ; it is
not, as in Paul, the foundation of the whole teaching ; in itself it is
only the will of the Father and, as the act of Christ, a proof of
love ; the thought of the Evangelist has become accustomed to it,

and he has treated it in such a way that it is not at all terrifying or disquieting; Christ speaks of it and passes through it with such calmness that the reader only receives an impression of life; the idea of life clearly outweighs that of death, and the death is only the condition of life.

"This view of Baptism and the Eucharist inaugurates the doctrine of the Sacraments. Baptism and the Supper are the two Christian mysteries, the two essential acts of worship and two elements of the faith. The Johannine Gospel and First Epistle associate them still more directly than Paul had done. They are represented together in the water and the blood which are the object of so solemn a witness in the account of the passion; they return again joined to the Spirit in the First Epistle; they are, with the Spirit and by the Spirit, the inheritance which Christ has left to those who are His; and in the thought of the Evangelist Christian Baptism corresponds to the baptism of Jesus, the Eucharist to His death; by the water the Spirit comes; by the blood comes life, the fruit of the death; the one completes the other, and the two are the means by which the Spirit comes; but the water communicates, the blood preserves, the life of the Spirit; the two extremities of the career of Christ mark the two poles between which the spiritual life of the Christian has its course." [1]

"If Jesus said . . . that the Spirit alone quickens and that the flesh profits nothing, this is not to retract what He had said before, and to give to His disciples an explanation which could also wholly remove the scandal of the multitude, but to show that the Eucharistic flesh and blood are communicated 'spiritually,' not by faith or by a mere influence of the divine Spirit, but as spiritualised in the glorifying of Christ." [2]

"The antithesis [in 'My words are spirit, they are life'] is not between the letter and the idea hidden under the letter, between the metaphor and the abstract truth, but between the spiritual and life-giving reality of the communion with Jesus, communion which had its effective symbol and its earthly consummation in the Eucharist, and the wholly material way in which the Jews understood the teaching of the Saviour and the Christian Sacrament." [3]

In 1907 an open letter was addressed to Pope Pius X. by a group of Italian priests and privately printed and circulated under the title *Quello che Vogliamo*. A translation of it was published and publicly sold in England entitled *What we want*.

---

[1] Pp. 114-16.   [2] Pp. 456, 457.   [3] P. 472.

It contained the following passage relating to the Eucharist:—

"To explain the Eucharistic mystery, we cannot . . . adopt the theory of Transubstantiation, unless no one is to understand. But we shall say that the faithful after the words of consecration, while with the senses of their bodily life they will see only bread and wine, will yet with the soul by means of a superphenomenal experience—of faith, in short—be in contact with the real and living Christ, who, before He died, gathered His disciples to a fraternal feast to communicate to them for the last time the 'bread of eternal life,' will be in contact with the Christ suspended on the cross, the Victim of justice and of peace." [1]

This statement had much in common with the passages already quoted from M. Loisy, and with the treatment of the Eucharist by M. le Roy in his *Dogma and Criticism*, which also appeared in 1907.

In this work M. le Roy wrote as follows on the subject of Eucharistic doctrine :—

"I shall say the same about the real presence. The doctrine does not at all commit me to a theory of that presence, nor does it teach me in what the presence consists. But the doctrine tells me very clearly that the presence must not be understood in some of the ways which have formerly been suggested, for instance, the consecrated host must not be held to be merely a symbol or figure of Jesus." [2]

"Is it more difficult for common sense to admit the resurrection in spite of the continuance of the body in the tomb than to admit the Trinity or the unlimited multiplication of the sacramental body?" [3]

"I do not think that I am rash in maintaining that a body, however distant, makes its presence known by its perceptible effects, even though it habitually be not perceived ; if there is no perceptible effect, I should say without hesitation that the body does not exist, for matter is not in itself. As for the presence of God in everything, I repeat with St. Paul [4] and with the fathers of the Vatican,[5] 'the invisible things of Him since the creation of the world are clearly seen, being perceived through the things that are made' ; and I add moreover that the fulness of that presence cannot be

[1] Pp. 42, 43, English translation. [2] P. 20. [3] P. 250.
[4] Rom. i. 20. [5] *Const. Dogm. de fid. Cath.* cap. ii.

defined except in terms of action (in the same sense as the divine personality) if we wish to avoid the error of pantheism. And this last resource is the only one which allows us certainly to grasp the fact of the real presence in the Eucharist, since as to this there is no perception or possibility of perception, in any degree or under any form. Consider for a minute! Who would dare to say that the statements of Trent relating to the Eucharist ought to be understood as dogmas according to the propositions of philosophy in the technical sense of the word? Who would dare to say, for instance, that the second canon of the thirteenth session imposes on the faith of the faithful the scholastic theory of matter or any theory at all on the relation between substance and accidents? The use of the word Transubstantiation does not imply anything of all this, nor does it imply that the idea of substance elaborated by the schoolmen is in any way necessarily connected with the revealed doctrine. The word simply means that we continue to perceive the bread and the wine, that the most penetrating scientific methods of analysis do not enable us to perceive anything else, and that nevertheless we ought not to behave in the presence of the consecrated host in any such way as we should behave in the presence of bread and wine, because it has become something of which this change of relation and conduct is the consequence reasonably obligatory on us. 'Let us notice first,' says M. Sertillanges,[1] 'that the definition quoted says nothing about accidents; it uses the word species, a word which our catechisms uniformly translate by the word appearances. Is not this to show that there is not involved any philosophy properly so called? Where shall we be, if we are to impose to-day on everybody in the name of dogma the division of being into categories, the actual distinction between substance and accidents, a theory of place, a theory of absolute or local quantity, and so on? Who should we allow to make his Easter?' The same writer says again,[2] 'How is a plain man to behave in relation to a dogma which he is bound to hold, of which he ought therefore to know the meaning, if the formula in which the meaning is expressed has an aim which he cannot understand? The positive side of the dogma ought to be accessible to all the world; the anathemas can only have their place in a system because they are addressed, so far as they are so placed, to those believers among whom the system is in vogue.' If the word substance in the definitions of Trent is interpreted in a properly philosophic sense, the

[1] *Revue du Clergé Français*, 1st Nov. 1905, p. 542.
[2] *Op. cit.* 1st Oct. 1905, p. 314.
28 *

definitions will have nothing to do with all the world, but only with those who accept the principles and ideas of that scholastic philosophy which was commonly professed at the time of the Council, and moreover for these they have only a negative meaning, proscribing certain theories without directly imposing any other.   It is then elsewhere that we ought to look for the positive meaning of the doctrine which ought to be accepted by all.

"From the point of view of history, it is quite certain that the fathers of Trent professed the scholastic philosophy ; on the methods of that philosophy they thought out the dogma, and in its language they expressed themselves.   But the psychology of a council is one thing ; the judicial force of its decrees as an official teaching proposition of the Church is another thing.   Do not let us confuse the vehicle of the faith with its object.   We must not fasten on the ideology any more than on the terminology of the definition ; 'is not the body,' says the Gospel, 'more than raiment?'   What we must look for is the real direction of the intention of the definition. Now let us consider the decrees of Trent from this point of view. It is unquestionable that the fathers of the Council never dreamed of canonising one philosophy in opposition to another.   The scholastic philosophy was the only philosophy with which they were acquainted, the only philosophy in vogue among them, one might almost say the only philosophy which existed in their time.   They therefore made use of it, as they spoke the language of their time, but without their attention being fastened on it.   We can say that the philosophy was not the point, that it was something else at which they were aiming.   From this it results that, whatever might be the learned interpretation which they on their part assigned to the word substance, we ought to understand it—we, I say—in a sense pragmatically clear and intellectually obscure, which is enough to signify that there is a gift, and which leaves the door open for all the researches of theory." [1]

In a note M. le Roy stated no less definitely his view of the sense in which he regarded the decrees of the Council of Trent as binding :—

"Neither the words nor the ideas are imposed on faith, but the reality which they signify and clothe in expressions which are human and therefore inadequate and incomplete." [2]

By a decree dated 26th July, 1907, the Congregation of the Index placed this book of M. le Roy, together with four other

[1] Pp. 259-62.   [2] P. 262.

works, three French and one Italian, also regarded as of an extreme "Liberal" character, in the list of condemned and prohibited books.

On 3rd July, 1907, the Congregation of the Inquisition agreed on a *Syllabus* of sixty-five condemned propositions ; and on the following day this *Syllabus* was confirmed by Pope Pius X. Five of the propositions thus condemned contained teaching bearing on the Eucharist held by or ascribed to theologians of the "Liberal" school. They were as follows :—

"39. The opinions concerning the origin of the Sacraments with which the fathers of Trent were imbued and which certainly influenced their dogmatic canons are very different from those which now rightly obtain among historians who examine into Christianity.

"40. The Sacraments had their origin in the fact that the Apostles and their successors, swayed and moved by circumstances and events, interpreted some idea and intention of Christ.

"41. The Sacraments are merely intended to bring before the mind of man the ever beneficent presence of the Creator.

"45. Not everything which Paul narrates concerning the institution of the Eucharist is to be taken historically.

"49. As the Christian Supper gradually assumed the nature of a liturgical action, those who were wont to preside at the Supper acquired the sacerdotal character."

The *Syllabus* was followed by the *Encyclical Letter* of Pope Pius X., dated 14th September, 1907, beginning *Pascendi dominici gregis* and entitled *On the Teaching of the Modernists*. This *Letter* contained the following passage :—

"Concerning worship it would not be necessary to say much, if it were not that the Sacraments come under this head, and that the gravest errors of the Modernists relate to them. The Modernists regard worship as the result of a twofold impulse or need ; for, as we have seen, everything in their system is explained by inward impulses or needs. In the present case, the first need is that of giving some sensible manifestation to religion ; the second is that of expressing it, which could not be done without some sensible form and consecrating acts, and these are called Sacraments. But for the Modernists Sacraments are bare symbols or signs, although not without efficacy, an efficacy, they tell us, like that of certain phrases commonly said to have caught the popular ear, inasmuch as they have the power of putting certain ideas into circulation,

and of making a marked impression on the mind. What these
phrases are to the ideas, that the Sacraments are to the religious
sense, that and nothing more. They would express their mind
more clearly if they were to affirm that the Sacraments were instituted solely to foster faith. But this has been condemned by the
Council of Trent,[1] 'If any one say that these Sacraments were
instituted solely to foster faith, let him be anathema'." [2]

It is obvious that in the condemnations of the *Syllabus* and
the *Encyclical* the opinions expressed by M. Loisy were largely
in view. This was recognised by M. Loisy himself. In 1908 he
published a book entitled *Simple Reflections on the Decree of the
Holy Office Lamentabili sane exitu and on the Encyclical Pascendi dominici gregis*, and a huge treatise, the work of years, on
The Synoptic Gospels. In the *Reflections* he commented on the
propositions condemned in the *Syllabus* one by one. As to the
influence on the Tridentine divines of views about the origin of
the Sacraments asserted to be now discredited, he said that,
the facts being so, they could not be honestly denied by those
who knew them. As to the origin of the Sacraments being an
interpretation by the Apostles and their successors of an idea
and intention of Christ, he wrote :—

"Taken exactly, as the Holy Office understood it, this statement
is inaccurate, for Jesus had not any idea or intention in regard to
the Sacraments of the Church. But the Church none the less
organised her sacramental system in consequence of certain postulates in the Gospels (*données évangéliques*) or traditional events, the
baptism of John, the recollection of the Last Supper, the mission of
the Apostles."

As to the alleged view that the Sacraments are only a means
of bringing to mind the presence of God, he explained that his
point had been to repudiate such a notion as that the Sacraments
are " a magical means of grace intervening between God and man ".
As to the unhistorical character of the account of the institution
of the Eucharist in the First Epistle to the Corinthians, he
said :—

"Neither the words 'This is My body' nor the words 'This is
My blood' belong to the primitive tradition about the Last Supper.
Jesus only gave the bread and the wine to His disciples, saying to

---

[1] Sess. vii. *De sacr. in gen.* can. 5.   [2] Pp. 24, 25.

them that He would not eat or drink with them again henceforth except in the feast of the kingdom of heaven."

On the forty-ninth proposition he simply re-asserted his view that the Supper gradually became a liturgical action, and the presidents gradually became priests and bishops.[1] M. Loisy's *Reflections* also contained comments on the *Encyclical*. In the course of these he said :—

"Sacraments do not only arouse the remembrance of saving truths, but they suggest moral impressions in connection with their proper object. It is difficult to see in what way general considerations on the necessity of religious rites can be among the gravest errors ; for a long time past Catholic apologists have laid stress on them to prove the necessity of outward and public worship, and certainly no one pretends that the institution of sensible signs, like the Sacraments, does not correspond to any need of human nature but proceeds only from the arbitrary will of Him who established them."[2]

In the parts relating to the Eucharist in his book *The Synoptic Gospels* M. Loisy explained and defended his view that at the Last Supper our Lord gave to His disciples bread and wine, and said "I will not drink from henceforth of the fruit of the vine until the kingdom of God shall come" with reference to His contemplated feast with His disciples on the establishment of the Messianic kingdom of God, and that the gradual and unhistorical enlargement of the accounts of this event may be traced through the First Epistle to the Corinthians, the shorter text of St. Luke, St. Mark, St. Matthew, and the longer text of St. Luke.[3] The original Eucharistic idea was that of the presence of Christ at a common meal in the kingdom. This was closely connected with the thought of the glorified Christ present with His disciples after His death by virtue of that abiding life of which the accounts of His appearances in His risen state are the witness. St. Paul, in consequence of his view of the Person and the work of Christ, added the idea of the memorial of the Crucified, who had given His body and shed His blood for the salvation of the world. The Fourth Gospel shows a further addition in the synthesis of Communion and sacrifice on the lines of the usual ancient ideas

---

[1] Pp. 83-85, 90, 95.   [2] Pp. 184, 185.
[3] For these texts, see vol. i. pp. 4-6, *supra*.

of the connection between sacrifice and communion with deity. Thus was reached the conception of the Eucharist as at once the memorial of a sacrifice which is itself a sacrifice, and the means of the Communion of Christians with their Lord.[1]

The writing of the *Reflections* and the publication of the long contemplated *The Synoptic Gospels* were obviously acts of defiance of the authorities of Rome. There is no doubt that M. Loisy intended them to be so. The reply of the authorities quickly followed. On 7th March, 1908, M. Loisy was excommunicated with the greater excommunication by name and in person, and declared to be subject to the penalties inflicted on those publicly excommunicated, and sentenced to be avoided by all.

To the instances which have been given of teaching of "Liberal" Roman Catholics abroad it may be well to add a passage of a different kind from the English writer Father George Tyrrell, whose attempt to frame a new apologetic theology led to his exclusion from the Society of Jesus and his eventual excommunication. The essay from which it is taken was originally written in 1899, and later formed part of the book entitled *The Faith of the Millions*. It was reprinted in 1907 in the work *Through Scylla and Charybdis, or the Old Theology and the New;* and Father Tyrrell then stated that it marked "a turning-point in" his "own theological experience," and gave "as it were in a brief compendium or analytical index" the main features of all his thought since it was first written.[2] In developing a contention as to "the abstract character of certain theological conclusions, and the superiority of the concrete language of revelation as a guide to truth," he wrote :—

"When we are told that Christ's sacramental body is not referred to space *ratione sui,* but only *ratione accidentis ;* that it is not moved when the species are carried in procession ; that we are not nearer to it at the altar than at the North Pole ; we can only say that this '*ratione sui*' consideration does not concern us, nor is it any part of God's revelation. It does well to remind us that our Lord's body is not to be thought of carnally and grossly ; that our natural imagination of this mystery is necessarily childish and inadequate. But it does not give us a more, but, if anything, a less adequate conception of it. 'This is My body' is nearer the mark

---

[1] i. 7, 9, 100, 167, 218, 219 ; ii. 522-44, 763.
[2] *Through Scylla and Charybdis,* p. 85.

than metaphysics can ever hope to come ; and, of the two superstitions, that of the peasant who is too literally anthropomorphic is
less than that of the philosopher who should imagine his part of the
truth to be the whole.

" Again, what is called the Hidden Life of our Lord in the
Sacrament is a thought upon which the faith and devotion of many
saints and holy persons has fed itself for centuries ; yet it is one
with which a narrow metaphysic plays havoc very disastrously.
The notion of the loneliness, the sorrows, and disappointments of
the neglected Prisoner of Love in the Tabernacle may be crude
and simple ; but it is assuredly nearer the truth than the notion of
a now passionless and apathetic Christ, who suffered these things by
foresight two thousand years ago, and whose irrevocable pains cannot possibly be increased or lessened by any conduct of ours. I
have more than once known all the joy and reality taken out of a
life that fed on devotion to the sacramental presence by such a
flash of theological illumination ; and have seen Magdalens left
weeping at empty tombs and crying, ' They have taken away my
Lord, and I know not where they have laid Him '." [1]

X.

The chief mark in the attitude of the authorities of the
Church of Rome since the time of the Council of Trent has been
their careful adherence to the decrees of that Council. It has
been held necessary to maintain undeviatingly the doctrine of
Transubstantiation and that the Eucharist is a real and proper
sacrifice. Very varying opinions as to the character of the sacrifice have been left uncondemned. No censure has been passed
on opinions which have minimised or eliminated the idea of destruction, or on those which have maximised it ; on opinions
which have ignored or made little of the heavenly offering of
Christ, or on those which have strongly emphasised it and the
connection of it with the Eucharist. Ideas about the Eucharistic presence of a somewhat different character and tending in
somewhat different directions in regard to the continuance and
nature of the accidents and to the spiritual manner wherein the
body of Christ is present have not been suppressed. On the
other hand, the rejection by the Council of Pistoia of that element in the sacrifice whereby the celebrant is able to make
special application of its fruits, the attempt of the same Council

[1] *Op. cit.* pp. 99, 100.

to avoid the affirmation of Transubstantiation, the opinion ascribed to Rosmini with its apparent modification of the same doctrine, the endeavour of the extreme section of the " Liberal " theologians who have become known as the Modernists to utilise critical hypotheses and philosophical theories as a way of attaching a changed meaning to the doctrine of the Eucharist, have all met with condemnation. There does not appear to have been any desire on the part of the authorities to elaborate further definitions, or to exact too closely particular interpretations of the words of the Tridentine decrees, or to press too hardly the philosophy accepted by those who framed them, provided that philosophical opinions be not made a screen for the rejection of the theology which they were drawn up to teach. On this subject, alike in what it said and in what it did not say, the Council of Trent has been taken and used as the standard.

CHAPTER XV.

POST-REFORMATION THEOLOGY.

PART II.

In the Church of England the dividing line between the Reformation period and the period of post-Reformation theology is rightly placed at the completion and authorisation of the Book of Common Prayer in 1662. During the time between 1662 and the beginning of the twentieth century there have been great differences of opinion and teaching in regard to the Holy Eucharist in the Church of England. The scope of the present chapter is to the end of the eighteenth century.

I.

An instance of a type of teaching probably widely prevalent in the Church of England between 1662 and the end of the first quarter of the eighteenth century may be seen in the writings of the profoundly learned theologian Bishop Bull. George Bull was born at Wells in 1634. Before he was fourteen he went into residence at Exeter College, Oxford, but left Oxford in 1649, while only fifteen, in consequence of his refusal to take the oath required by the "Engagement" to "be true and faithful to the Government established without King and House of Peers". In 1655 he was ordained deacon and priest by Dr. Skinner, the ejected Bishop of Oxford; and during the Commonwealth he did much to maintain the services of the Church, using the Church prayers, which he knew by heart, without book. Before and after the Restoration he was occupied in study and writing and pastoral work. In 1705 he was appointed Bishop of St. Davids. In 1710 he died. Concerning the Eucharist he appears to have combined a rejection of what he understood to be the Roman Catholic doctrine of the sacrifice with the assertion of a commemorative sacrifice, and the rejection of Transubstantiation with the assertion of some kind of virtual presence of the body and blood of Christ. The chief passages bearing on his Eucharistic beliefs are the following :—

"The consent of all the Christian Churches in the world, however distant from one another, in the prayer of oblation of the Christian sacrifice in the Holy Eucharist or Sacrament of the Lord's Supper, which consent is indeed wonderful. All the ancient liturgies agree in this form of prayer almost in the same words but fully and exactly in the same sense, order, and method, which whosoever attentively considers must be convinced that this order of prayer was delivered to the several Churches in the very first plantation and settlement of them. Nay, it is observable that this form of prayer is still retained in the very canon of the Mass at this day used in the Church of Rome, though the form doth manifestly contradict and overthrow some of the principal articles of their new faith. For from this very form of prayer still extant in their canon a man may effectually refute those two main doctrines of their Church, the doctrine of purgatory and that of Transubstantiation." 1

"We have an entire Sacrament, the cup of blessing in the Holy Eucharist, which was sacrilegiously taken from us by the Church of Rome, being happily restored to us. The ridiculous pageantry and fopperies of that Church are laid aside, and we have the Holy Sacrament purely, reverently, and decently administered." 2

"Who sees not that the sacrilege is here chargeable on the Church of Rome, which hath robbed the faithful of one half of the Blessed Sacrament, the cup of our Lord, to which they had a right by the institution of Christ, and the happy enjoyment and possession whereof they were invested with by the prescription and practice of the Catholic Church for many ages together after the Apostles? For when they tell us that the people receive a perfect Sacrament only in one kind, because both the body and blood of Christ are truly and perfectly contained under each species of the Sacrament, they egregiously prevaricate in a matter of great concernment to the souls of men. For, 1. If this be true, then our Saviour did superfluously institute the Sacrament to be received in both kinds; for if there be a perfect Sacrament in one kind only, to what purpose did Christ institute the other? 2. It is most false that the body and blood of Christ are sacramentally in each element; for it

1 Sermon xiii., on *Prescribed Forms of Prayer*, preached later than 1661 (*Works*, 1827, Oxford edition, vol. i. p. 333).
2 *Op. cit.* i. 344.

is the bread only that doth sacramentally signify and exhibit the body of Christ, and the wine only that doth sacramentally signify and exhibit the blood of Christ. 3. That which doth not perfectly represent and set forth the death and passion of our Lord is no perfect Sacrament; . . . but Communion only in one kind, namely, the bread, doth not perfectly represent the death and passion of our Lord Jesus. . . . The effusion and shedding of Christ's blood on the cross . . . is in the Communion only of the bread so far from being perfectly that it is not at all represented but totally obscured." [1]

" If I can be infallibly certain that my senses, rightly disposed and all due requisites to sensation supposed, are infallible, and cannot be deceived about their proper objects, . . . then I may be infallibly certain that the Church of Rome is not infallible, yea, that she hath grossly erred in her doctrine of Transubstantiation, teaching the bread and wine after the words of consecration to be turned into the very flesh and blood of Christ, which yet all my senses assure me to remain still the same in nature and substance, that is, bread and wine." [2]

"They [that is, the Tridentine divines] anathematise and damn all those who shall dare so far to trust all their senses wherewith God hath blessed them as to believe that the bread and wine in the Sacrament do after the words of Consecration still remain in substance the same (though they confess them transcendently changed in use), that is, bread and wine. And consequently . . . they anathematise and damn all those who shall teach that the consecrated bread and wine ought not to be worshipped with divine worship (such as is due to the only-begotten Son of God Himself), or to be carried about in solemn procession to be so worshipped and adored by the people. A hard case ! All our senses infallibly assure us of the truth of the former proposition, and upon the supposal thereof the papists do themselves confess the truth of the latter, and yet, nevertheless, we must be damned for thus teaching.", [3]

" Christ hath instituted two Sacraments in His Church, Baptism and His holy Supper, and both to seal the forgiveness of our sins. Of Baptism, that it is instituted for the forgiveness of sins, no one doubts ; of the cup also in the Lord's Supper, the Lord Himself hath said that it is His ' blood of the New Testament, shed for the remission of sins,' Matt. xxvi. 27, 28. Hence the Catholic Church in her prayers at the altar prays for the forgiveness of sins on account

---

[1] A *Vindication of the Church of England*, being a Letter to the Countess of Newburgh, written in 1671 (*op. cit.* ii. 180, 181).

[2] *Op. cit.* ii. 185, 186.   [3] *Ibid.* 221.

of the merit of the sacrifice of Christ commemorated in the Eucharist."[1]

"These superadded articles of the Trent creed are so far from
being certain truths that they are most of them manifest untruths,
yea, gross and dangerous errors. To make this appear, I shall not
refuse the pains of examining some of the chief of them. The first
article I shall take notice of is this, ' I profess that in the Mass is
offered to God a true, proper, and propitiatory sacrifice for the
living and the dead; and that in the most holy Sacrament of the
Eucharist there is truly and really and substantially the body and
blood together with the soul and divinity of our Lord Jesus Christ ;
and that there is wrought a conversion of the whole substance of
the bread into the body, and of the whole substance of the wine
into the blood, which conversion the Catholic Church calls Transubstantiation '. Where this proposition ('That in the Mass there
is offered to God a true, proper, and propitiatory sacrifice for the
living and the dead '), having that other of the ' substantial presence
of the body and blood of Christ in the Eucharist' immediately annexed to it, the meaning of it must necessarily be this, that in the
Eucharist the very body and blood of Christ are again offered up
to God as a propitiatory sacrifice for the sins of men. Which
is an impious proposition, derogatory to the one full satisfaction of
Christ made by His death on the cross, and contrary to express
Scripture, Heb. vii. 27, and ix. 12, 25, 26, 28, and x. 12, 14. It is
true that the Eucharist is frequently called by the ancient fathers
προσφορά, θυσία, an oblation, a sacrifice. But it is to be remembered
that they say also it is θυσία λογικὴ καὶ ἀναίμακτος, a reasonable
sacrifice, a sacrifice without blood, which how can it be said to be if
therein the very blood of Christ were offered up to God ? They held
the Eucharist to be a commemorative sacrifice, and so do we. This
is the constant language of the ancient liturgies, ' We offer by way of
commemoration' (μεμνημένοι προσφέρομεν : Commemorantes or Com-
memorando offerimus); according to our Saviour's words when He
ordained this holy rite, ' Do this in commemoration of Me'.[2] In
the Eucharist then, Christ is offered, not hypostatically, as the Trent
fathers have determined (for so He was but once offered) but commemoratively only ; and this commemoration is made to God the
Father, and is not a bare remembering, or putting ourselves in mind
of Him. For every sacrifice is directed to God, and the oblation

[1] *Examen Censuræ*, xvii. 24, published in 1675 (*op. cit.* iv. 234 ; in
Anglo-Catholic Library, ii. 179).

[2] St. Luke xxii. 19.

therein made, whatsoever it be, hath Him for its object, and not man.[1] In the Holy Eucharist therefore, we set before God the bread and wine, as 'figures or images of the precious blood of Christ shed for us, and of His precious body' (they are the very words of the Clementine Liturgy [2]), and plead to God the merit of His Son's sacrifice once offered on the cross for us sinners, and in this Sacrament represented, beseeching Him for the sake thereof to bestow His heavenly blessings on us. To conclude this matter: the ancients held the oblation of the Eucharist to be answerable in some respects to the legal sacrifices ; [3] that is, they believe that our blessed Saviour ordained the Sacrament of the Eucharist as a rite of prayer and praise to God instead of the manifold and bloody sacrifices of the law. . . . Instead therefore of slaying of beasts and burning of incense, whereby they praised God and called upon His name under the Old Testament, the fathers, I say, believed our Saviour appointed this Sacrament of bread and wine as a rite whereby to give thanks and make supplication to the Father in His name. . . . This Eucharistical sacrifice, thus explained, is indeed λογικὴ θυσία, a reasonable sacrifice, widely different from that monstrous sacrifice of the Mass taught in the Church of Rome. The other branch of the article is concerning Transubstantiation, wherein the ecclesiastic professeth upon his solemn oath his belief that in the Eucharist 'there is made a conversion of the whole substance of the bread into the body, and of the whole substance of the wine into the blood of Christ,' a proposition that bids defiance to all the reason and sense of mankind, nor, God be praised, hath it any ground or foundation in divine revelation. Nay, the text of Scripture on which the Church of Rome builds this article, duly considered, utterly subverts and overthrows it. She grounds it upon the words of the institution of the Holy Sacrament by our Saviour. . . . Now whatsoever our Saviour said was undoubtedly true ; but these words could not be true in a proper sense ; for our Saviour's body was not then given or broken, but whole and inviolate, nor was there one drop of His blood yet shed. The words therefore must necessarily be understood in a figurative sense ; and then, what becomes of the doctrine of Transubstantiation? The meaning of our Saviour is plainly this : What I now do is a representation of My death and

---

[1] A passage from *The Christian Sacrifice*, chap. ix., by Joseph Mede, Fellow of Christ's College, Cambridge (born 1586, died 1638), is here reproduced by Bishop Bull.

[2] *Const. Ap.* vii. 25.

[3] Compare a passage in Hooker, quoted on p. 247, *supra*.

passion near approaching ; and what I now do, do ye hereafter, ' Do
this in remembrance of Me '; let this be a standing, perpetual ordinance in My Church to the end of the world ; let My death be
thus annunciated and shown forth till I come to judgment. . . . As
little foundation hath this doctrine of Transubstantiation in the
ancient Church, as appears sufficiently from what hath been already
said concerning the notion then universally received of the Eucharistical sacrifice. It was then believed to be an ἀνάμνησις, or commemoration, by the symbols of bread and wine, of the body and
blood of Christ, once offered up to God on the cross for our redemption ; it could not therefore be then thought an offering up again to
God of the very body and blood of Christ, substantially present
under the appearance of bread and wine ; for these two notions are
inconsistent, and cannot stand together. The ancient doctors, yea,
and liturgies of the Church, affirm the Eucharist to be *incruentum
sacrificium,* ' a sacrifice without blood,' which it cannot be said to
be if the very blood of Christ were therein present and offered up
to God. In the Clementine Liturgy the bread and wine in the
Eucharist are said to be *antitypa,* ' correspondent types,' figures,
and images of the precious body and blood of Christ. And divers
others of the fathers speak in the same plain language.[1] . . . We
are not ignorant that the ancient fathers generally teach that the
bread and wine in the Eucharist, by and upon the consecration of
them, do become and are made the body and blood of Christ. But
we know also that, though they do not all explain themselves in the
same way, yet they do all declare their sense to be very dissonant
from the doctrine of Transubstantiation. Some of the most ancient
doctors of the Church, as Justin Martyr and Irenaeus, seem to have
had this notion, that by or upon the sacerdotal benediction, the
Spirit of Christ, or a divine virtue from Christ, descends upon the
elements, and accompanies them to all worthy communicants, and
that therefore they are said to be, and are the body and blood of
Christ, the same divinity, which is hypostatically united to the body
of Christ in heaven, being virtually united to the elements of bread
and wine on earth. Which also seems to be the meaning of all the
ancient liturgies, in which it is prayed, ' that God would send down
His Spirit upon the bread and wine in the Eucharist '. And this
doubtless is the meaning of Origen in his eighth book against Celsus.
. . . But that neither Justin Martyr, nor Irenaeus, nor Origen ever

[1] The passages from St. Gregory of Nazianzus, St. Cyril of Jerusalem,
and *De Sacramentis,* to which Bishop Bull here gives references, are quoted
on vol. i. p. 64, *supra.*

dreamed of the Transubstantiation of the elements is most evident. For Justin Martyr and Irenaeus do both of them plainly affirm that by eating and drinking the bread and wine in the Eucharist 'our bodies are nourished,' and that 'the bread and wine are digested and turned into the substance of our bodies,' which to affirm of the glorified body of Christ were impious and blasphemous, and to affirm the same of the mere accidents of the bread and wine would be very absurd and ridiculous. And Origen expressly saith that ‹ what we eat in the Eucharist is bread, but bread sanctified and made holy by prayer, and which by the divine virtue that accompanies it sanctifieth all those who worthily receive it '." [1]

"Come we now to the principal part of the Christian worship, the Holy Sacrament of the Eucharist. How lamentably hath the Church of Rome vitiated the primitive institution of that most sacred rite! She hath taken from the laity the blessed cup, contrary to our blessed Saviour's express command as expounded by the practice of the Apostles and of the Universal Church of Christ for the first ten centuries, as hath been above observed. . . . Besides, the whole administration of it is so clogged, so metaphorized and defaced by the addition of a multitude of ceremonies, and those some of them more becoming the stage than the Table of our Lord that, if the blessed Apostles were alive and present at the celebration of the Mass in the Roman Church, they would be amazed, and wonder what the meaning of it was; sure I am they would never own it to be that same ceremony which they left to the Churches. But the worst ceremony of all is the elevation of the host to be adored by the people as very Christ Himself under the appearance of bread, whole Christ, Θεάνθρωπος, God and Man, while they neglect the old *sursum corda*, the lifting up of their hearts to heaven, where whole Christ indeed is. A practice this is which nothing can excuse from the grossest idolatry but their gross stupidity, or rather infatuation, in thinking that a piece of bread can by any means whatsoever, or howsoever consecrated and blessed, become their very God and Saviour. A very sad excuse indeed. Moreover, by what reason, by what Scripture, by what example or practice

---

[1] *The Corruptions of the Church of Rome*, section iii. (*Works*, Oxford edition, 1827, ii. 250-56), written in consequence of the wonder expressed by Bossuet that the writer of the *Defensio Fidei Nicænæ*, published in 1685, and the *Judicium Ecclesiæ Catholicæ*, published in 1694, could remain separated from the Church of Rome. The passages from St. Justin Martyr and St. Irenæus and the liturgies and Origen which Bishop Bull here refers to are quoted on vol. i. pp. 34, 35, 38, 86, 151, *supra*.

of the primitive Churches, can the Romanists defend their carrying about the Holy Sacrament in procession, or the mockery of their solitary Masses ? " [1]

The life of Bishop William Beveridge was almost exactly contemporary with that of Bishop Bull.   He was born in 1637, became a sizar of St. John's College, Cambridge, in 1653, took the degree of B.A. in 1656 and of M.A. in 1660, and was ordained deacon and priest in 1661.   After holding the benefices of Ealing and of St. Peter's, Cornhill, and being Archdeacon of Colchester, he was offered the Bishopric of Bath and Wells in 1691, when Bishop Ken had been deposed from that see.[2]   After hesitation and once accepting, he eventually declined it.   In 1704 he was appointed Bishop of St. Asaph.   In 1708 he died.   His Eucharistic teaching is much the same as that of Bishop Bull, though he affirms that those who communicate worthily receive the body and blood of Christ, and lays stress on the realisation by faith that in the administration of the Communion the gifts are received from our Lord Himself.   His opinions are shown in the following extracts :—

"Scripture and fathers holding forth so clearly that whosoever worthily receives the Sacrament of the Lord's Supper doth certainly partake of the body and blood of Christ, the devil thence took occasion to draw men into an opinion that the bread which is used in that Sacrament is the very body that was crucified on the cross, and the wine after consecration the very blood that gushed out of His pierced side. . . . The words ' This is My body ' prove no more than that the bread was the sign or Sacrament of His body, not at all that it is really changed into His body. . . . The very words of institution themselves are sufficient to convince any rational man, whose reason is not darkened by prejudice, that that of which our Saviour said ' This is My body ' was real bread, and so His body only in a figurative or sacramental sense ; and by consequence that the bread was not turned into His body, but His body was only represented by the bread. . . . That which we eat at the Sacrament is bread, and not the very body of Christ ; that which we drink, the cup or wine, and not the very blood of Christ. . . . It being so clear a truth that the bread and wine are not turned into the very body and blood of Christ in the Holy Sacrament, we need not heap up many arguments to prove that it is only after a spiritual, not after

<hr>

[1] *Op. cit.* section iv, (ii, 309, 310).   [2] See p. 455, *infra*.

a corporal manner, that the body and blood of Christ are received and eaten in the Sacrament. . . . If the primitive Church was against the reservation, surely it was much more against the adoration of the Sacrament, holding . . . that no person or thing under any pretence whatsoever ought to be worshipped besides God. I know it is not bare bread our adversaries say they worship, but Christ in the bread, or the bread in the name of Christ. But I wish them to consider what Gregory Nyssen long ago said, 'He that worshippeth a creature, though he do it in the name of Christ, is an idolator, giving the name of Christ to an idol'.[1] And therefore let them not be angry at us for concluding them to be idolators, whilst they eat one piece of the bread, and worship the other. . . . Though godly and spiritual men may feed upon the body and blood of Christ out of the Sacrament as well as in it, yet wicked and carnal men miss of the body and blood of Christ in the Sacrament as well as out of it. . . . The papists . . . agree, . . . avouching that in this Mass they offer up a true and perfect sacrifice to God, propitiatory for the sins of the people, even as Christ did when He offered up Himself to God as a propitiation for our sins. This, I say, is that which the Church of Rome confidently affirms, and which our Church in this article doth as confidently deny. . . . As this doctrine is contrary to Scripture, so is it repugnant to reason too, there being so vast a difference betwixt a Sacrament and a sacrifice; for in a Sacrament God offereth something to man, but in a sacrifice man offers something to God. What is offered in a sacrifice is wholly or in part destroyed, but what is offered in a Sacrament still remaineth. And there being so great a difference betwixt the one and the other, if it be a Sacrament it is not a sacrifice, and if it be a sacrifice it is not a Sacrament, it being impossible it should be both a Sacrament and a sacrifice too. . . . It is Transubstantiation that is the ground of this fond opinion, therefore do they say the body of Christ is really offered up to God, because the bread is first really turned into the body of Christ; but now it being proved before that the bread is bread still after as well as before consecration, and not the very body of Christ, though the bread be consecrated by man, the very body of Christ cannot be offered to God in the Sacrament; and therefore, if they will still call it a sacrifice, they must acknowledge it is such a sacrifice wherein there is nothing but bread and wine offered to God, and by consequence no propitiatory sacrifice; for, as we have seen, 'without shedding of blood there is no remis-

[1] St. Gregory of Nyssa, *Orat. fun. de Placilla* (*Opera*, Paris, 1638, iii. 533; P.G. xlvi. 892).

29 *

sion,'[1] and in the breaking and pouring forth of bread and wine there is no shedding of blood, and not, therefore, any remission of sin. . . . We may see in what sense the ancients called the Eucharist a sacrifice, not as if it were a true or proper sacrifice itself, but only the commemoration or representation of that one and only true and proper sacrifice offered up by Christ Himself; and so all the sacrifices of Mass are at the best but dangerous deceits."[2]

"The outward part or sign in this Sacrament is only bread and wine, which the Lord commanded to be received, that is, to be received into our bodies. . . . But the inward part, or thing signified by that sign in the Lord's Supper, is 'the body and blood of Christ, which are verily and indeed taken and received by the faithful in the Lord's Supper'. . . . He [that is, our Lord] plainly signified that what He now gave them to eat and drink, He would have them look upon it and receive it, not as common bread and wine, but as His body and blood, the one as broken, the other as shed, for their sins. Which therefore are not in show and appearance but verily and indeed (according to the sense wherein the Lord instituting the Sacrament spoke those words) taken and received by the faithful in the Lord's Supper; by the faithful, even by all such, and only such, as believe the Gospel, and what our Lord said, and accordingly receive what He now gives them with a true faith. Which being 'the substance of things hoped for' as well as 'the evidence of things not seen,'[3] it causeth that which our Lord said, and what they therefore hope for and receive upon His word, to subsist really and effectually in them, to all intents and purposes to which the body and blood of Christ can possibly be communicated and received. . . . Though the thing signified in the Sacrament of the Lord's Supper be the body and blood of Christ, yet it is not received, as the sign is, into our bodies only, but into our souls. It is the inward and spiritual part in the Sacrament, and therefore hath respect only to the inward and spiritual part of him that receives it. . . . Our souls are strengthened by the body and blood of Christ

---

[1] Heb. ix. 22.

[2] *Discourse upon the Thirty-nine Articles,* on Articles xxviii. xxix. xxxi. (*Works, Anglo-Catholic Library,* vii. 470, 475, 477, 478, 482, 490, 491, 505, 506, 507, 509). This treatise was first published in an incomplete form, containing only the comments on the first thirty Articles, in 1716, eight years after Beveridge's death. The whole of it was first published in the *Anglo-Catholic Library* from the original MS.

[3] Heb. xi. 1.

received by faith in this Sacrament, because by this means we have Christ Himself to dwell in our hearts by faith." [1]

"The Apostle doth not say that Christ's death is repeated, or that He is offered up again every time this Sacrament is administered, but only that the Lord's death is shown by it. And therefore, that this is not, as the papists absurdly imagine, a 'propitiatory sacrifice for the living and the dead,' but only 'commemorative' and 'declarative' of that one sacrifice which Christ once offered to be a propitiation for the sins of the whole world. . . . We do not eat the very body that hung upon the cross, nor drink the blood which was there spilt for us, but only in a sacramental sense, which quite overthrows the 'doctrine of Transubstantiation'. . . . The elements are not transubstantiated into the body and blood of Christ, as the papists absurdly imagine, but the substance of the bread and wine still continues the same; and therefore without faith no man can receive any more than plain, though consecrated, bread and wine. But they who have, and at the same time act, that faith which is the substance of things hoped for do by that verily and indeed receive the body and blood of Christ according to His word when He said 'This is My body, and this is My blood'. This Christ said, and this they believe, and by their believing it have it verified to them. It is to them that body which was broken, and that blood which was shed, for their sins : they receive it as such upon Christ's word, and accordingly partake of all the merits of it, whereby their sins are all as fully remitted to them as if they themselves had already undergone all the punishments which the law had threatened against them ; for Christ having undergone them all in their stead, and He having now communicated that body and blood in which He did it unto them, and they having by faith accordingly received it, the law is now satisfied as to them, and can no more require that they should suffer the punishments which were due to their sins than it can require that Christ's body and blood, which they have received, should be broken and shed again for them. . . . When we hear the words of consecration repeated as they came from our Lord's own mouth, . . . we are then steadfastly to believe that, although the substance of the bread and wine still remain, yet now it is not common bread and wine as to its use, but the body and blood of Christ in that sacramental sense wherein He spake the words, insomuch that whosoever duly receives these His creatures of bread and wine according to Christ's

[1] *The Church Catechism Explained*, issued for the use of the clergy of the diocese of St. Asaph in 1704 (*Works, op. cit.* viii. 119-21).

holy institution in remembrance of His death and passion are partakers of His most precious body and blood, as it is expressed in the prayer of consecration. When we see the minister distributing the sacramental bread and wine to the several communicants, we are then by faith to look upon our Lord as offering His blessed body and blood and all the benefits of His death to all that will receive them at His hands, entertaining ourselves all the while others are receiving with these or suchlike meditations : Behold the Lamb of God, which taketh away the sins of the world! Behold the Son of God, the only-begotten of the Father, who loved us and gave Himself for us, who Himself bare our sins in His own body on the tree, and washed us from them in His own blood ! . . . Methinks I see Him yonder going about by His minister from one to another, and offering His most blessed body and blood with all the merits of His most precious death to all that will receive them faithfully. . . . Thus we may employ our thoughts while others are receiving ; but when it comes to our turns to receive it, then we are to lay aside all thoughts of bread and wine and minister and everything else that is or can be seen, and fix our faith, as it is ʻ the evidence of things not seen,' wholly and solely upon our blessed Saviour as offering us His own body and blood, to preserve our bodies and souls to everlasting life, which we are therefore to receive by faith, as it is ʻthe substance of things hoped for,'[1] steadfastly believing it to be, as our Saviour said, ʻ His body and blood,' ʻ which,' as our Church teacheth us, ʻare verily and indeed taken and received by the faithful in the Lord's Supper,' by which means, whatsoever it is to others, it will be to us who receive it with such a faith the body and blood of Christ our Saviour, the very ʻsubstance of all things hoped for,' upon the account of His body that was broken, and His blood that was shed, for us. . . . Our Church requires us to receive the Holy Sacrament kneeling, not out of any respect to the creatures of bread and wine, but to put us in mind that Almighty God, our Creator and Redeemer, the only object of all religious worship, is there specially present, offering His own body and blood to us, that so we may act our faith in Him, and express our sense of His goodness to us, and our unworthiness of it, in the most humble posture that we can. . . . How can I pray in faith to Almighty God to preserve both my body and soul to everlasting life, and not make my body as well as soul bow down before Him ? How can I by faith behold my Saviour coming to me, and offering me His own body and blood, and not fall down and worship Him ?

[1] Heb. xi. 1,

How can I by faith lay hold upon the pardon of my sins, as there sealed and delivered to me, and receive it any otherwise than upon my knees ? " [1]

Similarly, in the *Thesaurus Theologicus*, a series of notes on passages of Holy Scripture composed by Bishop Beveridge for his own use and published in 1711, three years after his death, he rejects Transubstantiation, denies that what we receive is " the real body and blood of Christ," affirms that those who receive worthily feed spiritually on the body and blood of Christ, and interprets the word " body " in the sentence " This is My body " to mean the figure or sign or Sacrament of the body.[2]

II.

Another contemporary of Bull and Beveridge was Bishop Ken. Thomas Ken was born in 1637. He was a Fellow of New College, Oxford, and a Fellow of Winchester. After holding several ecclesiastical preferments, he was consecrated Bishop of Bath and Wells in 1685. He was one of the " seven bishops " imprisoned in the Tower in 1688 for refusing to proclaim the " Declaration for Liberty of Conscience " ordered by King James II. On the accession of William and Mary he refused to take the new oath of allegiance, and was in consequence deprived of his see in 1691. He was opposed to the continuance of a Non-juring body by the consecration of bishops, and in 1701 suggested that he and Bishop Lloyd of Norwich, the only two deprived bishops then living, should resign their canonical claims on the sees of Bath and Wells and Norwich. In 1702 he declined the offer of Queen Anne to

---

[1] *The Great Necessity and Advantage of Frequent Communion,* first printed in 1710, two years after Beveridge's death (*Works, op. cit.* viii. 534, 546, 547, 604-7). In this discourse Beveridge mentions the great neglect of Communion in the Church of England, and says that in all parts of the kingdom there are a great many church-goers of all ages who have never once received Communion (p. 536). He expresses his own wish for daily Celebrations, and adds that in the Church of England, " if a sufficient number of parishioners, against whom there is no just exception, desire to receive " the Holy Communion " every Sunday, or every day in the year, the minister of their parish not only may, but " " is bound to consecrate and administer it to them, the want of such a number being, as far as I can perceive, the only reason that can ever justify the omission of it " (pp. 567, 568).

[2] *Works, op. cit.* ix. 432-34, 486-88, x. 83, 84, 87.

restore to him the bishopric of Bath and Wells; and in 1703, when Bishop Kidder, the occupant of the see, was killed by an accident, and it was offered to George Hooper, then Bishop of St. Asaph, he urged Hooper to accept, and ceded his rights to him. Ken died in 1711. His *Manual of Prayers for the Use of Winchester Scholars*, first published in 1674, shows his belief in a " mysterious presence " of the body and blood of Christ " in the Holy Sacrament," and that the body and blood are communicated to those who receive worthily.

"I know, O my God, that I must look through the outward elements, and fix my faith on that which they signify, and which is the inward and invisible grace, even Thy own blessed body and blood, which is verily and indeed taken and received of the faithful in the Lord's Supper.

" But tell me, O Thou whom my soul loveth, how canst Thou give us Thy flesh to eat?

" Lord, Thou hast told me that Thy words, they are spirit and they are life, and are therefore not carnally to be understood ; Lord, I believe, help Thou mine unbelief.

"I believe Thy body and blood to be as really present in the Holy Sacrament, as Thy divine power can make it, though the manner of Thy mysterious presence I cannot comprehend.

" Lord, I believe that the bread that we break, and the cup that we drink, are not bare signs only, but the real communication of Thy body and Thy blood, and pledges to assure me of it; and I verily believe that, if with due preparation I come to Thy altar, as certainly as I receive the outward signs, so certainly shall I receive the thing signified, even Thy most blessed body and blood, to receive which inestimable blessing, O merciful Lord, do Thou fit and prepare me."

"I adore Thee, O blessed Jesu, my Lord and my God, when I consider the benefits which through Thy mercy we receive by Thy Holy Sacrament.

"Glory be to Thee, O Lord, who there makest Thy own body and blood to become our spiritual food to strengthen and refresh our souls.

"Glory be to Thee, O Lord, who by this heavenly food dost mystically unite us to Thyself; for nothing becomes one with our bodies more than the bodily food we eat, which turns into our very substance ; and nothing makes us become one with Thee more than when Thou vouchsafest to become the very food of our souls.

"Glory be to Thee, O Lord, who by this immortal food dost

nourish our souls to live the life of grace here, and dost raise us up to life everlasting hereafter. Lord, do Thou evermore give me this bread." [1]

In his *An Exposition on the Church Catechism, or the Practice of Divine Love*, first published in 1685, Ken wrote:—

" Glory be to Thee, O adorable Jesus, who under the outward and visible part, the bread and wine, things obvious and easily prepared, both which Thou hast commanded to be received, dost communicate to our souls the mystery of divine love, the inward and invisible grace, Thy own most blessed body and blood, which are verily and indeed taken and received by the faithful in Thy Supper, for which all love, all glory be to Thee.

" O God incarnate, how the bread and wine, unchanged in their substance, become Thy body and Thy blood, after what extraordinary manner Thou, who art in heaven, art present throughout the whole sacramental action to every devout receiver, how Thou canst give us Thy flesh to eat and Thy blood to drink, how Thy flesh is meat indeed and Thy blood is drink indeed, how he that eateth Thy flesh and drinketh Thy blood dwelleth in Thee and Thou in him, how he shall live by Thee and be raised up by Thee to life eternal, I can by no means comprehend, but I firmly believe all Thou hast said, and I firmly rely in Thy omnipotent love to make good Thy word, for which all love, all glory, be to Thee.

" I believe, O crucified Lord, that the bread which we break in the celebration of the holy mysteries is the communication of Thy body, and the cup of blessing which we bless is the communication of Thy blood, and that Thou dost as effectually and really convey Thy body and blood to our souls by the bread and wine as Thou didst Thy Holy Spirit by Thy breath to Thy disciples, for which all love, all glory, be to Thee." [2]

A devotional book entitled *A Week's Preparation towards a Worthy Receiving of the Lord's Supper* was published anony-

[1] Pp. 42, 43, 47, edition 1675.

[2] Pp. 75, 76, edition 1686. In the first edition (1685) the paragraph quoted above beginning " O God incarnate," began " O God incarnate, how Thou canst give us Thy flesh to eat and Thy blood to drink, how Thy flesh is meat indeed and Thy blood is drink indeed, how he that eateth Thy flesh and drinketh Thy blood dwelleth in Thee and Thou in him, how he shall live by Thee and shall be raised up by Thee to life eternal, how Thou, who art in heaven, art present on the altar, I can by no means explain ". This was altered so as to be as above in the " revised " edition published in 1686.

mously in 1679. It became a standard book of the time, had
passed through twenty-five editions before 1700, and reached
a fifty-first edition in 1751. The meditations and prayers which
it contains are of great devotion and fervour ; they assume that
those who partake of the Sacrament worthily obtain the benefits
of the life and death of Christ and spiritually receive His body
and blood.

"O my Jesus, Thou savedst me by Thy blood! In this Thy
Sacrament Thou art set forth crucified, and I behold Thy wounds,
from whence by the hand of faith I pluck forth these comfortable
words of life, 'My Lord and my God'. My God! Mine, for Thou
hast partaken of my human nature, and Thou hast made me to
partake of Thy divine nature; Thou hast taken upon Thee my
flesh, and Thou hast communicated unto me of Thy Spirit. In this
Thy Holy Sacrament Thou communicatest body and blood, flesh
and spirit, Thy whole manhood, yea, Thy very Godhead too. . . .
The bread and wine I eat and drink is not more really my food
than Thou, my Jesus, in whom I believe and trust, art my God. . . .
The faithful communicant doth receive that which the Word found,
to wit, preservation unto life everlasting both to his body and
soul. For the humbled sinner, believing in the Incarnation, death,
and passion of Jesus, and receiving this bread and wine in token
that God hath given Him for our sins, and relying on Him as his
only Redeemer; this doth convey to such a penitent believer all
the benefits of the birth and the death of Jesus. And, as the
bread and wine, being received, do communicate to us all the
strength and comfort that they contain, so the worthy receiver, by
apprehending and embracing a crucified Saviour, draws persuasions
of his pardon and encouragement to his graces, and so spiritually
eats the flesh of Christ, and drinks His blood. . . . Christ, to show
His love towards us, has given us of His own bread, and of His
own cup; nay, He hath given us His own body as bread, His own
blood as wine, for the nourishment of our souls." [1]

"O most good and gracious Jesus, Thou before Thy sufferings
and death didst bequeath a most excellent gift unto Thy children
as a pledge of Thy love, leaving for us Thy most sacred body to
be our meat, and Thy most precious blood to be our drink. O
Thou true food of my soul, receive me, who am to receive Thee,
quicken me with Thy Spirit, feed me with Thy flesh, satisfy me

[1] Pp. 4, 5, 8, 12, 13, edition 1855.

with Thy blood, and let me receive life from Thee to act and to live unto Thee." [1]

"I am not worthy, O Lord, I am not worthy to come into Thy presence, much less to eat at Thy Table the flesh of the sacrificed Lamb. . . . Vouchsafe, good Lord, I humbly beseech Thee, so to work in my heart by Thy grace and Holy Spirit that I may worthily receive these heavenly mysteries to the reviving and refreshing of my sinful soul; that I may purge out the old leaven of my corrupt and wicked nature by hearty and unfeigned repentance; that I may spiritually eat Christ's flesh, and drink His blood by a true and lively faith; that I may effectually feed upon the merits of His Incarnation, passion, resurrection, and ascension by virtue of Thy sweet and comfortable promises made unto us in the word of Thy Holy Gospel; finally, that I may be partaker of all the fruits and benefits of that most precious and perfect sacrifice which He in the body of His flesh offered up once for all upon the cross for the redemption and salvation of mankind." [2]

"O Almighty and eternal God, what worthy praise can I give unto Thee, . . . especially for feeding me this day with the precious body and blood of Jesus Christ." [3]

In 1681 was published a book entitled *The Whole Duty of a Communicant, being Rules and Directions for a Worthy Receiving the Most Holy Sacrament of the Lord's Supper* which was ascribed to John Gauden, who had been appointed Dean of Bocking in 1641, was made Bishop of Exeter in 1660 and Bishop of Worcester in 1662, and died in 1662. This book also appears to have been much used, since it reached a seventh edition in 1698. The following passages show the doctrinal beliefs of the writer:—

"We deny not a true and real presence and perception of Christ's body and blood in the Sacrament, which in reality even they of the other gross opinion do not imagine is to sense, but to faith; which perceives its objects as really according to faith's perception as the senses do theirs after their manner. I believe, therefore, that in the Sacrament of the Lord's Supper there are both objects presented to and received by a worthy receiver. First, the bread and wine in their own nature and substances distinct do remain as well as their accidents, which are the true objects of our sense. . . . Also there are spiritual, invisible, and credible, yet most true and really present, objects of faith, the body and blood of Christ, that is, Christ Jesus Himself." [1]

"I adore Thee, O most righteous Redeemer, that Thou art pleased to convey unto my soul Thy precious body and blood, with all the benefits of Thy death and passion; I am not worthy, O Lord, to receive Thee, but let Thy Holy and Blessed Spirit, with all His purities, prepare for Thee a lodging in my soul, where Thou mayest unite me to Thyself for ever." [2]

Anthony Horneck, a native of Germany, was born in 1641 and came to England twenty years later. He became a member of Queen's College, Oxford, in 1663, and an incorporated M.A. of the University of Oxford in the following year. He held the benefices of All Saints, Oxford, and of Dolton in Devonshire, and was Prebendary of Exeter and Westminster and Wells, and preacher at the Savoy. He died in 1697. His devotional works, *The Fire of the Altar*, first published in 1683, and *The Crucified Jesus*, first published in 1686, were popular and influential in the Church of England in the latter part of the seventeenth century and the early years of the eighteenth, and went through many editions. The acts of spiritual communing with our Lord at the time of Communion are of intense feeling; his belief was clearly a form of Virtualism. He rejects Transubstantiation and Consubstantiation, explains the word "body" in the sentence "This is My body" as meaning a sign or figure or memorial of the body, and interprets the eating of Christ's body to be effected by the subjective acts of the soul.

"Transubstantiation is a thing which neither the Scripture nor the primitive Church did ever acknowledge; and, there being nothing in the word of God to establish it, and being besides contrary to all sense and reason, we must be first given up to believe a lie, as some men it seems are (2 Thess. ii. 11), before we can give assent unto it. . . . As these words 'This is My body' do not infer a Transubstantiation, so neither do they import a Consubstantiation, a word as hard as the former, and which have been taken up by the Lutheran Protestants to express their opinion that Christ's glorified body is in, with, and under the element of the bread in the Holy Sacrament, or hid under it, a doctrine which they ground upon the ubiquity of Christ's body, or being everywhere or in all places, which privilege they fancy was communicated to Christ's

---

[1] P. 20, edition 1698.   [2] P. 136.

human nature by its being joined with the divine. . . . Christ is present in the Holy Sacrament by His power and influence and gracious assistances, which sincere believers feel in their worthy receiving; but from hence it can never be made out that His body therefore is hid under the bread. . . . In what sense the bread in this Sacrament is the body of Christ, we may easily guess, if we explain Scripture by Scripture, and compare this expression with others not unlike it. 1. ' This is My body,' that is, This is a significant emblem or sign or figure of My body ; or this bread, thus broken, represents My body, that shall be crucified for the sins of the world. . . . 2. ' This is My body,' that is, This bread is My body as the roasted lamb in the great festival of the Jews was the passover, that is, the memorial of it. . . . 3. That Christ's Church is often called His body none can be ignorant that peruses these passages, Col. i. 18, Eph. v. 23, Eph. iv. 12, 1 Cor. x. 16, 1 Cor. xii. 27 ; and though that sense we have already alleged be the principal thing aimed at in these words, ' This is My body,' yet to show how little need there is to have recourse either to Transubstantiation or Consubstantiation, rather than run into such absurdities, we might very well say that the bread is an emblem or adumbration of Christ's body, that is, of Christ's Church." [1]

" From what hath been said it is easy to conclude what it is to eat Christ's body in this Holy Sacrament. 1. It is to contemplate Christ's crucified body, and the cause and reasons of that crucifixion, to view all this with our warmest thoughts, to make serious reflections on His death and agonies, and the bitterness of His passion. . . . 2. To eat Christ's body is to apply the benefits of His death and passion to our souls, and to rejoice in them as our greatest treasure. . . . 3. To make this crucified body a persuasive and motive to holiness and obedience." [2]

" In all writings, both ancient and modern, about this Holy Sacrament there are various rhetorical expressions used which we must not understand literally, but as flowers strewed upon the hearse of our blessed Redeemer, and as ornaments of speech, to represent the greatness of the mystery. There is nothing more common among the fathers than to call the bread and wine in the Lord's Supper the body and blood of Christ, and the cup the vessel in which Christ's blood is contained ; and many times Christ is said to stand at the altar, and all the holy angels standing at the Table ; that Christ offers His body to be bruised by the people's teeth,

[1] *The Crucified Jesus*, chap. xi. sect. 1-3.
[2] *Op. cit.* chap. xi. sect. 4.

and dyes them red with His blood ; that the elements are changed, and become the body and blood of the Lord Jesus ; and that after prayer and thanksgiving they are no more what they were before ; and a thousand such expressions besides ; from which the Church of Rome presently infers that they believed a Transubstantiation or a conversion of the elements into the substance of Christ's body and blood, than which nothing can be more absurd ; for, if a man compare these sayings of the ancients with other passages in their writings, it plainly appears that they meant no more than that the elements are representative of all this, and that the expressions they use are nothing but rhetorical flourishes to raise the people's affections, and to render their devotions brisk, lively, fervent, affectionate, and vigorous.   We do the same at this day when we tell you that you come to feast with Christ ; that in this Sacrament He is crucified before your eyes ; that you may see His blood run down ; that you hear Him groan under the burden of your sins ; that you see here His body hanging on the cross ; that you are to stand under the tree, and catch the precious gore as balsam for your souls ; all which is true in a spiritual sense, and we do it to make you more attentive, and set this passion out in such lively characters that your souls may be touched and enlivened ; and, as things represented in brighter colours strike the senses more, so we speak of these things as if they were visible and perceptible by the outward eyes, that your souls may more cheerfully feed on the kernel that lies in those shells, and with greater life embrace the glorious benefits, which come to you by that precious sacrifice." [1]

III.

John Tillotson was born in 1630.   He was a Fellow of Clare Hall, Cambridge.   In 1660 or 1661 he was ordained by Bishop Thomas Sydserff. [2]   After holding various posts, and being successively Dean of Canterbury and St. Paul's, he became Archbishop of Canterbury in 1691.   He died in 1694.   He was strongly opposed to the doctrine of Transubstantiation on the grounds that it was taught neither in Holy Scripture nor in the fathers, and is contrary to reason, and gives rise to scandals and absurdities.   His own opinion appears to have been that those

[1] *Op. cit.* chap. xi. consid. 1.

[2] Sydserff had been consecrated Bishop of Galloway in 1635.   With the other Scottish bishops he was deposed and excommunicated by the General Assembly in 1638.   In 1661, when he was the only survivor of the bishops deposed in 1638, he was appointed Bishop of Orkney.

who communicate worthily keep in memory the death of Christ and receive the benefits of His work. In the preface prefixed to the *Discourses* which he himself published, he wrote :—

"Supposing the thing to be believed to be Transubstantiation, this indeed is a very profound mystery, and is . . . of its own nature so seemingly impossible that I know no argument in the world strong enough to cope with it." [1]

In his sermon *On the Hazard of being saved in the Church of Rome* he spoke of Transubstantiation and adoration as follows :—

"The doctrine of Transubstantiation. A hard word, but I would to God that were the worst of it ; the thing is much more difficult. I have taken some pains to consider other religions that have been in the world, and I must freely declare that I never yet in any of them met with any article or proposition imposed upon the belief of men half so unreasonable and hard to be believed as this is. And yet this in the Romish Church is esteemed one of the most principal articles of the Christian faith, though there is no more certain foundation for it in Scripture than for our Saviour's being substantially changed into all those things which are said of Him, as that He is a rock, a vine, a door, and a hundred other things. . . . If the testimony of sense is to be relied upon, then Transubstantiation is false ; if it be not, then no man is sure that Christianity is true. For the utmost assurance that the Apostles had of the truth of Christianity was the testimony of their own senses concerning our Saviour's miracles ; and this testimony every man hath against Transubstantiation. From whence it plainly follows that no man (no, not the Apostles themselves) had more reason to believe Christianity to be true than every man to believe Transubstantiation to be false. . . . Supposing the Scripture to be a divine revelation, and that these words ' This is My body,' if they be in Scripture, must necessarily be taken in the strict and literal sense, I ask now what greater evidence any man has that these words ' This is My body ' are in the Bible than every man has that the bread is not changed in the Sacrament. Nay, no man has so much ; for we have only the evidence of one sense that these words are in the Bible, but that the bread is not changed we have the concurring testimony of several of our senses. In a word, if this be once admitted that the senses of all men are deceived in one of the most plain sensible matters that can be, there is no certain means left either to convey

<hr>

[1] Preface, p. iv, *Works*, vol. i, edition 1728.

or prove a divine revelation to men, nor is there any way to confute the grossest impostures in the world." [1]

"The worshipping of the bread and wine in the Eucharist out of a false and groundless persuasion that they are substantially changed into the body and blood of Christ. Which, if it be not true (and it hath good fortune if it be, for certainly it is one of the most incredible things in the whole world) then by the confession of several of their own learned writers they are guilty of gross idolatry." [2]

In the sermon entitled *A Persuasive to Frequent Communion* Tillotson mentions the belief about the Eucharist which he himself held :—

"If this be the end and use of this Sacrament, to be a solemn remembrance of the death and sufferings of our Lord during His absence from us, that is, till His coming to judgment, then this Sacrament will never be out of date till the second coming of our Lord. The consideration whereof should mightily strengthen and encourage our faith in the hope of eternal life so often as we partake of this Sacrament, since our Lord hath left it to us as a memorial of Himself till He come to translate His Church into heaven, and as a sure pledge that He will come again at the end of the world, and invest us in that glory which He is now gone before to prepare for us." [3]

In the sermon entitled *A Discourse against Transubstantiation* Tillotson maintains at length that the language of Holy Scripture and of the fathers does not mean more than that the Sacrament is a sign and pledge of the body and blood of Christ ; that the doctrine of Transubstantiation causes scandal through its "stupidity" and "barbarousness" and "cruel and bloody consequences" and "danger of idolatry" ; and that it is absurd as being contradictory to sense.

"Infidelity were hardly possible to men, if all men had the same evidence for the Christian religion which they have against Transub-

---

[1] *Works, op. cit.* i. 95, 96.   [2] *Op. cit.* i. 97.

[3] *Op. cit.* i. 226. It is of interest to notice that Tillotson, in spite of his strong opposition to Roman Catholic doctrine and practice, says in this sermon, in regard to those who exclude themselves from Communion for "months" or "years," that attacks on the Church of Rome for withholding one part of the Sacrament do not come well from those who deprive themselves of the whole (p. [236]).

stantiation, that is, the clear and irresistible evidence of sense. He that can once be brought to contradict or deny his senses is at an end of certainty ; for what can a man be certain of, if he be not certain of what he sees ? " [1]

In *A Discourse to His Servants Concerning Receiving the Sacrament*, which was published after his death, Tillotson shortly explains his positive belief.

" It is the most solemn institution of our religion ; and, as we are Christians, we are obliged to the frequent receiving of it, and we cannot neglect it without a great contempt of our blessed Saviour and His religion. He hath appointed it for a solemn remembrance of His great love for us in laying down His life for us ; and therefore He commands us to do it in remembrance of Him ; and St. Paul tells us that ' as often as we eat this bread, and drink this cup, we do show forth the Lord's death till He come '.[2] Both the comfort and the benefit of it are great. The comfort of it, because it does not only represent to us the exceeding love of our Saviour in giving His body to be broken, and His blood to be shed, for us, but it like-wise seals to us all those blessings and benefits which are purchased and procured for us by His death and passion, the pardon of sins, and power against sin. The benefit of it is also great, because hereby we are confirmed in goodness, and our resolutions of better obedience are strengthened, and the grace of God's Holy Spirit to enable us to do His will is hereby conveyed to us." [3]

IV.

During the reign of James II. many pamphlets were pub-lished in England attacking the Church of Rome. Some of these were wholly or partly directed against the doctrines ascribed to the Church of Rome in regard to the Eucharist. Instances may be seen in those entitled *A Discourse Concerning the Adoration of the Host as it is Taught and Practised in the Church of Rome*, published in 1685 ; *A Discourse against Transubstantiation*, published in 1685 ; and *The Necessity of Reformation with Respect to the Errors and Corruptions of the Church of Rome*, in two parts, both published in 1686. The writers of these pamph-lets reject Transubstantiation ; the definition of the Council of Trent that the Eucharist is a " proper sacrifice " ; and the view, supposed to be accepted by some Roman Catholics, that in the

[1] *Op. cit.* i. 243.   [2] 1 Cor. xi. 26.   [3] *Op. cit.* iii. 639.

Mass Christ died anew. Their positive opinions are less clearly stated. It is probable that they believed in a special degree of spiritual communion with our Lord which the reception of the Sacrament made possible for those who partook of it worthily; and held that the Eucharist was in some sense a setting forth of the sacrifice of the death of Christ. An illustration of the extent to which the teaching of the Church of Rome was misunderstood by such writers, possibly not without excuse from some statements made by Roman Catholics not well acquainted with theology, may be seen in the following quotation :—

"The Church of England doth not quarrel at the name of sacrifice ; she not only grants, but asserts, that the Eucharist is a commemorative and representative sacrifice. And this was the meaning of the ancient fathers, who frequently call it a remembrance or commemoration, a resemblance or representation, of the sacrifice which Christ once offered upon the cross. And this is as much as Cassander [1] seems to mean by it. But this will not satisfy the present Church of Rome ; but Christ (as they will have it) is truly and properly sacrificed ; that is, according to their own notion of a sacrifice, Christ is truly and properly put to death as oft as the priest says Mass. For in a true sacrifice (as Bellarmine tells us) the thing sacrificed must be destroyed ; and, if it be a thing that hath life, it must be killed. And so indeed many of the Romanists roundly assert that Christ every day is by the Mass-priest." [2]

In 1687 and 1688 respectively two treatises entitled *Two Discourses concerning the Adoration of our Saviour in the Eucharist* and *A Compendious Discourse of the Eucharist* were issued from the private printing press of Obadiah Walker, the

[1] George Cassander, a Belgian theologian of the Church of Rome, born 1515, died 1566, who attempted to promote a mediating position on some of the Reformation controversies. His most famous book, *Consultatio de articulis religionis intra Catholicos et Protestantes controversis*, was published in 1577, eleven years after his death, and, some think, against his wish. As regards the Eucharist he falls short of the explicit assertion of Transubstantiation, but maintains that, while Christ is visibly present at the right hand of the Father, His real body and blood are invisibly and incomprehensibly in the Sacrament, in which there is a conversion and change of the elements, and that the flesh and blood of Christ are received by all communicants, though beneficially only by those who communicate worthily. His view of the Eucharist as a commemorative sacrifice probably did not differ from that of many Roman Catholic theologians.

[2] *The Necessity of Reformation*, part i. p. 41.

Master of University College, Oxford, who had long been suspected of being a Roman Catholic, and had since 1686 arranged
for the saying of Mass after the Roman Catholic rite at University College. They were the work of Abraham Woodhead, who
had been a Fellow of University College, had been ejected from
his Fellowship in 1648, had become a Roman Catholic by 1654,
had been re-instated in his Fellowship in 1660, who died in 1678.
These treatises contain careful and moderate statements of the
ordinary theology of the Church of Rome in regard to the
Eucharist. In defending Transubstantiation, and the adoration
of our Lord in the Sacrament, and the doctrine of the Eucharistic sacrifice, the writer takes pains to repudiate gross ideas of
a presence of a carnal kind; to explain that by adoration he
means " adoration of Christ's body as present with the symbols
before communicating," not simply " adoration of Christ's body
or of Christ as in heaven in the act of communicating"; and to
emphasise that the sacrifice in the Eucharist does not involve
any repetition of the sacrifice of the cross or of Christ's death.[1]
The publication of these two treatises elicited a number of
replies. One of the most noteworthy was the answer to the first
of the two treatises entitled *A Discourse of the Holy Eucharist
in the Two Great Points of the Real Presence and the Adoration
of the Host*, which was published anonymously in 1687 but
ascribed to William Wake, who afterwards became Dean of
Exeter in 1701, Bishop of Lincoln in 1705, and Archbishop of
Canterbury in 1716. The opinion maintained in this work
appears to be a form of Receptionism. The following quotations are representative of the teaching contained in it:—

" Whilst we thus oppose the errors of some by asserting the
continuance of the natural substance of the elements of bread and
wine in this Holy Eucharist, let not any one think that we would
therefore set up the mistakes of others, as if this Holy Sacrament
were nothing more than a mere rite and ceremony, a bare commemoration only of Christ's death and passion. Our Church indeed
teaches us to believe that the bread and wine continue still in their
true and natural substance, but it teaches us also that it is the
body and blood of Christ which every faithful soul receives in that
Holy Supper, spiritually indeed and after a heavenly manner, but
yet most truly and really too. The primitive fathers, of whom we

[1] See *e.g.*, *A Compendious Discourse on the Eucharist*, pp. 14-16, 50, 75.

have before spoken, sufficiently assure us that they were strangers to that corporeal change that is now pretended; but for this divine and mystical, they have openly enough declared for it. Nor are we therefore afraid to confess a change, and that a very great one too, made in this Holy Sacrament. The bread and the wine which we here consecrate ought not to be given or received by any one in this mystery as common ordinary food. Those holy elements which the prayers of the Church have sanctified, and the divine words of our Blessed Saviour applied to them, though not transubstantiated, yet certainly separated to a holy use and signification, ought to be regarded with a very just honour by us; and, whilst we worship Him whose death we herein commemorate, and of whose grace we expect to be made partakers by it, we ought certainly to pay no little regard to the types and figures by which He has chosen to represent the one and convey to us the other. Thus therefore we think we shall best divide our piety if we adore our Redeemer in heaven, yet omit nothing that may testify our just esteem of His Holy Sacrament on earth, nor suffer the most zealous votary for this new opinion to exceed us in our care and reverence of approaching to His Holy Table. We acknowledge Him to be no less really present, though after another manner than they, nor do we less expect to communicate of His body and blood with our souls than they who think they take Him carnally into their mouths." [1]

"To state the notion of the real presence as acknowledged by the Church of England. I must observe, first, that our Church utterly denies our Saviour's body to be so really present in the Blessed Sacrament as either to leave heaven or to exist in several places at the same time. . . . Secondly, that we deny that in the sacred elements which we receive there is any other substance than that of bread and wine distributed to the communicants, which alone they take into their mouths and press with their teeth. In short, 'all which the doctrine of our Church implies by this phrase is only a real presence of Christ's invisible power and grace so in and with the elements as by the faithful receiving of them to convey spiritual and real effects to the souls of men. As the bodies assumed by angels might be called their bodies while they assumed them, or rather, as the Church is the body of Christ because of His Spirit quickening and enlivening the souls of believers, so the bread and wine after consecration are the real but the spiritual and mystical body of Christ.' [2] Thus has that learned man, to whom T. G. first

---

[1] Pp. 37-39.
[2] Quoted from *Answer to T. G.'s Dialogues*, published in 1679, p. 66.

made this objection, stated the notion of the real presence professed
by us; and that this is indeed the true doctrine of the Church of
England in this matter is evident not only from the plain words of
our twenty-eighth Article and of our Church Catechism, but also
from the whole tenor of that Office which we use in the Celebration
of it. . . . I will not deny but that some men may possibly have
advanced their own private notions beyond what is here said; but
this, I am sure, is all that our Church warrants, or that we are therefore concerned to defend. And, if there be any who, as our author
here expresses it, do believe Christ's natural body to be, as in heaven,
so in the Holy Sacrament, they may please to consider how this
can be reconciled with the rubric of our Church, 'That the natural
body and blood of our Saviour Christ are in heaven and not here,
it being against the truth of Christ's natural body to be at one time
in more places than one'." [1]

" I know but one objection more that is, or can be, offered against
what I have said, and, which having answered, I shall close this point,
' For, if this be all the Church of England understands when it
speaks of a real presence, namely, a real sacramental presence of
Christ's body and blood in the holy signs, and a real spiritual presence in the inward Communion of them to the soul of every worthy
receiver, will not this precipitate us into downright Zwinglianism,
and render us after all our pretences as very Sacramentaries as they
are?' Indeed, I am not able directly to say whether it will or no,
because I find the opinion of Zwinglius very variously represented
as to this matter. But yet, first, if by Zwinglianism he means that
which is more properly Socinianism, namely, a mere commemoration
of Christ's death, and a thanksgiving to God for it, it is evident it
does not, forasmuch as we positively confess that in this Holy Sacrament there is a real and spiritual grace communicated to us, even
all the benefits of that death and passion which we there set forth.
And this, or something like it, I find sometimes to have been maintained by Zwinglius. But now, secondly, if by Zwinglianism he
understands such a real presence as denies only the co-existence of
Christ's natural body now in heaven at the same time in this Holy
Sacrament, but denies nothing of that real and spiritual Communion
of it we have before mentioned, this is indeed our doctrine, nor
shall we be ashamed to own it for any ill names he is able to put
upon it. . . . I shall close up this discourse of the real presence
acknowledged by us in this Holy Sacrament with a plain familiar
example, and which may serve at once both to illustrate and confirm

[1] Pp, 43-46,

the propriety of it. A father makes his last will, and by it be-
queaths his estate and all the profits of it to his child. He delivers
it into the hands of his son, and bids him take there his house and
his lands, which by this his last will he delivers to him. The son
in this case receives nothing but a roll of parchment with a seal tied
to it from his father ; but yet by virtue of this parchment he is entituled to his estate performing the conditions of his will and to all
the benefits and advantages of it; and in that deed he truly and
effectually received the very house and lands that were thereby conveyed to him. Our Saviour Christ in like manner, being now about
to leave the world, gives this Holy Sacrament as His final bequest
to us ; in it He conveys to us a right to His body and blood, and to
all the spiritual blessings and graces that proceed from them. So
that as often as we receive this Holy Eucharist as we ought to do,
we receive indeed nothing but a little bread and wine into our
hands, but by the blessing and promise of Christ we by that bread
and wine as really and truly become partakers of Christ's body and
blood as the son by the will of his father was made inheritor of his
estate ; nor is it any more necessary for this that Christ's body should
come down from heaven, or the outward elements which we receive
be substantially turned into it than it is necessary in that other
case that the very houses and lands should be given into the hands
of the son to make a real delivery or conveyance of them, or the
will of the father be truly and properly changed into the very nature
and substance of them." [1]

A further illustration of the Eucharistic doctrine held by
Archbishop Wake may be seen in his *The Principles of the
Christian Religion Explained in a Brief Commentary upon the
Church Catechism*, which he wrote when a parish priest for the
use of his parish, and republished when he was Bishop of Lincoln
for the benefit of the clergy of his diocese. It contains the
following passages :—

"Q. Can Christ any more suffer or die now since His rising from
the dead ?

"A. No, St. Paul expressly tells us that He can not. . . .

"Q. How then do those of the Church of Rome say that He is
again offered for us as a true and proper sacrifice in this Holy Sacrament ?

[1] Pp. 82-85. The same illustration is used by Cosin in his *History of
Popish Transubstantiation*, chap. v. sect. 5 (*Works, Anglo-Catholic Library*,
iv. 58, 180). For Cosin's teaching, see pp. 321-28, *supra*.

"*A.* This Sacrament is not a renewal or repetition of Christ's sacrifice, but only a solemn memorial and exhibition of it. To talk of an expiatory sacrifice for sin without suffering is not only contrary to Scripture but is in the nature of the thing itself absurd and unreasonable, every sacrifice being put in the place of the person for whom it is offered, and to be treated so as that person in rigour ought to have been, had not God admitted of a sacrifice in his stead. And therefore the Apostle from hence concludes that Christ could not be more than once offered because He could but once suffer.[1] But to suppose that Christ in His present glorified state can suffer is such a contradiction to all the principles of our religion that the papists themselves are ashamed to assert it.

"*Q.* What do you think of the sacrifice, as they call it, of the Mass ?

"*A.* We do not deny but that in a large sense this Sacrament may be called a sacrifice, as the bread and wine may be called the body and blood of Christ. But that this Sacrament should be a true and proper sacrifice, as they define the sacrifice of the Mass to be, it is altogether false and impious to assert.

"*Q.* What was then the design of our Saviour in this institution ?

"*A.* To leave to His Church a perpetual, solemn, and sacred memorial of His death for us : that as often as we come to the Lord's Table and there join in the Celebration of this Holy Sacrament, we might be moved by what is there done at once both to call to our remembrance all the passages of His passion (to consider Him as there set forth crucified before our eyes) and to meditate upon the love of Christ thus dying for us, and upon the mighty benefits and advantages which have accrued to us thereby, and have our hearts affected after a suitable manner towards Him."[2]

"*Q.* Are the body and blood of Christ really distributed to every communicant in this Sacrament ?

"*A.* No, they are not ; for then every communicant, whether prepared or not for it, would alike receive Christ's body and blood there. That which is given by the priest to the communicant is as to its nature the same after consecration that it was before, namely, bread and wine, only altered as to its use and signification.

"*Q.* If the body and blood of Christ be not really given and distributed by the priest, how can they be verily and indeed taken and received by the faithful communicant ?

"*A.* That which is given by the priest is as to its substance

---

[1] Heb. ix. 25, 26, x, 10-12.　　[2] Sect. xlvi,

bread and wine ; as to its sacramental nature and signification it is the figure or representation of Christ's body and blood, which was broken and shed for us. The very body and blood of Christ as yet it is not. But, being with faith and piety received by the communicant, it becomes to him by the blessing of God and the grace of the Holy Spirit the very body and blood of Christ. . . .

"Q. How does the bread and wine become to the faithful and worthy communicant the very body and blood of Christ ?

" A. As it entitles him to a part in the sacrifice of His death, and to the benefits thereby procured to all His faithful and obedient servants.

" Q. How does every such communicant take and receive the body and blood of Christ in this Sacrament ?

" A. By faith ; and by means whereof he who comes worthily to the Holy Table is as truly entitled to a part in Christ's sacrifice by receiving the sacramental bread and wine which is there delivered to him as any man is entitled to an estate by receiving a deed of conveyance from one who has a power to deliver it for his use." [1]

" Q. Is this the only way in which you suppose Christ's body and blood to be really present in this Sacrament ?

" A. It is the only way in which I conceive it possible for them to be present there. As for His divine nature, that being infinite, He is by virtue thereof everywhere present. But in His human nature and particularly His body, He is in heaven only, nor can that be any otherwise present to us on earth than by figure and representation, or else by such a Communion as I have before been speaking of.

" Q. Does not Christ expressly say that the bread is His body, and the cup His blood ?

" A. He does say of the bread and wine, so taken, blessed, broken, and given as they were by Him in that sacred action, that ' This is My body,' etc., and so they are. The bread which we break is not only in figure and similitude, but by a real spiritual Communion, His body ; the cup of blessing which we bless is by the same Communion His blood. But this does not hinder but that as to their own natural substances they may and indeed do still continue to be what they appear to us, the same bread and wine that before they were." [2]

" Q. What do you call the host ?

" A. It is the wafer which those of the Church of Rome make use of instead of bread in this Sacrament.

[1] Sect. xlviii,   [2] Sect. xlix,

"*Q.* Do those of that Church adore the consecrated wafer?

"*A.* They do, and that as if it were really what they pretend to believe it is, our Saviour Christ Himself.

"*Q.* Is there any great harm in such a worship?

"*A.* Only the sin of idolatry; for so it must needs be to give divine worship to a piece of bread.

"*Q.* Ought not Christ to be adored in this Sacrament?

"*A.* Christ is everywhere to be adored, and therefore in the receiving of the Holy Communion as well as in all our other religious performances.

"*Q.* How can it then be sinful for those who believe the bread to be changed into the body of Christ upon that supposition to worship the host?

"*A.* As well as for a heathen who believes the sun to be God upon that supposition to worship the sun." [1]

"*Q.* May not a person who only looks on and sees the priest officiate commemorate Christ's death and mediate upon the benefits of it as well as if he received the elements of bread and wine?

"*A.* I will answer your question with another. May not a person who is not baptised, when he sees that Holy Sacrament administered, be truly penitent for his sins and believe in Christ, and desire to be regenerated and adopted into the communion of His Church as well as if he were himself washed with the water of Baptism? But yet the bare looking on in this case would not entitle such a one to the grace of regeneration; nor will it any more entitle the other to the Communion of Christ's body and blood."

"*Q.* . . . . Is not this Sacrament as perfect in one kind as in both?

"*A.* Can a thing be perfect which wants one half of what is required to make it perfect?

"*Q.* Yet it cannot be denied but that he who receives the body of Christ does therewith receive the blood too.

"*A.* Though that be not the question, yet it not only may be but in this case is absolutely denied by us; nor indeed can it without a manifest absurdity be affirmed, It was the design of our Saviour Christ in this Sacrament to represent His crucified body, His body as it was given for us. Now we know that when He suffered, His blood was shed and let out of His body; and that to represent His blood thus separated from His body, the cup was consecrated apart by Him. And how then can it be pretended that he who communicates in such a body must partake of the blood together with it?" [2]

[1] Sect. l.   [2] Sect. xlvii.

V.

The accession of William and Mary in 1689 led to the formation of the religious body separated from the Church of England
known as the Nonjurors. Archbishop Sancroft of Canterbury
and eight other bishops refused to take the oath of allegiance to
the new king and queen. Three of these bishops died shortly
afterwards. The rest, including Archbishop Sancroft, were deprived of their sees by process of law. At the same time about
four hundred of the clergy were deprived of their benefices. The
Nonjurors included very many of the best men in the Church
of England; and the separation caused a grievous loss to the
Church.

An excellent instance of teaching about the Holy Eucharist
current both among the Nonjurors and among some of those
who remained in the Church of England may be found in the
book by John Johnson, Vicar of Cranbrook in Kent, entitled
*The Unbloody Sacrifice and Altar, Unvailed and Supported, in
which the Nature of the Eucharist is explained according to the
Sentiments of the Christian Church in the four first Centuries.*
Johnson had previously published *The Propitiatory Oblation in
the Holy Eucharist* in 1710. The first edition of the first part
of his larger and more elaborate book, *The Unbloody Sacrifice*,
was published in 1714, and the first edition of the second part in
1718; the second edition appeared in 1724, while Johnson, who
died in 1725, was still alive. Johnson himself was not a Nonjuror,
but took the oaths and remained in possession of his benefice to the
end of his life. He was on friendly terms with the leading Nonjurors, and his doctrinal position appears to have been the same
as theirs. His definition of sacrifice is as follows :—

" Sacrifice is, 1. some material thing, either animate or inanimate,
offered to God, 2. for the acknowledging the dominion and other
attributes of God, or for procuring divine blessings, especially remission of sin, 3. upon a proper altar (which yet is rather necessary for the external decorum than for the internal perfection of
the sacrifice), 4. by a proper officer, and with agreeable rites, 5. and
consumed or otherwise disposed of in such a manner as the Author
of the sacrifice has appointed." [1]

[1] *Works, Anglo-Catholic Library,* i. 71,

Johnson maintains at great length that the five points specified are necessary to sacrifice; and that the Eucharist has them
all, and is therefore a " proper sacrifice ". He states :—

"That material bread and wine, as the sacramental body and
blood of Christ, were by a solemn act of oblation in the Eucharist
offered to Almighty God in the primitive Church, and that they
were so offered by Christ Himself in the institution " ; [1]

" That the Eucharistical bread and wine, or body and blood, are
to be offered for the acknowledgment of God's dominion and other
attributes, and for procuring divine blessings, especially remission
of sins " ; [2]

" That the Communion Table is a proper altar " ; [3]

" That bishops and priests are the only proper officers for the
solemn offering and consecrating of the Christian Eucharist" ; [4]

" That the sacrifice of the Eucharist is rightly consumed by being
solemnly eaten and drunk by the priest, clergy, and people." [5]

In the course of this long discussion Johnson describes the
Eucharist as an " expiatory" and " propitiatory," as well as a
" proper," sacrifice. For instance, he says :—

" The other end [6] of this sacrifice is to procure divine blessings,
and especially pardon of sin. In the first respect it is propitiatory,
in the second expiatory, by virtue of its principle, the grand sacrifice." [7]

The subject of the book, as the name denotes, is the sacrifice
in the Eucharist, not the Eucharistic presence ; but the treatment
of the doctrine of the sacrifice naturally involves some consideration of the doctrine of the presence also. Johnson says many
times that the elements are after consecration the "body and
blood " of Christ, or His " spiritual body and blood," or " sacramental body and blood," or " Eucharistical body and blood ".[8]
But he further explains that Christ does not " personally " or
" literally " " offer Himself in the Eucharist"; that he is not
" personally there present in His human nature " ; [9] and that the
consecrated bread and wine are His " very body and blood " " not

[1] *Op. cit.* i. 86.   [2] *Op. cit.* i. 360.   [3] *Op. cit.* i. 402.
[4] *Op. cit.* i. 418.   [5] *Op. cit.* i. 441.
[6] The " primary end " is that described as " the acknowledgment of
God's dominion and other attributes " : see i. 361.
[7] *Op. cit.* i. 384.   [8] *Op. cit.*, *e.g.*, i. 266, 267, 341.
[9] *Op. cit.* i. 200, 201.

in substance, but in power and effect," or "in inward life and spirit ".[1]   Thus, in one passage he writes :—

"That which renders the Eucharist the most excellent and valuable sacrifice that was ever offered except the personal sacrifice of Christ, is this, that the bread and wine then offered are in mystery and inward power, though not in substance, the body and blood of Christ. This raises the dignity of the Christian sacrifice above those of the law of Moses and all that were ever offered by mere men. As it is natural bread and wine, it is the sacrifice of Melchizedek and of the most ancient philosophers : as it is the sacrifice of the sacramental body and blood of Christ, it is the most sublime and divine sacrifice that men or angels can offer." [2]

Johnson then held the consecrated elements to be the body and blood of Christ in virtue and mystery and power and effect, but not actually. That this virtual presence was conferred at consecration, and permanently bestowed on the elements, he thought proved by the language in which writers of antiquity refer to the Sacrament, by the ancient methods of administration, and by the practice of the primitive Church in reserving it.

"They believed the Eucharist to be made the body and blood, not by the faith of the communicant, but by the power of the Holy Ghost, or divine benediction, imparted to it by means of the invocation (I mean perfectly and finally imparted by this means, not exclusively of the words of institution and the oblation). And this I suppose fully appears from those authorities above cited ; and, if any doubt of it, I must desire him to give himself the leisure of reviewing the passages produced to show that the ancients esteemed the symbols to be made the body and blood by the supervening energy of the Spirit, and those under the last head, which prove that they thought the words of institution, the oblation, and invocation to be effectual for rendering the elements the spiritual mysterious body and blood. And this further appears from their way of distributing the Communion, which has before been mentioned. The administrator affirms what he gives to be the body or blood without any certain knowledge whether the receiver had faith or not ; the receiver answers 'Amen,' and by this gives his assent and consent to the affirmation of the administrator, before he had actually received what was held forth to him. And indeed, if the Eucharist were not the body and blood before distribution, it could

---

[1] *Op. cit., e.g.,* i. 251, ii. 73.   [2] *Op. cit.* ii. 86.

not be made so by any post-fact of the communicants; for faith can give existence to nothing, cannot alter the nature of things. But I apprehend that this may be further proved from the practice of the primitive Church in reserving some part of the Eucharistical bread and wine; for this proves not only that they thought it the body and blood without any respect to the faith of the receiver, but that its consecration was permanent and remained after the holy action was at an end. What was not received by any at the Holy Table could not there be made the body and blood by the faith of the communicant; and yet, if they did not believe it to be the body and blood, for what purpose should they reserve it?"[1]

In a postscript to the preface to the second part of *The Un-bloody Sacrifice*, dated 14th June, 1716, Johnson denies in very vehement language an insinuation that it was his practice to elevate the elements after consecration.

"Dr. Wise slily insinuates that it is my practice to elevate the bread and wine. And it is true that I did sometimes, about four or five years ago, in the act of consecration lift up the bread and wine higher than usual, that the people might see the bread broken and the cup taken into my hand as the rubric directs, and for no other reason, some people who seemed desirous to see the holy action sitting at a great distance from the Lord's Table in this very large church. But I never elevated the elements after consecration; nay, I believe it horrible superstition in those that do it, if any such there be; and I do further solemnly declare it to be my sentiment that to elevate and adore the Sacrament according to the practice of the Church of Rome is downright idolatry."[2]

Like Eucharistic doctrine to that maintained in Johnson's writings is found also in a treatise by Robert Nelson entitled *The Great Duty of Frequenting the Christian Sacrifice*, published in 1707, in which he regards the Eucharistic sacrifice as a presentation to God the Father of the consecrated bread and wine as the symbols of the body and blood of Christ, and so a means of imploring His favour by pleading the merits of the passion. Nelson, as a layman, held no office which necessitated his taking the oath of allegiance; but he felt unable to recognise William and Mary as lawful sovereigns, and after some hesitation he threw in his lot in Church matters also with the Non-jurors. Eventually, however, though he never ceased to hold

[1] *Op. cit.* i. 341, 342. [2] *Op. cit.* ii. 25.

the right of the descendants of King James II. to the throne, he
conformed to the Established Church, and he received the Holy
Communion from the hands of Archbishop Sharp of York in
1710. He died in 1715.

During the years from 1716 to 1725 the correspondence between the Nonjurors and the bishops of the Greek Church,
already mentioned in connection with the East,[1] took place. A
list of " proposals " made by the Nonjurors, dated 18th August,
1716, contained a statement of points of agreement and disagreement between them and the Easterns. Among the points of disagreement was included :—

"Though they [the Nonjurors] believe a divine mystery in the
Holy Eucharist through the invocation of the Holy Spirit upon the
elements, whereby the faithful do verily and indeed receive the
body and blood of Christ, they believe it yet to be after a manner
which flesh and blood cannot conceive. And, seeing no sufficient
ground from Scripture or tradition to determine the manner of it,
are for leaving it indefinite and undetermined ; so that every one
may freely, according to Christ's own institution and meaning, receive the same in faith, and may also worship Christ in spirit as
verily and indeed present without being obliged to worship the
sacred symbols of His presence." [2]

In reply to the objections of the Greek bishops to this statement, the Nonjurors in a document completed on 19th May,
1722, said :—

"As to their patriarchal lordships' sentiment maintaining the
bread and wine in the Holy Eucharist being changed after consecration into the natural body and blood of our Saviour, nothing of
the elements remaining excepting the bare accidents void of substance, we can by no means agree with their lordships' doctrine,
such a corporal presence, which they call Transubstantiation, having
no foundation in Scripture, and being by implication, and sometimes
plainly, denied by the most celebrated fathers of the primitive

---

[1] See vol. i. pp. 183, 184, *supra.*

[2] Williams, *The Orthodox Church of the East in the Eighteenth Century,*
pp. 9, 10. The above quotation is from the English draft preserved by Dr.
Thomas Brett. The Greek letter actually sent is substantially the same,
though the emphasis in the last sentence (αὐτῷ ὥσπερ ἀληθῶς παρόντι
ἐμβλέπων, ἅγια δὴ τῆς παρουσίας αὐτοῦ σύμβολα οὐ προσκυνῶν οὔτε προσκυνεῖν
δεδεμένος) is slightly different: see Martin and Petit, *Coll. Conc. Recent.
Eccl. Univ.* i. 389-92.

Church.   As to the Scripture, it is true our Blessed Saviour calls the
Eucharistic bread and wine His body and blood; but that these
words are not to be restrained to a literal sense we may collect from
other passages of Scripture, where our Saviour calls Himself a door
and a vine; and in other places of Holy Writ He is called the
Lamb of God and the Lion of the tribe of Judah.   All which texts
we doubt not but the Oriental Church will allow must be construed
in a metaphorical sense; and, if these places are to be figuratively
interpreted, why not the other at the institution of the Holy Eucharist, which, if restrained to the letter, is no less shocking than the
rest?   Farther, St. Paul calls the Eucharistic element bread, even
after consecration, when it was to be received (1 Cor. xi. 28).   And
now to allege some testimonies from the primitive fathers.[1] . . .
Pope Gelasius . . . plainly declares, the substance and nature of
the bread and wine remains after consecration.[2]   It is true he then
tells us, the elements are changed into a divine thing, that is, raised
to a divine efficacy by the operation of the Holy Spirit.   Which
change we most willingly confess, namely, that there is a mystic
virtue and supernatural force transfused upon the Eucharistic elements by the priest's pronouncing the words of institution and his
prayer for the descent of the Holy Ghost."[3]

In 1717 some of the Nonjurors published an edition of the
First Prayer Book of King Edward VI. with some alterations;
and in 1718 this was followed by the publication of *A Communion Office taken partly from Primitive Liturgies and partly
from the First English Reformed Common-Prayer-Book: Together with Offices for Confirmation and the Visitation of the Sick.*
The publication of these books proved the occasion for a division
of the Nonjurors into the Usagers, who adopted the use of them,
and those who kept to the Prayer Book of the Church of England, avoiding the name of the actual reigning sovereign.   In the
Book of 1717[4] the Prayer for the Church, the Prayer of Consecration, and the Prayer of Oblation are identical with those in

[1] The passages quoted are from St. Justin Martyr, St. Irenæus, St.
Cyril of Jerusalem, St. Chrysostom, Theodoret, Tertullian, St. Augustine.
For the teaching of these writers, see vol. i. chap. ii. iii. *supra.*

[2] The passage from Gelasius is quoted on vol. i. p. 102, *supra.*

[3] Williams, *op. cit.* pp. 93-98.   The Greek document actually sent is
substantially the same as Dr. Brett's English draft quoted above, except
that it has τὸ ἴδιον σῶμα καὶ αἷμα for "the natural body and blood":
see Martin and Petit, *op. cit.* i. 481-88.

[4] This Book is printed in Hall, *Fragmenta Liturgica,* i. 101-47.

the First Prayer Book of King Edward VI.[1] In the Book of
1718,[2] besides other alterations, the Prayer for the Church was
placed after the Consecration and Oblation, the invocation of the
Holy Ghost was placed after the words of institution, and the
words "these Thy gifts and creatures of bread and wine, that
they may be unto us the body and blood of Thy most dearly
beloved Son Jesus Christ," were altered to "this sacrifice, that
He may make this bread the body of Thy Christ, and this cup
the blood of Thy Christ". The whole piece between the Sanctus
and the Prayer for the Church was as follows :—

"Holiness is Thy nature and Thy gift, O eternal King. Holy
is Thine only-begotten Son our Lord Jesus Christ, by whom Thou
hast made the worlds; holy is Thine ever-blessed Spirit, who
searcheth all things, even the depths of Thine infinite perfection.
Holy art Thou, Almighty and merciful God ; Thou createdst man in
Thine own image, broughtest him into Paradise, and didst place him
in a state of dignity and pleasure ; and when he had lost his happiness by transgressing Thy command, Thou of Thy goodness didst
not abandon and despise him. Thy providence was still continued,
Thy law was given to revive the sense of his duty, Thy prophets
were commissioned to reclaim and instruct him. And when the
fulness of time was come, Thou didst send Thine only-begotten Son
to satisfy Thy justice, to strengthen our nature, and renew Thine
image within us. For these glorious ends Thine eternal Word
came down from heaven, was incarnate by the Holy Ghost, born of
the Blessed Virgin, conversed with mankind, and directed His life
and miracles to our salvation. And when His hour was come to
offer the propitiatory sacrifice upon the cross, when He, who had no
sin Himself, mercifully undertook to suffer death for our sins, in the
same night that He was betrayed, He took bread ; and when He
had given thanks, He brake it, and gave it to His disciples, saying,
Take, eat, this is My bo✠dy, which is given for you : do this in
remembrance of Me.

"*Here the people shall answer*, Amen.
"*Then shall the priest say* :—
"Likewise after supper He took the cup : and when He had given
thanks, He gave it to them, saying, Drink ye all of this; for this
is My blo✠od of the New Testament, which is shed for you and

---

[1] See pp. 136-39, *supra*.
[2] This Book is printed in Hall, *op. cit.* v. 1-78.

for many for the remission of sins : Do this, as oft as ye shall drink it, in remembrance of Me. [1]

" *Here the people shall answer*, Amen.

" *Then shall the priest say* :—

"Wherefore, having in remembrance His passion, death, and resurrection from the dead, His ascension into heaven, and second coming with great power to judge the quick and the dead, and to render to every man according to his works, we offer to Thee, our King and our God, according to His holy institution, this bread and this cup, giving thanks to Thee through Him that Thou hast vouchsafed us the honour to stand before Thee, and to sacrifice unto Thee. And we beseech Thee to look favourably on these Thy gifts, which are here set before Thee, O Thou self-sufficient God ; and do Thou accept them for the honour of Thy Christ ; and send down Thine Holy Spirit, the witness of the passion of our Lord Jesus, upon this sacrifice, that He may make this bread the body of Thy Christ, and this cup the blood of Thy Christ ; [2] that they who are partakers thereof may be confirmed in godliness, may obtain remission of their sins, may be delivered from the devil and his snares, may be replenished with the Holy Ghost, may be made worthy of Thy Christ, and may obtain everlasting life; Thou, O Lord Almighty, being reconciled unto them through the merits and mediation of Thy Son our Saviour Jesus Christ, who with Thee and the Holy Ghost liveth and reigneth ever, one God, world without end."

A clear statement of Eucharistic doctrine, which is probably representative of the teaching of many of the Nonjurors, may be quoted from the *Shorter Catechism* contained in Thomas Deacon's book *A Full, True, and Comprehensive View of Christianity*, which was published in 1747. Deacon was born in 1697 and died in 1753. He was consecrated a Nonjuring bishop in

[1] There are rubrical directions: at "took bread," "Here the priest is to take the paten into his hands " ; at " brake," " And here to break the bread " ; at "this," "And here to lay his hand upon all the bread " ; at "took the cup," " Here he is to take the cup into his hands " ; and at " this," " And here to lay his hand upon every vessel (be it chalice or flagon) in which there is any wine and water to be consecrated ".

[2] There are rubrical directions : at "-bread," " Here the priest shall lay his hand upon the bread " ; at " cup," " And here upon every vessel (be it chalice or flagon) in which there is any wine and water ". It should be observed that these manual acts are ordered in connection with both the words of institution and the invocation of the Holy Ghost.

1747. The doctrine taught in the following passages is that at the recital of the words of institution the bread and wine are made symbols and representatives of Christ's body and blood; that, as such symbols, they are offered in sacrifice; and that at the invocation of the Holy Ghost they become the spiritual and life-giving body and blood of Christ in life and power and virtue and efficacy.

"The Eucharist is a sacrifice and a Sacrament. As a sacrifice, it is the offering the representative body and blood of Christ to God the Father; as a Sacrament, it is a feast upon that sacrifice. It was at the institution of the Eucharist that our Saviour began to offer Himself to His Father for the sins of all men. The sacrifice which He then offered was His natural body and blood, as separate from each other, because His body was considered as broken, and His blood as shed, for the sins of the world. But because it would have been unnatural for Him to have broken His own body and shed His own blood, and because He could not as a living High Priest offer Himself when He was dead, therefore, before He was so much as apprehended by His enemies, He offered to the Father His natural body and blood voluntarily and really though mystically under the symbols of bread and wine mixed with water; for which reason He called the bread at the Eucharist His body, which was then broken, given, or offered for the sins of many, and the cup His blood, which was then shed or offered for the sins of many. All the sacrifices of the old law were figures of this great one of Christ; and the Eucharist or sacrifice of thanksgiving, which we celebrate according to His institution, is a solemn commemorative oblation of it to God the Father, and procures us the virtue of it." [1]

"The consecration of the Eucharist is thus performed. The priest, after having placed the bread and mixed cup upon the altar, first gives God thanks for all His benefits and mercies conferred upon mankind, especially those of creation and redemption: he then recites how Jesus Christ instituted this Sacrament the night before His passion, and performs His command by doing what He did, he takes the bread into his hands and breaks it, which broken bread represents the dead body of Christ pierced upon the cross: he takes the cup into his hands, which cup, consisting of wine and water, represents the blood and water that flowed from the dead body of Christ upon the cross: he then repeats our Saviour's powerful words over them, by which the bread and cup are made authori-

[1] Part II. Lesson xxvii.

tative representations or symbols of Christ's crucified body and offered blood : and being thus in a capacity to be offered to God, he accordingly makes the oblation, which is the highest and most proper act of Christian worship. After God has accepted of this sacrifice, He is pleased to return it to us again to feast upon, that we may thereby partake of all the benefits of our Saviour's death and passion ; in order to which the priest prays to God the Father to send His Holy Spirit upon the bread and cup offered to Him, that He may enliven those representations of Christ's dead body and effused blood, and make them His spiritual life-giving body and blood in virtue and power, that the receivers thereof may obtain all the blessings of the institution. After which he continues his prayer and oblation in behalf of the whole world, particularly of the Church, bishops, clergy, king, and in general of all the faithful, whether living or dead. Thus we see that by the consecration of the Eucharist the bread and mixed wine are not destroyed, but sanctified ; they are changed not in their substance but in their qualities ; they are made not the natural but the sacramental body and blood of Christ ; so that they are both bread and wine and the body and blood of Christ at the same time but not in the same manner. They are bread and wine by nature, the body and blood of Christ in mystery and signification ; they are bread and wine to our senses, the body and blood of Christ to our understanding and faith ; they are bread and wine in themselves, the body and blood of Christ in power and effect. So that whoever eats and drinks them as he ought to do, dwells in Christ and Christ in him, he is one with Christ and Christ with him." [1]

"The Eucharist as a Sacrament is a feast upon the sacrifice of the body and blood of Christ. . . . This Sacrament is necessary for all baptised Christians, infants as well as others. . . . It is by the Eucharist alone that Christians are made one body with Christ, and reckoned to be His flesh, and are so united to Him as the body is to the head ; it is the Eucharist alone that renders their bodies incorruptible, instilling a principle of life into them, by virtue of which they shall be raised to a blessed immortality." [2]

It is probable that the Eucharistic beliefs of Bishop Thomas Wilson, who was consecrated Bishop of Sodor and Man in 1698 and continued Bishop of that see until 1755, resembled those of

[1] Part II. Lesson xxviii.
[2] Part II. Lesson xxix. For further illustrations of Deacon's Eucharistic teaching, see *Longer Catechism*, Part II. Lessons lxv.-cxxxvi.

some Nonjurors. Bishop Wilson lays great stress on the necessity
of receiving the Holy Communion, and on the spiritual blessings
of pardon and grace and salvation which may thereby be obtained ; and on the Eucharist as a means of remembering Christ
and His death and of receiving Christ as "food and sustenance,"
and as a pledge and seal of His gifts. It is

"an ordinance appointed by Christ Himself, and for this reason,
that Christians being often called upon to remember the love of their
dying Saviour, and the occasion of His death, which was to make
their peace with God, they might love Him with all their soul, and
remember to observe the commands He has given them in order to
fit them for heaven " ;

" the only way to render our persons and our prayers acceptable to
God ; of obtaining the pardon of our sins, the grace of God, and
everlasting life after death." [1]

Of it he says :—

" All Christians are bound at the peril of their souls to observe
this ordinance of Christ. The blessings which attend the worthy
receiving of this Sacrament are invaluable : no less than the pardon
of all our past sins ; the continuance of God's Holy Spirit ; the increase of His graces here, and eternal happiness hereafter. And,
lastly, the neglect or abuse of this ordinance will be punished with
judgments in this world, and in the world to come with misery unspeakable." [2]

The Eucharist is

"that very ordinance" "which Jesus Christ Himself appointed
on purpose to keep up the remembrance of what He has done and
suffered for us, that our own death, whenever it shall happen, may
be a comfort to us, and when nothing in this world, nothing but a
firm faith in Jesus Christ, can support or comfort our dying spirit ".[3]

One of the prayers which he suggests is :—

[1] *Serm.* i. (*Works, Anglo-Catholic Library*, ii. 12); *cf. Serm.* vi. xiii.
xxxv. lxv. lxvi. lxix. lxxv. lxxvii., *Works*, ii. 79, 158, 391, iii. 152, 156, 166,
167, 193, 267, 268, 291, 292 ; *A Plain Instruction for such as have learned the
Church Catechism, Works*, iv. 81, 85, 88 ; *Plain and Short Directions and
Prayers, Works*, iv. 117 ; *An Instruction for the Indians, Works*, iv. 275,
276 ; *Sacra Privata, Works*, v. 320, 334, 336, 337 ; *Parochialia, Works*,
vii. 5 ; *A Catechetical Instruction for Candidates for Holy Order, Works*,
vii. 165 ; *Maxims of Piety and Morality, Works*, v. 412.
[2] *Serm.* ix., *Works*, ii 108.   [3] *Serm.* xxvi., *Works*, ii. 294.

"I adore Thine infinite mercy and goodness, Blessed God, for that Thou hast given Thy Son, our Saviour Jesus Christ, not only to die for us, but to be our food and sustenance in this Holy Sacrament." [1]

Of the consecrated bread and wine he says :—

"These being pledges to assure us that, as certainly as bread and wine do nourish our bodies, so do these seal to us all the benefits which Jesus Christ hath purchased for us by His sacrifice and death." [2]

Further, Bishop Wilson regards the bread and wine as being made by the Holy Ghost at the consecration representatives of the body and blood of Christ, and His sacramental or spiritual body and blood ; he expresses a wish for the restoration of the First Prayer Book of Edward VI. ; he suggests the use of the invocation of the Holy Ghost after the Prayer of Consecration of the Book of Common Prayer ; he describes the Eucharist as the " true Christian sacrifice ".

"Let a man, I say, be never so unlearned, yet he will easily understand that he is not to look upon and receive this bread and wine as common food, but as holy representatives of Christ's body and blood, made such by an especial blessing of God." [3]

"'Do this,' that is, this that I do, offer bread and wine as a sacrifice to God (when consecrated). They could not offer His real body, but only His sacramental body, as a memorial of His real body. . . . When the bread and wine are by consecration made the sacramental body and blood of Christ, we have then a sacrifice to offer which is worthy to be received and to prevail with God. . . . The power of the Holy Spirit accompanies these elements, and makes them effectual means of grace and salvation. . . . Christ's spiritual body, that is, made such by the Spirit of God. Not by the faith of the receiver, for they were such before." [4]

"The priest by doing what Christ did, by prayer and thanksgiving, by breaking the bread and pouring out the wine, obtaineth of God that these creatures by the descent of the Holy Ghost be-

---

[1] *A Short and Plain Instruction for the Better Understanding of the Lord's Supper, Works*, iv. 393 ; cf. *Sacra Privata, Works*, v. 342 ; *Private Thoughts, Works*, vii. 92 ; *Collectanea, Works*, vii. 237, 238.

[2] *A Short and Plain Instruction for the Better Understanding of the Lord's Supper, Works*, iv. 347 ; cf. *A Further Instruction for such as have learned the Church Catechism, Works*, iv. 80.

[3] *Serm.* lxxvi., *Works*, iii. 277.   [4] *Sacra Privata, Works*, v. 339.

come after a spiritual manner the body and blood of Christ, by receiving of which our souls shall be strengthened and refreshed, as our bodies are by bread and wine." [1]

" Private devotions at the altar, taken out of the most ancient offices of the Church, to render our present Communion-service more agreeable to apostolic usage, and more acceptable (I hope) to God, and beneficial to all that partake thereof. Until it shall please Him to put it into the hearts and power of such as ought to do it to restore to us the First Service of Edward VI. or such as shall be more conformable to the appointment of Christ and His Apostles and their successors. Which may the Divine Majesty vouchsafe to grant for His sake who first ordained this Holy Sacrament." [2]

" Immediately after the Consecration. We offer unto Thee, our King and our God, this bread and this cup. We give Thee thanks for these and for all Thy mercies, beseeching Thee to send down Thy Holy Spirit upon this sacrifice, that He may make this bread the body of Thy Christ, and this cup the blood of Thy Christ ; and that all we who are partakers thereof may thereby obtain remission of our sins, and all other benefits of His passion. . . . May I atone Thee, O God, by offering to Thee the pure and unbloody sacrifice, which thou hast ordained by Jesus Christ." [3]

" Say secretly, [that is, after the Prayer of Consecration,] Send down Thy Spirit and blessing upon this means of grace and salvation, which Thou Thyself, O Jesus, hast ordained. Most merciful God, the Father of our Lord Jesus Christ, look graciously upon the gifts now lying before Thee ; and send down Thy Holy Spirit on this sacrifice, that He may make this bread and this wine the body and blood of Thy Christ, that all they who partake of them may be confirmed in godliness, may receive remission of their sins, may be delivered from the devil and his wiles, may be filled with the Holy Ghost, may be worthy of Thy Christ, and obtain everlasting life." [4]

"This is the true Christian sacrifice, without which there is no remission of sins ; it was appointed by Jesus Christ Himself to be done in remembrance of His death until His coming again to judgment." [5]

"Give me such holy dispositions of soul whenever I approach

[1] *Parochialia, Works*, vii. 20, 21 ; *cf. Plain and Short Directions and Prayers, Works*, iv. 119, 120.

[2] *Sacra Privata, Works*, v. 73, 74.

[3] *Sacra Privata, Works*, v. 74, 75.

[4] *A Short and Plain Instruction for the Better Understanding of the Lord's Supper, Works*, iv. 403.

[5] *Serm.* lxix., *Works*, iii. 203.

Thine altar in some measure proportionable to the holiness of the work I am about,—of presenting the prayers of the faithful, of offering a spiritual sacrifice to God, in order to communicate the true bread of God to all His members." [1]

"He then, at that instant, [that is, at the institution of the Eucharist,] gave His body and blood a sacrifice for the sins of the world. He then offered as a priest Himself under the symbols of bread and wine, and this is the sacrifice which His priests do still offer. And let it be observed that Jesus Christ did this before He was apprehended, when He was at His own disposal; it was then that He offered Himself a sacrifice to God." [2]

VI.

Instances of somewhat different kinds of Eucharistic teaching may be given from three devotional books of the early part of the eighteenth century. In *The Reasonable Communicant*, the third edition of which was published in 1708, an explanation is given of the statement in the Catechism that "the body and blood of Christ" "are verily and indeed taken and received by the faithful in the Lord's Supper" which appears to define the body and blood of Christ as the power and grace of Christ.

"The real presence maintained by the Church of England is not the presence of Christ's natural body, but of His spiritual and mystical one, that is, the real presence of Christ's invisible power and grace so in and with the creatures of bread and wine as to convey spiritual and real effects to the souls of such as duly receive them." [3]

In *The Orthodox Communicant*, published by the famous engraver John Sturt in 1721, the gift in Communion is thus described :—

"The banquet thou art now about to feed on is no less than the pure and immaculate body and precious blood of Thy Saviour, which He instituted to support and comfort thee until His coming again. It is not a feast of earthly dainties, which give but an imperfect momentary pleasure, but it is a divine and spiritual banquet, which, if thou comest duly prepared, and with true faith feedest on it, will for ever satiate thy hunger and allay thy thirst. . . . With most profound gratitude and humility adore the divine goodness,

[1] *Sacra Privata, Works*, v. 160.
[2] *Notes on the Holy Scriptures*, on St. Matt. xxvi. 28, *Works*, vi. 423; cf. on Ezra vi. 10 and 1 Tim. ii. 1, *Works*, vi. 174, 643.
[3] P. 12.

which offers thee this cup of reconciliation, this healing draught, which will cure thy infirmities and reconcile thee to thy offended God. With steadfast faith believe and be assured (for thy Saviour hath said it) 'This is His blood of the New Testament, which was shed for thee and for many for the remission of sins'. This is the heavenly draught, which alone can cleanse thee from all impurity and make thee white as snow. Drink this in pious memory of thy Blessed Saviour, that thou mayest obtain the grand benefit which He hath purchased for thee at the expense of His most precious blood. Implore the Father of mercies to impart such a share of grace to thee that thou mayest immediately feel the happy effects of it in a perfect and complete reformation of life ; and beg of God such a continual supply of it that thou mayest enjoy the blessed presence of thy Saviour till the next opportunity of renewing this covenant with Him."[1]

In *The Communicant Instructed how to Examine Himself in some Necessary Interrogatives for Worthy Receiving of the Lord's Supper*, by Thomas Trott, the Rector of Barkston in Lincolnshire, which was published at Dublin in 1723, one of the questions in preparation for Communion was :—

"Do I know the Lord's Supper as part of God's instituted worship? As a token, pledge, or seal of the covenant of grace, as representing Jesus Christ, and Him crucified, as having two parts, namely, the outward signs, bread and wine, with the actions thereunto belonging ; the inward mysteries signified by those signs and sacramental actions, the nourishing, cleansing, enriching of my soul by the death of Christ?"[2]

VII.

In 1735 a book was published entitled *A Plain Account of the Nature and End of the Sacrament of the Lord's Supper*. It was anonymous, but was understood to be the work of Benjamin Hoadly. Hoadly had been appointed Bishop of Bangor in 1716, Bishop of Hereford in 1721, Bishop of Salisbury in 1723, and Bishop of Winchester in 1734. He continued Bishop of Winchester until his death in 1761. He was a prominent member of the Latitudinarian party which by 1735 had become influential in the Church of England. There is little doubt that the *Plain Account of the Nature and End of the Sacra-*

[1] Pp. 71, 73, 74.   [2] P. 7.

ment of the Lord's Supper was written by him. The main object of the book was practical. Its aim was to show that an exaggerated stress was laid by many on the need of preparation and devotion in connection with Communion, and that scruples which held back those who might otherwise communicate were unnecessary and groundless. In maintaining this thesis the writer stated his view of the doctrine of the Sacrament. He rejected any assertion of the presence of Christ or of a gift of grace. He advocated the purely Zwinglian position that our Lord's words at the institution of the Sacrament were wholly figurative, that an act done in remembrance of Christ required the bodily absence of Christ, and that a memorial could not be a sacrifice. He asserted that the Lord's Supper was a token and pledge of the promises of Christ and of the duties and privileges of Christians, and denied that it was anything more. Among the statements about doctrine which the book contained were the following :—

" This remembrance of Christ, during the time of His bodily absence, was by Himself and His Apostles declared to be the end of this positive institution." [1]

" The very essence of this institution being remembrance of a past transaction, and this remembrance necessarily excluding the corporal presence of what is remembered, it follows that, as the only sacrifice and the only sacrificer in the Christian dispensation are remembered, and therefore not present in the Lord's Supper, so the only Christian altar (the cross upon which Christ suffered) being also by consequence to be remembered, it cannot be present in this rite, because that presence would destroy the very notion of remembrance." [2]

" Christians, meeting together for religious worship, and eating bread and drinking wine in remembrance of Christ's body and blood, and in honour of Him, do hereby publicly acknowledge Him to be their Master, and themselves to be His disciples ; and by doing this in an assembly own themselves, with all other Christians, to be one body or society under Him the Head ; and consequently profess themselves to be under His government and influence, to have communion or fellowship with Him as Head, and with all their brethren as fellow-members of that same body of which He is the Head." [3]

" As bread and wine, taken at an ordinary meal, are the food of

---

[1] P. 30.   [2] P. 54.   [3] P. 58.

our bodies, so this bread and wine, taken in a serious and religious remembrance of Christ as our Master, may (in a figurative, spiritual, or religious sense) be styled the food of our souls, or the nourishment of us considered as Christians ; as the receiving them duly implies in it our believing and receiving the whole doctrine of Christ, which is the food of the Christian life ; and leads our thoughts to all such obligations and engagements on our part, and all such promises on God's part, as are most useful and sufficient for our improvement in all that is worthy of a Christian. And Almighty God on His part requiring and accepting our due performance of this part of our duty, does by this assure us who come to profess ourselves the disciples of Christ that we are in His favour. Or, in other words, the Lord's Supper, being instituted as the memorial of His goodness towards us in Christ Jesus, may justly be looked upon as a token and pledge to assure us of what it calls to our remembrance, namely, that God is ready to pardon and bless us upon the terms proposed by His Son ; and consequently that we are received by Him as the disciples of Christ, members of His body the Church, and heirs of His heavenly kingdom ; in a word, as persons entitled to all the happiness promised to Christians, if we be not wanting to ourselves in other parts of our duty." [1]

" This bread and wine, considered and taken as memorials of the body and blood of Christ our Master, lead us by their peculiar tendency to all such thoughts and practises as are indeed the improvement and health of our souls." [2]

The publication of this book was followed by a vigorous controversy. Out of the large number of pamphlets which appeared in attack on and in defence of the *Plain Account*, it may be sufficient to mention only a few, selecting those which are representative of different lines of thought. Much of the controversy had to do with the practical questions which the writer of the *Plain Account* had raised, or with the allegations of disbelief in the doctrines of the Atonement and of the deity of our Lord which were brought against him ; and it is often difficult to ascertain the opinions with regard to the doctrine of the Eucharist of those who took part in it. Several of the pamphleteers who attacked the *Plain Account* asserted with greater or less definiteness a gift in Communion. At any rate two of them took up a position practically the same as that of John Johnson. [3] Some of those who defended the *Plain Account* advocated Zwinglian views.

[1] Pp. 130, 131.   [2] P. 162.   [3] See pp. 474-77, *supra*.

The writer of *Remarks on a Book lately published entituled A Plain Account of the Nature and End of the Sacrament of the Lord's Supper*, published in 1735, is one of the opponents of the *Plain Account* whose doctrinal views are expressed with little definiteness ; but he held a fuller belief than the author of the *Plain Account* in regard to the Eucharist and the Eucharistic elements as sealing the covenant of God. In his first pamphlet just mentioned he says :—

"It is true the blood of Christ is not itself present, but there is that present which is appointed by Christ to represent it, and which He Himself calls His blood. And why the bread and wine may not be called the seal of the new covenant for the same reason that they are called Christ's body and blood, I cannot for the heart of me see. Nothing is more common than to call the representatives of things by the names of the things themselves which they represent. If then the bread and wine are representatives of the seal of the new covenant, what forbids that they should be termed the seal ? And, since we receive these by the express command of God, why may it not be said that we receive His seal, or that God puts to His seal ? " [1]

And in his *A Second Letter to the Author of a Book entituled A Plain Account of the Nature and End of the Sacrament of the Lord's Supper*, published in 1735, he implies that the elements become "the representative body and blood of Christ" when "the Eucharistical Prayer" is said over them ;[2] and he calls them "the representatives of the great Christian sacrifice".[3]

A differently expressed explanation of the gift in Communion emphasising that Communion is the means not only of "a renewal of the new covenant between God and man"[4] but also of bestowing immortality, through the union of the Spirit of God with our spirits, is given by the author of *A Letter to a Lord in Answer to his late Book entitled A Plain Account of the Nature and End of the Sacrament of the Lord's Supper*, published in 1736. After quoting passages from St. Ignatius and St. Irenæus,[5] he goes on :—

"The assistance of God's Spirit is in them annexed by the promise of our Lord to the due partaking of the Sacrament of the

---

[1] P. 33.   [2] P. 37.   [3] P. 51.   [4] P. 31.

[5] See *Ad Eph.* 20, and *Adv. Haer.* IV. xviii. 5, quoted on vol. i. pp. 25, 35, *supra*.

Lord's Supper. This is grounded on (St. John vi. 56) 'He that
eateth My body and drinketh My blood dwelleth in Me, and I in
him'. 'And hereby,' says the same St. John (explaining these his
words in another place) (1 Ep. iv. 13), 'Hereby know we that we
dwell in Him, and He in us, by His Spirit which He hath given us'.
Here the Evangelist plainly tells us that by those His words,
namely, 'our dwelling in Christ and Christ in us,' we are to understand God's Spirit united to our spirit ; or, which is the same thing,
as we are told by the great Apostle (Rom. viii. 9), 'the Spirit of
Christ' (united to our souls) 'which if any want, he is none of His '.
'For know ye not,' saith the same Apostle (1 Cor. iii. 16), 'that ye
are the temple of God, and that the Spirit of God dwelleth in you ?'
And (2 Cor. xiii. 5) 'know ye not that Jesus Christ is in you, unless
ye be reprobates?' But I suggested that something more (if
possible) is promised to us by our Lord in this passage of St. John's
Gospel ; and is it not plainly affirmed in it by our Lord, and by those
first Christian writers which we cited, interpreting His words, that
the Sacrament of the Lord's Supper produces in us the principles of
immortality? Is not this plainly and fairly inferred from these
words (verse 54), 'He that eateth My body and drinketh My blood
hath eternal life, and I will raise him up at the last day'?   Is it
not plainly affirmed that the Eucharist duly received is the medicine
of immortality, the antidote against eternal death, that will make
us live alway in God through Jesus Christ? For, as the great
Apostle speaks to the Romans (viii. 11), 'If the Spirit of Him that
raised up Jesus from the dead dwell in you, He that raised up Christ
from the dead shall also quicken your mortal bodies by His Spirit
that dwelleth in you'." [1]

In the first of the three dialogues entitled *The Winchester
Converts*, published in 1735 as a satirical attack on the *Plain
Account*, the position of the writer is evidently stated when the
Eucharist is described as

" An awful and tremendous institution designed not only for
a bare remembrance of the death of Christ, but also a seal of that
pardon which God had promised to repenting sinners, and a renewal of that covenant which He first made with them in Baptism,
and a means of conveying to them that spiritual grace and assistance
which was the thing covenanted to be granted, and which the
Church in all ages has declared the very best of men to stand in
need of and must necessarily obtain before they can offer up to
God any sacrifice that will be truly acceptable " ; [2]

[1] Pp. 12, 13.   [2] P. 16.

and as the means through which "sins" are "blotted out by" the

"Partaking of the body and blood of Christ in some such mysterious manner as the original sin of our first parents is washed away by Baptism."[1]

One of the pamphlets in which a position resembling that of John Johnson is taken up is entitled *The Sacrament of the Altar : or the Doctrine of a Representative Sacrifice in the Holy Eucharist vindicated : in Answer to a late Book entituled A Plain Account of the Nature and End of the Sacrament of the Lord's Supper*. It was published in 1735. The writer speaks of the consecrated elements as being "in power and effect" the body and blood of Christ ;[2] and in his preface gives the following clear statement of his views :—

"The primitive doctrine, which I have endeavoured to vindicate in the following tract, is most directly opposite to the present doctrine of the corrupt Church of Rome. The Church of Rome in their sacrifices of the Mass pretend to offer up to God very Christ, whole Christ, God and Man hypostatically. Hence, according to them the sacrifice of the Mass is propitiatory in its own nature, and to be worshipped as being the very natural substantial body and blood of Christ. On the other hand, the primitive doctrine maintains that not the very natural substantial body and blood of Christ is offered to God in the Eucharist, but that bread and wine, as the appointed representatives of Christ's body and blood, are to be offered according to Christ's own institution, and that this representative sacrifice is therefore propitiatory, not in its own nature, not from any intrinsic worth in itself, but by institution by virtue of the grand, personal sacrifice of Christ, which by His institution it is appointed to commemorate and represent ; and that therefore the materials of this representative sacrifice are not to be worshipped, as not being substantially the body and blood of Christ, though they are indeed made so in power and effect by the presence and blessing of the life-giving, eternal Spirit."[3]

A similar view was advocated in *A True Scripture Account of the Nature and Benefits of the Holy Eucharist, in Answer to a Book entituled A Plain Account of the Nature and End of the Sacrament of the Lord's Supper*, by the famous Dr. Thomas

[1] P. 17.   [2] *E.g.*, pp. 32, 91.   [3] Preface, p. iii.

Brett, which was published in 1735. Dr. Brett was born in 1667. He was ordained in 1690, and took the oath of allegiance to William and Mary with some scruple, although in his case there was not, as in the case of many, the complication of having taken an oath to King James II. . When George I. came to the throne in 1714, he had made up his mind that he could no longer give allegiance to a sovereign of the new succession; and he consequently vacated his benefices of Betshanger and Ruckinge. He was admitted to the communion of the Nonjurors in 1715, and was consecrated a Nonjuring bishop in 1716. He died in 1743. In his pamphlet against the *Plain Account* Brett, whose earlier work *A Discourse concerning the Necessity of discerning the Lord's Body in the Holy Communion* had been published in 1720, fifteen years before, closely follows John Johnson, from whom he quotes largely. He vigorously attacks the *Plain Account* as contrary to Scripture, the fathers, and the Catechism of the Church of England. He maintains that the consecrated elements are "in some sense the body and blood of Jesus Christ,"[1] and His "body and blood in power and virtue";[2] and that the Eucharist is

"A commemorative sacrifice, or sacrifice of remembrance, a sacrifice whose whole virtue and efficacy is derived from that sacrifice of which it is the memorial."[3]

These and other attacks on the *Plain Account* led to much being written in defence of it. Some of the writers who thus replied to the attacks did not deal with matters of doctrine touching the Holy Eucharist. Others frankly avowed the Zwinglian tenet that the Holy Communion is merely a sign. The authors of two pamphlets published in 1735 entitled *A Defence of the Plain Account of the Nature and End of the Sacrament of the Lord's Supper against the Objections contained in the Remarks on that Book* and *A Proper Answer to a Late Abusive Pamphlet Entitled The Winchester Converts*, both quote at length as expressive of their own opinion a definitely Zwinglian statement of John Hales, the famous Latitudinarian divine of the seventeenth century.[4] The writer of *An Apologetical Defence, or a Demonstration of the Usefulness and Expediency of a Late Book Entitled A*

---

[1] *E.g.*, p. 35.   [2] *E.g.*, p. 138.   [3] P. 69.
[4] This statement of Hales is quoted on pp. 314, 315, *supra*.

Plain Account of the Nature and End of the Sacrament of the Lord's Supper, which was published in 1735, defended the *Plain Account* on explicitly doctrinal grounds, and described that book as necessary because of what he considered extravagant teaching about preparation for Communion which was current; to refute ideas contained in such books as Horneck's *The Crucified Jesus, The Christian Sacrament and Sacrifice*, and the *Week's Preparation*, that in the Sacrament Christ gives Himself, that there is the "most true and real presence" of "Christ's body and blood" and the reception of the "very Godhead" of Christ,[1] and that the Eucharist is "a propitiatory sacrifice";[2] to make clear that the Church of England does not favour "the absurd doctrine of a true and real presence,"[3] and that "to teach any bodily presence of Christ in this holy Supper is to pervert the very nature of the institution which was appointed to be observed in remembrance of Christ";[4] and because he had himself frequently seen "persons bow down in the humblest posture of adoration" "as the minister officiating drew near to them with the bread or wine".[5] This writer interpreted the manuals which he condemned as teaching "Transubstantiation," and a doctrine equivalent to that of the Council of Trent;[6] his own opinion evidently was that the Eucharist is a mere memorial, in which the remembrance made of Christ is inconsistent with His presence.[7]

This war of pamphlets which followed the appearance of the *Plain Account* is of considerable importance as illustrating that the Latitudinarian movement in the Church of England in the first half of the eighteenth century, like the position taken up by John Hales in the seventeenth,[8] included Zwinglian opinions about the Holy Eucharist. A work from the pen of William Law, which also resulted from the publication of the *Plain Account*, is of interest for a different reason.

William Law was born in 1686 and died in 1761. From 1711 to 1713 he was a Fellow of Emmanuel College, Cambridge; and he was ordained in 1711. Before the death of Queen Anne on 1st August, 1714, he appears to have doubted the lawfulness of the rule of the existing dynasty; and he refused to take the oaths of allegiance and abjuration on the accession of George I.

---

[1] Pp. 18, 19.   [2] P. 34.   [3] P. 25.   [4] P. 27.   [5] P. 22.
[6] This was by no means the case: see pp. 457-62, *supra*.
[7] P. 19.   [8] See pp. 313-15, *supra*.

In 1735, when the *Plain Account* appeared, he was already known as an acute controversialist and as a writer on practical religion; and as early as 1717 he had sharply attacked Bishop Hoadly in his famous *Letters*. His work *A Demonstration of the Gross and Fundamental Errors of a Late Book Called a Plain Account of the Nature and End of the Sacrament of the Lord's Supper*, which was published in 1735, was one of the most important of the answers to the *Plain Account*. In this work Law severely criticises the arguments used by the author of the *Plain Account*, and charges him with disbelief in the "great foundation doctrine that Christ was truly and essentially God, very God of very God," and in the doctrines that Christ is "a true and real atonement for sins" and "a true and real principle of life to us".[1] He shows signs of the mystical theology which he afterwards more fully developed. The following are among the passages which express his own beliefs in regard to the Eucharist:—

"When our Saviour says, 'Do this,' it is the same thing as if He had said, Do these two things appointed in the Sacrament as your act of faith that I am both the atonement for your sins and a principle of life to you. Don't say bare and outward words when you say, 'This is My body which is given for you,' and 'This is My blood which is shed for the remission of sins'; but let faith say them and acknowledge the truth of them. When you eat My body and drink My blood, don't let your mouth only eat or perform the outward action, but let faith, which is the true mouth of the inward man, believe that it really partakes of Me, and that I enter in by faith. And, when you thus by faith perform these two essential parts of the Sacrament, then, and then only, may what you do be said to be done in remembrance of Me, and of what I am to you. . . . Since our Saviour says, 'This is My body which is given for you,' 'This is My blood which is shed for the remission of sins,' what He says, that we are to say, and what we say, that we are to believe, and therefore what we are here to do is an act or exercise of faith. And, since in these words He says two things, the one, that He is the atonement for our sins; the other, that this bread and this wine are the signification or application of that atonement, or that which we are to take for it; therefore we in doing this are by faith to say and believe these two things; and therefore all that we here do is faith, and faith manifested in this twofold manner. Again, seeing our Saviour commands us to eat His body and drink

[1] Pp. 99, 100 (second edition, 1738).

His blood, we are to say and believe that His body and blood are
there signified and exhibited to us; and that His body and blood
may be eaten and drunk as a principle of life to us; and therefore
faith is all, or all is faith, in this other essential part of the Sacrament; and we cannot possibly do that which our Saviour commands
us to do unless it be done by faith." [1]

"The institution consists of those two essential parts just mentioned; that is, in offering, presenting, and pleading before God by
faith the atonement of Christ's body and blood, and in owning Him
to be a principle of life to us by our eating His body and blood:
this is the entire, whole institution." [2]

"This poor man (for so I must call one so miserably insensible
of the greatness of the subject he is upon) can find nothing in the
institution but, first, bread and wine, not placed and offered before
God as first signifying and pleading the atonement of His Son's
body and blood, and then eaten and drank in signification of having
our life from Him, but bread and wine set upon a Table to put
the people that see it in mind that by and bye they are to exercise
an act of the memory. And then, secondly, this same bread and
wine afterwards brought to every one in particular, not for them to
know or believe that they are receiving anything of Christ or partaking of anything from Him, but only to let them know that the
very instant they take the bread and wine into their mouth is the
very time for them actually to excite that act of the memory for
the exciting of which bread and wine had been before set upon a
Table." [3]

"If we are in covenant with Christ, and have an interest in Him,
as our atonement and life, not because He once said that this was
His body and blood given and shed for our sins, or because we once
owned it and pleaded it before Him, but because He continues to
say the same thing in the Sacrament and to present Himself there
to us as our atonement and life, and because we continue to own
and apply to Him as such, it necessarily follows that the Sacrament
rightly used is the highest means of finishing our salvation, and puts
us in the fullest possession of all the benefits of our Saviour, both as
He is our atonement and life, that we are then at that time capable
of." [4]

"Do not the Scriptures plainly and frequently enough tell us of
the benefit of the new birth in Christ, of the putting on Christ, of
having Christ formed in us, of Christ's being our life, of our having
life in Him, of His being that bread from heaven, that bread of life,

---

[1] Pp. 91-93.   [2] P. 94.   [3] P. 95.   [4] Pp. 106, 107.

of which the manna was only a type, of His flesh being meat indeed and His blood drink indeed, of our eating His flesh and drinking His blood, and that without it we have no life in us; and are not all these things so many plain and open declarations of that which we seek to obtain by eating the body and blood of Christ? For we eat the sacramental body and blood of Christ to show that we want and desire and by faith lay hold of the real spiritual nature and being of Christ; to show that we want and desire the progress of the new birth in Christ; to put on Christ, to have Christ formed and revealed in us, to have Him our life, to partake of Him, our second Adam, in the same fulness and reality as we partake of the nature of the first Adam. And therefore all that the Scripture says of the benefits and blessings of these things, so much it says of the benefits and blessings that are sought and obtained by the eating the body and blood of Christ in the Lord's Supper. For to eat the body and blood of Christ is neither more nor less than to put on Christ, to receive birth and life and nourishment and growth from Him, as the branch receives its being and life and nourishment and growth from the vine." [1]

"You must therefore consider the Sacrament purely as an object of your devotion, that is to exercise all your faith, that is to raise, exercise, and inflame every holy ardour of your soul that tends to God. It is an abstract or sum of all the mysteries that have been revealed concerning our Saviour from the first promise of a seed of the woman to bruise the serpent's head to the Day of Pentecost. As you can receive or believe nothing higher of our Saviour than that He is the atonement for our sins and a real principle of life to us, so every height and depth of devotion, faith, love, and adoration which is due to God as your Creator is due to God as your Redeemer. Jacob's ladder that reached from earth to heaven, and was filled with angels ascending and descending between heaven and earth, is but a small signification of that communion between God and man which this Holy Sacrament is the means and instrument of. Now here it may be proper for you to observe that whatever names or titles this institution is signified to you by, whether it be called a sacrifice propitiatory or commemorative, whether it be called an holy oblation, the Eucharist, the Sacrament of the body and blood of Christ, the Sacrament of the Lord's Supper, the heavenly banquet, the food of immortality, or the Holy Communion, and the like, matters not much. For all these words or names are right and good, and there is nothing wrong in them but the

[1] Pp. 108-10.

striving and contention about them. For they all express something that is true of the Sacrament, and therefore are every one of them in a good sense rightly applicable to it; but all of them are far short of expressing the whole nature of the Sacrament, and therefore the help of all of them is wanted." [1]

"The reason why this Sacrament is said in one respect to be a propitiatory or commemorative sacrifice is only this, because you there offer, present, and plead before God such things as are by Christ Himself said to be His body and blood given for you. But, if that which is thus offered, presented, and pleaded before God is offered, presented, and pleaded before Him only for this reason, because it signifies and represents both to God and angels and men the great sacrifice for all the world, is. there not sufficient reason to consider this service as truly a sacrifice?" [2]

Law expressed his Eucharistic beliefs more fully in his work entitled *An Appeal to All that Doubt or Disbelieve the Truths of the Gospel, whether they be Deists, Arians, Socinians, or Nominal Christians*, which was published in 1742. He alluded in passing to "the reality of Christ's flesh and blood in the Sacrament under the notion of the Transubstantiation of the bread and wine" in a way which implied that he held the doctrine of Transubstantiation to be untrue. [3] He explained that in our Lord's incarnate life there was "a holy humanity of heavenly flesh and blood veiled under" His "outward flesh and blood"; and that this "heavenly flesh and blood" is the gift in Communion.

"This great and glorious Redeemer had in Himself the whole humanity both as it was before and after the Fall, namely, in His inward man the perfection of the first Adam, and in His outward the weakness and mortality of the fallen nature." [4]

"By the Fall of our first father we have lost our first glorious bodies, that eternal celestial flesh and blood which had as truly the nature of paradise and heaven in it as our present bodies have the nature, mortality, and corruption of this world in them. If therefore we are to be redeemed, there is an absolute necessity that our souls be clothed again with this first paradisical or heavenly flesh and blood, or we can never enter into the kingdom of God. Now, this is the reason why the Scriptures speak so particularly, so frequently, and so emphatically of the powerful blood of Christ, of the

[1] Pp. 121-23.   [2] P. 127.   [3] Pp. 180, 181.   [4] Pp. 188, 189.

32 *

great benefit it is to us, of its redeeming, quickening, life-giving virtue ; it is because our first life, or heavenly flesh and blood, is born again in us, or derived again into us from this blood of Christ. Our Blessed Lord . . . had not only that outward flesh and blood which He received from the Virgin Mary, and which died upon the cross, but . . . also a holy humanity of heavenly flesh and blood veiled under it, which was appointed by God to quicken, generate, and bring forth from itself such a holy offspring of immortal flesh and blood as Adam the first should have brought forth before his Fall. . . . Our common faith, therefore, obliges us to hold that our Lord had the perfection of the first Adam's flesh and blood united with and veiled under that fallen nature which He took upon Him from the Blessed Virgin Mary. . . . Our Blessed Lord had a heavenly humanity, which clothed itself with the flesh and blood of this world in the womb of the Virgin ; and from that heavenly humanity or life-giving blood it is that our first heavenly immortal flesh and blood is generated and formed in us again ; and therefore His blood is truly the atonement, the ransom, the redemption, the life of the world, because it brings forth and generates from itself the paradisical immortal flesh and blood as certainly, as really, as the blood of fallen Adam brings forth and generates from itself the sinful vile corruptible flesh and blood of this life.   Would you farther know what blood it is that has this atoning life-giving quality in it ?   It is the blood which is to be received in the Holy Sacrament. . . . There is but one redeeming, sanctifying, life-giving blood of Christ, and it is that which gave and shed itself under the veil of that outward flesh and blood that was sacrificed upon the cross ; it is that holy and heavenly flesh and blood which is to be received in the Holy Sacrament ; it is that holy immortal flesh and blood which Adam had before the Fall, of which blood if we had drank, that is, if we had been born of it, we had not wanted a Saviour, but had had such flesh and blood as could have entered into the kingdom of heaven. . . . Does not the Holy Sacrament undeniably prove to us that He had a heavenly flesh entirely different from that which was seen nailed to the cross, and which was to be a heavenly substantial food to us ; that He had a blood entirely different from that which was seen to run out of His mortal body, which blood we are to drink of, and live for ever ? . . . Here therefore is plainly discovered to us the true nature, necessity, and benefit of the Holy Sacrament of the Lord's Supper, both why, and how, and for what end we must of all necessity eat the flesh and drink the blood of Christ.   No figurative meaning of the words is here to be sought for, we must eat Christ's flesh and drink His blood in the same reality as He took upon Him the real flesh and blood of the Blessed Virgin; we can have no real relation to Christ, can be no true members of His mystical body, but by being real partakers of that same kind of flesh and blood which was truly His, and was His for this very end, that through Him the same might be brought forth in us. . . . What flesh and blood are we to eat and drink? Not such as we have already, not such as any offspring of Adam hath, not such as can have its life and death by and from the elements of this world; and therefore not that outward visible mortal flesh and blood of Christ which He took from the Virgin Mary and was seen on the cross, but a heavenly immortal flesh and blood, which came down from heaven, which hath the nature, qualities, and life of heaven in it. . . . As the flesh and blood which we lost by his [Adam's] Fall was the flesh and blood of eternal life, so it is the same flesh and blood of eternal life which is offered to us in the Holy Sacrament, that we may eat and live for ever. This is the adorable height and depth of this divine mystery, which brings heaven and immortality again into us, and gives us power to become sons of God. . . . Thus is this great Sacrament, which is a continual part of our Christian worship, a continual communication to us of all the benefits of our Second Adam; for in and by the body and blood of Christ, to which the divine nature is united, we receive all that life, immortality, and redemption which Christ, as living, suffering, dying, rising from the dead, and ascending into heaven, brought to human nature, so that this great mystery is that in which all the blessings of our redemption and new life in Christ are centred. And they that hold a Sacrament short of this reality of the true body and blood of Jesus Christ cannot be said to hold that Sacrament of eternal life which was instituted by our Blessed Lord and Saviour." [1]

VIII.

One result of the Eucharistic controversy which arose in consequence of the publication of the *Plain Account* may be seen in the various works about the Eucharist from the pen of Dr. Daniel Waterland. Waterland was born in 1683, became Master of Magdalene College, Cambridge, in 1713, was subsequently Canon of Windsor and Archdeacon of Middlesex, and

[1] Pp. 202-14. On such theories as that thus expressed by Law about the twofold humanity of Christ, see Oxenham, *The Catholic Doctrine of the Atonement*, pp. 358-62 (fourth edition).

held other preferments. He died in 1740. Before the out-
break of the controversy occasioned by the publication of the
Plain Account he had in 1730 published three tracts entitled
*Remarks upon Dr. Clarke's Exposition of the Church Catechism;
The Nature, Obligation, and Efficacy of the Christian Sacraments Considered;* and *A Supplement to the Treatise on the
Nature, Obligation, and Efficacy of the Christian Sacraments.*[1]
In these tracts the nature of the Holy Eucharist was necessarily
in view; but they did not contain any complete or detailed con-
sideration of it. The controversy excited by the *Plain Account*
led to Dr. Waterland delivering his *Charge* on *The Doctrinal
Use of the Christian Sacraments Considered*[2] in 1736, and to his
writing the elaborate treatise, *A Review of the Doctrine of the
Eucharist as laid down in Scripture and Antiquity,*[3] which appeared in 1736. He continued the treatment of the same subject in the *Charges* on *The Christian Sacrifice Explained,*[4] *The
Sacramental Part of the Eucharist Explained,*[5] and *Distinctions
of Sacrifice,*[6] delivered in 1738, 1739, and 1740. In the treatise
and in the *Charges* the doctrines of the presence and of the
sacrifice are considered with great seriousness, thoroughness, and
learning. The arguments both of the author of the *Plain Account* and of such theologians as Johnson and Brett are kept
well in view. The conclusions accepted throughout are the
same as those in the latest position of Cranmer,[7] namely, that
those who communicate worthily receive, not Christ's body and
blood, but the virtue and grace of them; and that the sacrificial
character of the Eucharist is completely described when there is
said to be a remembrance of Christ's sacrifice, a sacrifice of praise
and thanksgiving, and the oblation of the lives of the communicants. Waterland explicitly rejects the "Romanist," "Lutheran,"
"Calvinist," and "Zwinglian" opinions about the presence, and
also that of Johnson; and in his careful enumeration of the
sacrificial characteristics of the Eucharist, which he calls "a true
and proper sacrifice," he does not include the presentation to
God the Father of the body and blood of our Lord. The main
features of his teaching may be seen in the following quotations:—

[1] These tracts are in Waterland, *Works* (Oxford, 1843), iv. 1-50, 51-
104, 105-48.
[2] *Op. cit.* v. 105-19. [3] *Op. cit.* iv. 459-802. [4] *Op. cit.* v. 121-84.
[5] *Op. cit.* v, 185-230. [6] *Op. cit.* v, 231-96. [7] See pp. 127-29, 184, *supra.*

"Whatever God is once pleased to sanctify by His more peculiar presence, or to claim a more special property in, or to separate to sacred uses, that is relatively holy as having a nearer relation to God; and it must of course be treated with a reverence and awe suitable. . . . The thrones, or sceptres, or crowns, or presence-rooms of princes are, in this lower sense, relatively sacred; and an offence may be committed against the majesty of the sovereign by an irreverence offered to what so peculiarly belong to him. . . . The things are in themselves just what they before were; but now they are considered by reasonable creatures as coming under new and sacred relations, which have their moral effect, insomuch that now the honour of the divine majesty in one case, or of royal in the other case, becomes deeply interested in them. Let us now apply these general principles to the particular instance of relative holiness supposed to be conveyed to the symbols of bread and wine by their consecration. They are now no more common bread and wine (at least not during this their sacred application), but the communicants are to consider the relation which they bear, and the uses which they serve to." [1]

"Come we then directly to consider the words, 'This is My body,' and 'This is My blood'. What can they, or what do they mean?

"1. They cannot mean that this bread and this wine are really and literally that body in the same broken state as it hung upon the cross, and that blood which was spilled upon the ground 1700 years ago. Neither yet can they mean that this bread and wine literally and properly are our Lord's glorified body, which is as far distant from us as heaven is distant; all sense, all reason, all Scripture, all antiquity, and sound theology reclaim against so wild a thought.

"2. Well, then, since the words cannot be understood literally, or with utmost rigour, they must be brought under some figure or other, some softening explication, to make them both sense and truth.

"3. . . . There appears to be something very solemn and awful in our Lord's pointed words, 'This is My body,' and 'This is My blood'. Had He intended no more than a bare commemoration or representation, it might have been sufficient to have said, 'Eat this bread broken,' and 'Drink this wine poured out,' in remembrance of Me and My passion, without declaring in that strong manner that the bread and wine are His body and blood, at

[1] *Op. cit.* iv. 527, 528.

the same time commanding His disciples to take them as such. We ought to look out for some as high and significant a meaning as the nature of the thing can admit of, in order to answer such emphatical words and gestures.

"4. Some, receding from the letter, have supposed the words to mean, this bread and this wine are My body and blood in power and effect, or in virtue and energy; which is not much amiss, excepting that it seems to carry in it some obscure conception either of an inherent or infused virtue resting upon the bare elements, and operating as a mean, which is not the truth of the case; excepting also that it leaves us but a very dark and confused idea of what the Lord's body and blood means in that way of speaking, whether natural or sacramental or both in one.

"5. It appears more reasonable and more proper to say that the bread and wine are the body and blood, namely, the natural body and blood, in just construction put upon them by the Lawgiver Himself, who has so appointed, and who is able to make it good. The symbols are not the body in power and effect, if those words mean efficiency; but, suitable dispositions supposed in the recipient, the delivery of these symbols is, in construction of Gospel law, and in divine intention, and therefore in certain effect and consequence, a delivery of the thing signified. If God hath been pleased so to order that these outward elements, in the due use of the Eucharist, shall be imputed to us, and accepted by Him, as pledges of the natural body of our Lord, and that this constructional intermingling His body and blood with ours shall be the same thing in effect with our adhering inseparably to Him as members or parcels of Him; then those outward symbols are, though not literally, yet interpretatively and to all saving purposes, that very body and blood which they so represent with effect; they are appointed instead of them." [1]

"Sacramental or symbolical feeding in the Eucharist is feeding upon the body broken and the blood shed under the signs and symbols of bread and wine; the result of such feeding is the strengthening or perfecting our mystical union with the body glorified; and so, properly speaking, we feed upon the body as dead, and we receive it into closer union as living, and both in the Eucharist when duly celebrated. . . .

"1. To the Romanists, who plead warmly for the very body and blood in the Eucharist, we make answer that we do receive the very body and blood in it and through it as properly as a man

[1] *Op. cit.* iv. 573, 574.

receives an estate and becomes possessed of an inheritance by any deeds or conveyances. . . .

"2. To the Lutherans, who seem to contend for a mixture of the visible elements with the body invisible, we have this to reply, that we readily admit of a symbolical delivery, or conveyance, of one by the other. . . .

"3. To the Calvinists of the ancient stamp, if any such remained now, we might reply that, though we eat not Christ's glorified body in the Eucharist, yet we really receive it, while we receive it into closer mystical union than before. . . .

"4. To the Zwinglian Sacramentarians, old Anabaptists, Socinians, and Remonstrants, who will not admit of any medium between local corporal presence and no presence at all as to beneficial effects, no medium between the natural body itself and mere signs and figures, to them we rejoin that there is no necessity of falling in with either extreme, because there is a medium, a very just one, and where indeed the truth lies. For, though there is no corporal presence, yet there is a spiritual one, exhibitive of divine blessings and graces; and, though we eat not Christ's natural glorified body in the Sacrament, or out of it, yet our mystical union with that very body is strengthened and perfected in and through the Sacrament by the operation of the Holy Spirit. . . .

"5. To those who admit not that the natural body of Christ is in any sense received at all, but imagine that the elements, as impregnated or animated with the Spirit, are the only body received, and are made our Lord's body by such union with the Spirit, I say, to those we make answer that the union of the Spirit with the elements (rather than with the persons) appears to be a gross notion and groundless; and, if it were admitted, yet could it not make the elements in any just sense our Lord's body, but the notion would resolve itself into a kind of impanation of the Spirit for the time. Besides, that the consequence would be that the Lord's body is received by all communicants, worthy or unworthy, which is not the truth of the case. Wherefore, to avoid all such needless suppositions and needless perplexities, let us be content to teach only this plain doctrine, that we eat Christ crucified in this Sacrament as we partake of the merits of His death; and, if we thus have part in His crucified body, we are thereby *ipso facto* made partakers of the body glorified; that is, we receive our Lord's body into a closer union than before, and become His members by repeated and stronger ties, provided we come worthily to the Holy Table, and that there is no just obstacle on our part to stop the current of divine graces." [1]

"The service therefore of the Eucharist . . . is both a true and a proper sacrifice . . . and the noblest that we are capable of offering, when considered as comprehending under it many true and evangelical sacrifices: 1. The sacrifice of alms to the poor and oblations [2] to the Church. . . . 2. The sacrifice of prayer from a pure heart. . . . 3. The sacrifice of praise and thanksgiving to God the Father through Christ Jesus our Lord. . . . 4. The sacrifice of a penitent and contrite heart. . . . 5. The sacrifice of ourselves, our souls and bodies. . . . 6. The offering up the mystical body of Christ, that is, His Church. . . . 7. The offering up of true converts or sincere penitents to God by their pastors. . . . 8. The sacrifice of faith and hope and self-humiliation in commemorating the grand sacrifice and resting finally upon it." [3]

An illustration of the wide prevalence in the middle and latter part of the eighteenth century of some such way of regarding the Eucharist as that advocated by Waterland is in the devotional manual entitled *The New Week's Preparation for a Worthy Receiving of the Lord's Supper*, the first edition of which was published in 1749. This book was avowedly designed to counteract and supersede the old *Week's Preparation;* [4] and it appears to have gradually taken the place of that work as a popular manual; it continued to be much used to the end of the eighteenth century and for some part of the nineteenth. The doctrine assumed in the prayers and meditations is that the Eucharist is a commemorative sacrifice appointed as a means of representing the passion and presenting its merits to God the Father on earth, as our Lord presents them in heaven; and that the consecrated bread and wine are symbols through the reception of which those who communicate worthily obtain spiritual benefits and spiritually feed on Christ.

[1] *Op. cit.* iv. 608-10.

[2] The word "oblations" appears to be used here in the sense of contributions of money for the support of the clergy. For the two ways in which the word is used, see Frere, *A New History of the Book of Common Prayer*, p. 482; and the Bishop (Dowden) of Edinburgh's article in the *Journal of Theological Studies*, April, 1900, pp. 321-46.

[3] *Op. cit.* iv. 730, 731.

[4] See Preface, pp. iii-ix, edition 1810: for the old *Week's Preparation* see pp. 457-59, *supra*.

"Lord, who are we, unworthy sinners, that Thou thus regardest our wretched dust ? . . . It was for our sakes, and to draw us up to Thy love, that Thou hast commanded us to commemorate and represent Thy passion, and present the merits of it before Thy Father on earth, as Thou dost present them to Him in heaven. It was for our sakes, and to help the infirmities of our nature, that Thou didst appoint a commemorative sacrifice of that one oblation of Thyself once offered upon the cross, and bread and wine so offered and blessed as symbols of Thy body and blood." [1]

"Now, O my God, prostrate before Thine altar, I dare not so much as look upon this mystery of our salvation if Thou hadst not invited me : I beseech Thee, therefore, accept of this representation we make before Thee of that all-sufficient sacrifice which Thy Son our Saviour Jesus Christ made upon the cross : let the merit of it plead effectually for the pardon and forgiveness of all my sins, and render Thee favourable and propitious to me a miserable sinner ; let the power of it prevail against all the powers of darkness ; let the wisdom of it make me wise unto salvation ; and let the peace of it reconcile me unto Thee, and bring to me peace of conscience. And then, O Blessed Jesus, my Redeemer, I shall be enabled to adore Thee, who didst endure the painful and shameful death of the cross to recover me from the state of sin and misery. . . . With all my soul, O dear Jesus, I love and praise Thee for the stupendous expression of Thy bounty and goodness towards me. O Lamb of God, that takest away the sins of the world, have mercy upon me ; O Lamb of God, that takest away the sins of the world, grant me Thy peace. Amen, Lord Jesus. Amen." [2]

"I beseech Thee, O Lord, to cure my infirmities, and let me not only receive the outward and visible sign, but the inward and spiritual grace, the body and blood of Thy Son Jesus Christ." [3]

"O Blessed Jesu, who vouchsafest to be my food, nourish my soul to eternal life ; create in me a mighty hunger after righteousness, and let this divine food instil into my weak and languishing soul new supplies of grace, new life, new vigour, and new resolutions, that I may never again faint or droop or tire in my duty." [4]

"Consider, O my soul, how by divine providence we have escaped the dangers of this night, and are continued together under a deep sense of our duty, which we yesterday acknowledged

[1] Part i. pp. 21, 22, edition 1810.
[2] Part i. pp. 128, 129. For use after the Prayer of Consecration.
[3] Part i. p. 130. For use before receiving the species of bread.
[4] Part i. pp. 132, 133. For use after receiving the species of bread.

and confirmed in the receiving of that Holy Sacrament which in its outward part is only bread and wine which the Lord hath commanded to be received, that is, to be eaten and drank by all such as come to His Table, in remembrance of the body and blood of Christ, which are verily and indeed taken and received by the faithful in the Lord's Supper. A Sacrament which at once by the bread broken signifies the body of Christ broken on the cross and by the wine poured out signifies the blood of Christ shed at His crucifixion. But guard against that doctrine which teaches that we eat the natural body and drink the natural blood of Christ; for the natural body and blood of Christ are in heaven and not here, it being against the truth of Christ's natural body to be at one time in more places than one; and therefore we cannot eat and drink Christ's natural body and blood in the Sacrament.

"2. We are well assured by Christ Himself as well as by His Apostle that the Lord's Supper was expressly designed for the remembrance of Christ after He should be taken away; therefore Christ, who is to be remembered, cannot be corporally present at the time of such remembrance. And as the bread and wine were ordained for memorials of His body broken and blood shed for us, His natural body and blood must be absent in order to be remembered by means of such memorials. They themselves cannot be the memorials of themselves in this rite; for nothing can be eaten or drank in remembrance of itself. They who argue for the contrary doctrine run into the greatest absurdities. For,

"3. The doing any act in remembrance of a person implies his bodily absence; and we are never said, nor can we be said, to perform that action in order, if he be corporally present, to remember him. And therefore, the end of this institution being the remembrance of Christ, it must follow from hence that to eat and drink in the Lord's Supper must be to eat and drink in a sense consistent with the notion of this remembrance, and, consequently, that to suppose or teach that Christians eat His real natural body in remembrance of His real natural body, and drink His real blood in remembrance of His real blood, is to teach that they are to do something in order to remember Him which at the same time supposes Him to be corporally present, and destroys the very notion of that remembrance, and so directly contradicts the most important words of the institution itself. Therefore,

"4. It cannot be the natural body and blood of Christ which is eaten and drank in the Lord's Supper, but something else, namely, bread and wine, in remembrance of them. All this is founded upon the plain notion of the word remembrance; and this remembrance is expressly mentioned in the original institution as a part thereof, and consequently it is this remembrance which constitutes the very nature of this Holy Sacrament. So that,

" 5. The real presence maintained by Protestants is not the presence of Christ's natural body, but the real presence of Christ's invisible power and grace so in and with the elements of bread and wine as to convey spiritual and real effects to the souls of such as duly receive them; for Christ did not only give His Son Jesus Christ to die for us but also to be our spiritual food and sustenance in that Holy Sacrament. Now, spiritual food and sustenance is doubtless the food and sustenance of the spirit; so to eat and drink spiritually is a figurative expression, and signifies the feeding upon Christ's body with our heart by faith. See John vi. 63.

" 6. Therefore, the benefits whereof we are made partakers of this Sacrament, to the strengthening and refreshing of our souls by the body and blood of Christ, as our bodies are by the bread and wine. O happy soul, that feeds on such celestial food, that art refreshed with the bread that came down from heaven, if with a true penitent heart and lively faith thou receive that Holy Sacrament, for then we spiritually eat the flesh of Christ and drink His blood. And,

" 7. Consider that bread and wine (or anything else which it might have pleased Christ to have chosen) may by the blessing and appointment of God be as communicative of grace as the true natural flesh and blood of Christ itself can be; for even that, if you could indeed eat it with your teeth, would no more communicate grace or any blessing to the receiver without such institution and appointment of God than any other food in the world that you can eat.

" 8. Wherefore it is my firm belief that, as this Sacrament is matter of mere institution and appointment, I am concerned to know no more either what the Sacrament is, or how it operates, than it hath pleased God to reveal in the Holy Scriptures. And it will be sufficient for me to believe that the consecrated elements are both called and made the body and blood of Christ so verily and indeed to all spiritual intents and purposes as to convey to the faithful receiver whatever grace and blessing Christ hath annexed to the due performance of those holy rites which He hath ordained as pledges of His love and for our joy and comfort." [1]

[1] Part ii. pp. 33-37.

IX.

The *Hymns on the Lord's Supper* published by John and
Charles Wesley [1] in 1745 give devotional expression to belief in
a spiritual communion with the body and blood of Christ by
means of the reception of the Sacrament, and in a sacrificial
commemoration of the death of Christ in union with His pleading of His sacrifice in heaven. The hymns are one hundred and
sixty-six in number, and of very varied character. Their doctrinal teaching is represented in the following quotations :—

> " Then let us go, and take and eat
> The heavenly, everlasting meat,
>   For fainting souls prepared ;
> Fed with the living bread divine,
> Discern we in the sacred sign
>   The body of the Lord.
>
> .   .   .   .
>
> The oblation sends as sweet a smell,
> Even now it pleases God as well,
>   As when it first was made ;
> The blood doth now as freely flow
> As when His side received the blow
>   That showed Him newly dead.
>
> Then let our faith adore the Lamb,
> To-day as yesterday the same,
>   In Thy great offering join ;
> Partake the sacrificial food,
> And eat the flesh, and drink the blood,
>   And live for ever Thine." [2]

> " O Thou eternal Victim, slain
> A sacrifice for guilty man,
>   By the eternal Spirit made,
> An offering in the sinner's stead ;
> Our everlasting Priest art Thou,
> And pleadest Thy death for sinners now.

---

[1] John Wesley was born in 1703, and died in 1791. Charles Wesley
was born in 1708, and died in 1788.

[2] Hymn 3.

Thy offering still continues new,
Thy vesture keeps its bloody hue ;
Thou stand'st the ever-slaughtered Lamb,
Thy priesthood still remains the same ;
Thy years, O God, can never fail,
Thy goodness is unchangeable." [1]

" The tokens of Thy dying love,
   O let us all receive,
And feel the quickening Spirit move,
   And sensibly believe.

The cup of blessing, blest by Thee,
   Let it Thy blood impart ;
The bread Thy mystic body be,
   And cheer each languid heart.

The grace which sure salvation brings,
   Let us herewith receive ;
Satiate the hungry with good things,
   The hidden Manna give.

The living bread sent down from heaven,
   In us vouchsafe to be ;
Thy flesh for all the world is given,
   And all may live by Thee.

Now, Lord, on us Thy flesh bestow,
   And let us drink Thy blood,
Till all our souls are filled below
   With all the life of God." [2]

" O the depth of love divine,
   The unfathomable grace !
Who shall say how bread and wine
   God into man conveys !
How the bread His flesh imparts,
How the wine transmits His blood,
Fills His faithful people's hearts
   With all the life of God ! " [3]

[1] Hymn 5.   [2] Hymn 30.   [3] Hymn 57.

" Draw near, ye blood-besprinkled race,
    And take what God vouchsafes to give,
The outward sign of inward grace,
    Ordained by Christ Himself, receive ;
The sign transmits the Signified,
The grace is by the means applied.

Sure pledges of His dying love,
    Receive the sacramental meat,
And feel the virtue from above,
    The mystic flesh of Jesus eat ;
Drink with the wine His healing blood,
And feast on the incarnate God.

Gross misconceit be far away !
    Through faith we on His body feed,
Faith only doth the Spirit convey,
    And fills our souls with living bread ;
The effects of Jesu's death imparts,
And pours His blood into our hearts." [1]

" 'Tis God we believe who cannot deceive ;
        The witness of God
Is present and speaks in the mystical blood.

Receiving the bread, on Jesus we feed ;
        It doth not appear
His manner of working ; but Jesus is here !

With bread from above, with comfort and love,
        Our spirit He fills,
And all His unspeakable goodness reveals." [2]

"Take, and eat, the Saviour saith,
    This My sacred body is !
Him we take and eat by faith,
    Feed upon that flesh of His ;
All the benefits receive,
    Which His passion did procure,
Pardoned by His grace we live,
    Grace which makes salvation sure.

        [1] Hymn 71.   [2] Hymn 92.

Title to eternal bliss,
    Here His precious death we find,
This the pledge, the earnest this
    Of the purchased joys behind:
Here He gives our souls a taste,
    Heaven into our hearts He pours,
Still believe, and hold Him fast,
    God, and Christ, and all is ours!" [1]

"Victim divine, Thy grace we claim,
    While thus Thy precious death we show,
Once offered up a spotless Lamb,
    In Thy great temple here below,
Thou didst for all mankind atone,
And standest now before the throne.

Thou standest in the holiest place,
    As now for guilty sinners slain,
Thy blood of sprinkling speaks and prays,
    All-prevalent for helpless man ;
Thy blood is still our ransom found,
And speaks salvation all around.

The smoke of Thy atonement here
    Darkened the sun, and rent the veil,
Made the new way to heaven appear,
    And showed the great Invisible:
Well pleased in Thee our God looked down,
And called His rebels to a crown.

He still respects Thy sacrifice,
    Its savour sweet doth always please,
The offering smokes through earth and skies,
    Diffusing life and joy and peace:
To these Thy lower courts it comes,
And fills them with divine perfumes.

We need not now go up to heaven
    To bring the long-sought Saviour down,
Thou art to all already given,
    Thou dost e'en now Thy banquet crown:
To every faithful soul appear,
And show Thy real presence there." [2]

[1] Hymn 103.   [2] Hymn 116.

"Father, Thy feeble children meet,
  And make Thy faithful mercies known ;
Give us through faith the flesh to eat,
  And drink the blood of Christ Thy Son ;
Honour Thine own mysterious ways,
  Thy sacramental presence show,
And all the fulness of Thy grace,
  With Jesus, on our souls bestow.

Father, our sacrifice receive,
  Our souls and bodies we present,
Our goods and vows and praises give,
  Whate'er Thy bounteous love hath lent ;
Thou canst not now our gift despise,
  Cast on that all atoning Lamb,
Mixt with the bleeding sacrifice,
  And offered up through Jesu's name." [1]

X.

The Eucharistic beliefs held in the Church of England between 1662 and the end of the eighteenth century were thus of
very varied kinds. The author of the *Plain Account of the
Nature and End of the Sacrament of the Lord's Supper* and his
followers were avowedly Zwinglian. A more usual opinion was
that those who communicate worthily receive at their Communion the benefits of the body and blood of Christ. Ken and
the author of the widely used manual called *A Week's Preparation towards a Worthy Receiving of the Lord's Supper* appear to
have believed that the gift in Communion was not simply the
benefits of Christ's body and blood, but the body and blood
themselves. Some of the Nonjuring divines and of those who to
a large extent sympathised with them held that the elements
were made by consecration to be in power and effect, though not
actually, the body and blood of Christ. William Law, dis-
tinguishing between the heavenly immortal flesh and blood of
Christ and His outward and visible and mortal flesh and blood,
both of which were in His incarnate life on earth, maintained
the presence and gift of the heavenly and immortal flesh and
blood. A belief in a commemorative sacrifice was ordinarily
held by those who adopted some doctrine other than the Zwinglian denial of any sacramental presence or gift.

[1] Hymn 153.

CHAPTER XVI.

POST-REFORMATION THEOLOGY.

PART III.

In the early years of the nineteenth century the prevailing Eucharistic doctrine in the Church of England was probably identical with or approximating to that taught by Waterland, whose *Review of the Doctrine of the Eucharist* has been described as " a treatise which was once considered almost as the text-book of the Church of England ".[1] Yet other views were held, some of them carrying on the Zwinglian lines of teaching promoted by the *Plain Account of the Nature and End of the Sacrament of the Lord's Supper*, others continuing the type of theology congenial to Bishop Ken and the author of the old *Week's Preparation towards a Worthy Receiving of the Sacrament of the Lord's Supper*, or to the Nonjurors.

I.

The work entitled *Remains of Alexander Knox, Esq.* contains very much of interest on theological matters, and not least in regard to the Eucharist. Mr. Knox was private secretary to Lord Castlereagh in the closing years of the eighteenth century, and was engaged in political life, which, however, he abandoned in his desire for study and retirement. He died in 1831. The second volume of the *Remains*, published in 1834, contains an

---

[1] See a preface by the late Bishop Jackson of London to the volume issued by the Clarendon Press containing the *Review of the Doctrine of the Eucharist* and the four *Charges* on the Eucharist, p. v. Bishop Jackson added that the doctrine asserted and defended by Waterland "as the true doctrine of the Eucharist" was "the *via media* between two extremes, which, though not excluded by the tolerant moderation of our Articles and formularies, have each too facile a tendency to pass into serious error".: see p. vii.

undated *Treatise on the Use and Import of the Eucharistic Symbols* and a *Letter to John S. Harford, Esq., prefatory to the Treatise on the Eucharist,* dated 19th July, 1826. Mr. Knox lays great stress on the Eucharist as the appointed means of conveying to Christians the benefits of the Incarnation. He regards the consecrated elements as the "representatives" of Christ, and the "vehicles" of His "power," and the means whereby He is "personally present" and is communicated to those who receive the Sacrament. He rejects " Transubstantiation," and the " gross sense " of " the term of the Lord's body " which "has been fancied in the Church of Rome"; and does not appear to consider the elements to be made by consecration more than "to be in virtue and efficacy" Christ's "body and blood". The most probable interpretation of his teaching is that it is a combination of Receptionism and of the theory of which John Johnson is a good representative.[1]

" The ancient writers of the Church were agreed in ascribing to the consecrated elements in the Eucharist an unutterable and efficacious mystery in virtue of our Saviour's words of institution, by which He had made those elements, when consecrated after His example, the vehicles of His saving and sanctifying power, and in that respect the permanent representatives of His incarnate Person. But, notwithstanding this exalted estimate of the Eucharist, the notion of a literal Transubstantiation, such as was subsequently introduced into the Western Church, would appear never to have entered into their mind." [2]

"To understand the mysterious term of the Lord's body in any such gross sense as has been fancied in the Church of Rome would be to overlook our Redeemer's expressions, already in part quoted, ' It is the spirit which quickeneth, the flesh profiteth nothing. The words which I speak unto you, they are spirit, and they are life.' [3] But let us not therefore rush into an opposite extreme, nor treat the words of an inspired Apostle as we would not treat those of any common intelligent writer. Let us observe that every expression St. Paul uses tends, as it were, more and more, to invest the sacramental symbols with an ineffable measure of derivative dignity and instrumental virtue. He gives no shadow of pretext for any carnal interpretation ; but he says all that could be said to make us regard ' that bread and that cup ' not only as the visible pledge, but the

---

[1] See pp. 474-77, *supra.*   [2] II. 139.   [3] St. John vi. 63.

effective organ, of a vital communication from the invisible, but then specially operative and therefore specially present, Redeemer. For He alone it is who could make those symbols to be in virtue and efficacy His body and blood." [1]

"Contemplated as the actual vehicle of Christ's own ineffable influences to the capable receiver, it becomes a matter of intrinsic interest, to neglect which would be to neglect both present and everlasting salvation." [2]

"Our incarnate Saviour is described as the Second Adam, who was to be to us the fountain of a spiritual and heavenly nature, as the first Adam has been to us the fountain of an animal and earthly nature ; and we are instructed that, as by the Fall of our earthly progenitor sin entered into the world, and death by sin, and thus one man was to all the source of corruption and mortality, so by the grace of the one Man Jesus Christ a gift of righteousness is given to all who will receive it, which destroys the reign of sin, and is at once the earnest and the principle of a blessed immortality. . . . In these divine energies and influences of the incarnate Word the co-operation of the Holy Spirit is so expressly and uniformly stated to bear a part as to make this a point of Christian faith ever to be kept in view. . . . The richest treasures of grace and virtue are provided for us in the adorable Person of our incarnate Saviour, and . . . not only in virtue of His union with our nature, but of His being crucified, His dying, and His rising again; and . . . those treasures are communicated to our minds and hearts by the continued agency of the Holy Spirit, who, as it were, passes from the Second Adam into all who aspire to a spiritual union with this ineffable source of a new and heavenly life, and makes them at once His own temple and living members of the great Head of the Church, to whom He unites them in a vital, and (if they faithfully concur) a still advancing and, at length, beatific incorporation. . . . Such then being the special and peculiar blessing of the Gospel, it might be inferred on general grounds, if even direct evidence were wanting, that the peculiar rite of the Gospel must have a special relation and subserviency to that blessing.   But the express designation of the Holy Eucharist by our Lord Himself as His own virtual body and blood, and St. Paul's appeal to the received belief of the Church that the blessed cup was the communion of the blood of Christ, and that the broken bread was the communion of the body of Christ, established beyond question that the Sacrament of the Lord's Supper is to serve as the external and visible medium

[1] II. 201.   [2] II. 210.

through which the disciples of Christ in all ages are to expect, through the co-operation of the Eternal Spirit, the divinely vivifying influences of His incarnate Person, and the ineffable virtues of His crucifixion and death. The fact being undeniable that there are in the evangelic dispensation such influences and such virtues, and those influences and virtues being denominated by our Lord Himself His flesh and His blood, we are obliged by the terms of St. Paul and by the still stronger terms (if that be possible) of our Lord Himself to identify the internal grace and virtue of the Eucharist with those quickening, strengthening, and purifying communications which are promised to Christians as proceeding from the Person and death of Christ through the ever-co-operative agency of the Holy Ghost. . . . Is it not, then, with this highest and fullest communication of divine grace that the Sacrament of the Lord's Supper has been specifically connected by the very words of institution? It could have been no other than that highest and fullest communication of divine grace which our Lord has promised, and so emphatically dwelt on, in the sixth chapter of St. John. When, therefore, he applies those very terms which He had declared to be in the highest degree significant of spirit and life to those sanctified elements which He was pleased to appoint as sacramental symbols, and when He enjoins that very eating and drinking which in that discourse He had pronounced indispensable to be carried into act in a visible manner, but with such profoundly significant import, in this perpetuated institution, what can we conclude but that the Sacrament of the Lord's Supper is eminently, and in a way of peculiar appropriation, the visible conduit through which, by the invisible operation of Him who appointed it, is conveyed that special evangelical grace with which the Father, Son, and Holy Ghost have conjointly distinguished and blessed the Christian dispensation?" [1]

"The height of beatific purity and virtue, then, to which as Christians we are called to rise, and the influences from above by which alone we can thus by anticipation dwell in God's tabernacle and rest upon His holy hill, are the two grand points to which all the devotional forms of our Church are directed. Concluding the matter of our true happiness to consist in a virtual but vital commencement of our future heaven, and the indispensable means of that happiness not less to consist in a really divine communication, our Church aims at forming us to such habits and feelings of devotion as must imply a constant commerce of the heart with heaven,

[1] II. 228-30, 232-35.

and a gradual approximation to its purity, its serenity, and its happiness through fresh and fuller infusion of that eternal life, which God has given us in His Son.

"Such, I say, is the uniform import and design of all our established services. Their object is to raise us to everything for which we were created, which can make us well pleasing to God, acceptable to men, and happy in ourselves, substantially happy even while in the body, with the assurance of unalloyed and consummate happiness hereafter. And for this exalted purpose, while every possible degree of fidelity and vigilance is to be exercised on our part, we are continually taught to look upward, and expect all increase of wisdom, fortitude, or virtue from the boundless provision made for us in the mystery of redemption. Of this mystery, then, the Church considers the Sacrament of the Eucharist not only to be expressly and profoundly significant, but to constitute in some sort an instrumental organ. That grace of our Lord Jesus Christ, by which alone we can live, much more grow up and advance, as Christians is, according to our Church, eminently and peculiarly conveyed to us in and through this visible ordinance. As it is that special and appropriate grace of the Gospel which she always has in view, that grace which raises every living member of Christ's kingdom above even Christ's distinguished forerunner, so is it this crowning blessing of the Gospel, this concentration of all its lights, and verification of its most precious promises, which she unites indissolubly with the right reception of the Eucharistic symbols; ' For then,' says she, ' we spiritually eat the flesh of Christ, and drink His blood; then, we dwell in Christ, and Christ in us; we are one with Christ, and Christ with us '." [1]

II.

The first edition of *The Christian Year* was published anonymously by John Keble in 1827. It contained signs that its author regarded the Eucharist as a sacrifice and as the means whereby our Lord is received to be the food of the soul. The poem for " Holy Communion " included the verses :—

> " Fresh from th' atoning sacrifice
> The world's Creator bleeding lies,
> That man, His foe, by whom He bled,
> May take Him for his daily bread.

[1] II. 244, 245.

> O agony of wavering thought
> When sinners first so near are brought!
> 'It is my Maker—dare I stay?
> My Saviour—dare I turn away?'"

That headed "Commination" referred to the Eucharist as "our glorious sacrifice". Six poems added to the third edition in 1828 included one for 5th November, then entitled "An Address to Converts from Popery," afterwards headed "Gunpowder Treason". The twelfth and thirteenth stanzas of this poem were :—

> "If with thy heart the strains accord,
>   That on His altar-throne
> Highest exalt thy glorious Lord,
>   Yet leave Him most thine own;
>
> O come to our Communion Feast:
>   There, present in the heart,
> Not in the hands, th' eternal Priest
>   Will His true self impart."

In later years, at any rate, the words "present in the heart, not in the hands" were understood by Mr. Keble to mean that the presence in the hands is of no profit unless there is the presence in the heart also, on the analogy of such passages as "I will have mercy, and not sacrifice"; and that this was the sense intended from the first is to some extent supported by the fact that in one copy of the original poems he had written "There, treasured in the heart".[1] Before his death, "fearing," as his brother Mr. Thomas Keble wrote,[2] "that he was misleading others," he altered the words to "There present, in the heart as in the hands," the form in which they stand in editions of *The Christian Year* published since that time.[3]

Though it is possible that Dr. Pusey may have unconsciously read back some of his later beliefs to an earlier time, yet it was

[1] See Lock, *John Keble*, p. 56.

[2] See a note by him, dated 25th April, 1866, added to editions of *The Christian Year* since published.

[3] There is a very full and careful statement of the various reasons which led Mr. Keble to determine on the alteration in a letter from Dr. Pusey to Dr. Liddon, dated 20th May, 1878, which was printed in the *Church Quarterly Review*, July, 1878, pp. 539-44.

his belief, expressed in 1879, that in the early years of the nine-teenth century he had as a child "learnt" "the doctrine of the real presence" from his "mother's explanation of the Catechism, which she had learned to understand from older clergy ".[1]

III.

An illustration of Eucharistic belief on the part of those whose Churchmanship was of a different kind from that of Mr. Keble and Dr. Pusey may be seen in a volume of lectures entitled *The Doctrine of the Church of England, as contrasted with that of the Church of Rome.* The lectures contained in the volume were delivered in Manchester in 1839 and 1840; they are bitterly hostile to, and denunciatory of, the Church of Rome; their general standpoint is that of "Low Churchmen"; the first and last of the series are by the famous "Evangelical" leader Mr. Hugh Stowell. In the lecture on *The Sacrifice of the Mass*, there is a violent repudiation of Transubstantiation and of the statements of the Council of Trent in regard to the sacrifice of the Mass; and the lecturer does not suggest that the Eucharist is in any sense a sacrifice, or that the consecrated bread and wine are more, or convey more, than a "representation" of the body and blood of Christ.[2] The lecturer on *The Lord's Supper* joins to his emphatic and indignant reprobation of the doctrine of the Church of Rome, as he understood it, a no less emphatic assertion of what he calls "the Catholic doctrine of the real presence of the Saviour," the doctrine, that is, that "Christ is really present to the true believer," that the "faithful" "receive verily and indeed, in truth and in fact," "after a spiritual manner," "the body and blood of Christ ".[3]

IV.

One part of the work of the Oxford Movement was to give theological expression and devotional setting to the doctrine which Dr. Pusey regarded himself as having learnt from his mother's instruction.

One of the most solid of the literary productions associated with the Movement was the elaborate and learned work, *A*

---

[1] Liddon, *Life of E. B. Pusey*, i. 7.   [2] Lecture ix. p. 21.
[3] Lecture viii. pp. 6, 7, 10, 11, 53.

Treatise on the Church of Christ, by Mr. William Palmer, after-wards Sir William Palmer, of Worcester College, the Rector of Whitchurch Canonicorum. The first edition of this book was published in 1838, the second in 1839, and the third in 1842. In discussing the documents of the Reformation in England, Mr. Palmer wrote :—

"In 1562 the Convocation authorised the *Thirty-nine Articles of Religion*, the only formulary of doctrine established by competent authority in England since the publication of the *Necessary Doctrine* in 1543. It may be well to remark the points of doctrine in which the two formularies agreed and differed. Baptism and the Eucharist alone are in the *Articles* accounted ' Sacraments of the Gospel' ; but Matrimony, Ordination, and other rites are termed Sacraments in our *Homilies* approved by the *Articles;* so that there is no very marked difference as to the number of Sacraments between the two formularies; for the *Necessary Doctrine* does not pronounce the lesser Sacraments or rites of the Church to be ' Sacraments of the Gospel'. It seems, in fact, that the Church of England has refrained from limiting the use of the word ' Sacrament,' and left her theologians, in this respect, to that ancient liberty of which the Synod of Trent has deprived the Roman Theologians. If the *Necessary Doctrine* maintains a change of substance in the Eucharist without affirming Transubstantiation, the Article in denying Transubstantiation does not condemn absolutely all change of substance in any sense, but the particular change called by the Romanists Transubstantiation, which supposes the bread to cease to exist. The article condemning ' the sacrifices of Masses, in which it was commonly said that Christ was offered for the quick and dead, for the remission of pain or guilt,' rightly censures that erroneous view of the sacrifice, but does not declare against the doctrine of the Eucharistic sacrifice rightly understood, and therefore does not differ from the *Necessary Doctrine*, which merely acknowledges a sacrifice. . . . Altogether I see not that there is any very great contradiction between these two formularies in matters of doctrine. I dispute not that several of those who composed the one differed in some points from several of those who composed the other; but their formularies are not so worded as to evince any great or irreconcilable opposition between the public and authorised faith of the Church of England in the reign of Henry VIII. and in that of Elizabeth.

"The Church of England is said to have varied again when, in the time of Charles II., she readmitted the declaration on kneeling at the Sacrament, which not only maintains the existence of the substance of the bread and wine after consecration, but denies the corporal presence. But there is no inconsistency; for the former assertion only amounts to a denial of Transubstantiation, already rejected by the Articles; and the latter is not opposed to the real, spiritual, and heavenly presence of Christ's body.

"This Catholic and Apostolic Church has always avoided any attempt to determine too minutely the mode of the true presence in the Holy Eucharist. Guided by Scripture, she establishes only those truths which Scripture reveals, and leaves the subject in that mystery with which God for His wise purposes has invested it. Her doctrine concerning the true presence appears to be limited to the following points:—

"Taking as her immovable foundation the words of Jesus Christ, 'This is My body. . . . This is My blood of the new covenant,' and 'Whoso eateth My flesh and drinketh My blood hath eternal life,' she believes that the body, or flesh, and the blood of Jesus Christ, the Creator and Redeemer of the world, both God and Man united indivisibly in one Person, are verily and indeed given to, taken, eaten, and received by the faithful in the Lord's Supper under the outward sign or form of bread (and wine), which is on this account the 'partaking or Communion of the body and blood of Christ'. She believes that the Eucharist is not the sign of an absent body, and that those who partake of it receive not merely the figure, or shadow, or sign of Christ's body, but the reality itself. And, as Christ's divine and human natures are inseparably united, so she believes that we receive in the Eucharist, not only the flesh and blood of Christ, but Christ Himself, both God and Man.

"Resting on these words, 'The bread which we break, is it not the Communion of the body of Christ?' and again, 'I will not drink henceforth of this fruit of the vine,' she holds that the nature of the bread and wine continues after consecration, and therefore rejects Transubstantiation, or 'the change of the substance' which supposes the nature of bread entirely to cease by consecration.

"As a necessary consequence of the preceding truths, and admonished by Christ Himself, 'It is the Spirit that quickeneth, the flesh profiteth nothing : the words that I speak unto you, they are spirit and they are life,' she holds that the presence (and therefore the eating) of Christ's body and blood, though true, is altogether 'heavenly and spiritual,' of a kind which is inexplicable by any carnal or earthly experience or imagination, even as the Sonship of the eternal Word of God, and His Incarnation, and the procession of the Holy Spirit are immeasurable by human understandings.

"Believing, according to the Scriptures, that Christ ascended in His natural body into heaven, and shall only come from thence at the end of the world, she rejects for this reason, as well as for the last, any such real presence of Christ's body and blood as is 'corporal' or organical, that is, according to the known and earthly mode of the existence of a body.

"Resting on the divine promise, 'Whoso eateth My flesh and drinketh My blood hath eternal life,' she regards it as the most pious and probable opinion that the wicked, those who are totally devoid of true and living faith, do not partake of the holy flesh of Christ in the Eucharist, God withdrawing from them so 'divine' a gift, and not permitting His enemies to partake of it. And hence she holds that such a faith is 'the means by which the body of Christ is received and eaten,' 'a necessary instrument in all these holy ceremonies,' because it is the essential qualification on our parts, without which that body is not received, and because 'without faith it is impossible to please God'.

"Following the example of our Lord Jesus Christ and of the Apostles, and supported by their authority, she believes that 'the blessing' or 'consecration' of the bread and wine is not without effect, but that it operates a real change ; for, when the Sacrament is thus perfected, she regards it as so 'divine a thing,' so 'heavenly a food' that we must not 'presume' to approach it with unprepared minds, and that sinners, although they only partake of the bread and wine, partake of them to their own condemnation, because they impiously disregard the Lord's body, which is truly present in that Sacrament. Hence it is that the Church, believing firmly in the real presence of the 'precious and blessed body and blood of our Saviour Jesus Christ,' speaks of the Eucharist as 'high and holy mysteries,' exhorts us to consider the 'dignity of that holy mystery,' that 'heavenly feast,' that 'holy table,' 'the banquet of that most heavenly food,' even 'the King of kings' table'.

"Such is the simple, the sublime, and, what is more, the true and Scriptural doctrine of our Catholic and Apostolic Church. . . . Our doctrine leaves this subject in the sacred mystery with which God has enveloped it. It is not to be denied that the Roman doctrine of Transubstantiation facilitates the mental conception of that mystery ; but it has the fatal defect of being opposed to the plain language of Scripture." [1]

[1] I. 399-405. On several occasions Dr. Pusey expressed his approval of this statement, except the part relating to reception by the wicked: see e.g., *Letter to the Bishop of London*, p. 41 ; *Eirenicon*, part i. pp. 23, 24.

In this careful statement Mr. Palmer, following what he believed to be the teaching of the Church of England, rejected
Transubstantiation, and any view of the presence of Christ's
body as would represent it as being "according to the known
and earthly mode of the existence of a body"; and affirmed that
"a real change" is effected by the "consecration of the bread
and wine," and that the "reality" of Christ's body and blood is
"given to," "taken" and "received" and "eaten" "by the
faithful" "under the outward sign or form of bread and wine".
Of the Communions made by the wicked, he said, the wicked
"do not partake of the holy flesh of Christ [1] in the Eucharist,
God withdrawing from them so 'divine' a gift". Without explaining his meaning, he alluded to "the doctrine of the Eucharistic sacrifice rightly understood".

Elsewhere in his book, Mr. Palmer referred to the doctrine
of the Eucharistic sacrifice in the part of his defence of English
Ordinations in which he was replying to the objection that the
Church of England denies "that there is any sacrifice in the
Eucharist". Speaking of "Eucharistic sacrifice, understood in
an orthodox sense," he said:—

"The Church of England has always acknowledged such a
sacrifice. The thirty-first Article is directed against the vulgar and
heretical doctrine of the reiteration of Christ's sacrifice in the
Eucharist. It was those 'missarum sacrificia quibus vulgo dice-
batur sacerdotem offerre Christum in remissionem poenæ aut culpæ
pro vivis et defunctis' which are pronounced 'blasphema figmenta
et perniciosæ imposturæ,' but not 'missarum sacrificia' as understood by the fathers and in an orthodox sense. The article was
directed against the errors maintained or countenanced by such
men as Soto, Hardinge, etc., who, by rejecting the doctrine of a
sacrifice by way of commemoration and consecration, and not literally identical with that on the cross, and by their crude and objec-
tional mode of expression, countenanced the vulgar error that the
sacrifice of the Eucharist or Mass was in every respect equal to that
of Christ on the cross, and that it was in fact either a reiteration
or a continuation of that sacrifice. The article was not directed

---

[1] It will be observed that Mr. Palmer, who for the most part follows
closely the words of the English formularies, here alters the phrase of
Article xxix., "in no wise are they partakers of Christ," into "do not
partake of the holy flesh of Christ".

against the doctrine of the Eucharistic sacrifice as explained by Bossuet, Veron, and others, with which we have no material fault to find." [1]

Reference has already been made to the indications of Eucharistic belief in *The Christian Year*, published by Mr. Keble in 1827. On the question of the Communions of the wicked there are some important letters of his, written in the years 1854, 1855, and 1856. In March, 1854, Archdeacon Denison, the Archdeacon of Taunton, in consequence of charges made against his Eucharistic teaching, set out eight propositions declaring :—

"1. That the bread and wine become, by the act of consecration, 'the outward part or sign of the Lord's Supper'; and, considered as objects of sense, are unchanged by the act of consecration, 'remaining still in their very natural substances'.

"2. That 'the inward part or thing signified' is 'the body and blood of Christ'.

"3. That 'the body and blood of Christ,' being present naturally in heaven, are supernaturally and invisibly but really present in the Lord's Supper through the elements by virtue of the act of consecration.

"4. That by 'the real presence of the body and blood in the Lord's Supper' is not to be understood the presence of an influence emanating from a thing absent, but the supernatural and invisible presence of a thing present, of His very body and very blood present 'under the form of bread and wine'.

"5. That the 'outward part or sign' and 'the inward part or thing signified,' being brought together in and by the act of consecration, make the Sacrament.

"6. That the Sacrament, that is, 'the outward part or sign' and 'the inward part or thing signified,' is given to, and is received by, all who communicate.

"7. That 'in such only as worthily receive the same [the Sacraments of the body and the blood of Christ] they have a wholesome effect or operation; but they that receive them unworthily purchase to themselves damnation as St. Paul saith'.

"8. That worship is due to 'the body and blood of Christ' supernaturally and invisibly but really present in the Lord's Supper 'under the form of bread and wine' by reason of that Godhead with which they are personally united. But that the elements,

_____
[1] II. 347.

through which 'the body and blood of Christ' are given and received, may not be worshipped."[1]

With Archdeacon Denison's general position, and with most of his detailed statements, Mr. Keble was in complete agreement; but he felt some doubt in regard to the assertion that "the inward part" of the Sacrament "is received by all who communicate". On 18th January, 1855, he wrote to Dr. Pusey:—

"Surely some of our friends are putting themselves in a wrong position in maintaining so earnestly reception by the wicked as an integral part of the doctrine. I am afraid of the consequences when they find they have less sympathy than they had imagined. For myself, I must confess that if I were forced to decide I think there is more to be said against that tenet than for it, especially looking to St. Augustine, and most especially to *Tractate* 26 *on St. John*, and to the passage in *Ep.* xcviii. § (I think) 17,[2] in which he speaks of calling Sacraments by the names of the things of which they are Sacraments. But surely our Church permits us to leave it open, and surely she is right in so doing, and we are wrong to close it either way."[3]

After a condemnation of Archdeacon Denison's teaching by the Archbishop (Sumner) of Canterbury, Mr. Keble, while strongly dissenting from the decision of the Archbishop both as to the reception by the wicked and as to adoration, wrote about the reception by the wicked, "as you know, I do not see my way in that point so clearly as Denison thinks he does";[4] and a lengthy and elaborate correspondence on this matter took place between him and Dr. Pusey, who agreed with Archdeacon Denison.[5] In October, 1856, he was one of those who signed a declaration of protest, which was chiefly written by Dr. Pusey, in which, after making some references to the teaching of Anglican divines, the signatories said :—

"We, therefore, being convinced :—

"1. That the doctrine of the real presence of 'the body and blood of our Saviour Christ under the form of bread and wine,' has

---

[1] *The Defence of the Archdeacon of Taunton*, pp. 19-21.
[2] The passage referred to *Ep.* xcviii. 9.   For it and that from *In Joh. Ev. Tract.* xxvi. see vol. i. pp. 84, 92-94, *supra*.
[3] Liddon, *Life of E. B. Pusey*, iii. 433.
[4] *Op. cit.* iii. 435.   [5] *Op. cit.* iii. 460-69.

528 THE DOCTRINE OF THE HOLY EUCHARIST

been uniformly accepted by General Councils, as it is also embodied in our own formularies ;

" 2. That the interpretation of Scripture most commonly held in the Church has been that the wicked, although they can 'in no wise be partakers of Christ,' nor 'spiritually eat His flesh and drink His blood,' yet do in the Sacrament not only take, but eat and drink unworthily to their own condemnation the body and blood of Christ which they do not discern ;

" 3. That the practice of worshipping Christ then and there especially present, after consecration and before communicating, has been common throughout the Church. And, moreover, that the *Thirty-nine Articles* were intended to be, and are, in harmony with the faith and teaching of the ancient undivided Church ;

" Do hereby protest earnestly against so much of the opinion of his Grace the Archbishop of Canterbury, in the case of Ditcher *v.* Denison, as implies, directly or indirectly, that such statements as we have cited above are repugnant to the doctrine of the *Thirty-nine Articles.*

" And we appeal from the said opinion, decision, or sentence of his Grace, in the first instance, to a free and lawful Synod of all the Churches of our communion, when such by God's mercy may be had." [1]

In the following year, 1857, Mr. Keble published his book *On Eucharistical Adoration; or the Worship of Our Lord and Saviour in the Sacrament of Holy Communion,* a second edition of which appeared in 1859. In 1858, in consequence of some controversies in the Scottish Church,[2] he published his *Considerations Suggested by a Late Pastoral Letter on the Doctrine of the Most Holy Eucharist.* Some extracts from these works will show clearly his beliefs in regard to the Eucharist.

" The Person . . . of Jesus Christ our Lord, wherever it is, is to be adored—to be honoured, acknowledged, sought unto, depended on, with all possible reverence, with the most entire and single-hearted devotion, incommunicable to any finite being—by all creatures whom He has brought to know Him. This proposition, though in the heat of theological warfare it may seem to have been denied, and that recently, cannot, I conceive, be really and advisedly denied by any one who believes the divinity of our Lord. Taking it for granted, I will state it once again. The Person of Jesus Christ our

---

[1] The whole of this protest is printed in Liddon, *op. cit.* iii. 440-42.
[2] See pp. 624-27, *infra.*

Lord, wherever it is, is to be adored. And now I will add the next proposition in the argument, namely, Christ's Person is in the Holy Eucharist by the presence of His body and blood therein. From which, as will be seen, follows by direct inference that the Person of Christ is to be adored in that Sacrament, as there present in a peculiar manner, by the presence of His body and blood.

" It is on the second or minor of these three propositions, if on any, that opposition is to be expected, and explanation is necessary. It raises, evidently, the whole question of that which is denominated ' the real objective presence ' of Jesus Christ in the Holy Eucharist. That is to say, whereas the divine nature in Christ is everywhere and always equally present, and so everywhere and always alike adorable ; but to us frail children of men He has condescended at certain times and places to give especial tokens of His presence, which it is our duty to recognise, and then especially to adore ; thus far, I suppose, all allow who in any sense believe the creeds of the Church, that in the Holy Eucharist we are very particularly bound to take notice of His divine presence as God the Word, and to worship Him accordingly. That which some in modern times have denied is, that He is then and there present according to His human nature, really and substantially present, as truly present as He was to any of those with whom He conversed when He went in and out among us ; or, again, as He is now present in heaven interceding for us. Both of these two last mentioned are modes of His human presence, acknowledged by all who confess Him come in the flesh. But that which some affirm, some deny, as part of the Catholic doctrine of the Eucharist, is a third and special mode of presence of the holy humanity of our Lord, denoted and effected by His own words, ' This is My body, this is My blood,' a presence the manner of which is beyond all thought, much more beyond all words of ours, but which those who believe it can no more help adoring than they could have helped it had they been present with St. Thomas, to see in His hands the print of the nails ; or, again, with so many sick persons to touch the hem of His garment, and so to be made whole. It is no more natural for them to think, one way or the other, of worshipping the bread and wine than it was for the woman with the issue of blood to think of worshipping the garment which she touched instead of Him who was condescending to wear it and make it an instrument of blessing to her.

" If we may reverently say it, . . . ' as the reasonable soul and flesh is one man,' and as ' God and Man is one Christ,' so the consecrated bread and wine, and the body and blood of our Lord Jesus

Christ, are one Sacrament. And as we know the soul of a man, which we cannot see, to be present by the presence of his living body, which we can see, so the presence of that bread and wine is to us a sure token of the presence of Christ's body and blood. . . . And, as persons of common sense are not apt to confound a man's soul with his body because of the intimate and mysterious connection of the two, . . . nor yet can you easily bring them to doubt whether meat and drink serve to keep the two together, whether life can come by bread, because they cannot understand how, so no plain and devout reader of Holy Scripture and disciple of the Church would of his own accord find a difficulty in adoring the thing signified, apart from the outward sign or form; or in believing that the one may surely convey the other by a spiritual and heavenly process known to God, but unknown to him and to all on earth." [1]

"Where His flesh and blood are, there is He by a peculiar and personal presence, in His holy humanity; and being there, . . . He must needs be adorable." [2]

"The Eucharist . . . is the unbloody sacrifice of the New Testament; unbloody, though it be in part an offering of blood; ἀναιμακτός not ἄναιμος. No blood shed in it, but the living blood of Christ with His living body offered up to the Father, for a memorial of the real blood-shedding, the awful and painful sacrifice once for all offered on the cross.

"This memorial Christ offers in heaven, night and day, to God the Father, His glorified body with all its wounds, His blood which He poured out on the cross but on His resurrection took again to Himself, and with it ascended into heaven. With that body and blood He appears continually before the throne, by it making intercession for us, by it reminding God the Father of His one oblation of Himself once offered on the cross." [3]

"If the Holy Eucharist as a sacrifice be all one with the memorial made by our High Priest Himself in the very sanctuary of heaven, where He is both Priest after the order of Melchizedek and Offering by the perpetual presentation of His body and blood, then, as the blessed inhabitants of heaven cannot but be thought of s adoring Him in both His aspects of Priest and Sacrifice, so how hould His Holy Church throughout all the world not adore Him in like manner as often as she 'goeth up to the reverend Communion' to offer up spiritual sacrifices, and 'to be satisfied with spiritual

[1] *On Eucharistical Adoration*, pp. 57-59, edition 1867.
[2] P. 65.   [3] Pp. 66, 67.

meats'? For there He is in His holy and perfect manhood virtually present as our Priest with him that ministereth, being one of those to whom He said, 'Lo, I am with you alway, even unto the end of the world,' and really present as our sacrifice according to that other word, 'This is My body, and this is My blood,' 'Do this in remembrance of Me'." [1]

"If we really believe that that which He declares to be His own flesh and blood is Jesus Christ giving Himself to us under the form of bread and wine, how can we help thanking, and therefore adoring (for to thank God is to adore) the unspeakable Gift as well as the most bountiful Giver? seeing that in this case both are one." [2]

"The *rationale* of the Holy Eucharist is to be a sacrifice offered by the Son to the Father; it is the transference for the time to earth of the great perpetual commemorative sacrifice in heaven." [3]

"At the risk of officiousness and unnecessary repetition, I am tempted to set down here a series of dogmatical statements, which I had occasion not long since to draw up for private use. They may perhaps help to relieve some of tedious, haunting, bewildering thoughts, setting forth, as they endeavour to do, the special bearing of the doctrine of the Incarnation on these Eucharistical questions.

"1. I believe that there is one, and only one, true body of the Lord Jesus, in the sense in which any man's natural body is called his own. That body, I mean, which He took of the Blessed Virgin Mary when He came into the world.

"2. That neither this body nor the reasonable soul which He took to Himself at the same time, nor His manhood consisting of both together, have or ever had any distinct personality, but have subsisted, and ever will subsist, as taken into the Person of the Eternal Son of God.

"3. That, as the divine Word or Person of Christ is everywhere and always present and adorable, so ever since the Incarnation the presence of the body of Christ, or the presence of the soul of Christ, or of both united, whenever and wherever and however He wills to notify it, is to be taken as a warrant and call for especial adoration on the part of all His reasonable creatures, to whom the knowledge of the two natures has been revealed, adoration to Him as to God most high, and to His holy manhood, not separately but as subsisting in His divine Person. I believe, therefore :—

"4. That His sacrificed body, hanging on the cross and laid in the grave, was adorable.

[1] Pp. 72, 73.   [2] P. 76.   [3] P. 114.
34 *

" 5. I understand the words, 'This is My body which is given (broken) for you,' literally taken, to affirm that what He gives us in the Sacrament is the same body which was sacrificed on the cross.

" 6. And I believe that those words ought to be literally taken. Therefore :—

" 7. I believe that what He gives us in the Sacrament, under the name of His body, is adorable." [1]

" The objections usually taken to such statements as the above are taken, some to their evidence, some to their substance. The latter may be referred (speaking broadly) to one or more of the following heads :—

" 1. Men cannot in their own minds separate what is said from notions of a carnal and natural presence, as of an earthly body among earthly things ; or :—

" 2. They are religiously afraid of encroaching on the verity of Christ's human nature by believing His body to be verily and indeed present anywhere but in one place in heaven.

" With the principle of both these objections, I need hardly say, the maintainers of the presence have entire and perfect sympathy. They would rather die than accept a carnal heathenish doctrine as against the one, or as against the other a notion which would spiritualise away the whole Gospel. But they claim to be believed when they say that they cannot of themselves discern, nor has it ever been enforced on them by any authority to which they are bound to defer, that their doctrine involves either of these notions." [2]

To these extracts from Mr. Keble's published works may be added a portion of a letter printed in the volume entitled *Letters of Spiritual Counsel and Guidance by the late Rev. J. Keble* on the subject of the obligation of Eucharistic doctrine.

" I have long had an opinion that, in respect of the Holy Sacrament of the Eucharist, we are bound to be especially careful how we make doctrinal statements in such sense as to charge dissentients with heresy, for this reason, that, while the great truths of the creeds have been settled, even as to the wording connected with them, by true Œcumenical Councils (in which statement I include the doctrine of Baptism, as connected with the Pelagian contro-

---

[1] *Considerations*, pp. 206, 207, edition 1867.   *Cf. Letters of Spiritual Counsel and Guidance*, pp. 209-11, edition 1875.

[2] Pp. 207, 208.

versy), it has so happened in the providence of God that the doctrine of the Holy Eucharist has never been subject to similar enactments until the eleventh or twelfth century, after the separation of East and West. Well therefore may each person, or each portion of the Church, for himself or itself, form strong opinions, and express them strongly, as God shall guide them, on the several points involved in the doctrine; but to impose them as articles of faith, making those heretics who demur to them, they are not, I conceive, competent, except the point be such an one as can be shown to have been unequivocally received by the whole Church from the beginning, such (for example) as the inspiration of Holy Scripture. What is the authority for the saying that 'whole Christ' remains in 'each particle of either kind' other than that it was deduced by certain great divines in the middle ages from certain formulæ which had been accepted by certain portions of the Church, and that one or two very exceptional cases occur in early Church History which might be explained on that supposition, but may also be explained in other ways? Where, again, do you find in so many words that the wicked eat and drink the body and blood of Christ in the same sense that the penitent do? The *onus probandi* surely lies with those who affirm it, considering, (1) our Lord's express words in St. John vi. and (2) St. Augustine's words in *Tr.* xxvi. §§ 15, 18 ; considering also that when St. Augustine seems to affirm the contrary, he may be using the names of the sacred things for the sacred symbols only, in the way indicated by him in *Ep.* xcviii. 9.[1] And the apparent separation of the 'inward part' from the 'benefits partaken of' (in the Catechism) may be due to its being felt by the framers of the Catechism that it was necessary, with a view to the doctrine of the sacrifice, to state the objective presence previous to reception. I own that to me the Catechism and Communion Service appear to be silent as to what the wicked receive, and, indeed, the Articles also, rightly taken." [2]

[1] See p. 527, *supra.*

[2] Pp. 212, 213, edition 1875. In another letter in the same volume (p. 223) Mr. Keble mentioned that the holders of " the tenet of reception by the wicked " hold it " as the most probable interpretation of Holy Scripture, especially of 1 Cor. xi. 29," and because of " the great and manifest preponderance of patristical authority for it," as well as because of " logical arguments or physical analogies ". In 1856 he signed the statement that " the interpretation of Scripture most commonly held in the Church has been that the wicked " " do in the Sacrament " " eat and drink unworthily to their own condemnation the body and blood of Christ ". See pp. 527, 528, *supra.*

Thus Mr. Keble, while not prepared to make definite statements as to the presence of the " whole Christ " in "each particle of either kind" or as to the reception of the body of Christ by the wicked, was convinced that in the Sacrament—that is, as the context shows, in the consecrated bread and wine—is the body of Christ which He took of the Blessed Virgin Mary, which was sacrificed on the cross; that this presence of the body of Christ is not after a carnal or natural manner ; that Christ thus present is to be adored; and that the Eucharist is a sacrifice offered by Christ to the Father, being a sacrifice of the body and blood which were offered on the cross, and a transference to earth and in time of the abiding sacrifice in heaven.

The teaching of Dr. Pusey about the Eucharist is very voluminous, is contained in writings of different kinds, and is spread over many years.   It will promote clearness to give some characteristic instances in, so far as is possible, chronological order.   In 1839 Dr. Pusey published a treatise entitled *A Letter to the Right Rev. Father in God, Richard, Lord Bishop of Oxford,*[1] *on the Tendency to Romanism imputed to Doctrines held of old, as now, in the English Church.*   In this *Letter* he expressed his belief that—

" In the Communion there is a true, real, actual, though spiritual (or rather the more real because spiritual), communication of the body and blood of Christ to the believer through the holy elements ; that there is a true, real, spiritual presence of Christ at the Holy Supper, more real than if we could with Thomas feel Him with our hands, or thrust our hands into His side ; that this is bestowed upon faith, and received by faith, as is every other spiritual gift, but that our faith is but a receiver of God's real, mysterious, precious gift; that faith opens our eyes to see what is really there, and our hearts to receive it; but that it is there independently of our faith. . . . We see not why we need avoid language used by the fathers, as well as by the ancient liturgies, and quoted with approbation by great divines of our Church, that 'the bread and wine is made the body and blood of Christ,' seeing that its being spiritually the body and blood of Christ interferes not with its being still corporeally what the Apostle calls it, 'the bread and wine,' nor with the nature of a Sacrament, but rather the better agrees thereto." [2]

---

[1] Bishop Bagot.   [2] Pp. 128, 131, 132.

To these positive statements, and to an assertion that "we do not think that our Lord is less really and spiritually present than" "the Romanists,"[1] Dr. Pusey added in the same *Letter* a careful and explicit rejection, not only of "modern novelties" of "Zurich or Geneva," but also of the definitions of the Council of Trent and of Bellarmine, and spoke several times of the Roman Catholic doctrine as "carnal".[2] Thus, he says:—

"We maintain . . . that Rome has grievously erred by explaining in a carnal way the mode of this presence, and requiring this her carnal exposition to be received as an article of faith. She anathematises us in our Church for holding that 'in the most holy Sacrament of the Eucharist there remains the substance of bread and wine,' and 'denying that wonderful and remarkable conversion of the whole substance of bread into the body, and of the whole substance of wine into the blood, so that there remain only the appearances of bread and wine,' 'which,' it proceeds, 'the [Roman] Catholic Church most aptly terms Transubstantiation'.[3] We suppose also that they meant it in a carnal and erroneous sense that they say 'that the body and blood of Christ is' not only 'really,' but 'substantially present in the Sacrament of the Holy Eucharist'; for 'substantially' they explain to be not simply equivalent to 'really,' but 'corporeally,'[4] that 'the body of the Lord is sensibly touched by the hands, broken and bruised by the teeth'.[5] Further, we think it presumptuous to define, as they do, that 'Christ is wholly contained under each species,'[6] whereby they would excuse their modern innovation of denying the cup to the laity, and would persuade themselves by a self-invented and unauthorised theory of modern days that they receive no detriment thereby. Again, we hold it rash to define peremptorily 'that the body and blood of Christ remain in the consecrated elements which are not consumed or are reserved after the Communion'[7] (meaning thereby that they so remain independently of any subsequent participation, as of the sick, or by the communicants), although doubtless they are not common bread and wine, but hallowed. Then also we reject what Rome maintains under an anathema, 'that in the Holy Sacrament of the Eucharist Christ the only-begotten Son of God is to be adored with the outward adoration of divine

---

[1] P. 129.

[2] Pp. 114, 115, 130, 133, 140.

[3] Quoted from Council of Trent, sess. xiii. can. 2.

[4] Quoted from Bellarmine, *De Sacram. Euch.* i. 12.   [5] *Ibid.* iii. 24.

[6] Quoted from Council of Trent, sess. xiii. can. 3.   [7] *Ibid.* 4.

worship, and to be set forth publicly to the people in order to be adored,' [1] nay, 'that this most holy Sacrament rightly received the same divine worship as is due to the true God, and that it was not therefore the less to be adored because instituted by Christ the Lord to be received. For that the same Eternal God was present in it whom, when the Eternal Father brought into the world, He said, And let all the angels of God worship Him.' [2] Lastly, as connected with and dependent upon Transubstantiation, we cannot but hold that the ' Sacrifice [3] of Masses, in the which it was commonly said that the priest did offer Christ for the quick and dead, to have remission of pain and guilt, were blasphemous fables and dangerous deceits,' and interfere ' with the offering of Christ once made ' upon the cross." [4]

In 1841 Dr. Pusey wrote his treatise *The Articles treated on in Tract Ninety Reconsidered and Their Interpretation Vindicated in a Letter to the Rev. R. W. Jelf.* The positive doctrine here affirmed does not appear to differ in any way from that in the *Letter* of 1839. As regards the Church of Rome, Dr. Pusey still speaks of " the received doctrine " as " carnal," and as involving the annihilation of the bread and wine ; but he differs from the *Letter* of 1839 in adding "though happily (one must in candour add) not so defined in the Council of Trent ". [5] In his sermon *The Holy Eucharist a Comfort to the Penitent*, preached in 1843, and in the preface to this sermon, written in the same year, he spoke of " the consecrated elements " as " being," and " becoming " the " body and blood " of Christ, of the " bread which is His flesh," and described the words of institution as " the form which consecrates the sacramental elements into His body and blood ". [6] In the treatise *A Letter to the Right Hon. and the Right Rev. the Lord Bishop of London in Explanation of some Statements Contained in a Letter by the Rev. W. Dodsworth*, published in 1851, he described the Eucharist as " a pleading of our Lord's passion in act, a memorial of it, not to ourselves, but to God "; he said that in it " We present before Him not mere bread and wine, but that which, without physical change of substance, consecrated by the words of our Lord and the power and grace of God, is verily and indeed, not carnally, but mystically,

[1] Quoted from Council of Trent, sess. xiii. can. 6.   [2] *Ibid.* cap. 5.
[3] Apparently a slip or misprint for "sacrifices ".
[4] Pp. 133-35.   [5] P. 48.   [6] Preface, p. v, pp. 12, 18, 22.

sacramentally, spiritually, and in an ineffable and supernatural way, the body and blood of our Lord," and that "we are admitted, as it were, to see in image" "what in truth" "the one High Priest" "ever doth in heaven," and that "the Church pleadeth as a suppliant that same sacrifice which He presenteth as High Priest efficaciously"; he excepted from his agreement with Mr. Palmer's statement [1] the inference that "God withdraws the presence of the body and blood of Christ" from those who communicate unworthily, and said he "should prefer to leave" this question "as a mystery," since those who communicate unworthily cannot be "partakers of Christ" and "yet" that which they receive "must in some sense be the body and blood of Christ"; he repudiated "a local confinement and humiliation" of Christ in the Eucharist, and maintained that Christ is "to be adored as present," "not as confined or contained in place," and not "so as to involve any worship of the consecrated elements".[2] In this *Letter* of 1851 he advanced a further step than in the *Letter* of 1841 towards allowing that the differences between the Church of England and the Church of Rome were not crucial.

"I have never taught anything physical, corporeal, carnal, but spiritual, sacramental, divine, ineffable. And, when I have said, as I could not but acknowledge, that I could not see how the Roman Catholics could mean less by 'the accidents of bread and wine' than we by the substance, this was not to draw our doctrine to theirs, but theirs to ours. If it be granted, as they must grant, that all the natural properties remain, size, form, solidity, the same distribution of particles, whereof the elements are composed, the same natural powers of nourishment or exhilaration, the same effect upon the nervous system and every other physical property, I do not know what remains which we mean to affirm and they to deny. But I have said this, not as adopting their mode of explanation, which is not acknowledged by the Greek Church any more than by our own, but as hoping that our differences were not irreconcilable, and that we are condemning a popular physical interpretation which they cannot consistently hold. . . . I have said that it appears from our Article itself that it condemns Transubstantiation in the sense

[1] See pp. 524, 525, *supra*.
[2] Pp. 25, 31, 41, 42, 51, 54, small 8vo edition of 1851. *Cf.* the Advertisement to the *Paradise for the Christian Soul*, p. vii.

of implying a physical change. . . . If any imply not a physical change, the Article does not apply to them." [1]

In the following year, 1852, Dr. Pusey appears to have temporarily returned to his former view that the doctrine of the Church of Rome was "physical" and "carnal"; for on 16th October in that year he wrote to Mr. Keble, with reference to a forthcoming book by Archdeacon R. I. Wilberforce,[2] "R. W. is writing what I think is quite untenable, that the Roman Church by Transubstantiation does not mean a physical change, which I believe to be contrary to fact".[3]

The sermon preached in 1853, *The Presence of Christ in the Holy Eucharist*, contained the same positive teaching as earlier writings. Dr. Pusey spoke of the presence as " sacramental, supernatural, mystical, ineffable, as opposed not to what is real, but to what is natural," as " a presence without us, not within us only," as parallel to the passing of our Lord's "spiritual body" " on the morning of the resurrection through the sealed tomb" and to the passing of His body "*illæsa virginitate* through the doors of the Virgin's womb," as " above nature," and as consequently not inconsistent with the continued existence of the bread and wine notwithstanding the law of " physical nature that two bodies cannot be in the same place at the same time".[4]   Our Lord's words "This is My body," are to be taken "solemnly and literally".[5]   What is consecrated and what we receive are the " body and blood of Christ " " not in any physical or carnal way, but spiritually, sacramentally, divinely, mystically, ineffably, through the operation of the word of Christ and of God the Holy Ghost ".[6]

In 1855 Dr. Pusey published his great treatise *The Doctrine of the Real Presence as contained in the Fathers from the Death of St. John the Evangelist to the Fourth General Council vindicated*. It was a voluminous and elaborate *catena* of evidence in the form of notes to his sermon preached in 1853, *The Presence of Christ in the Holy Eucharist*. While thus for the most part a statement of evidence and not of his own beliefs, the whole structure of the book and occasional sentences made it clear that the doctrine maintained by him was that the elements con-

[1] Pp. 49, 50.   [2] See pp. 549-51, *infra*.
[3] Liddon, *Life of E. B. Pusey*, iii. 423.
[4] Pp. 21-25.   [5] P. 26.   [6] P. 46.

tinue to exist after consecration, that the body and blood of Christ are present in and under them, and that this presence is of a supernatural kind. ' For instance, he said :—

"The term 'in,' as used by the fathers, does not express any 'local' inclusion of the body and blood of Christ; it denotes their presence there after the manner of a Sacrament. . . . The presence of our Lord's body and blood in the Holy Eucharist is in a supernatural, divine, ineffable way, not subject to the laws of natural bodies. The word 'in,' like the word of our *Book of Homilies,* 'under the form of bread and wine,'[1] only expresses a real presence under that outward veil. But the term does imply the existence of the elements, in which the body and blood of our Lord are said to be."[2]

"What is consecrated upon the altars for us to receive, what under the outward elements is there present for us to receive, is the body and blood of Christ, by receiving which the faithful in the Lord's Supper do verily and indeed take and receive the body and blood of Christ, by presuming to approach which the wicked . . . become guilty of the body and blood of the Lord, that is, become guilty of a guilt like theirs who laid hands on His divine Person, while yet in the flesh among us, or who shed His all-holy blood."[3]

The treatise published in 1857, *The Real Presence of the Body and Blood of Our Lord Jesus Christ the Doctrine of the English Church, with a Vindication of the Reception by the Wicked and of the Adoration of our Lord Jesus Christ Truly Present,* was, like the book of 1855, mainly a statement of evidence, but it also contained abundant signs of Dr. Pusey's own beliefs. He explicitly stated that "there is no physical union of the body and blood of Christ with the bread and wine"; that "where the consecrated bread is, there sacramentally is the body of Christ; where the consecrated wine is, there sacramentally is the blood of Christ"; "the heavenly part is conveyed to us through the earthly symbol consecrated by His word of power".[4] There were some passages of special interest on the questions of the reception by the wicked and of adoration, subjects both of which were emphasised by being mentioned in the title of the book. As to the reception by the wicked, Dr. Pusey referred to his former "suspense" of judgment, and ex-

---

[1] See p. 214, note 2, *supra.*   [2] Pp. 131, 132.
[3] Pp. 719, 720.   [4] Preface, p. xix, and p. 183.

plained that he now felt clear that those who communicate unworthily receive the body and blood of Christ.

"I was myself long in suspense about these words, partly de-
ferring to the apparent authority of St. Augustine, partly withheld
by the difficulty which St. Augustine states, that the wicked cannot 'dwell in Christ, or Christ in them'. . . . Now, having seen
more accurately that St. Augustine does agree with that great body
of Christian fathers who believe that the wicked do receive His
body and blood, I have yielded my belief to what before seemed to
me the plainest meaning of St. Paul's words, that the wicked, while
they 'are in no ways partakers of Christ' Himself, yet receive
within them sacramentally His body and blood, which they do not
discern nor discriminate." [1]

Among the passages relating to adoration was the following :—

"Believing as we believe, we should with the magi have fallen
down and worshipped the speechless Infant, knowing Him to be
God the Word. We should have thought His raiment as Man no
hindrance to our adoring Him. Why then should we think it too
strange a thing for His marvellous condescension that He should
now give us 'His blessed body and blood under the form of bread
and wine'? Or how should His body, which He gives us, not be
His living, life-giving body? Or how should His life-giving body
be apart from His Godhead, which makes it life-giving? Or how,
since His Godhead is present there, should we not adore? We do
not adore the Sacrament,[2] as, when He was upon the earth, we
should not have adored His raiment, even though the touch of it
conveyed the hidden virtue from Him, the Source of life and healing. But Himself, wheresoever or howsoever He is present, we are
bound to adore." [3]

In the preface to the first volume of his collected *Sermons
Preached before the University of Oxford*, dated Easter, 1859,
Dr. Pusey implied that he had returned to the opinion which
he appears to have temporarily abandoned in 1852,[4] that the

---

[1] Pp. 307, 308.

[2] "Sacrament" is here evidently used in the sense of the outward
part of the Sacrament, as is shown by the comparison with the raiment of
our Lord : *cf.* the statement in the Tridentine *Catechism* quoted on p. 101,
supra.

[3] Pp. 336, 337.   [4] See p. 538, *supra.*

difference between the Church of England and the Church of Rome on the subject of Transubstantiation is not of importance. To the sentence "the teaching of the English Church, in contrast with that of the schoolmen, as to the continuance of the visible elements in their natural substances," he added a footnote:—

"I say the schoolmen, because the Roman Church has tacitly modified the meaning of the word 'substance' by allowing that the elements retain their natural power of nourishing (*Catech. Conc. Trid.*) which all the schoolmen denied.[1] The Church of Rome has not explained what it means by a change of substance, while it allows that everything remains which we understand by the word 'substance'." [2]

In an appendix, dated Vigil of St. Matthias, 1867, to the sermon *Will ye also go away?* preached in 1867, Dr. Pusey wrote with reference to an opinion expressed in the preamble of a resolution passed by the Upper House of the Convocation of Canterbury, in February, 1867, that there was a danger lest "certain ritual observances" should "favour errors deliberately rejected by the Church of England":—

"I cannot for a moment believe that the bishops who passed this resolution meant to condemn as 'errors deliberately rejected by the Church of England' those truths which I spoke of as being 'set before the eyes' by that ritual.[3] But it becomes necessary for me for my own position and for that character of unreserve and straightforwardness which every one who would benefit the Church of England must maintain, to state what those doctrines are which I believe to be included in it. These are:—

"1. That the Holy Eucharist is the great and central act of Christian worship, our closest nearness to God.

"2. That—while repudiating any materialistic conception of the mode of the presence of our Lord in the Holy Eucharist, such as I believe is condemned in the term 'corporal presence of our

[1] For teaching of schoolmen on this point, and for Dr. Pusey's apparent misunderstanding, see vol. i. pp. 310, 316, 318, 319, 330, 335, *supra*, pp. 544, 547, *infra*.
[2] P. vii.
[3] The allusion is to a speech delivered by Dr. Pusey at a meeting of the English Church Union on 14th June, 1866; see Liddon, *Life of E. B. Pusey*, iv. 212, 213.

Lord's natural flesh and blood,' that is, as though His precious body
and blood were present in any gross or carnal way, and not rather
sacramentally, really, spiritually—I believe that in the Holy Eucharist the body and blood of Christ are sacramentally, supernaturally, ineffably, but verily and indeed, present 'under the form
of bread and wine,' and that, 'where His body is, there is Christ'.

" 3. That—thankfully believing that the 'offering of Christ
once made is that perfect redemption, propitiation, and satisfaction
for the sins of the whole world, both original and actual,' and that
our Blessed Lord Himself, having 'finished upon the cross that one
oblation of Himself,' doth now, while ever living to make intercession for us, add nothing to the infinite merits of the super-
abundant satisfaction of that His one sacrifice which would suffice
to redeem a thousand worlds—I also believe that, as in all our
prayers 'through Jesus Christ our Lord' we plead in word that one
meritorious sacrifice, so in the celebration of the Holy Eucharist the
priest presents and pleads to the Father that same body which was
broken for us, and the blood which was shed for us, therein sacramentally present by virtue of the consecration, which our great
High Priest in His perpetual intercession for us, locally present in
His natural body at the right hand of the Father, evermore exhibits
before the Father for us. . . .

" 4. I do not know the 'ritual observances' well enough to say
whether the adoration of Christ, truly present, is symbolised in
them.   But, while I hold the literal meaning of the words of the
Articles, 'The Sacrament of the Lord's Supper was not by Christ's
ordinance reserved, carried about, lifted up, or worshipped,' I hold
also, in the words of Bishop Andrewes, that 'Christ Himself, the
Substance (*res*) of the Sacrament, in and with the Sacrament, out
of and without the Sacrament, is, wherever He is, to be adored, that
is, the Substance of the Sacrament, but not the Sacrament, that is,
the earthly part, as Irenaeus, the visible, as Augustine '.[1]

"These truths I hold, not as 'opinions,' but as matters of faith,
for which, if need were, I would gladly 'suffer the loss of all
things'.

"These truths I would thankfully have to maintain, by the help
of God, on such terms that, if (*per impossibile*, as I trust) it should
be decided by a competent authority that either the real objective
presence, or the Eucharistic sacrifice, or the worship of Christ there
present (as I have above stated those doctrines) were contrary to

---

[1] Quoted from Andrewes, *Resp. ad Apol. Bell.*; see the passage on
p. 265, *supra*.

the doctrine held by the Church of England, I would resign my office." [1]

Dr. Pusey maintained the same position in his sermon *This is My Body*, preached in 1871.

"The senses can tell us of form, size, colour, weight, taste, smell. Experience tells us of the power of nourishing. They cannot tell us more than these phenomena. Since then they cannot tell the hidden cause of these phenomena, neither are they entitled to deny the hidden presence of the life-giving body of Jesus, because they cannot discern it. The miracle, through which Jesus by His word of power makes His body really present under these bodily forms, is above, but it is no more against, our senses than those equally miraculous operations of His love, whereby He, through His infused grace or the outpouring of His Spirit, converts the averted soul, and, uniting, binds it to Himself with the indissoluble bond of love, or turned the fiery persecutor of all who called upon His Name into the devoted Apostle, whose life was the life of Christ within him." [2]

" He [St. Paul] does not say, a communion, or communication, or what men will, of a grace, or a virtue, or a power, or an efficacy, or an influence from Christ's absent body in heaven, even apart from the fact that no such influence from our Lord's all-holy body in heaven is ever in the remotest degree hinted at. Our dear Lord in His glorious body does ever in the presence of the Father make intercession for us ; His meritorious sacrifice and passion live on there ; those scars, more glorious than all created light, shine with the effulgence of His Godhead through all the compass of heaven, and pleading His atoning death obtain mercy and pardon for us sinners. But to us He hath given the Communion of His body, not in heaven as yet, but here on earth." [3]

" Finding that the words ' real presence ' were often understood of what is in fact a ' real absence,' we added the word ' objective,' not as wishing to obtrude on others a term of modern philosophy, but to express that the life-giving body, the *res sacramenti*, is by virtue of the consecration present without us, to be received by us. . . . The doctrines of the Eucharistic sacrifice and of Eucharistic adoration are involved in the doctrine of the real presence." [4]

In 1865 Dr. Pusey published his *The Church of England a Portion of Christ's One Holy Catholic Church, and a Means of*

[1] Pp. 26-28.   [2] Pp. 13, 14.   [3] Pp. 25, 26.   [4] P. 40.

Restoring Visible Unity, an Eirenicon, in a Letter to the Author of The Christian Year, usually known as his *Eirenicon, Part 1.* In this work he expressed more fully and clearly than before his previous opinion that there is no necessary difference between the Eucharistic doctrine of the Church of England and that of the Church of Rome, as defined in the Council of Trent and by Roman Catholic theologians since the time of that Council.

"With regard to the term Transubstantiation, there must be a real difference between the meaning which it had in the minds of the schoolmen and that which it must now have since the *Catechism* of the Council of Trent. For it is there taught with authority that 'the Eucharist has been called bread because it has the appearance, and still retains the quality natural to bread of supporting and nourishing';[1] but the schoolmen thought that with the 'change of substance' that power of nourishing ceased.[2] Yet, this being granted, I know not what can be included in our term 'substance,' which the English Church affirms to remain, which is not also included in the Roman term 'accidents,' which they also affirm to remain. Clearly the doctrine which the Church of England rejects under the term 'Transubstantiation, or the change of the substance of bread and wine,' is only one which 'overthroweth the nature of a Sacrament' in that the sign and the thing signified became the same. This was so according to the doctrine of the schoolmen, in which 'substance' was equivalent to 'matter'.[3] The meaning of the word 'substance' being changed, the Roman doctrine must be so far changed too. Archbishop Plato in the Greek Church admits the term μετουσίωσις in a sense which, if proposed to it, the English Church must accept. 'The Eastern and Greek-Russian Church admits the word Transubstantiation, in Greek μετουσίωσις, not that physical and carnal Transubstantiation, but the sacramental and mystical, and receives that word Transubstantiation in the same sense in which the oldest fathers of the Greek Church received the words μεταλλαγή, μετάθεσις, μεταστοιχείωσις.'[4] A sacramental or a

---

[1] Quoted from *Cat. Con. Trid.* II. iv. 38; see the passage on p. 103, *supra.*

[2] See p. 541, n. 1, *supra,* and references to earlier pages there given. Dr. Pusey does not appear at this time or earlier to have fully understood the doctrine of the schoolmen, or to have realised the differences between them. For his later realisation of this, see p. 547, *infra.*

[3] See the last note.

[4] Quoted from an answer of Plato, Archbishop of Moscow, to M. Dutens, given in Dutens, *Œuvres Mêlées,* part ii. p. 171, edition 1797.

hyperphysical change no English Churchman, who believes the real presence as his Church teaches, could hesitate to accept.

"The doctrine of the Eucharistic sacrifice depends upon the doctrine of the real objective presence. Where there is the apostolic succession and a consecration in our Lord's words, there, it is held by Roman authorities too, is the Eucharistic sacrifice. The very strength of the expressions used of 'the sacrifices of Masses,' that 'they were blasphemous fables and dangerous deceits,' the use of the plural, and the clause 'in the which it was commonly said,' show that what the Article speaks of is not 'the sacrifice of the Mass,' but the habit (which, as one hears from time to time, still remains) of trusting to the purchase of Masses when dying, to the neglect of a holy life, or repentance, and the grace of God and His mercy in Christ Jesus, while in health. . . . In the Holy Eucharist we do in act what in our prayers we do in words. I am persuaded that, on this point, the two Churches might be reconciled by explanation of the terms used. The Council of Trent, in laying down the doctrine of the sacrifice of the Mass, claims nothing for the Holy Eucharist but an application of the one meritorious sacrifice of the cross. An application of that sacrifice the Church of England believes also. Many years have flowed away since we have taught this, and have noticed how the words 'sacrifice,' 'proper,' or 'propitiatory sacrifice' have been alternately accepted or rejected according as they were supposed to mean that the Eucharistic sacrifice acquired something propitiatory in itself, or only applied what was merited once and for ever by the one sacrifice of our Lord upon the cross." [1]

"Since the meaning of the word 'substance' has been changed since the word Transubstantiation was adopted in the Latin Church to express the 'change' produced by consecration in the Holy Eucharist, it is not too much to ask the Roman Church to explain what that 'substance' is which they believe to be changed. For, since they require a belief in Transubstantiation as terms of communion, and since the meaning has been changed since the times of the schoolmen, it is but reasonable that they should explain the meaning of that which they require us to express belief in. My own conviction is, that our Articles deny Transubstantiation in one sense, and that the Roman Church, according to the explanation of the *Catechism* of the Council of Trent, affirms it in another." [2]

See Palmer, *A Treatise on the Church of Christ*, i. 172, third edition. For Eastern teaching on this point, see vol. i. pp. 173-91, *supra*.

[1] Pp. 24-26, 28, 29.   [2] P. 229.

In 1870 Dr. Pusey published his *Is Healthful Re-union Impossible ? A Second Letter to the Very Rev. J. H. Newman*, usually known as his *Eirenicon, Part III.* which was re-issued in 1876 with the title *Healthful Re-union as Conceived Possible before the Vatican Council.* In this treatise he still further emphasised his conviction that the Eucharistic doctrines of the Church of England and the Church of Rome were not necessarily in opposition to one another. On the subject of the real presence, as distinct from Transubstantiation, he wrote :—

" Reserving the question of Transubstantiation for the present, since the Council of Trent states the two doctrines separately, we cannot doubt that the Council of Trent, in regard to the real presence, expresses the ancient faith, and we could willingly accept its terms as expressing our belief." [1]

On the subject of Transubstantiation, he wrote :—

" Since then the body and blood of Christ are present in their substance (for otherwise they could not be present at all), but the presence of that ' substance ' does not involve the presence of any of the ordinary properties of a body, so neither does the conversion of the substance of the bread and of the wine into the substance of the body and blood of Christ involve the conversion of any of the properties of the bread or wine. We may then (as I said) think that by ' substance " is meant the ' essence ' or οὐσία of a thing, that which it is (whatever it is), its *quidditas ;* and under the ' species ' which remain, and which are the veil of the unseen presence, we may understand ' the φύσις or nature, including all those properties of which the senses are cognizant, and with them, or among them, the natural power of supporting and nourishing our bodies '. For although the *Catechism* of the Council of Trent is not authoritative, yet it has, I suppose, more authority than any individual doctor, or than many doctors ; and it distinctly asserts that ' by this name bread the Eucharist has been called, because it has the appearance and still retains the quality natural to bread, of supporting and nourishing '.[2] Whatever may have been the value of the Aristotelian philosophy to Christian theology, it has, I think, in this particular instance, introduced needless difficulty into the divine mystery, difficulty which relates, not to the mystery declared

---

[1] P. 76.

[2] Quoted from *Cat. Conc. Trid.* II. iv. 38 ; see the passage on p. 103, *supra.*

by our Lord, but attaching to the use of the word 'substance'. For, while affirming that the substance of the bread had ceased to be, they following that philosophy for the most part assumed that the power of nourishing ceased also, and that it was restored by a miracle,[1] for which miracle there is no authority in our Lord's words which are the foundation of the mystery, nor has the Church ever laid down anything upon it. But, if the species, that is, that which the Roman Church also believes to remain as the outward veil of our Blessed Lord's presence, retains those natural powers of nourishing and refreshing, then, as I have for many years said, I can see no contradiction; there is nothing, the existence of which the Church of England, while she says that 'the bread and wine remain in their very natural substances,' can mean to affirm, the existence whereof the Council of Trent can mean to deny, when it affirms 'the conversion of the whole substance of the bread into the substance of the body of Christ our Lord, and of the whole substance of the wine into the substance of His blood'. For, in addition to those qualities which, in philosophic language, were termed 'accidents,' the *Catechism* of Trent includes a property which is not cognizable by sight, or touch, or taste, that whereby the body is strengthened and refreshed. . . . However, then, in ordinary controversy or explanations, we seem to be almost hopelessly met with the contrast of 'substance' and 'accidents,' yet the contrast belongs to the schools, not to the Church." ?

In 1851 Dr. Henry Phillpotts, the Bishop of Exeter, published *A Pastoral Letter to the Clergy of the Diocese of Exeter on the Present State of the Church*. It contained the following passage :—

. "I see the same high authority number among the errors of Rome, which our own Church has renounced, that 'a propitiatory virtue is attributed to the Eucharist'. I am not aware of our Church having anywhere condemned such a doctrine. That it has condemned (as we all from our hearts condemn) as 'blasphemous fables and dangerous deceits' 'the sacrifices of Masses, in the which it was commonly said that the priest did offer Christ for the quick and dead to have remission from pain or guilt,' we know and heartily rejoice. But this is very far indeed from saying or meaning that the Eucharist hath not 'a propitiatory virtue'; and we must be very careful how we deny that virtue to it. The con-

[1] See p. 541, note 1, and p. 544, note 2, *supra*.
[2] Pp. 80-82.

35 *

secrated elements ought not to be separated in our minds from the
propitiation for our sins, continually presented for us before the
throne of God.   Whether we regard them in correspondence with
the meat-offerings and drink-offerings of the Old Testament as memorials of the one great sacrifice, and so, in union with that sacrifice, by virtue of Christ's appointment, representing and pleading
to the Father the atonement finished on the cross, or as answering
to those portions of the typical sacrifice which were eaten by the
priests and offerers, in either case they are intimately united with
the altar in heaven, and with its propitiatory virtue.   ' In these
holy mysteries ' in an especial manner heaven and earth are brought
together. . . . The partakers of the sacrifice are partakers of the
altar, and of all its inestimable benefits, the first of which is the
propitiation of our sins.   For in the Eucharist, as a Sacrament,
' we eat our ransom,' as St. Augustine says,[1] we receive spiritually
'the body of our Lord Jesus Christ which was given for,' ' His
blood which was shed for us ' ; in the same Eucharist, as a sacrifice,
we, in representation, plead the one great sacrifice, which our great
High Priest continually presenteth for us in heaven.   In heaven
He presenteth ever before the Father in Person Himself, mediating
with the Father as our Intercessor ; on earth He invisibly sanctifies
what is offered, and makes the earthly elements which we offer to
be sacramentally and ineffably—but not in a carnal way—His body
and His blood.   For, although once for all offered, that sacrifice, be
it remembered, is ever living and continuous, made to be continuous by the resurrection of our Lord.   Accordingly St. John tells us
in Rev. v. 6, 12, that he ' beheld, and lo, in the midst of the throne
stood a Lamb as it had been slain,' and to Him is continually
addressed the triumphal song of the heavenly hosts, ' Worthy is the
Lamb that was slain to receive power, and riches, and wisdom, and
strength, and honour, and glory, and blessing '.   To Him His
Church on earth in the Eucharistic service in like manner continually cries, ' O Lord God, Lamb of God, Son of the Father, that
takest away the sins of the world '.   Not that tookest away, but
still takest, *Agnus Dei, qui tollis peccata mundi*.   As, then, the sacrifice is continuous, its propitiatory virtue is continuous, and the fulness of the propitiation is pleaded for the whole Church whensoever
the commemoration of it is exhibited in the Eucharist." [2]

[1] Bishop Phillpotts does not give any reference.   The phrase occurs
in *e.g. Conf.* x. 70 ; *Serm.* cxxxi. 1,
[2] Pp. 53-55.

Allusion has already been made in passing, in connection with a letter by Dr. Pusey,[1] to the book by Robert Isaac Wilberforce, Archdeacon of the East Riding, who became a Roman Catholic in 1854. This book was entitled *The Doctrine of the Holy Eucharist*. It was published in 1853. The treatment adopted in it was very full and careful, and for the most part followed the general lines of scholastic theology. Archdeacon Wilberforce maintained that the glorified body and blood of Christ are sacramentally present in the Eucharist under the form of bread and wine by virtue of the consecration ; that questions relating to Transubstantiation may be left open, pending any authoritative decision in regard to them ; and that the Eucharist is a sacrifice of Christ. The following quotations supply indications of the positions stated and defended at length in the book :—

"The manner in which Christ's presence is bestowed, whether it be by Transubstantiation, or according to any other law, is a point which did not come under consideration during the first eight centuries. On this subject therefore it will not be necessary to enter. But that Christ's presence in the Holy Eucharist is a real presence ; that the blessings of the new life are truly bestowed in it through communion with the New Adam ; that consecration is a real act, whereby the inward part or thing signified is joined to the outward and visible sign ; and that the Eucharistic oblation is a real sacrifice—these points it will be attempted to prove by the testimony of Scripture and of the ancient fathers."[2]

"Our Lord's human body is not subject to the laws of material existence, because His body is a glorified body, and therefore not an object to our senses, unless such be His own will. That we do not commonly discern it is not owing, surely, to distance of place, but to the fact that glorified beings cannot be discerned by those who are in our present state, except at their own pleasure. . . . Our Lord is present in heaven in a particular place and under an especial form, that form, namely, under which His Apostles beheld Him, and that place to which they saw Him depart, at the right hand of God. This is our Lord's natural presence, in which He is a fitting object, when it pleases Him, to the senses of men. In this form He showed Himself to St. Stephen at his death, to St. Paul at his conversion, and to St. John in his exile. But our Lord's presence in the Holy Eucharist is not natural, but supernatural ; it

[1] See p. 538, *supra*.   [2] Pp. 4, 5, edition 1885.

is a sacramental presence, the presence, that is, of a *res sacramenti*, which is not in itself an object to the senses of men. We have no reason therefore to suppose that form and outline belong to it, because these are the conditions through which things become an object to the senses of men. And yet there is a way in which our Lord's body may be said to be present with form and place in the Holy Eucharist. For there is a connection between the *sacramentum* and *res sacramenti ;* and form and place belong to the first, though they do not belong to the second. So that, though the *res sacramenti* in itself has neither place nor form, yet it has them in a manner through the *sacramentum* with which it is united. Christ's body therefore may be said to have a form in this Sacrament, namely, the form of the elements, and to occupy that place through which the elements extend. As the spirit may be said to be present in that place where the body is situated, and as light may be said to assume the shape of the orifice through which it passes, so it may be said that the *res sacramenti* borrows place and shape from the *sacramentum* with which it is united by consecration. . . . His will is to be present in the Holy Eucharist, not indeed as an object to the senses of the receiver, but through the intervention of consecrated elements. So that His presence does not depend upon the thought and imaginations of men, but upon His own supernatural power, and upon the agency of the Holy Ghost. He is present Himself, and not merely by His influence, effects, and operation ; by that essence, and in that substance, which belongs to Him as the true Head of mankind." [1]

"If it were made a question, in what manner our Lord's presence in the Holy Eucharist was supposed to be brought about, and still more if it were requisite to explain this process in terms which all parties in the ancient Church would have been prepared to accept, the inquiry would involve considerable difficulty. It would be necessary to find some mode of adjustment between the tendency of the Eastern school, as it has been called, on one side, and that of the opponents of Eutychianism on the other. The former tendency went so far in some instances as to imply that the outward part retained no real existence at all ; the latter led to language which might be represented to mean that it was wholly unaltered. The more scientific statements of the school of St. Augustine did not harmonise exactly with either. And consequently the theory subsequently maintained by Aquinas, that the substance of our Lord's body and blood supersedes that of the

[1] Pp. 108, 109, 116, 117, 126.

bread and wine, while, so far as the senses go, the latter remain wholly unaltered, was an explanation of the mode in which our Lord's presence is brought about which did not exactly accord with the statement of any early party. . . . There can be no necessity therefore for admitting this expression of the manner in which our Lord's presence is brought about, unless it is commended to us by some later authority to which we are bound to submit. And, therefore, while it is accepted by those who admit the authority of the Council of Trent, it is not accepted by English Churchmen, by whom that council is not recognised. They withhold their assent from this account of the manner in which our Lord's presence is brought about in the Holy Eucharist, and allow nothing but that in which all parties in the ancient Church were accordant. They hold, of course, as our Article declares, and as Aquinas would not have denied, that according to that popular sense of the word substance, which implies it to be an object of the senses of men, the substance of the elements remains unchanged. But in reference to that more subtle explanation, which was designed by Aquinas,[1] they simply withhold their judgment, and affirm nothing respecting the Holy Eucharist but that which was affirmed by the whole Church, both in the East and West, during the first seven centuries of its existence."[2]

"The Eucharistic sacrifice is not the offering of the *sacramentum* only, the first-fruits of nature, but much more that of the *res sacramenti*, the reality, or thing signified. It is the offering up of the collective Church, Christ's mystical body, but it is also the offering up of Christ Himself, by whom that body is sanctified. Yet He is not offered up as though anything could be added to the sacrifice of the cross, or as though that sacrifice required renewal. The blood-stained sacrifice which the One Great High Priest for ever pleads before the Father's throne, admits neither of increase nor repetition. . . . . He who has been consecrated a Priest for ever after the order of Melchizedek, chooses this medium for giving effect to His perpetual intercession. That acceptance which he purchased by the sacrifice of the cross, He applies through the sacrifice of the altar. He Himself it is, who through the voice of His ministers consecrates these earthly gifts, and thus bestows the mystery of His real presence. By Himself, again, is the precious Victim presented before the Father's throne; and the intervention of their heavenly Head gives reality to the actions of his earthly ministers."[3]

[1] The "more subtle explanation" is really older than Aquinas; see *e.g.* vol. i. p. 304, *supra*.
[2] Pp. 208-10. [3] Pp. 278, 279.

In 1867 a *Charge* which excited much attention was delivered by the Bishop of Salisbury, Dr. Walter Kerr Hamilton.   The Bishop maintained that the inward part of the Eucharist, present by means of the consecration under the veil of the outward part of bread and wine, is the body and blood of Christ ; that the Eucharist is a sacrifice, in which that which was offered on the cross and is pleaded by our Lord in heaven is presented to God the Father in a sacrificial action ; and that these doctrines are the doctrines of the Church of England.   In the course of his careful and argumentative *Charge* he said :—

"As our Lord's representatives, and so in the Person of Christ putting forth some of His delegated powers, and by His own words, we bless the elements, or rather He blesses them through us.   Through such blessing the oblation becomes a Sacrament, and as such has not only an outward, but an inward part.   The outward part, the bread and wine, remains in its appearance, form, and essence or substance, what it was before the act of consecration, but still by consecration it has been made the veil and channel of an ineffable mystery.   The inward part is that which our Blessed Lord took from the Blessed Virgin, which He offered to God as an atoning sacrifice on the cross, which the Almighty Father has glorified, has, that is, endowed, 'not with the actual properties, but with the supernatural gifts, graces, and effects of Godhead,' and out of which wells forth every blessing of the new covenant.   The inward part of the Sacrament of the Lord's Supper is Christ's precious body and blood, and so, by virtue of the hypostatic union, Christ Himself. . . . This inward part of the Sacrament, this presence of the body and blood of Christ, and of Christ Himself, is not after the manner or laws of a body, according to which ordinary laws our Lord's body is in heaven only, but is a supernatural, heavenly, invisible, incomprehensible, and spiritual presence. . . . The gifts receive an inward part, even the presence of the *res sacramenti*, the body and blood of Christ. . . . This consecration of the gifts stands in closest relation to another great function.   That sacrificial action, which is the counterpart of Christ's perpetual pleading and presentation of His body and blood in our behalf, is consummated when the bread and wine are made the Sacrament of the Lord's body and blood. . . . It should seem to us to be only according to the analogy of faith that our Lord should in His own Person ever present the sacrifice, that which was once for all offered up to God as a sacrifice for ever, and that His representatives here on earth should also plead,

in a way appointed by Himself, that same sacrifice which the Great
Mediator evermore pleadeth in heaven. . . . Christians keep a feast
where they strengthen and refresh their souls on that which is presented to God, in commemoration of His Son's atoning work, namely,
the *res sacramenti*, the precious body and precious blood, whereby we
are made one with Christ, and Christ with us. . . . The Apostles
and those who have received the commission from them, have min-
istrations entrusted to them, through which the bread and wine
become at Holy Communion the body and blood of Christ, and the
Church presents before the throne of grace that which is present,
namely, Christ's body and blood in the Sacrament, and by such
offering pleads with Christ and through Christ with the Father. . . .
The effect of your blessing the elements is that there becomes a
real presence of the Lord's body and blood in the Sacrament. . . .
You are to call to the remembrance of your God, even as your
Saviour is doing in heaven, by pleading His precious body and blood,
the new covenant which He has made with man. . . . Every one
who is enabled to receive the doctrine held in the apostolical and
literal meaning of our Lord's words, ' This is My body,' ' This is My
blood,' will almost instinctively pass on to unite himself to the inter-
cessory, mediatorial action of our Lord as the one Priest in heaven." [1]

"Through consecration the body and blood of Christ become
really present, and by this I mean ' present without us,' and not
only ' in the soul of the faithful receiver '." [2]

"If . . . I desire for you and for myself that we should not give
any occasion to have the charge brought against us, that we do not
honestly teach the doctrine of the Church of England on its positive side, I am not less anxious that we should with equal honesty
distinctly contradict those doctrines which our Church negatives.
. . . These negations may be summed up in some such words as
these : ' The substance of bread and wine is not changed '. The
sacrifice of Christ's natural body is not re-iterated and repeated in
that most effectual act of pleading which is called the commemorative sacrifice. Adoration is not due to the consecrated bread and
wine, although ' Christ our Lord (as Bishop Andrewes says) in or
without the Sacrament is to be adored '.[3] The presence of Christ
is not that of an organical body and of a material character." [4]

In 1867 the Rev. William J. E. Bennett, then Vicar of
Froome-Selwood, published a pamphlet entitled *A Plea for*

---

[1] Pp. 31-39, edition 1885.   [2] P. 51.
[3] For the passage by Bishop Andrewes, see p. 265, *supra*.
[4] Pp. 61, 62.

Toleration in the Church of England, in a Letter to the Rev. E. B. Pusey. The pamphlet was chiefly on ritual and ceremonial observances, and on episcopal legislation ; but these were treated from a doctrinal standpoint ; and the following statement, afterwards the subject of much controversy, was made by Mr. Bennett in the course of it :—

"I am one of those who burn lighted candles at the altar in the day-time, who use incense at the holy sacrifice, who use the Eucharistic vestments, who elevate the Blessed Sacrament, who myself adore, and teach the people to adore, the consecrated elements, believing Christ to be in them, believing that under their veil is the sacred body and blood of my Lord and Saviour Jesus Christ." [1]

Mr. Bennett also used the expression "the real, actual, and visible presence of our Lord upon the altars of our churches".[2]

It is obvious that in the phrases "adore the consecrated elements" and "visible presence" Mr. Bennett had carelessly expressed a meaning which would have been better conveyed in such words as "adore the inward part of the Sacrament" and "presence under visible species"; and at the instance of Dr. Pusey [3] he altered the passages quoted so as to run in the third edition of his pamphlet :—

"I am one of those who . . . myself adore, and teach the people to adore, Christ present in the Sacrament under the form of bread and wine, believing that under their veil is the sacred body and blood of my Lord and Saviour Jesus Christ" ;

"the real and actual presence of our Lord upon the altars of our churches."

A prosecution of Mr. Bennett for the doctrine about the Eucharist held by him, chiefly as stated in the *Plea for Toleration,* led to a decision of the Court of Arches on 23rd July, 1870, confirmed on appeal by the Judicial Committee of the Privy Council on 8th June, 1872, that the statements as corrected in the third edition of Mr. Bennett's pamphlet were not unlawful in the Church of England.[4]

In 1867 a memorial was presented to the Archbishop of

[1] P. 14, first and second editions.
[2] P. 3, first and second editions.
[3] See Liddon, *Life of E. B. Pusey,* iv. 217.
[4] See *Guardian,* 27th July, 1870 ; 12th June, 1872.

Canterbury on the doctrine of the Eucharist by twenty-one of the more prominent clergy who accepted the teaching which had been promoted by the Oxford Movement. The signatories included Dr. Pusey, Dr. Liddon, Archdeacon Denison, Mr. Carter of Clewer, and Dr. Littledale. It contained the following repudiations and affirmations :—

" (1) We repudiate the opinion of a 'corporal presence of Christ's natural flesh and blood,' that is to say, of the presence of His body and blood as they 'are in heaven,' and the conception of the mode of His presence which implies the physical change of the natural substances of bread and wine, commonly called 'Transubstantiation '.

" We believe that in the Holy Eucharist by virtue of the consecration through the power of the Holy Ghost the body and blood of our Saviour Christ, 'the inward part or thing signified,' are present really and truly but spiritually and ineffably under 'the outward visible part or sign ' or ' form of bread and wine '.

" (2) We repudiate the notion of any fresh sacrifice, or any view of the Eucharistic sacrificial offering as of something apart from the one all-sufficient sacrifice and oblation on the cross, which alone ' is that perfect redemption, propitiation, and satisfaction for all the sins of the whole world, both original and actual,' and which alone is ' meritorious '.

" We believe that, as in heaven Christ our great High Priest ever offers Himself before the eternal Father pleading by His presence His sacrifice of Himself once offered on the cross, so on earth in the Holy Eucharist that same body once for all sacrificed for us and that same blood once for all shed for us, sacramentally present, are offered and pleaded before the Father by the priest, as our Lord ordained to be done in remembrance of Himself when He instituted the Blessed Sacrament of His body and blood.

" (3) We repudiate all 'adoration' of 'the sacramental bread and wine,' which would be 'idolatry,' regarding them with the reverence due to them because of their sacramental relation to the body and blood of our Lord ; we repudiate also all adoration of a ' corporal presence of Christ's natural flesh and blood,' that is to say, of the presence of His body and blood as they 'are in heaven '.

" We believe that Christ Himself, really and truly but spiritually and ineffably present in the Sacrament, is therein to be adored." [1]

[1] See *Guardian*, 5th June, 1867.

With this memorial may be compared a clear statement in an undated tract by Dr. Richard Frederick Littledale, entitled *The Real Presence*.

"The Christian Church teaches, and has always taught, that in the Holy Communion, after consecration, the body and blood of the Lord Jesus Christ are 'verily and indeed' present on the altar under the forms of bread and wine.

"The Church also teaches that this presence depends on God's will, not on man's belief, and therefore that bad and good people receive the very same thing in communicating, the good for their benefit, the bad for their condemnation.

"Further, that, as Christ is both God and Man, and as these two natures are for ever joined in His one Person, His Godhead must be wherever His body is, and therefore He is to be worshipped in His Sacrament.

"The body and blood present are that same body and blood which were conceived by the Holy Ghost, born of the Virgin Mary, suffered under Pontius Pilate, ascended into heaven, but they are not present in the same manner as they were when Christ walked on earth. He, as Man, is now naturally in heaven, there to be till the Last Day, yet He is supernaturally, and just as truly, present in the Holy Communion in some way which we cannot explain, but only believe, knowing, as we do, that since He rose from the dead His body has more than human powers, as He showed by passing through closed doors." [1]

One of the most eminent of the younger contemporaries of Dr. Pusey was Dr. William Bright, who became Regius Professor of Ecclesiastical History in the University of Oxford in 1868, and held that office until his death in 1901. Most of his published writings deal with historical subjects ; but it may be well to quote from the volume of *Selected Letters* which was edited by Dr. Kidd, and from a note in his collection of *Ancient Collects*, a few passages of some special interest in which he alluded to Eucharistic doctrine.

"As for the sacrifice, I should begin by sweeping off the ground all notions of a repetition of the atonement, of a new redemption, 'satisfaction,' etc., so as to show that nothing like that is intended. Then, and only then, would it be opportune to show that our Lord, as the Lamb that was slain, must always be still pleading His

[1] P. 1.

atonement, and thus acting as our propitiation, and that the Eucharistic memorial is a form of such pleading, inasmuch as He is in an especial manner present in the Eucharist, and if present must be present as the Lamb." [1]

"The distinction to be taken between our partaking of Christ in Baptism and our partaking of Him through His body and blood in the Eucharist is that the recipient of Baptism is incorporated into Christ's body mystical, which is itself formed and sustained by His body and blood, but that He does not directly come into spiritual contact with the body and blood till he communicates. Why does he need such contact? What is the *rationale* of this further privilege? Must we not find it in the Incarnation? The Word became flesh, as for other reasons so for this, that His flesh, being the 'flesh of God the Word who is the Life-giver,' [2] may become a medium of imparting a fresh energy of spiritual life to believers. As it has an efficacy which no other 'flesh' could have, so it has power of contact or of presence which belong to no other. These powers are exercised, this efficacy is imparted, in the Eucharist. I think, then, that although the phrase 'sacred humanity' is quite sound, yet one might add a little by way of bringing out the idea of a mysterious participation of the sacred body and blood of Christ, present or imparted under conditions belonging to their spiritualised or glorified state, and this for the purpose of sustaining spiritual life in the whole being of the faithful or devout receivers. I am sure that the best way of removing or lessening difficulties as to the Eucharistic presence is by linking it as closely as possible to the Incarnation, regarded as in order to the sustentation of spiritual life in Christians. This will help people to see how those great verses in John vi. are the legitimate carrying out of John i. 14-16, and to see, that is, that not Christ's spirit only, or His grace, has a function in regard to their spiritual life, but His body and flesh also, as being His." [3]

"I deeply regret that the point of 'adoration' was so prominently urged; but, since it has been put forward, I cannot think Denison's view wrong." [4]

In other letters Dr. Bright spoke of "the peculiar and unsatisfactory, because unreal, view which Hooker takes of the Euchar-

[1] Kidd, *Selected Letters of William Bright*, p. 88 (from a letter written in 1894).

[2] Quoted from St. Cyril of Alexandria, see vol. i. pp. 75, 76, *supra*.

[3] *Op. cit.* pp. 89, 90 (from a letter written in 1897).

[4] *Op. cit.* p. 97 (written in 1857). For "Denison's view," see pp. 526, 527, *supra*.

istic presence,"[1] and of "the mistake which" "the Roman
theology made when it placed the sacrifice of the Mass in a line
with that of the cross instead of in a line with the heavenly presentation".[2] The note in Dr. Bright's collection of *Ancient Collects* was also on the Eucharistic sacrifice being "in a line with
the heavenly presentation". He there said :—

"This and the preceding Syrian prayer bear witness to the great
truth that the Eucharistic sacrifice, even in its highest aspect, must
be put in one line (if we may say so), not with what Christ did once
for all upon the cross, but with what He is doing continually in
heaven ; that, as present naturally in heaven, and sacramentally in
the Holy Eucharist, the Lamb of God exhibits Himself to the
Father, and pleads the atonement as once finished in act, but ever
living in operation ; that in neither case does He repeat it or add to
it. The notion that it was not unique or perfect, but could be re-
iterated or supplemented in heaven or on earth, was justly denounced
as a 'blasphemous fable' in Article xxxi. But this should not lead
us to forget that 'the Lamb as It had been slain,' 'appearing in the
presence of God for us,' 'is the propitiation for our sins,' and even
now *tollit peccata mundi* by an intercession consisting in the presentation of Himself."[3]

A short statement of belief, which was adopted by a unanimous vote at the annual meeting of the members of the English
Church Union on 21st June, 1900, affords a convenient instance
of the doctrine of the Eucharistic presence held by those who
were influenced by the Oxford Movement.

"We, the members of the English Church Union, holding fast
to the faith and teaching of the one Holy Catholic and Apostolic
Church—that in the Sacrament of the Lord's Supper the bread and
wine, through the operation of the Holy Ghost, become, in and by
consecration, according to our Lord's institution, verily and indeed
the body and blood of Christ, and that Christ our Lord, present in
the same Most Holy Sacrament of the altar under the form of bread
and wine, is to be worshipped and adored—desire, in view of pre-

---

[1] *Op. cit.* p. 139 (written in 1865); *cf.* pp. 106-9 (written in 1899).

[2] *Op. cit.* pp. 258, 259 (written in 1896).

[3] *Ancient Collects*, pp. 144, 145. *Cf.* Dr. Bright's well-known hymns,
" And now, O Father, mindful of the love " (*Hymns Ancient and Modern*,
new edition, 1904, no. 267 ; *The English Hymnal*, no. 302); " Once, only
once, and once for all " (*Hymns Ancient and Modern*, no. 283 ; *The English
Hymnal*, no. 327).

sent circumstances, to re-affirm, in accordance with the teaching of the Church, our belief in this verity of the Christian faith, and to declare that we shall abide by all such teaching and practice as follow from this doctrine of the whole Catholic Church of Christ." [1]

V.

The teaching of Dr. Pusey and others met with great opposition, much denunciation, and some carefully considered and formulated argument. Among the more important works which thus appeared was a treatise, published in 1856, entitled *The Nature of Christ's Presence in the Eucharist, or the True Doctrine of the Real Presence Vindicated in Opposition to the Fictitious Real Presence asserted by Archdeacon Denison, Mr. (late Archdeacon) Wilberforce, and Dr. Pusey,* written by Mr. William Goode, then Rector of St. Margaret Lothbury, afterwards Dean of Ripon. Mr. Goode discussed at length and with much care the teaching of the fathers and of the authoritative documents of the Church of England. He stated and defended his belief that in the Eucharist there is a real presence to the receiver, not to the elements; that in the case of those who communicate worthily this presence is connected with the reception of the elements; that the faithful communicant receives in his soul at the time of his Communion the body and blood of Christ; and that Christ Himself is spiritually present, as the host at a feast, giving His crucified body and shed blood to the souls of those who communicate worthily. There was no detailed treatment of the Eucharistic sacrifice, but Mr. Goode shortly observed that, since the presence is to the receiver, not to the elements, there can be no sacrifice in the sense affirmed by Archdeacon Wilberforce and others.

"The doctrine . . . maintained in the formularies of the Church of England and, speaking generally, by all her great divines . . . is that, though the act of consecration makes the bread and wine sacred symbols or Sacraments of the body and blood of Christ, in the participation of which by the faithful there is vouchsafed a real

[1] See *Guardian*, 13th and 27th June, 1900. For some criticisms on this statement because of the want of "considerateness" and explanation in the phraseology used, and because of its failure to co-relate the belief expressed with "full Eucharistic ideas," see a letter by Dr. Bright in Kidd, *Selected Letters of William Bright*, pp. 329-31.

spiritual presence to the soul of the body and blood of Christ, which
are verily and indeed received and spiritually eaten and drunk to
the soul's health, yet that the presence of the body and blood of
Christ is not communicated to (though in the case of the faithful
connected with the participation of) the bread and wine, and His
body and blood are not given to, or partaken of by, the faithless.
In short, it is a real presence to the receiver and not to the elements." [1]

"The direction that we are to eat and drink the consecrated
elements 'in remembrance of' Christ is hardly reconcilable with the
notion that there is a real bodily presence of Christ, though unseen,
in the elements. . . . Our Lord's bodily absence is also clearly indicated by the phrase that in the celebration of His Supper we are
to show His death 'till He come'. The bread and wine represent
His body as dead, the body broken and the blood shed, and we are
thus to represent His death 'till He come,' which words necessarily
imply His bodily absence. And, further, the admonition that in
this rite we are to exhibit the Lord's death till He come leads us
again to the remark that the bread and wine, as representing the
crucified body and the shed blood, cannot have the actual presence
of that body and blood united to them; for our Lord rose with a
glorified body, a body numerically the same but in condition very
different, and therefore we cannot now have that body that was
crucified and that blood which was shed actually and substantially
with us. But it was that body and that blood that made the
atonement, and it is of that body that we are to eat, and of that
blood that we are to drink. And they are given to us by God that
we may eat and drink them. It is therefore altogether a spiritual
transaction, one in which our spirits only can take part. The eating and drinking are by that faith which is, as it were, the mouth
of the soul. And the body broken and the blood shed 1800 years
ago are made present to our faith by God, and given to our souls
that we may be nourished by them, for that 'flesh is meat indeed,
and that blood is drink indeed'. And by thus partaking of the
body broken and the blood shed upon the cross we are brought
to union and communion with that living, exalted, and glorified
Saviour who now sitteth on the right hand of God. And, while He
is thus eaten as crucified and dead, He is also present as living and
glorified. For the glorified Saviour is present with us in the rite.
His human nature is, in a spiritual sense, really present with us,
though not bodily. As the sun, though bodily far away from us, is

[1] I. 29, 30.

really present with us when we have the presence of his light and
heat, so the human nature of Christ, though bodily far away from
us, is enabled by that Spirit to which it is united to be present in
power and influence throughout the earth, and thus to communicate
to those who by a living faith are united to it, as the members of a
body to the head, those spiritual energies and graces that dwell in
it abundantly for communication to the members of His mystical
body, the true Church. If any man ask, What is the meaning of
the phrase that the crucified body and the shed blood of our
Blessed Lord are given to our souls for their nourishment, I would
ask him again whether the acts of faith have never obtained for
him, when by faith eating and drinking that body and blood,
nourishment and strength for the spiritual life of his soul, and
whether this has not arisen from our Lord having set before him, as
a host sets food before his guests, His own broken body and shed
blood for his soul to feed upon. . . . To help our weak faith, we
are assisted by sensible objects, suited to impress us with some idea
of the nature and character of the spiritual blessings derived to us
thereby, but which, alas! some of Christ's ministers would fain
boast, to their own glorification, that they turn into the things
which they represent, so that they instead of God should be the
dispensers of the heavenly gift." [1]

"The body of Christ is as truly present to the soul, and given to
and received by the soul, when the soul is enabled to feed upon it
by faith and is spiritually united to it and made partaker of its life-
giving efficacy by the Holy Spirit, as meat is truly present to the
body and given to it and received by it, when the body receives it
into the mouth and stomach, and there derives from it, by a natural
process, the virtue which it contains. To spiritual union and communion, and therefore real presence to our spirits, local separation,
if it so please God, need cause no bar. The agency of the Holy
Spirit can render it complete, whatever the distance may be." [2]

"There is to the faithful a real, though not substantial, presence
of Christ's body in the Lord's Supper, and a true spiritual eating
and drinking of His body and blood, not because the elements are
made by consecration to include within themselves, either locally
or superlocally or spiritually or supernaturally or in any other way
which men may like to imagine, a real substantial presence of the
body and blood of Christ, for then the wicked would be partakers
of the same, but because the faithful in receiving the consecrated
elements do, through faith on their part and a gracious gift on

Christ's part, become in a spiritual way partakers of the body and blood of Christ." [1]

" If the views maintained in the preceding pages are correct, it is evident that there can be no such sacrifice in the Eucharist as Archdeacon Wilberforce supposes,[2] because there is no such bodily presence as is required for that purpose. . . . If there is any validity in the arguments of the preceding work, they overthrow the foundations on which it [that is, the doctrine of the sacrifice maintained by Archdeacon Wilberforce] rests, the actual presence of Christ's body and blood in or under the elements." [3]

Another important book was published in 1871 by Dr. Thomas S. L. Vogan, Canon of Chichester, entitled *The True Doctrine of the Eucharist*, being an enlargement of a book published in 1849 with the title *Nine Lectures on the Holy Sacrament of the Lord's Supper.* Dr. Vogan contended that the consecrated bread is the body of Christ, and the consecrated wine is His blood, by representation and in spiritual power and effect, but not in literal fact ; that the body denoted is the dead, not the glorified, body of Christ; that there is no real presence either of the dead or of the glorified body ; that the body and blood are not received by the wicked ; that Christ is not to be adored as present in the elements; and that the Eucharist is not a sacrifice but a feast on a sacrifice.

" The letter [that is, in the words of institution] does not speak of the Lord's body in any other condition than in that of ' being given for us,' or of His blood in any other condition than in that of being poured out for sin. The letter sets forth the Lord's body as a sacrifice for sin ; it sets forth His blood as poured out from His body for sin. It sets forth His body and His blood separated from each other ; and, since blood is the life of the body, the body from which the blood is poured out has its life taken away, and is dead. . . . As the bread and the wine were distinct things, and were given separately from each other, so He gave His body and His blood separately from each other, and therefore it was His dead body which He gave. . . . The bread is the body of Christ, and the wine is the blood of Christ, in a way beyond the nature of earthly things. The bread and the wine are the body and blood of Christ so far as one thing can be another, the nature of each being unchanged. They are what He called, and by calling made, them

---

[1] II. 689.   [2] See p. 551, *supra.*   [3] II. 973, 978.

to all the intents and purposes for which He so made them. The
wine is His blood poured out, the bread is His body given, the life
being taken from it, and the body therefore dead, but both in
spiritual effect, not in positive and absolute reality. . . . The dead
body of our Lord, and His blood shed, cannot be, and therefore are
not, present either in the Eucharist or in its elements. The letter
speaks only of the given body and the poured out blood. It says
nothing of our Lord's living body or of His glorified body. It says
nothing, and implies nothing, of His soul or His Godhead. . . . The
ancient fathers of the Church for many centuries and . . . the great
divines of the Church of England . . . agree that it is the body of
our Lord Jesus Christ which was given for us which we receive, and
that it is His blood which was shed for us which we receive. They
do not teach that it is the living glorified body of our Lord, His
living glorified body present in the bread and wine, which we receive. But they teach us that by receiving His body given, and
His blood shed for us, we are made one with Him, are united to
His glorious body, dwell in Him, and have Him also dwelling in us.
. . . The letter . . . shows that our Lord was not, and is not,
present in the bread and wine of the Eucharist, and therefore it
compels the conclusion that He is not to be adored as present in
them. . . . The literal interpretation admits of no sacrifice to be
offered by us, in fulfilling His words that we should do as He did,
but that which is comprehended in the sacrifice of thanksgiving. . . .
Since there is not, nor can be, any real presence of the body and
blood of Christ in or with or under the elements or their form, no
sacrifice can be offered of Him, or of His body and blood, in or with
or under them, whether they remain in their proper natural substances or do not. The Eucharistic sacrifice, therefore, which is
offered by us is not of Christ or of His body and blood or of His
presence. The letter has nothing of any such oblation to be made
by us. He only could, He only Himself did, offer that all-sufficient
sacrifice. And, having made it, He now makes us not offerers but
partakers of it. And we plead that sacrifice before the throne of
God. We rely on it as all-sufficient and all-prevailing with the
Father. We embrace its benefits, and render all the return we can
make for it, in the oblation of ourselves, our souls and bodies, as a
reasonable, holy, and acceptable sacrifice to God."[1]

"There is . . . no real presence of the glorified body of Christ
in the Eucharist for the one sufficient reason that He neither gave
nor promised to give His glorified body. And there is no real pres-

[1] Preface, pp. ix-xiv ; *cf.* pp. 104, 105, 116, 288, 289, 500-509.
36 *

ence of His dead body in the Eucharist for the one sufficient reason
that His dead body now is not, and therefore cannot be present.
That which is not cannot have a real presence." [1]

"They who have not faith are not ' verily and indeed ' partakers
of the inward part, the inward and spiritual grace, of the Sacrament;
they do not receive or partake of that body of Christ which the
bread is not, or of that blood of Christ which the wine is not." [2]

" We feast upon the sacrifice which He once made, upon a past
and not upon a present sacrifice ; and we are therein worshippers of
God, and have communion in its benefits." [3]

" When we come to commemorate and feast upon the sacrifice
of Christ, we also must bring corresponding sacrifices. . . . We
offer ' the sacrifice of God, a troubled spirit '. . . . Secondly, we
offer the sacrifice of faith. . . . Thirdly, we make the sacrifice of
thanksgiving. . . . Fourthly, . . . there is the offering up of ourselves to God. . . . Fifthly, we offer up all that we have, to hold it
in God's service, to use it to His glory. . . . Sixthly, we offer up the
sacrifice of prayers, intercessions, and thanks for all men. . . . To
these spiritual sacrifices we may add material oblations of our substance, for the house and service of God, for the sustentation of His
ministers, for the succour of our fellow Christians, and for other
' pious and charitable uses'. . . . The spiritual sacrifices are the
true Eucharistic sacrifice. They are comprehended in the whole
service of the Eucharist, which, therefore, in this sense is to be
called and is a sacrifice. It is a thankful commemoration of the
death of Christ, in which by the breaking of the bread and the
pouring out of the wine, we declare our faith to God that the body
of Christ was broken and His blood was shed, and by eating and
drinking the symbols of His body and blood we declare also our
faith that His body was given and His blood was shed for us. And
we cannot doubt, but must be most certainly assured, that with this
sacrifice of faith and thanksgiving God is well pleased. But as for
a sacrifice of the bread and wine in that service, after all that can be
said, it is not an actual, and therefore if a sacrifice it must be merely
an imaginary sacrifice." [4]

In 1871 Dr. John Harrison, then Vicar of Fenwick, published
*An Answer to Dr. Pusey's Challenge Respecting the Doctrine of
the Real Presence, in which the Doctrines of the Lord's Supper, as
held by Him, Roman and Greek Catholics, Ritualists, and High
Anglo-Catholics, are Examined and Shown to be Contrary to the*

[1] P. 133.   [2] P. 276.   [3] P. 308.   [4] Pp. 476, 477.

Holy Scriptures, and to the Teaching of the Fathers of the First Eight Centuries, with the Testimony of an Ample Catena Patrum of the same Period. This elaborate work was wholly devoted to the examination and discussion of evidence, and to controversial handling of the inferences from evidence which had been drawn by Dr. Pusey and others. It did not contain any positive construction of Dr. Harrison's own position. But the whole character of the book and the treatment adopted in it show clearly that the author regarded the consecrated elements as nothing more than memorials and representatives of the crucified body and the shed blood of Christ, and held that the faithful recipients by means of their faith using the picture thus presented to their minds were enabled to enter into a spiritual union with Christ at the time of their Communion.

A book of considerable learning and ability, though unfortunately greatly marred by want of accuracy, was published in 1879 by Dr. Charles Hebert, formerly Vicar of Ambleside, with the title *The Lord's Supper : Uninspired Teaching*. Notwithstanding many deficiencies, it contained a very valuable collection of passages bearing on the doctrine of the Eucharist. Dr. Hebert's own opinions are stated incidentally only. He maintained that the Eucharist is a means of the mental and spiritual realisation of the thought of Christ's body and blood, and that even the faithful communicants do not receive the body and blood at their Communion. Thus, he writes :—

" The body and blood of Christ are now in heaven, and not here, except in thought. I can grasp no more than that the thought of the body and blood of Christ given and shed is in my mind, and moves my heart to gratitude and love, and in calling upon God in such deeply affecting meditations I receive all blessing and grace to enable me to feel my union with Him and with all His people in every age, and to supply me with power to overcome sin and to act after His pattern till He comes to earth again or I go to Him. The more I read and the more I meditate on the subject, and the longer my experience of this present earthly conflict continues, the more do I find this view fill the whole horizon." [1]

" I am once more obliged openly to confess that I cannot reconcile one answer in our Catechism [2] with the rubric on kneeling

[1] II. 698.

[2] That is, the answer that "the body and blood of Christ" "are verily and indeed taken and received by the faithful ",

and the rest of our Church's utterance both in her services and her articles." [1]

A shorter and less important book than any of the four works last mentioned was published in 1885 by Mr. Frederick Meyrick, who was Rector of Blickling and Non-residentiary Canon of Lincoln, under the title *The Doctrine of the Church of England on the Holy Communion Restated as a Guide at the Present Time*, to which a preface was contributed by Dr. Edward Harold Browne, the Bishop of Winchester. There are features of Mr. Meyrick's treatment of evidence which lessen the value of his book ; but his clear summary of the doctrine which he held may be cited as a good instance of the teaching of those who, while rejecting the theology of the Oxford Movement, affirmed that the Eucharist is in some sense a sacrifice, and that it is a means whereby the soul may feed spiritually on Christ.

"The Holy Communion is a remembrance, a sacrifice, a means of feeding, a means of incorporation, a pledge.

"It is a remembrance in so far as its object is to recall to the minds of Christians the love of Christ as exhibited in the sacrifice of His death ; in so far as it commemorates by an outward act that divine sacrifice ; and in so far as it is a memorial of Christ and His death before man and before God.

"It is a sacrifice inasmuch as it is an offering made to God as an act of religious worship—a spiritual sacrifice, as being a sacrifice of prayer and praise to God for the benefits received by the sacrifice of the death of Christ ; a material sacrifice, in so far as the bread and wine are regarded as gifts of homage to God in acknowledgment of His creative and sustaining power ; a commemorative sacrifice, inasmuch as it commemorates the great sacrifice of the cross— the words ' commemorative sacrifice ' meaning in this acceptation a commemoration of the sacrifice. But it is not a sacrifice of Christ to His Father, whereby God is propitiated and man's sins expiated.

"It is a means of feeding upon Christ ; but this feeding is not effected by the elements to be eaten being changed into Christ. . . . Nor is our feeding on Christ effected by our eating His material body together with the bread and wine. . . . But it is effected by the spiritual presence of Christ, and the benefits of the blood-shedding on the cross being conveyed to the soul of the humble recipient qualified by faith and love towards God and man.

[1] II, 699.

"It is a means of incorporation, inasmuch as by it we are more and more made part of the mystical body of Christ, and united with its other members.

"It is a pledge inasmuch as it serves to the humble Christian as a symbolical assurance of God's past forgiveness, and of His present favour towards Him, and of a future inheritance graciously reserved for him." [1]

There are clear statements in the undated book *A Sacrament of Our Redemption*, and the manual *The Catholic Faith* published in 1905, both by Dr. W. H. Griffith Thomas, the Principal of Wycliffe Hall. Dr. Thomas holds that the change effected by the consecration is a change only of use and purpose; that faithful communicants receive grace directly from Christ and feed upon Him in their hearts; and that the Eucharist is not a sacrifice but the commemoration of a sacrifice. The following quotations from the latter of these two books illustrate the teaching contained in them both : —

"Our faith looks back on Calvary as the bread is broken and the wine poured out; our love looks up to the throne and holds fellowship and sweet communion as we appropriate to ourselves the spiritual benefits of our Lord's redemption ; our hope looks forward to the day of our Master's coming as we in union with our fellow-Christians 'do this in remembrance of' Him 'until the day dawn and the shadows flee away'. Thus the whole of our Christian life and experience may be said to be summed up, symbolised, and expressed in the Supper of the Lord. The three great truths of union, communion, and reunion are all found here, and past, present, and future are all beautifully included and summed up in this holy ordinance. We remember our Lord, we appropriate Him, we confess Him, and we expect Him. The Lord's Supper appeals to every part of our nature, to our intellect, to our imagination, to our heart, to our conscience, to our soul, to our will, to our life, to our social instincts, and to our steadfast hope. Truly, then, it is a means of grace. Our souls are undoubtedly strengthened with the power and grace of God, and refreshed by the joy and peace and hope of the Gospel of our Lord and Saviour. . . . Our Church always clearly distinguishes between the outward and the inward parts of the Lord's Supper, otherwise it could not possibly be a Sacrament according to the definition of the Catechism and the

[1] Pp. 241-43, edition 1908.

Article. This distinction is plainly seen in the language of the Catechism already quoted, and it is as evidently brought before us in Article xxviii. In the Holy Communion Service we are said to receive 'these Thy creatures of bread and wine,' and we pray to be made 'partakers of His most blessed body and blood'. The words of administration said to the communicant make the same clear distinction. First, the minister speaks of 'the body of our Lord Jesus Christ, which was given for thee,' and 'the blood of our Lord Jesus Christ, which was shed for thee,' clearly referring to the sacrifice of our Lord, the inward part or thing signified in the Holy Communion. Then He says, 'Take and eat this in remembrance that Christ died for thee'; 'Drink this in remembrance of Christ's blood that was shed[1] for thee'. This clear distinction between the outward and the inward is maintained from first to last in our Communion Service. The prayer of consecration which immediately precedes the reception of the Holy Communion teaches the same truth. The bread and wine are then set apart or consecrated for the special purpose of being symbols, pledges, and seals of the grace of God in Christ. Consecration involves no change in the substance of the bread and wine, only a change of use and purpose, the ordinary bread and wine being thus separated from common use for the purpose already indicated. There are thus two givers in the Holy Communion; the minister gives the elements which are received into the body, the Lord gives direct from heaven His own grace and power, 'the body and blood of Christ,' and these are received into the soul. These two gifts are never to be identified or confused. The minister cannot possibly give the body and blood of Christ, for this is a spiritual act which the Lord Jesus Christ has never delegated, and cannot delegate, to any human being. In the case of worthy receivers, the reception of the wine and bread into the body, and the grace of our Lord into the soul, are always parallel and concurrent, but never identical. Our faith must, therefore, be ever occupied with the Lord Jesus Christ; the visible sign of bread and wine has annexed to it the promise of grace and blessing, and, if only our faith looks up to Christ on the throne and feeds upon Him in our hearts, blessing always comes. We can see this truth still more plainly set before us in Article xxix. . . . Faith remembers Calvary and finds peace with God. Faith rests on Him who once died and who now lives for ever. Faith receives the gift of the Holy Spirit as the indwelling divine fount of holiness. Faith

[1] The words in the Book of Common Prayer are "in remembrance that Christ's blood was shed".

realises our fellowship with God the Father, Son, and Holy Ghost. Faith rejoices in our Lord Jesus Christ as Prophet, Priest, and King; and the language of the adoring, trusting, grateful soul is 'O my God, Thou art true! O my soul, thou art happy!'" [1]

"The only sacrifices other than that of Calvary known to our Church formularies are the sacrifices of ourselves, our substance and our praises. . . . Strictly and accurately, the Lord's Supper is not a sacrifice, but a Sacrament. It has sacrificial aspects and relations because it is so closely associated in thought and purpose with the atoning sacrifice of Christ, and because it is the standing testimony to the world and to ourselves of our constant need of and perpetual dependence on that sacrifice in all our near approach to God. But the ordinance in itself and alone cannot with accuracy be called a sacrifice. It is a Sacrament of a sacrifice, 'the Sacrament of our redemption by Christ's death'. . . . It is a feast on that sacrifice. The essential difference between a sacrifice and a Sacrament is that in the former God is the Receiver (or the *terminus ad quem*), while in the latter God is the Giver (or the *terminus a quo*). In a sacrifice we give, we yield up; in a Sacrament we receive, we appropriate. . . . The ideas of a sacrifice and a Sacrament are so distinct and different that the Lord's Supper, unless Scripture warrants it, cannot be both at the same time. The passover was both sacrificial and sacramental; but the proper antitype to that is not the Lord's Supper, but the Lord Himself, who is at once our sacrifice and our feast. . . . The Lord's Supper is not strictly and fully the antitype of the passover; it is the rite of our life and worship which is analogous to it in the sacramental but not in the sacrificial aspect. . . . The Lord's Supper is not a commemorative sacrifice; it is the commemoration of a sacrifice; and, if the words Eucharistic sacrifice mean some sacrifice which is offered only at and in the Lord's Supper, then we assert that no such idea occurs in Bible or Prayer Book. The cardinal error of the Church of Rome and those who think with her on this subject is that the Sacraments 'contain' grace, that by the consecration the elements contain the grace they signify, and that by the reception of the elements grace is conveyed in them. . . . The whole position is un-Scriptural, un-Anglican, un-historical, unreal, untrue. It ministers to superstition, tends to materialism, and is perilous to the soul in relation to God and Christ." [2]

---

[1] Pp. 172-77. The concluding words are quoted from Hooker, *Eccl. Pol.* V. lxvii. 12; see p. 243, *supra.*

[2] Pp. 418-20.

A clear statement of the positive side of the doctrine held by many who reject the teaching associated with the Oxford Movement occurred in a *Charge* delivered in 1906 by Dr. Edmund Arbuthnott Knox, the Bishop of Manchester.

"The true keynote to the service seems to be that of union with the living Christ by the spiritual and faithful partaking of His body and His blood. Such a reception, and such union, has no meaning apart from the idea of sacrifice. Nor is the thought of sacrifice obliterated, rather is it strengthened, by the fact that our Lord Jesus Christ, by His death upon the cross, made there a full, perfect, and sufficient sacrifice for the sins of the whole world. That solemn truth we neither wish nor dare to question. But for the partaker the conception is that by the act of consuming he becomes one with the Victim, its death is his death, its life-blood is his life. In this sense, and in this only, is it true that the sacrifice offered once for all, and once for all accepted, yet remains for us an ever-continued life-giving sacrificial feast. We are partakers of the sacrifice that was offered upon the cross, partakers not merely by an effort of memory, or by an effort of imagination, but by an act of faith. The Lamb of God is, spiritually but really, the food of which we are partakers in that heavenly banquet; and the Sacrament, with its signs, is the means whereby we are thus fed. The sacrifice has been offered and accepted; but the sacrificial feast, which is part of the sacrifice, must continue and be carried on into the marriage supper of the Lamb." [1]

VI.

One of the most independent minds of the nineteenth century was that of Frederick Denison Maurice. Maurice was for ten years Chaplain of Guy's Hospital; he was deposed from his two chairs of Theology and of English Literature and History at King's College, London, for supposed unorthodoxy on eschatological questions in 1853; he was appointed Professor of Moral Philosophy in the University of Cambridge in 1866, and held this office until his death in 1872. His work *The Kingdom of Christ; or Hints to a Quaker Respecting the Principles, Constitutions, and Ordinances of the Catholic Church*, the first edition of which was published in 1838, contained a discussion on the doctrine of the Eucharist of considerable length. Maurice criti-

[1] Pp. 77, 78.

cised with some severity the views of Quakers, Zwinglians, Calvinists, and Lutherans in regard to the Eucharist, the objections of Rationalists, and the teaching of Roman Catholics; he himself maintained a doctrine that the Eucharist is a sacrificial feast, that Christ is there really present, that the words of institution are to be literally understood in a true and spiritual meaning, and that the partaking of the Sacrament enables communicants to enter into fellowship with Christ in His glory at the right hand of the Father.

" They [that is, the words of institution] might only signify that a person who had been deeply beloved was leaving with the friends from whom He was about to be separated a token and memorial of His intercourse with them. The words, indeed, 'This is My body, this is My blood,' might sound strange and hyperbolical, especially in a moment of what seemed final separation, for then the utterances of such a friend would be especially simple and awful, as we know that His other utterances were; but yet they might only signify, This will remind you of My Person, and this of the blood which is about to be so unrighteously shed. Such an explanation, however embarrassing, would be the easiest, nay, it would be the only possible one, unless there were some circumstances connected with the whole character of Him who spake the words, with His other acts and purposes, with the time when they were spoken, which determined them to a different sense. Suppose now that the Person who spoke these words was the Son of Man and the Son of God; suppose at the very time He spoke them He had been declaring Himself to be the way through which men must come to the unseen Father, to be the truth, to be the life, to be in that relation to His disciples in which the vine is to its branches, to be about to bestow upon them a Spirit who should guide them into the knowledge of the Father and of the Son; suppose Him to have told His disciples that they were the appointed messengers of these truths to men; suppose Him to have prayed that not only they, but all who should believe in Him through their word might be one in Him as He and the Father were one; suppose Him to have connected all these mysterious words with the giving up of Himself to death; suppose death to have been felt in all ages and in all countries to be the great barrier between the visible and the invisible world; suppose sacrifice, or the giving up of certain animals to death, and the offering them to some unseen Ruler, had been felt in all countries which attained to anything like national fellowship

and consistency to be the means whereby they could approach that
Ruler's presence, obtain His favour, remove His wrath ; suppose
sacrifices to have been the most essential part of the Jewish insti-
tutions, the most important element in their worship, the only way
whereby they could draw nigh, as members of a nation, to the God
of their nation ; suppose them, however, to have been taught, both
by the law ¡which appointed those sacrifices and by the prophets
who expounded it, that they were not valuable for their own sakes,
but were accepted when they were performed by God's appointment through His priests as a confession on the part of the offerer
that he had violated his relation to the head of the commonwealth
and to its members, as a submission of the will, as a prayer to be
restored to that position which through self-will had been lost, or
else as a means of expressing that entire self-surrender which was
implied in the fact of belonging to the divine society ; suppose that
the feast which the disciples were keeping with their Master was
the most purely national and strictly sacrificial of all the feasts,
that one which celebrated the first deliverance and establishment
of the nation, and which recalled the fact that it was a nation
based upon sacrifices in which every Jew realised the blessings of
His covenant, rejoiced that God was His King, knew that he was
indeed an Israelite ; suppose all this, and then consider whether
that which seemed the only possible interpretation of Christ's words,
though a most difficult and perplexing one, do not become actually
irrational and monstrous ? Consider whether any one who believed
what we know the Apostles did believe respecting their Master,
His Person, His Kingdom, could attach any but the very highest
significance to language concerning His body and blood. ` Consider
whether any persons who believed what we know they believed
respecting their own office and work, could imagine that this
significance was limited and temporary. Consider whether persons
who connected, as we know they did connect, the kingdom whereof
they were ministers with the earlier dispensations, could believe
otherwise than that, by the same simple, wonderful method that
had been used in all countries, and had been appointed, as they
believed, by the authority of God Himself in their own, by the
method which had enabled the Jews to enter into the fruition of
their covenant and its privileges, and the neglect of which had again
and again cheated them of it, He meant to put them in possession
of all the substantial good things which He came to bestow upon
mankind ? Could they doubt that, when they ate this bread and
drank this wine, He meant that they should have the fullest par-

ticipation of that sacrifice with which God had declared Himself well-pleased, that they should really enter into that presence, into which the Forerunner had for them entered, that they should really receive in that Communion all the spiritual blessings which, through the union of the Godhead with human flesh, the heirs of this flesh might inherit ? Could they doubt that the state of individual death which they had claimed for themselves in Baptism was here to be practically attained by fellowship with Christ's death ; that the new life which they had claimed for themselves, as members of Christ's body, was here to be attained through the communication of His life ? Could they doubt that, if their spirits were to be raised up to behold the infinite and absolute glory, here they were admitted into that blessedness ? that, if their hearts and affections desired a manifested and embodied King, here they became united to Him ? that, if spirit, soul, and body were to be subjected to the government of God's Spirit, that each might be delivered from its own corruption, receive its own quickening, and exert its own living powers, here each received that strength and renewal by which it was enabled to do its appointed work, to overcome its peculiar temptations, to be fitted for its future perfection ? Could they doubt that, if they were baptised into the name of the Father, the Son, and the Holy Ghost, and if this deepest unity were the foundation of such a union among men as no barrier of time, or space, or death could break, here they were actually received into communion with that awful name, and into communion with all the saints who live by beholding it and delighting in it ? Could they doubt that here the partial views, and one-sided words, and opposing thoughts of men, found their meeting-point, and complete reconciliation ? that here lay the clear vital expression of those distinctions which in verbal theology become dry, hard, dogmatic oppositions ? that here it is apprehended how faith alone justifies, and how faith without works is dead ? how it is we that act, and yet not we, but Christ in us ? how he that is born of God cannot commit sin, and yet if we say we have no sin we deceive ourselves ? how we may be persuaded that neither death nor life, nor things present, nor things to come, shall separate us from the love of God which is in Christ, yet may tremble lest we should be castaways ? Could they doubt that it was their office to present Christianity in its different aspects to the different wants and circumstances of their own age and of ages to come ; that it was the office of this Sacrament to exhibit it as a whole truth, at once transcendent and practical, surpassing men's thoughts, independent of men's faith and opinions, and yet essentially belonging to man, the governing law of his being, the actuating power of his life ? Could they doubt that they were to lay the foundation of the Church on earth, and that this Sacrament was to give it permanency, coherency, vitality throughout all generations ? And, if this were their faith, why, I ask, is it not to be ours ? " [1]

" Our Lord says, ' This is My body '. St. Paul addresses the Ephesian converts as sitting in the heavenly places with Christ. He tells the Philippians that their bodies shall be made like unto Christ's glorious body. Surely this is Christianity. It is the Gospel of the deliverance of the spirit and soul and body from all the fetters by which they are held down and prevented from fulfilling each its own proper function, from maintaining their right relations to each other. And this emancipation is connected with and consequent upon our union as members of one body with Christ, the crucified, the risen, the glorified Lord of our race. Now, if these be the privileges of Christian men, and if these privileges, whatever they be, are in this Sacrament asserted and realised, what a low notion it is that we are invited to hold communion, not with Christ as He is, not with His body exalted at the right hand of God, but with a body consubstantiated in the elements. . . . What we need is that they [the bread and wine] should be made a perfectly transparent medium through which His glory may be manifested, that nothing should be really beheld by the spirit of the worshippers save He into whose presence they are brought. For this end the elements require a solemn consecration from the priest, through whom Christ distributes them to His flock, not that they may be clothed with some new and peculiar attributes, not that they may acquire some essential and miraculous virtue, but that they may be diverted from their ordinary uses, that they may become purely sacramental. . . . We need some pure untroubled element which has no significancy except as the organ through the which the voice of God speaks to man, and through which he may answer, ' Thy servant heareth '. Such we believe are this bread and wine when redeemed to His service: let us not deprive them of their ethereal whiteness and clearness by the colours of our fancy or the clouds of our intellect." [2]

" I have maintained that the character of the Eucharistic feast is sacrificial, that Christ is really present in it, and that the words of institution are to be taken literally." [3]

" I have maintained that in order to the full acknowledgment of Christ's spiritual presence, we must distinctly acknowledge that He it clothed with a body ; that, if we lose this belief, we adopt a vague

[1] II. 74-80, edition 1842.   [2] II. 107-9.   [3] II. 126.

pantheistic notion of a presence hovering about us somewhere in the air in place of a clear spiritual apprehension of a Person in whom all truth and love dwell; that the spiritual organ therefore does demand an actual body for its nourishment; that through that spiritual organ our bodies themselves are meant to be purified and glorified; that this Sacrament meets and satisfies the needs both of the human spirit which is redeemed and of the body which is waiting for its redemption. But all these admissions only bring out the difference with the Romanist into stronger relief. To enter into fellowship with Christ as He is, ascended at the right hand of God, in a body of glory and not of humiliation, this must be the desire of a Christian man, if he seek the presence of a real not an imaginary object, if he desire his body as well as his spirit to be raised and exalted. On this ground then he must reject all theories which involve the imagination of a descent into the elements; on this ground, also, he must feel that the intellectual contradiction which such theories contain, and even boast of, is the counterpart of a spiritual contradiction still more gross and dangerous." [1]

VII.

A lecture on *The Holy Eucharist* delivered sometime between 1871 and 1877 by Dr. J. B. Mozley, then Regius Professor of Divinity in the University of Oxford, and included in the posthumous volume *Lectures and Other Theological Papers*, was an attempt to estimate the result of the "review of the doctrine of the Eucharist" by the Church of England "at the Reformation". According to Dr. Mozley's view, the Church of England at the Reformation accepted the position that "the undefined form of the doctrine" was "the designed form," and that "incompleteness was intended"; and "restored the doctrine to its original and more undefined state".[2] Adopting the attitude of the Church of England as he understood it, he maintained that by consecration a virtue is joined to the elements through which they become to the faithful recipients a means of participation in the body and blood of Christ; that the body and blood are received by faith in the soul; that they are not received by the wicked; that Christ is to be adored in the rite through His body and blood but not under the elements; and that the Eucharist has a sacrificial virtue borrowed from the sacrifice of the cross. He expressed his agreement with the con-

[1] II. 131, 132.　　　　[2] P. 200.

tention of Hooker[1] that the fundamental truth is the assertion of the participation of the body and blood, and that the question whether the Sacrament is the body and blood before reception does not concern necessary belief.

"Our Church . . . at the Reformation rejected Transubstantiation, and fell back upon the earlier and more indefinite idea of a change in the elements, as a change, namely, which was true and real for all the purposes of the Sacrament, by which the elements became, from being mere physical food, spiritual food."[2]

"The ground taken by the early Church with respect to the spiritual part of the Sacrament of the Lord's Supper, the body and blood of our Lord, was not that that spiritual part was only an internal matter, a moral effect of the act of participation upon the mind. The Lord's body and blood was regarded as a reality external to the mind, even as the bread and wine was ; it was considered as joined to the bread and wine, and co-existing with it in one Sacrament."[3]

"The body and blood of Christ is not a natural, but a spiritual substance. It can only therefore be eaten spiritually. To suppose that a man's natural mouth and teeth can eat a spiritual thing would be a simple confusion of ideas. The eating of it must be wholly in the sense of, and correspond to the nature of, the food. It is in a spiritual sense alone that a spiritual substance can be eaten. Although, then, the natural mouth and teeth can eat the bread and wine, which is the sign of the body and blood, and the sign to which it is by divine ordinance joined, the natural organs cannot eat the body and blood of Christ, which is wholly spiritual. Only the soul or spirit of man can take in and feed upon a spiritual nutriment. Faith, therefore, as being the spiritual faculty in man, must in its own nature be the medium by which the body of Christ is eaten ; and that body, though present in the Sacrament, must remain uneaten by the partaker of the Sacrament unless he has faith. Without faith it can only be eaten sacramentally, by eating the bread which is the sign or Sacrament of it."[4]

"To partake of our Lord's body and blood implies union with our Lord ; it implies the fruition of Him, it implies a cognateness of the eater to the food. The body and blood of our Lord are not spiritual food in the immaterial sense only, but they are spiritual food in the moral sense, as being moral aliment and nutrition, the goodness and holiness of our Lord infusing itself into the

[1] See pp. 239-49, *supra.*   [2] P. 201.   [3] P. 202.   [4] Pp. 204, 205.

human soul. But to eat what is in this sense spiritual requires a state of mind which is spiritual in this sense. . . . The wicked then cannot eat them spiritually, but the spiritual is the only way in which they can be eaten ; the wicked therefore cannot eat them at all." [1]

" It is not, however, to be inferred, because the wicked do not eat the very body and blood of Christ in the Sacrament, that therefore they only eat common bread and wine. They eat consecrated material elements, to which the mysterious property has been imparted that the faithful receive and eat in them the body and blood of Christ. Common bread has not this property imparted to it, but the bread in the Sacrament has. When the wicked eat the sacramental bread, then, though they do not eat the Lord's body, they eat bread which is in a certain intimate and mystical relation to our Lord's body. . . . The wicked eat that to which a divine virtue is joined, even the property of becoming to the faithful the body of our Lord. This virtue is joined to the consecrated bread independently of our faith, and the wicked who eat it eat it with this virtue attaching to it, which cannot leave it, namely, that the very same bread, if eaten by the faithful, would be spiritual nourishment to them, which common bread could not be. . . . The material symbols are ever accompanied by a divine virtue and property, which adheres to them by the very nature of the Sacraments, and . . . therefore, even when the wicked eat and drink them, that virtue still belongs to and accompanies them, the invisible part is still joined to the visible, but it does not imply that the wicked eat the thing signified itself, that they eat the body and blood which is the inward part of the Sacrament." [2]

" There are . . . two wholly different kinds of statements mixed together in the general language relating to adoration of our Lord in the Eucharist. One of these kinds of statement expresses only an adoration accompanying the act of receiving, the other expresses an adoration of Him as contained in some sense in that which is received : one denotes only the worship of Christ as generally present in and at the Eucharistic rite; the other signifies a worship of Him as specially present under the species of bread and wine. Of these two kinds of statement one, as I have just said, has no real bearing upon the particular question of adoration in the Eucharist, as that phrase is understood in controversy. All Christians, of whatever Church or party, would admit the adoration of our Lord in this general sense in the Eucharist, namely, that, when a man partakes

[1] P. 206. [2] Pp. 208, 209.

of the Eucharist, he does worship Christ.   But this is not worshipping Him as present or in any way contained in the bread and wine.
. . . The body and blood in the Sacrament is not the object of the
worship, but only the occasion of it. . . . There is a great difference
of course between a general presence of Christ in the act of Communion, and a particular presence united to the bread and wine.
Separating this general language then from that particular body of
language which asserts an adoration in special connection with the
material elements, we find in the first place that in all earlier language, and in the language of our own divines which represents the
earlier ages, adoration is addressed to the body and blood of our
Lord, and that that, and that only, is the object to which it is addressed.   Our divines, indeed, when speaking of the partaking in
Communion, speak of Christ simply being received, not making
any distinction between the body and blood and the divinity of
Christ ; nor is such an extension of the *res sacramenti* other than
natural, nor can any injurious consequence follow it, in connection
with the Sacrament as spiritual food ; the boundaries and limitations
of mystical language are not to be very accurately restricted where
no practical danger can ensue.   But as regards the adoration in the
Eucharist, the act of adoration has been assigned specially to the
body and blood of Christ as its object, that being the strict and
proper *res sacramenti*, and not to the divinity of Christ, which is not
properly or strictly the *res sacramenti* or united with the material
elements.   The whole language of antiquity establishes the body
and blood as that which is in sacramental connection with the bread
and wine.   The divinity is not represented as placed in this sacramental union with the material elements.   It is quite true indeed
that wherever the body and blood of Christ are, there by strict
reasoning must be the human soul and the divinity of Christ ; it is
impossible to separate what are in their own nature united.   But it
must be remembered that this is a mystical subject, and that in
mystical doctrine we cannot proceed in this way by logical steps.
In mystical doctrine we must take the form of statement which is
given to us, and not exceed it ; because if the truth is given in a
certain form and measure, and with certain limits and confines, we
must assume that it is intentionally so given, and for a divine purpose.   Earlier writers and our own divines then adhere cautiously
and faithfully to Scripture in speaking of the body and blood of
Christ as the *res sacramenti* in the Eucharist, and in assigning the
act of adoration in the Eucharist to the body and blood.   It was
therefore a qualified and conditioned kind of adoration which patris-

tic theology connected specially with the Eucharist. For the body. and blood of Christ are not in themselves objects of divine adoration and worship; they only admit of a worship which is paid to them indirectly by reason of their intimate connection with that which is an object of direct adoration, namely, the divinity of Christ; they can only receive that reflected divinity which comes from the Person of Christ, and consequently only a secondary worship. . . . The reverence . . . that is paid to sacred signs and symbols, and to all objects which are associated with the divine majesty, is a worship or adoration in a secondary sense; and *a fortiori* may our Lord's body and blood, as being joined not by association but by the truth of nature with His divinity, receive that worship. But the worship given specially in the Eucharist was such subordinate worship, worship paid to that which was intimately connected with divinity, not to the divinity itself. The mind of the worshipper was necessarily carried indeed to the direct worship of the divinity of Christ, but in so doing it went out of the area and limits of the Sacrament, and worshipped the God of God, Light of Light, Very God of Very God, by whom all things were made. But, when later theology took up the subject of the adoration in the Eucharist, it instituted a very different kind of adoration. In later theology, in the first place, the *res sacramenti* was not only the body and blood of Christ, but was the whole Christ, body, soul, and Godhead. . . . But, the inward part of the Sacrament being thus defined, when it came to the adoration of the *res sacramenti*, that adoration necessarily became, not the indirect worship of what was in natural conjunction with the divinity, but the direct adoration of the Godhead itself existing under the species of bread and wine. But, without entering into the question of the criterion by which we define idolatry, or at all asserting that the worship of the true God, though under an unauthorised material form, is idolatry, we must still see that this express adoration of the Godhead, as subsisting under the visible material form of bread, holds a place very distinct from, and is divided by a great interval from, the primitive adoration of the body and blood." [1]

" There are two distinct senses in which an act may be said to be propitiatory. The act of Christ's sacrifice on the cross had an original propitiatory power, that is to say, it was the cause of any other act, or any act of man, or any rite, being propitiatory, that is, appeasing God's anger, and reconciling Him to the agent. We

[1] Pp. 211-15.

37 *

may allow that in common language a man may do something which will reconcile God to him, and restore him to God's favour; but then all the power that any action of man can have for this end is a derived power, derived from Christ's sacrifice, from which any other sacrifice, the Eucharistic one included, borrows its virtue, and without which it would be wholly null and void. There is, then, an original propitiation and a borrowed propitiation, a first propitiation and a secondary one." [1]

"Our Church at the Reformation recalled the doctrine of the Eucharist to its proper proportions, and corrected the errors and extravagances into which later theology had been led. She relieved the change in the elements from the interpolation of Transubstantiation, and from that false, rigid completeness and system which the schools of the middle ages had given it. She restored faith as the medium by which the body of Christ is eaten. She restored the true limits of the adoration in the Eucharist, and of the sacrifice of the Eucharist." [2]

"Amid the various explanations of the manner in which the mystery of the Sacrament is to be expressed, the mode of change, the kind of change, the relation of the material element or sign to the inner part or thing signified, the relation of the whole Sacrament to the mind and faith of the partaker, one central truth remains, retaining which we retain the true substance of the doctrine of the Eucharist, namely, that it is a true participation of the body and blood of Christ, which are verily and indeed taken and received by the faithful in that Sacrament. Various degrees of importance may attach to circumstantial points, to Transubstantiation in the Romanist's view, to Consubstantiation in the Lutheran, and different ideas may be entertained among ourselves as to the sense in which the body and blood are contained in the Sacrament, or the Sacrament transmuted into them, antecedently to the participation of the receiver. I do not by any means intend to say that upon this latter question there is not a grave truth and a grave error; but I must say with Hooker that the question does not relate to necessary belief in regard to the doctrine of the Sacrament, and that a true participation of the body and blood of Christ is the fundamental truth of the Eucharist." [3]

VIII.

In the closing years of the nineteenth century several attempts were made to lessen the acuteness of the controversies

[1] Pp. 216, 217.   [2] P. 217.   [3] Pp. 217, 218.

concerning the Eucharist in the Church of England. The most notable were the *Charge* delivered in 1898 by the Archbishop of Canterbury, Dr. Frederick Temple, and a Conference appointed by the Bishop of London, Dr. Mandell Creighton, at the instance of the London Diocesan Conference, which met at Fulham Palace in October, 1900. With them may be associated a Conference held at Oxford in December, 1899, under the chairmanship of Dr. Sanday, the Margaret Professor of Divinity in the University of Oxford, in which both Churchmen and Nonconformists took part, at which, although the discussion of the doctrine of the Eucharist was not prominent, questions relating to priesthood and sacrifice were considered.[1]

The salient point of Archbishop Temple's Visitation *Charge* of 1898 in regard to the Eucharist was the contention that the Church of England has expressly affirmed that the Sacrament is a means of conveying to communicants the spiritual gift of union with Christ, but, while rejecting Transubstantiation, has left open the question whether the effect of consecration is to make the body and blood of Christ present under the form of bread and wine.

" Concerning the Holy Eucharist there are two distinct opinions which have for a long time divided Christians from one another. There are those who hold that no special gift is bestowed in the Sacrament, but that the value of it, mainly if not entirely, resides in the effect produced on the soul of the receiver by the commemoration of that wonderful act of love, our Lord's sacrifice of Himself on the cross. . . . On the other hand, there are, and always have been, those who believe that this Sacrament conveys to the receivers a special mysterious gift, uniting us to Christ in a special manner and degree, giving new power, new cleansing, new life, and even new insight into spiritual things, leavening the whole being with a heavenly infection. . . . Between these two opinions there can be no question that the Church [that is, the Church of England] holds the latter. . . . It is hardly necessary to add that the doctrine of the reality of the gift bestowed in the Holy Communion is universal in the writings of the early Christians, and is still maintained not only by the Anglican Communion, but also by the Greek and other Churches in the East, by the Romans, and by the Lutherans.

[1] The proceedings of this Conference are reported in the volume entitled *Different Conceptions of Priesthood and Sacrifice*, edited by Dr. Sanday.

" Having come to this point, we reach a further question and
another division of opinion. For it may be asked, When is the gift
bestowed, and how ? It is clear that, if we confine this question to
make it mean when is the gift bestowed on the individual communicant, only one answer is possible. It is bestowed on the communicant when he receives the consecrated elements. He cannot receive
it before, for till that moment he has not fulfilled the necessary
conditions ; but the consuming of the bread and wine is the means
whereby he receives the gift, and the pledge to him that he has received it. Nor, indeed, is there any dispute upon this point. But,
if the question be, not when does the communicant receive the gift,
but when does the congregation in which the Holy Eucharist is
celebrated receive it, not as individuals but as congregation, the
answer may be very different, and on the answer to this question
there have been the angriest and longest controversies, and this is
the dispute which is commonly called the dispute concerning the
real presence. The Church of England has given no answer to this
question ; and Hooker, undeniably a very high authority on the
doctrine of the Church of England, maintains that the real presence
should not be looked for in the consecrated elements, but in the receivers. They certainly receive a real gift, and, knowing this, why
should we ask any further question ? Knowing the reality of the
gift, we know all that is needed for our spiritual life. The Church
certainly teaches Hooker's doctrine, but to this it must be added
that the Church nowhere forbids the further doctrine that there is
a real presence in some way attached to the elements at the time of
consecration and before the reception. If there be no real presence
until their reception, it may be asked what is the effect of consecration, and may not the consecration be omitted ? The answer is
obvious. On the theory that the real presence is bestowed in the
reception, and not before, then the effect of the prayer of consecration is to attach to the elements, not a presence, but a promise.
The bread has been blessed according to our Lord's command, and
the Lord's promise is that, when the communicant partakes of this
bread, so blessed, he shall be a partaker of the Lord's body. But,
though this explanation entirely satisfies all the language of the
Articles and the Prayer Book, it is nowhere explicitly asserted so
as to exclude altogether the other opinion, namely, that in some
mysterious way there is a presence attached to the elements from
the moment of their consecration. This was the question raised by
the case of Mr. Bennett, of Frome. He had asserted ' the real and
actual presence of our Lord under the form of bread and wine upon

the altars of our churches '. He had said of himself, ' Who myself
adore and teach the people to adore Christ present in the Sacrament
under the form of bread and wine, believing that under their veil is
the sacred body and blood of my Lord and Saviour Jesus Christ '.[1]
This doctrine, so expressed, the Privy Council refused to condemn.
Though it be not explicitly taught in our formularies, there is nothing
in those formularies which explicitly forbids a man to hold or to teach
it. It is difficult, if not impossible, really to distinguish between
this doctrine and the Lutheran doctrine commonly called Consubstantiation,[2] and it is important that it should be clearly understood
that it is not unlawful to hold it and to teach it within the Church
of England. Up to this point the Church of· England leaves the
question open. But the Roman Church has gone a step beyond this,
and has endeavoured to lay down, not only the time when, but also
the mode whereby the great gift is given, and here the Church of
England has distinctly negatived the Roman teaching. The doctrine of Transubstantiation is expressed in terms taken from the
philosophy of the schoolmen. The fullest exposition of it is to be
found in the *Summa Theologiæ* of Thomas Aquinas. According to
this doctrine, the substance of the bread and wine is by the prayer
of consecration miraculously converted into the body and blood of
our Lord. After that prayer has been said the bread is gone and so
is the wine. They have been converted into the Lord's body and
blood. The accidents, as the schoolmen called them, that is, the
size, the shape, the colour, the feel, the taste, the smell, the weight,
remain unchanged. · : . . Most assuredly, if ever human inventions
have been allowed to supersede the teaching of Scripture, this is
among the number of such inventions. There is not a word in the
New Testament which can be wrested into a support for the doctrines of the conversion of the substance of the bread into the body
of the Lord or of the substance of the wine into His blood ; and the
prayer in some of the early liturgies beseeching the Holy Ghost
to make the bread and wine into the body and blood of the Lord
for us is an absurdly weak foundation for this highly metaphysical
structure of a change of the substance without disturbing the accidents and the maintenance of the accidents as accidents of nothing." [3]

"It is allowed to a man to adore Christ present in the Sacra-

[1] See pp. 553, 554, *supra*.
[2] This identification with "Consubstantiation" would not usually be
allowed by advocates of the doctrine described as not unlawful in the Church
of England. For the Lutheran doctrine, see pp. 10-37, *supra*.
[3] Pp. 6-12.

ment if he believes Him to be there present, but it is not allowed
to any one to use any other external mark of adoration except that
of kneeling to receive the consecrated elements.   The priest is not
allowed to elevate the elements before the people, lest, perchance,
they should be tempted to worship those elements, and not only
Christ Himself." [1]

At the Conference held at Fulham Palace in October, 1900,
it was found impossible to agree on any statement of doctrine;
but the Conference extracted from the minutes and formally recorded three statements which had been put forward by members
of the Conference with eirenic intentions, although unable as a
body to assent to any one of them.   The first of these statements was by Dr. Handley Moule, then Norrisian Professor of
Divinity in the University of Cambridge, now Bishop of
Durham.   It was a reverent and devout expression of the line of
thought found in particular in Bishop Beveridge [2] and other
post-Reformation Anglican divines that our Lord is present in
the rite of the Eucharist to bless and distribute the bread and
wine, and as so present in the rite and as giving us the signs of
His body and blood is rightly to be worshipped.

"I believe that, if our eyes, like those of Elisha's servant at
Dothan, were opened to the unseen, we should indeed behold our
Lord present at our Communions.   There and then, assuredly, if
anywhere and at any time, He remembers His promise, 'Where
two or three are gathered together in My name, there am I in the
midst of them'.   Such special presence, the promised congrega-
tional presence, is perfectly mysterious in mode, but absolutely true
in fact, no creation of our imagination or emotion, but an object for
our faith.   I believe that our Lord, so present, not on the Holy
Table, but at it, would be seen Himself, in our presence, to bless
the bread and wine for a holy use, and to distribute them to His
disciples, saying to all and each, 'Take, eat, this is My body which
was given for you: Drink ye all of this; this is My blood of the
new covenant which was shed for you for the remission of sins'.   I
believe that we should worship Him thus present in the midst of us
in His living grace, with unspeakable reverence, thanksgiving, joy,
and love.   We should revere the bread and the wine with a profound sense of their sacredness as given by Him in physical assurance of our joyful part, as believers in Him, and so as members of

[1] P. 15.   [2] See p. 454, *supra*.

Him, in all the benefits of His passion. Receiving them, while beholding Him, we should, through them as the equivalent signs of His once sacrificed body and blood, take deep into us a fresh certainty of our perfect acceptance in Him our sacrifice, and also of our mystical union with Him as He, once dead, now lives for us and in us, thus feeding on Him in the heart, by faith, with thanksgiving. Receiving His signs, we should look up with renewed and inexpressible confidence through Him to the Father. I do not think that the Holy Scriptures give us reason to believe that this sacred procedure (which we cannot see, but which is truly present to faith) involves any special attachment of His presence to the sacred signs, albeit called His body and His blood by reason of their equivalence as divine tokens." [1]

The second statement was a carefully worded expression by Lord Halifax of the spiritual change of the bread and wine into the body and blood of Christ, following the lines of the great mediæval theologians and the post-Tridentine Roman Catholic divines, though without touching on the questions as to the substance and the accidents in the Sacrament.

" That the bread and wine, by virtue of our Lord's institution, become sacramentally the body and blood of Christ.

" That this change is sacramental, in a sphere outside the cognisance of sense, to be accepted and therefore to be apprehended by faith, that is, that to the eye of faith, since 'faith is not imagination, but believes only what is objectively true,' the bread and wine are the body and blood of Christ, but that in the natural order they remain what they were before.

" That expressed devotionally in the words of Professor Moule, ' I see in the Holy Eucharist, which is primarily and before all things the memorial of the Lord's death, Christ my Lord at the Holy Table coming to me and saying, "This is My body which was broken for you, this is My blood which was shed for you," ' or, as was expressed by Canon Gore, Canon Newbolt, and Lord Halifax, ' That in every Eucharist Christ is the real Consecrator,' who in the service which He has instituted for the perpetual memory of His death gives to His faithful people His body as broken, His blood as poured out, mystically represented and exhibited under the aspect of death by the separate consecration of the bread and wine.

[1] The Doctrine of Holy Communion and Its Expression in Ritual (Report of a Conference held at Fulham Palace in October, 1900, edited by Dr. Wace), pp. 72, 73, 91.

"That Christ is present in the Holy Eucharist not in a corporal
or natural manner, not locally as if He descended from heaven upon
our altars, but sacramentally only, spiritually, after the manner of
a spirit." [1]

The third statement was by Dr. Charles Gore, then Canon
of Westminster, now Bishop of Birmingham. It to a large extent reproduced the teaching of St. Irenæus [2] as to the co-ordinate
presence in the consecrated Sacrament of the natural reality of
the bread and wine, and the spiritual reality of the body and
blood of Christ.

"I believe that 'the bread which is of the earth receiving the
invocation of God is no longer common bread, but Eucharist, made
up of two realities (πραγμάτων), an earthly and a heavenly,' that
is, the bread and wine in all their natural reality and the spiritual
realities of the body and blood of Christ, which are inseparable from
Christ Himself in His whole Person. Therefore, as truly as with
the eye of sense I behold the bread and wine, so truly with the eye
of faith I am henceforth to behold Jesus Christ present to feed me
with His own body and blood, sacramentally identified with the bread
and wine." [3]

IX.

Among those who have accepted the main positions of the
Oxford Movement, Father R. M. Benson, the Founder and first
Superior of the Society of St. John the Evangelist, the Bishop
(Gore) of Birmingham, and Father P. N. Waggett, of the
Society of St. John the Evangelist, have been notable for the
emphasis laid by them on particular aspects of Eucharistic doc-
trine.

A characteristic feature of Father Benson's teaching has been
the importance attached by him to the spiritual nature of the
risen body of Christ, and to the part played by the spiritual risen
body in the life of Christians in union with their Lord. [4] An
instance of this teaching and of the application of it to the
Eucharist may be seen in a letter which Father Benson wrote in
1907, in which he said :—

[1] *Op. cit.* pp. 68, 69, 91, 92.
[2] See vol. i. pp. 34, 35, *supra.*
[3] *Op. cit.* pp. 74, 92.
[4] See *e.g., The Life beyond the Grave,* pp. 398-401, 429-33.

"I hear that some persons . . . are striving to laugh the true doctrine of our Lord's presence out of court by representing it as a miracle. Of course, it is a miracle; all the operations of the living God in this material world are a miracle; birth, nourishment, growth, all are miracles, 'but seen too oft are miracles in vain'. They are not miracles in the sense of being acts contrary to nature, wrought by divine power in order to attest the divine mission of One whom God has sent, but they are miracles as being acts of God's continuous though secret power by which He raises the things of nature to become the channels of operations which in their original nature they could not have effected. God's work must be supernatural. He acts by infusing some new law, by which the lower creation is raised to do the higher work. . . . Christ takes the bread and wine into His glorified body. If He did not do so, the Church, which is His body in its earthly form, would die. The Church requires as an earthly organisation to be nourished by earthly elements, but those elements must have a heavenly substance. Christ must take them into the substance of His glorified body. Otherwise, they would not be capable of nourishing His body upon the earth. Without this continuous feeding upon the body of Christ, the Church upon earth would die of starvation. . . . The word 'Transubstantiation,' true of our natural food, fails to express the truth of the change which is effected in the bread and wine when they become the body and blood of Christ. The true bread is given to us 'from heaven'. It has a heavenly nature in itself; the bread and wine acquire a heavenly virtue by incorporation into His glorified substance. We are made Christ's members, and need to feed upon Christ's glorified body. . . . From Christ, the Head, must come the life of each successive generation of the Church, which is His body. His body has nourishment administered to it by sacramental joints and bands from Himself, the Head, as St. Paul teaches us. . . . Christ comes to us in this Holy Sacrament, not leaping down from His central throne of divine love, as He will do at His second coming, when the number of His elect is complete, and He will return to judge the world, moving all the majesty of heaven, while He brings along with Himself the souls of the saints that are in Him, that they may take up their bodies, which are in Him by sacramental fellowship, though now they are sleeping. But He comes by an onflow of divine force—substantive, for it is in His human nature that He comes to be the food of man; personal, for in Christ the humanity cannot be without the divine Person; affectionate, for He comes with the love of God; spiritual, for He acts in the power of the Holy Ghost ; regenerating, for He lifts us up into a heavenly life ; nutritive, for He makes His members to grow in grace by this feeding upon Him ; purifying, for our sinful bodies are made clean by His body ; divine, because our souls are washed by His ever-living blood; sanctifying, for He, of God, is therein made to us sanctification and redemption ; glorifying, for His hidden presence shall be revealed in us hereafter in the glory of His kingdom. . . . In such a stream of supernatural power, surely the provision of the food by which this grace streams forth cannot but be a miracle. If it were not, it would be an act altogether unworthy of its relation as ordained by God to raise us from earth to heaven. The consecration of the sacred elements is not a tentative action; from which great things may follow, but it is a covenant, ordained in all things, and sure. Hereby, Christ comes to us. Hereby, we, as His members, appeal to God, that God may remember us as speaking to Him in Christ's name. . . . People talk about Christ's body as if it were the body of any other man. They do not realise that it is ascended to the right hand of God. They think of Christ sitting in heaven as He may be represented in a picture, with the form which He might have had during His earthly life. They do not realise what is meant by His ascension. He did not ascend to some place in the sky miles and miles away from earth. He ascended by passing up from an earthly form of existence, measured by space and outline, to an entirely new sphere and manner and capacity of life. He ascended up a little way above the heads of the bystanders, and then He vanished out of their sight. He was not lost in distance. Nor did He cease to exist. He was crucified in a natural body. He rose again as a spiritual body. That spiritual body is incapable of any earthly measurement or form. It is a heavenly power such as we can in no wise apprehend. It is no longer in space, but is at the right hand of God, exercising a power by the inherent glory of the Holy Ghost. It is no longer in space, but it acts independently of space, so that however many may be the altars on which the Holy Eucharist is celebrated, there is no multiplication of Christ's body. His body, being now a spiritual body, is a force divinely operating in every crumb of the consecrated bread, communicating the existence of its glorified state to each one who feeds thereon. This is what people are too apt to ignore, so that it seems as if each individual received into himself a separate Christ, and not the divine undivided Christ. One Christ, one living Force acting throughout the whole of the Church, which is His body, and acting completely in every individual communicant. . . . We must not think of the sacred elements as if they were transubstantiated into human flesh like our own, but as being lifted up by the divine indwelling so as to be the mediatorial channel of life uniting us as the members of Christ to a vital fellowship with Christ, the Head of the body. . . . The Sacraments are the means through which the Spirit acts. The bread and wine consecrated by the Spirit are taken into the body of Christ, so as to be a channel of communication. If the bread and wine were an empty symbol, they could not effect bodily union between ourselves and Christ. Our bodies are made members of Christ's body, of His flesh, and of His bones. There must be a material substance to act upon our bodies, as there must be a spiritual substance with which we are united. . . . The miracle is not our work. It is the work of the Holy Ghost in the body of Christ. We cannot work the miracle, it is not we who consecrate the bread and wine. There is only one Priest in the Church of God. One Victim, one Altar. The priest who celebrates can neither help the miracle, nor can he nullify it. However little he believes in the sacramental change, that change is just the same as if he believes in it most fully. . . . We must realise that it is by the power of the Holy Ghost descending from heaven at Pentecost that we are called to consecrate the bread and wine, and make them channels of mediatorial grace by their identification with the mediatorial Head of the covenant." [1]

The Bishop (Gore) of Birmingham's work *The Body of Christ* was published in 1901, when the writer was still a Canon of Westminster. It was an attempt to state the Scriptural and historical doctrine of the Holy Eucharist in its fulness and its balance, to indicate its relation to widespread or universal instincts of natural religion, to place it in its due position in regard to Christian thought and life as a whole, and by a combination of frankness and caution and consideration in statement to tend towards "the promotion of mutual understanding and unity among Christians". In this book great stress was laid on the harmony between Eucharistic doctrine and the rest of Christian theology. The fundamental idea is the gift of the spiritual principle of the manhood of Christ, and therefore of Christ Himself, to Christians. The flesh and blood thus given are the flesh and blood of the glorified Christ. This presence of Christ is effected by means of the act of consecration, and through con-

[1] This letter was printed in *The Cowley Evangelist* for July, 1907.

secration the bread and wine are identified with His body and blood.   Christ is Himself present through the Eucharistic service, and He Himself consecrates the elements.   Transubstantiation in its cruder form is contrary to reason and instinct, and in its technical form is philosophically unsound and not free from un-spiritual tendencies.   Since the presence is of the spiritual risen and ascended body of Christ, it is not subject to conditions of space, nor again to the sacramental elements.   Hence caution must be observed as to dogmatic statements in regard to the Sacrament when reserved as a centre of worship, and as to what those who communicate unworthily receive.   Yet the presence is not dependent on the precarious faith of an individual.   The Eucharist is a sacrifice, and has points of contact with the general sacrificial ideas of communion with deity and with the special emphasis in the Jewish religion on propitiation in sacrifice.   As a sacrifice, it is the exercise of the Church's privilege of sonship and the Church's commemoration of the passion and death and resurrection and ascension and second coming of Christ; it is united with the sacrifice of Christ in heaven ; it is the offering of the Church as itself the body of Christ ; and it culminates in the Communion and self-oblation of the worshippers.

" Shall we say . . . that by His flesh we understand the spiritual principle or essence of His manhood, as distinguished from its material constituents ? and by His blood, according to the deeply-rooted Old Testament idea, the 'life thereof,' the human life of Jesus of Naza-reth in His glory ? Whether these phrases are thought to be satisfac-tory or no, in some sense it is the manhood which must be meant by the flesh and blood.   At the same time, it is equally evident that it is only because of the vital unity in which the manhood stands with the divine nature that it can be 'spirit' and 'life'.   It is the humanity of nothing less than the divine Person which is to be, in some sense, communicated to us, and not (what would be the worst materialism) a separated flesh and blood.   What the Father is spoken of as giving us is the whole Christ, the whole of His indivisible and living self." [1]

"The communication of this spiritual life to us by means of a material and social ceremony is quite analogous to the whole of what we know about the relation of the human spirit to bodily conditions,

[1] Pp. 24-26.   All the quotations and references are from the fourth edition, published in 1907.

about the relation of the individual to the society, and about the principles of the pre-eminently human and social religion of the Son of Man." [1]

"It stands to reason that, if there be thus, as the Christian Church so constantly believed, a real communication to us of the flesh and blood of Christ, it must be the 'flesh' and 'blood' of the glorified Christ, for no other exists. These mysterious things are given to us in the Eucharist under conditions which recall a past state, the state of sacrificial death. It is our Lord as dying that faith recalls; it is His death for us that we 'proclaim till He come' [2] in the breaking of the bread. But those very words of St. Paul, 'till He come,' suggest that He is no longer dead, that He is alive and in heaven. The Person who now feeds us with His own very life, divine and human, is He who is set before us in a vision of the Apocalypse as a 'Lamb as it had been slain,' [3] but alive for evermore in the heavenly places." [4]

"I do not think it is disputable that the Church from the beginning did, as a whole, believe that the Eucharistic elements themselves in some real sense became by consecration, and prior to reception, the body and blood of Christ in the midst of the worshipping assembly; and that the body and blood thus made present objectively, in undefinable identification with the bread and wine, were the same body (or flesh) and blood as the faithful hoped to receive, that is, the flesh and blood of the living and glorified Christ, the flesh and blood which are spirit and life, and are quite inseparable from the living Person of Christ Himself." [5]

"Whatever was done in the Eucharist in His name, He was believed to be present and the doer of it. He was there to speak the words and consecrate the gifts. This belief in Christ already present as unseen Minister anticipated and so weakened the emotion following upon the consecration. What was brought about was not the presence of Christ—He was already there—but His adoption of the Church's gifts to become His body and His blood. Henceforth an attention and a worship already given to Christ as present among the worshippers was more or less focussed upon these holy symbols and instruments. But, if the ancients associated His 'coming' with any moment in the service, it was with the first solemn entrance of the elements, and the whole order and ritual of the service fell in with this conception. Now Catholics with one consent still believe that Christ is in some special sense present in the

[1] P. 47.   [2] 1 Cor. xi. 26.   [3] Rev. v. 6.
[4] P. 66.   [5] Pp. 93, 94.

whole Eucharistic service as the invisible Celebrant and consecrating Priest; and the more this belief is realised the less can His coming and presence be represented to the imagination as merely the result of consecration. The difference is not one of doctrine, but of practical emphasis on different parts of truth." [1]

"Transubstantiation in its first form, as for example the weak and unhappy Berengar was forced by the dominant power in the Church to subscribe to it,[2] was indeed a gross and horrible doctrine. . . . Most of the contemporary writers against Berengar assert that the body and blood of Christ are to be eaten and drunken ' with the mouth of the body as well as the mouth of the heart'; and, like some of the earlier Greeks, they deny that the elements after consecration retain their natural properties of nourishing or becoming corrupted or being digested.[3] The nature of the bread and wine was understood to be destroyed in everything but appearance. Miracles were recklessly postulated, and it was sufficient objection to any more reasonable treatment of the mystery that in diminishing the difficulty of belief it reduced the merit of faith. Certainly the atmosphere in which the doctrine of Transubstantiation grows into a dogma is calculated to send a shiver through one's intellectual and moral being. But the rising scholasticism, or perhaps the evidence of facts, very quickly corrected this extreme tendency. The use indeed of the distinction of substance and accidents, for the purpose of assisting the doctrine of Transubstantiation, was already familiar to Berengar, and he excellently combats the proposed use of it, denying that accidents can exist apart from their substance (or 'subject'), or apart from that of which they are attributes. But the later scholastics used the distinction with a more laborious precision to formulate the doctrine. By the act of consecration the substrata or substances of the bread and the wine were changed into the substances of the body and blood of Christ; but the accidents or qualities of bread and wine—all that we are cognizant of in our experience of bread and wine—remained with all their natural properties and defects, remained (in the compassion of God) as veils under which the awful realities should be screened. In later days a still further refinement has led Roman theologians to say that the remaining species or accidents of the bread and wine constitute a real object, 'something objectively real'.[4] But this is in fact to explain away the doctrine and the phrase. Plainly modern philosophy of all schools recognises no distinction between substance

---

[1] Pp. 105, 106.
[2] See vol. i. p. 247, *supra*.
[3] See vol. i. p. 254, *supra*.
[4] See pp. 413-15, *supra*.

and accident, knows no substance other than that 'something objectively real' which is constituted by the qualities or relations under which alone any object is known in experience. Thus the modern Roman theologians allow to the consecrated bread and wine all the reality which any one believes bread and wine to possess, or, in other words, explain away Transubstantiation till it remains as little more than a verbal incumbrance due to an inopportune intrusion into Church doctrine of a temporary phase of metaphysics. In its original and more natural meaning, Transubstantiation—the overthrowing of the natural substance by the spiritual—is truly contrary to a fundamental Christian philosophy, and really 'overthroweth the nature of a Sacrament'. But even in its minimised sense Transubstantiation does not remain only as an incumbrance in terminology, witnessing to a mistake in the dogmatic action of the mediæval Church; for its really materialistic and unspiritualising effects cannot be done away. As soon as the accidents or species have reached a certain stage in the process of being digested by the communicant, or of being destroyed in some other way, it is felt to be irreverent to imagine that they can still be veils of the divine substances. . . . The result of so materialistic a way of conceiving the relation of the spiritual gift to the outward part of the Sacrament is that the corruption of the material elements involves the withdrawal of the divine gift. . . . Apart from the degree of authority which Transubstantiation has obtained in the West, and to a certain extent in the East, there is truly on the grounds of antiquity, or Scripture, or reason, nothing to be said for it." [1]

"The risen body of Christ was spiritual . . . not because it was less than before material, but because in it matter was wholly and finally subjugated to spirit, and not to the exigencies of physical life. Matter no longer restricted Him or hindered. It had become the pure and transparent vehicle of spiritual purpose. . . . The spirituality of the risen body of Christ lies not so much in any physical qualities as in the fact that His material presence is absolutely controlled by His spiritual will. . . . If all subjection to conditions of space was over for the body of the resurrection, even more certainly was it over for the glorified body (if any distinction is to be drawn), the body in which He through His whole Person has become 'quickening spirit,' and even His flesh and blood are 'spirit and life'. As to what the 'body of glory' is, silence is our best wisdom. . . . In claiming spirituality for Christ's presence we claim for it that, though He condescends to use material means,

[1] Pp. 116-21, 123.

the sacramental elements, yet He is never subject to them.   As in the risen and glorified body in itself, so in its sacramental applica_ tion to our necessities, spiritual freedom dominates everything with an absolute freedom.   The presence is controlled by the purpose· And in a matter where the evidence of the senses is denied us, our only right to be confident that the presence abides with us depends on our remaining under the shelter of the purpose.   Thus it seems to me to be illegitimate and insecure to argue that because the pre- sence, admitted to be spiritual, is vouchsafed to us (so to speak) under conditions of bread and wine, therefore I am justified in as- suming that it abides under those conditions so long as the bread subsists, or till I am informed to the contrary." [1]

"Metaphysical study makes us conscious how much the mind . . . has to do with actually constituting the objects of the out- ward world, the trees, the animals, the persons.   Mind, as it is in me and in all men, not only perceives these things as ready-made, but also has to do with making them to be. . . . Relations are the work of mind, and relations are necessary to make objects.   On the other hand, it is only the sensations given from outside which enable the mind to perceive and know, and so to become a mind at all. . . . It would be of a piece with this if we are to suppose that a similar relation exists between the spiritual presence of Christ in the Eucharist and our corresponding faculties of spiritual percep- tion, if we are to suppose that, though it is God who makes the bread to be the body of Christ and not man (as it is God who makes the objects in the natural world and not man), yet He makes this spiritual reality to exist relatively, not absolutely, in such sense as to exist only for faith, the faith of the believing and worshipping Church, just as He creates the world relatively, not absolutely, that is, to exist for rational beings and by the action of thought. . . . The spiritual presence of Christ in His body and His blood (and all that goes with it) rests not on the precarious faith of any individual, but is so relative to the faith of the Church as a whole— that common faculty which rests at bottom on the activity of the Holy Ghost—as that apart from faith, or for one who in no way shares it, it can no more in any intelligible sense be said to exist than the beauty of nature can be said to exist for what is quite without reason.   For here again existence proves to mean a rela- tion to a consciousness, only now it is not mere rational sensibility, but spiritual faith." [2]

"Recent investigation has tended to show that at least one

[1] Pp. 127, 129, 131, 132.   [2] Pp. 150-53.

deep root of sacrificial customs, if not *the* root, is the idea of communion or common sharing in a life believed to be divine. . . .
The development of the sacrificial system among the Jews tended
to bring to the front the idea of giving to God in homage and
recognition, and propitiating Him by victims, at the expense of the
idea of communion with Him." [1]

"The Eucharist is a sacrifice because in it the Christian Church
—the great priestly body, and 'soul of the world'—exercises her
privilege of sonship in free approach to the Father in the name
of Christ. She comes before the Father with her material offerings of bread and wine, and of those things wherein God has
prospered her, bearing witness that all good things come of Him ;
and, though He needs nothing from man, yet He accepts the
recognition of his Fatherhood from loyal and free hearts. She
comes with her wide-spreading intercessions for the whole race of
mankind,[2] and for her members living and departed. She offers
her glad sacrifice of praise and thanksgiving for all the blessings
of creation and redemption. She solemnly commemorates the
passion in word and in symbolic action, through the bread broken
and the wine outpoured, the appointed tokens of Christ's sacrificed
body and blood, reciting before God His own words and acts in
instituting the Holy Eucharist. This is the Church's sacrifice ; and
it is all that she can do. She can but make the appointed remembrance of Christ's passion and death and resurrection and of
His second coming which she awaits, and offer to the Father the
appointed symbols, praying Him by the consecrating power of the
Holy Ghost to fill the sacrifice with a divine power by accepting
the earthly elements at the heavenly altar. This is the time for
God's response to the Church's uplifting of her hearts and gifts ;
and He by His Spirit consecrates the gifts to be, in the midst of
the worshipping Church, the body and blood of the Lord. Now
the Eucharist is a sacrifice in a second and deeper sense, for God
has united the offerings of the Church to the ever-living sacrifice
of the great High Priest in the heavenly sanctuary, or has given
His presence among them who is their propitiation and their
spiritual food. Then, once more, united afresh in one body to
God by the Communion in Christ's body and blood, the Church
offers herself, one with Christ as a body with its head, living in
the same life and indwelt by the same Spirit ; she offers herself
that her whole fellowship, both the living and the dead, having
their sins forgiven through the propitiation of Christ, may be

---

[1] Pp. 12, 15.   [2] See p. 602, n. 1, *infra*.

accepted with all their good works and prayers 'in the beloved'. And in the self-oblation of the Church is the culmination of the sacrifice." [1]

In the preface to the fourth edition of this book, published in 1907, Bishop Gore makes an interesting reference to the question of possible compatibility between the Eucharistic doctrine of the Church of England and that of the Church of Rome which has already been referred to in connection with writings in the nineteenth century.[2] In 1906 a Report of a Royal Commission on Ecclesiastical Discipline, which had been appointed in 1904, appeared. The Report, which was signed by all the Commissioners, who included the Archbishop (Davidson) of Canterbury, the Bishop (Paget) of Oxford, and the Bishop (Gibson) of Gloucester, dealt chiefly, in accordance with the terms of reference, with matters of discipline and ceremonial, but was not without incidental statements on the subject of doctrine. Among these it was recognised that the Church of England allows the teaching of "a presence which is" "'real, actual, objective,' a presence in the Sacrament, a presence upon the altar, under the form of bread and wine," and teaching in which "the word 'sacrifice'" is applied "in the sense in which Bishop Bull has used it [3] to the ordinance of the Lord's Supper".[4] The practices of "the interpolation of the prayers and ceremonies belonging to the canon of the Mass," "the use of the words 'Behold the Lamb of God,' accompanied by the exhibition of a consecrated wafer or bread," the "reservation of the Sacrament under conditions which lead to its adoration," the "Mass of the Præ-sanctified," "Corpus Christi processions with the Sacrament," "Benediction with the Sacrament," and "Celebration of the Holy Eucharist with the intent that there shall be no communicant except the celebrant" were declared to be "clearly inconsistent with and subversive of the teaching of the Church of England as declared by the Articles and set forth in the Prayer Book," and "plainly significant of teaching repugnant to the doctrine of the Church of England"; and these were among the practices which were said to "lie on the Rome-ward side of a line of deep cleavage between the Church of England and that of Rome".[5] These

---

[1] Pp. 210-13.   [2] See pp. 535-47, supra.   [3] See pp. 443-50, supra.
[4] Pp. 16, 17.   [5] Pp. 44, 53, 75, 76, 77.

condemnations on grounds of doctrine necessarily raised again
the question whether Dr. Pusey's later opinion that the Eucharistic doctrine of the Church of Rome was not irreconcilable with
the Eucharistic doctrine of the Church of England[1] was correct; and in view of the condemnations of the Commissioners
and of the controversy which ensued the Bishop of Birmingham
wrote :—

"The main object of this book is to set the specifically Anglican
teaching of our formularies on a larger background, by going back
behind the Reformation and the middle age upon the ancient Catholic teaching and upon the Bible. I seek to elaborate the Eucharistic doctrine in what I think the truest and completest form. I
have to admit that Anglican standards are in certain respects
defective, and even misleading when taken by themselves. But
after all the Anglican Church does not claim to stand by itself. It
refers back behind itself to the ancient and Catholic Church. Thus
I am most thankful to believe that it admits a great deal which it
does not, in its present formularies, explicitly teach. It admits the
doctrine of Dr. Bright's popular hymn, 'And now, O Father,'
though it assuredly does not explicitly teach it; though, in fact, our
liturgy, more perhaps than any other, leaves out of regard the
heavenly altar. Moreover, in the direction of mediæval teaching, it
has no careful definitions such as might easily enough have excluded
approximations to the teaching of the Roman schools. The 'anti-
Roman' utterances of the Articles[2] are, as is well known, so
vaguely or ambiguously worded that, as weapons of discipline, they
would break in our hands. Thus it came about that the Judicial Committee acquitted Mr. Bennett[3] of teaching what the Church of
England could be said positively to reject. But it is quite certain
that Mr. Bennett's teaching, even in its revised form, was so similar
to current Roman teaching as to afford a perfectly natural background for those practices in connection with the Sacrament which
the Commissioners claim should be 'promptly made to cease' because they are significant of doctrine condemned by the Church of
England. Now it is precisely this that I believe to be untrue. I
believe that some practices connected with the Tabernacle and the
Monstrance involve an extension of the use of the Sacrament which

[1] See pp. 544-47, *supra*.

[2] There is here a footnote, "The same applies to the Declaration
about kneeling as revised in 1662".

[3] See pp. 553, 554, *supra*.

diverges so widely from Christ's intention as to be illegitimate. I
would prohibit them in the Church of England for this reason; and
every Bishop can legitimately prohibit any rite or service or prayer
which is not in the Prayer Book. I should be, therefore, quite
prepared, apart from any suggestion of a Royal Commission, to cause
to cease almost all the practices scheduled. But not—precisely not
—on the ground that they involve a doctrine which the Church of
England excludes. It does not exclude Mr. Bennett's doctrine.
So the Commissioners recognise. And I am sure that Mr. Bennett's
doctrine, neither more nor less, affords a natural basis for these (devotionally most attractive) practices, unless indeed the devotional
logic is restrained by reverent adherence to the purpose of Christ in
the institution of the Sacrament. . . . It is quite true that, if we
take a typical Anglican teacher and a typical Roman, we may find
'a line of deep cleavage' between them. But, if we take the least
Protestant types of Anglican teaching and the most moderate
Roman types, the line is hardly apparent; and, if we take the
doctrinal requirement of Rome at its minimum, and at the same
time recognise how vague are the limits of Anglican Eucharistic
theology, we shall come to the conclusion that no such line of deep
cleavage exists at all." [1]

Father Waggett's volume *The Holy Eucharist with Other
Occasional Papers*, which was published in 1906, contains an
address and four shorter papers on the Eucharist. Their special
feature is the presentation and treatment of the Eucharistic doctrine taught by Dr. Pusey and others in such a way as to appeal
to those who are interested in the science and philosophy of the
time. Theologically, the most characteristic thought is that of
the uplifting of the earthly elements and of the worshippers into
the heavenly life of our Lord.

"By the power of God there is communicated to the earthly
elements the reality and power and substance of the glorified body
and blood. The earthly things which we bring remain after consecration what they were before, and they become that which they
were not before; and, being named naturally and reverently according to their higher reality, according to that 'inward part' which is
communicated to them from above, according to that which in the
highest sense of their being they 'are,' the holy gifts are said, as
they have in every age been said, to 'become' the body and blood

[1] Pp. vii-x.

of Christ. . . . The empty reality of the earthly things is filled by
the truer and indeed absolute reality of the heavenly things." [1]

"The body and blood of our Lord Jesus Christ . . . are now
permanent, imperishable, and full of glory and life; and accordingly they are contrasted with all the so-called reality of this lower
scene, and their true substance is, in the mystery of the Eucharist,
placed under the relative and imperfect reality of the consecrated
bread and wine. In the eternal light, therefore, of God's contemplation, and in the sphere regarded by that divine faith which is
planted in man, the bread is the body, the wine is the blood of the
Lord." [2]

" Christ has ascended into heaven. There in heaven, in the unseen world, in glory, at the right hand of the Father are now His
once mortal body and blood. We are not to drag down this holy
reality into the earthly sphere, that the Treasure of the unseen
world and the Light of the heavenly Jerusalem may become the
ornament of a circle of carnal experience. This is to bring Christ
down from above. No : our thoughts are to rise to heaven, seeking
Him beyond the skies, and to press on continually to find these
unseen and glorified realities which are the sole food of our souls
and even of our bodies in the order of their redemption. But, on
the other hand, that bread and wine, those earthly things we knew,
are really lifted up into a heavenly use. We brought 'the best and
purest wheaten bread that can be gotten'; and that which we
brought, as in another application the rubric says, is allowed to
suffice. God accepts it, and it is really taken, translated, exalted,
used, filled, sanctified, and empowered with the realities of the
kingdom of heaven, of the throne of God's love." [3]

" The presence in the Holy Eucharist is the presence of the real
body and blood, of the really created and glorified humanity of the
Lord. It is a presence not in the regenerate alone, for it *is* before
the regenerate receive it. It is a presence not in the regenerate,
but yet it is a presence *unto* the regenerate; and the encounter
which it implies takes place, if we may so say, in that region which
is no place, in that plane, in that sphere, in that unspeakable possibility of experience which is the 'wherein' in which the man
walks with God ; in the conversation which is in heaven, in the love
of the Spirit, in the energy of the blessed into which we are brought
by the new birth, to which entrance is obtained by the precious
blood, and in which life is sustained by this very God-filled humanity of which we speak. . . . Bear with me, therefore, when I

[1] Pp. 9, 10.   [2] P. 12.   [3] P. 19.

say that the presence is 'unto the regenerate,' that it stands as a condemnation indeed in the bodily presence of the unbelieving, but shines as a divine manifestation to the heart which reacts to the vibrations of the life of Jesus. And therefore let us not be afraid of the old word which states that the mode and means whereby we receive this heavenly gift is faith." [1]

" As to our bodily eyes the bread is present, and the media of that presence are the luminiferous ether and so forth ; as to our bodily sense earthly foods are given according to the communications of a physical process ; so also to our inmost being and to its outer regions of soul and mind and thought and will there is given the heavenly reality of the body and blood of Christ, filled with the power of an endless life." [2]

" We know that the Lord's sacrifice is an offering of His whole life to the Father, and that it is such that His divinely unbegun life had already this character of presentation to the Father, from whom, as from the Fount of deity, it springs. So the Incarnation itself is from the first an offering, because it is a bringing of the creature into the great stream of the Son's love towards the Father, by the Holy Spirit. Now in the Incarnation the Creature also is offered by the same Spirit to the Father, and the whole life of Christ from the conception to the end is one effectual sacrifice. This sacrifice finds its seal in the accomplished work on the cross, its utterance in the outpouring of the blood, where the obedience reached to the climax of self-oblation. But we know that it continues evermore, that our Lord, bearing with Him the blood of an everlasting Testament, has entered in once into the holy place made without hands, not once because He goeth in no more, but once because He never more cometh forth. Having once entered into the holy place, not once because less than twice, but once because for ever, He abides there eternally, rich in the merits of an everlasting sacrifice, showing forth and offering continually the love of created humanity to the Father of all, pouring evermore into the treasury of God's love and acceptance the abundance which God Himself has insinuated into the stream of human life. That is the eternal sacrifice, Christ appearing ever before the Father for us, appearing in the glory of His love, appearing in the unchanged power of the God-given life, a Lamb as it had been slain, yet living for evermore, upon the altar in the midst of the throne. . . . By virtue . . . of the heavenly Treasure put within our reach our actions are in heaven; we also, by that substance given

[1] Pp. 28, 29.   [2] P. 30.

to us, with that substance which we minister standing in the
heavenly place, are brought in to be coheirs, to be communicants
of that heavenly service, and are made partakers of the eternal
mystery of Christ offered to the Father. Through His humanity
bestowed upon us we offer with Him, by Him, and through His
Spirit, that same offering which He makes by the one Spirit to
the Father. This then is our sacrifice. It is all one with the
sacrifice of Christ, which embraces in its unfaltering obedience and
charity the whole sweep of His experience from His conception
unto now; and it is conscious of this union in the memory of
Calvary, where the witness of the blood and the water spoke out
the hitherto for us unspoken devotion of the Son to the Father." [1]

A further instance of teaching which lays stress on the relation of the Eucharist to the heavenly offering of Christ may be
taken from a *Charge*, delivered in 1901, by Dr. C. C. Grafton,
the Bishop of Fond du Lac, in America, formerly, like Father
Benson and Father Waggett, a member of the Society of St.
John the Evangelist. After explaining the need of sacrifice in
religion, and the different aspects and modes of sacrifice, Bishop
Grafton says:—

"Christ . . . offered Himself on Calvary with shedding of
blood for the reconciliation of mankind as the victim on the brazen
altar. He is offered in the Eucharist for His covenanted people
without shedding of blood like as the shew bread was placed on the
holy table and the blood on the altar. Christ presents Himself in
glory as the life that has passed through death just as the blood
was presented before the mercy seat. Christ's offices being eternal,
in all these cases He is the Priest and Victim, the High Priest for
ever and the Lamb. In all three He is the Offerer and the Offered.
What is their relation to one another ? Let us consider first that of
the sacrifice of the altar to that of Calvary. In that the Priest and
the Victim are in each case the same, the two are identical. If the
actual immolation of the victim is the essence of sacrifice, then,
since there is no actual slaying of the Victim in the Eucharist, the
Eucharist is not a sacrifice. If sacrifice is an ordained oblation
which man offers to God, and through which God gives back some
gift to man, it is a true and proper sacrifice. At the altar there is
by the breaking of the bread and separate consecration of the cup a
mystical immolation of Christ's body and blood. In this same sense
it may be termed a sacrifice. Granting it to be a true and proper

[1] Pp. 32-34.

sacrifice, and so far alike with Calvary, in what way is it like and in what way does it differ from it? It is like it in all of its fourfold aspects. It is a sacrifice of praise and thanksgiving. . . . It is also a sacrifice of prayer. . . . It is also . . . a propitiatory sacrifice. . . . The Eucharistic sacrifice is one with that of Calvary in all its four aspects. In what do they differ? In one the Victim is actually slain, in the other there is only a mystical immolation. One is the bloody, the other the unbloody sacrifice. One was unique and can never be repeated, the other is capable of continued repetition. One was offered for humanity, for our race, the other is offered for those in covenant with Christ.[1] One was a sufficient sacrifice, the other is an efficient sacrifice. . . . Our Lord representing humanity made for humanity on the cross the fourfold offering due from humanity, and God and man by His action were reconciled. By offering the Eucharistic sacrifice, we appropriate and plead Christ's sacrifice on Calvary for our individual needs. . . . What is the relation of the sacrifice of the altar to that in heaven? In heaven Christ as ever a High Priest, must have somewhat eternally to offer, and Holy Scripture declares what that offering is when He is seen there as the Lamb of God. If the essence of sacrifice is an actual or mystical oblation, then there is no sacrifice in heaven. But, if sacrifice is the law of the creature's relation to God wherever he may be, then the worship of heaven must express that law. It may be objected that sacrifice is an act, that the sacrifice on Calvary was an

---

[1] This restriction of those for whom the Eucharist is offered to those who are "in covenant with Christ" would not be universally allowed by those who regard the Eucharist as a sacrifice. The Liturgy of the *Apostolic Constitutions* contains prayers both before the dismissal of the catechumens and after the consecration for persecutors and those without the Church and in error; see *Const. Ap.* viii. 10, 12. In a letter written about 427 St. Augustine mentions prayer at the altar for unbelievers as well as for catechumens and the faithful, though about 419 he had restricted those for whom the sacrifice is offered to members of Christ: see *Ep.* ccxvii. 2; *De Anima*, i. 10, 13, ii. 15, 21, iii. 18; *Retract.* i. 19 (7). See also the restriction in St. Thomas Aquinas, *S.T.* III. lxxix. 7. In the present Roman Missal the prayers in the canon are all for members of the Church, but at the offering of the chalice the priest speaks of the sacrifice as being "for our salvation and for that of the whole world". It is taught in the Church of Rome that prayers for living unbaptised or excommunicated persons may be connected with the Mass, if the object is their conversion or restoration: see St. Thom. Aq. *Sent. IV.* xii. 2 (2, 2, ad 4), cit. vol. i. p. 327, *supra*; Lehmkuhl, *Theol. Mor.* ii. §§ 175-81; Schouppe, *Elem. Theol. Dogm.* xiii. §§ 326, 327. *Cf.* the Bishop (Wordsworth) of Salisbury's *The Holy Communion*, pp. 63-65, and the present writer's *The Holy Communion*, pp. 274-77.

act, but that the oblation of Christ in heaven is a state, and hence cannot be a sacrifice. But it is not with God or our Lord as with us creatures. We must either be in action or in repose. It is not so with God. As cause rightly understood connotes the two ideas of action and finality or rest, so it is with the great first Cause. God is at once unceasing activity and eternal rest. So it is with our Lord. He abides in the passionless tranquillity of the eternal life, yet His saints will follow the Lamb in all the marvellous developments of His majestic operations wherever He goeth. He who is at once action and repose is the Priest and Oblation in the glory of the Blessed Trinity. The sacrifice of the altar is one with that in glory, because it is the same oblation." [1]

X.

The formularies of the Scottish Church, the American Church, and the Irish Church are in the main the same as those of the Church of England; but there are in each case one or more distinctive features in regard to the Eucharist.

1. In 1764, a revision of the Scottish Liturgy by the Primus, Bishop William Falconer of Moray, afterwards Bishop of Edinburgh, and Bishop Robert Forbes of Ross and Caithness, was printed with the title *The Communion-Office for the Use of the Church of Scotland, as far as concerneth the Ministration of that Holy Sacrament*.[2] This is the recognised standard text of the Scottish Communion Office. The authority for the use of this Office in the Scottish Church has to some extent varied. The fifteenth of the canons of 1811, while giving liberty to retain the English Office wherever it had previously been in use, enacted that "the Scottish Communion Office shall be used in all consecrations of bishops; and that every bishop, when consecrated, shall give his full assent to it as being sound in itself, and of primary authority in Scotland, and therefore shall not permit its being laid aside, where now used, but by the authority of the College of Bishops". In the revised canons of 1828 the twenty-sixth canon, which corresponded to the fifteenth canon of 1811, gave power to the bishop of the diocese to approve a change from one Office to the other, and no longer required

[1] Pp. 14-18.
[2] This edition is reprinted in reduced facsimile in the Bishop (Dowden) of Edinburgh's *The Annotated Scottish Communion Office*, pp. 133-56.

the authority of the College of Bishops for laying aside the
Scottish Office. The twenty-first canon of 1838 declared the
Scottish Office to be "the authorised service of the Episcopal
Church in the administration of the Sacrament"; ratified the
permission "to retain the use of the English Office in all congregations where" it "had been previously in use"; forbade any
alteration from one Office to the other without the approval
of the bishop of the diocese; and enacted that the Scottish
Office "continue to be held of primary authority in this Church,
and that it shall be used not only in all consecrations of bishops,
but also at the opening of all general synods". In 1863 the
twenty-ninth canon declared the English Book of Common
Prayer to be the service book of the Scottish Church "for all
the purposes to which it is applicable," and forbade any departure from it "except so far as the circumstances of this
Church require, and as specified in the canons of this Church".
The thirtieth of the same canons enacted that the adoption
of the English Book of Common Prayer as the service book of
the Scottish Church should not affect the use of the Scottish
Office where previously existing; that such a previously existing
use of the Scottish Office should be continued "unless the in-
cumbent and a majority of the communicants shall concur in
disusing it"; that the English Office should be used in all new
congregations unless the majority of the applicants desiring
the formation of the new congregation should ask the bishop
of the diocese to sanction the use of the Scottish Office, in which
case the bishop shall sanction the use of the Scottish Office,
and the use of it shall continue "unless the clergyman and a
majority of the communicants shall concur in disusing it"; that
the bishop of the diocese, "subject to an appeal to the episcopal
synod," may refuse an application for the use of the Scottish
Office, if he think that "any undue influence has been exercised";
and that the English Office should be used "at all consecrations,
ordinations, and synods". In 1876 these canons were re-enacted.
In 1890 the twenty-ninth canon of 1863 and 1876, which became the thirty-third canon, was to some extent altered, but
still enacted that the English Book of Common Prayer is "the
duly authorised service book of this Church for all the purposes
to which it is applicable," and forbade any departure from it
"except so far as the circumstances of this Church require and

as specified in these canons"; the thirtieth canon of 1863 and 1876 was excluded from the consideration of the synod, and remained in force, and was printed without alteration as the thirty-fourth canon. It appears, therefore, that from 1811 to 1863 the Scottish Office was of primary authority in the Scottish Church, and the use of the English Office was in certain circumstances allowed; and that from 1863 to the present time the English Office has been of primary authority, and the use of the Scottish Office has been in certain circumstances allowed. In point of fact the use of the Scottish Office seems to have first declined and then, at any rate on some occasions, increased while in point of law it has had a reduced degree of authority. It has been stated that in 1850, out of 118 congregations forty used the Scottish Office; in 1888, out of 275 congregations, fifty-nine used the Scottish Office only, and thirty-three used both the Scottish and the English Offices; and in 1899 the Scottish Office was used either jointly or solely in nearly half the congregations, the chief use of the Scottish Office being in the dioceses of Aberdeen, Argyll, and Brechin, and the chief use of the English Office being in the dioceses of Edinburgh and Glasgow.[1] In the Scottish Office the Sursum corda and Preface and Sanctus follow the Offertory, and are followed by the recital of the institution, the oblation, the invocation of the Holy Ghost, the prayer for the whole state of Christ's Church, and the Lord's prayer in the following form :—

"All glory be to Thee, Almighty Father, for that Thou of Thy tender mercy didst give Thy only Son Jesus Christ to suffer death upon the cross for our redemption; who (by His own oblation of Himself once offered) made[2] a full, perfect, and sufficient sacrifice, oblation, and satisfaction, for the sins of the whole world, and did institute, and in His holy gospel command us to continue a perpetual memorial of that His precious death and sacrifice until His coming again. For in the night that He was betrayed, He took bread; and

[1] These statistics are given in Proctor and Frere, *A New History of the Book of Common Prayer*, pp. 229, 230.

[2] It is suggested with much probability by the Bishop (Dowden) of Edinburgh in his *The Annotated Scottish Communion Office*, p. 338, that the omission of "there," which is in the English Office and the Scottish Office of 1637, is due to the view that Christ did not offer Himself on the cross : see pp. 610, 611, 617, 621, 622, *infra*.

when He had given thanks, He brake it, and gave it to His disciples, saying, Take, eat, THIS IS MY BODY, which is given for
you: DO this in remembrance of Me.   Likewise after supper He
took the cup; and when He had given thanks, He gave it to them,
saying, Drink ye all of this, for THIS IS MY BLOOD of the new
testament, which is shed for you and for many for the remission of
sins: DO this as oft as ye shall drink it in remembrance of Me.
Wherefore, O Lord, and heavenly Father, according to the institution of Thy dearly beloved Son our Saviour Jesus Christ, we Thy
humble servants do celebrate and make here before Thy divine
majesty, with these Thy holy gifts, WHICH WE NOW OFFER UNTO THEE,
the memorial Thy Son hath commanded us to make; having in remembrance His blessed passion, and precious death, His mighty resurrection, and glorious ascension; rendering unto Thee most hearty
thanks for the innumerable benefits procured unto us by the same.
And we most humbly beseech Thee, O merciful Father, to hear us,
and of Thy almighty goodness vouchsafe to bless and sanctify, with
Thy word and Holy Spirit, these Thy creatures of bread and wine,
that they may become the body and blood of Thy most dearly beloved Son.   And we earnestly desire Thy fatherly goodness mercifully to accept this our sacrifice of praise and thanksgiving, most
humbly beseeching Thee to grant that by the merits and death of
Thy Son Jesus Christ, and through faith in His blood, we (and all
Thy whole Church) may obtain remission of our sins, and all other
benefits of His passion.   And here we humbly offer and present
unto Thee, O Lord, ourselves, our souls and bodies, to be a reasonable, holy, and lively sacrifice unto Thee, beseeching Thee, that
whosoever shall be partakers of this Holy Communion may worthily
receive the most precious body and blood of Thy Son Jesus Christ,
and be filled with Thy grace and heavenly benediction, and made
one body with Him, that He may dwell in them, and they in Him.
And, although we are unworthy through our manifold sins to offer
unto Thee any sacrifice, yet we beseech Thee to accept this our
bounden duty and service, not weighing our merits, but pardoning
our offences, through Jesus Christ our Lord: by whom, and with
whom, in the unity of the Holy Ghost, all honour and glory be
unto Thee, O Father Almighty, world without end.   Amen."
   " Let us pray for the whole state of Christ's Church.
   "Almighty and everliving God, who by Thy holy Apostle hast
taught us, . . .[1] truly serving Thee in holiness and righteousness

   [1] The part here omitted is identical with the corresponding part of the
prayer "for the whole state of Christ's Church militant here on earth"

all the days of their life. And we commend especially to Thy merciful goodness the congregation which is here assembled in Thy name, to celebrate the commemoration of the most precious death and sacrifice of Thy Son and our Saviour Jesus Christ. And we most humbly beseech Thee of Thy goodness, O Lord, to comfort and succour all those who in this transitory life are in trouble, sorrow, need, sickness, or any other adversity. And we also bless Thy holy name for all Thy servants, who, having finished their course in faith, do now rest from their labours. And we yield unto Thee most high praise and hearty thanks for the wonderful grace and virtue declared in all Thy saints, who have been the choice vessels of Thy grace, and the lights of the world in their several generations, most humbly beseeching Thee to give us grace to follow the example of their steadfastness in Thy faith, and obedience to Thy holy command-ments, that at the day of the general resurrection we, and all they who are of the mystical body of Thy Son, may be set on His right hand, and hear that His most joyful voice, Come, ye blessed of My Father, inherit the kingdom prepared for you from the foundation of the world. Grant this, O Father, for Jesus Christ's sake, our only Mediator and Advocate. Amen.

" *Then shall the presbyter say* :—

" As our Saviour Christ hath commanded and taught us, we are bold to say :—

Our Father . . . For ever and ever. Amen."

After the short exhortation, confession, absolution, comfort-able words, and prayer of humble access, the directions for the administration are given. The species of bread is called "the sacrament of the body of Christ". The words of administration are "The body of our Lord Jesus Christ, which was given for thee, preserve thy soul and body [1] unto everlasting life"; "The blood of our Lord Jesus Christ, which was shed for thee, pre-serve thy soul and body [2] unto everlasting life"; and in each case the person receiving was directed to [say "Amen". After the

used at an earlier point in the English Office, except that in the Scottish Office (1) no name is added to the words "Thy servant our king"; (2) "bishops, priests, and deacons" occurs instead of "bishops and curates"; and (3) the words "and specially to this congregation here present" do not occur. In later editions the name of the reigning sovereign has been inserted in the Scottish Office.

[1] In later editions the words are "body and soul".

[2] Here also "body and soul" in later editions.

administration the use of the words "Having now received the
precious body and blood of Christ, let us give thanks to our
Lord God" is ordered. In the event of a further consecration
being needed, the use of the whole prayer from "All glory be
to Thee" to "that they may become the body and blood of
Thy most dearly beloved Son" is directed.

2. In 1784 Samuel Seabury was consecrated as first Bishop
of the American Church, to be Bishop of Connecticut, by the
Primus of the Scottish Church, Bishop Robert Kilgour of Aberdeen, Bishop Arthur Petrie of Moray and Ross, and Bishop
John Skinner, then Coadjutor Bishop of Aberdeen. He recom-
mended to his congregations in Connecticut a Communion Office
differing very slightly from the Scottish Office. In 1789 the
American Communion Office was drawn up and agreed to by
the Convention of the American Church. In the American
Office the prayer "for the whole state of Christ's Church militant" follows the Offertory; the short exhortation, confession,
absolution, and comfortable words precede the Sursum corda;
and the prayer of humble access follows the Sanctus, as in the
English Office. As in the English Office too, the words of administration include the additions "Take and eat this in remembrance that Christ died for thee, and feed on Him in thy heart
by faith, with thanksgiving," "Drink this in remembrance that
Christ's blood was shed for thee, and be thankful"; and there is
no direction for the words "Having now received the precious
body and blood of Christ" after the administration. In other
respects, it is based on the Scottish Office, though with some
important difference. In the recital of the institution "one
oblation" is substituted for "own oblation"; and in the invocation of the Holy Ghost the words "that they may become the
body and blood of Thy most dearly beloved Son" are altered to
"that we, receiving them according to Thy Son our Saviour
Jesus Christ's holy institution, in remembrance of His death and
passion, may be partakers of His most blessed body and blood".
In the Catechism the answer to the question "What is the inward part, or thing signified," is "The body and blood of
Christ, which are spiritually taken and received by the faithful
in the Lord's Supper".

In connection with the American Prayer Book it is interesting to notice a careful account by Bishop Seabury of the doctrine

which he held in the sermon *On the Holy Eucharist* in his book *Discourses on Sacred Subjects,* which was published at New York in 1793. It is the same as that of many of the Nonjurors, for instance as that of Thomas Deacon,[1] namely that the effect of the recital of the institution is to make the bread and wine representations of the body and blood of Christ; that after being made such symbols they are presented to God the Father as a sacrificial oblation; and that through the invocation of the Holy Ghost they become the body and blood of Christ in power and efficacy. Seabury regards the sacrifice of Himself by our Lord as having been offered at the institution of the Eucharist, and considers His crucifixion as having been merely passive, not an act of sacrifice. Like some of the writers of the Reformation period,[2] he uses the phrase "natural body," to denote the body of Christ which was born of the Virgin and suffered on the cross in its present glorious state in heaven as well as in its state of humiliation during His mortal life on earth. His teaching of the Nonjuring doctrine is linked with his explicit rejection of Transubstantiation, Consubstantiation, Receptionism, and Zwinglianism. He claims that the beliefs which he expresses are those of " the early writers and first liturgies of the Christian Church," " the first Reformers in England," " the First Prayer Book of King Edward VI.," " a great number of eminent divines of the Church of England," and " the present doctrine and practice of the venerable remains of the old Apostolical Church of Scotland ".[3]

"When those Christian sects who retain the institution come to explain its nature and design, they differ widely in their sentiments, . . . one teaching that the bread and cup are by the priest's repeating the words of Christ, 'This is My body; this is My blood,' over them converted or transubstantiated into the natural body and blood of Christ, that very body and blood which He assumed in the womb of the Virgin, and which suffered on the cross. Another denies Transubstantiation, and affirms that the bread and wine are not changed into the natural body and blood of Christ upon the minister's pronouncing, 'This is My body; this is My blood'; but only that the body and blood of Christ are thereby consubstantially united to the bread and wine. A third teaches that upon the repetition of those

---

[1] See pp. 481-83, *supra.*   [2] See *e.g.* pp. 37, 57, 135, *supra,*
[3] I. 180, note.

words no alteration at all is made in the bread and wine; but that they are only made or designated to be memorials or symbols of Christ's body and blood, on the receiving of which the souls of believers by and through the energy of their own faith receive spiritually the flesh and blood of Christ, are made partakers of the benefits of His passion, and of that Holy Spirit with which His humanity was anointed. Lastly, some who call themselves Christians do consider the bread and wine merely as remembrances to put us in mind of the death of Christ, and seem to require no qualifications in the recipients but to remember at the instant that Christ died on the cross to attest the truth of the doctrines He taught, nor do they appear to expect either grace or remission of sins from this Holy Sacrament. Attentive consideration will, I think, convince us that neither of these opinions is reconcilable with the institution of the sacred ordinance; and a very moderate acquaintance with primitive Christianity will make us sensible that neither of them can be reconciled to the sentiments which the first Christians entertained of it." [1]

"That there was . . . a great and real change made in the bread and the cup by our Saviour's blessing and thanksgiving and prayer cannot be doubted. Naturally they were only bread and wine, and not the body and blood of Christ. When He had blessed them, He declared them to be His body and blood. They were therefore by His blessing and word made to be what by nature they were not. That Christ offered Himself, His natural body and blood, His humanity, to God, a sacrifice for the sin of the world, will, I presume, be readily acknowledged to be a Scripture doctrine. But, as the Scripture has not in direct terms told us when He did so, it becomes a matter of inquiry when it was done. I know it is commonly said that He offered Himself on the cross. But, however common the opinion may be, it does not appear to me to have either Scripture or fact to support it. That He bore our sins in His own body on the tree, and that He was once offered to bear the sin of many, are expressions of Scripture. [2] But I know not that it is said in Scripture that Christ offered Himself on the cross. As far as I can perceive, the representation which the Scriptures give of the fact is decidedly against such an opinion. . . . It being admitted that Christ did offer Himself, His natural body and blood, His whole humanity, to God, a sacrifice for the sins of the world; and having been shown that He did not offer Himself on the cross, but was in everything that related to His crucifixion merely passive, it may be

[1] I. 165-67.   [2] 1 St. Pet. ii. 24; Heb. ix. 28.

asked, When did He offer Himself? I answer, In the institution of the Holy Eucharist." [1]

"As He could not wound and kill His own natural body, and shed His own blood, He made this offering in a mystery, that is, under the emblems of bread and wine. Therefore He took bread, and having blessed and consecrated it to be His representative body, He brake it to signify and represent the wounding and piercing of His body on the cross, which was then soon to happen; also the cup of wine and water mixed to signify and represent the blood and water which flowed from His dead body on the cross when the soldier pierced His precious side." [2]

"It having now been proved that Christ did at the institution of the Eucharist offer His natural body and blood to God an expiatory sacrifice for sin under the symbols and representation of bread broken and wine poured out, and consecrated by blessing and thanksgiving, and His Apostles being commanded to do this, that is, what He had done, in remembrance of Him, I ask, In what sense can this command be understood but as an injunction on them to offer bread broken and wine poured out, and consecrated by blessing and thanksgiving, to God as symbols of Christ's body and blood, and for a representation or memorial of His offering His natural body and blood to God, which He then made under the same representation? . . . Hence it will follow that the Eucharist is not only a memorial of the passion and death of Christ for the sin of the world but also of that offering of Himself, His natural body and blood, which under the representation of bread and wine He made to God at the institution of the holy ordinance. . . . Hence also it appears that the Eucharist is a memorial not so much before men as before the Almighty Father." [3]

"It appears therefore that the Eucharist is not only a sacrament in which under the symbols of bread and wine according to the institution of Christ the faithful truly and spiritually receive the body and blood of Christ, but also a true and proper sacrifice commemorative of the original sacrifice of Christ for our deliverance from sin and death, a memorial made before God to put Him in mind, that is, to plead with Him the meritorious sacrifice and death of His dear Son, for the forgiveness of our sins, for the sanctification of His Church, for a happy resurrection from death, and a glorious immortality with Christ in heaven. From this account the priesthood of the Christian Church evidently appears. As a Priest Christ offered Himself a sacrifice to God in the mystery of the

[1] I. 168-70.   [2] I. 172.   [3] I. 175, 176.

Eucharist, that is, under the symbols of bread and wine; and He commanded His Apostles to do as He had done. If His offering were a sacrifice, theirs was also. His sacrifice was original; theirs commemorative. His was meritorious through His merit who offered it; theirs drew all its merit from the relation it had to His sacrifice and appointment. His, from the excellence of its own nature, was a true and sufficient propitiation for the sins of the whole world; theirs procures remission of sins only through the reference it has to His atonement." [1]

"We may see in what sense the consecrated or eucharistised bread and wine are the body and blood of Christ. They are so sacramentally or by representation, changed in their qualities, not in their substance. They continue bread and wine in their nature; they become the body and blood of Christ in signification and mystery; bread and wine to our senses, the body and blood of Christ to our understanding and faith; bread and wine in themselves, the life-giving body and blood of Christ in power and virtue, that is, by the appointment of Christ and through the operation of the Holy Ghost, and the faithful receive in them the efficacy of Christ's sacrifice and death to all spiritual intents and purposes. There is therefore in this holy institution no ground for the errors of Transubstantiation, Consubstantiation, or the bodily presence of Christ, with which the Church of Rome, Luther, and Calvin have deceived, beguiled, and perplexed the Church. The bread and wine are in their nature still bread and wine. They are not transubstantiated into the natural body and blood of Christ, as the Papists teach. The natural body and blood of Christ are not consubstantiated with them, so as to make one substance, as the Lutherans teach. Nor are the natural body and blood of Christ infused into them, nor hovering over them, so as to be corporally received with them, as Calvin and his followers seem to teach, for they are far from being intelligible on the subject. The natural body and blood of Christ are in heaven, in glory and exaltation; we receive them not in the Communion in any sense. The bread and wine are His body and blood sacramentally and by representation. And, as it is an established maxim that all who under the law did eat of a sacrifice with those qualifications which the sacrifice required were partakers of its benefits, so all who under the Gospel eat of the Christian sacrifice of bread and wine with those qualifications which the holy solemnity requires are made partakers of all the benefits and blessings of that sacrifice

[1] I. 177.

of His natural body and blood which Christ Jesus made when under the symbols of bread and wine He offered them to God a propitiation for the sin of the world." [1]

" The officiating bishop or priest [2] first gave thanks to God for all His mercies, especially for those of creation and redemption. Then, to show the authority by which he acts and his obedience to the command of Christ, he recites the institution of the Holy Sacrament which he is celebrating, as the holy evangelists have recorded it. In doing this he takes the bread into his hands and breaks it, to represent the dead body of Christ torn and pierced on the cross, the cup also of wine and water mixed representing the blood and water which flowed from the dead body of Christ when wounded by the soldier's spear. Over the bread and the cup he repeats Christ's powerful words, 'This is My body, This is My blood'. The elements being thus made authoritative representations or symbols of Christ's crucified body and blood are in a proper capacity to be offered to God as the great and acceptable sacrifice of the Christian Church. Accordingly, the oblation, which is the highest, most solemn, and proper act of Christian worship, is then immediately made. Continuing his prayer, the priest intercedes with the Almighty Father to send upon them (the bread and wine) the Holy Spirit, to sanctify and bless them, and make the bread the body, and the cup the blood, of Christ, His spiritual life-giving body and blood in power and virtue, that to all the faithful they may be effectual to all spiritual purposes. Nor does he cease his prayer and oblation till he has interceded for the whole Catholic Church, and all the members of it, concluding all in the name and through the merit of Jesus Christ the Saviour. The Eucharist being, as its name imports, a sacrifice of thanksgiving, the bread and wine, after they have been offered or given to God, and blessed and sanctified by His Holy Spirit, are returned by the hand of His minister to be eaten by the faithful as a feast upon the sacrifice, the priest first partaking of them himself, and then distributing them to the communicants, to denote their being at peace and in favour with God, being thus fed at His Table, and eating of His food, and also to convey to the worthy receivers all the benefits and blessings of Christ's natural body and blood, which were offered and slain for their redemption. For this reason the Eucharist is also called the Communion of the body and blood of Christ, not only because by communicating together we declare our mutual love and good-will, and our unity in the

[1] I. 178-80.   [2] That is, in the early liturgies.

Church and faith of Christ, but also because in that holy ordinance we communicate with God through Christ the Mediator by first offering or giving to Him the sacred symbols of the body and blood of His dear Son, and then receiving them again, blessed and sanctified by His Holy Spirit, to feast upon at His Table for the refreshment of our souls, for the increase of our faith and hope, for the pardon of our sins, for the renewing of our minds in holiness by the operation of the Holy Ghost, and for a principle of immortality to our bodies as well as to our souls. . . . It is a sensible pledge of God's love to us, who, as He hath given His Son to die for us, so hath He given His precious body and blood in the Holy Eucharist to be our spiritual food and sustenance." [1]

3. The English Book of Common Prayer was approved by the Irish Convocation in 1662; and the use of it was enjoined by the Irish ·Parliament in 1666. There are some allusions to Eucharistic doctrine in the Irish *Form of Consecration or Dedication of Churches and Chapels, together with what may be used in the Restauration of Ruined Churches, and Expiation of Churches Desecrated or Prophaned*, which was published in 1666 with the *imprimatur* of the Archbishop of Armagh and the Archbishop of Dublin.[2] The name of the compiler is not known; and, though the *Form* was to some extent used, it does not appear to have received any official sanction on the part of the Irish Church. The allusion to the eternal sacrifice perpetually presented in heaven in the prayer said before the altar is of considerable interest :—

" *Then the bishop arising from his chair shall kneel before the altar or Communion Table, and say* :—

" Let us pray.

" O Eternal God : who in an infinite mercy to mankind, didst send Thy holy Son to be a sacrifice for our sins and the food of our souls, the Author and Finisher of our faith, and the great Minister of eternal glory ; who also now sits at Thy right hand, and upon the heavenly altar perpetually presents to Thee the eternal sacrifice, a never ceasing prayer, be present with Thy servants, and accept us in the dedication of a ministerial altar, which we humbly have pro-

---

[1] I. 181-83.

[2] Copies of the original edition are extremely rare. The *Form* is printed at the end of many editions of the Irish Prayer Book. It is reprinted in *Hierugia Anglicana*, iii. 194-225, edition 1904.

vided for the performance of this great ministry, and in imitation of Christ's eternal priesthood, according to our duty and His commandment. Grant that all the gifts which shall be presented on this Table may be acceptable unto Thee, and become unto Thy servants a savour of life unto life. Grant that all who shall partake of this Table may indeed hunger after the bread of life, and thirst for the wine of elect souls, and may feed upon Christ by faith, and be nourished by a holy hope, and grow up to an eternal charity. Let no hand of any that shall betray Thee be ever upon this Table; let no impure tongue ever taste of the holy body and blood which here shall be sacramentally represented and exhibited. But let all Thy servants that come hither to receive these mysteries come with prepared hearts, and with penitent souls, and loving desires, and indeed partake of the Lord Jesus, and receive all the benefits of His passion. Grant this for His sake, who is the Priest and the Sacrifice, the Feeder and the Food, the Physician and the Physic of our souls, our most Blessed Lord and Saviour Jesus. Amen."

After the passing of the Act for the Disestablishment of the Irish Church in 1869, the formularies of that Church were revised by the Representative Body of the Church. No alteration was made in the Thirty-nine Articles. The Communion Office of the English Book of Common Prayer was not altered, except in some rubrics [1] and by the provision of additional collects at the end of the Office. Nothing in the Catechism was omitted or altered, but the following question and answer were added :—

"*Question.* After what manner are the body and blood of Christ taken and received in the Lord's Supper?

"*Answer.* Only after a heavenly and spiritual manner; and the mean whereby they are taken and received is faith."

The fourth of the *Constitutions and Canons Ecclesiastical* decreed in 1871, 1877, and 1899 forbids the wearing of any vestment or ornament other than surplice, bands, scarf, hood, and for preaching a plain black gown if the minister shall wish; and the thirty-fourth, thirty-fifth, thirty-sixth, and thirty-seventh for-

---

[1] The most important changes in the rubrics are the direction that the priest shall say the Prayer of Consecration "standing at the north side of the Table," which is explained in canon 5 to mean "that side or end of the Table which in churches lying east and west is towards the north," and the requirement of "three (or two at the least) of the people to communicate with the priest".

bid the Communion Table to be other than "a movable Table of wood," the use of lights "except when they are necessary for the purpose of giving light," the use of a cross on or behind the Communion Table or on the covering of it, "the elevation of the paten or cup beyond what is necessary for taking the same into the hands of the officiating minister, the use of wine mixed with water, or of wafer bread, and all acts, words, ornaments, and ceremonies other than those that are prescribed by the Order of the Book of Common Prayer". In the preface of the Revised Book it was said :—

"As concerning the Holy Communion, some of our brethren were at first earnest that we should remove from the Prayer Book certain expressions, which they thought might seem to lend some pretext for the teaching of doctrine concerning the presence of Christ in that Sacrament repugnant to that set forth in the Articles of Religion, wherein it is expressly declared that the body of Christ is given, taken, and eaten in the Supper only after an heavenly and spiritual manner, and that the mean whereby it is therein received and eaten is faith ; but, upon a full and impartial review, we have not found in the formularies any just warrant for such teaching, and therefore in this behalf we have made no other change than to add to the Catechism one question with an answer taken out of the twenty-eighth of the said Articles. As for the error of those who have taught that Christ has given Himself or His body and blood in the Sacrament, to be reserved, lifted up, carried about, or worshipped, under the veils of bread and wine, we have already in the canons prohibited such acts and gestures as might be grounded on it, or lead thereto ; and it is sufficiently implied in the Note at the end of the Communion Office (and we now afresh declare) that the posture of kneeling prescribed to all communicants is not appointed for any purpose of such adoration, but only for a signification of our humble and grateful acknowledgment of the benefits of Christ, which are in the Lord's Supper given to all worthy receivers, and for the avoiding of such profanation and disorder as might ensue if some such reverent and uniform posture were not enjoined."

This preface, although expressed with great caution and apparently intended to be such as could be accepted by any who were accepting the English formularies, appears to interpret the Declaration on Kneeling at the end of the Communion Office in such a way as to make "adoration" "unto any corporal presence of Christ's natural flesh and blood" equivalent to "adoration" of "Christ" "Himself or His body and blood in the Sacrament" "under the veils of bread and wine".[1]

XI.

It is probable that the Eucharistic doctrine of the Scottish theologians of the eighteenth century, who were chiefly responsible for the Communion Office of 1764, greatly resembled that of the Nonjuring divines.[2] The revision of 1764 was perhaps chiefly due to the effect of the influence of Bishop Thomas Rattray,[3] who became Bishop of Dunkeld in 1727, whose work *The Ancient Liturgy of the Church of Jerusalem*, with an appendix *An Office for the Sacrifice of the Holy Eucharist, being the Ancient Liturgy of the Church of Jerusalem*,[4] was published in 1744 after the death of its author. His opinions may be seen in his book *Some Particular Instructions Concerning the Christian Covenant*, which was published posthumously in 1748. His Eucharistic doctrine was that the Eucharist is a sacrifice of the body and blood of Christ in the sense that the elements are made to be the "symbols" and "antitypes" of the body and blood at the recital of the institution, are then offered to God the Father in the oblation as the representatives of the body and blood, and have "the virtue and power and efficacy" of the body and blood communicated to them at the invocation of the Holy Ghost; he also speaks of the elements after the invocation of the Holy Ghost as being "verily and indeed" Christ's "body and blood," and made "one with" Christ's body. Like Bishop Seabury,[5] he held that our Lord "did" "offer up Himself a free and voluntary sacrifice" at the institution of the Eucharist, that "this sacrifice of Himself was immediately after slain on the cross," that He "entered into heaven" "to present this His sacrifice to God the Father and in virtue of it to make continual intercession for the Church". He writes :—

[1] For the meaning of the Declaration on Kneeling, see pp. 318-21, *supra*.

[2] See pp. 474-83, *supra*.

[3] See the Bishop (Dowden) of Edinburgh's *The Annotated Scottish Communion Office*, pp. 93-96.

[4] Reprinted in Hall, *Fragmenta Liturgica*, i. 151-78.

[5] See pp. 610-14, *supra*.

"It is by the virtue of these words spoken by Christ [that is, the words of institution] that the following prayer of the priest is made effectual for procuring the descent of the Holy Ghost upon them whereby they become the spiritual and life-giving body and blood. . . . As Christ offered up His body and blood to God the Father under the symbols of bread and wine as a sacrifice to be slain on the cross for our redemption, so here the priest offereth up this bread and cup as the symbols of this sacrifice of His body and blood thus once offered up by Him, and thereby commemorateth it before God with thanksgiving; after which He prays that God would favourably accept this commemorative sacrifice by sending down upon it His Holy Spirit, that by His descent upon them He may make this bread and this cup (already so far consecrated [that is, by the recital of the words of institution] as to be the symbols or anti_ types of the body and blood of Christ and offered up as such [that is, in the oblation]) to be verily and indeed His body and blood, the same divine Spirit by which the body of Christ was formed in the womb of the Blessed Virgin, and which is still united to it in heaven, descending on and being united to these elements, and invigorating them with the virtue, power, and efficacy thereof, and making them one with it.   Then the priest maketh intercession in virtue of this sacrifice thus offered up in commemoration of, and union with, the one great personal sacrifice of Christ, for the whole Catholic Church, and pleadeth the merits of this one sacrifice in behalf of all estates and conditions of men in it, offering this memorial thereof not for the living only but for the dead also." [1]

A document entitled *A Catechism Dealing Chiefly with the Holy Eucharist* dated " Leith, February 25th, 1737-8," which exists in a manuscript in the Library of the Theological College at Edinburgh,[2] has the interest and importance of being the work of Robert Forbes, who was born in 1708, became Bishop of Ross and Caithness in 1769, and died in 1775, to whom, as mentioned above,[3] together with Bishop Falconar, the compilation of the

---

[1] *Some Particular Instructions Concerning the Christian Covenant*, pp. 23, 24. The author sought in vain for a copy of this book in many libraries. He has to thank the Bishop of Edinburgh for telling him of one in the Library of the Edinburgh Theological College, and the Principal, Canon Mitchell, for allowing him to read and make extracts from it. This copy has the interest that it was the property of Bishop Alexander Jolly (see pp. 620-23, *infra*) and has his signature on the title page.

[2] Printed by the Bishop (Dowden) of Edinburgh in 1904.

[3] See p. 603, *supra*.

Scottish Communion Office of 1764 is due. The doctrine taught in this *Catechism* is that the consecrated bread and wine are the body and blood of Christ in power and virtue and effect. The most important parts are the following :—

"*Q.* What is the end and design of its institution ?

"*A.* To keep up a constant lively remembrance in our minds of the sacrifice of the death of Christ, and of the benefits which we receive thereby, which only can be done by frequent communicating.

"*Q.* What does the breaking of the bread represent ?

"*A.* The breaking or piercing of the body of Christ.

"*Q.* What does the pouring out of the wine represent ?

"*A.* The shedding of the most precious blood of Christ.

"*Q.* Is this Sacrament only a bare remembrance or memorial of Christ's death and sufferings ?

"*A.* No, it is more than that ; for by receiving of it we solemnly renew our baptismal vow ; and, if we partake worthily, we therein have the pardon of our former sins sealed unto us, and we receive new supplies of the grace of God to repair those breaches the enemies of our salvation have made, and to assist us to perform our duty for the time to come." [1]

"*Q.* Are not Christians to believe the consecrated bread in the Holy Eucharist to be the body of Christ, and the consecrated wine to be the blood of Christ ?

"*A.* Yes, certainly they are ; because our Saviour. Himself in His institution of this most holy Sacrament has expressly declared the bread to be His body and the wine to be His blood. . . .

"*Q.* In what sense are we to believe this mysterious doctrine ?

"*A.* Though we cannot believe that the bread and wine are the very natural and substantial body and blood of Christ that were upon the cross, yet we are to believe them to be so in a spiritual manner, that is to say, that the consecrated bread and wine are the body and blood of Christ in power, virtue, and effect.

"*Q.* By what power is this wonderful change made upon these weak elements of bread and wine ?

"*A.* 'Tis certain (as I have already said) from the words of institution that Christ did make the elements to be His body and blood ; for He expressly tells us they are so ; but no power inferior to His own could make them so. As therefore the Holy Ghost is His divine Substitute upon earth, by which He is present with His Church unto the end of the world, so whatever operations He now

---

[1] Pp. 7, 8 of Bishop Dowden's edition.

performs in His Church are wrought by that divine Spirit. Therefore, that the bread and wine may become His body and blood,
though not in substance, yet in power, virtue, and effect, it is necessary that this Holy Spirit should bless and sanctify them, and work
in them and with them. . . . The bread and wine are the body
and blood, not in themselves considered, nor merely by their resembling or representing the sacred body and blood of the adorable
Jesus, but by the invisible power and operation of the Holy Ghost,
by which the sacramental bread and wine, in the act of consecration, are made as powerful and as effectual for the ends of religion
as the natural body and blood themselves could be, if they were
present before our eyes.

" Q. Are there any similitudes in Scripture from the consideration of which this interpretation of our Saviour's words can receive
any light ?

" A. There are several similitudes to be found there which
might be condescended upon to clear up this point ; but there is
one in particular so much to the purpose that I shall pitch upon it
without mentioning any of the rest ; and it is this. St. John the
Baptist is by our Saviour . . . called the prophet Elias,[1] who had
flourished so many hundred years before his time, for this could
not readily be believed, seeing the time and place of St. John the
Baptist's birth were so well known. But the reason assigned why
he is called Elias is this, namely, Because he came in the spirit and
power of Elias.[2] . . . Even so, in the Holy Eucharist the consecrated bread and wine are called by Christians, and believed to be,
the body and blood of Christ according to His own positive declaration because attended with the same power, virtue, and effect for
the ends of religion that His natural body and blood could be, were
they existing with us." [3]

Like teaching is expressed by Dr. Alexander Jolly, who became Bishop of Moray in 1796 and died in 1838, in his book entitled *The Christian Sacrifice in the Eucharist Considered as it is
the Doctrine of Holy Scripture, Embraced by the Universal
Church of the First and Purest Times, by the Church of England, and by the Episcopal Church in Scotland.* Bishop Jolly
there maintains, in opposition to the doctrine of Transubstantiation and to the view that the Eucharist is a merely figurative
rite, that by the recital of the words of institution the bread and

---

[1] St. Matt. xvii. 12, 13 ; St. Mark ix. 13 ; Mal. iv. 5.
[2] St. Luke i. 17.   [3] Pp. 10-12.

wine are made the representative body and blood of Christ, that as such they are presented to God the Father in sacrifice, and that at the invocation of the Holy Ghost as placed in the ancient liturgies and in the Scottish Communion Office they are made the virtual life-giving body and blood of Christ, the body and blood of Christ in power and virtue and efficacy. He maintains also that Christ offered Himself in sacrifice at the institution of the Eucharist, and not on the cross, where He was simply the passive Victim.

"If we examine the whole sacred history of His life and death, we shall nowhere find this act [that is, the oblation of Himself] performed by Him but at His Last Supper, when He made this oblation, or gave Himself to suffer and die, under the symbols or substitutes of bread and wine. We cannot without shuddering horror think that He would lay violent hands on Himself, wound or break His own body, or shed out His own blood; and therefore He did—under representatives of His own appointment, authoritative figures of His body and blood, sure pledges of the real substance— give His body to be broken, and His blood to be shed by the hands of His crucifiers. And, in order to show, of His transcendent love to lost mankind, that His death in their stead, to redeem them from death, was voluntary, and entirely of His own free will, He made the oblation of Himself while to the eye of the world He was perfectly at liberty. . . . That this sacrificed passover might be eaten as a feast to His household the Church ever after, He performed the oblation of it in bread and wine, which He made His virtual flesh and blood. . . . The sacrifice was first offered, and then it was slain, as our Redeemer, the true and only meritorious sacrifice in reality, was once offered to bear our sins, offered by His own voluntary oblation of Himself in the institution of the Eucharist, that He might passively bear our sins in His own body on the tree of the cross." [1]

"Making the voluntary oblation or sacrifice of Himself under the symbols of bread and wine, and calling them, and in effect making them, His body and blood, broken and shed, while His natural substantial body, with His blood in His veins, unbroken and unshed, stood divinely ministering, and as yet untouched by any hostile hand." [2]

"Our divine adorable Redeemer did of His own free will with love unspeakable give Himself for us under substituted symbols or

[1] Pp. 52-55, edition 1831.   [2] P. 58.

representations, giving way and yielding Himself to the actual performance of the mactation or slaying of the sacrifice. In virtue of what He then did, and had given Himself up to suffer in His bitter agony and bloody death, He devoutly said in that most solemn prayer in the seventeenth chapter of St. John's Gospel—the prayer for the whole state and perfect unity of His Church, as it may well be called—which followed the oblation of Himself, ' I have finished the work which Thou gavest Me to do'. His part, by His thus willingly offering Himself to suffer and die, He had then finished. The remaining part was the bloody and malicious work of men and devils." [1]

"In the history of this divine institution, then, we clearly trace these three things which our Saviour did: 1. He took bread, and the cup of the Jewish paschal supper, and set them apart; separated or consecrated them so far as to be the representative figures, symbols, or substitutes of His body and blood. 2. He offered them in sacrifice to God, and thereby, or by these pledges, voluntarily gave or offered to God His body and blood as a sacrifice to be slain upon the cross for the sins of the whole world. 3. He blessed them that they might become His body and blood, not in bare figure or representation only, as they were made by His separation of them before, but in efficacy, power, and life-giving virtue. And as such He gave them with those words of delivery, which are the ground of our faith and hope, ' This is My body, which is given for you ' ; ' This is My blood, which is shed for you '." [2]

"The rehearsal of these words [that is, the words of institution], declaring the original institution, makes the first part of the consecration. The bread and wine are thereby separated and set apart from all common use, and raised to value beyond all the bread and wine in the universe, being by Christ's institution and authority made the figures and symbols of His body and blood who, of His wondrous love and desire for our salvation, offered Himself a sacrifice for our redemption under such tokens or substitutes, and commanded that we should by the apostolic priesthood plead the merits of His death under these representations to the end of the world. This most ancient Liturgy [that is, the Clementine] goes on accordingly to offer the Christian sacrifice of bread and wine—not as bread and wine, but as the representative body and blood of Christ—in the following words, ' Wherefore, having in remembrance His passion. . . .' [3] These are the oblatory words, by which the Eucharistic sacrifice is actually offered and presented to

---

[1] Pp. 58, 59.   [2] Pp. 68, 69.   [3] See vol. i. p. 86, *supra*.

the Father as the memorial of the infinitely meritorious passion and death of His Son, in whom He is ever well pleased, and for His sake looks propitiously upon us. This then is the second step or degree of the consecration, by which the elements are still farther sanctified as being presented and given to God and made His in a special manner, the image of His Son, as the Council of Constantinople (assembled in the year 754 to repress image-worship) called the bread and cup of the Eucharist.[1] And the office accordingly proceeds to beg His acceptance of them, and divine blessing upon them, thereby imparting to them the highest degree of consecration. . . . A prayer to this purpose [that is, the invocation of the Holy Ghost] and in this place we find in all the ancient liturgies, and we instantly see the piety and propriety of it. For surely that bread and wine, which have no natural virtue to that purpose, may be the means of conveying such inestimable blessings, they must have a supernatural virtue communicated to them by the Holy Ghost the Sanctifier, the Author of all benediction and grace." [2]

" By the almighty power and grace of this Spirit these elements without any change of their substance become the body and blood of Christ in spirit and power, in divine virtue and life-giving efficacy, to all intents and purposes of grace and glory." [3]

" Communion consists in giving and receiving ; and this representative sacrifice of the Eucharist, accordingly, is, first, by Christ's commissioned servant the priest offered or given to God as the mysterious body and blood of His Son, in whom He is ever well pleased, and then again given by God to us, the same bread and wine that were offered to Him, without any change of substance, but highly enriched and consecrated by the Holy Spirit, the Author of all consecration, and thus made Christ's body and blood in virtue, power, and efficacy, conveying to the well-disposed receiver all the benefits purchased by the sacrifice of His death, pardon of sins, increase of grace, and pledge of eternal glory, upon the condition of repentance, faith, and future obedience." [4]

An instance of teaching which thus appears to have been traditional among some Scottish Churchmen is in *The Christian Sacrifice in the Eucharist, or the Communion Office of the Church of Scotland Conformable to Scripture and to the Doctrine and*

[1] See vol. i. pp. 148, 149, *supra*. Bishop Jolly makes a similar reference to this council also on p. 189 of his book. It is of some importance that he appeals to this iconoclastic council and not to the Second Council of Nicæa : see vol. i. pp. 149, 150, *supra*.

[2] Pp. 98-100.   [3] P. 101.   [4] Pp. 176, 177.

Practice of the Church of Christ in the First Four Centuries, an unfinished work by Mr. George Hay Forbes, the first part of which was published in 1844, the second in 1851, and the third in 1854. The doctrine affirmed by Mr. Forbes is that by the recital of the institution the bread and wine are made pledges and representatives of the crucified body and shed blood of Christ; that they are then offered as a memorial and sacrifice; and that they are made the body and blood of Christ in energy and spirit and power and efficacy and by some unique and incomprehensible change at the invocation of the Holy Ghost.

"The Catholic doctrine . . . is that the bread and mixed wine are solemnly devoted to God's service, and offered as a thank-offering to Him for having bestowed upon us the fruits of the earth, by being placed upon His altar by a priest, with or without a verbal oblation, the want of which is supplied by the significant action. . . . By the recital of the institution our commission to celebrate this mystery is declared; and by the words used by our Lord at the delivery of the gifts the bread and mixed wine are deputed to be, and are made, the pledges and representatives of Christ's natural body crucified and dead, and of His blood shed for us; as such they are straightway, in accordance with Christ's command, which had just before been recited, offered or given to God as a memorial of our Lord's own oblation of Himself, with a thankful commemoration of what He did and suffered, and thus become truly a sacrifice of praise and thanksgiving. God the Father is then besought to accept the sacrifice, and to send down upon the gifts the co-eternal Comforter, the Source and Fountain of all sanctification, by whom the body of Christ was formed in the womb of the ever-blessed Virgin, that He may perfectly sanctify and hallow them, and make the bread the body of Christ, and the mixed wine His blood, not only in symbol, type, and figure, but also in quickening energy, in spirit and power and efficacy, nay more, in such wise as no other thing in the whole creation, retaining its own proper substance and nature, can become another thing, and the precise mode and manner of which change is far above the comprehension, not only of men, but of angels also." [1]

In the middle of the nineteenth century the controversies which were going on in England were not unknown in Scotland; and they became acute in 1857. In that year Dr. Alex-

[1] I. 19-21.

ander Penrose Forbes, who had been appointed Bishop of Brechin in 1847, delivered his *Primary Charge*. In this *Charge* Bishop Forbes maintained that "the bread of the Eucharist is the flesh of the incarnate Jesus"; rejected Transubstantiation as involving "the terminology of a philosophy which may be wrong," and, though "capable of an innocent interpretation," yet tending "to promote a very material view" "as if a physical change took place in the consecration," and not allowing for the testimony of the fathers concerning the continued existence of the outward part of the Sacrament; rejected also "the rationalistic theory of the real presence which makes it one of power and efficacy only," albeit "the later Nonjurors and some of the ornaments of our own Church have used language which seems to advocate this imperfect view"; affirmed that "in some sense the wicked do receive Christ" at their Communion "to their condemnation and loss"; affirmed that "supreme adoration is due to the body and blood of Christ mysteriously present in the gifts which yet retain their own substance," and that "worship is due not to the gifts but to Christ in the gifts"; and declared that "the Eucharistic sacrifice is the same substantially with that of the cross".[1] The Bishop strongly defended the use of the Scottish Office, though saying:—

"My own attachment to this Office is not a bigoted one. I have no sympathy with those few earnest men who scruple to use the English Office, nor with those who look upon the question as a national one. I use the English Office constantly myself; I believe its consecration is valid, and in validity there can be no question of degree. As it stands at present, I regard it as a sad mutilation of the first Office of the Reformers, as an Eucharistic service 'more marred than any,' but still, thanks be to God, preserving all the essentials of a true Sacrament."[2]

A protest against the teaching contained in the *Charge* of Bishop Forbes was issued by Bishop Terrot of Edinburgh, Bishop Ewing of Argyll, and Bishop Trower of Glasgow; and in 1858,

[1] Pp. 3, 17, 18, 26, 27, 28, 40, third edition. For Bishop Forbes's later explanation of the sense in which he used the word "substantially," see p. 627, note 2, *infra*.

[2] P. 53

after a synod held at Edinburgh, a *Pastoral Letter* signed by those three bishops and by Bishop Eden of Moray and Ross, Bishop Wordsworth of St. Andrews, and Bishop Suther of Aberdeen, that is, all the Scottish Bishops except Bishop Forbes, was addressed to " all faithful members of the Church in Scotland ". Parts of the *Pastoral* commented in severe terms on the *Charge* of Bishop Forbes ; it contained the following instructions to the clergy :—

" 1. Instructed by Scripture and the formularies of the Church, you will continue to teach that the consecrated elements of bread and wine become in a mystery the body and blood of Christ, for purposes of grace to all who receive them worthily, and for condemnation to those who receive the same unworthily. But you will not, we trust, attempt to define more nearly the mode of this mysterious presence. You will remember that, as our Church has repudiated the doctrine of Transubstantiation, so she has given us no authority whereby we can require it to be believed that the substance of Christ's body and blood, still less His entire Person as God and Man, now glorified in the heavens, is made to exist with, in, or under the material substances of bread and wine.

"2. You will continue to teach that this sacrifice of the altar is to be regarded no otherwise than as the means whereby we represent, commemorate, and plead, with praise and thanksgiving, before God the unspeakable merits of the precious death of Christ, and whereby He communicates and applies to our souls all the benefits of that one full and all-sufficient sacrifice once made upon the cross.

" 3. You will continue to teach that the consecrated elements, being the Communion of the body and blood of Christ, are to be received with lowly veneration and devout thankfulness. And inasmuch as doubts have been raised with regard to the true interpretation of the rubric affixed to the Communion Office in the Book of Common Prayer,[1] we desire to remind you of a canon which was passed by the Convocations of both provinces of the Church of England in 1640, and which we are satisfied to accept meanwhile for our own guidance in determining the sense of the aforesaid rubric, the matter not having been ruled by a general synod of our own Church. According to that canon, it was resolved that gestures of adoration in the celebration of the Holy Eucharist are to be performed ' not upon any opinion of a corporal presence of the body of Jesus Christ

---

[1] That is, the English Book of Common Prayer.

on the Holy Table, or in mystical elements, but only for the advancement of God's majesty, and to give Him alone that honour and glory that is due to Him, and no otherwise'." [1]

In 1859 Bishop Forbes was formally presented to the Episcopal College of the Scottish Church for teaching

"doctrines contrary and repugnant to, unsanctioned by, and subversive of certain of the said Articles of Religion, and by consequence contrary and repugnant also to the word of God ; and also contrary and repugnant to, unsanctioned by, and subversive of certain parts of the said formularies for public worship in use in the said Episcopal Church in Scotland contained as aforesaid in the said Book of Common Prayer, and also contrary and repugnant to, unsanctioned by, and subversive of the said Scotch Communion Office " ;

and, in particular, for his teaching in regard to the Eucharistic sacrifice, Eucharistic adoration, and the reception by the wicked. At the trial in 1860, Bishop Forbes put in an elaborate *Theological Defence*, in which he maintained at length the consistency of his beliefs with the teaching of the fathers, and with Anglican writings and formularies.[2] The judgment of the court, which was delivered on 15th March, 1860, was to the effect that the teaching of Bishop Forbes in regard to the Eucharistic sacrifice and to Eucharistic adoration was " unsanctioned by the Articles and formularies of the Church " and " to a certain extent inconsistent therewith " ; that the third charge relating to the reception by the wicked was "not proven " ; and that the duty of the College of Bishops would be best discharged by limiting their sentence on Bishop Forbes to "a declaration of censure and admonition ".[3] In his work entitled *An Explanation of the Thirty-*

. [1] For this canon, see p. 254, *supra*. It was in consequence of the *Pastoral* quoted above that Mr. Keble wrote his *Considerations ;* see pp. 528-32, *supra*.

[2] His explanation that in the sentence "the Eucharistic sacrifice is the same substantially with that of the cross," he had used the word "substantially " " in its strict theological sense," meaning that "the sacrifice, in respect to its substance, namely, the body and blood of Christ, is the same as that of the cross," is of some importance : see *Theological Defence*, p. 13.

[3] See *Guardian*, 21st March, 1860. The Bishop (Ewing) of Argyll, who had signed the protest against Bishop Forbes's *Charge* and the *Pastoral Letter* of the Scottish bishops (see pp. 625, 626, *supra*), was prevented by illness from attending the trial, and wrote on 12th March to the Primus that

40 *

nine Articles, the first edition of which was published in 1867, Bishop Forbes gave fresh expression to the doctrines which he had maintained in his *Primary Charge* and *Theological Defence ;* and, to illustrate his position, it may be well to quote some passages from this book on the Eucharistic presence and sacrifice :—

"The word κοινωνία everywhere in Holy Scripture means an actual participation or communion of that which is spoken of. The Scripture word κοινωνία, as applied to the body and blood of Christ, means not only that we receive that body and blood, but that we become one body and blood with Him. . . . This patristic explanation of the word κοινωνία disposes of the formula whereby Calvin endeavoured to steer a middle course between the Lutheran teaching on the one hand, and that of Zwingli and Oecolampadius on the other.[1] He taught that the body of Christ is truly present in the Lord's Supper, and that the believer partakes of it ; but he only meant that simultaneously with the bodily participation of the material elements, which in every respect remained what they were, and merely signified the body and the blood, a power emanating from the body of Christ, which is now in heaven only, is communicated to the spirit. Framed originally under the pressure of the confusions among the Reformed, this middle opinion made its way among them, and included many of the Lutherans themselves, as its advocates employed without hesitation the expression that Christ is really present in the Eucharist, and His body and blood given to believers for participation. In England, in consequence of the great authority of Richard Hooker, who, in the gradual process of working himself out of Puritanism, had on this mysterious doctrine attained to Catholic feeling, while he adhered to Calvinistic definition,[2] this view has obtained to an extent remarkable in view of its intrinsic inanity. . . . The word κοινωνία disposes also of what has been termed the theory of virtualism or equivalence.[3] . . . It is not said in the

he could not concur in any judgment which should go " beyond exhorting " Bishop Forbes "to abstain from speculative teaching on the subject of the Holy Communion," and expressed some doubt as to whether even so much in the way of censure as this would be just in all the circumstances of the case. See *Guardian,* 21st March, 1860.

[1] For the teaching of Luther, Zwingli, Oecolampadius, and Calvin, see pp. 9-24, 37-43, 50-56, *supra.*

[2] For Hooker's teaching, see pp. 239-49, *supra.*

[3] For instances of this theory, see *e.g.* pp. 127-29, 501-06, *supra.*

Article that we are partakers of Christ, or of a grace from Christ, but the bread which we break, that is, the bread which has been blessed and consecrated by our Lord's words, 'This is My body,' through the operation of the Holy Ghost is the communion or participation of the body of Christ; and the cup of blessing, that is, the cup blessed by the words, 'This is My blood,' is the partaking of or communication of the blood of Christ." [1]

"The doctrine of the real objective presence being certainly true, as being contained in our Blessed Lord's words, 'This is My body,' and attested by the whole Christian Church from the times of the Apostles, it follows that some sort of change must have taken place as to the elements through consecration. . . . This change was in the oldest time expressed by the simplest terms, 'It is,' 'It becomes,' or in prayer to God 'consecrate,' 'perfect,' 'appoint,' 'make'. The Liturgy of St. Chrysostom, and others following him, use the words, 'changing by Thy Spirit'. There are also other more emphatic, yet rare words, occurring once or twice only in each father who used them, 'transmake,' 'transelement,' 'transfashion,' 're-order,' 'transfigure,' 'transfer'.[2] Against any of these the English Church has never made any exception, but only to a specified sense of the word 'transubstantiate,' which is popularly taken, not as implying a change in the οὐσία or 'essence' of a material thing, but the desition of the material substances of which that creature of God is composed." [3]

"The Article does not charge Transubstantiation with the common incorrect argument that it contradicts the senses, but that it overthrows the nature of a Sacrament. Now this greatly helps us in our view that it is not the abstract theory of a change, but the incorrect physics which are condemned. Such a change only is excepted against as would involve a physical desition of what before existed in such wise that the visible sign of That which is invisible should have no real existence." [4]

"There is but one belief [that is, of the Church of England and the Church of Rome] as to the presence of Christ, that He, 'our Saviour, who now sitteth at the right hand of the Father in heaven according to His natural mode of existence, is yet present to us by His substance sacramentally '.[5] The question [that is,

---

[1] Pp. 500-4, edition 1878.

[2] For instances of such phraseology, see vol. i. pp. 102-5, *supra.*

[3] Pp. 538, 539.   [4] Pp. 550, 551.

[5] Quoted from the Council of Trent, sess. xiii. cap. 1 : see p. 90, *supra.*

whether there is difference between the Church of England and the Church of Rome] has relation only to the bread and wine, what the Roman Church means by the '*substantia*' which it affirms to cease to remain, and we by the 'substances' which we affirm to remain. If ' substance' means no more than its Greek equivalent, οὐσία, 'essence'; and if the term 'is transubstantiated' means no more than those old words, 'becomes,' 'is'; and if, by it, the Roman Church only means to guard with greater accuracy our Blessed Lord's words, 'This is My body,' not contradicting anything which we know by experience, not basing a theology upon a supposed illusion of our senses, but only asserting that that '*quidditas*' (whatever it be) whereby the bread was bread is removed, leaving all those forces of which alone we are cognisant, then God be thanked, who has said to a great mountain which stood between us, 'Be thou a plain'. There is nothing in such a statement which our Article denies, or which could form a difficulty to any soul which believed the blessed presence of our Saviour, of His body and His blood." [1]

"The sacrifice in the Eucharist is substantially [2] the same as the sacrifice of the cross, because the Priest is the same in both, and the Victim is the same in both, just as the sacrifice which Christ the eternal Priest is now presenting to His Father in heaven is the same which He offered upon the cross, because He Himself is the same Victim and Priest both in one. But there is a difference. There is a difference in the manner of offering. In heaven Christ is not offering Himself in the same manner as He did upon the cross." [3]

"That one sacrifice [that is, the sacrifice of the cross] and its all-sufficient merits live on, as in our Lord's perpetual presentation of Himself in heaven, so in our Eucharistical oblation of His body and blood sacramentally present on our altars. We have nothing apart from that one sacrifice; our Eucharistic oblation is not something in and for itself, something independent of that one sacrifice, even while it pleaded it. Such is its union with that sacrifice that it is a perpetual application of its virtue, yet not as something distinct, but as united with it through the oneness of that which is offered, that same body of Christ offered on the cross to make atonement for the sins of the whole world and for each one of us, offered and presented to the Father in heaven and in the Church

---

[1] Pp. 558, 559.

[2] For the sense in which Bishop Forbes used this word in this connection, see p. 627, note 2, *supra*.

[3] P. 609.

below, on the 'altar above' and on the Holy Table, in pleading and for application of the atonement once wrought upon the holy cross. On the cross that offering was made once for all with shedding of blood; on earth the offering is made in an unbloody manner, as the ancient Church attests. On the cross that offering merited the salvation of the world; on the altar Christ being risen from the dead dieth no more, but the fruit of that death is made over to the faithful. On the cross the full satisfaction was paid; on the altar the memorial of that satisfaction is made to the Father in correspondence with the memorial made upon the celestial altar." [1]

" He offered Himself by anticipation at the Last Supper; He offered Himself in deed by His meritorious death on the cross; He offereth Himself by presenting Himself, our High Priest for ever, in the presence of the Father in heaven; He mystically offereth Himself in the Holy Eucharist, not only in that He consecrateth by His word the gifts which He has taught us to offer for a memorial of Himself, but that being sacramentally present He is 'precious in the eyes of the Father'. Yet because He is the agent in all, it follows not that He acts in the same way in all. On the cross He made the offering; in heaven He presents it, and as God-Man pleads it; on earth He giveth it to us to plead in that He consecrates that offering whose very presence pleads, in that it is in a mystery the body which was broken, the blood which was shed for us." [2]

" He is not in such wise a High Priest that He can be imagined separate from the sacrifice which He once offered. For that sacrifice was Himself. That sacrifice is His manhood, never to be divided from His Godhead. He has carried within the veil that holy body, once wounded for our transgressions, and those very wounds, which He showed to St. Thomas, now resplendent in glory, still move the Father to look upon the face of His anointed, and for His sake freely to give us all things. And as this is no derogation from the oneness and completeness of our Lord's atoning act on Calvary, so neither is a derogation therefrom that we in the Holy Eucharist with all our prayers present unto the Father the same holy body present in an ineffable way by the words of consecration." [3]

At the time of the presentation of Bishop Forbes to the Episcopal College of the Scottish Church for alleged false teaching in 1859, as already mentioned, all the other Scottish bishops were opposed to the Eucharistic doctrines advocated by him; and, although the diocesan synod of the diocese of Brechin passed a resolution approving his teaching with only two dissentients in 1860, it is probable that the opinions of the majority of the bishops were shared by very many Scottish Churchmen. In the years which have elapsed since, acceptance of the doctrines taught by Bishop Forbes has become more widely prevalent, though resisted or not assented to by a large part of the whole number of members of the Scottish Church; and some instances of like belief may be given from the *Book of the Charges* of the late Bishop of Argyll and the Isles, Dr. Chinnery Haldane, who died in 1906, which was published after his death.

"Have we realised that the sacrifices of the Old Testament, though they were divinely appointed and graciously accepted, were in comparison with the Eucharist, poor and weak? Have we realised that upon our altars we have no mere type or figure of an absent Christ, but the real presence of the Lamb of God who once for all died upon the cross, but who now ever lives, the abiding propitiation for our sins? Remembering all this, have we been eager on every possible occasion to offer up this holy sacrifice and to plead continually with the Eternal Father the merits and death of His dear Son, in order that we and all His whole Church, both the living and the departed, may obtain remission of our sins and all the other benefits of His passion?"[1]

"As to the Blessed Sacrament itself, what reverent care should we not exercise! Can we believe the words of our Lord Himself, 'This is My body, This is My blood,' and yet allow ourselves to be guilty of the very least act of irreverence or of carelessness with regard to that bread and that cup? What is true of the whole is true of every particle on the paten, and of every drop in the chalice. When, therefore, we think or speak about taking the ablutions, or about cleansing the sacred vessels, let us not allow ourselves to imagine that we are merely considering some minute details of ritual, to be observed only for form's sake, or ancient custom's sake, but let us realise that by doing or not doing our duty in this matter, we are honouring or dishonouring the sacred body and the precious blood of our Lord and only Saviour."[2]

"We cannot insist too earnestly on the objective reality of the presence of the body and blood of Christ our Lord in His Holy

[1] Pp. 4, 5.   [2] P. 32.

Sacrament, a reality which makes that holy mystery life and salvation to those who draw near with humility and penitent faith, but
condemnation and death to those who in unbelief or pride presume
to receive the same most Holy Sacrament unworthily, and who are
thus in no wise partakers of Christ.   But all this relates to what we
may call the manward aspect of the Eucharist.   There is, however,
another aspect of that holy mystery, of which we must never lose
sight, an aspect concerning which I think I may venture to say that
it is the more prominent of the two in the words uttered by our
.divine Lord at its institution, and in the general teaching of His
Church.   For the Holy Eucharist is not only a feast; it is also a
memorial.   Regarded in this light, we have its Godward aspect, and
we thus recognise it as an act of worship, or rather as the one great
and divinely appointed act of worship, the pure sacrifice of the
Church foretold by the prophet Malachi, the sacrifice which im-
measurably exceeds in reality and power the figurative sacrifices
of the Old Testament, even as the blood of Christ our God, who
once for all suffered upon the cross, is infinitely more precious than
the blood of bulls and goats shed in those sacrifices of the law of
.Moses, which could never make the comers thereunto perfect.   And
this brings us to the root of the matter.   The Eucharist is what it
is because it is the showing of the Lord's death, the pleading of
His all-prevailing merits. . . .   It cannot be denied that both
anciently and modernly there has been the disposition . . . to deny
or to obscure the vital truth of redemption through the sacrificial
death of Jesus Christ.   Now, against all such baneful tendencies
the Holy Eucharist has been a perpetual witness from the beginning.
. . . The sacrifice of the Holy Eucharist is thus essentially the
divinely appointed memorial of Christ's propitiatory death.   Here
is its prominent characteristic.   There can be in the Holy Eucharist
no communion with our risen and ascended Lord, nor with one
another as members of His mystical body, no partaking of His flesh
and blood, no eating and drinking at His Table, apart from that
sacrifice. . . .   All our hopes as sinners are built upon that sacrifice
which our Blessed Saviour has offered for us by His death upon the
cross, and which He ever lives to plead on our behalf in the heavenly
. sanctuary." [1]

"The thought of the Holy Eucharist, in which we thus show
the Lord's death till He shall come again, very naturally leads us
on to the thought of His second and glorious appearing.   The Lamb
of God, to whom we now offer worship in the Blessed Sacrament,

[1] Pp. 119, 120, 122, 123, 124, 125.

hidden beneath the veils of bread and wine, and seen only by the eye of faith, will then be manifested to all, for every eye shall see Him." [1]

"It is a certain truth that at all times and under all circumstances we live and move and have our being in the divine presence of our Blessed Saviour, because He is true God as well as true Man. For, if we believe that He is one with the Father and the Holy Spirit in the undivided glory of the ever-blessed Trinity, we must also of necessity believe that He is omnipresent. But, guided by His holy word and by His Church, we believe something besides this. For we believe that, though He has ascended into heaven in His human nature—in which nature He there lives and reigns according to His natural mode of existing (*juxta modum existendi naturalem*) —yet that in His condescending love He, the same Lord Jesus Christ, gives to us under the forms of bread and wine, and through the operation of the Holy Ghost, a supernatural presence of His most blessed body and of His most precious blood. . . . It is in response to this great love and divine condescension on the part of our Blessed Saviour that His people are impelled to render to Him in His Holy Sacrament, and in all that concerns that Holy Sacrament, I will not say reverence merely—for that would be too cold a word—but every token of adoring love by which it is possible to manifest the most entire devotion of which the human heart is capable. For He, the Lamb that was slain, is worthy to receive honour and glory and blessing for ever and for ever both in the unveiled majesty of His heavenly kingdom and also wherever on this poor earth, which is the footstool of His throne, He manifests to the faith of His humble disciples the sacramental presence of His most holy body and of His most precious blood." [2]

XII.

A brief statement is needed as to the Eucharistic doctrine of non-episcopal religious bodies. Since the time of the Westminster Assembly [3] and of the foreign Protestant Confessions of the Reformation period [4] most of the non-episcopal bodies in England and abroad, except those Lutherans who have maintained the beliefs of Luther, [5] have held opinions either Calvinist [6] or Zwinglian. [7] The very remarkable attempts of the Lutheran

---

[1] P. 126.   [2] Pp. 209-11.   [3] See pp. 308-12, *supra.*
[4] See pp. 24-37, 48-50, 56-61, *supra.*
[5] See pp. 9-24, *supra.*   [6] See pp. 50-56, *supra.*
[7] See pp. 37-43, *supra.*

theologian Godfrey William Leibnitz towards the end of the seventeenth century to promote a reconciliation between Roman Catholic and Protestants abroad, which should include the allowance of the doctrine of Transubstantiation or a doctrine not strongly distinguished from it, wholly failed.[1] As to the teaching of the non-episcopal theologians in the nineteenth century and at the present time, a very few representative instances may suffice.

Among the more eminent Lutheran theologians of the nineteenth century were the Danish Dr. Martensen and the German Dr. Dorner. Both these writers adopt the later Lutheran doctrine of a gift of the body and blood of Christ under the veil of the elements, but not so closely associated with the elements as to imply that they are the body and blood apart from the administration and reception of the Sacrament. Dr. Dorner in his *System of Christian Doctrine* says :—

"In the Supper . . . believers are to be made directly partakers of the body and blood of Christ as the true Paschal Lamb, and therewith of His Personality, His merit and life. Certainly it is founded also in memory of Him, and this element ought not to be undervalued, precisely because it recalls most definitely the intention of Jesus, that it should be repeated. It is ordained in remembrance of Him, and therefore for the future. . . . What is the more precise meaning of the words of institution? They are not handed down to us in uniform terms, from which it may justly be inferred, since the early Church received these different forms without opposition, that they all contain what is essential. At least the essential part must not be discovered in that in which they vary. Now, that ἐστί may mean 'signifies' is beyond question, and ought never to have been denied. In proof, it is enough to refer to the interpretation of the parables. The meaning then certainly is : The bread is a figure of My body. . . . Since . . . the elements in the sacred act exist to be partaken of, and are partaken of, denoting consequently a gift to be received, and since the words 'Eat, drink,' cannot mean a past or future gift, all that

[1] Leibnitz was born in 1646 and died in 1716. For his attempts at reconciliation alluded to above, see his book, probably written about 1684 but not published till 1819, over a hundred years after his death, usually known as *Systema Theologicum*. In Leibnitz's MS. the book is without title, and it has also been called *Expositio Doctrinae Ecclesiae Catholicae*, and *Examen Religionis Christianae*.

is left to be said is : The symbolism denotes a present gift offered
to be partaken of ; the elements are aliments.   But that which is
offered under the symbolic veil of the elements is described by
Christ in the words ' My body,' and ' My blood,' by which, in
opposition to anything merely ideal or merely material, is meant
the entire reality of His Personality, Christ Himself with body
and blood ; and in order to understand the full meaning of the
act instituted for all future time, we must go back to the import
of Christ's Person in general, and its relation to believers as their
Head, to His parable of the vine and branches, to His words of
promise, such as, ' Where two or three are gathered together in
My name, there am I in the midst of them' ; ' Lo, I am with you
always, even to the end of the world' ;[1] further, to His exaltation to be the Head of the Church and the glorification of His
entire Person ; finally, in general to His loving purpose, which
desires to give Himself with princely generosity unreservedly to
His people. . . . It was in keeping with the indefiniteness and
looseness of the relation of the elements to the thing that the
elements played an independent part alongside the Sacrament as
a Communion, and were specially employed in divine worship.
Since sacrificial gifts were also joined with the Supper as thank-
offerings for the benefits of Christ, the Holy Supper became a
' Eucharist,' and a sacrifice, certainly not of Christ, but of the
earthly sacrificial gifts.   The Supper was only changed into the
Sacrificium of the Mass after the earthly elements had vanished
into a mere semblance through the Transubstantiation-doctrine of
Paschasius Radbert and Lanfranc.   Christ's body and blood were
put in their place, and treated in just the same way as the elements
had been before, namely, as a sacrifice. . . . The view taken by
the Lutheran Church of the connexion of Christ with the elements
is not so rigid that it approves the above expressions[2] (which are
rather expressly rejected), or that it makes a material imprisonment
of Christ (*impanatio*) take place.   Further, the *unio sacramentalis*
with the elements is not made so indissoluble as to take place also
extra usum.   The presence of Christ is not to be conceived after
the manner of the presence of the elements (not locally), but a
modus supernaturalis of the presence obtains ; and the view is
earnestly repudiated that the *manducatio oralis* is a *Capernaitica* one,

---

[1] St. Matt. xviii. 20, xxviii. 20.

[2] That is, such expressions as that the body of Christ *dilaniatur et
dentibus laceratur*.   For Luther's acceptance of such phraseology, see p.
21, *supra*.

for only the elements, not Christ's body and blood, experience a
lacerari dentibus. . . . Not merely does the universal Lutheran
doctrine affirm that the unworthy do not receive the spiritual blessing annexed to faith, although the sacramental contents are objectively present to man along with the elements, and are presented,
that is, offered, to every one, but a difference is made between the
spiritual and material eating. . . . The notion of partaking of Christ,
or at least of His body and blood, as a punitive Judge is incongruous,
because partaking affirms a union or assimilation, whereas the Judge
stands outside and above Him who is punished. . . . Every theory
must in the end go back to the promise of Christ, to the effect
that He desires to be the present gift in the Supper. That promise
implies, therefore, that the present Christ really offers Himself
through the entire act to every one taking the outward elements,
consequently to unbelievers also. As Christ truly and earnestly
offers grace in the word, and as far as He is concerned not merely
to believers, so is it in the Holy Supper. The objective grace exists
for all, and this is the essential point; but there is a difference in
the taking, and hence in the effect also. As unbelief only receives
the sensible word with the bodily ear, while the inner ear or heart
is closed to the meaning and truth of the word, so too may it be
in the Holy Supper. The saving blessing is rejected by the unbeliever, therefore not accepted. And since the unbeliever takes
the elements like the believer, and Christ offered Himself in the
act in which the unbeliever takes part under the guise of a believer,
unbelief renders void Christ's promise and purpose, which held
good also to him, by this wicked, hypocritical conduct; and whereas
he receives nothing but the elements, thus making the Sacrament
a common eating or empty ceremony, he sins against the Lord and
draws down judgment on himself. . . . The God-man received by
faith through the Holy Spirit is the real power that reconciles all
antitheses, the antitheses of nationalities and individuals, in the
last resort even the antithesis between nature and spirit. In Him
is given the new and true humanity, in which likeness to God is
realised also in the world, appearing in His glorified corporeity.
Hence the Holy Supper is also a real bond of communion between
all the members. Every individuality is destined to be trans-
figured through Him, and made a reflex of His glory. And for
this very reason, through the instrumentality of the faith that
receives Christ, the Holy Supper operates also as the principle of
reconciliation between all antitheses in the individual personality,

and therefore as the principle of pneumatic corporeity such as will be exhibited in the resurrection-body." [1]

Like teaching to this of Dr. Dorner's is contained in Dr. Martensen's *Christian Dogmatics.*

"The Lutheran doctrine is opposed not only to the doctrine of Transubstantiation, but to the Calvinistic separation of heaven and earth likewise.   Christ is not in a literal manner separate from His believing people, so that they must go to heaven in order to find Him.   Christ is on the right hand of God; but the right hand of God is everywhere.   *Dextera Dei ubique est.*   And therefore He is present wholly and entirely (*totus et integer*) in His Supper, wherein He in an especial manner wills to be.   There are not in the ordinance two acts, one heavenly and one earthly, distinct from each other, but the heavenly is comprehended in the earthly and visible act, and is organically united therewith, thus constituting one sacramental act.   The heavenly substance is communicated in, with, and under the earthly substances.   And as the sacramental Communion is not a partaking of the corporeal nature of Christ apart from His spiritual nature, no more is it a mere partaking of the spiritual nature of Christ apart from His corporeity.   It is one and undivided, a spiritual and corporeal communion. . . . The idea which lies at the foundation of the Lutheran doctrine regarding the Lord's Supper . . . is . . . the idea of Christ as the Head of that new creation whose final end is the redemption and perfecting of human nature as a whole, as undivided body and soul. . . . The Lutheran view of the Lord's Supper . . . sees . . . not only, like Calvin, an aliment for the soul, but an aliment for the whole new man, for the future man of the resurrection, who is germinating and growing in secret, and who shall be manifested in glory in exact likeness with the glorified humanity of his Lord. . . . The whole and undivided Christ gives Himself as the aliment of the new man in the Lord's Supper. . . . The act here in question is not a literal eating of Christ according to the notion of the Jews at Capernaum, but it is one whereby we are made partakers of Christ as the principle of the entire new creation of man, and of the future humanity of the resurrection which shall be revealed in that day.   Here we have to do, not with a presence of Christ literally defined according to the category of place, but with a presence in which the higher heavenly sphere invisibly penetrates the lower

---

[1] §§ 143-45 (vol. iv. pp. 308, 311-15, 319, 320, 329, 330, English translation).

and the earthly, a presence in power, in working, in gift; for in His gifts He gives Himself. . . . It follows . . . that the Calvinistic notion that Christ is present only for the faithful must be rejected. For the word and command of God, not the faith or devotion of man, make the Sacrament; and as the seed-corn is the same, whether it fall into good or into bad ground, so is it with the Sacrament. . . . Unbelievers also who partake of the Sacrament come into actual relation with the All-holy; and, though we cannot say of them that they eat the Sacrament, that is, make it their food, yet we must say that they receive it. . . . It is not weakness of faith, nor deficiency in doctrinal insight, which causes a person to eat condemnation to himself. It is the unhallowed sense which fails to discern the Lord's body, to discern between the holy and the profane, and which draws nigh to the Table of the Lord without preparation or self-examination. As we oppose the Calvinistic principle that the presence of Christ is conditional upon faith, we equally reject the Romish representation that the consecrated bread and the consecrated wine are the body and blood of Christ apart from the receiving thereof. For the presence of Christ in the Eucharist extends only so far as the words of institution extend; but the words of institution are inseparable from the distribution and the receiving of the bread and wine. The Lord has instituted His Supper as one undivided act, and to separate one single element from the ordinance for a holy use is arbitrary and without promise. We therefore reject the adoration of the host in the Romish Church, a rite which depends upon the doctrine of Transubstantiation and the notion connected therewith of the sacrifice of the Mass. . . . The doctrine of Transubstantiation expresses a false relation of unity of the kingdom of nature and of grace, because the former is interwoven with the latter. . . . The Calvinistic doctrine regarding the Lord's Supper rests upon an overt principle of dualism between the kingdom of grace and that of nature, a dualism so thorough that the Lord's Supper is literally divided into two distinct acts, the one in heaven, the other on earth. . . . The Lutheran doctrine regarding the Lord's Supper rests neither upon a dualism between nature and grace nor upon a transformation of the one into the other, but upon an inner marriage of the heavenly and earthly substance. But this inner marriage of the supernatural and the natural, of the heavenly and earthly, is the fundamental feature of Lutheranism, and is reflected in its whole worship, in all its services, in its poetry, in its customary world-life." [1]

[1] §§ 264-69 (pp. 436-42, English translation).

A representative instance of the kind of Eucharistic doctrine prevalent among many non-episcopal Christians is to be seen in the teaching of the eminent Wesleyan theologian of the nineteenth century, Dr. William Burt Pope, in his treatise entitled *A Compendium of Christian Theology*. The Eucharist is there described as a memorial among Christians of the sacrifice of Christ, and a sign and pledge of the salvation and nourishment received from Christ. Dr. Pope writes :—

"The Lord's Supper is a rite ordained by our Lord for perpetual observance in His Church as a sacramental feast in which bread and wine are signs of His sacred body and blood offered in one oblation on the cross, and seals of the present and constant impartation to the believer of all the benefits of His passion. In this Supper the Church joyfully and thankfully celebrates before the world the sacrifice once presented in the past, until He come again without sin unto salvation. Moreover, the Lord's people partake of the elements as the symbol of a common Christian life and sustentation, as the mutual pledge of union and brotherly fellowship, with all its enjoyments and obligations. Thus, this ordinance is the Sacrament, as it signifies and seals the mystical nourishment of Christ; the Eucharist, as commemorating the sacrifice of redemption ; and the Communion, as the badge of united Christian profession." [1]

"The true doctrine generally is that which bears in mind the design of the ordinance to be a sign to the believing Church of all the blessings purchased by the oblation of the one sacrifice for sins, and a seal to the believer of his constant and present interest in those blessings. Whatever other ends it subserves, as a perpetual memorial of the life and death of Christ, as a badge of union among Christian people, and as a sacred service in which all holy affections and purposes are quickened, it is also the abiding exhibition to the eye, in sensible emblems, of the blood of atonement and the bread of life, and also a pledge to those who accept the propitiation, as it is offered to penitent and believing faith, of their present and constant and eternal heritage of life in Jesus. Each of the terms sign and seal must have its full meaning preserved, while they are made one to the eye and hand and experience of living faith. That which the sign represents and the seal pledges is a benefit proceeding from Christ which must not be separated from Christ Himself. It is not the Holy Spirit save as He is the Spirit of Jesus." [2]

[1] III. 325, second edition.   [2] III. 334, second edition.

As an instance of modern Presbyterian teaching, some passages from Dr. J. C. Lambert's *The Sacraments in the New Testament*, the *Kerr Lectures* for 1903,[1] may be quoted :—

"We feel bound to maintain, on the plain evidence of the New Testament, and on every ground of historic probability as well, that Jesus both intended and instructed that the Supper should be repeated, and that His purpose was that it should become a regular ordinance for the Christian Church. So regarded, its meaning in the mind of Christ appears, in the main, to have been threefold :—

"(1) In the first place, it was designed to be a commemoration of His own death of sacrifice, by which the new covenant was established. This is shown by its connection with the memorial feast of the old dispensation out of which it sprang, as well as by the express injunction in which its chief purpose is clearly summed up, 'This do in remembrance of Me'.

"(2) In the next place, it was meant to be a means of communion. There was to be a real communion in it with Christ Himself, a truth which is indicated by the fact that Jesus not only used the bread and wine as symbols of His body and blood, but gave them to His disciples to eat and drink ; and, further, by the circumstance that, as His death was represented as the sacrifice of the new covenant, the Supper was thereby shown to be the covenant meal of the new dispensation, in which, as in other covenant meals, a genuine fellowship was established between the members of the covenant and their Head. In this latter aspect of it as a covenant feast, the Lord's Supper was also intended to be the occasion of a communion not only of Christians with Christ, but of fellow-Christians with one another.

"(3) Once more, it was the pledge of Christ's promised return, and a foretaste of a fuller fellowship between Him and His disciples in the consummated kingdom of God."[2]

"To sum up the doctrinal teaching of Paul with regard to the Lord's Supper, we may say :—

"1. In the first place, and this is his fundamental conception, the Supper is a commemoration of the Lord's death. This does not mean, however, that the celebration of the rite is nothing but

[1] It is of some interest that the Kerr Lectureship was originally a United Presbyterian Foundation attached to the United Presbyterian College in Edinburgh, and that Dr. Lambert's were the first lectures on the foundation delivered at the Glasgow College of the United Free Presbyterians after the union of the United and Free Presbyterians in 1900.

[2] Pp. 316, 317.

the raising of a monument beside the highway of time to a great historic fact of the past.   On Paul's lips the proclamation of the Lord's death on the part of Christians is the proclamation of His redeeming sacrifice, and so includes faith in Christ Himself as the Redeemer of His people.   And, as this faith, which the Apostle certainly assumes, is the basis of all communion with Christ, whatever special forms communion may take, it is absurd to attempt to make out any contradiction between the thought of the Supper as a commemoration and the thought of it as a communion and participation. Rather, in the very proclamation of the Lord's death there is a communion by faith with the Lord Himself, and an appropriation of the blessings that flow from His sacrifice.

"2. But, further, Paul looked upon the Supper as a communion with the Lord in a sense that is special and peculiar.   He did not imagine that Christ was objectively present in the elements, or that there was some specific religious content in the bread and wine, whether sensible or supersensible, which is communicated in no other way to the bodies and souls of Christian people.   But He believed that in this ordinance of His own appointing the Lord draws near to offer Himself with all the fruits of His redeeming death to faithful hearts, and that faith, quickened by seeing and touching and tasting the outward symbols, through which it is brought into direct historical contact with Him who first put the bread and the wine into the hands of His disciples, may be drawn out at the Supper with unusual warmth and freeness to conscious fellowship with the Saviour and conscious appropriation of His saving gifts.   And, further, He believed that in the Lord's Supper Christians may realise as nowhere else, not only their communion with Christ Himself, but their fellowship with one another in the unity of the body, of which Christ Jesus is the Head.

"3. Once more, although this is a thought to which he only alludes, Paul conceived of the Supper as containing within it the promise of the Lord's glorious return." [1]

With these expositions of Dr. Lambert may be compared some statements by Mr. R .M. Adamson of Ardrossan in his book *The Christian Doctrine of the Lord's Supper*, published in 1905 :—

"That at least in this great Action communicants make loving remembrance of their Lord is admitted upon all hands.   But, however precious this mode of remembrance may be (so precious is it that there can be no true Communion without it), we cannot

[1] Pp. 383, 384.

emphasise too strongly the fact that Christendom as a whole has ever been strenuous in maintaining that the Sacrament means a great deal besides, and that far more important than any devout or loving act on our part is the substantial gift bestowed upon us by God through this holy ordinance. . . . A supper enjoyed by guests is essentially something given by the host. . . . What exactly is the divine gift? . . . The nature and the greatness of that gift can be expressed only by saying that it consists of Christ Himself. The real gift to be obtained through the Sacrament is the Lord Jesus Christ Himself. . . . The expression 'the body and blood of Christ' signifies His whole Personality. . . . The richest and most liberal nature ever known among men is that of Jesus Christ. All who come in vital contact with Him know themselves to be gainers. In proportions largely conditioned by their own receptivity and faith, they feel that the divine life so abundant in Him tends to infuse itself into them. . . . If, then, this experience of Christ as properly a gift be found peculiarly real in the Supper, there should be no difficulty in attaching definite meaning to the assertion that what Christ gives therein is truly Himself, Himself in all the offices and relationships which He has sustained and does sustain towards mankind collectively and individually. In the Last Supper with His disciples, the first of the new covenant, He gave Himself to them in a manner conditioned by the circumstances. He being not yet crucified and risen, not yet perfected and glorified, the gift of Himself could not have that completed character which it afterwards assumed. Yet the first Communion was a true one, in that the partakers enjoyed a fresh reception of Christ through the sacramental medium. After the Lord had been sacrificed, after He had risen and ascended and shed forth His Pentecostal Spirit, after His disciples' eyes were opened to the significance of all that, the gift of God in His Son became unspeakably amplified. Henceforward the exalted Saviour carries within Himself the gathered force of all His redemptive achievement, and communicates that force to His people through all the media of grace, specially the Sacrament of His body and blood. And, finally, however little we may be able to imagine the precise mode in which the perfect communion of eternity is to be realised, it is promised that the heavenly period shall be gladdened by a blessed Marriage Supper, in which the affiance of Christ and His own shall be as intimate, as mutual, and as indissoluble as is the most ideal union between bridegroom and bride, the most unimpeded marriage of true minds. The proper gift, then, of the Sacrament is the manifold

41 *

entity of the God-Man as He now exists. . . . To assert the reality
of such a gift in the Sacrament is in some sort to assert the real
presence of Christ. . . . There should be no difficulty regarding the
general statement that Christ is present with His people in the
sacred action.   To state that fact is to affirm a real presence. . . .
To be conscious of Christ's presence is simply to be conscious of the
living energy of the Lord.   And, if the vital powers of His nature
are felt in the Eucharistic service, there can be no disadvantage but
rather a gain in predicating His presence.   Further, it would be
consistent with this to call such a presence objective. . . . The
theory which the present writer is endeavouring to construct certainly demands an objective presence of Christ amongst the communicants of His body and blood. . . . This is not to view the
Sacrament as a mode of existence for Christ apart from the presence
of communicating souls.   The simple idea of presence implies a
subject as well as an object.   It is to communicants as subjects
that Christ is objectively present: take away the subjects, and to
speak of presence at all is a meaningless use of words.   Hence our
insistence upon the necessity of faith on the part of communicants;
and hence the truth of the statement that it is in the believer's
heart that Christ's presence is realised.   When, therefore, we say
that Christ is in the Sacrament, we can only mean that He is mediately present therein. . . . We have consistently spoken of Christ
being present in the Sacrament as contrasted with the elements
merely.   The distinction is one of the highest importance ; and, if
it had more frequently been kept in mind, a considerable deal of
superstition might have been avoided.   When we say that Christ is
present in the Sacrament, what we strictly mean is that the Sacrament is a means whereby Christ makes Himself felt by His people.
. . . A real Communion involves faith in the Gospel of the Son of
God together with a whole series of ritual actions.   Of these actions
the principal are the gathering together in the name of Jesus, the
worship of God in prayer and praise, the hearing of His word read
and declared, the confession of sins and of faith in Christ, adhesion
to the Church as the body of Christ, recognition of the unity of the
members of the Church, the offerings of the faithful ; and then the
consecration of the elements by thanksgiving, blessing, or invocation, together with the pronouncement of Christ's words, followed
by the fraction and distribution ; also on the part of the communicants the believing reception, the dividing perhaps among themselves, along with all interior acts of devotion.   Here we have the
process of a great spiritual function, in the course of which Christ

makes Himself specially present as a Power and a Gift. . . . There is . . . no warrant for singling out bread and wine, or both together, and attempting to view them as the particular centres of the Lord's presence. Certainly within the Sacrament the things that answer pictorially to Christ's body and blood are the bread and wine, but the analytic attempt to press the identification is really a kind of afterthought which causes us to part company with the informing idea of the whole." [1]

" A great many outward and inward acts go to make up the great sacred action called the Lord's Supper, and every one of these acts is of the nature of those 'spiritual sacrifices acceptable to God by Jesus Christ'.[2] . . . If all prayer be . . . sacrificial, especially so is that prayer which is offered in the peculiarly holy circumstances of the Supper. . . . The element of thanksgiving, whether in praise, prayer, gifts, or services, is especially described in Scripture as being sacrificial, and the Eucharist is *the* Thanksgiving. . . . While the more real sacrifice of persons consists in character and conduct, yet Christians present their persons to God as they approach the Lord's Table. That aspect of sacrifice in which a material gift is prominent finds some place in the Eucharist. Every material thing necessary to its celebration, and devoted to that sacred purpose, is an offering or sacrifice to God. . . . The most costly of the material oblations consists in the money gifts made at Communion. . . . With regard to all such acts of worship and offering there is . . . express Scriptural sanction for speaking of them as sacrifices. Needless to say, however, they are on a plane altogether inferior, and in a category altogether different from the one and only sacrifice of the world's Redeemer. . . . True as it is that Christ's mediatory life in heaven is a life for us, the introduction of the appellation sacrifice is somehow not altogether happy. And, even if it were from some points of view appropriate, the Eucharist cannot under this head be called sacrificial. At best it could only be a means of grace in dependence upon Christ's heavenly mediation." [3]

The teaching of Dr. Lambert and that of Mr. Adamson are not wholly identical, and both of them are expressed in view of the circumstances of recent times. In their essential features they closely resemble the doctrine which has been taught by many Anglican divines, as, for instance, by Bishop Beveridge.[4]

An interesting treatment from a Presbyterian source of the

---

[1] Pp. 149-56, 163-67.   [2] 1 St. Pet. ii. 5.
[3] Pp. 179-82, 187.   [4] See pp. 450-55, *supra.*

idea of the heavenly sacrifice of Christ and the connection of the
Eucharist with it rejected by Mr. Adamson in the last two of
the sentences quoted above is in the *Baird Lecture* for 1891,
The Ascension and Heavenly Priesthood of our Lord, by Dr.
William Milligan, then Professor of Divinity and Biblical Critic-
ism in the University of Aberdeen.

"There can be no doubt that in" "the Eucharistic Service of the
Church" "the idea of offering is more fully and forcibly expressed than
in any other Christian ordinance, or that the Church has throughout
her history felt this to be the case. With the exception of a com-
paratively small number in recent times, her members have never
been able to rest in the idea that the Sacrament of the Supper is
simply a memorial of the death of Christ. They have beheld in it,
in one sense or another, an offering which they make to God, as well
as a remembrance of what God has done for them. . . . The offering . . . made in the Eucharist is not an offering of death. . . .
The Eucharist is an oblation in which the offerer, offering himself,
lives, having accepted death as the penalty of sin in Him who died
upon the cross ; but having now through death entered into life, the
life of Him who died once, and dieth no more. As the Lord's
offering of Himself to His heavenly Father never ends, or can end,
so in that offering His people, organically united to Him, one with
Him, must be offered, and must offer themselves ; and this they do
in the expressive and touching symbols of the Eucharist. They do
not simply remember what Jesus did on earth. They bring to remembrance as a present fact what He is doing in heaven. They
commemorate, they hold communion with, they accept, and at His
Table are nourished by, a living Lord,—'in remembrance of Me,' of
Me, not as I was, but as I am, to the end of time. Christ Himself,
spiritually present with them, is the life of their souls ; His body
and blood there given them are the substance of their feast ; and
living in Him, and obtaining in Him pardon, peace, and strength,
they transact here below what He is transacting in the heavenly
sanctuary. In the Sacrament of the Supper, in short, they offer
themselves in Him who is now and for ever an offering to the
Father." [1]

XIII.

One of the chief marks of the history of Eucharistic doctrine
in the Church of England in the nineteenth century was the re-

[1] Pp. 265, 266.

vival of clear and definite teaching that the body and blood of Christ are present in the Sacrament under the form of bread and wine, and that the Eucharist is a sacrifice of the body and blood so present. Emphasis has been laid by some writers who have adopted this general standpoint on the spiritual character of the body of Christ since His resurrection, and therefore in heaven and in the Eucharist; and on the identity between the sacrifice offered by our Lord in heaven since His ascension and the sacrifice offered in the Church on earth. The most prominent and best equipped teachers who have advocated positions opposed to this theology have not maintained Zwinglian doctrines such as had been widespread in the Church of England since the time of the *Plain Account* ascribed to Bishop Hoadly, or merely virtualistic doctrines which had been frequent both before and after that time; but have asserted the spiritual presence of Christ throughout the celebration of the rite and the spiritual reception of Christ by the souls of the communicants on making their Communion. While Zwinglianism and mere Virtualism have been more widely held among non-episcopal bodies, still, at any rate among some Lutherans abroad and some Presbyterians at home, there has been much teaching of a real spiritual gift and a real feeding of the soul on Christ in the reception of the Eucharist.

CHAPTER XVII.

CONCLUSION.

THE aim of this book is historical. It has been the purpose of the writer to tabulate and classify facts. He has tried to record opinion, and, so far as has been possible, to abstain from passing judgments on it. To him it has seemed that the collection of evidence has in itself been a work which is worth some little pains. But he may be allowed to point out that the historical treatment of doctrine has also its practical value as it aids towards an estimate of the right methods of interpreting Holy Scripture and towards knowledge of the authoritative decisions of the Church, of the judgments of the collective Christian consciousness, of the beliefs of representative teachers, of the extent and limits of agreement at notable periods of Church life. And, further, at the conclusion of his historical survey, he may be allowed to express his mind on three practical topics which emerge from it.

I.

A significant fact in Christian history is the width of the appeal made by the rite of the Eucharist. In times so different as the first century and the tenth and the twentieth, at every intervening moment of Christian life, the Eucharist is seen to be acknowledged as the chief privilege of the Christian religion. In whatever ways it may have been used, and however it may have been explained, its pre-eminence is unquestionable. What is true about times is true also about places. The men of the East and of the West, the men of Northern Europe and of Southern Europe differing in some respects not less than Westerns and Easterns, those who are the devoted adherents of the Pope and those who have renounced or never acknowledged his distinctive claims, those who cherish the name of Catholic and those who delight to describe themselves as Protestant, alike

648

regard the Eucharist as an essential element in the religion of Christ. They would agree that, where a sect exists which excludes it, or if a national religion should arise which should make no provision for it, there must be recognised a departure from Christian principles so grave as to make the sect or the religion other than Christian.[1] It is touching to notice the language of devotion which men of most divergent beliefs have used in reference to the rite as to the explanation of which they have widely disagreed.[2] This unanimity tells its own tale as to the needs of human thought and life.

II.

Notwithstanding much present controversy, there are some grounds for hope that disagreement in regard to the doctrine of the Eucharist may decrease. Something may be anticipated as a result of that calmer way of viewing religious problems which is increasingly found. The scientific study of history with all that it manifests in regard to the past and its exhibition of the real mind of the best representatives of different points of view may do much. Old crudities of thought as to the nature of presence and the conception of reality are less influential than they were. It is being recognised that the relation of matter to spirit and of spirit to matter is a more complex problem than once was thought. The essential feature in sacrifice is being seen to lie deeper than death or destruction, as it is understood that the dedication of abiding life is no less sacrificial than the death which in some circumstances is a necessary part of the oblation of the will.[3] All fuller understanding of the spiritual character and power of the risen body of Christ and of the mystery of His ascended glory tends towards the removal of misunderstandings of manifold kinds.

[1] For the significance of this fact, see Maclear, *The Evidential Value of the Holy Eucharist*, pp. 46-61.

[2] For two instances out of many which might be cited of this appreciation among those who would not usually be thought to lay much emphasis on Eucharistic Doctrine, see the death-bed addresses of Mons. A. Monod in 1855 and 1856, published under the title of *Les Adieux*, and an address by Dr. A. Saphir reported in *The Christian* of 6th July, 1882.

[3] See, *e.g.*, Westcott, *Epistles of St. John*, pp. 34-37 ; *Epistle to the Hebrews*, pp. 281-95.

III.

There is great need of a generous temper and an ungrudging way of viewing the opinions and expressions which are least congenial. Rough methods of controversy have done little to promote real understanding of the questions with which they have dealt. The denunciations of the sixteenth century, however excusable in their own day, bear across them the mark of failure. Not to recognise that crude ways of speech were a practical necessity of certain times for the preservation of spiritual doctrines, or that every age has its own imperfections of thought and expression and life, or that the great schoolmen used the intellectual methods which were of force for their own day, is simply to be false to history. To put out of court the explanations by theologians of the doctrines to which they are pledged is really an offence against plain and honest dealing. To insist on fixing a carnal and unspiritual view of divine and supernatural things on the utterances and acts of those who protest in their theology that their doctrines are spiritual and uncarnal is even more unjust than it would be to charge a theologian like Bishop Pearson with carnal teaching because he may have thought that the identical material particles of our present bodily life will be re-assembled in the body of the resurrection, and that our Lord in His ascension passed through local divisions of material space to a circumscribed heaven. Whole series of volumes of controversial theology leave the student wondering over the want of insight and imagination and candour and justice which led to their being penned. And, if it is true that champions of Protestant controversy have utterly failed to understand that which they have attacked, it is also true that there have been misunderstandings and consequent misrepresentations on another side. The rejection of a particular method of the presence of Christ has too often been understood as if it were the rejection of the presence of Christ altogether. The separation of His special presence from the elements has too often been thought to mean the assertion of His absence from the rite. The repudiation of particular notions of sacrifice has often been regarded as the denial of sacrifice in any true sense. Because many have avowed less than others would desire, they have often been supposed to acknowledge nothing at all. The warning that want of generosity will usually mean failure to understand comes from opposite camps. It is a reasonable conclusion that the official language and the official ceremonial of great Christian bodies call for a liberal and a considerate interpretation. The practical ecclesiastic no less than the theological student will do well to pause before he binds any such language or any such ceremonial to the narrowest interpretation of which it is capable, and to be quite sure of his ground before he says that a document or an action has closed a door. In the mystery of the Eucharist, where human thought is so apt to go astray, and human language is so inadequate to express even human thought, the interpreter will be most likely to be right who is patient of a wide latitude of interpretation and gentle towards what seem to him offending expressions. To press on the Thirty-nine Articles the narrowest interpretation of which they are capable, and to extend as widely as possible the condemnations which they contain is to refuse to appreciate the lessons of history on the imperfections of the divines of the Reformation period. To make out that they impose as of obligation doctrines which they fall short of explicitly condemning is to be no less blind to opinions which prevailed among their compilers. To fail to see in the decisions of the Council of Trent the influence of a cautious and moderate policy is to be without recognition of the history and meaning of its work. Given the more generous estimate of the English Articles and the Tridentine canons, and there are ways open towards inner life and missionary enterprise on the part of both England and Rome, and perhaps towards ultimate re-union, which else must be closed.[1] The temper which thus weighs the official documents and actions of the West is not unneeded also in all that concerns the relations of West and East. There is much in the East which wears a strange aspect to Western eyes. There is much in the West, and not least in the Church of England, which requires justification to Eastern minds. Here too power to understand and hope of friendship will make large demands on generosity of interpretation. And among all sections of Christians there is need of the remembrance that it is the positive and not the negative, the devotion and not the denunciation, which helps the soul.

[1] See, *e.g.*, Carson, *An Eucharistic Eirenicon*, and the references to Bishop Alexander Forbes and Dr. Pusey on pp. 544-47, 629, 630, *supra*.

INDEX OF SUBJECTS.

653

INDEX OF PASSAGES IN HOLY SCRIPTURE
REFERRED TO.

INDEX OF AUTHORS, COUNCILS, AND BOOKS REFERRED TO.